Literary Criticism: Pope to Croce

LITERARY CRITICISM

Pope to Croce

by

Gay Wilson Allen
Professor of English
New York University

and

Harry Hayden Clark
Professor of English
University of Wisconsin

Detroit   Wayne State University Press   1962

135635

A Few Errata

Page 604, footnote 6 should read *La Tour de Nesle* by Alexandre Dumas Père (1832) and footnote 8, *Le Chapeau de paille d'Italie* by E. Labiche (1851).

Page 609, footnote 22 should read: *Faramond, ou l'Histoire de France,* by La Calprenède (1661). *Faramons* in line 24 of this page should read *Faramonds.*

PREFACE

oᏫooᏫo

THE EDITORS OF THIS BOOK of criticism have brought together a collection of writings sufficiently varied and comprehensive to indicate the main trends and developments of critical thought in the Western World from Pope through Croce. Since the seventeenth century the number of critics and the volume of their works have increased so rapidly that choice for an anthology is a difficult task, and many favorites of each editor have reluctantly been excluded in order to make room for the major selections which teachers and students might be expected to seek in this book. Though we have tried not to neglect any country, we have chosen heavily from France, Germany, and England simply because during the past two and a quarter centuries these countries have produced the majority of the critics; but we have not ignored other countries, and we have included five American critics. Of twentieth-century critics we have included only Bergson and Croce because we believe their ideas have been more influential than those of their contemporaries. Perhaps at the present time the most flourishing critical school is the Marxist, but the fact that Plekhanov and other Marxists are so easily obtainable in cheap editions makes it seem unwise to crowd them into this book of established critics.

We have attempted to represent each writer with an extract of sufficient length to give an accurate indication of his main point of view. Likewise, in order to illustrate the history of critical thought, we have preferred general theories to specific judgments on individual works. Aesthetics and philosophy are so closely allied to literary theories that it is not always possible to draw a line between them, but we have tried to make a distinction so far as practicable. Sometimes, however, philosophers like Nietzsche, Schopenhauer, and Bergson have contributed more to critical theory than a practicing literary critic like Sainte-Beuve. But our primary intention has been to represent the most important critical ideas of the past two centuries whether they were written by a poet, a novelist, a literary critic, or a philosopher, and we trust that we have succeeded.

Our original plan was to give fully annotated bibliographies for each critic, but this scheme had to be modified in order to economize on space. We have, therefore, tried to give annotations where most needed. And we have also endeavored to make the introductory notes

of practical benefit to the student without attempting to eliminate the
need for lectures by the professor of literary criticism.

In this volume, Mr. Allen assumes responsibility for all parts except
the American selections, which Mr. Clark edited; but Mr. Allen received the generous advice of Mr. Clark, who is an experienced editor,
and the able assistance of several friends, whose efforts deserve specific
acknowledgment. First on the list is Dean Helena Brawley Watts, of
Webber College, Florida, who not only did a large part of the editing of
the eighteenth-century English selections but also translated the extracts from Madame de Staël and Voltaire. The editors are deeply
indebted for her scholarly help.

Others who made special translations for this volume are Dr. Allan H. Gilbert, professor of English at Duke University, who translated the extract from Croce's *La Poesia*, with the kind permission of
Mr. Croce and the Macmillan Company; Mr. Samuel Putnam, the distinguished professional translator, who provided the English version of
Belinski; Mr. Field Horine, Newscaster in German, CBS, New York,
who translated Lessing; and Professor E. Gustav Johnson, of North
Park College, who translated Thorild.

The editors are also grateful to the many academic friends who have
offered valuable suggestions, especially Professor Spencer Wood, of
Grinnell College; Professor Henry Lilly, of Davidson College; Professor Earl Griggs, of the University of Pennsylvania; and Professor
Cecil Rew, of Bowling Green State University. The staff of the University of Michigan has assisted the work in many ways. Miss Evelyn
Simmons has generously helped in checking proof and assisting with
the Index.

The editors likewise wish to offer their thanks to all those persons
and publishing houses which have kindly permitted the use of copy-
righted material, specific acknowledgment of which has been made in
the text.

G. W. A.
H. H. C.

CONTENTS

CONTENTS

Literary Criticism: Pope to Croce

°◯°○°◯°

LA PREMIÈRE CONDITION pour bien apprécier les anciens critiques et leurs productions de circonstance, c'est donc de se remettre en situation et de se replacer en idée dans l'esprit d'un temps.

SAINTE-BEUVE

ALEXANDER POPE

(1688–1744)

o◯ooo◯o

An Essay on Criticism, published in 1711, was probably written in 1709, before Pope was twenty-one years of age. Although he is generally considered today as the greatest English poet of his age, Pope in the eighteenth century shared with Dryden and Johnson the position of critical authority. *An Essay on Criticism*, one of his earliest poems, served as the basis upon which his later critical reputation was founded.

The poem is a brilliant application of neoclassical doctrines to criticism.[1] It is at once both familiar and original: familiar in that it is consciously founded on the classical theories of Aristotle, Longinus, Horace, Quintilian, and their followers Vida, Boileau,[2] Rapin, Le Bossu, and Bouhours; original in that it shifts the emphasis of such materials from the poet to the critic. However, as Professor Sherburn says—

> Pope was not beguiled by any itch of originality; his method was scientific and inductive: the experience of the past could be codified into guiding rules and could show the proper temper and behavior for the critic. In general, his object was to restate accepted wisdom (or commonplace), but to restate it in that compelling form which is the magic of true wit.[3]

Criticism in the early eighteenth century was in general disrepute, as Swift's *Tale of a Tub*, published in 1704, indicates in its contempt

---

[1]Earlier English metrical treatises on the art of poetry include Mulgrave's *Essay on Poetry* (1682), Roscommon's *Essay on Translated Verse* (1684), and Lord Lansdowne's *Essay upon Unnatural Flights in Poetry* (1701). These works, however, were addressed to the poet, not the critic.

[2]Pope's copy of Boileau is in the Huntington Library. Professor Root has examined the book and describes it as "a thin quarto volume entitled: '*The Art of Poetry*, written in French by The Sieur de Boileau, made English by Sir William Solmes, London, Printed for R. Bentley, and S. Magnes, in Russel-street in Covent Garden, 1683.' . . . In the lower margins of Cantos I and IV Pope has in a very neat printing hand analyzed Boileau's matter." For a list of Pope's annotations, see Robert Kilburn Root, *The Poetical Career of Alexander Pope* (Princeton, 1938), p. 231, n. 5.

[3]George Sherburn, *The Early Career of Alexander Pope* (Oxford, 1934), p. 86.

for the pedantic critic and the Grub Street hack writer.[4] *An Essay on Criticism*, appearing in the next decade, also contains satiric portraits of bad critics. Pope was following a literary convention as well as his own personal bent when he turned his couplets against the fop who considered it fashionable to damn new books, the narrow-minded critical poetaster who led others astray by arbitrary pronouncements on literary subjects, and the carping scholastic critic. Pope's couplet on the pedantic critic

> The bookful blockhead, ignorantly read,
> With loads of learnèd lumber in his head,

deserves to be placed beside Ben Jonson's caustic denunciation of the type, as "those common torturers that bring all wit to the rack; whose noses are ever like swine spoiling and rooting up the Muses' gardens; and their whole bodies like moles, as blindly working under earth, to cast any, the least, hills upon virtue." [5]

An Essay on Criticism, aside from the attacks on false critics, seems to be an honest attempt to set up practical rules for judging literature. Pope points out the qualifications of mind necessary to the critic, suggests ways by which such modes of judgment may be developed, and stresses the importance of taste above all other criteria in literary matters. To him, as to Joubert, "le goût est la conscience littéraire de l'âme."

BIBLIOGRAPHY

TEXT

Collins, John Churton, *An Essay on Criticism*. London, 1896.
Elwin and Courthope, *The Works of Alexander Pope*. 10 vols. London, 1871–1889.
Sherburn, George, *The Best of Pope*. New York, 1929.

BIOGRAPHY AND CRITICISM

Audra, E., *L'Influence française dans l'œuvre de Pope*. Paris, 1931.
Addison, Joseph (a review of *An Essay on Criticism*), *Spectator*, no. 253. December 20, 1711.
Bobertag, Felix, "Zu Popes Essay on Criticism," *Englische Studien*, III (1880), 43–91.

[4]See also Sir Richard Blackmore's *Satyr against Wit* (1700) and Wycherley's preface to his *Miscellany Poems* (1704). Cited by Sherburn, *op. cit.*, p. 86. Pope's informal paper, "On False Criticks," published in the *Guardian*, no. 12, Wednesday, March 25, 1713, is another attack on hasty and ill-considered criticism.

[5]Ben Jonson, "To the Readers," prefixed to *Sejanus*.

Courthope, W. J., "Life of Alexander Pope," in *The Works of Alexander Pope*, V. London, 1889.

De la Harpe, Jacqueline, *Le Journal des savants et la renommée de Pope en France au XVIIIᵉ siècle*. University of California Press, 1933.

Dennis, John, *The Age of Pope*. London, 1928.

Mackail, John William, *Pope* (the Leslie Stephen lecture delivered before the University of Cambridge, 10 May 1919). Cambridge University Press, 1919.

Root, Robert Kilburn, *The Poetical Career of Alexander Pope*. Princeton University Press, 1938.

Sherburn, George, *The Early Career of Alexander Pope*. Oxford, Clarendon Press, 1934.

Spence, Joseph, *Anecdotes, Observations, and Characters of Books and Men*. Collected from the conversation of Mr. Pope and other eminent persons of his time, by Samuel W. Singer. London, 1820.

Sitwell, Edith, *Alexander Pope*. London, 1930.

Stephen, Sir Leslie, *Alexander Pope*. London, 1880. (English Men of Letters.)

Tillotson, Geoffrey, *On the Poetry of Pope*. Oxford, Clarendon Press, 1938.

Warton, Joseph, *An Essay on the Genius and Writings of Pope*. 2 vols. London, 1756, 1782.

Warren, Austin, *Alexander Pope as Critic and Humanist*. Princeton University Press, 1929.

AN ESSAY ON CRITICISM

1711

Part I

[On the formation of taste and judgment in critics and poets]

'Tis hard to say if greater want of skill
Appear in writing or in judging ill;
But, of the two, less dang'rous is th' offense
To tire our patience, than mislead our sense.
Some few in that, but numbers err in this,
Ten censure wrong for one who writes amiss;
A fool might once himself alone expose,
Now one in verse makes many more in prose.
'Tis with our judgments as our watches, none
Go just alike, yet each believes his own.
In poets as true genius is but rare,   10
True taste as seldom is the critic's share;

Both must alike from heaven derive their light,
These born to judge, as well as those to write.
Let such teach others who themselves excel,
And censure freely who have written well.
Authors are partial to their wit, 'tis true,
But are not critics to their judgment too?
   Yet, if we look more closely, we shall find
Most have the seeds of judgment in their mind.   20
Nature affords at least a glimm'ring light;
The lines, though touched but faintly, are drawn right:
But as the slightest sketch, if justly traced,
Is by ill coloring but the more disgraced,
So by false learning is good sense defaced:
Some are bewildered in the maze of schools,
And some made coxcombs nature meant but fools:
In search of wit, these lose their common sense,
And then turn critics in their own defense:
Each burns alike, who can, or cannot write,   30
Or with a rival's, or an eunuch's spite.
All fools have still an itching to deride,
And fain would be upon the laughing side.
If Maevius [1] scribble in Apollo's spite,
There are who judge still worse than he can write.
   Some have at first for wits, then poets passed,
Turned critics next, and proved plain fools at last.
Some neither can for wits nor critics pass,
As heavy mules are neither horse nor ass.
Those half-learned witlings, num'rous in our isle,   40
As half-formed insects on the banks of Nile;
Unfinished things, one knows not what to call,
Their generation's so equivocal;
To tell 'em would a hundred tongues require,
Or one vain wit's, that might a hundred tire.
   But you who seek to give and merit fame,
And justly bear a critic's noble name,
Be sure yourself and your own reach to know,
How far your genius, taste, and learning go;
Launch not beyond your depth, but be discreet,[2]   50
And mark that point where sense and dullness meet.

[1] Inferior Roman poet of the first century who attacked the writings of Vergil and Horace.   [2] Cf. Horace, *Ars poetica*, 38–41; Vida, *De arte poetica*, I, 39–40.

Nature to all things fixed the limits fit,
And wisely curbed proud man's pretending wit.[3]
As on the land while here the ocean gains,
In other parts it leaves wide sandy plains;
Thus in the soul while memory prevails,
The solid power of understanding fails;
Where beams of warm imagination play,
The memory's soft figures melt away.
One science only will one genius fit;   60
So vast is art, so narrow human wit:
Not only bounded to peculiar arts,
But oft in those confined to single parts.
Like kings we lose the conquests gained before,
By vain ambition still to make them more:
Each might his sev'ral province well command,
Would all but stoop to what they understand.
    First follow NATURE, and your judgment frame
By her just standard, which is still the same:
Unerring nature! still divinely bright,[4]   70
One clear, unchanged, and universal light,
Life, force, and beauty, must to all impart,
At once the source, and end, and test of art.[5]
Art from that fund each just supply provides;
Works without show, and without pomp presides:
In some fair body thus th' informing soul
With spirits feeds, with vigor fills the whole;
Each motion guides, and every nerve sustains,
Itself unseen, but in the effects remains.[6]
Some, to whom heaven in wit has been profuse,   80
Want as much more, to turn it to its use;

[3]Cf. Boileau, *L'Art poétique*, I, 13–14.
    [4]There is nothing more elusive in the *Essay* than the use of the critical catchword
"nature." Under the influence of the eighteenth-century critics, the Aristotelian
maxim that the poet was to imitate nature received a very realistic interpretation.
"Nature" not only meant the universal element in the world but the life and society
of the times. See also ll. 89, 243, and 297.
    [5]Cf. Horace, *Ars poetica*, 317; Boileau, *L'Art poétique*, III, 359; Vida, *De arte poetica*,
455–456. Pope urges in the Preface to his translation of the *Iliad* (*Works*, VI,
357): "For Art is only like a prudent steward that lives on managing the riches
of Nature."
    [6]Elwin gives a reference to Mulgrave's *Essay on Poetry:*
        A spirit which inspires the work throughout,
        As that of nature moves the world about;
        Itself unseen, yet all things by it shown.

For wit and judgment often are at strife,
Though meant each other's aid, like man and wife.
'Tis more to guide, than spur the Muse's steed;
Restrain his fury, than provoke his speed:
The wingèd courser, like a gen'rous horse,
Shows most true mettle when you check his course.
 Those RULES of old discovered, not devised,
Are nature still, but nature methodized: [7]
Nature, like liberty, is but restrained   90
By the same laws which first herself ordained.
 Hear how learned Greece her useful rules indites,
When to repress, and when indulge our flights:
High on Parnassus' top her sons she showed, [8]
And pointed out those arduous paths they trod;
Held from afar, aloft, th' immortal prize,
And urged the rest by equal steps to rise.
Just precepts thus from great examples given,
She drew from them what they derived from heaven;
The generous critic fanned the poet's fire,   100
And taught the world with reason to admire.
Then criticism the Muses' handmaid proved,
To dress her charms, and make her more beloved:
But following wits from that intention strayed;
Who could not win the mistress, wooed the maid;
Against the poets their own arms they turned,
Sure to hate most the men from whom they learned.
So modern 'pothecaries, taught the art
By doctor's bills to play the doctor's part,
Bold in the practice of mistaken rules,   110
Prescribe, apply, and call their masters fools.
Some on the leaves of ancient authors prey;
Nor time nor moths e'er spoiled so much as they:
Some dryly plain, without invention's aid,
Write dull receipts how poems may be made;
These leave the sense, their learning to display,
And those explain the meaning quite away.
 You then whose judgment the right course would steer,
Know well each ANCIENT's proper character; [9]

[7] Boileau, *L'Art poétique*, IV, 229; Horace, *De orat.*, I, i, c. 41.
[8] Cf. Vida, *De arte poetica*, III, 8–14.
[9] Cf. *ibid.*, I, 71–74, 409–414; III, 185.

His fable, subject, scope in every page;   120
Religion, country, genius of his age:
Without all these at once before your eyes,
Cavil you may, but never criticize.
Be Homer's works your study and delight,
Read them by day, and meditate by night;
Thence form your judgment, thence your maxims bring,
And trace the Muses upward to their spring.
Still with itself compared, his text peruse;
And let your comment be the Mantuan Muse.[10]
   When first young Maro in his boundless mind   130
A work t' outlast immortal Rome designed,
Perhaps he seemed above the critic's law,
And but from nature's fountains scorned to draw:
But when t' examine every part he came,
Nature and Homer were, he found, the same.
Convinced, amazed, he checks the bold design,
And rules as strict his labored work confine
As if the Stagirite [11] o'erlooked each line.
Learn hence for ancient rules a just esteem;
To copy nature is to copy them.   140
   Some beauties yet no precepts can declare,
For there's a happiness as well as care.
Music resembles poetry; in each
Are nameless graces which no methods teach,
And which a master hand alone can reach.
If, where the rules not far enough extend,
(Since rules were made but to promote their end)
Some lucky license answer to the full
Th' intent proposed, that license is a rule.
Thus Pegasus, a nearer way to take,   150
May boldly deviate from the common track.
From vulgar bounds with brave disorder part,
And snatch a grace beyond the reach of art,[12]
Which, without passing through the judgment, gains
The heart, and all its end at once attains.
In prospects thus some objects please our eyes,
Which out of nature's common order rise,

[10]Vergil was born in the vicinity of Mantua.
[11]Aristotle was born at Stagira in Macedonia. References to the "mighty Stagirite" were the literary fashion.   [12]Boileau, *L'Art poétique*, I, 75–76; IV, 77–80.

The shapeless rock, or hanging precipice.   160
Great wits sometimes may gloriously offend,
And rise to faults true critics dare not mend;
But though the ancients thus their rules invade,
(As kings dispense with laws themselves have made)
Moderns, beware! or if you must offend
Against the precept, ne'er transgress its end;
Let it be seldom, and compelled by need;
And have, at least, their precedent to plead;
The critic else proceeds without remorse,
Seizes your fame, and puts his laws in force.
  I know there are, to whose presumptuous thoughts
Those freer beauties, even in them, seem faults.   170
Some figures monstrous and misshaped appear,
Considered singly, or beheld too near,
Which, but proportioned to their light, or place,
Due distance reconciles to form and grace.
A prudent chief not always must display
His powers in equal ranks, and fair array,
But with th' occasion and the place comply,
Conceal his force, nay, seem sometimes to fly.
Those oft are stratagems which errors seem,
Nor is it Homer nods but we that dream.   180
  Still green with bays each ancient altar stands,
Above the reach of sacrilegious hands;
Secure from flames, from envy's fiercer rage,
Destructive war, and all-involving age.
See, from each clime, the learned their incense bring;
Hear, in all tongues consenting paeans ring!
In praise so just let every voice be joined,
And fill the general chorus of mankind.
Hail, bards triumphant! born in happier days;
Immortal heirs of universal praise!   190
Whose honors with increase of ages grow,
As streams roll down, enlarging as they flow;
Nations unborn your mighty names shall sound,
And worlds applaud that must not yet be found!
O may some spark of your celestial fire,
The last, the meanest of your sons inspire
(That on weak wings, from far, pursues your flights;
Glows while he reads, but trembles as he writes),

To teach vain wits a science little known,
T' admire superior sense, and doubt their own!   200

Part II

[On principles of poetry and critics' attention to them]

Of all the causes which conspire to blind
Man's erring judgment, and misguide the mind,
What the weak head with strongest bias rules,
Is *pride*, the never-failing vice of fools.[13]
Whatever nature has in worth denied,
She gives in large recruits of needful pride;
For as in bodies, thus in souls, we find
What wants in blood and spirits, swelled with wind:
Pride, where wit fails, steps in to our defense,
And fills up all the mighty void of sense: 210
If once right reason drives that cloud away,
Truth breaks upon us with resistless day.
Trust not yourself; but, your defects to know,
Make use of every friend—and every foe.
    A *little learning* is a dang'rous thing;
Drink deep, or taste not the Pierian spring:
There shallow draughts intoxicate the brain,
And drinking largely sobers us again.
Fired at first sight with what the Muse imparts,
In fearless youth we tempt the heights of arts,   220
While from the bounded level of our mind,
Short views we take, nor see the lengths behind;
But more advanced, behold with strange surprise,
New distant scenes of endless science rise!
So pleased at first the tow'ring Alps we try,
Mount o'er the vales, and seem to tread the sky,
Th' eternal snows appear already past,
And the first clouds and mountains seem the last:
But, those attained, we tremble to survey
The growing labors of the lengthened way;   230
Th' increasing prospect tires our wand'ring eyes,
Hills peep o'er hills, and Alps on Alps arise!

[13]Cf. Roscommon, *An Essay on Translated Verse* (1684):
        "Pride, of all others the most dangerous Fault,
        Proceeds from want of Sense or want of Thought."

A perfect judge will read each work of wit
With the same spirit that its author writ;
Survey the WHOLE, nor seek slight faults to find
Where nature moves, and rapture warms the mind;
Nor lose for that malignant dull delight,
The gen'rous pleasure to be charmed with wit.[14]
But in such lays as neither ebb nor flow,[15]
Correctly cold, and regularly low,
That, shunning faults, one quiet tenor keep,   240
We cannot blame indeed—but we may sleep.
In wit, as nature, what affects our hearts
Is not th' exactness of peculiar parts;
'Tis not a lip, or eye, we beauty call,
But the joint force and full result of all.
Thus when we view some well-proportioned dome,
(The world's just wonder, and even thine, O Rome!)
No single parts unequally surprise,
All comes united to th' admiring eyes;   250
No monstrous height, or breadth, or length appear;
The whole at once is bold, and regular.
    Whoever thinks a faultless piece to see,
Thinks what ne'er was, nor is, nor e'er shall be.[16]
In every work regard the writer's end,
Since none can compass more than they intend;
And if the means be just, the conduct true,
Applause, in spite of trivial faults, is due.
As men of breeding, sometimes men of wit,
T' avoid great errors, must the less commit;   260
Neglect the rules each verbal critic lays,
For not to know some trifles is a praise.
Most critics, fond of some subservient art,
Still make the whole depend upon a part:

[14] This liberal attitude of Pope's may be found in several other places, although he succeeded in disregarding the sentiments after he expressed them. See Preface to the *Edition of Shakespeare* (*Works*, VI, 399): "To judge therefore Shakespear by Aristotle's rules, is like trying a man by the laws of one country, who acted under those of another."

[15] Boileau, *L'Art poétique*, I, 71–72:

> A frozen style that neither ebbs nor flows,
> Instead of pleasing makes us gape and doze.

[16] Cf. Horace, *Ars poetica*, ll. 347–353, and the Earl of Mulgrave, *An Essay on Poetry*, ll. 67–69.

They talk of principles, but notions prize,
And all to one loved folly sacrifice.
   Once on a time, La Mancha's [17] knight, they say,
A certain bard encount'ring on the way,
Discoursed in terms as just, with looks as sage,
As e'er could Dennis [18] of the Grecian stage;   270
Concluding all were desperate sots and fools,
Who durst depart from Aristotle's rules.
Our author, happy in a judge so nice,
Produced his play, and begged the knight's advice;
Made him observe the subject, and the plot,
The manners, passions, unities; what not?
All which, exact to rule, were brought about,
Were but a combat in the lists left out.
"What! leave the combat out?" exclaims the knight.
Yes, or we must renounce the Stagirite.   280
"Not so by heaven!" (he answers in a rage)
"Knights, squires, and steeds, must enter on the stage."
So vast a throng the stage can ne'er contain.
"Then build a new, or act it in a plain."
   Thus critics of less judgment than caprice,
Curious, not knowing, not exact but nice,
Form short ideas, and offend in arts
(As most in manners) by a love to parts.
   Some to *conceit* alone their taste confine,
And glitt'ring thoughts struck out at every line;   290
Pleased with a work where nothing's just or fit;
One glaring chaos and wild heap of wit.
Poets, like painters, thus unskilled to trace
The naked nature and the living grace,
With golds and jewels cover every part,
And hide with ornaments their want of art.
True wit is nature to advantage dressed;
What oft was thought, but ne'er so well expressed;

[17] Don Quixote de la Mancha. Pope alludes to an episode in the second part of *Don Quixote*.
[18] See below, ll. 584–587 of this *Essay*, for another reference to Dennis. John Dennis replied to Pope's lines with *Reflections critical and satyrical upon a late rhapsody call'd an Essay upon Criticism* (London [1711]). For a history of this malicious but entertaining quarrel, see George Sherburn, *The Early Career of Alexander Pope* (Oxford, 1934), pp. 87–95, 104–112; and H. G. Paul's dissertation, *John Dennis: His Life and Criticism* (Columbia University Press, 1911), pp. 86–100.

Something, whose truth convinced at sight we find,
That gives us back the image of our mind.   300
As shades more sweetly recommend the light,
So modest plainness sets off sprightly wit:
For works may have more wit than does 'em good,
As bodies perish through excess of blood.
   Others for *language* all their care express,
And value books, as women men, for dress:
Their praise is still—the style is excellent;
The sense, they humbly take upon content.
Words are like leaves, and where they most abound,
Much fruit of sense beneath is rarely found.   310
False eloquence, like the prismatic glass,
Its gaudy colors spreads on every place;
The face of nature we no more survey,
All glares alike, without distinction gay;
But true expression, like th' unchanging sun,
Clears and improves whate'er it shines upon,
It gilds all objects, but it alters none.
Expression is the dress of thought, and still
Appears more decent, as more suitable:
A vile conceit in pompous words expressed   320
Is like a clown in regal purple dressed:
For diff'rent styles with diff'rent subjects sort,
As several garbs with country, town, and court.
Some by old words to fame have made pretense,
Ancients in phrase, mere moderns in their sense;
Such labored nothings, in so strange a style,
Amaze th' unlearned, and make the learnèd smile.
Unlucky, as Fungoso [19] in the play,
These sparks with awkward vanity display
What the fine gentleman wore yesterday;   330
And but so mimic ancient wits at best,
As apes our grandsires, in their doublets dressed.
In words, as fashions, the same rule will hold;
Alike fantastic, if too new, or old:
Be not the first by whom the new are tried,
Nor yet the last to lay the old aside.
   But most by numbers judge a poet's song,

[19] A poor scholar who aped the dress of a gentleman of the court, in Ben Jonson's
Every Man out of His Humor.

And smooth or rough, with them, is right or wrong:
In the bright Muse, though thousand charms conspire,
Her voice is all these tuneful fools admire;   340
Who haunt Parnassus but to please their ear,
Not mend their minds; as some to church repair,
Not for the doctrine, but the music there.
These equal syllables alone require,
Though oft the ear the open vowels tire;
While expletives their feeble aid do join,
And ten low words oft creep in one dull line:
While they ring round the same unvaried chimes,
With sure returns of still expected rhymes;
Where'er you find "the cooling western breeze,"   350
In the next line, it "whispers through the trees":
If crystal streams "with pleasing murmurs creep,"
The reader's threatened (not in vain) with "sleep":
Then, at the last and only couplet fraught
With some unmeaning thing they call a thought,
A needless Alexandrine ends the song,
That, like a wounded snake, drags its slow length along.
Leave such to tune their own dull rhymes, and know
What's roundly smooth, or languishingly slow;
And praise the easy vigor of a line   360
Where Denham's strength, and Waller's sweetness join.
True ease in writing comes from art, not chance,
As those move easiest who have learned to dance.
'Tis not enough no harshness gives offense;
The sound must seem an echo to the sense.
Soft is the strain when zephyr gently blows,
And the smooth stream in smoother numbers flows;
But when loud surges lash the sounding shore,
The hoarse, rough verse should like the torrent roar:
When Ajax strives some rock's vast weight to throw,   370
The line too labors, and the words move slow:
Not so when swift Camilla [20] scours the plain,
Flies o'er th' unbending corn, and skims along the main.
Hear how Timotheus' [21] varied lays surprise,
And bid alternate passions fall and rise,
While, at each change, the son of Libyan Jove

[20] Cf. Dryden's translation of the *Aeneid*, VII, 1094–1113.
[21] Cf. Dryden's *Alexander's Feast*.

Now burns with glory, and then melts with love;
Now his fierce eyes with sparkling fury glow,
Now sighs steal out, and tears begin to flow:
Persians and Greeks like turns of nature found,   380
And the world's victor stood subdued by sound!
The power of music all our hearts allow,
And what Timotheus was, is DRYDEN now.
   Avoid extremes, and shun the fault of such
Who still are pleased too little or too much.
At every trifle scorn to take offense,
That always shows great pride, or little sense:
Those heads, as stomachs, are not sure the best,
Which nauseate all, and nothing can digest.
Yet let not each gay turn thy rapture move;   390
For fools admire, but men of sense approve:
As things seem large which we through mists descry,
Dullness is ever apt to magnify.
   Some foreign writers, some our own despise;
The ancients only, or the moderns prize.[22]
Thus wit, like faith, by each man is applied
To one small sect, and all are damned beside.
Meanly they seek the blessing to confine,
And force that sun but on a part to shine,
Which not alone the southern wit sublimes,   400
But ripens spirits in cold northern climes;
Which, from the first has shone on ages past,
Enlights the present, and shall warm the last;
Though each may feel increases and decays,
And see now clearer and now darker days;
Regard not then if wit be old or new,
But blame the false, and value still the true.
   Some ne'er advance a judgment of their own,
But catch the spreading notion of the town;
They reason and conclude by precedent,   410
And own stale nonsense which they ne'er invent.
Some judge of authors' names, not works, and then
Nor praise nor blame the writings, but the men.
Of all this servile herd, the worst is he
That in proud dullness joins with quality;

---

[22]A slight quip at the expense of the men who were involved in the battle over the Ancients and the Moderns.

A constant critic at the great man's board,
To fetch and carry nonsense for my lord.
What woeful stuff this madrigal would be,
In some starved hackney sonneteer, or me?
But let a lord once own the happy lines, 420
How the wit brightens! how the style refines!
Before his sacred name flies every fault,
And each exalted stanza teems with thought!
   The vulgar thus through imitation err,
As oft the learned by being singular;
So much they scorn the crowd, that if the throng
By chance go right, they purposely go wrong:
So schismatics the plain believers quit,
And are but damned for having too much wit.
Some praise at morning what they blame at night, 430
But always think the last opinion right.
A muse by these is like a mistress used,
This hour she's idolized, the next abused;
While their weak heads, like towns unfortified,
'Twixt sense and nonsense daily change their side.
Ask them the cause; they're wiser still, they say;
And still tomorrow's wiser than today.
We think our fathers fools, so wise we grow;
Our wiser sons, no doubt, will think us so.
   Once school-divines this zealous isle o'erspread; 440
Who knew most Sentences,[23] was deepest read:
Faith, gospel, all, seemed made to be disputed,
And none had sense enough to be confuted.
Scotists and Thomists,[24] now, in peace remain,
Amidst their kindred cobwebs in Duck Lane.[25]
If faith itself has diff'rent dresses worn,
What wonder modes in wit should take their turn?
Oft leaving what is natural and fit,
The current folly proves the ready wit;
And authors think their reputation safe, 450
Which lives as long as fools are pleased to laugh.
   Some, valuing those of their own side or mind,

[23]Peter Lombard, pupil of Abelard, wrote the *Sententiae*. They were a summary of theological doctrine and were taught in the schools.
[24]Thomas Aquinas and Duns Scotus, rival philosophers in the Middle Ages.
[25]Famous for its secondhand book shops.

Still make themselves the measure of mankind:
Fondly we think we honor merit then,
When we but praise ourselves in other men.
Parties in wit attend on those of state,
And public faction doubles private hate.
Pride, malice, folly, against Dryden rose,
In various shapes of parsons, critics, beaus;
But sense survived when merry jests were past;   460
For rising merit will buoy up at last.
Might he return, and bless once more our eyes,
New Blackmores and new Milbournes [26] must arise:
Nay, should great Homer lift his awful head,
Zoilus [27] again would start up from the dead.
Envy will merit, as its shade, pursue;
But, like a shadow, proves the substance true:
For envied wit, like Sol eclipsed, makes known
Th' opposing body's grossness, not its own.
When first that sun too powerful beams displays,   470
It draws up vapors which obscure its rays;
But even those clouds at last adorn its way,
Reflect new glories, and augment the day.
    Be thou the first true merit to befriend;
His praise is lost, who stays till all commend.
Short is the date, alas! of modern rhymes,
And 'tis but just to let them live betimes.
No longer now that golden age appears,
When patriarch wits survived a thousand years;
Now length of fame (our second life) is lost,   480
And bare threescore is all even that can boast;
Our sons their fathers' failing language see,
And such as Chaucer is,[28] shall Dryden be.
So when the faithful pencil has designed
Some bright idea of the master's mind,
Where a new world leaps out at his command,
And ready nature waits upon his hand;

[26]The Reverend Luke Milbourne had planned a translation of Vergil before Dryden's and had attacked Dryden's. Sir Richard Blackmore had attacked Dryden for "irreligion and folly." Dryden mentions these men in his Preface to the *Fables*. [27]Greek critic famous for his attack on Homer.

[28]Spence, *Anecdotes* (1820), p. 19, quotes Pope: "I read Chaucer still with as much pleasure as almost any of our poets. He is a master of manners, of description, and the first tale-teller in the true enlivened natural way.—P."

When the ripe colors soften and unite,
And sweetly melt into just shade and light;
When mellowing years their full perfection give,   490
And each bold figure just begins to live,
The treach'rous colors the fair art betray,
And all the bright creation fades away! [29]
    Unhappy wit, like most mistaken things,
Atones not for that envy which it brings;
In youth alone its empty praise we boast,
But soon the short-lived vanity is lost;
Like some fair flower the early spring supplies,
That gaily blooms, but even in blooming dies.
What is this wit, which must our cares employ?   500
The owner's wife, that other men enjoy;
Then most our trouble still when most admired,
And still the more we give, the more required;
Whose fame with pains we guard, but lose with ease,
Sure some to vex, but never all to please;
'Tis what the vicious fear, the virtuous shun,
By fools 'tis hated, and by knaves undone!
    If wit so much from ign'rance undergo,
Ah let not learning too commence its foe!
Of old, those met rewards who could excel,   510
And such were praised who but endeavored well:
Though triumphs were to generals only due,
Crowns were reserved to grace the soldiers too.
Now, they who reach Parnassus' lofty crown,
Employ their pains to spurn some others down;
And while self-love each jealous writer rules,
Contending wits become the sport of fools;
But still the worst with most regret commend,
For each ill author is as bad a friend.
To what base ends, and by what abject ways,   520
Are mortals urged through sacred lust of praise!
Ah ne'er so dire a thirst of glory boast,
Nor in the critic let the man be lost.
Good nature and good sense must ever join;
To err is human, to forgive, divine.

[29]See Geoffrey Tillotson, *On the Poetry of Pope* (Oxford, 1938), pp. 100–102, for a short discussion of Pope's fear that the English language would change again at the "end of one Age."

But if in noble minds some dregs remain
Not yet purged off, of spleen and sour disdain,
Discharge that rage on more provoking crimes,
Nor fear a dearth in these flagitious times.
No pardon vile obscenity should find,   530
Though wit and art conspire to move your mind;
But dullness with obscenity must prove
As shameful sure as impotence in love.
In the fat age of pleasure, wealth, and ease,
Sprung the rank weed, and thrived with large increase:
When love was all an easy monarch's care;
Seldom at council, never in a war,
Jilts ruled the state, and statesmen farces writ;
Nay, wits had pensions, and young lords had wit;
The fair sat panting at a courtier's play,   540
And not a mask went unimproved away;
The modest fan was lifted up no more,
And virgins smiled at what they blushed before.
The following license of a foreign reign
Did all the dregs of bold Socinus drain;
Then unbelieving priests reformed the nation,
And taught more pleasant methods of salvation;
Where heaven's free subjects might their rights dispute,
Lest God himself should seem too absolute:
Pulpits their sacred satire learned to spare,   550
And vice admired to find a flatt'rer there!
Encouraged thus, wit's Titans braved the skies,
And the press groaned with licensed blasphemies.
These monsters, critics! with your darts engage,
Here point your thunder, and exhaust your rage!
Yet shun their fault, who, scandalously nice,
Will needs mistake an author into vice:
All seems infected that th' infected spy,
As all looks yellow to the jaundiced eye.

Part III

[Advice to critics]

Learn then what MORALS critics ought to show,   560
For 'tis but half a judge's task, to know.
'Tis not enough, taste, judgment, learning, join;

In all you speak, let truth and candor shine,
That not alone what to your sense is due
All may allow, but seek your friendship too.
   Be silent always when you doubt your sense,
And speak, though sure, with seeming diffidence:
Some positive, persisting fops we know,
Who, if once wrong, will needs be always so;
But you with pleasure own your errors past,   570
And make each day a critique on the last.
   'Tis not enough your counsel still be true;
Blunt truths more mischief than nice falsehoods do;
Men must be taught as if you taught them not,
And things unknown proposed as things forgot.
Without good breeding truth is disapproved;
That only makes superior sense beloved.
   Be niggards of advice on no pretense,
For the worst avarice is that of sense.
With mean complacence ne'er betray your trust,   580
Nor be so civil as to prove unjust.
Fear not the anger of the wise to raise;
Those best can bear reproof, who merit praise.
   'Twere well might critics still this freedom take,
But Appius [30] reddens at each word you speak,
And stares, tremendous, with a threat'ning eye,
Like some fierce tyrant in old tapestry.
Fear most to tax an Honorable fool,
Whose right it is, uncensured, to be dull:
Such, without wit, are poets when they please,   590
As without learning they can take degrees.
Leave dangerous truths to unsuccessful satires,
And flattery to fulsome dedicators,
Whom, when they praise, the world believes no more,
Than when they promise to give scribbling o'er.
'Tis best sometimes your censure to restrain,
And charitably let the dull be vain;
Your silence there is better than your spite,
For who can rail so long as they can write?
Still humming on, their drowsy course they keep,   600
And lashed so long, like tops, are lashed asleep.

[30]John Dennis had written a tragedy, *Appius and Virginia*. See above, note 18,
l. 270 of this *Essay*.

False steps but help them to renew the race,
As, after stumbling, jades will mend their pace.
What crowds of these, impenitently bold,
In sounds and jingling syllables grown old,
Still run on poets in a raging vein,
Even to the dregs and squeezings of the brain,
Strain out the last dull droppings of their sense,
And rhyme with all the rage of impotence.

[Concerning bad critics]

Such shameless bards we have; and yet 'tis true,   610
There are as mad, abandoned critics too.
The bookful blockhead, ignorantly read,
With loads of learnèd lumber in his head,
With his own tongue still edifies his ears,
And always list'ning to himself appears:
All books he reads, and all he reads assails,
From Dryden's *Fables* down to Durfey's [31] *Tales*.
With him most authors steal their works, or buy;
Garth did not write his own *Dispensary*.[32]
Name a new play, and he's the poet's friend,   620
Nay, showed his faults—but when would poets mend?
No place so sacred from such fops is barred,
Nor is Paul's church more safe than Paul's churchyard: [33]
Nay, fly to altars; there they'll talk you dead;
For fools rush in where angels fear to tread.
Distrustful sense with modest caution speaks,
It still looks home, and short excursions makes;
But rattling nonsense in full volleys breaks,
And never shocked, and never turned aside,
Bursts out, resistless, with a thund'ring tide.   630

[Definition of a good critic]

But where's the man, who counsel can bestow,
Still pleased to teach, and yet not proud to know?
Unbiased, or by favor, or by spite,
Not dully prepossessed, nor blindly right;
Though learned, well-bred; and though well-bred, sincere;

---

[31]Thomas D'Urfey (1653–1723), doggerel poet, *Tales, Tragical and Comical* (1704).
[32]Sir Samuel Garth, poet and physician, published *The Dispensary*, a mock-heroic,
in 1699.   [33]Before the Great Fire famous for its book stalls.

Modestly bold, and humanly severe;
Who to a friend his faults can freely show,
And gladly praise the merit of a foe?
Blest with a taste exact, yet unconfined;
A knowledge both of books and human kind;   640
Gen'rous converse; a soul exempt from pride;
And love to praise, with reason on his side?

[History of criticism]

Such once were critics; such the happy few
Athens and Rome in better ages knew.
The mighty Stagirite first left the shore,
Spread all his sails, and durst the deeps explore;
He steered securely, and discovered far,
Led by the light of the Maeonian [34] star.
Poets, a race long unconfined and free,
Still fond and proud of savage liberty,   650
Received his laws, and stood convinced 'twas fit,
Who conquered nature, should preside o'er wit.
Horace still charms with graceful negligence,
And without method talks us into sense;
Will, like a friend, familiarly convey
The truest notions in the easiest way.
He who supreme in judgment, as in wit,
Might boldly censure, as he boldly writ,
Yet judged with coolness, though he sung with fire;
His precepts teach but what his works inspire.   660
Our critics take a contrary extreme,
They judge with fury, but they write with phlegm:
Nor suffers Horace more in wrong translations
By wits, than critics in as wrong quotations.
See Dionysius [35] Homer's thoughts refine,
And call new beauties forth from every line!
Fancy and art in gay Petronius [36] please,
The scholar's learning, with the courtier's ease.
In grave Quintilian's [37] copious work, we find
The justest rules, and clearest method joined.   670

[34]Homer was supposedly born in the province of Maeonia.
[35]Greek rhetorician and critic of the first century B.C.
[36]Petronius Arbiter, supposed author of the *Satirae*, attached to the court of Nero.
[37]Reference to Quintilian's renowned work on oratory, *Institutio oratoria*.

'Thus useful arms in magazines we place,
All ranged in order, and disposed with grace;
But less to please the eye, than arm the hand,
Still fit for use, and ready at command.
    Thee, bold Longinus! [38] all the Nine inspire,
And bless their critic with a poet's fire:
An ardent judge, who, zealous in his trust,
With warmth gives sentence, yet is always just;
Whose own example strengthens all his laws;
And is himself that great Sublime he draws.   680
    Thus long succeeding critics justly reigned,
License repressed, and useful laws ordained.
Learning and Rome alike in empire grew,
And arts still followed where her eagles flew;
From the same foes, at last, both felt their doom,
And the same age saw learning fall, and Rome.
With tyranny, then superstition joined,
As that the body, this enslaved the mind;
Much was believed, but little understood,
And to be dull was construed to be good;   690
A second deluge learning thus o'er-run,
And the monks finished what the Goths begun.
    At length Erasmus, that great injured name,
(The glory of the priesthood, and the shame!)
Stemmed the wild torrent of a barb'rous age,
And drove those holy vandals off the stage.
    But see! each Muse, in Leo's golden days,[39]
Starts from her trance, and trims her withered bays;
Rome's ancient genius, o'er its ruins spread,
Shakes off the dust, and rears his rev'rend head.   700
Then sculpture and her sister arts revive;
Stones leaped to form, and rocks began to live;
With sweeter notes each rising temple rung;
A Raphael painted, and a Vida sung.
Immortal Vida! on whose honored brow
The poet's bays and critic's ivy grow:
Cremona [40] now shall ever boast thy name,
As next in place to Mantua, next in fame!

[38]For Longinus see Gilbert, *Literary Criticism, Plato to Dryden,* pp. 144–198.
[39]Leo X's papacy (1513–1521) was in the "golden days" of the Italian Renaissance.
[40]Bishop Vida, author of the treatise on epic poetry, was born at Cremona.

But soon by impious arms from Latium chased,
Their ancient bounds the banished Muses passed: 710
Thence arts o'er all the northern world advance,
But critic-learning flourished most in France;
The rules a nation, born to serve, obeys;
And Boileau still in right of Horace sways.
But we, brave Britons, foreign laws despised,
And kept unconquered, and uncivilized;
Fierce for the liberties of wit, and bold,
We still defied the Romans, as of old.
Yet some there were, among the sounder few
Of those who less presumed, and better knew,   720
Who durst assert the juster ancient cause,
And here restored wit's fundamental laws.
Such was the Muse whose rules and practice tell
"Nature's chief masterpiece is writing well."
Such was Roscommon, not more learned than good,
With manners gen'rous as his noble blood;
To him the wit of Greece and Rome was known,
And every author's merit, but his own.
Such late was Walsh [41]—the Muse's judge and friend,
Who justly knew to blame or to commend;   730
To failings mild, but zealous for desert;
The clearest head, and the sincerest heart.
This humble praise, lamented shade! receive;
This praise at least a grateful Muse may give:
The Muse whose early voice you taught to sing,
Prescribed her heights, and pruned her tender wing,
(Her guide now lost) no more attempts to rise,
But in low numbers short excursions tries;
Content if hence th' unlearned their wants may view,
The learned reflect on what before they knew: 740
Careless of censure, nor too fond of fame;
Still pleased to praise, yet not afraid to blame;
Averse alike to flatter or offend;
Not free from faults, nor yet too vain to mend.

[41]William Walsh, minor poet, one of Pope's personal friends. Undoubtedly
Pope's friendship colored his overly enthusiastic praise.

JOSEPH ADDISON

(1672–1719)

o☾ooo☽o

ADDISON WROTE FOR A WIDE AUDIENCE through the medium of the popular journals, particularly the *Tatler*, the *Spectator*, and the *Guardian*. Aside from the essays published in these magazines, there is some critical discussion in the *Remarks on Italy*, the *Dialogues on Medals*, the essays on Vergil's *Georgics*, the notes on Ovid's *Metamorphoses*, and the *Discourse on Ancient and Modern Learning*. The "Account of the Greatest English Poets" was written in 1694,[1] and he continued writing until his death in 1719.

It is to the *Spectator* papers that the student turns for Addison's mature criticism. A study of these essays might serve as a summary of the subject matter of aesthetics in early eighteenth-century England. Some of the papers ran continuously from issue to issue or week to week; others were complete within themselves. Among the more carefully constructed criticisms are those on the stage,[2] True and False Wit,[3] the Ballads,[4] *Paradise Lost*,[5] and the Pleasures of the Imagination.[6]

Addison's comments on comedy are, in the main, ethical in content; like Steele he disapproved of the corrupt drama written in imitation of Congreve and Wycherley. Some of the points discussed in the essays on tragedy are the use of the double plot, which Addison disliked; tragicomedy, which he termed "one of the most monstrous inventions that ever entered into a poet's thought"; and the use of rhyme in plays, with which he was not in sympathy.

The essays dealing with *Paradise Lost* have been edited by Professor Cook.[7] Early in the first paper of this series, Addison declares himself in sympathy with a freer and more historical type of criticism. The

---

[1]Addison was twenty-two when this poem was written and was none too well informed on his subject. Spence quotes Pope as saying that Addison himself thought it "a poor thing."

[2]The papers on tragedy are *Spectator*, nos. 39, 40, 42, and 44; on comedy 446; and isolated comments as in no. 35.

[3]*Spectator*, nos. 58–63.   [4]*Spectator*, nos. 70 and 74.

[5]*Spectator*, no. 267 and continuing with every Saturday paper through no. 369.

[6]*Spectator*, nos. 411–421.

[7]For a discussion of these papers see the introduction to *Criticisms on Paradise Lost*, ed. A. S. Cook (Boston, 1892).

genre of the epic at the moment seemed to mean little to him. "It will be sufficient to its perfection," he writes of *Paradise Lost*, "if it has in it all the beauties of the highest kind of poetry; and as for those who allege it is not a heroic poem, they advance no more to the diminution of it than if they should say Adam is not Aeneas, nor Eve, Helen."[8] Yet, in the next sentence, he turns his back on this more liberal attitude and returns to the classical rules. In general, throughout these papers Addison judges the poem by comparing it with the *Iliad* and the *Aeneid*.

In 1897 Basil Worsfold wrote enthusiastically of Addison's papers on the Pleasures of the Imagination[9]—too enthusiastically, in fact, later scholars have thought. Quite recently Clarence D. Thorpe has written on these papers, suggesting a more conservative estimate of the essays as original work but pointing out particularly their value as early psychological criticism.[10]

Addison's critical code was drawn from Aristotle, Horace, and Longinus, some of their tenets being considerably altered by having been filtered through such books as Le Bossu's *Traité du poéme épique*, Rapin's *Reflexions sur la poétique*, and Boileau's *L'Art poétique*. Still there are many evidences in his criticism of beliefs which are not in accord with neoclassical laws. Genius is above rules; poetic justice need not be observed in the drama; the old ballads have positive literary value; the wilder aspects of nature are the more interesting: these ideas were all promulgated by Addison, and they are more definitely of the late eighteenth and early nineteenth centuries than of the Queen Anne period. Also, Addison adapted philosophical material for critical purposes. Particularly is this true in the papers on the Pleasures of the Imagination, where he borrows from Locke's *Essay on Human Understanding* and occasionally from Bacon and Hobbes.

Addison wrote with little thought of setting up a new critical code. His primary aim was to improve the literary taste of the English public. Dr. Johnson explains the purpose of Addison's criticism. It was, he says, "to infuse literary curiosity, by gentle and unsuspected conveyance, into the gay, the idle, and the wealthy: he therefore presented knowledge in the most alluring form, not lofty and austere, but accessible and familiar. When he showed them their defects, he showed them likewise that they might be easily supplied. His attempt succeeded, inquiry was awakened, and comprehension expanded."[11] The arrangement

[8]*Spectator*, no. 267.
[9]Basil Worsfold, *Principles of Criticism* (London, 1897), pp. 55–107.
[10]Clarence D. Thorpe, "Addison's Theory of the Imagination as 'Perceptive Response'," *Papers of the Michigan Academy of Science, Arts, and Letters*, XXI (1935), 509–530.   [11]*Lives of the English Poets* (ed. Hill, Oxford, 1905), II, 146.

of material to suit a general audience was an important factor in shaping the form and spirit of Addison's criticism. He was primarily the teacher, and his criticism is adapted to suit that purpose.

BIBLIOGRAPHY

TEXT

Spectator, carefully corrected. 8 vols. London, 1754.

Spectator, with introduction and notes by G. A. Aitken. 8 vols. London, 1898.

Works, with notes by Richard Hurd. 6 vols. London, 1863–1869.

CRITICISM

Broadus, Edward Kemper, "Joseph Addison as a Literary Critic," *University Magazine* (Montreal), February, 1909.

Courthope, W. J., *Addison*. London, 1884. (English Men of Letters.)

Dobrée, Bonamy, "The First Victorian, Joseph Addison," in *Essays in Biography, 1680–1726*. London, 1925.

Johnson, Samuel, *Life of Addison*, with introduction and notes by F. Ryland. London, 1893.

Kabelmann, Karl, *Joseph Addisons litterarische Kritik im "Spectator."* Rostock, 1900.

Sande, C. L. E., *Die Grundlagen der literarischen Kritik bei Joseph Addison.* Weimar, 1906.

Thorpe, Clarence D., "Addison's Theory of the Imagination as 'Perceptive Response'," *Papers of the Michigan Academy of Science, Arts, and Letters*, XXI (1935), 509–530.

Tickell, Thomas, "Life of Joseph Addison," in Edward Arber, *An English Garner*, VI, 513–522. The Preface to the first edition of Addison's *Works*, 1721.

THE SPECTATOR (selections)

[Concerning Original Genius][1]

. . . Cui mens divinior, atque os
Magna sonaturum, des nominis hujus honorem.</i>[2]
Horace, <i>Satires</i>, I, iv, 43–44.</div>

There is no character more frequently given to a writer than that of being a genius. I have heard many a little sonneteer

---

[1] *Spectator*, no. 160, Monday, September 3, 1711.

[2] "To him who possesses a mind more divinely inspired and whose lips are about to resound great things, give honor to his name."

called a *fine genius*. There is not an heroic scribbler in the nation that has not his admirers who think him a *great genius;* and as for your smatterers in tragedy, there is scarce a man among them who is not cried up by one or other for a *prodigious genius.*

My design in this paper is to consider what is properly a great genius, and to throw some thoughts together on so uncommon a subject.

Among great geniuses, those few draw the admiration of all the world upon them, and stand up as the prodigies of mankind, who by the mere strength of natural parts and without any assistance of art or learning have produced works that were the delight of their own times and the wonder of posterity.[3] There appears something nobly wild and extravagant in these great natural geniuses that is infinitely more beautiful than all the turn and polishing of what the French call *bel esprit*, by which they would express a genius refined by conversation, reflection, and the reading of the most polite authors. The greatest genius which runs through the arts and sciences, takes a kind of tincture from them and falls unavoidably into imitation.

Many of these great natural geniuses, that were never disciplined and broken by rules of art, are to be found among the ancients, and in particular among those of the more eastern parts of the world. Homer has innumerable flights that Vergil was not able to reach, and in the Old Testament we find several passages more elevated and sublime than any in Homer. At the same time that we allow a greater and more daring genius to the ancients, we must own that the greatest of them very much failed in, or, if you will, that they were much above the nicety and correctness of the moderns. In their similitudes and allusions, provided there was a likeness, they did not much trouble themselves about the decency of the comparison. Thus, Solomon resembles the nose of his beloved to the tower of Lebanon which looketh toward Damascus; as the coming of a thief in the night is a similitude of the same kind in the New Testament. It would be endless to make collections of this nature. Homer illustrates

---

[3]Cf. Pope, Preface to the translation of the *Iliad* for another discussion of innate genius; also compare Dryden's lines—

> Time, place, and action may with pains be wrought,
> But genius must be born, and never can be taught.

from the prefatory poem for *The Double Dealer* (1693), ll. 59–60.

one of his heroes encompassed with the enemy, by an ass in a field of corn that has his sides belabored by all the boys of the village without stirring a foot for it; and another of them tossing to and fro in his bed and burning with resentment, to a piece of flesh broiled on the coals. This particular failure in the ancients opens a large field of raillery to the little wits, who can laugh at an indecency but not relish the sublime in these sorts of writings. The present Emperor of Persia, conformable to this eastern way of thinking, amidst a great many pompous titles, denominates himself the *Sun of Glory*, and the *Nutmeg of Delight*. In short, to cut off all caviling against the ancients, and particularly those of the warmer climates, who had most heat and life in their imaginations, we are to consider that the rule of observing what the French call the *bienséance* [4] in an allusion, has been found out of latter years and in the colder regions of the world; where we would make some amends for our want of force and spirit by a scrupulous nicety and exactness in our compositions. Our countryman Shakespeare was a remarkable instance of this first kind of great geniuses.

I cannot quit this head without observing that *Pindar* was a great genius of the first class, who was hurried on by a natural fire and impetuosity to vast conceptions of things and noble sallies of imagination. At the same time, can anything be more ridiculous than for men of a sober and moderate fancy to imitate this poet's way of writing in those monstrous compositions which go among us under the name of Pindarics? [5] When I see people copying works, which, as Horace has represented them, are singular in their kind and inimitable; when I see men following irregularities by rule, and by the little tricks of art straining after

[4] Cf. Boileau, *L'Art poétique*, III, 122–123.

[5] For other criticisms of these odes, see *Spectator*, nos. 58 and 147. Later Johnson was to say of Prior that "his poems are written without regularity of measure, for when he commenced poet we had not recovered from our Pindaric infatuation." (*Lives, op. cit.*, II, 210); and of Watts that his odes were "deformed by the Pindaric folly then prevailing, and written with such neglect of all metrical rules as it is with-out example among the ancients" (*ibid.*, III, 303).

Cf. Sidney, Sonnet III:

> Let dainty wits cry on the Sisters nine,
> That, bravely masked, their fancies may be told;
> Or, Pindar's apes, flaunt they in phrases fine,
> Enam'ling with pied flowers their thoughts of gold;
> Or else let them in statelier glory shine,
> Ennobling new-found tropes with problems old;
> Or with strange similes enrich each line
> Of herb or beast with Ind or Afric hold.

the most unbounded flights of nature, I cannot but apply to them
that passage in Terence:

> . . . *incerta haec si tu postules*
> *Ratione certa facere, nihilo plus agas,*
> *Quam si des operam, ut cum ratione insanias.*[6]

In short, a modern Pindaric writer compared with Pindar is
like a sister among the Camisars [7] compared with Vergil's
Sybil. There is the distortion, grimace and outward figure, but
nothing of that divine impulse which raises the mind above
itself and makes the sounds more than human.

There is another kind of great geniuses which I shall place in
a second class, not as I think them inferior to the first, but only
for distinction's sake as they are of a different kind. This second
class of great geniuses are those that have formed themselves by
rules and submitted the greatness of their natural talents to the
corrections and restraints of art. Such among the Greeks were
Plato and Aristotle; among the Romans, Vergil and Tully;
among the English, Milton and Sir Francis Bacon.

The genius in both these classes of authors may be equally
great, but shows itself after a different manner. In the first it is
like a rich soil in a happy climate that produces a whole wilderness of noble plants rising in a thousand beautiful landscapes
without any certain order or regularity. In the other it is the
same rich soil under the same happy climate that has been laid
out in walks and parterres, and cut into shape and beauty by the
skill of the gardener.

The great danger in these latter kind of geniuses is lest they
cramp their own abilities too much by imitation and form themselves altogether upon models, without giving the full play to

[6]"If you would ask to do these uncertain things in a certain way, you would no
more accomplish it than if you should try to be insane with reason" (Terence, *Eunu-
chus*, I, i, 16–18).

[7]Members of a fanatic religious sect, originally of the Cevennes in France, but
known in England as the French Prophets. See *Tatler*, nos. 11 and 257; also Shaftesbury, *Characteristics* (edited by John M. Robertson, New York, 1900, I, 21–22):
"I am told, for certain, that they are at this very time [1707] the subject of a choice
droll or puppet-show at Bart'lemy Fair. There, doubtless, their strange voices and
involuntary agitations are admirably well acted, by the motions of wires and inspiration of pipes. . . . And whilst Bart'lemy Fair is in possession of this privilege,
I dare stand security to our National Church that no sect of enthusiasts, no new
venders of prophecy or miracles, shall ever get the start, or put her to the trouble
of trying her strength with them."

their own natural parts. An imitation of the best authors is not to compare with a good original, and I believe we may observe that very few writers make an extraordinary figure in the world who have not something in their way of thinking or expressing themselves that is peculiar to them and entirely their own.

It is odd to consider what great geniuses are sometimes thrown away upon trifles.

"I once saw a shepherd," says a famous Italian author, "who used to divert himself in his solitudes with tossing up eggs and catching them again without breaking them. In which he had arrived to so great a degree of perfection that he would keep up four at a time for several minutes together playing in the air, and falling into his hands by turns. I think," says the author, "I never saw a greater severity than in this man's face; for by his wonderful perseverence and application, he had contracted the seriousness and gravity of a privy councilor; and I could not but reflect with myself that the same assiduity and attention, had they been rightly applied, might have made him a greater mathematician than Archimedes."

[Concerning the Development of Fine Taste][1]

Musaeo contingens cuncta lepore.[2]

Lucretius, I, 933

Gratian[3] very often recommends the *fine taste* as the utmost perfection of an accomplished man. As this word arises very often in conversation, I shall endeavor to give some account of it, and to lay down rules how we may know whether we are possessed of it, and how we may acquire that fine taste of writing, which is so much talked of among the polite world.[4]

Most languages make use of this metaphor to express that faculty of the mind which distinguishes all the most concealed faults and nicest perfections in writing. We may be sure this metaphor would not have been so general in all tongues, had

[1] *Spectator*, no. 409, Thursday, June 19, 1712.
[2] "Touching everything with the charm of the Muses."
[3] Gratian (1601–1658), author of *Agudeza y arte de ingenio* and *El Oráculo manual*. *The Courtier's Oracle* (1685) and *The Art of Prudence* (1702) were translations of the *El Oráculo*. The style of Lyly is associated with the type of writing advocated in Gratian's works.
[4] See *Covent Garden Journal*, no. 10, in which Fielding deals with the question of taste. He describes it as a "nice harmony between the imagination and the judgment."

there not been a very great conformity between that mental taste which is the subject of this paper, and that sensitive taste which gives us a relish of every different flavor that affects the palate. Accordingly we find there are as many degrees of refinement in the intellectual faculty as in the sense which is marked out by this common denomination.

I knew a person who possessed the one in so great a perfection that, after having tasted ten different kinds of tea, he would distinguish, without seeing the color of it, the particular sort which was offered him; and not only so, but any two sorts of them that were mixed together in an equal proportion; nay, he has carried the experiment so far as, upon tasting the composition of three different sorts, to name the parcels from whence the three several ingredients were taken. A man of a fine taste in writing will discern, after the same manner, not only the general beauties and imperfections of an author, but discover the several ways of thinking and expressing himself which diversify him from all other authors, with the several foreign infusions of thought and language, and the particular authors from whom they were borrowed.

After having thus far explained what is generally meant by a fine taste in writing, and shown the propriety of the metaphor which is used on this occasion, I think I may define it to be *that faculty of the soul which discerns the beauties of an author with pleasure and the imperfections with dislike.* If a man would know whether he is possessed of this faculty, I would have him read over the celebrated works of antiquity, which have stood the test of so many different ages and countries; or those works among the moderns which have the sanction of the politer part of our contemporaries. If upon the perusal of such writings he does not find himself delighted in an extraordinary manner, or if, upon reading the admired passages in such authors, he finds a coldness and indifference in his thoughts, he ought to conclude, not (as is too usual among tasteless readers) that the author wants those perfections which have been admired in him, but that he himself wants the faculty of discovering them.

He should, in the second place, be very careful to observe whether he tastes the distinguishing perfections, or—if I may be allowed to call them so—the specific qualities of the author whom he peruses; whether he is particularly pleased with Livy for his manner of telling a story, with Sallust for his entering into those internal principles of action which arise from the characters and manners of the persons he describes, or with Tacitus for his displaying those outward motives of safety and interest which gave birth to the whole series of transactions which he relates.

He may likewise consider how differently he is affected by the same thought which presents itself in a great writer, from what he is when he finds it delivered by a person of an ordinary genius. For there is as much difference in apprehending a thought clothed in Cicero's language and that of a common author as in seeing an object by the light of a taper or by the light of the sun.

It is very difficult to lay down rules for the acquirement of such a taste as that I am here speaking of. The faculty must in some degree be born with us, and it very often happens that those who have other qualities in perfection are wholly void of this. One of the most eminent mathematicians of the age has assured me that the greatest pleasure he took in reading Vergil was in examining *Aeneas* his voyage by the map; as I question not but many a modern compiler of history would be delighted with little more in that divine author than the bare matters of fact.

But, notwithstanding this faculty must in some measure be born with us, there are several methods for cultivating and improving it, and without which it will be very uncertain, and of little use to the person that possesses it. The most natural method for this purpose is to be conversant among the writings of the most polite authors. A man who has any relish for fine writing either discovers new beauties, or receives stronger impressions from the masterly strokes of a great author every time he peruses him; besides that he naturally wears himself into the same manner of speaking and thinking.

Conversation with men of a polite genius is another method for improving our natural taste. It is impossible for a man of the greatest parts to consider anything in its whole extent and in all its variety of lights. Every man, besides those general observations which are to be made upon an author, forms several reflections that are peculiar to his own manner of thinking; so that conversation will naturally furnish us with hints which we did not attend to, and make us enjoy other men's parts and reflections as well as our own. This is the best reason I can give for the observation which several have made, that men of great genius in

the same way of writing seldom rise up singly, but at certain
periods of time appear together, and in a body; as they did at
Rome in the reign of Augustus, and in Greece about the age
of Socrates.   I cannot think that Corneille, Racine, Molière,
Boileau, La Fontaine, Bruyère, Bossu, or the Daciers would have
written so well as they have done, had they not been friends and
contemporaries.

It is likewise necessary for a man who would form to himself a
finished taste of good writing to be well versed in the works of
the best critics both ancient and modern.   I must confess that I
could wish there were authors of this kind who, besides the
mechanical rules which a man of very little taste may discourse
upon, would enter into the very spirit and soul of fine writing,
and show us the several sources of that pleasure which rises in
the mind upon the perusal of a noble work.   Thus although in
poetry it be absolutely necessary that the unities of time, place,
and action, with other points of the same nature, should be
thoroughly explained and understood; there is still something
more essential to the art, something that elevates and astonishes
the fancy, and gives a greatness of mind to the reader, which
few of the critics besides Longinus[5] have considered.

Our general taste in England is for epigram, turns of wit, and
forced conceits[6] which have no manner of influence, either for

[5]See Samuel H. Monk, *The Sublime: A Study of Critical Theories in Eighteenth-Century England* (New York, 1935) and A. Rosenberg, *Longinus in England bis zum Ende des 18. Jahrhunderts* (Weimar and Berlin, 1917), for discussions of the influence of Longinus.   The first English translation of Longinus, "*Peri Hupsous, or Dionysius Longinus of the Height of Eloquence* rendered out of the originall by J[ohn] H[all]," appeared in 1652.   Some idea of the enormous appeal of the treatise may be had from the number of references made to it by literary men.   Pope parodied it in *Peri Bathos: or, Of the Art of Sinking in Poetry* (1727), and Swift added his *On Poetry: A Rhapsody* (1733), in which he satirized the current vogue for the work:

> A forward critic often dupes us
> With sham quotations *Peri Hupsous:*
> And if we have not read Longinus,
> Will magisterially outshine us.
> Then lest with Greek he over run ye,
> Procure the book for love or money,
> Translated from Boileau's translation,
> And quote quotation on quotation.

See Gilbert, *Literary Criticism, Plato to Dryden*, pp. 144–198.
[6]Mulgrave writes, "They sigh in simile, and die in rhyme" (*An Essay on Poetry*, 201).   Voltaire attempted to change his style in *An Essay on Epick Poetry* (1727) to conform with what he believed to be the accepted English vogue.   "The style besides is after the English fashion; so many similes, so many things which appear but easy and familiar here, would seem too low to your wits of Paris" (Foulet, *Correspondance de Voltaire*, pp. 145 ff).

the bettering or enlarging the mind of him who reads them, and have been carefully avoided by the greatest writers, both among the ancients and moderns. I have endeavored in several of my speculations to banish this Gothic taste which has taken possession among us. I entertained the town for a week together with an essay upon wit,[7] in which I endeavored to detect several of those false kinds which have been admired in the different ages of the world; and at the same time to show wherein the nature of true wit consists. I afterwards gave an instance of the great force which lies in a natural simplicity of thought to affect the mind of the reader, from such vulgar pieces as have little else besides this single qualification to recommend them. I have likewise examined the works of the greatest poet which our nation or perhaps any other has produced, and particularized most of those rational and manly beauties which give a value to that divine work.[8] I shall next Saturday enter upon an essay *On the Pleasures of the Imagination*,[9] which, though it shall consider the subject at large, will perhaps suggest to the reader what it is that gives a beauty to many passages of the finest writers both in prose and verse. As an undertaking of this nature is entirely new, I question not but it will be received with candor.

[7]*Spectator*, nos. 58–63. [8]See above, Addison, page 24, n. 5. [9]*Spectator*, nos. 411–421.

FRANÇOIS MARIE AROUET
de VOLTAIRE

(1694–1778)

o◯○○◯o

VOLTAIRE WROTE his *Essay on Epic Poetry* under interesting and complicated circumstances. Dr. Florence Donnell White has painstakingly traced out the story for us and the best we can do in a brief note is to summarize a few of her discoveries and conclusions.[1]

Following a quarrel with the Chevalier de Rohan-Chabot in 1726, when Voltaire was in his thirty-second year and a very successful man, he was thrown into the Bastille and finally exiled from Paris. He asked permission to go to England and arrived there in 1726. Voltaire's epic poem, *Henriade*, had been acclaimed in France and was known among a few literary men across the Channel. Since this poem deals with Henry IV's visit to England and the part played by Queen Elizabeth, it was natural that Voltaire should attempt to interest the English in his work and thereby make some amends for his severe financial losses.

It now seems certain that in order to prepare the English audience for his epic, and of course to advertise the poem itself, Voltaire wrote two essays, published in a single volume in 1727, under the title: *An Essay upon the Civil Wars of France, extracted from curious Manuscripts and also upon the Epick Poetry of the European Nations, from Homer down to Milton, by Mr. de Voltaire.* In all, this work seems to have passed through five editions, four English and one Irish, between 1727–1761. And it did accomplish its immediate object of selling the English edition of the *Henriade*.

That Voltaire should be able to write the essay in English seems surprising at first, but Dr. White has established the fact that Voltaire did write it himself, with probably only a minimum of assistance. The

---

[1] *Voltaire's Essay on Epic Poetry: A Study and an Edition* (Albany, New York, 1915). (A Bryn Mawr doctor's dissertation.) The edition is of the English version, with footnote comments on the differences between this and the French version.

following year it was translated into French, much against Voltaire's wishes, by a hack translator, Abbé Guyot Desfontaines. Voltaire probably objected chiefly because he had so lavishly praised the English, particularly the great epic poet of England, Milton, and contrasted the lack of freedom in France with the existing freedom in England. The essay would, he knew, offend the French church, state, and public. But Voltaire also claimed that Desfontaines had made a poor translation and that he had already begun a French version himself.[2]

Aside from these practical considerations, there seems little doubt that Voltaire did wish to give the French a longer, more systematic version which would contribute to the lasting fame which he hoped to achieve with his epic poem. After many delays, Voltaire brought out his French version in 1733, though retaining parts (which he apparently did not regard as important enough to revise) of the Desfontaines translation.

It is not necessary to summarize the argument of the essay here, for our translated extract of the French version given below contains the main themes of both the English and French essays. Suffice it to say, therefore, that, aside from the superiority in organization and presentation, the French version differs from the English primarily in its less fulsome, but probably more sincere, praise of England, shows some hostility toward Milton now that the writer is back in France, is less critical of Italian taste, and tries in various ways to conciliate the French people. The indiscreet contrast of English and French liberty is omitted, and he even accounts for the lack of a great French epic by saying that no great French writer has ever attempted the epic.

Even in the final version, Voltaire's *Essay on Epic Poetry* is inconsistent, incomplete, and not one of the world's great contributions to literary criticism, but as the product of one of the world's greatest writers and of considerable importance in the history of criticism, it is well worth serious study today. In his sections on Homer, Vergil, Tasso, Trissino, Ariosto, Camoëns, Ercilla, and Milton, Voltaire made, as he intended, a lasting contribution to comparative literature—and the essay is a forerunner of literary cosmopolitanism in France, which it did much to bring about.

Miss Helena Brawley Watts's translation of the French version of the *Essay on Epic Poetry*, which follows, is the only one in English which, to our knowledge, has been published.

[2]White, *op. cit.*, 41.

BIBLIOGRAPHY

TEXT

Œuvres complètes. 70 vols. Paris, 1784–1789.
——, ed. by L. Moland. 52 vols. Paris, 1877–1885.

TRANSLATIONS

Critical Essays on Dramatic Poetry, with notes. London, 1761.
Essay on Epic Poetry, ed. by Florence Donnell White (version by Voltaire himself). Albany, New York, 1915. (A Bryn Mawr dissertation.)
Letters Concerning the English Nation. London, 1733.
——, with introduction by Charles Whibley. London, 1926.
Selections; with Explanatory Comment upon His Life and Works, by George R. Havens. New York, 1925.
Voltaire and the Enlightenment; selections newly tr. with an introduction by N. L. Loney. New York, 1931.
Works, tr. by T. Smollett and others. 35 vols. London, 1770.

BIOGRAPHY AND CRITICISM

Ballantyne, Archibald, *Voltaire's Visit to England.* London, 1919.
Barr, Mary Margaret, *A Century of Voltaire Study; a Bibliography of Writings on Voltaire, 1825–1925.* New York, 1929.
Brandes, Georg, *Voltaire,* tr. by Otto Kruger and Pierce Butler. New York, 1930.
Chase, Cleveland Bruce, *The Young Voltaire.* New York, 1926.
Collins, John Churton, *Voltaire, Montesquieu, and Rousseau in England.* London, 1908.
Harper, Henry H., *Voltaire.* Boston, 1934.
Lounsbury, Thomas R., *Shakespeare and Voltaire.* New York, 1902.
Lowenstein, Robert, *Voltaire as an Historian of Seventeenth-Century French Drama,* in *Studies in Romance Literatures and Languages,* Vol. XXV. Johns Hopkins Press, 1935.
MacDonald, Mrs. Frederika, *Studies in the France of Voltaire and Rousseau.* London, 1895.
Maurois, André, *Voltaire,* tr. by Hamish Miles. New York, 1932.
Morley, John Viscount, *Voltaire.* London, 1919.
Noyes, Alfred, *Voltaire.* New York, 1936.
Parton, James, *Life of Voltaire.* 2 vols. Boston, 1882. A most detailed biography.
Sainte-Beuve, Charles Augustin, *Portraits of the Eighteenth Century, Historic and Literary,* with a critical introduction by Edmond Sherer. New York, 1905.

ESSAY ON EPIC POETRY (*selection*)[1]

1733

Chapter I

Concerning the Different Tastes of People

Almost all the arts are encumbered by rules, which are for the most part useless and false. There are books of directions everywhere but very few practical examples. Nothing is easier than to speak with authority of things which one cannot perform; there are a hundred poetics for every poem.[2] There are always teachers of oratory but almost never an orator. The world is filled with critiques, which, by the aid of commentaries, definitions, and distinctions, have succeeded in obscuring the simplest and clearest knowledge. . . . Each science and art has its own unintelligible jargon which appears to have been devised only to make it inaccessible. How many barbarous names, how many pedantic trivialities were recently stuffed into the head of a young man, in giving him in one or two years an utterly false conception of eloquence, when he might have acquired a real knowledge of it in a comparatively short time through the reading of a few excellent books. The method of teaching the art of reasoning, which has been used so long, is quite opposed to the talent of reasoning.

The commentators and critics have been particularly lavish with their books of directions to the poets. They have written volumes of criticism on a few lines of poetic fancy. . . . They have talked learnedly concerning things which should be felt with ecstasy; and, even if their rules were correct, of what little benefit they are! Homer, Vergil, Tasso, and Milton have followed almost entirely their own genius. Many rules and limitations would have served only to encumber the progress of these great men and would have been of little assistance to those who

---

[1] The French text used for this translation is that of *Œuvres complètes* (Paris, 1877–1885), VIII, 305–314. All citations in this anthology are to that edition.

[2] This is not to be taken as a quip at Boileau's *Art of Poetry*, which Voltaire admired. ". . . we have very few poets who are always elegant and always correct. Perhaps there are in France only Racine and Boileau who have a continued elegance . . . you will not find a defective word nor a word out of place [in the *Art of Poetry*]" ("Vers et poésie," in *Dictionnaire philosophique*, *Œuvres*, XX, 562). Later in the same article he urges his readers: "Let us not tire of citing the *Art of Poetry;* it is the code not only of poets but also of prose writers" (*Œuvres*, XX, 569).

lacked talent. Those who run in a race should not be hobbled. Many critics have sought for rules in Homer which are assuredly not there. Since the *Iliad* and the *Odyssey* are of entirely different types, the critics have had much difficulty in reconciling Homer with himself. To make the confusion even greater, Vergil used the plan of the *Iliad* and the *Odyssey* in composing the *Aeneid*, forcing the critics to establish still other rules to make Vergil agree with Homer. . . .

If a savant or one presuming to that title, and there are many such, should tell you: "An epic poem is a long story invented to teach a moral truth; in it the hero performs some lofty deed, with the aid of the gods, in the space of a year," you would be forced to answer: "Your definition is entirely false; the *Iliad* of Homer may fit your rules; but the English have an epic poem whose hero, far from succeeding in such a noble enterprise in a year, even by divine assistance, is deceived by both the Devil and his wife in one day and is thereupon expelled from terrestrial paradise." This poem, nevertheless, is ranked by the English as the equal of the *Iliad;* in fact, many people prefer it to Homer, with some apparent justification.[3]

But, you ask me, could not an epic poem then be the narration of a disastrous enterprise? No, that definition would be more false than the other. The *Oedipus* of Sophocles, the *Cinna* of Corneille, the *Athalie* of Racine, the *Julius Caesar* of Shakespeare,[4] the *Cato* of Addison, the *Merope* of Marquis Scippion Massei, and the *Roland* of Quinault are all excellent tragedies, and, I dare say, all of different styles. A critic would have to vary his definition of tragedy to fit each of them.

It is necessary in all of the arts to guard against fallacious definitions which exclude the unknown for which custom has not yet set a standard. The arts, especially those which depend upon imagination, are not like the material universe. We can define metals, minerals, elements, and animals because their nature is always the same; the works of man change like the imaginations which produce them. . . . The same nation is not recognizable at the end of three or four centuries. In the arts which depend purely on the imagination, there are as many revolutions as in

[3]See Voltaire's article on "Homer" in "Épopée," in *Dictionnaire philosophique* (*Œuvres*, XVIII, 567–570).
[4]For Voltaire's part in the Shakespearian controversy, see Thomas R. Lounsbury, *Shakespeare and Voltaire* (1920); Jusserand, *Shakespeare en France* (1898).

governments; they change in a thousand ways while one is trying to fix them. . . .

But to return to examples which have a closer connection with our subject. What was Greek tragedy?—a chorus which was on the stage almost continually, no division of acts, very little action, and still less plot. In France tragedy is ordinarily a series of conversations in five acts, containing a love intrigue. In England, tragedy is purely a matter of action; and, if the authors of that country were to combine more natural style, propriety, and regularity with the activity which gives life to their plays, they would soon surpass the Greek and the French. When one examines all of the other arts, there is not one which does not receive some particular twist which typifies the genius of the countries which have cultivated them.

What idea then should we form of epic poetry? The word *epic* comes from the Greek ἔπος, which means *discourse*. Custom alone has connected the word with the narration of heroic adventures in verse; as the Latin word *oratio*, which first meant discourse, later came to mean only formal speeches; and so the title of *Imperator*, which used to belong only to generals in the army was later conferred only on the sovereigns of Rome.

The epic poem, examined in itself, is thus a narration in verse of heroic adventures. Whether the action is simple or complex; whether it is completed in a month or in a year; or whether it lasts for a longer time; whether the scene is fixed in one place, as in the *Iliad*, or whether the hero sails the seven seas, as in the *Odyssey;* whether the action is fortunate or unfortunate; whether the hero is as angry as Achilles or as devoted as Aeneas; whether the poem has one principal character or many; whether the action takes place on land or on sea; upon the shore of Africa as in the *Lusiad*,[5] or in America as in the *Araucana;*[6] in Heaven, in Hell, or beyond the limits of our world as in *Paradise Lost*—it is of no consequence. It will still be an epic poem, an heroic poem unless one finds a new title adapted to its particular merits. If you have scruples, said the celebrated Mr. Addison, about giving the title of epic to the *Paradise Lost* of Milton, call it, if you like, a divine poem. Give it any name you please, provided you admit that it is a work as admirable in its type as the *Iliad*.[7]

[5]Don Luiz de Camoëns (1524–1580), *Lusiadas* (1572).
[6]Alonso Ercilla y Zúñiga (1533–1596), *Araucana* (1569–1590).
[7]Addison, *Spectator*, no. 267. See above, introductory note to Addison.

Never quarrel over names. Shall I refuse to call the plays of Congreve or of Calderon comedies because they do not conform to our rules? [8] The scope of the arts is very broad. A man who has read only the classical authors is contemptuous of all that is written in the modern languages. One who knows only the language of his own country is like the man who has never left the court of France and who declares that the rest of the world is a sorry trifle and that whoever has seen Versailles has seen everything.

But the point of the controversy is in understanding upon what the cultured nations agree. An epic poem should be founded upon judgment and embellished by imagination. Anything that has good sense belongs to all the nations of the world. Nations agree that a single and simple action, which is developed easily and gradually and which does not require tiresome attention, is more pleasing than a confused collection of unrelated adventures. It is generally desirable to add to this unity a variety of episodes which are developed and well-proportioned like the limbs of the body. [9] The more elevated the action is, the more it will delight everyone who is fascinated by things that lie beyond the bounds of ordinary life. It is necessary for the action to be moving, for all hearts want to be touched. . . . The epic should be complete, because no one would be satisfied if he received only part of what was promised. These are some of the principal rules which nature dictates to all of the nations which cultivate literature. But the choice of the fable, the intervention of celestial power, the nature of the episodes depend on custom and taste. It is here that there are a thousand opinions and no general rules.

But, you ask, are there no canons of taste equally accepted by all nations? There are without doubt a very great number of them. Since the Renaissance of literature, when the ancients were taken for models, Homer, Demosthenes, Vergil, and Cicero have, in some manner, united all the people of Europe under their government and have made all the different nations a single republic of letters. But in the midst of this general agreement each country has introduced a particular taste of its own.

[8] Cf. "rules" in the index.

[9] Cf. Addison, *Spectator*, no. 267: "The second qualification required in the action of an epic poem is, that it should be an entire action. An action is entire when it is complete in all its parts; or as Aristotle describes it, when it consists of a beginning, a middle and an end." See also Le Bossu, *Traité du poème épique* (1675), I, 119, 142.

In the best modern writers, the character of their country is
discernible through the imitation of the ancients; their flowers
and fruits are warmed and ripened by the same sun, but they
receive different tastes, colors, and forms from the land which
nourishes them. An Italian, a Frenchman, an Englishman, or a
Spaniard is as easily recognized by his style as by the contours of
his face, his pronunciation, and his manners. The softness and
the sweetness of the Italian language are insinuated into the
genius of the Italian authors. Pomp of words, metaphors, and
majesty of style are, it appears to me, generally speaking the
characteristics of the Spanish writers. Force, energy, and boldness are more particular to the English, who love allegories and
similes above everything else. The French have clarity, exactness, and elegance. They have neither the force of the English,
which appears to them as gigantic and monstrous violence, nor
the Italian softness, which seems to them an effeminate quality.
All these differences result from the dislike and scorn which
nations have for one another. In order to see the differences in
taste of neighboring peoples, consider their style.

The Italians approve of the verses from the first canto of *Jerusalem Delivered*, which are in imitation of Lucretius.

> So we, if children young diseased we find,
> Anoint with sweets the vessel's foremost parts
> To make them taste the portions sharp we give;
> They drink deceived, and so deceived, they live (Fairfax).[10]

This comparison of the charms of a fable with the bitter medicine given to children in a cup edged with sweet would not be
allowed by the French in an epic poem. We read with pleasure
in Montaigne that it is necessary to season food to the taste of a
child. This figure pleases us in familiar writing, but it does not
have sufficient dignity to suit the majesty of an epic.

Here is another quotation universally approved, and which
merits to be; it is in the thirty-sixth stanza of canto sixteen of
Jerusalem Delivered, where Armida begins to suspect that her
lover has deserted her.

> "Whither, O cruel! leavest thou me alone?"
> She would have cried, her grief her speeches stayed,

[10]*Così all' egro fanciul porgiamo aspersi*
Di soave licor gli orli del vaso:
Succhi amari ingannato intanto ei beve,
E dall' inganno suo vita riceve.

So that her woeful words are backward gone,
And in her heart a bitter echo made; (Fairfax).[11]

These lines are very touching and natural in the Italian; but
when one translates them exactly into French, they are nonsense.
"Elle voulait crier: Cruel, pourquoi me laisses-tu seule? Mais
la douleur ferma le chemin à sa voix; et ces paroles douloureuses
reculèrent avec plus d'amertume, et retentirent sur son cœur."
Take another example from one of the most sublime parts of
that singular poem of Milton of which I have already spoken.
It is the description of Satan and of the infernal regions.

> . . . round he throws his baleful eyes
> That witnessed huge affliction and dismay
> Mixed with obdúrate pride and steadfast hate:
> At once, as far as angels ken, he views
> The dismal situation waste and wild,
> A dungeon horrible, on all sides round
> As one great furnace flamed; yet from those flames
> No light, but rather darkness visible
> Served only to discover sights of woe,
> Regions of sorrow, doleful shades, where peace
> And rest can never dwell, hope never comes
> That comes to all.[12]

"Il promène de tous côtés ses tristes yeux, dans lesquels sont
peints le désespoir et l'horreur, avec l'orgueil et l'irréconciliable
haine. Il voit d'un coup d'œil, aussi loin que les regards des
chérubins peuvent percer, ce séjour épouvantable, ces déserts
désolés, ce donjon immense, enflammé comme une fournaise
énorme. Mais de ces *flammes il ne sortait point de lumière; ce sont des
ténèbres visibles,* qui servent seulement à découvrir des spectacles
de désolation; des régions de douleur, dont jamais n'approchent
le repos ni la paix, où l'on ne connaît point l'espérance connue
partout ailleurs."
Antonio de Solís, in his excellent *History of the Conquest of
Mexico,*[13] after describing the place in which Montezuma consulted his gods as a large subterranean vault, adds: "O permitian

---

[11]*Volea gridar: Dove, o crudel, me sola
Lasci? Ma il varco al suon chiuse il dolore:
Si che torno la flebile parola
Piu amara indietro a rimbombar sul core.*

[12]*Paradise Lost,* I, 56–67.

[13]Antonio de Solís y Rivadeneyra (1610–1686), Spanish poet, historian, and
dramatist.

solamente la [luz], que bastava, para que se viesse la obscuri-
dad." [14] "Ou laissaient entrer seulement autant de jour qu'il en
fallait pour voir l'obscurité." These visible shades of Milton are
not condemned in England, and the Spanish do not criticize the
same expression in Solis. The French would certainly not allow
similar liberties. There may be an excuse for these licenses in
expression, but the French admit nothing that needs an excuse.

In order to illustrate this difference in taste further, I shall take
an example from the church. When Father Bourdaloue preaches
before an assemblage of the Anglican faith, he enlivens his discourse with pathos and noble gestures. He cries: "Yes, Christians, you have had good intentions; but the blood of the widow
whom you have abandoned; but the blood of the poor whom you
have allowed to be oppressed; but the blood of the miserable
whose cause you have not championed; that blood will fall upon
you, and your good intentions will only serve to strengthen its
voice in asking vengeance from God for your infidelity. Oh! My
dear listeners,—." These pathetic words spoken with vigor and
accompanied by eloquent gestures would force an English congregation to laughter; for, although they like bombastic torrents
of eloquence and high-sounding speeches on the stage, they want
unadorned simplicity in their sermons. In France a sermon is a
long declamation, carefully divided into three parts and delivered
with fervor; in England a sermon is a weighty dissertation, sometimes dry, which a man reads to his congregation with no gestures and without raising his voice.[15] In Italy it is a witty comedy.
This is to show the great difference in the tastes of nations.

There are many people who will not admit this; they will say
that reason and passion are the same everywhere. That is true,
but they are expressed differently. In every land, men have a
nose, two eyes, and a mouth; however, the combination of
features which is beautiful in France will not be considered
beautiful in Turkey; what is most charming in Asia and in Europe
will be looked upon as monstrous in Guinea. Since nature varies
so within herself, how can she be subjected to the general laws of
arts which are entirely governed by custom? This is in itself
inconstancy. If, then, we wish to understand the arts thoroughly,

[14]*Historia de la conquista de Méjico*, III, chap. XIV, col. 271, edition of 1704, folio
(first published in 1684): "Where only sufficient light to see the gloom was allowed
to enter."

[15]See Jonathan Swift, *A Letter to a Young Gentleman Lately Entered into Holy Orders*
(1721).

it is necessary first to understand the manner of their development in the different countries. It is not sufficient, in order to know the epic, to have read Vergil and Homer, as it is not sufficient from the viewpoint of tragedy to have read only Sophocles and Euripides.

We should admire that part of the ancients that is universally beautiful, and we should appropriate for ourselves all that is beautiful in their language and customs. It would be a ridiculous blunder to follow them literally in everything. We do not speak the same language; and our religion, which is nearly always the foundation of epic poetry, is opposed to the pagan mythology. Our customs are as different from those of the Trojan heroes as they are from those of the Americans. Our battles, our military maneuvers, and our fleets have not the slightest resemblance to theirs, and our philosophy is altogether contrary to the old. The invention of gunpowder, the compass, the printing press, and many other accomplishments have changed the universe for us. It is necessary to paint with true colors, as did the ancients, but it is not necessary to paint the same things.[16]

Homer pictures the gods drunk with wine and laughs at the ill grace with which Vulcan serves them with drinks. That was all very well in his time when the gods represented what fairies do in ours; but certainly no poet today would dare to describe a band of angels and saints drinking at a table. On the other hand, what would be said of an author who followed Vergil by using harpies to carry off the food of his heroes, or who transformed battered ships into beautiful nymphs? In short, let us admire the ancients, but let us not allow our admiration to become a deluded superstition. And let us not injure ourselves and nature by closing our eyes to the beauties which she scatters around, in order to look back and admire her ancient productions which we cannot judge with any degree of accuracy.

There are no Italian literary monuments which merit more attention than the *Jerusalem Delivered* of Tasso. Milton has as much honor in England as the great Newton; Camoëns is in Portugal what Milton is in England. It would doubtless be a great pleasure, as well as a great benefit, to a student of literature to examine all the epic poems of different kinds, created in

---

[16]This line in the English *Essay* first read "and an Epic Poet, being surrounded with so many novelties, must have but a small share of Genius, if he durst not be new himself" (White, *op. cit.*, p. 87).

periods and countries widely separated from each other. It seems to me that there is a profound satisfaction in considering living portraits of these illustrious personages—Greeks, Romans, Italians, English, all clothed, if I dare say it, in the manner of their countries.

It is an enterprise far above my abilities, so that I do not claim to portray them; I shall only attempt to sketch imperfectly a rough outline of their principal traits. It is for the reader to strengthen the frailties of the pattern; I shall only indicate. It will be his duty to judge; and his judgment will be just if he reads with impartiality, and if he disregards his academic prejudices and that false vanity which causes us to scorn everything that is not according to our customs. He will see the birth, progress, and decadence of art. . . . He will distinguish eternal and universal beauties from local and transient beauties which are admired in one country and scorned in another. He will not require of Ariosto what he would of an English or a Portuguese author, nor will he judge the *Iliad* by Perrault's comments. He will not allow himself to be tyrannized by Scaliger or Le Bossu, but he will draw his conclusion from nature and the examples which he has before his eyes; he will judge between the gods of Homer and the God of Milton, between Calypso and Dido, between Armida and Eve.

If the nations of Europe, instead of despising one another, would give less superficial consideration to the works and customs of their neighbors, not for the purpose of laughing at them but in order to profit by them, perhaps through this mutual exchange and observation there would be developed that general taste which is so futilely sought after.

HENRY FIELDING

(1707–1754)

∘◯∘∘◯∘

HENRY FIELDING did not write any work dealing exclusively with critical theory. It is even doubtful whether his incidental prefaces, dedications, and articles would have been given the consideration which they deserve had he not included the majority of them in *Tom Jones* and *Joseph Andrews* and claimed for himself the prerogative of setting up his own laws for the new medium in which he wrote. In the Preface to *Joseph Andrews* (1742) he gives his reasons for considering the book a comic prose epic.

> The epic, as well as the drama, is divided into tragedy and comedy. Homer, who was the father of this species of poetry, gave us a pattern of both these, though that of the latter kind is entirely lost; which, Aristotle tells us,[1] bore the same relation to comedy which his *Iliad* bears to tragedy. And perhaps, that we have no more instances of it among the writers of antiquity, is owing to the loss of this pattern, which had it survived, would have found its imitators equally with the other poems of this great original.
>
> And farther, as this poetry may be tragic or comic, I will not scruple to say it may be likewise either in verse or prose: for though it wants one particular, which the critic enumerates in the constituent parts of an epic poem, namely meter; yet, when any kind of writing contains all its other parts, such as fable, action, characters, sentiments, and diction, and is deficient in meter only; it seems, I think, reasonable to refer it to the epic, at least, as no critic hath thought proper to range it under other head, or to assign it a particular name to itself.

Each of the eighteen books of *Tom Jones* begins with a critical chapter in the serio-comic vein. In these Fielding gives several crusts to the critics and further explains the type of book he is writing, pointing out that it is the first time it has been attempted in English. He held a supreme contempt for the Grub Street critics, "the beaux, rakes,

[1]Aristotle, *Poetics*, IV.

Templars, wits, lawyers, mechanics, schoolboys, and fine ladies" who attempted to pass judgment on literary works,[2] but he constantly acknowledged his indebtedness to "Aristotle, Horace, and Longinus, among the ancients, . . . Dacier and Bossu among the French."

Fielding was a thorough rationalist, and if he could discover no reason for a classical rule, he was extremely apt to ridicule it. His various comments on the adherence to the unities of time and place in the drama are typical of his method of dealing with a rule which he thought unreasonable. "If Shakespeare had observed them," he writes of the unities, "he would have flown like a paper kite, not soared like an eagle."[3] The essence of Fielding's criticism was trained personal judgment.

BIBLIOGRAPHY

TEXT

Works, ed. with a biographical essay by Leslie Stephen.   10 vols. London, 1882.

CRITICISM

[Anon.], *An Essay on the New Species of Writing Founded by Mr. Fielding: with a Word or Two upon the Modern State of Criticism.* London, 1751.

Bissell, Frederick Olds, Jr., *Fielding's Theory of the Novel.* Ithaca, New York, 1933.

Blanchard, Frederick, *Fielding the Novelist: A Study in Historical Criticism.* Yale University Press, 1926.

Bosdorf, E., *Einstehungsgeschichte von Fieldings Joseph Andrews.* Weimar, 1908.

Cross, Wilbur L., *The Development of the English Novel.* New York, 1899.

——, *The History of Henry Fielding.* Yale University Press, 1918.

Dobson, Austin, *Fielding.* New York, 1907. (English Men of Letters.)

——, "Fielding's Library," *Eighteenth Century Vignettes.* London, 1892.

---

[2]See the *Covent Garden Journal*, no. 2. "I well know the present dreadful Condition of the great Empire of Letters; the State of Anarchy that prevails among Writers; and the great Revolution which hath lately happened in the Kingdom of Criticism; that the Constitutions of Aristotle, Horace, Longinus, and Bossu, under which the State of Criticism so long flourished, have been entirely neglected, and the Government usurped by a Set of Fellows entirely ignorant of all these Laws."

Laurence Sterne maintained the same skeptical attitude toward the modern critics. In *Tristram Shandy* (Bk. III, chap. XII), he writes that "a work of genius had better go to the devil at once, than stand to be pricked and tortured to death" by the race of critics who are "so hung round and *befetished* with the bobs and trinkets of criticism" that they are incapable of correct judgment. He sums up his opinion of the critics: "Of all the cants which are canted in this canting world—though the cant of hypocrites may be the worst—the cant of criticism is the most tormenting!"

[3]*Covent Garden Journal*, no. 62; see also introductory chapter of Bk. v of *Tom Jones.*

Morgan, C. E., *The Rise of the Novel of Manners: 1600–1740*. New York, 1911.

Radtke, B., *Henry Fielding als Kritiker*. Berlin, 1926.

Thornbury, Ethel M., *Henry Fielding's Theory of the Comic Prose Epic*, in *University of Wisconsin Studies in Language and Literature*, no. 30. Madison, 1931.

TOM JONES (*selections*)

1749

Book V, Chapter I

Of the Serious in Writing, and For What Purpose It Is Introduced

Peradventure there may be no parts in this prodigious work which will give the reader less pleasure in the perusing than those which have given the author the greatest pains in composing. Among these probably may be reckoned those initial essays which we have prefixed to the historical matter contained in every book; and which we have determined to be essentially necessary to this kind of writing, of which we have set ourselves at the head.

For this our determination we do not hold ourselves strictly bound to assign any reason, it being abundantly sufficient that we have laid it down as a rule necessary to be observed in all prosai-comi-epic writing. Who ever demanded the reasons of that nice unity of time or place which is now established to be so essential to dramatic poetry? What critic hath been ever asked why a play may not contain two days as well as one? Or why the audience (provided they travel, like electors, without any expense) may not be wafted fifty miles as well as five? Hath any commentator well accounted for the limitation which an ancient critic hath set to the drama, which he will have contain neither more nor less than five acts?[1] Or hath anyone living attempted to explain what the modern judges of our theaters mean by that word *low*, by which they have happily succeeded in banishing all humor from the stage, and have made the theater as dull as a drawing room? Upon all these occasions the world seems to have embraced a maxim of our law, viz. *cuicunque in arte sua perito credendum est;*[2] for it seems perhaps difficult to conceive that

[1] Cf. Johnson, Preface to Shakespeare, below, pp. 68–85.
[2] "Belief is to be given to every man who is skilled in his art."

anyone should have had enough of impudence to lay down dog-matical rules in any art or science without the least foundation. In such cases, therefore, we are apt to conclude there are sound and good reasons at the bottom, though we are unfortunately not able to see so far.

Now, in reality, the world have paid too great a compliment to critics, and have imagined them men of much greater pro-fundity than they really are. From this complacence, the critics have been emboldened to assume a dictatorial power, and have so far succeeded that they are now become the masters, and have the assurance to give laws to those authors from whose predeces-sors they originally received them.

The critic, rightly considered, is no more than the clerk, whose office it is to transcribe the rules and laws laid down by those great judges whose vast strength of genius hath placed them in the light of legislators, in the several sciences over which they presided. This office was all which the critics of old aspired to; nor did they ever dare to advance a sentence without supporting it by the authority of the judge from whence it was borrowed.

But in process of time, and in ages of ignorance, the clerk be-gan to invade the power and assume the dignity of his master. The laws of writing were no longer founded on the practice of the author, but on the dictates of the critic. The clerk became the legislator, and those very peremptorily gave laws whose business it was, at first, only to transcribe them.

Hence arose an obvious, and perhaps an unavoidable, error; for these critics, being men of shallow capacities, very easily mis-took mere form for substance. They acted as a judge would who should adhere to the lifeless letter of law and reject the spirit. Little circumstances, which were perhaps accidental in a great author, were by these critics considered to constitute his chief merit, and transmitted as essentials to be observed by all his successors. To these encroachments, time and ignorance, the two great supporters of imposture, gave authority; and thus many rules for good writing have been established which have not the least foundation in truth or nature; and which commonly serve for no other purpose than to curb and restrain genius, in the same manner as it would have restrained the dancing master had the many excellent treatises on that art laid it down as an essential rule that every man must dance in chains.

To avoid, therefore, all imputation of laying down a rule for posterity founded only on the authority of *ipse dixit*—for which, to say the truth, we have not the profoundest veneration—we shall here waive all the privilege above contended for, and proceed to lay before the reader the reasons which have induced us to intersperse these several digressive essays in the course of this work.

And here we shall of necessity be led to open a new vein of knowledge, which, if it hath been discovered, hath not, to our remembrance, been wrought on by any ancient or modern writer. This vein is no other than that of contrast, which runs through all the works of the creation, and may probably have a large share in constituting in us the idea of all beauty, as well natural as artificial: for what demonstrates the beauty and excellence of anything but its reverse? Thus the beauty of day, and that of summer, is set off by the horrors of night and winter. And, I believe, if it was possible for a man to have seen only the two former, he would have a very imperfect idea of their beauty.

But to avoid too serious an air; can it be doubted but that the finest woman in the world would lose all benefit of her charms in the eye of a man who had never seen one of another cast? The ladies themselves seem so sensible of this that they are all industrious to procure foils: nay, they will become foils to themselves; for I have observed (at Bath particularly) that they endeavor to appear as ugly as possible in the morning in order to set off that beauty which they intend to show you in the evening.

Most artists have this secret in practice, though some, perhaps, have not much studied the theory. The jeweler knows that the finest brilliant requires a foil; and the painter, by the contrast of his figures, often acquires great applause.

A great genius among us will illustrate this matter fully. I cannot, indeed, range him under any general head of common artists, as he hath a title to be placed among those

> *Inventas qui vitam excoluere per artes,*[3]
> Who by invented arts have life improved.

I mean here the inventor of that most exquisite entertainment called the English Pantomime.

This entertainment consisted of two parts, which the inventor distinguished by the names of the serious and the comic. The serious exhibited a certain number of heathen gods and heroes,

---

[3]Vergil, *Aeneid*, VI, 663.

who were certainly the worst and dullest company into which an audience was ever introduced, and (which was a secret known to few) were actually intended so to be, in order to contrast the comic part of the entertainment and to display the tricks of harlequin to the better advantage.

This was, perhaps, no very civil use of such personages; but the contrivance was, nevertheless, ingenious enough, and had its effect. And this will now plainly appear, if, instead of *serious* and *comic*, we supply the words *duller* and *dullest;* for the comic was certainly duller than anything before shown on the stage, and could be set off only by that superlative degree of dullness which composed the serious. So intolerably serious, indeed, were these gods and heroes that harlequin (though the English gentleman of that name is not at all related to the French family, for he is of a much more serious disposition) was always welcome on the stage, as he relieved the audience from worse company.

Judicious writers have always practiced this art of contrast with great success. I have been surprised that Horace should cavil at this in Homer; but indeed he contradicts himself in the very next line:

> *Indignor quandoque bonus dormitat Homerus;*
> *Verùm opere longo fas est obrepere somnum.*[4]

> I grieve if e'er great Homer chance to sleep,
> Yet slumbers on long works have right to creep.

For we are not here to understand, as perhaps some have, that an author actually falls asleep while he is writing. It is true that readers are too apt to be so overtaken; but if the work was as long as any of Oldmixon, the author himself is too well entertained to be subject to the least drowsiness. He is, as Mr. Pope observes,

> Sleepless himself to give his readers sleep.[5]

[4]Horace, *Art of Poetry*, 359–360:
Roscommon was not quite so kind as Horace:

> For who, without a qualm, hath ever looked
> On holy garbage, though by Homer cooked?
> Whose rayling heroes, and whose wounded Gods,
> Make some suspect, he snores, as well as nods.
> *Essay on Translated Verse*

[5]*Dunciad*, I, 94, paraphrased. John Oldmixon (1673–1742), historian and pamphleteer, had annoyed Pope by the critical essay prefixed to his *Critical History of England*.

To say the truth, these soporific parts are so many scenes of serious artfully interwoven in order to contrast and set off the rest; and this is the true meaning of a late facetious writer who told the public that whenever he was dull they might be assured there was a design in it.

In this light, then, or rather in this darkness, I would have the reader to consider these initial essays. And after this warning, if he shall be of opinion that he can find enough of serious in other parts of this history, he may pass over these, in which we profess to be laboriously dull, and begin the following books at the second chapter.

Book VIII, Chapter I

A Wonderful Long Chapter concerning the Marvelous; Being Much the Longest of All Our Introductory Chapters

As we are now entering upon a book in which the course of our history will oblige us to relate some matters of a more strange and surprising kind than any which have hitherto occurred, it may not be amiss, in the prolegomenous or introductory chapter, to say something of that species of writing which is called the marvelous. To this we shall, as well for the sake of ourselves as of others, endeavor to set some certain bounds, and indeed nothing can be more necessary, as critics[6] of different complexions are here apt to run into very different extremes; for while some are, with M. Dacier, ready to allow that the same thing which is impossible may be yet probable,[7] others have so little historic or poetic faith that they believe nothing to be either possible or probable the like to which hath not occurred to their own observation.

First, then, I think it may very reasonably be required of every writer that he keeps within the bounds of possibility, and still remembers that what it is not possible for man to perform, it is scarce possible for man to believe he did perform.[8] This conviction perhaps gave birth to many stories of the ancient

[6] By this word here, and in most other parts of our work, we mean every reader in the world. (Fielding's note.)

[7] It is happy for M. Dacier that he was not an Irishman. (Fielding's note.)

[8] Cf. Hobbes, "As truth is the bound of Historical, so the Resemblance of truth is the utmost limit of Poeticall Liberty. . . . Beyond the actual works of nature a Poet may now go; but beyond the conceived possibility of nature, never" (Spingarn, *Critical Essays of the Seventeenth Century*, II, 62). Also, see Gilbert, *Literary Criticism: Plato to Dryden*, Index, truth, verisimilitude.

heathen deities (for most of them are of poetical original). The poet, being desirous to indulge a wanton and extravagant imagination, took refuge in that power, of the extent of which his readers were no judges, or rather which they imagined to be infinite, and consequently they could not be shocked at any prodigies related of it. This hath been strongly urged in defense of Homer's miracles; and it is perhaps a defense; not, as Mr. Pope would have it, because Ulysses told a set of foolish lies to the Phaeacians, who were a very dull nation, but because the poet himself wrote to heathens, to whom poetical fables were articles of faith. For my own part, I must confess, so compassionate is my temper, I wish Polypheme had confined himself to his milk diet and preserved his eye; nor could Ulysses be much more concerned than myself, when his companions were turned into swine by Circe, who showed, I think, afterwards, too much regard for man's flesh to be supposed capable of converting it into bacon. I wish, likewise, with all my heart that Homer could have known the rule prescribed by Horace, to introduce supernatural agents as seldom as possible. We should not then have seen his gods coming on trivial errands, and often behaving themselves so as not only to forfeit all title to respect, but to become the objects of scorn and derision. A conduct which must have shocked the credulity of a pious and sagacious heathen; and which could never have been defended, unless by agreeing with a supposition to which I have been sometimes almost inclined, that this most glorious poet, as he certainly was, had an intent to burlesque the superstitious faith of his own age and country.

But I have rested too long on a doctrine which can be of no use to a Christian writer; for as he cannot introduce into his works any of that heavenly host which make a part of his creed, so it is horrid puerility to search the heathen theology for any of those deities who have been long since dethroned from their immortality. Lord Shaftesbury observes that nothing is more cold than the invocation of a muse by a modern; he might have added that nothing can be more absurd. A modern may with much more elegance invoke a ballad, as some have thought Homer did, or a mug of ale, with the author of *Hudibras;* which latter may perhaps have inspired much more poetry, as well as prose, than all the liquors of Hippocrene or Helicon.

The only supernatural agents which can in any manner be allowed to us moderns are ghosts; but of these I would advise an author to be extremely sparing. These are, indeed, like arsenic and other dangerous drugs in physic, to be used with the utmost caution; nor would I advise the introduction of them at all in those works, or by those authors, to which, or to whom, a horse-laugh in the reader would be any great prejudice or mortification.

As for elves and fairies, and other such mummery, I purposely omit the mention of them, as I should be very unwilling to confine within any bounds those surprising imaginations for whose vast capacity the limits of human nature are too narrow, whose works are to be considered as a new creation, and who have consequently just right to do what they will with their own.

Man, therefore, is the highest subject (unless on very extraordinary occasions indeed) which presents itself to the pen of our historian, or of our poet; and, in relating his actions, great care is to be taken that we do not exceed the capacity of the agent we describe.

Nor is possibility alone sufficient to justify us; we must keep likewise within the rules of probability. It is, I think, the opinion of Aristotle; or if not, it is the opinion of some wise man, whose authority will be as weighty when it is as old, "That it is no excuse for a poet who relates what is incredible, that the thing related is really a matter of fact." This may perhaps be allowed true with regard to poetry, but it may be thought impracticable to extend it to the historian; for he is obliged to record matters as he finds them, though they may be of so extraordinary a nature as will require no small degree of historical faith to swallow them. Such was the successful armament of Xerxes described by Herodotus, or the successful expedition of Alexander related by Arrian. Such of later years was the victory of Agincourt obtained by Harry the Fifth, or that of Narva won by Charles the Twelfth of Sweden. All which instances, the more we reflect on them, appear still the more astonishing.

Such facts, however, as they occur in the thread of the story, nay, indeed, as they constitute the essential parts of it, the historian is not only justifiable in recording as they really happened, but indeed would be unpardonable should he omit or alter them. But there are other facts not of such consequence nor so necessary which, though ever so well attested, may nevertheless be sacrificed to oblivion in complacence to the skepticism of a reader. Such is that memorable story of the ghost of George Villiers, which might with more propriety have been made a present of to Dr. Drelincourt, to have kept the ghost of Mrs. Veale company, at the head of his *Discourse upon Death*, than have been introduced into so solemn a work as the *History of the Rebellion*.

To say the truth, if the historian will confine himself to what really happened, and utterly reject any circumstance which, though never so well attested, he must be well assured is false, he will sometimes fall into the marvelous, but never into the incredible. He will often raise the wonder and surprise of his reader, but never that incredulous hatred mentioned by Horace. It is by falling into fiction, therefore, that we generally offend against this rule of deserting probability which the historian seldom if ever quits till he forsakes his character and commences a writer of romance. In this, however, those historians who relate public transactions have the advantage of us who confine ourselves to scenes of private life. The credit of the former is by common notoriety supported for a long time; and public records, with the concurrent testimony of many authors, bear evidence to their truth in future ages. Thus a Trajan and an Antoninus, a Nero and a Caligula, have all met with the belief of posterity; and no one doubts but that men so very good, and so very bad, were once the masters of mankind.

But we who deal in private character, who search into the most retired recesses, and draw forth examples of virtue and vice from holes and corners of the world are in a more dangerous situation. As we have no public notoriety, no concurrent testimony, no records to support and corroborate what we deliver, it becomes us to keep within the limits not only of possibility, but of probability too; and this more especially in painting what is greatly good and amiable. Knavery and folly, though never so exorbitant, will more easily meet with assent; for ill-nature adds great support and strength to faith.

Thus we may, perhaps, with little danger, relate the history of Fisher; who, having long owed his bread to the generosity of Mr. Derby, and having one morning received a considerable bounty from his hands, yet, in order to possess himself of what remained in his friend's scrutoire, concealed himself in a public office of the Temple, through which there was a passage into Mr. Derby's chambers. Here he overheard Mr. Derby for many hours solacing himself at an entertainment which he that evening gave his friends, and to which Fisher had been invited. During all this time, no tender, no grateful reflections arose te restrain his purpose; but when the poor gentleman had let his company out through the office, Fisher came suddenly from his lurking place, and, walking softly behind his friend into his chamber, discharged a pistol ball into his head. This may be believed when the bones of Fisher are as rotten as his heart. Nay, perhaps, it will be credited that the villain went two days afterwards with some young ladies to the play of *Hamlet;* and with an unaltered countenance heard one of the ladies, who little suspected how near she was to the person, cry out, "Good God! if the man that murdered Mr. Derby was now present!"[9] manifesting in this a more seared and callous conscience than even Nero himself, of whom we are told by Suetonius "that the consciousness of his guilt, after the death of his mother, became immediately intolerable, and so continued; nor could all the congratulations of the soldiers, of the senate, and the people allay the horrors of his conscience."

But, now, on the other hand, should I tell my reader that I had known a man whose penetrating genius had enabled him to raise a large fortune in a way where no beginning was chalked out to him; that he had done this with the most perfect preservation of his integrity, and not only without the least injustice or injury to any one individual person, but with the highest advantage to trade, and a vast increase of the public revenue; that he had expended one part of the income of this fortune in discovering a taste superior to most, by works where the highest dignity was united with the purest simplicity, and another part in displaying a degree of goodness superior to all men, by acts of charity to objects whose only recommendations were their merits, or their wants; that he was most industrious in searching after merit in distress, most eager to relieve it, and then as careful (perhaps too careful) to conceal what he had done; that his house, his furniture, his gardens, his table, his private hospitality, and his public beneficence, all denoted the mind from which they flowed, and were all intrinsically rich and noble, without tinsel, or external ostentation; that he filled every relation in life with the most adequate virtue; that he was most piously religious to his Creator, most zealously loyal to his sovereign; a most tender husband to his wife, a kind relation, a munificent patron, a

---

[9] See Gilbert, *Literary Criticism: Plato to Dryden*, pp. 563–564. Heywood relates a story of "domestic and home-born truth" in which a murderess sees a murder committed in a play and is so conscience-stricken that she confesses her crime.

warm and firm friend, a knowing and a cheerful companion, indulgent to his servants, hospitable to his neighbors, charitable to the poor, and benevolent to all mankind. Should I add to these the epithets of wise, brave, elegant, and indeed every other amiable epithet in our language, I might surely say,

> — *Quis credet? nemo Hercule! nemo;*
> *Vel duo, vel nemo,* [10]

and yet I know a man who is all I have here described. But a single instance (and I really know not such another) is not sufficient to justify us while we are writing to thousands who never heard of the person nor of anything like him. Such *rarae aves* should be remitted to the epitaph writer, or to some poet who may condescend to hitch him in a distich, or to slide him into a rhyme with an air of carelessness and neglect without giving any offense to the reader.

In the last place, the actions should be such as may not only be within the compass of human agency, and which human agents may probably be supposed to do; but they should be likely for the very actors and characters themselves to have performed; for what may be only wonderful and surprising in one man may become improbable, or indeed impossible, when related of another.

This last requisite is what the dramatic critics call conservation of character; and it requires a very extraordinary degree of judgment, and a most exact knowledge of human nature.

It is admirably remarked by a most excellent writer that zeal can no more hurry a man to act in direct opposition to itself than a rapid stream can carry a boat against its own current. I will venture to say that for a man to act in direct contradiction to the dictates of his nature is, if not impossible, as improbable and as miraculous as anything which can well be conceived. Should the best parts of the story of M. Antoninus be ascribed to Nero, or should the worst incidents of Nero's life be imputed to Antoninus, what would be more shocking to belief than either instance! whereas both these, being related of their proper agent, constitute the truly marvelous.

Our modern authors of comedy have fallen almost universally into the error here hinted at; their heroes generally are notorious rogues and their heroines abandoned jades during the first four

---

[10] "Who would believe? No one, by Hercules, no one; perhaps two, or none."

acts; but in the fifth, the former become very worthy gentlemen, and the latter women of virtue and discretion: nor is the writer often so kind as to give himself the least trouble to reconcile or account for this monstrous change and incongruity. There is, indeed, no other reason to be assigned for it than because the play is drawing to a conclusion; as if it was no less natural in a rogue to repent in the last act of a play than in the last of his life; which we perceive to be generally the case at Tyburn, a place which might indeed close the scene of some comedies with much propriety, as the heroes in these are most commonly eminent for those very talents which not only bring men to the gallows, but enable them to make an heroic figure when they are there.

Within these few restrictions, I think, every writer may be permitted to deal as much in the wonderful as he pleases; nay, if he thus keeps within the rules of credibility, the more he can surprise the reader the more he will engage his attention, and the more he will charm him. As a genius of the highest rank observes in his fifth chapter of the *Bathos*,[11] "The great art of all poetry is to mix truth with fiction, in order to join the credible with the surprising."

For though every good author will confine himself within the bounds of probability, it is by no means necessary that his characters or his incidents should be trite, common, or vulgar, such as happen in every street, or in every house, or which may be met with in the home articles of a newspaper. Nor must he be inhibited from showing many persons and things which may possibly have never fallen within the knowledge of great part of his readers. If the writer strictly observes the rules above mentioned, he hath discharged his part, and is then entitled to some faith from his reader, who is indeed guilty of critical infidelity if he disbelieves him. For want of a portion of such faith, I remember the character of a young lady of quality which was condemned on the stage for being unnatural, by the unanimous voice of a very large assembly of clerks and apprentices; though it had the previous suffrages of many ladies of the first rank, one of whom, very eminent for her understanding, declared it was the picture of half the young people of her acquaintance.

[11]Pope, *Bathos: or, Of the Art of Sinking in Poetry*, printed in *Miscellanies* (1727).

SAMUEL JOHNSON

(1709–1784)

o◯oo◯o

THE PREFACE TO JOHNSON'S EDITION of Shakespeare is his most important piece of criticism. In 1745 he wrote the *Miscellaneous Observations on the Tragedy of Macbeth*, and in 1753 the Dedication prefixed to Mrs. Charlotte Lennox's *Shakespear Illustrated;*[1] the *Proposals for Printing the Dramatick Works of William Shakespeare* appeared in 1756, and nine years later the edition was finally published. The Preface to this edition, writes D. Nichol Smith, is "by common consent nowadays . . . one of the greatest essays on Shakespeare that has ever been written, but it has not won this pre-eminence by any novelty in its method or its object. It gives us the general estimate, and it gives us the final statement of the old commonplaces of Shakespearian criticism."[2]

Johnson's comments on Shakespeare are less touched by prejudice than much of his other criticism, which was sometimes weakened by his predetermined ideas.[3] Neither Boswell nor Garrick was able to provoke him into a tirade against Shakespeare. "Sir," he said to Garrick, who accused him of not having enough reverence for the dramatist, "I will stand by the lines I have written on Shakespeare in my Prologue at the opening of your Theatre."[4]

[1]Mrs. Lennox's *Shakespear Illustrated: or the Novels and Histories, on which the Plays of Shakespear are Founded, Collected and Translated from the Original Authors* was a valuable contribution to a study of Shakespeare's sources. Gerard Langbaine's *Account of the English Dramatick Poets* (1691) contains the only examination of Shakespeare's sources worth mentioning which appeared before Mrs. Lennox's compilation.

[2]David Nichol Smith, *Shakespeare in the Eighteenth Century* (Oxford, 1928), p. 68. As to the edition itself it was not only "the best which had yet appeared, it is still one of the few editions which are indispensable" (David Nichol Smith, ed., *Eighteenth Century Essays on Shakespeare* [Glasgow, 1903], p. xxxi).

[3]The prejudices in brief are: dislike of imitative verse, such as pastorals, odes, ballads, and adaptations; the combative weakness (which Johnson owned to himself) of arguing against his better judgment when too lavish praise was bestowed on a writer; annoyance with an author who mingled Christian themes and pagan mythology; dislike of antique words and forms which the poets of his time were using; and an inability to treat a man's writing fairly when he disapproved of the man's moral life.

[4]James Boswell, *The Life of Johnson*, IV, 25. The lines referred to in the Prologue for the opening of Garrick's management at Drury Lane contain Johnson's most

Johnson approved of the historical method of criticism. He believed that it was necessary to understand the manners, habits of thought, traditions, language, and literature of the Elizabethan period in order to interpret Shakespeare.[5] In the opening sentence of the *Miscellaneous Observations on the Tragedy of Macbeth*, he states his belief that "in order to make a true estimate of the abilities and merit of a writer, it is always necessary to examine the genius of his age and the opinions of his contemporaries."[6] The approach was excellent; the flaw in the criticism was, of course, the fact that Johnson knew very little about pre-Shakespearian drama, and was acquainted with only the work of Shakespeare, some of Ben Jonson, and Beaumont and Fletcher among the Elizabethan dramatists.[7] Johnson's dislike for reading drama probably operated to a large extent in weakening his background knowledge of the period. A contributing factor in this weakness was the existence of the major part of the Elizabethan dramatic work only in copies over a hundred years old. Aside from this, the criticism of Shakespeare as a closet dramatist was already well begun; and Johnson, like some of his predecessors and the early nineteenth-century critics, almost completely ignored the fact that the stage was the medium of Shakespeare's art.

The criticism of the late seventeenth and eighteenth centuries influenced Johnson to a large extent.[8] The most commonly censured faults and excellencies which the earlier critics found in Shakespeare are summed up by Joseph Warton: "As Shakespeare is sometimes blamable for the conduct of his fables, which have no unity; and sometimes for

famous tribute to Shakespeare:

> When learning's triumph o'er her barbarous foes
> First reared the stage, immortal Shakespeare rose;
> Each change of many-colored life he drew,
> Exhausted worlds, and then imagined new;
> Existence saw him spurn her bounded reign,
> And panting time toiled after him in vain.
> His powerful strokes presiding truth impressed
> And unresisted passion stormed the breast.

[5]This is one of the underlying ideas in the *Proposals for Printing the Dramatick Works of Shakespeare*.

[6]See also Boswell, *op. cit.*, I, 270; *Lives*, I, 143, 411; III, 238–240.

[7]See W. B. C. Watkins, *Johnson and English Poetry before 1660* (Princeton, 1936), chap. IV, for a study of Johnson's knowledge of the Elizabethans. Watkins points out that even the quotations from Beaumont and Fletcher which Johnson used in the Dictionary are transcribed from Warburton's edition of Shakespeare (1747), as are the two quotations from Marston's plays. However, Johnson did own an edition of Beaumont and Fletcher, listed in the catalogue of his library as "'Plays of Beaumont and Fletcher,' 10 vols., 1750."

[8]For example, compare the Preface with Dryden's *Essay of Dramatic Poesy* (Gilbert, *Literary Criticism: Plato to Dryden*, pp. 600–658), and the passage on the unities with Lord Kames's chapter (chap. XXIII) on the unities in *Elements of Criticism* (1762).

diction which is obscure and turgid; so his characteristical excellencies may possibly be reduced to these three general heads: his lively creative imagination, his strokes of nature and passion, and his preservation of the consistency of his characters."[9] This list includes many of the points with which Johnson is concerned. After the publication of the Preface, the question of the violation of the unities of time and place ceased to be discussed;[10] the mixture of tragedy and comedy was never again to be of such vital importance.[11] The extreme and slavish reliance upon classical rules in judging a drama received almost as great a blow as the unities. Johnson dealt no less decisively with the problem of historical accuracy; bickerings over how true Shakespeare's Romans were to history were "petty cavils of petty minds." The issues he disposed of are dead; the faults which he mentioned are still discussed.

BIBLIOGRAPHY

TEXT

The Critical Opinions of Samuel Johnson, arr. and comp. with an introduction by Joseph Epes Brown. Part I: A Compilation and Interpretation of Dr. Johnson's Principles of Criticism. Part II: His Opinions of Authors and Works. Princeton University Press, 1926.

Lives of the English Poets, ed. by George Birkbeck Hill. 3 vols. Oxford, 1905.

Preface to *Edition of Shakespeare's Plays*. London, 1765.

Prefaces and Dedications, ed. by Allen T. Hazen. Yale University Press, 1937.

Works. 12 vols. London, 1820.

——. 9 vols. Oxford, 1825. (Oxford English Classics.) Supplementary volumes ten and eleven contain the *Debates*.

BIBLIOGRAPHY

Bibliography of Johnson, compiled by William Prideaux Courtney and D. Nichol Smith, in *Oxford Historical and Literary Studies*, Vol. IV. Oxford, 1915.

BIOGRAPHY AND CRITICISM

Arnold, Matthew, *Essays in Criticism;* third series; with an introduction by Edward J. O'Brien. Boston, 1910.

Bosker, A., *Literary Criticism in the Age of Johnson*. The Hague, 1930.

[9]*Adventurer*, no. 93.
[10]For references to prior discussions of the unities, see below, p. 79, note 12.
[11]See *Rambler*, no. 156, for earlier comments of Johnson on tragicomedy.

Boswell, James, *Life of Johnson, together with Boswell's Journal of a Tour to the Hebrides and Johnson's Diary of a Journey into North Wales*, ed. by George Birkbeck Hill. 6 vols. Oxford, 1887. Revised and enlarged by L. F. Powell. 4 vols. to date. Oxford, 1928–1934.

Christiani, Sigyn, *Samuel Johnson als Kritiker im Lichte von Pseudo-klassizismus und Romantik*. Leipzig, 1931.

Evans, Bergen, "Dr. Johnson's Theory of Biography," *Review of English Studies*, X (1934), 301–310.

Houston, Percy Hazen, *Doctor Johnson: a Study in Eighteenth Century Humanism*. Harvard University Press, 1923.

[Lunn], Hugh Kingsmill, *Samuel Johnson*. New York, 1934.

Potter, Robert, *The Art of Criticism; as exemplified in Dr. Johnson's Lives of the Most Eminent English Poets*. London, 1789.

Raleigh, Sir Walter, *Six Essays on Johnson*. Oxford, 1910.

——, *Johnson on Shakespeare*. Oxford, 1908.

Roscoe, Edward Stanley, *Aspects of Dr. Johnson*. New York, 1928.

Roberts, Sydney Castle, *Doctor Johnson*. London, 1926.

Smith, David Nichol, ed., *Eighteenth Century Essays on Shakespeare*. Glasgow, 1903.

——, *Shakespeare in the Eighteenth Century*. Oxford, 1928.

Spittal, John Ker, ed. and comp., *Contemporary Criticisms of Dr. Samuel Johnson*. London, 1923.

Stephen, Leslie, *Samuel Johnson*. New York, 1878. (English Men of Letters.)

Watkins, W. B. C., *Johnson and English Poetry before 1660*, in *Princeton Studies in English*, no. 13. Princeton University Press, 1936.

THE RAMBLER (*selections*)

[The Modern Novel][1]

1750

Simul et jucunda et idonea dicere vitae.[2]

The works of fiction with which the present generation seems more particularly delighted are such as exhibit life in its true state, diversified only by accidents that daily happen in the world

---

[1] *The Rambler*, no. 4, Saturday, March 31, 1750.

[2] Horace, *Art of Poetry*, 334. One line from the famous passage on the aim of poetry. For the section, Howes's translation reads:

> To teach—to please—comprise the poet's views,
> Or else at once to profit and amuse.

Byron, *Hints from Horace*, translates the lines:

> Two objects always should the poet move,
> Or one or both,—to please or to improve.

See Gilbert, *Literary Criticism: Plato to Dryden*, p. 139.

and influenced by passions and qualities which are really to be found in conversing with mankind.

This kind of writing may be termed not improperly the comedy of romance, and is to be conducted nearly by the rules of comic poetry. Its province is to bring about natural events by easy means and to keep up curiosity without the help of wonder: it is therefore precluded from the machines and expedients of the heroic romance, and can neither employ giants to snatch away a lady from the nuptial rites nor knights to bring her back from captivity; it can neither bewilder its personages in deserts nor lodge them in imaginary castles.[3]

I remember a remark made by Scaliger upon Pontanus that all his writings are filled with the same images; and that if you take from him his lilies and his roses, his satyrs and his dryads, he will have nothing left that can be called poetry. In like manner, almost all the fictions of the last age will vanish if you deprive them of a hermit and a wood, a battle and a shipwreck.

Why this wild strain of imagination found reception so long in polite and learned ages, it is not easy to conceive; but we cannot wonder that while readers could be procured, the authors were willing to continue it; for when a man had by practice gained some fluency of language, he had no further care than to retire to his closet, let loose his invention, and heat his mind with incredibilities; a book was thus produced without fear of criticism, without the toil of study, without knowledge of nature, or acquaintance with life.

The task of our present writers is very different; it requires, together with that learning which is to be gained from books, that experience which can never be attained by solitary diligence, but must arise from general converse and accurate observation of the living world. Their performances have, as Horace expresses it, *"plus oneris quantum veniae minus,"*[4] little indulgence, and therefore more difficulty. They are engaged in portraits of which everyone knows the original, and can detect any deviation from exactness of resemblance. Other writings are safe, except from the malice of learning, but these are in danger from every common reader; as the slipper ill executed was censured by a shoemaker who happened to stop in his way at the Venus of Apelles.

But the fear of not being approved as just copiers of human

---

[3]See the introductory chapter to Bk. viii of *Tom Jones* and the Preface to *Joseph Andrews*.   [4]"The less indulgence, the more weight" (*Epistles*, II, i, 170).

manners is not the most important concern that an author of this sort ought to have before him. These books are written chiefly to the young, the ignorant, and the idle, to whom they serve as lectures of conduct, and introductions into life. They are the entertainment of minds unfurnished with ideas, and therefore easily susceptible of impressions; not fixed by principles, and therefore easily following the current of fancy; not informed by experience, and consequently open to every false suggestion and partial account.

That the highest degree of reverence should be paid to youth and that nothing indecent should be suffered to approach their eyes or ears are precepts extorted by sense and virtue from an ancient writer by no means eminent for chastity of thought. The same kind, though not the same degree, of caution is required in everything which is laid before them, to secure them from unjust prejudices, perverse opinions, and incongruous combinations of images.

In the romances formerly written, every transaction and sentiment was so remote from all that passes among men that the reader was in very little danger of making any applications to himself; the virtues and crimes were equally beyond his sphere of activity; and he amused himself with heroes and with traitors, deliverers and persecutors, as with beings of another species, whose actions were regulated upon motives of their own, and who had neither faults nor excellencies in common with himself.

But when an adventurer is leveled with the rest of the world, and acts in such scenes of the universal drama as may be the lot of any other man, young spectators fix their eyes upon him with closer attention and hope, by observing his behavior and success, to regulate their own practices when they shall be engaged in the like part.

For this reason these familiar histories may perhaps be made of greater use than the solemnities of professed morality, and convey the knowledge of vice and virtue with more efficacy than axioms and definitions. But if the power of example is so great as to take possession of the memory by a kind of violence, and produce effects almost without the intervention of the will, care ought to be taken that, when the choice is unrestrained, the best examples only should be exhibited; and that which is likely to operate so strongly should not be mischievous or uncertain in its effects.

The chief advantage which these fictions have over real life is that their authors are at liberty, though not to invent, yet to select objects, and to cull from the mass of mankind those individuals upon which the attention ought most to be employed; as a diamond, though it cannot be made, may be polished by art, and placed in such situation as to display that luster which before was buried among common stones.

It is justly considered as the greatest excellency of art, to imitate nature; but it is necessary to distinguish those parts of nature which are most proper for imitation: greater care is still required in representing life, which is so often discolored by passion or deformed by wickedness. If the world be promiscuously described, I cannot see of what use it can be to read the account; or why it may not be as safe to turn the eye immediately upon mankind as upon a mirror which shows all that presents itself without discrimination.[5]

It is therefore not a sufficient vindication of a character that it is drawn as it appears; for many characters ought never to be drawn: nor of a narrative, that the train of events is agreeable to observation and experience; for that observation which is called knowledge of the world will be found much more frequently to make men cunning than good. The purpose of these writings is surely not only to show mankind, but to provide that they may be seen hereafter with less hazard; to teach the means of avoiding the snares which are laid by TREACHERY for INNOCENCE, without infusing any wish for that superiority with which the betrayer flatters his vanity; to give the power of counteracting fraud, without the temptation to practice it; to initiate youth by mock encounters in the art of necessary defense, and to increase prudence without impairing virtue.

Many writers, for the sake of following nature, so mingle good and bad qualities in their principal personages that they are both equally conspicuous; and as we accompany them through their adventures with delight, and are led by degrees to interest ourselves in their favor, we lose the abhorrence of their faults, because they do not hinder our pleasure, or perhaps regard them with some kindness for being united with so much merit.

[5]This and the following paragraphs are evidently an unfavorable discussion of novels of the type of Smollett's *Roderick Random* (1748) and Fielding's *Tom Jones* (1749). See *The Critical Opinions of Samuel Johnson*, arranged and compiled with an introduction by Joseph Epes Brown (Princeton, 1926), pp. 346–348, for Johnson's remarks on Fielding.

There have been men indeed splendidly wicked, whose endowments threw a brightness on their crimes, and whom scarce any villainy made perfectly detestable, because they never could be wholly divested of their excellencies; but such have been in all ages the great corrupters of the world, and their resemblance ought no more to be preserved than the art of murdering without pain.

Some have advanced, without due attention to the consequences of this notion, that certain virtues have their correspondent faults, and therefore that to exhibit either apart is to deviate from probability. Thus men are observed by Swift to be "grateful in the same degree as they are resentful." This principle, with others of the same kind, supposes man to act from a brute impulse and pursue a certain degree of inclination without any choice of the object; for, otherwise, though it should be allowed that gratitude and resentment arise from the same constitution of the passions, it follows not that they will be equally indulged when reason is consulted; yet, unless that consequence be admitted, this sagacious maxim becomes an empty sound, without any relation to practice or to life.

Nor is it evident that even the first motions to these effects are always in the same proportion. For pride, which produces quickness of resentment, will obstruct gratitude, by unwillingness to admit that inferiority which obligation implies; and it is very unlikely that he who cannot think he receives a favor will acknowledge or repay it.

It is of the utmost importance to mankind that positions of this tendency should be laid open and confuted; for while men consider good and evil as springing from the same root, they will spare the one for the sake of the other, and, in judging, if not of others at least of themselves, will be apt to estimate their virtues by their vices. To this fatal error all those will contribute who confound the colors of right and wrong, and, instead of helping to settle their boundaries, mix them with so much art that no common mind is able to disunite them.

In narratives where historical veracity has no place, I cannot discover why there should not be exhibited the most perfect idea of virtue; of virtue not angelical, nor above probability— for what we cannot credit we shall never imitate—but the highest and purest that humanity can reach, which, exercised in such trials as the various revolutions of things shall bring upon it,

may, by conquering some calamities and enduring others, teach
us what we may hope and what we can perform. Vice, for vice
is necessary to be shown, should always disgust; nor should the
graces of gaiety or the dignity of courage be so united with it as
to reconcile it to the mind. Wherever it appears, it should raise
hatred by the malignity of its practices, and contempt by the
meanness of its stratagems: for while it is supported by either
parts or spirit, it will be seldom heartily abhorred. The Roman
tyrant was content to be hated if he was but feared; and there
are thousands of the readers of romances willing to be thought
wicked if they may be allowed to be wits. It is therefore to be
steadily inculcated that virtue is the highest proof of understanding, and the only solid basis of greatness; and that vice is the
natural consequence of narrow thoughts; that it begins in mistake
and ends in ignominy.

PREFACE TO SHAKESPEARE (*selections*)[1]

1765

. . . The poet of whose works I have undertaken the revision
may now begin to assume the dignity of an ancient and claim the
privilege of an established fame and prescriptive veneration. He
has long outlived his century, the term commonly fixed as the
test of literary merit. Whatever advantages he might once derive from personal allusions, local customs, or temporary opinions have for many years been lost; and every topic of merriment or motive of sorrow which the modes of artificial life
afforded him, now only obscure the scenes which they once illuminated. The effects of favor and competition are at an end;
the tradition of his friendships and his enmities has perished;
his works support no opinion with arguments nor supply any
faction with invectives; they can neither indulge vanity nor
gratify malignity; but are read without any other reason than
the desire of pleasure, and are therefore praised only as pleasure
is obtained. Yet, thus unassisted by interest or passion, they
have passed through variations of taste and changes of man-

---

[1]Johnson published "Proposals for a New Edition of Shakespeare" in 1745, and
after having postponed the project for eleven years, he renewed his "proposals" in
1756. He finally published the completed work, *The Plays of Shakespeare in Eight
Volumes*, in 1765. This extract from his famous Preface includes the core of his
Shakespeare criticism.

ners, and, as they devolved from one generation to another, have received new honors at every transmission.

But because human judgment, though it be gradually gaining upon certainty, never becomes infallible, and approbation, though long continued, may yet be only the approbation of prejudice or fashion, it is proper to inquire by what peculiarities of excellence Shakespeare has gained and kept the favor of his countrymen.

Nothing can please many and please long but just representations of general nature.[2] Particular manners can be known to few, and therefore few only can judge how nearly they are copied. The irregular combinations of fanciful invention may delight a while by that novelty of which the common satiety of life sends us all in quest, but the pleasures of sudden wonder are soon exhausted and the mind can only repose on the stability of truth.

Shakespeare is, above all writers—at least above all modern writers—the poet of nature; the poet that holds up to his readers a faithful mirror of manners and of life. His characters are not modified by the customs of particular places unpracticed by the rest of the world; by the peculiarities of studies or professions which can operate but upon small numbers; or by the accidents of transient fashions or temporary opinions: they are the genuine progeny of common humanity, such as the world will always supply and observation will always find. His persons act and speak by the influence of those general passions and principles by which all minds are agitated and the whole system of life is continued in motion. In the writings of other poets a character is too often an individual; in those of Shakespeare it is commonly a species.[3]

It is from this wide extension of design that so much instruction is derived. It is this which fills the plays of Shakespeare with practical axioms and domestic wisdom. It was said of Euripides that every verse was a precept; and it may be said of Shakespeare that from his works may be collected a system of civil and economical prudence. Yet his real power is not shown

[2] Johnson had delivered this dictum before. *Rambler*, no. 59: "He that writes upon general principles, or delivers universal truths, may hope to be often read, because his work will be equally useful at all times and in every country."

[3] For Hazlitt's comments on this and other passages of Johnson's Preface, see the Preface to the *Characters of Shakespeare's Plays* in *Complete Works*, ed. P. P. Howe (London, 1931–1933), IV, 174–178.

in the splendor of particular passages, but by the progress of his
fable and the tenor of his dialogue; and he that tries to recommend him by select quotations will succeed like the pedant in
Hierocles[4] who, when he offered his house to sale, carried a brick
in his pocket as a specimen.

It will not easily be imagined how much Shakespeare excels
in accommodating his sentiments to real life but by comparing
him with other authors. It was observed of the ancient schools
of declamation that the more diligently they were frequented,
the more was the student disqualified for the world, because he
found nothing there which he should ever meet in any other
place. The same remark may be applied to every stage but that
of Shakespeare. The theater, when it is under any other direction, is peopled by such characters as were never seen, conversing in a language which was never heard, upon topics which
will never arise in the commerce of mankind. But the dialogue
of this author is often so evidently determined by the incident
which produces it and is pursued with so much ease and simplicity, that it seems scarcely to claim the merit of fiction, but
to have been gleaned by diligent selection out of common conversation and common occurrences.

Upon every other stage the universal agent is love, by whose
power all good and evil is distributed and every action quickened or retarded. To bring a lover, a lady, and a rival into the
fable; to entangle them in contradictory obligations, perplex
them with oppositions of interest, and harass them with violence
of desires inconsistent with each other; to make them meet in
rapture and part in agony; to fill their mouths with hyperbolical
joy and outrageous sorrow; to distress them as nothing human
ever was distressed; to deliver them as nothing human ever was
delivered—is the business of a modern dramatist. For this,
probability is violated, life is misrepresented, and language is
depraved. But love is only one of many passions; and as it has
no great influence upon the sum of life, it has little operation in
the dramas of a poet who caught his ideas from the living world
and exhibited only what he saw before him. He knew that any
other passion, as it was regular or exorbitant, was a cause of
happiness or calamity.

[4]From a collection of witticisms formerly attributed to Hierocles of Alexandria, the
commentator on the *Golden Verses* of Pythagoras. See *Hieroclis commentarius in
aurea carmina* (ed. Needham, 1709), p. 462.

Characters thus ample and general were not easily discriminated and preserved, yet perhaps no poet ever kept his personages more distinct from each other. I will not say with Pope [5] that every speech may be assigned to the proper speaker, because many speeches there are which have nothing characteristical; but, perhaps, though some may be equally adapted to every person, it will be difficult to find any that can be properly transferred from the present possessor to another claimant. The choice is right when there is reason for choice.

Other dramatists can only gain attention by hyperbolical or aggravated characters, by fabulous and unexampled excellence or depravity, as the writers of barbarous romances invigorated the reader by a giant and a dwarf; and he that should form his expectations of human affairs from the play or from the tale would be equally deceived. Shakespeare has no heroes; his scenes are occupied only by men who act and speak as the reader thinks that he should himself have spoken or acted on the same occasion. Even where the agency is supernatural, the dialogue is level with life. Other writers disguise the most natural passions and most frequent incidents, so that he who contemplates them in the book will not know them in the world. Shakespeare approximates the remote and familiarizes the wonderful; the event which he represents will not happen, but, if it were possible, its effects would probably be such as he has assigned; and it may be said that he has not only shown human nature as it acts in real exigencies but as it would be found in trials to which it cannot be exposed.

This, therefore, is the praise of Shakespeare, that his drama is the mirror of life; that he who has mazed his imagination in following the phantoms which other writers raise up before him, may here be cured of his delirious ecstasies by reading human sentiments in human language; by scenes from which a hermit may estimate the transactions of the world, and a confessor predict the progress of the passions.

[5] See Pope's Preface to his edition of *Shakespeare:*
"His characters are so much nature herself, that 'tis a sort of injury to call them so distant a name as copies of her. . . . But every single character in Shakespeare is as much an individual as those in life itself; it is as impossible to find any two alike; . . . To this life and variety of character, we must add the wonderful preservation of it; which is such throughout his plays, that had all the speeches been printed without the very names of the persons, I believe one might have applied them with certainty to every speaker."

His adherence to general nature has exposed him to the censure of critics who form their judgments on narrower principles. Dennis and Rymer think his Romans not sufficiently Roman,[6] and Voltaire censures his kings as not completely royal. Dennis is offended that Menenius, a senator of Rome, should play the buffoon; and Voltaire perhaps thinks decency violated when the Danish usurper is represented as a drunkard.[7] But Shakespeare always makes nature predominate over accident; and, if he preserves the essential character, is not very careful of distinctions superinduced and adventitious. His story requires Romans or kings, but he thinks only on men. He knew that Rome, like every other city, had men of all dispositions; and wanting a buffoon, he went into the senate house for that which the senate house would certainly have afforded him. He was inclined to show an usurper and a murderer not only odious but despicable; he therefore added drunkenness to his other qualities, knowing that kings love wine like other men and that wine exerts its natural power upon kings. These are the petty cavils of petty minds; a poet overlooks the casual distinction of country and condition, as a painter, satisfied with the figure, neglects the drapery.[8]

[6]Thomas Rymer, *A Short View of Tragedy* (1692), cites the buffoonery of Menenius Agrippa. His hostile criticism of Shakespeare had appeared before in *The Tragedies of the Last Age* (1678). John Dennis wrote *The Impartial Critic* (1693) in defense of Shakespeare against Rymer's strictures, although he was far from believing that Shakespeare was without faults. See *On the Genius and Writings of Shakespeare* published by Dennis in 1711: "For want of this poetical art, Shakespeare has introduced things into his tragedies which are against the dignity of that noble poem, as the rabble in *Julius Caesar* and that in *Coriolanus;* though that in *Coriolanus* offends not only against the dignity of tragedy but against the truth of history likewise, and the customs of ancient Rome, and the majesty of the Roman people."

[7]Voltaire's criticism of Shakespeare appeared in *Discours sur la tragédie à Milord Bolingbroke* (1730); *Lettres philosophiques* (dix-huitième lettre, "sur la tragédie," 1734); and *Du Théâtre anglais, par Jérôme Carré* (1764). Apparently Johnson refers only to the last essay.

[8]Voltaire replied to this criticism in the *Dictionnaire philosophique*, "Art dramatique," section "Du Théâtre anglais": "I do not wish to suspect Mr. Johnson of being a poor jester, and of being too fond of wine; but I find it a bit extraordinary that he considers buffoonery and drunkenness among the beauties of the tragic theatre; the reason which he gives is no less singular. 'The poet,' he says, 'overlooks the casual distinction of country and condition as a painter, satisfied with the figure, neglects the drapery.' The comparison would be more just if he was speaking of a painter who, in a noble subject, would introduce ridiculous grotesques, painting in the battle of Arbela, Alexander the Great mounted on a donkey, and the wife of Darius drinking with a hod carrier in a tavern. . . . The genius of Shakespeare could be only the disciple of the manners and the spirit of the time" (*Œuvres*, XVII, 398).

The censure which he has incurred by mixing comic and tragic scenes, as it extends to all his works, deserves more consideration. Let the fact be first stated and then examined.

Shakespeare's plays are not, in the rigorous and critical sense, either tragedies or comedies but compositions of a distinct kind, exhibiting the real state of sublunary nature, which partakes of good and evil, joy and sorrow, mingled with endless variety of proportion and innumerable modes of combination, and expressing the course of the world, in which the loss of one is the gain of another; in which, at the same time, the reveler is hasting to his wine and the mourner burying his friend; in which the malignity of one is sometimes defeated by the frolic of another, and many mischiefs and many benefits are done and hindered without design.

Out of this chaos of mingled purposes and casualties the ancient poets, according to the laws which custom had prescribed, selected some the crimes of men, and some their absurdities; some the momentous vicissitudes of life, and some the lighter occurrences; some the terrors of distress, and some the gaieties of prosperity. Thus rose the two modes of imitation known by the names of tragedy and comedy, compositions intended to promote different ends by contrary means, and considered as so little allied that I do not recollect among the Greeks or Romans a single writer who attempted both.[9]

Shakespeare has united the powers of exciting laughter and sorrow not only in one mind but in one composition. Almost all his plays are divided between serious and ludicrous characters, and, in the successive evolutions of the design, sometimes produce seriousness and sorrow, and sometimes levity and laughter.

That this is a practice contrary to the rules of criticism will be readily allowed; but there is always an appeal open from criticism to nature. The end of writing is to instruct; the end of poetry is to instruct by pleasing. That the mingled drama may convey all the instruction of tragedy or comedy cannot be denied, because it includes both in its alternations of exhibition, and approaches nearer than either to the appearance of life by showing how great machinations and slender designs may promote or obviate one another, and the high and the low co-operate in the general system by unavoidable concatenation.

[9]But see the *Cyclops* of Euripides.

It is objected that by this change of scenes the passions are interrupted in their progression and that the principal event, being not advanced by a due gradation of preparatory incidents, wants at last the power to move, which constitutes the perfection of dramatic poetry. This reasoning is so specious that it is received as true even by those who in daily experience feel it to be false. The interchanges of mingled scenes seldom fail to produce the intended vicissitudes of passion. Fiction cannot move so much but that the attention may be easily transferred; and though it must be allowed that pleasing melancholy be sometimes interrupted by unwelcome levity, yet let it be considered likewise that melancholy is often not pleasing, and that the disturbance of one man may be the relief of another; that different auditors have different habitudes; and that upon the whole all pleasure consists in variety.

The players who in their edition divided our author's works into comedies, histories, and tragedies seem not to have distinguished the three kinds by any very exact or definite ideas. An action which ended happily to the principal persons, however serious or distressful through its intermediate incidents, in their opinion constituted a comedy. This idea of a comedy continued long amongst us; and plays were written which, by changing the catastrophe, were tragedies today and comedies tomorrow.[10] Tragedy was not, in those times, a poem of more general dignity or elevation than comedy; it required only a calamitous conclusion, with which the common criticism of that age was satisfied, whatever lighter pleasure it afforded in its progress. History was a series of actions with no other than chronological succession, independent of each other and without any tendency to introduce or regulate the conclusion. It is not always very nicely distinguished from tragedy. There is not much nearer approach to unity of action in the tragedy of *Antony and Cleopatra* than in the history of *Richard the Second*. But a history might be continued through many plays; as it had no plan, it had no limits.

Through all these denominations of the drama, Shakespeare's mode of composition is the same: an interchange of seriousness and merriment, by which the mind is softened at one time and exhilarated at another. But whatever be his purpose, whether to gladden or depress, or to conduct the story without vehemence

[10]As the *Aglaura* of Suckling and the *Vestal Virgin* of Sir Robert Howard.

or emotion through tracts of easy and familiar dialogue, he never fails to attain his purpose. As he commands us, we laugh or mourn or sit silent with quiet expectation, in tranquillity without indifference.

When Shakespeare's plan is understood, most of the criticisms of Rymer and Voltaire vanish away. The play of *Hamlet* is opened without impropriety by two sentinels; Iago bellows at Brabantio's window without injury to the scheme of the play, though in terms which a modern audience would not easily endure; the character of Polonius is seasonable and useful, and the gravediggers themselves may be heard with applause.

Shakespeare engaged in dramatic poetry with the world open before him. The rules of the ancients were yet known to few; the public judgment was unformed; he had no example of such fame as might force him upon imitation, nor critics of such authority as might restrain his extravagance. He therefore indulged his natural disposition; and his disposition, as Rymer has remarked, led him to comedy. In tragedy he often writes, with great appearance of toil and study, what is written at last with little felicity; but in his comic scenes he seems to produce, without labor, what no labor can improve. In tragedy he is always struggling after some occasion to be comic; but in comedy he seems to repose or to luxuriate as in a mode of thinking congenial to his nature. In his tragic scenes there is always something wanting, but his comedy often surpasses expectation or desire. His comedy pleases by the thoughts and the language, and his tragedy for the greater part by incident and action. His tragedy seems to be skill, his comedy to be instinct.

The force of his comic scenes has suffered little diminution from the changes made by a century and a half, in manners or in words. As his personages act upon principles arising from genuine passion, very little modified by particular forms, their pleasures and vexations are communicable to all times and to all places; they are natural and therefore durable. The adventitious peculiarities of personal habits are only superficial dyes, bright and pleasing for a little while, yet soon fading to a dim tinct, without any remains of former luster; but the discriminations of true passion are the colors of nature: they pervade the whole mass, and can only perish with the body that exhibits them. The accidental compositions of heterogeneous modes are dissolved by the chance that combined them, but the uniform simplicity of primitive qualities neither admits increase nor suffers decay. The sand heaped by one flood is scattered by another, but the rock always continues in its place. The stream of time, which is continually washing the dissoluble fabrics of other poets, passes without injury by the adamant of Shakespeare.

If there be, what I believe there is, in every nation a style which never becomes obsolete—a certain mode of phraseology so consonant and congenial to the analogy and principles of its respective language as to remain settled and unaltered—this style is probably to be sought in the common intercourse of life, among those who speak only to be understood, without ambition of elegance. The polite are always catching modish innovations, and the learned depart from established forms of speech in hope of finding or making better; those who wish for distinction forsake the vulgar when the vulgar is right. But there is a conversation above grossness and below refinement, where propriety resides, and where this poet seems to have gathered his comic dialogue. He is therefore more agreeable to the ears of the present age than any other author equally remote, and among his other excellencies deserves to be studied as one of the original masters of our language.

These observations are to be considered not as unexceptionably constant but as containing general and predominant truth. Shakespeare's familiar dialogue is affirmed to be smooth and clear yet not wholly without ruggedness or difficulty, as a country may be eminently fruitful though it has spots unfit for cultivation. His characters are praised as natural though their sentiments are sometimes forced and their actions improbable, as the earth upon the whole is spherical though its surface is varied with protuberances and cavities.

Shakespeare with his excellencies has likewise faults, and faults sufficient to obscure and overwhelm any other merit. I shall show them in the proportion in which they appear to me, without envious malignity or superstitious veneration. No question can be more innocently discussed than a dead poet's pretensions to renown, and little regard is due to that bigotry which sets candor higher than truth.

His first defect is that to which may be imputed most of the evil in books or in men. He sacrifices virtue to convenience, and is so much more careful to please than to instruct that he seems to write without any moral purpose. From his writings, indeed, a system of social duty may be selected, for he that thinks reasonably must think morally; but his precepts and axioms drop casually from him; he makes no just distribution of good or evil nor is always careful to show in the virtuous a disapprobation of the wicked. He carries his persons indifferently through right and wrong, and at the close dismisses them without further care, and leaves their examples to operate by chance. This fault the barbarity of his age cannot extenuate, for it is always a writer's duty to make the world better, and justice is a virtue independent on time or place.

The plots are often so loosely formed that a very slight consideration may improve them, and so carelessly pursued that he seems not always fully to comprehend his own design. He omits opportunities of instructing or delighting which the train of his story seems to force upon him, and apparently rejects those exhibitions which would be more affecting, for the sake of those which are more easy.

It may be observed that in many of his plays the latter part is evidently neglected. When he found himself near the end of his work, and in view of his reward, he shortened the labor to snatch the profit. He therefore remits his efforts where he should most vigorously exert them, and his catastrophe is improbably produced or imperfectly represented.

He had no regard to distinction of time or place, but gives to one age or nation without scruple the customs, institutions, and opinions of another, at the expense not only of likelihood but of possibility. These faults Pope has endeavored, with more zeal than judgment, to transfer to his imagined interpolators. We need not wonder to find Hector quoting Aristotle, when we see the loves of Theseus and Hippolyta combined with the Gothic mythology of fairies. Shakespeare, indeed, was not the only violator of chronology, for in the same age Sidney, who wanted not the advantages of learning, has, in his *Arcadia*, confounded the pastoral with the feudal times—the days of innocence, quiet, and security with those of turbulence, violence, and adventure.

In his comic scenes he is seldom very successful when he engages his characters in reciprocations of smartness and contests of sarcasm. Their jests are commonly gross, and their pleasantry licentious; neither his gentlemen nor his ladies have much delicacy, nor are sufficiently distinguished from his clowns by any appearance of refined manners. Whether he represented the real conversation of his time is not easy to determine; the reign of Elizabeth is commonly supposed to have been a time of stateliness, formality, and reserve, yet perhaps the relaxations of that severity were not very elegant. There must, however, have been always some modes of gaiety preferable to others, and a writer ought to choose the best.

In tragedy his performance seems constantly to be worse as his labor is more. The effusions of passion, which exigence forces out, are for the most part striking and energetic; but whenever he solicits his invention or strains his faculties, the offspring of his throes is tumor, meanness, tediousness, and obscurity.

In narration he affects a disproportionate pomp of diction and a wearisome train of circumlocution, and tells the incident imperfectly in many words which might have been more plainly delivered in few. Narration in dramatic poetry is naturally tedious, as it is unanimated and inactive and obstructs the progress of the action; it should therefore always be rapid, and enlivened by frequent interruption. Shakespeare found it an encumbrance, and instead of lightening it by brevity, endeavored to recommend it by dignity and splendor.

His declamations or set speeches are commonly cold and weak, for his power was the power of nature. When he endeavored like other tragic writers to catch opportunities of amplification and, instead of inquiring what the occasion demanded, to show how much his stores of knowledge could supply, he seldom escapes without the pity or resentment of his reader.

It is incident to him to be now and then entangled with an unwieldy sentiment which he cannot well express and will not reject. He struggles with it a while, and, if it continues stubborn, comprises it in words such as occur, and leaves it to be disentangled and evolved by those who have more leisure to bestow upon it.

Not that always where the language is intricate the thought is subtle, or the image always great where the line is bulky. The equality of words to things is very often neglected, and trivial sentiments and vulgar ideas disappoint the attention, to which they are recommended by sonorous epithets and swelling figures.

But the admirers of this great poet have most reason to complain when he approaches nearest to his highest excellence and seems fully resolved to sink them in dejection and mollify them with tender emotions by the fall of greatness, the danger of innocence, or the crosses of love. What he does best he soon ceases to do. He is not long soft and pathetic without some idle conceit or contemptible equivocation. He no sooner begins to move than he counteracts himself; and terror and pity, as they are rising in the mind, are checked and blasted by sudden frigidity.

A quibble is to Shakespeare what luminous vapors are to the traveler: he follows it at all adventures; it is sure to lead him out of his way and sure to engulf him in the mire. It has some malignant power over his mind, and its fascinations are irresistible. Whatever be the dignity or profundity of his disquisitions, whether he be enlarging knowledge or exalting affection, whether he be amusing attention with incidents or enchaining it in suspense, let but a quibble spring up before him and he leaves his work unfinished. A quibble is the golden apple for which he will always turn aside from his career or stoop from his elevation. A quibble, poor and barren as it is, gave him such delight that he was content to purchase it by the sacrifice of reason, propriety, and truth. A quibble was to him the fatal Cleopatra for which he lost the world, and was content to lose it.[11]

It will be thought strange that, in enumerating the defects of this writer, I have not yet mentioned his neglect of the unities,[12] —his violation of those laws which have been instituted and established by the joint authority of poets and critics.

For his other deviations from the art of writing I resign him to critical justice, without making any other demand in his favor than that which must be indulged to all human excellence—that his virtues be rated with his failings. But from the censure which this irregularity may bring upon him, I shall, with due reverence to that learning which I must oppose, adventure to try how I can defend him.

[11]See Thomas Warton, *The History of English Poetry*, sect. 61, on the "Elizabethan Age of Poetry": "In the same scene, he [Shakespeare] descends from his meridian of the noblest tragic sublimity, to puns and quibbles, to the meanest merriments of a plebeian farce. In the midst of his dignity, he resembles his own Richard the Second, the *skipping king*, who sometimes discarding the state of a monarch,

Mingled his royalty with capering fools."
Henry IV, Pt. I, iii, ii, 63.

[12]David Nichol Smith (*Eighteenth Century Essays on Shakespeare*, p. 322, n. 126) refers to this passage on the unities as the most brilliant in the entire preface. He cites as other references to the unities: *The Rambler*, no. 156; Farquhar, *Discourse upon Comedy* (1702) and *Some Remarks on the Tragedy of Hamlet* (1736); Upton, *Critical Observations* (1746); Fielding, *Tom Jones*, prefatory chapter of Book V; Alexander Gerard, *Essay on Taste* (1759); Daniel Webb, *Remarks on the Beauties of Poetry* (1762); Lord Kames, *Elements of Criticism* (1762); Hurd's defense of unity of design in *Letters on Chivalry* (1762).

His histories, being neither tragedies nor comedies, are not subject to any of their laws.[13] Nothing more is necessary to all the praise which they expect than that the changes of action be so prepared as to be understood; that the incidents be various and affecting, and the characters consistent, natural, and distinct. No other unity is intended, and therefore none is to be sought.

In his other works he has well enough preserved the unity of action. He has not, indeed, an intrigue regularly perplexed and regularly unraveled; he does not endeavor to hide his design only to discover it, for this is seldom the order of real events, and Shakespeare is the poet of nature. But his plan has commonly what Aristotle requires, a beginning, a middle, and an end; one event is concatenated with another and the conclusion follows by easy consequence. There are perhaps some incidents that might be spared, as in other poets there is much talk that only fills up time upon the stage; but the general system makes gradual advances and the end of the play is the end of expectation.

To the unities of time and place he has shown no regard; and perhaps a nearer view of the principles on which they stand will diminish their value and withdraw from them the veneration which, from the time of Corneille,[14] they have generally received, by discovering that they have given more trouble to the poet than pleasure to the auditor.

The necessity of observing the unities of time and place arises from the supposed necessity of making the drama credible. The critics hold it impossible that an action of months or years can be possibly believed to pass in three hours; or that the spectator can suppose himself to sit in the theater while ambassadors go and return between distant kings, while armies are levied and towns besieged, while an exile wanders and returns, or till he whom they saw courting his mistress shall lament the untimely

[13]Percy in *Reliques of Ancient English Poetry* (1765), I, introductory chapter to sect. 2, "Essay on the Origin of the English Stage": "Upon the whole we have abundant proof that both Shakespeare and his contemporaries considered his histories, or historical plays, as a legitimate distinct species, sufficiently separate from tragedy and comedy; a distinction which deserves the particular attention of his critics and commentators, who, by not adventing to it, deprive him of his proper defence and best vindication of his neglect of the unities, and departure from the classical dramatic forms."

[14]Pierre Corneille, *Discourses*, III (1660); for Castelvetro's discussion of the unities in his commentary on Aristotle (1571), see Gilbert, *Literary Criticism: Plato to Dryden*, pp. 318–319.

fall of his son. The mind revolts from evident falsehood, and fiction loses its force when it departs from the resemblance of reality.

From the narrow limitation of time necessarily arises the contraction of place. The spectator who knows that he saw the first act at Alexandria cannot suppose that he sees the next at Rome, at a distance to which not the dragons of Medea could in so short a time have transported him. He knows with certainty that he has not changed his place, and he knows that place cannot change itself—that what was a house cannot become a plain; that what was Thebes can never be Persepolis.

Such is the triumphant language with which a critic exults over the misery of an irregular poet and exults commonly without resistance or reply. It is time, therefore, to tell him by the authority of Shakespeare that he assumes as an unquestionable principle a position which, while his breath is forming it into words, his understanding pronounces to be false. It is false that any representation is mistaken for reality; that any dramatic fable in its materiality was ever credible, or for a single moment was ever credited.

The objection arising from the impossibility of passing the first hour at Alexandria, and the next at Rome, supposes that when the play opens the spectator really imagines himself at Alexandria and believes that his walk to the theater has been a voyage to Egypt and that he lives in the days of Antony and Cleopatra. Surely he that imagines this may imagine more. He that can take the stage at one time for the palace of the Ptolemies may take it in half an hour for the promontory of Actium. Delusion, if delusion be admitted, has no certain limitation. If the spectator can be once persuaded that his old acquaintance are Alexander and Caesar, that a room illuminated with candles is the plain of Pharsalia, or the bank of Granicus, he is in a state of elevation above the reach of reason or of truth, and from the heights of empyrean poetry may despise the circumscriptions of terrestrial nature. There is no reason why a mind thus wandering in ecstasy should count the clock, or why an hour should not be a century in that calenture of the brains that can make the stage a field.

The truth is that the spectators are always in their senses, and know, from the first act to the last, that the stage is only a stage and that the players are only players. They come to hear a cer-

tain number of lines recited with just gesture and elegant modu-
lation. The lines relate to some action, and an action must be in
some place; but the different actions that complete a story may
be in places very remote from each other; and where is the absurdity of allowing that space to represent first Athens and then
Sicily, which was always known to be neither Sicily nor Athens
but a modern theater?

By supposition, as place is introduced, time may be extended.
The time required by the fable elapses for the most part between
the acts; for, of so much of the action as is represented, the real
and poetical duration is the same. If, in the first act, preparations
for war against Mithridates are represented to be made in Rome,
the event of the war may, without absurdity, be represented in
the catastrophe as happening in Pontus. We know that there is
neither war nor preparation for war; we know that we are neither
in Rome nor Pontus; that neither Mithridates nor Lucullus are
before us. The drama exhibits successive imitations of successive
actions; and why may not the second imitation represent an
action that happened years after the first, if it be so connected
with it that nothing but time can be supposed to intervene?
Time is, of all modes of existence, most obsequious to the imagination; a lapse of years is as easily conceived as a passage of hours.
In contemplation we easily contract the time of real actions, and
therefore willingly permit it to be contracted when we only see
their imitation.

It will be asked how the drama moves, if it is not credited.
It is credited with all the credit due to a drama. It is credited,
whenever it moves, as a just picture of a real original; as representing to the auditor what he would himself feel if he were to
do or suffer what is there feigned to be suffered or to be done.
The reflection that strikes the heart is not that the evils before
us are real evils, but that they are evils to which we ourselves
may be exposed. If there be any fallacy, it is not that we fancy
the players but that we fancy ourselves unhappy for a moment;
but we rather lament the possibility than suppose the presence
of misery, as a mother weeps over her babe when she remembers
that death may take it from her. The delight of tragedy proceeds
from our consciousness of fiction; if we thought murders and
treasons real, they would please no more.

Imitations produce pain or pleasure, not because they are
mistaken for realities but because they bring realities to mind.

When the imagination is recreated by a painted landscape, the trees are not supposed capable to give us shade, or the fountains coolness; but we consider how we should be pleased with such fountains playing beside us and such woods waving over us. We are agitated in reading the history of *Henry the Fifth*, yet no man takes his book for the field of Agincourt. A dramatic exhibition is a book recited with concomitants that increase or diminish its effect. Familiar comedy is often more powerful on the theater than in the page; imperial tragedy is always less. The humor of Petruchio may be heightened by grimace; but what voice or what gesture can hope to add dignity or force to the soliloquy of Cato?

A play read affects the mind like a play acted. It is therefore evident that the action is not supposed to be real; and it follows that between the acts a longer or shorter time may be allowed to pass, and that no more account of space or duration is to be taken by the auditor of a drama than by the reader of a narrative, before whom may pass in an hour the life of a hero or the revolutions of an empire.

Whether Shakespeare knew the unities and rejected them by design, or deviated from them by happy ignorance, it is, I think, impossible to decide and useless to inquire. We may reasonably suppose that, when he rose to notice, he did not want the counsels and admonitions of scholars and critics, and that he at last deliberately persisted in a practice which he might have begun by chance. As nothing is essential to the fable but unity of action, and as the unities of time and place arise evidently from false assumptions and by circumscribing the extent of the drama lessen its variety, I cannot think it much to be lamented that they were not known by him or not observed. Nor, if such another poet could arise, should I very vehemently reproach him that his first act passed at Venice and his next in Cyprus. Such violations of rules merely positive become the comprehensive genius of Shakespeare, and such censures are suitable to the minute and slender criticism of Voltaire.

> *Non usque adeo permiscuit imis*
> *Longus summa dies, ut non, si voce Metelli*
> *Serventur leges, malint a Caesare tolli.*[15]

[15]"The long day has not so far confused the highest with the lowest that it is not preferable to have laws set aside by Caesar rather than have them preserved by the voice of Metellus" (Lucan, *Pharsalia*, III, 138–140).

Yet when I speak thus slightly of dramatic rules, I cannot but recollect how much wit and learning may be produced against me. Before such authorities I am afraid to stand; not that I think the present question one of those that are to be decided by mere authority, but because it is to be suspected that these precepts have not been so easily received, but for better reasons than I have yet been able to find. The result of my inquiries, in which it would be ludicrous to boast of impartiality, is that the unities of time and place are not essential to a just drama; that, though they may sometimes conduce to pleasure, they are always to be sacrificed to the nobler beauties of variety and instruction; and that a play written with nice observation of critical rules is to be contemplated as an elaborate curiosity, as the product of superfluous and ostentatious art, by which is shown rather what is possible than what is necessary.

He that without diminution of any other excellence shall preserve all the unities unbroken, deserves the like applause with the architect who shall display all the orders of architecture in a citadel without any deduction from its strength. But the principal beauty of a citadel is to exclude the enemy, and the greatest graces of a play are to copy nature and instruct life.

Perhaps what I have here not dogmatically but deliberately written may recall the principles of the drama to a new examination. I am almost frighted at my own temerity; and, when I estimate the fame and the strength of those that maintain the contrary opinion, am ready to sink down in reverential silence, as Aeneas withdrew from the defense of Troy when he saw Neptune shaking the wall and Juno heading the besiegers. . . .

Voltaire expresses his wonder that our author's extravagancies are endured by a nation which has seen the tragedy of *Cato*.[16] Let him be answered that Addison speaks the language of poets, and Shakespeare of men. We find in *Cato* innumerable beauties which enamor us of its author, but we see nothing that acquaints us with human sentiments or human actions. We place it with the fairest and the noblest progeny which judgment propagates

---

[16]The last sentence of Voltaire in "Du Mérite de Shakespeare," a subsection of "L'Art dramatique," in *Dictionnaire philosophique* (*Œuvres*, XVII, 403), offers a key to his attitude: "What is one to conclude from this contrast of grandeur and baseness, of sublime reason and gross folly, finally of all the contrasts which we have just seen in Shakespeare? that he would have been a perfect poet if he had lived in the time of Addison." Another interesting side light is the translation of passages from Shakespeare in "Sur la tragédie"—quite literally and in rhymed heroic couplets.

by conjunction with learning; but *Othello* is the vigorous and vivacious offspring of observation impregnated by genius. *Cato* affords a splendid exhibition of artificial and fictitious manners and delivers just and noble sentiments in diction easy, elevated, and harmonious, but its hopes and fears communicate no vibration to the heart; the composition refers us only to the writer. We pronounce the name of Cato, but we think on Addison.

The work of a correct and regular writer is a garden accurately formed and diligently planted, varied with shades and scented with flowers. The composition of Shakespeare is a forest in which oaks extend their branches and pines tower in the air, interspersed sometimes with weeds and brambles and sometimes giving shelter to myrtles and to roses; filling the eye with awful pomp and gratifying the mind with endless diversity. Other poets display cabinets of precious rarities minutely finished, wrought into shape, and polished into brightness. Shakespeare opens a mine which contains gold and diamonds in unexhaustible plenty, though clouded by incrustations, debased by impurities, and mingled with a mass of meaner minerals. . . .

GOTTHOLD EPHRAIM LESSING

(1729–1781)

o◯oo◯o

LESSING WROTE at the end of the neoclassical age, and his *Laokoon* is the product of neoclassical thinking, but in his *Hamburgische Dramaturgie* he took a liberal position which in some ways anticipated that of the romantic critics. He attacked mechanical rules, especially those of the classical French dramatists, and exalted Shakespeare, whose "unity of action" invalidated all other rules regarding the "unities."

The subject of *Laokoon* (1766), the confusion between the arts, had been discussed from the ancients down to Lessing's own day. Plutarch had quoted Simonides's definition of "painting as silent poetry, and poetry as speaking painting."[1] And Lessing quotes Voltaire's use of this same idea.[2] In fact, the neoclassical theory of "imitation" led many critics to regard the two arts as correlative.[3]

Lessing was likewise indebted to other writers to some extent for his own theory, particularly to Abbé Dubos.[4] But his main argument impressed his age as novel and profoundly true, and his chief sources seem to have been, as the work indicates in the quotations and allusions, the Greek statue, *Laocoön*, and Homer and Vergil's use of the fable. As the editor of the Bohn edition says, "The real originality of the work as a whole is patent, and the profound interest excited by it in minds most qualified to form a just estimate of it is the strongest proof of its merits. A book which filled Goethe, when a Leipzig student, with enthusiasm and which he unreservedly endorsed in later life, which Herder read three times through in a single afternoon and night, and from which Macaulay, as he told the late G. H. Lewes, learned more than he ever learned elsewhere, is one of which there is no room to question the intrinsic worth."[5]

---

[1]See Plutarch's *Comm. bellone an pace clariores fuerint Athenienses* (Reiske ed.), VII, 366.

[2]See Lessing's Preface to *Laokoon:* "Painting is dumb poetry, and poetry speaking painting."

[3]Cf. Dryden's *Parallel of Poetry and Painting* (1695).

[4]*Réflexions critiques sur la poésie et la peinture* (1719).

[5]*Laokoon* (London, 1914), p. xii.

Blümner, in his edition of the work, says that, "The tendency toward descriptive poetry . . . received through it its deathblow. . . . We may indeed affirm that the law forbidding the poet to paint has nowadays become a universally accepted doctrine."[6] But Blümner was undoubtedly wrong in this assertion in 1880, for soon after the publication of the *Laokoon* the whole romantic school, first in Germany and then in England, France, and America, achieved, as a doctrinary principle, the greatest "confusion" of the arts in the history of literature. Wackenroder believed that poetry lay conquered at the feet of music.[7] The whole school of the Schlegels, E. T. A. Hoffmann, and Novalis tried to make word-music, and most of the English romantic poets tried in the same way to paint word-pictures. The Pre-Raphaelite school drew its inspiration from painting, and, in the words of the late Professor Babbitt, Rossetti attempted "to paint sonnets and write his pictures."[8] Both Mallarmé and Lanier[9] tried to compose symphonies in words. Perhaps the latest spectacular attempt to combine painting and poetry was "Imagism," now dead as a movement but still influential as a technique in poetic style. But the fact that literary history has gone counter to Lessing's teachings need not therefore of necessity invalidate his doctrines. Nor has it, for *Laokoon* remains one of the great masterpieces in world literary criticism.

Professor Babbitt has written a searching analysis and invaluable supplement to Lessing's work, bringing the argument more or less up to date.[10] Lessing thought he was dealing with the pseudoclassic as opposed to the genuinely classic, but Professor Babbitt has shown that the conflict was really between what we today call "romantic" and "classic."

The extracts which we print below have been selected and translated by Mr. Field Horine.

BIBLIOGRAPHY

TEXT

Sämtliche Schriften, Hrsg. von Karl Lachmann, 3. neu durchgesehene und verm. aufl., besorgt durch Franz Muncker. 23 vols. Stuttgart, 1886–1924.
Laocoön, ed. with English notes by A. Hamann. Oxford, 1901. Authoritative edition of the German text.

[6]H. Blümner (1880), p. 138.
[7]Cf. Rudolf Haym, *Die romantische Schule* (Berlin, 1920), pp. 121 ff.
[8]Irving Babbitt, *The New Laokoön: An Essay on the Confusion of the Arts* (Boston, 1910), p. ix. [9]Cf. "The Symphony." [10]Babbitt, *op. cit.*

TRANSLATIONS

Laocoön, An Essay upon the Limits of Painting and Poetry, with Remarks Illustrative of Various Points in the History of Ancient Art, tr. by Ellen Frothingham. Boston, 1910.
——, tr. with preface and notes by the late Rt. Hon. Sir Robert Phillimore, Bart. London, 1905.
——, tr. by E. C. Beasley, and "How the Ancients Represented Death," tr. by Helen Zimmern. London, 1914.
Selected Prose Works, tr. by E. C. Beasley and Helen Zimmern. London, 1905.

CRITICISM

Babbitt, Irving, *The New Laokoön: An Essay on the Confusion of the Arts.* Boston, 1910.
Goddard, Eunice Rathbone, "Psychological Reasons for Lessing's Attitude toward Descriptive Poetry," *Publications of the Modern Language Association*, XXVI (1911), 593–603.
Meisnest, F. W., "Lessing and Shakespeare," *Publications of the Modern Language Association*, XIX (1904), 234–249.
Robertson, J. G., *Lessing's Dramatic Theory, being an Introduction to and Commentary on His Hamburgische Dramaturgie.* New York, 1939.
Rolleston, Thomas William Hazen, *Life of Gotthold Ephraim Lessing.* London, 1889.
Vail, C. C. D., *Lessing's Relation to the English Language and Literature.* Columbia University Press, 1936.

THE LAOKOON (*selections*) [1]

1766

Chapter XVI

But I shall attempt to derive the matter from its fundamental principles. I reason thus. If it is true that painting, in its imitations, makes use of means and symbols entirely different from those which poetry employs, the former using only forms and colors *in space*, and the latter articulated sounds *in time;* also, if these symbols must unquestionably be in proper relationship to that which is represented—then co-existent symbols can only express objects which are co-existent, or the parts of which co-exist; and symbols which are successive can only express objects which are successive, or the parts of which succeed one another in time.

[1] Translated for this anthology by Field Horine, from the authoritative edition of Lessing's *Laokoon*, edited with English notes by A. Hamann (Oxford, 1901).

Objects which co-exist, or the parts of which co-exist, are termed *bodies*. Consequently bodies, with their visible properties, are the proper objects of painting.

Objects which succeed one another in time, or the parts of which succeed one another in time, are generally termed *actions*. Hence, actions are the proper object of poetry.

But all bodies exist not only *in space* but also *in time*. They have continuous duration, and can, at any given moment of their duration, assume a different appearance, and stand in a different relationship to one another. Each of these momentary appearances and relationships is the effect of a preceding action, each can be the cause of a following action, and thus each represents, as it were, a center of action. It follows that painting can also express actions, but only by way of suggestion, by means of bodies. On the other hand, actions cannot subsist in and by themselves, but must invariably cling to certain beings. In so far, then, as these beings are bodies, or may be regarded as such, poetry also portrays bodies, but only indicatively, by means of actions.

Painting, in its compositions, in which the objects are necessarily co-existent, can make use of only a single moment of an action, and must therefore choose the most fertile one, the one out of which that which precedes and that which follows will be most intelligible. Similarly, poetry, in its progressive representations, can make use of only a single property of a body, and must therefore choose that one property which awakens the most vivid image of the body, from the point of view for which it is being employed. From this last is derived the rule of the singleness of picturesque epithets, and of frugality in the description of physical objects.[2]

I should have little confidence in this dry chain of argumentation if I did not find it fully corroborated by the practice of Homer, or rather, if it were not the practice of Homer that has introduced me to it. Only by means of these principles can we define and explain the great style of Homer, just as we can only in this way render justice to the exactly opposite style of so many modern poets who endeavor to rival the painter in a department in which they must inevitably be surpassed by him.

I find that Homer depicts nothing but progressive actions,

[2] I.e., the use of single descriptive epithets for single objects, such as Homer's "rosy-fingered dawn," "wine-dark sea," and so on.

and that he portrays all bodies, all individual things only in their relationship to these actions, usually with only *one* descriptive term for each. What wonder is it, then, that the painter sees little or nothing for himself to do with a descriptive passage from Homer; and that his harvest is to be gathered only where the story brings together a large group of beautiful bodies, in beautiful positions or attitudes, and in a space that is favorable to pictorial art, however little the poet may have described these bodies, these poses, and this space. One need only examine the whole series of paintings which were suggested to Caylus [3] by the poetry of Homer; in each one will be found ample proof of this observation.

Here I must leave the Count, who would make the color-grinding stone [4] of the painter into the touchstone of the poet, in order that I may explain further the style of Homer.

For *one thing*, I say, Homer usually gives only *one descriptive term*. A ship is, for him, now *the black ship*, now *the hollow ship;* now *the swift ship*, and at the most, *the well-rowed ship*. He does not enter further into a description of the ship; but the navigation, the weighing and the casting of the anchor—out of these he makes a detailed picture, from which the painter, if he wished to place all of it on his canvas, would have to make five or six separate paintings. If particular circumstances compel Homer to fix our attention for a longer time on one physical object, he nevertheless produces no painting which the actual painter could follow stroke for stroke with his brush. Rather, he knows how to place this single object, by means of innumerable artifices, into a series of moments in each of which it appears different. Thus only in the last one can the painter expect to show us, already completed, what the poet has shown us in the making. For example, when Homer wishes to show us the chariot of Juno, he has Hebe put it together piece by piece. We see the wheels, the axletrees, and the chariot-seat; the pole, the traces, and the straps, not as these parts are when fitted together but as they are being assembled by Hebe. To the description of the wheels alone does he apply more than one characterization, showing us the eight brazen spokes, the golden fellies, the tires of bronze, the silver hub—each individual part. One might almost say that, since there was more than one wheel,

[3]Count Caylus, (1692–1765), an art critic of considerable merit, is mentioned by Lessing here and on several other occasions.   [4]I.e., the palette.

Homer felt that he had to devote exactly as much more time, in their description, as their separate fastening required more time in the actual operation.

> Her golden-bridled steeds
> Then Saturn's daughter brought abroad; and Hebe, she proceeds,
> T' address her chariot instantly; she gives it—either wheel
> Beamed with eight spokes of sounding brass; the axle-tree was steel,
> The fell'ffs incorruptible gold, the upper bands of brass,
> Their matter most invalued, their work of wondrous grace.
> The naves in which the spokes were driven were all with silver bound;
> The chariot's seat, two hoops of gold and silver strengthened round
> With massy silver; on whose top, geres all of gold it wore,
> And golden poitrils.[5] . . .

But not only on those occasions on which Homer combines such ulterior purposes with his descriptions, but also when he is concerned primarily with the picture itself, will he disperse this picture over a sort of history of the object, in order to let the separate parts of it, which we see in nature as co-existent, follow each other naturally in his picture, and to allow them, as it were, to keep pace with the flow of language. For example, he wishes to paint for us the bow of Pandarus,—a bow of horn, of such and such a length, well polished and tipped at both ends with beaten gold. What does he do? Does he simply recount so dryly all these characteristics one after the other? By no means; that would be to give the order for such a bow and to describe how it was to be executed, but not to paint it. He begins with the hunt in which the wild goat was captured, from the horns of which the bow was made; Pandarus had lain in wait for it in the rocks and killed it; the horns were of extraordinary size, and for that reason he had determined to have a bow made from them; they are brought to the workshop, the artisan puts them together, polishes them, and decorates them. And thus with the poet, as I have said, we see in the making that which, with the painter, we can see only after it has already been put into its final form.

> Who instantly drew forth a bow most admirably made
> Of th' antler of a jumping goat, bred in a steep upland,
> Which archer-like (as long before he took his hidden stand

[5] *Iliad*, E. 722–731. This and the following passages from Homer, which Lessing quotes in the original Greek, are from Chapman's translation.

The doomed one skipping from a rock) into the breast he smote,
And headlong felled him from his cliff. The forehead of the goat
Held out a wondrous goodly palm that sixteen branches wrought,
Which piked and polished both the ends he hid with horns of gold.[6]

I should never finish if I wished to write out all the examples
of this sort. They will occur in multitudes to anyone who really
knows his Homer.

Chapter XVII

Yet, as you will object, the symbols of poetry are not simply
consecutive, but they are also arbitrary; and as arbitrary symbols they are, to be sure, capable of expressing bodies as they
exist in space. In Homer himself one could find examples of
this. One need only recollect Achilles' shield, in order to have the
most conclusive example of how discursively and yet poetically
one can depict a single object according to its co-existing parts.

I wish to make answer to this double objection—I call it
double because a correct conclusion must be considered as valid
even without an example; and, on the other hand, the example
from Homer is of importance to me, even though I am not yet
able to justify it by any conclusion. . . .

It is true that, since the symbols of speech are arbitrary, it is
as entirely possible to allow, through them, the parts of a body
to follow in succession, as it is possible, and frequent, to find
them co-existent in nature. This is, however, a characteristic of
speech and its symbols in general, but not in that relation which
is the most convenient to the purpose of poetry. The poet wishes
not merely to be understood, his ideas are not meant to be
simply clear and intelligible—with this the prose writer is content; but the poet wishes also to make the images which he
awakens in us so vivid that, from the rapidity with which they
arise, we shall believe ourselves to be really as conscious of their
objects as if they were actually presented to our senses; and at this
moment of illusion we cease to be conscious of the means he uses
for this purpose, namely, his words. This was the substance of the
definition of the poetic picture as given in the discussion above.

But the poet should always paint; and now we shall see how
well bodies, considered according to their co-existing parts,
adapt themselves to this type of painting.

[6]*Iliad*, D. 105, 111.

How do we obtain an adequate conception of a thing in space? First we observe its parts separately; then the connection between these parts; and finally we observe the object as a whole. Our senses perform these different operations with such astonishing rapidity that we are prone to think of them as but a single operation; and this rapidity is absolutely necessary if we are to gain an idea of the whole, which is nothing more than the result of the ideas of the parts and their relationships to each other. Assuming then also that the poet leads us from one part of the object to another in perfect order, assuming that he understands how to make the interrelationship of parts entirely evident: how much time is required for this? That which the poet gradually, and by degrees, reveals to us, the eye sweeps over at a single glance; and it not seldom occurs that we have forgotten the first feature of the description before we come to the last. We are, nevertheless, supposed to form from these several traits a picture of the object as a whole. To the eye these several parts remain constantly present; it can run over them again and again. For the ear, on the contrary, the parts which have once been heard are lost unless they remain clear in the mind. Yet even if we do remember them exactly, what pains, what tremendous exertion it costs us to renew all the impressions in the proper order, or to think back over them all even with moderate rapidity, in order to succeed in obtaining an approximate idea of the whole!

Let us make the experiment with an example which may be called a masterpiece of its kind:

> Thus does the noble Gentian raise his head
> High o'er the lower troop of common plants,
> Beneath its standard serve a tribe of flowers;
> Its own blue brother bows and honors it.
> While golden pyramids of brilliant flowers
> Cling round the stem and crown its robe of green,
> The leaves of brilliant white, with deepest green,
> Streaked and inlaid throughout, are seen to glow
> With the moist diamond's many-colored rays.
> Most righteous law! uniting strength with grace,
> In the fair body dwells the fairer soul.
> Here creeps a lowly plant like some grey mist,
> Its leaves by nature shaped as cruciform;
> Two gilded beaks formed by the lovely flower

Spring from a bird made out of amethyst.
Here a bright finger-fashioned leaf doth cast
Its green reflection in the limpid stream.
The flower of snow, with purple lightly tinged,
Environed by the white rays of a star;
Emeralds and roses deck the trodden heath,
And cliffs are covered with a purple robe.[7]

Here are plants and flowers which the learned poet paints with skill and according to nature. He paints, yes, but without producing any illusion. I will not say that a person who has never seen these flowers and plants could not gain any idea of their appearance. It may be that all poetic pictures require a previous acquaintance with their objects. I also do not deny that the poet might awaken a more vivid image of some parts of the picture in a person who does have the advantage of such a previous acquaintance. I only ask how it stands with the idea of the picture as a whole. If this, too, is to be more vivid, then no individual parts of the picture should predominate; but rather, the brighter light must be equally distributed over them all. The imaginative powers must be able to glance rapidly over all alike, in order to gain a unified impression of that which is seen in nature as a unified picture. Is that the case here? If it is not, how was it possible for someone to state "that the most accurate drawing of a painter must be quite flat and dark when compared with this poetical representation"?[8] It is definitely inferior to that which lines and colors on a plane surface can express, and the critic who gives it such exaggerated praise must have considered it from an entirely false point of view. He must have looked more at the extraneous embellishments which the poet has woven into his description, or at the exaltation over vegetable life, at the development of its inner completeness, to which the outward beauty of it serves only as a shell—all this he must have considered in more detail than the beauty itself and than the degree of vividness and the verisimilitude of the picture which the painter, and the true poet as well, can furnish us.

Here we are concerned, however, only with this last, and whoever would say that these lines alone:

[7]The translation of this passage from Haller's *Die Alpen* is that of Sir Robert Phillimore, *Laocoön* (London, 1905), pp. 140–141.
[8]Breitinger's *Critical Poetics*, II, p. 807. (Lessing's note.)

'While golden pyramids of brilliant flowers
Cling round the stem and crown its robe of green,
The leaves of brilliant white, with deepest green,
Streaked and inlaid throughout, are seen to glow
With the moist diamond's many-colored rays.

that those lines, in respect of the impression which they make, can rival a picture by Van Huysum—whoever would say that must either not have consulted his sensations, or must have wanted to contradict them deliberately. They may be well suited to recitation if one has the flower itself in one's hand; but in and for themselves they express little or nothing. In every word I hear the laboring poet, but the thing itself I am far from perceiving.

I repeat, then, that I do not deny to language generally the ability to depict an object as a whole by describing its component parts; language *can* do that because its symbols are arbitrary signs, even though they do follow each other consecutively. I do, however, deny this possibility to language as a means of poetry because that sort of verbal pictures of objects lacks the power of creating an illusion, upon which power poetry chiefly depends. This power of illusion, I say, must be lacking in such pictures due to the fact that the co-existence of bodies necessarily comes into conflict with the consecutiveness of language. Now, because the former is dissolved in the latter, the analysis of the whole into its constituent parts becomes exceedingly difficult indeed, often impossible.

Everywhere, therefore, where the creation of an illusion is not essential, and where the primary purpose of a writer is to appeal to the *understanding*, to the *intellect*, of the reader, and to express ideas which shall be clear and as complete as possible— wherever this is the case, these pictures of objects may indeed have a place, although they must be excluded from true poetry.

Chapter XXIII

One single unseemly part can mar the harmonious effect of many other parts used to create beauty; yet, even then, the object will not be ugly on that account alone. Even ugliness requires several disagreeable parts which we must be able to perceive at one and the same time (just as we have seen this to be true for the beautiful), if we are to feel the opposite of that which we feel on seeing beautiful objects.

Ugliness, therefore, considered according to its essential nature, cannot be an object of poetry; yet Homer pictures the most extreme ugliness in the person of Thersites, and he describes this ugliness by painting for us its co-existent aspects. Why, in picturing ugliness, was that conceded to him which, in portraying beauty, he himself so sedulously avoided? Will not the effect of ugliness be lessened by a successive enumeration of its elements, just as the effect of beauty is impaired by a similar enumeration of *its* elements?

This is most assuredly true; but in just that lies the justification of Homer's procedure. It is precisely because ugliness, in the description given of it by the poet, becomes less a disgusting appearance of bodily imperfection and, ceasing to be ugliness when seen from the point of view of its effect, is then useful to the poet. And that which he cannot use for itself he uses as an ingredient to cause, or to strengthen, certain mixed sensations, with which he must absorb our attention, lacking, as he does, the possibility of awakening in us purely pleasant sensations.

These mixed sensations are the *ridiculous* and the *horrible.*

Homer makes Thersites [9] ugly in order to make him ridiculous. He becomes ridiculous, however, not only as a result of his ugliness. For ugliness is imperfection; and for an effect that shall be ridiculous a contrast between perfection and imperfection is necessary.[10] This is the explanation which a friend of mine has given, and to it I should like to add that this contrast should not be too harsh and sharp; that the *opposita*, to continue in the painter's terminology, must be of such a kind as to melt into one another. The wise and just Aesop does not appear ridiculous, if one assigns to him the ugliness of Thersites. It was only the stupid whim of a monk to attempt to transfer also to his person the comical element in his instructive fables, by representing him as deformed. A misshapen body and a beautiful soul are like oil and vinegar, which remain separate to the taste even if they are mixed together. They do not furnish a third sensation. The body arouses feelings of displeasure; the soul, sensations of pleasure—each has its own sentiment for itself. It is only if the deformed body is at the same time weak and invalid, if it hinders the spirit in its functioning, if it becomes

---

[9] A slanderous quarreler among the Greeks before Troy.

[10] *Philos. Schriften des Herrn Moses Mendelssohn* (*Sämtliche Werke*, 7 vols. Leipzig, 1843-1844), II, 23.

the source of disadvantageous prejudices against the spirit—
then disgust and pleasure flow together; but the new sensation
arising from this is not the desire to laugh, but rather a feeling
of sympathy. And the object which we otherwise should have
respected becomes intriguing and interesting for us. The
deformed and sickly Pope must have been far more interesting to
his friends than the handsome and healthy Wycherley was to his.

As little as Thersites appears ridiculous as a result of his
ugliness alone, just as little would he be ridiculous without it.
Ugliness, the correspondence of this ugliness with his character,
the contradiction which both of these present to his ideas of his
own importance, the harmless effects of his malevolent garrulity,
by which he alone was humiliated—all this must work together
toward the end of his seeming ridiculous. This last element is
that *harmlessness* (Οὐ φθαρτικόν) which Aristotle[11] considers indispensable to the ridiculous. Similarly, my friend believes
it necessary that the contrast I have spoken of should be on the
whole of little importance, and should not especially arouse
our interest. If we only assume that Thersites' malicious dis-
paragement of Agamemnon had cost him dearly, that he had
had to pay for it with death rather than with a few bloody
stripes, then we should cease laughing at him. For this monster
of a man is still a man, whose death would always seem a greater
evil than all his deformities and vices. In order to experience
this we have only to read the account of his death as given by
Quintus Calaber.[12] Achilles regrets having killed Penthesilea;
her beauty, though she is now covered with her own blood so
bravely shed, demands the high esteem and the sympathy of the
hero; and high esteem and sympathy become love. But the
slanderous Thersites goes so far as to accuse him of this love as
though it were a crime. He rages against voluptuousness, which
can seduce, he says, even the bravest of men to follies (737 ff.):

> That deprives a man of his reason,
> Be he never so wise.[13]

Achilles grows furious, and without answering a word, strikes
him so ungently between the cheek and the ear, that his teeth, his
blood, and his soul are vomited up together. It is too dreadful!

---

[11]*Poetics*, chap. v. [12]*Paralipom.*, I, 720–778.
[13]Quoted in Greek by Lessing. The translation is that given by A. Hamann, *op.
cit.*, p. 287.

The hasty, murderous Achilles becomes more odious to me than
the crafty, grumbling Thersites; the shout of joy which the
Greeks raise at this deed insults me; I go over to the side of Dio-
medes, who is already brandishing his sword to take revenge on
the murderer for the crime committed against his kinsman; and
I feel that Thersites is also a kinsman of mine, a human being.

Let us assume, however, that, at the instigation of Thersites,
mutiny had broken out, that the rebellious army had boarded
the ships, and treacherously deserted its leaders, who had fallen
into the hands of a vengeful enemy; and that then a divine
punishment had sealed the fate of the army and the fleet, doom-
ing them to utter destruction. How would we then have been
affected by Thersites' ugliness? If harmless ugliness can become
ludicrous, harmful ugliness is always horrifying. . . .

Chapter XXIV

We have seen how the poet employs ugliness of forms. What
use of them is to be allowed for the painter?

Painting, regarded as dexterity in imitation, can express
ugliness; but, considered as an art of the beautiful, painting does
not wish to express ugliness. As the former, it has at its disposal
all visible objects; as the latter, it confines itself to those objects
which excite pleasant sensations.

But are not even unpleasant sensations pleasing when they
have their origin in imitations? Not all of them. A discerning
critic has already remarked this on the subject of disgust:

> Representations of fear, sadness, terror, compassion, etc., can
> excite aversion only insofar as we consider the evil as real.
> Through the recollection that it is an artificial deception, these
> feelings can be resolved into pleasant sensations. The revolting
> sensation of disgust, however, by virtue of the law of the imagi-
> native powers, arises in conjunction with a mere idea in the mind,
> whether the object is considered real, or not. Of what help, then,
> is it to an offended imagination when the art of imitation dis-
> closes its identity? The aversion arose not from the presumption
> that the evil was real, but from the mere idea of it; and this really
> is present. Sensations of disgust, therefore, always come from
> nature, and never from imitations of nature.[14]

[14]Moses Mendelssohn, *Briefe, die neueste Litteratur betreffend, Werke, op. cit.,* V, 102.
(Lessing's note.)

Just this holds true for ugliness of forms. Ugliness offends our sense of sight, runs counter to our taste for order and harmony, and arouses aversion, regardless of the actual existence of the object in which we perceive it. We may not like to see Thersites either in nature or in a description; and even if the description of him is less displeasing, still this is not because his bodily ugliness ceases to be ugliness when it is only an imitation, but because we are capable of withdrawing our thoughts from this ugliness, and of enjoying simply the art of the painter. But even this enjoyment will be interrupted every few moments by a consideration of how illy applied this art is. This consideration will seldom fail to bring about a contempt for the artist.

Aristotle assigns another reason [15] to the fact that things which we regard only with displeasure in *nature*, become pleasurable in a *representation*, even the most exact one. This reason is the universal curiosity of man. We are pleased if we can learn to know, through a representation, what each thing is, τi $\ddot{\epsilon}\kappa\alpha\sigma\tau\sigma\nu$, or if we can draw our own conclusions as to whether it is this or that other thing, $\sigma\tilde{\upsilon}\tau\sigma\varsigma$ $\dot{\epsilon}\kappa\epsilon\tilde{\iota}\nu\sigma\varsigma$. But no inference can be drawn from this in favor of the representation of ugliness. The pleasure which arises from the satisfaction of our curiosity is only momentary, and only by chance incident to the object over which the satisfaction is experienced. The displeasure, on the other hand, which accompanies the sight of ugliness, is permanent, and an essential characteristic of the object that arouses it. How, then, can the former counterbalance the latter? Still less can the momentary pleasant occupation which the observation of similarity affords us overcome the unpleasant effect of the ugliness. The more closely I compare the ugly imitation with the ugly original, the more do I expose myself to this effect, so that the pleasure of comparison soon vanishes, and nothing remains but the disagreeable impression of double ugliness. To judge by the examples which Aristotle gives, it would seem that even he himself did not wish to consider ugliness of form as one of the unpleasant objects that can afford diversion in their imitations. These examples are of savage beasts and of corpses. Wild beasts excite terror even though they may be ugly; and this terror, not their ugliness, is what is resolved into a pleasurable sensation when they are seen in an imitation. Thus also with corpses; the more nearly dominant feeling of

[15]*Poetics*, chap. IV.

compassion, or the awful contemplation of our own destruction is what renders, in nature, a corpse so disagreeable. In an imitation, however, this compassion loses its potency, convinced of the unreality of the death represented; and the addition of flattering circumstances can either remove us entirely from such a mournful contemplation of death, or is so inseparably connected with it, that we believe it to be more attractive than terrifying.

Thus ugliness of forms in and by itself cannot be an object of painting as a fine art, because the sensations aroused by it are displeasing and are also not of that sort of unpleasant sensations which are transformed by their imitations into pleasant ones. It now remains to be seen whether ugliness of forms can be used as an ingredient to strengthen other sensations, as is the case in poetry.

Can painting avail itself of ugly forms to attain the effect of the ludicrous or of the horrifying?

I should not dare to answer this with a definite and positive *No.* It is indisputable that harmless ugliness can become a means for the attainment of an effect of the ridiculous, especially if an affectation of grace and dignity be united with it. It is equally incontestable that harmful ugliness, just as in nature, so also in a painting, can arouse fear; and that that ridiculousness and this fearfulness, which are in themselves mixed sensations, receive through their imitation a new degree of attractiveness and pleasantness.

I must, however, emphasize the fact that painting and poetry are not in exactly the same situation, in this respect. In poetry, as I have remarked, ugliness of form loses its disagreeable effect almost entirely through the transformation of its actually coexistent parts into successive ones; and from this point of view it ceases, as it were, to be ugliness. It can for this reason be combined more intimately with other phenomena to facilitate the creation of a new and different effect. In painting, on the contrary, ugliness has all its forces gathered together, and produces an effect not much weaker than in nature itself. *Harmless* ugliness can consequently not well remain, for long, ridiculous. The unpleasant sensation gains the upper hand, and what was ludicrous in the first few moments becomes merely horrible in longer contemplation. And it is the same with *harmful* ugliness: the fearful aspect of it is soon lost, and deformity remains alone and unalterable. . . .

EDWARD YOUNG
1683—1765

o◯oo◯o

PERHAPS THE MOST POSITIVE mid-eighteenth-century reaction against the tyranny of the principle of imitation was Dr. Young's *Conjectures on Original Composition.*[1] The writers of the Augustan age considered imitation of the classics identical with imitation of nature;[2] they accepted Horace's dictum that a poet must have genius, but that he can do nothing without the assistance of learning and the labor of the file.[3] Furthermore, they did not look with favor on either an untutored genius[4] or a too luxuriant imagination.[5] Young insists that genius should be allowed freedom of expression unhampered by any regard for the forms and rules derived from the ancients, and that creative imagination should be considered one of the chief qualifications for poetic writing.

None of this is particularly startling or original. Other poets and critics of the second and third quarters of the eighteenth century were mulling over the same ideas. Dr. Johnson, the so-called bulwark of

---

[1]The essay was in the process of being written as early as 1756, although it was not published until 1759. The revisions and additions are discussed in a series of letters between Young and Richardson, to whom the essay was addressed. These letters explain the inclusion of moral sentiments in the piece. See Alan D. McKillop, "Richardson, Young, and the *Conjectures,*" *Modern Philology,* XX (May, 1925), 391–404.

[2]For Pope's expression of this idea, see above, *Essay on Criticism,* ll. 130–140 .

[3]This, like all unqualified generalities, is none too near the truth. The literary men of the first half of the eighteenth century were well aware of the existence of natural genius. Shakespeare was the great example of the poet who wrote without rules and with no thought of imitation. Pope readily granted that there was "a grace beyond the reach of art." He could write *Bathos; or, Of the Art of Sinking in Poetry* and Swift could write *Poetry: A Rhapsody,* both pieces satirizing the rules with which their period has come to be identified.

[4]Hogarth's comment on genius bears some imprint of the thought of the age: " 'I know of no such thing as genius,' said our Mr. Hogarth to Mr. Gilbert Cooper one day, 'genius is nothing but labor and diligence' " (William Seward, *Biographiana* [London, 1799], II, 293).

[5]See Donald Bond, " 'Distrust' of the Imagination in English Neo-Classicism" (*Philological Quarterly,* XIV [January, 1935], 54–69), for an appraisal of the early eighteenth-century attitude toward imagination, which was not so distrustful as is sometimes thought.

classicism, defended originality;[6] he was also opposed to imitative verse. "No man ever yet became great by imitation. Whatever hopes for the veneration of mankind must have invention in the design or the execution; either the effect must itself be new, or the means by which it is produced. . . . That which hopes to resist the blast of malignity, and stand firm against the attacks of time, must contain in itself some original principle of growth."[7] Joseph Warton declared his belief in imagination in the Dedication prefixed to *An Essay on the Genius and Writings of Pope:* "a clear head and acute understanding are not sufficient, alone, to make a POET; . . . it is a creative and glowing IMAGINATION, *acer spiritus ac vis,* and that alone, that can stamp a writer with this exalted and very uncommon character, which so few possess, and of which so few can properly judge."[8] The materials of the *Conjectures* are those which have interested philosophers and critics from earliest times,[9] and the reader of the essay is always conscious of the murmur of earlier voices [10] as well as the nearer speech of Young's contemporaries. This is necessarily true since Young wrote of the inspiration and the original genius of the poet, the materials of poetry, and the poet's force for moral good. The *Conjectures* is a fresh and stimulating interpretation of these concepts.

In his *Essay on Original Genius,* William Duff clarifies Young's discussion of imagination and genius. Duff describes imagination as "that faculty whereby the mind not only reflects on its own operations, but which assembles the various ideas conveyed to the understanding by the canal of sensation, and treasured up in the repository of the memory, compounding or disjoining them at pleasure; and which by its plastic power of inventing new associations of ideas, and of combining them with infinite variety, is enabled to present a creation of its own, and to exhibit senses and objects which never existed in nature." [11] The definition of imagination was coming closer to Shelley's

[6]*Rambler,* no. 143.   [7]*Rambler,* no. 154.

[8]*An Essay on the Genius and Writing of Pope* (London, 1756).

[9]See Gilbert, *Literary Criticism: Plato to Dryden,* Index, imitation, genius, imagination, inspiration.

[10]It is interesting to note that Philostratus (*c.* 170–245) includes a discussion of the relative importance of imitation and imagination in a debate in his *Life of Apollonius of Tyana.* The ideas expressed in the passage are similar to those of Young and Warton. "Imitation will fashion what it has seen, but imagination goes on to what it has not seen, which it will assume as the standard of reality; and imitation is often baffled by awe, but imagination by nothing, for it rises unawed to the height of its own ideal" (Bk. VI, chap. XIX, ed. Loeb; II, 77–81, for entire debate). Cited by Katharine Gilbert and Helmut Kuhn, *A History of Esthetics* (New York, 1939), p. 108.

[11]*An Essay on Original Genius and Its Various Modes of Exertion in Philosophy and the Fine Arts, Particularly Poetry* (London, 1767), p. 17.

concept of it as "the immortal God which should assume flesh for the redemption of mortal passion."[12] It was becoming Coleridge's "living power and prime agent of all human perception."[13]

BIBLIOGRAPHY

TEXT

Complete Works. 2 vols. Rev. ed. with *Life* by J. Doran. London, 1854.
Conjectures on Original Composition, ed. Edith J. Morley. Manchester, 1918.

CRITICAL

Bowen, Marjorie, "Edward Young," in *Transactions of the Royal Society of Literature*, N.S., VIII, 1928.

Brandl, Alois L., Preface to reprint in the *Jahrbuch der deutschen Shakespeare Gesellschaft*, XXXIX (1903).

Jahn, Kurt, ed., *Edward Young's Gedanken über die Originalwerke in einem Schreiben an S. R. übersetz v. H. E. von Teubern.* Bonn, 1910.

Kind, John Louis, *Edward Young in Germany.* New York, 1906.

Mann, Elizabeth L., "The Problem of Originality in English Literary Criticism, 1750–1800," *Philological Quarterly*, XVIII, 97–118 (April, 1939).

McKillop, Alan D., "Richardson, Young, and the *Conjectures*," *Modern Philology*, XXII (May, 1925) 391–404.

Steinke, M. W., *Edward Young's "Conjectures on Original Composition" in England and Germany.* New York, 1917.

CONJECTURES ON ORIGINAL COMPOSITION
(*selections*)
1759

It is with thoughts as it is with words; and with both as with men; they may grow old and die. Words tarnished, by passing through the mouths of the vulgar, are laid aside as inelegant, and obsolete. So thoughts, when become too common, should lose their currency; and we should send new metal to the mint, that is, new meaning to the press. The division of tongues at Babel did not more effectually debar men from *making themselves a name* (as the Scripture speaks) than the too great concurrence, or union of tongues, will do forever. We may as well grow good by another's virtue, or fat by another's food, as famous by

---

[12]Preface to *The Cenci.*   [13]*Biographia Literaria*, chap. XVIII.

another's thought. The world will pay its debt of praise but once; and, instead of applauding, explode a second demand, as a cheat.

If it is said that most of the Latin classics, and all the Greek, except perhaps Homer, Pindar, and Anacreon, are in the number of imitators, yet receive our highest applause; our answer is, that they, though not *real*, are accidental originals; the works they imitated, few excepted, are lost: they, on their father's decease, enter as lawful heirs on their estates in fame: the fathers of our copyists are still in possession and secured in it, in spite of Goths and flames, by the perpetuating power of the press. Very late must a modern imitator's fame arrive if it waits for their decease.

An original enters early on reputation: Fame, fond of new glories, sounds her trumpet in triumph at its birth; and yet how few are awakened by it into the noble ambition of like attempts? Ambition is sometimes no vice in life; it is always a virtue in composition. High in the towering Alps is the fountain of the Po; high in fame and in antiquity is the fountain of an imitator's undertaking; but the river, and the imitation, humbly creep along the vale. So few are our originals that, if all other books were to be burnt, the lettered world would resemble some metropolis in flames, where a few incombustible buildings, a fortress, temple, or tower, lift their heads in melancholy grandeur amid the mighty ruin. Compared with this conflagration, old Omar lighted up but a small bonfire when he heated the baths of the barbarians for eight months together with the famed Alexandrian library's inestimable spoils, that no profane book might obstruct the triumphant progress of his holy Alcoran round the globe.

But why are originals so few? not because the writer's harvest is over, the great reapers of antiquity having left nothing to be gleaned after them; nor because the human mind's teeming time is past, or because it is incapable of putting forth unprecedented births; but because illustrious examples engross, prejudice, and intimidate. They engross our attention, and so prevent a due inspection of ourselves; they prejudice our judgment in favor of their abilities, and so lessen the sense of our own; and they intimidate us with the splendor of their renown, and thus under diffidence bury our strength. Nature's impossibilities and those of diffidence lie wide asunder.

Let it not be suspected that I would weakly insinuate anything in favor of the moderns, as compared with ancient authors; no, I am lamenting their great inferiority. But I think it is no *necessary* inferiority; that it is not from divine destination, but from some cause far beneath the moon: I think that human souls, through all periods, are equal; that due care and exertion would set us nearer our immortal predecessors than we are at present; and he who questions and confutes this will show abilities not a little tending toward a proof of that equality which he denies.

After all, the first ancients had no merit in being originals: they could not be imitators. Modern writers have a choice to make, and therefore have a merit in their power. They may soar in the regions of liberty or move in the soft fetters of easy imitation; and imitation has as many plausible reasons to urge as pleasure had to offer to Hercules. Hercules made the choice of an hero and *so* became immortal.

Yet let not assertors of classic excellence imagine that I deny the tribute it so well deserves. He that admires not ancient authors betrays a secret he would conceal, and tells the world that he does not understand them. Let us be as far from neglecting, as from copying, their admirable compositions; sacred be their rights, and inviolable their fame. Let our understanding feed on theirs; they afford the noblest nourishment; but let them nourish, not annihilate, our own. When we read, let our imagination kindle at their charms; when we write, let our judgment shut them out of our thoughts; treat even Homer himself as his royal admirer was treated by the cynic; bid him stand aside, nor shade our composition from the beams of our own genius; for nothing original can rise, nothing immortal, can ripen in any other sun.[1]

Must we then, you say, not imitate ancient authors? Imitate them by all means; but imitate aright. He that imitates the divine *Iliad* does not imitate Homer, but he who takes the same method which Homer took for arriving at a capacity of accomplishing a work so great. Tread in his steps to the sole fountain

[1]See Samuel Daniel, *A Defense of Rhyme* (ed. by G. B. Harrison, Bodley Head Quarto Reprint, 1925, pp. 17–18): "Methinks we should not so soon yield our consents captive to the authority of antiquity, unless we saw more reason; all our understandings are not to be built by the square of Greece and Italy. We are the children of nature as well as they; we are not so placed out of the way of judgment, but that the same sun of discretion shineth upon us; we have our portion of the same virtues as well as of the same vices."

of immortality; drink where he drank, at the true Helicon, that is, at the breast of nature: imitate; but imitate not the composition, but the man. For may not this paradox pass into a maxim? viz., "The less we copy the renowned ancients, we shall resemble them the more."

But possibly you may reply that you must either imitate Homer, or depart from nature. Not so: for suppose you was to change place, in time, with Homer; then, if you write naturally, you might as well charge Homer with an imitation of you. Can you be said to imitate Homer for writing *so*, as you would have written if Homer had never been? As far as a regard to nature and sound sense will permit a departure from your great predecessors, so far ambitiously depart from them; the farther from them in similitude, the nearer are you to them in excellence; you rise by it into an original; become a noble collateral, not an humble descendant from them. Let us build our compositions with the spirit, and in the taste, of the ancients;[2] but not with their materials: thus will they resemble the structures of Pericles at Athens, which Plutarch commends for having had an air of antiquity as soon as they were built. All eminence and distinction lies out of the beaten road; excursion and deviation are necessary to find it; and the more remote your path from the highway, the more reputable, if, like poor Gulliver (of whom anon) you fall not into a ditch in your way to glory. . . .

A star of the first magnitude among the moderns was Shakespeare; among the ancients, Pindar; who (as Vossius tells us) boasted of his no-learning, calling himself the eagle for his flight above it. And such genii as these may, indeed, have much reliance on their own native powers. For genius may be compared to the natural strength of the body; learning to the superinduced accouterments of arms: if the first is equal to the proposed exploit, the latter rather encumbers than assists, rather retards than promotes the victory. *Sacer nobis inest Deus*,[3] says Seneca. With regard to the moral world, conscience, with regard to the intellectual, genius, is that god within. Genius can set us right in composition without the rules of the learned; as

[2] See the Preface to *Imperium Pelagi: A Naval Lyric* (1730), in which Young explains his aim in a line under the title: "Written in Imitation of Pindar's Spirit."

[3] "Holy is the God within us." Probably taken from *Epistulae morales*, XLI, 1–2, of Seneca the younger: "God is near you, he is with you, he is within. So I say . . . that the holy spirit resides within you."

conscience sets us right in life, without the laws of the land: *this*, singly, can make us good, as men: *that*, singly, as writers, can sometimes make us great.

I say, sometimes, because there is a genius which stands in need of learning to make it shine. Of genius there are two species, an earlier, and a later; or call them *infantine*, and *adult*. An adult genius comes out of nature's hand, as Pallas out of Jove's head, at full growth and mature: Shakespeare's genius was of this kind; on the contrary, Swift stumbled at the threshold and set out for distinction on feeble knees: his was an infantine genius; a genius which, like other infants, must be nursed and educated,[4] or it will come to nought: learning is its nurse and tutor; but this nurse may overlay with an indigested load, which smothers common sense; and this tutor may mislead, with pedantic prejudice, which vitiates the best understanding: as too great admirers of the fathers of the Church have sometimes set up their authority against the true sense of Scripture; so too great admirers of the classical fathers have sometimes set up their authority, or example, against reason.

Neve minor, neu sit quinto productior actu Fabula.[5]

So says Horace; so says ancient example. But reason has not subscribed. I know but one book that can justify our implicit acquiescence in it: and (by the way) on that book a noble disdain of undue deference to prior opinion has lately cast, and is still casting, a new and inestimable light.

But, superstition for our predecessors set aside, the classics are forever our rightful and revered masters in composition, and our understandings bow before them. But when? When a master is wanted, which sometimes, as I have shown, is not the case. Some are pupils of nature only, nor go farther to school:[6]

[4]See Addison's remarks on these two types of genius, *Spectator*, no. 160, above p. 27. Brandl, *op. cit.*, p. 4, refers to Shaftesbury's *Characteristics*, where a similar distinction is made between the two types of genius; one type is the "natural and simple genius of antiquity" and the other is developed from "the critical art itself, and from the more accurate inspection into the works of preceding masters."

[5]"Let your play be neither shorter nor longer than five acts" (Horace, *Art of Poetry*, 189).

Seneca followed the rule of Horace in his tragedies and they were imitated in the Renaissance period. The division of Shakespearian drama into five acts was probably due to this dictum of Horace.

[6]"Not but I think a painter may make a better face than ever was; but he must do it by a kind of felicity, as a musician that maketh an excellent air in music, and not by rule" (Bacon, Essay XLIII, "Of Beauty").

from such we reap often a double advantage; they not only rival the reputation of the great ancient authors but also reduce the number of mean ones among the moderns. For when they enter on subjects which have been in former hands, such is their superiority that, like a tenth wave, they overwhelm and bury in oblivion all that went before: and thus not only enrich and adorn, but remove a load and lessen the labor of the lettered world.

"But," you say, "since originals can arise from genius only, and since genius is so very rare, it is scarce worth while to labor a point so much, from which we can reasonably expect so little." To show that genius is not so very rare as you imagine, I shall point out strong instances of it in a far distant quarter from that mentioned above. The minds of the schoolmen were almost as much cloistered as their bodies; they had but little learning and few books; yet may the most learned be struck with some astonishment at their so singular natural sagacity and most exquisite edge of thought. Who would expect to find Pindar and Scotus, Shakespeare and Aquinas, of the same party? Both equally show an original, unindebted energy; the *vigor igneus* and *caelestis origo* burns in both, and leaves us in doubt whether genius is more evident in the sublime flights and beauteous flowers of poetry, or in the profound penetrations and marvelously keen and minute distinctions called the thorns of the schools. There might have been more able consuls called from the plow than ever arrived at that honor: many a genius, probably, there has been which could neither write nor read. So that genius, that supreme luster of literature, is less rare than you conceive.

By the praise of genius we detract not from learning; we detract not from the value of gold by saying that diamond has greater still. He who disregards learning shows that he wants its aid; and he that overvalues it shows that its aid has done him harm. Overvalued indeed it cannot be, if genius, as to composition, is valued more. Learning we thank, genius we revere; that gives us pleasure, this gives us rapture; that informs, this inspires, and is itself inspired; for genius is from heaven, learning from man: this sets us above the low and illiterate; that, above the learned and polite. Learning is borrowed knowledge; genius is knowledge innate, and quite our own. Therefore, as Bacon observes, it may take a nobler name, and be called wisdom; in which sense of wisdom, some are born wise.

. . . [Nature] brings us into the world all originals: no two faces, no two minds, are just alike; but all bear nature's evident mark of separation on them. Born originals, how comes it to pass that we die copies? That meddling ape, Imitation, as soon as we come to years of indiscretion (so let me speak), snatches the pen, and blots out nature's mark of separation, cancels her kind intention, destroys all mental individuality; the lettered world no longer consists of singulars, it is a medley, a mass; and a hundred books, at bottom, are but one. Why are monkeys such masters of mimicry? Why receive they such a talent at imitation? Is it not as the Spartan slaves received a license for ebriety that their betters might be ashamed of it?

. . . I will speak of one which is sure of your applause. Shakespeare mingled no water with his wine, lowered his genius by no vapid imitation. Shakespeare gave us a Shakespeare, nor could the first in ancient fame have given us more! Shakespeare is not their son, but brother—their equal—and that, in spite of all his faults. Think you this too bold? Consider, in those ancients what is it the world admires? Not the fewness of their faults, but the number and brightness of their beauties; and if Shakespeare is their equal (as he doubtless is) in that which in them is admired, then is Shakespeare as great as they; and not impotence, but some other cause, must be charged with his defects. When we are setting these great men in competition, what but the comparative size of their genius is the subject of our inquiry? And a giant loses nothing of his size, though he should chance to trip in his race. But it is a compliment to those heroes of antiquity to suppose Shakespeare their equal only in dramatic powers; therefore, though his faults had been greater, the scale would still turn in his favor. There is at least as much genius on the British as on the Grecian stage, though the former is not swept so clean; so clean from violations not only of the *dramatic*, but *moral* rule; for an honest heathen, on reading some of our celebrated scenes, might be seriously concerned to see that our obligations to the religion of nature were canceled by Christianity.

Jonson, in the serious drama, is as much an imitator as Shakespeare is an original. He was very learned, as Sampson was very strong, to his own hurt: blind to the nature of tragedy, he pulled down all antiquity on his head, and buried himself under it; we see nothing of Jonson, nor indeed, of his admired (but also murdered) ancients; for what shone in the historian is a cloud on the poet; and *Catiline* might have been a good play if Sallust had never writ.[7]

Who knows whether Shakespeare might not have thought less, if he had read more? Who knows if he might not have labored under the load of Jonson's learning, as Enceladus under Aetna? His mighty genius, indeed, through the most mountainous oppression would have breathed out some of his inextinguishable fire; yet possibly he might not have risen up into that giant, that much more than common man, at which we now gaze with amazement, and delight. Perhaps he was as learned as his dramatic province required; for, whatever other learning he wanted, he was master of two books unknown to many of the profoundly read, though books which the last conflagration alone can destroy; the book of nature and that of man. These he had by heart, and has transcribed many admirable pages of them into his immortal works. These are the fountain head, whence the Castalian streams of original composition flow; and these are often mudded by other waters, though waters in their distinct channel, most wholesome and pure: as two chemical liquors, separately clear as crystal, grow foul by mixture, and offend the sight. So that he had not only as much learning as his dramatic province required, but, perhaps, as it could safely bear. If Milton had spared some of his learning, his muse would have gained more glory than he would have lost by it.

Dryden, destitute of Shakespeare's genius, had almost as much learning as Jonson and, for the buskin, quite as little taste. He was a stranger to the pathos, and by numbers, expression, sentiment, and every other dramatic cheat strove to make amends for it; as if a saint could make amends for the want of conscience; a soldier, for the want of valor; or a vestal, of modesty. The noble nature of tragedy disclaims an equivalent; like virtue, it demands the heart; and Dryden had none to give. Let epic poets think, the tragedian's point is rather to feel; such distant things are a tragedian and a poet that the latter indulged destroys the former. Look on Barnwell, and Essex, and see how as to these distant characters Dryden excels, and is excelled. But the strongest demonstration of his no-taste for the buskin are

[7]Young's verses, published in *St. James Magazine* (March, 1763), p. 63 and in the *Universal Magazine*, XXXVII (1765), 209, contain almost the same comparison of Shakespeare and Jonson, as does also the Prologue to *Julius Caesar* (attributed to Dryden). See Robert Gale Noyes, *Ben Jonson on the English Stage, 1660–1776* (Cambridge, Mass., 1935), p. 9.

his tragedies fringed with rhyme; which, in epic poetry, is a sore disease, in the tragic, absolute death. To Dryden's enormity, Pope's was a light offense. As lacemen are foes to mourning, these two authors, rich in rhyme, were no great friends to those solemn ornaments which the noble nature of their works required.

Must rhyme then, say you, be banished? I wish the nature of our language could bear its entire expulsion; but our lesser poetry stands in need of a toleration for it; it raises that but sinks the great, as spangles adorn children but expose men. Prince Henry bespangled all over in his oylet-hole suit with glittering pins, and an Achilles, or an Almanzor, in his Gothic array, are very much on a level, as to the majesty of the poet and the prince. Dryden had a great, but a general capacity; and as for a general genius, there is no such thing in nature: a genius implies the rays of the mind concentered, and determined to some particular point; when they are scattered widely, they act feebly and strike not with sufficient force to fire, or dissolve, the heart. As what comes from the writer's heart reaches ours, so what comes from his head sets our brains at work and our hearts at ease. It makes a circle of thoughtful critics, not of distressed patients; and a passive audience is what tragedy requires. Applause is not to be given, but extorted; and the silent lapse of a single tear does the writer more honor than the rattling thunder of a thousand hands. Applauding hands and dry eyes (which during Dryden's theatrical reign often met) are a satire on the writer's talent and the spectator's taste. When by such judges the laurel is blindly given, and by such a poet proudly received, they resemble an intoxicated host, and his tasteless guests, over some sparkling adulteration, commending their champagne.

But Dryden has his glory, though not on the stage; what an inimitable original is his ode? A small one, indeed, but of the first luster, and without a flaw; and, amid the brightest boasts of antiquity, it may find a foil. . . .

RICHARD HURD

(1720–1808)

oᴑooᴑo

"Wɪᴛ ᴀɴᴅ ʀʜʏᴍᴇ, sentiment and satire, polished numbers, sparkling couplets, and pointed periods, having so long kept undisturbed possession in our poetry, would not easily give way to fiction and fancy, to picturesque description, and romantic imagery." Thus Thomas Warton wrote of the struggle to gain a place for the poetry of emotion and fancy. The scholars and poets of the mid-century had turned back to the medieval period and to the Renaissance. Much attention was being given to the old romance, the ballad, and early Germanic sagas. The critics, many of whom were poets, were seeking for a means of justifying their love for the antique, the imaginative, and the emotional.[1]

The *Letters on Chivalry and Romance* (1762) were presumably written to illustrate some of the remarks in the *Moral and Political Dialogues* (1759). The third and fourth of these dialogues deal with the Elizabethan period. Hurd gives his plan for the *Letters:* he is writing to explain the rise, progress, and genius of Gothic chivalry, the poetic appeal of the manners of that age and the decline of interest in Gothic work.

From a critical point of view the two most important letters are five and six, which give the three main points of his criticism: that Gothic and Greek literature were not written by the same rules and that it is impossible to judge them by the same standards; that unity of action is no more necessary than unity of design; that the essence of the life of one age differs from that of another; so it is impossible to consider nature as unchanging and to use it for a fixed rule of art.

Bɪʙʟɪᴏɢʀᴀᴘʜʏ

ᴛᴇxᴛ

Letters on Chivalry and Romance, with the "Third Elizabethan Dialogue," ed. with an introduction by Edith J. Morley. London, 1911.

[1]Not so Dr. Johnson, who turned on the antiquarian interest in "Lines Written in Ridicule of Certain Poems Published in 1777."

The Correspondence of Richard Hurd and William Mason, and Letters of Richard Hurd to Thomas Gray, with introd. and notes by E. H. Pearce; ed. with additional notes by Leonard Whibley. New York, 1932.
Works. 8 vols. London, 1811.

CRITICISM

Beers, H. A., *A History of English Romanticism in the Eighteenth Century.* New York, 1898.
Bosker, A., *Literary Criticism in the Age of Johnson.* The Hague, 1930.
Hamelius, Paul, *Die Kritik in der englischen Literatur des 17 und 18 Jahrhunderts.* Leipzig, 1897.
Kilvert, Francis, *Memoirs of the Life and Writings of Richard Hurd,* with a selection from his correspondence and unpublished papers. London, 1860.
Phelps, William Lyon, *The Beginnings of the English Romantic Movement.* Boston, 1893.

LETTERS ON CHIVALRY AND ROMANCE *(selections)*

1762

[Heroic and Gothic Manners][1]

Let it be no surprise to you that, in the close of my last letter, I presumed to bring the *Gerusalemme liberata* into competition with the *Iliad.*

So far as the heroic and Gothic manners are the same, the pictures of each, if well taken, must be equally entertaining. But I go further and maintain that the circumstances in which they differ are clearly to the advantage of the Gothic designers.

You see my purpose is to lead you from this forgotten chivalry to a more amusing subject, I mean the poetry we still read, and which was founded upon it.

Much has been said, and with great truth, of the felicity of Homer's age for poetical manners. But as Homer was a citizen of the world, when he had seen in Greece, on the one hand, the manners he has described, could he, on the other hand, have seen in the west the manners of the feudal ages, I make no doubt but he would certainly have preferred the latter. And the grounds of this preference would, I suppose, have been "the improved gallantry of the feudal times"; and the "superior solemnity of their superstitions."

[1]Letter vi.

If any great poet, like Homer, had lived amongst, and sung of, the Gothic knights (for after all Spenser and Tasso came too late, and it was impossible for them to paint truly and perfectly what was no longer seen or believed) this preference, I persuade myself, had been very sensible. But their fortune was not so happy.

> *—omnes illacrymabiles*
> *Urgentur, ignotique longâ*
> *Nocte, carent quia vate sacro.*[2]

As it is, we may take a guess of what the subject was capable of affording to real genius from the rude sketches we have of it in the old romancers. And it is but looking into any of them to be convinced that the gallantry which inspirited the feudal times was of a nature to furnish the poet with finer scenes and subjects of description in every view than the simple and un-controlled barbarity of the Grecian.

The principal entertainment arising from the delineation of these consists in the exercise of the boisterous passions, which are provoked and kept alive from one end of the *Iliad* to the other, by every imaginable scene of rage, revenge, and slaughter. In the other, together with these, the gentler and more humane affections are awakened in us by the most interesting displays of love and friendship; of love elevated to its noblest heights, and of friendship operating on the purest motives. The mere variety of these paintings is a relief to the reader as well as writer. But their beauty, novelty, and pathos give them a vast advantage on the comparison.

Consider, withal, the surprises, accidents, adventures which probably and naturally attend on the life of wandering knights; the occasion there must be for describing the wonders of different countries, and of presenting to view the manners and policies of distant states, all which make so conspicuous a part of the materials of the greater poetry.

So that, on the whole, though the spirit, passions, rapine, and violence of the two sets of manners were equal, yet there was a dignity, a magnificence, a variety in the feudal which the other wanted.

---

[2]["Many brave men lived before Agamemnon, but] all, unlamented and unknown, are oppressed by the long night, because they lack a divine poet" (Horace, *Odes*, IV, 9, 26–28).

As to religious machinery, perhaps the popular system of each was equally remote from reason, yet the latter had something in it more amusing, as well as more awakening to the imagination.

The current popular tales of elves and fairies were even fitter to take the credulous mind, and charm it into a willing admiration of the specious miracles which wayward fancy delights in, than those of the old traditionary rabble of pagan divinities. And then, for the more solemn fancies of witchcraft and incantation, the horrors of the Gothic were above measure striking and terrible. The mummeries of the pagan priests were childish, but the Gothic enchanters shook and alarmed all nature.

We feel this difference very sensibly in reading the ancient and modern poets. You would not compare the Canidia of Horace with the witches in *Macbeth.* And what are Vergil's myrtles dropping blood, to Tasso's enchanted forest?

Ovid, indeed, who had a fancy turned to romance, makes Medea, in a rant, talk wildly. But was this the common language of their other writers? The enchantress in Vergil says coolly of the very chiefest prodigies of her charms and poisons,

> *His ego saepe lupum fieri, et se condere sylvis*
> *Moerin; saepe animas imis excire sepulchris,*
> *Atque satas alio vidi traducere messes.*[3]

The admirable poet has given an air of the marvelous to his subject by the magic of his expression. Else, what do we find here, but the ordinary effects of melancholy, the vulgar superstition of evoking spirits, and the supposed influence of fascination on the hopes of rural industry?

> *Non isthic obliquo oculo mihi commoda quisquam*
> *Limat . . .*[4]

says the poet of his country seat, as if this security from a fascinating eye were a singular privilege, and the mark of a more than common good fortune.

Shakespeare, on the other hand, with a terrible sublime (which not so much the energy of his genius, as the nature of

[3] "Often have I seen Moeris, thanks to these [herbs], become a wolf and hide himself in the forest, often have I seen him evoke the spirits from the depths of the tombs, and transport the planted grain into the field of another" (Vergil, *Eclogues,* VIII, 97–99).

[4] "Where you are, no one with envious eye diminishes my good fortune" (Horace, *Epistles,* I, 14, 37).

his subject drew from him) gives us another idea of the rough
magic, as he calls it, of fairy enchantment:

> . . . I have bedimmed
> The noon-tide sun, called forth the mutinous winds,
> And 'twixt the green sea and the azure vault
> Set roaring war: to the dread rattling thunder
> Have I given fire, and rifted Jove's stout oak
> With his own bolt; the strong-based promontory
> Have I made shake, and by the spurs plucked up
> The pine and cedar: graves, at my command,
> Have opened, and let forth their sleepers . . . [5]

The last circumstance, you will say, is but the *animas imis excire
sepulchris*[6] of the Latin poet. But a very significant word marks
the difference. The pagan necromancers had a hundred little
tricks by which they pretended to call up the ghosts, or shadows
of the dead: but these, in the ideas of paganism, were quite
another thing from Shakespeare's sleepers.

This may serve for a cast of Shakespeare's magic; and I can't
but think that when Milton wanted to paint the horrors of that
night (one of the noblest parts in his *Paradise Regained*), which
the devil himself is feigned to conjure up in the wilderness, the
Gothic language and ideas helped him to work up his tempest
with such terror. You will judge from these lines:

> . . . nor yet stayed the terror there;
> Infernal ghosts and hellish furies round
> Environed thee; some howled, some yelled, some shrieked,
> Some bent at thee their fiery darts . . . [7]

but above all from the following:

> Thus passed the night so foul, till morning fair
> Came forth with pilgrim steps in amice gray,
> Who with her *radiant finger* stilled the roar
> Of thunder, chased the clouds, and laid the winds
> And *grisly specters* . . . [8]

where the radiant finger points at the potent wand of the
Gothic magicians, which could reduce the calm of nature, upon
occasion, as well as disturb it; and the grisly specters laid by the

---

[5] *The Tempest*, v, i, 41–49. Last line either misquoted or based on corrupt text.
[6] "To call forth spirits from the depths of the tombs" (Vergil, *Eclogues*, VIII, 98).
[7] *Paradise Regained*, IV, 421–424.   [8] *Paradise Regained*, IV, 426–430.

approach of morn were apparently of their raising, as a sagacious critic perceived when he took notice "how very injudicious
it was to retail the popular superstition in this place."

After all, the conclusion is not to be drawn so much from
particular passages, as from the general impression left on our
minds in reading the ancient and modern poets. And this is so
much in favor of the latter that Mr. Addison scruples not to say,
"The ancients have not much of this poetry among them; for,
indeed," continues he, "almost the whole substance of it owes its
original to the darkness and superstition of later ages. Our
forefathers looked upon nature with more reverence and horror
before the world was enlightened by learning and philosophy
and loved to astonish themselves with the apprehensions of
witchcraft, prodigies, charms, and enchantments. There was
not a village in England that had not a ghost in it, the church-
yards were all haunted, every large common had a circle of
fairies belonging to it, and there was scarce a shepherd to be
met with who had not seen a spirit."[9]

We are upon enchanted ground, my friend; and you are to
think yourself well used that I detain you no longer in this
fearful circle. The glimpse you have had of it will help your
imagination to conceive the rest. And without more words you
will readily apprehend that the fancies of our modern bards are
not only more gallant, but, on a change of the scene, more
sublime, more terrible, more alarming, than those of the classic
fablers. In a word, you will find that the manners they paint
and the superstitions they adopt are the more poetical for being
Gothic.

[9]*Spectator*, no. 419.

THOMAS THORILD

(1759–1808)

oᏅᎧᏅᎧ

THE LAST QUARTER OF THE EIGHTEENTH CENTURY is called in the history of Swedish literature the Gustavian period. The school of reason, with its polished French taste, flourished under the brilliant reign of Gustavus III, breaking the influence of English literature, which had a strong vogue earlier in the century. The intellectual lawgiver and final literary referee of the age was Johan Henrik Kellgren (1751–1795), a writer of satirical and didactic verse, but also of lyrics of true poetic feeling. In him the school of reason reached its climax. But the battle between the old expiring school of rhetoric and reason and the new forces of romanticism which were then making themselves felt throughout Europe had reached Sweden a decade before the death of Kellgren. Kellgren's first meeting with the new movement was in the form of an attack upon him and the dominating school of criticism by Thomas Thorild, who violently opposed the taste and practice of the Gustavian period and demanded complete liberty in literature and a return to nature. *A Critique of the Critics* established him as the first apostle of romanticism in Sweden. It was an unanswerable argument for the new school; it is the most able eighteenth-century defense extant in behalf of the movement in Sweden.

Thorild published a small periodical called *The New Critic* from 1784 to 1792. The *Critique* was first published in that periodical in 1791. Even the first numbers in 1784 contained attacks on the prevailing school of criticism; this essay is, as it were, a summary of these and the ones that followed in subsequent issues.

The translation is by E. Gustav Johnson, here published for the first time.

BIBLIOGRAPHY

TEXT

Bref, utgifna af Lauritz Weibull. 3 häften. Uppsala, 1899–1902.
Samlade skrifter, utgifna af E. G. Geijer. 4 bd. Stockholm, 1819–1835.
Samlade skrifter, utgifna af Stellan Arvidson. Stockholm, 1932.

Thorilds bref till C. F. Cramer, med inledning och anmärkningar, utgifna
af Martin Lamm. Uppsala, 1907.
Valda skrifter, utgifna af Ruben G:son Berg. Stockholm, 1910.

CRITICISM

Arvidson, Stellan, *Thorild: Studier i hans ungdomsutveckling*. Lund, 1931.
Beskow, B. V., "Om den estetiska betydelsen af Thorilds strid emot
Kellgren och Leopold," *Svenska akademiens handlingar från 1796*, del 48.
Geijer, E. G., "Thorild: En filosofisk eller ofilosofisk bekännelse,"
Samlade skrifter. Del III. Stockholm, 1820.
Hammarsköld, L., *Historiska anteckningar rörande fortgången och utvecklingen
af det filosofiska studium i Sverige*. Stockholm, 1821, pp. 347–374.
Karitz, Anders, "Tankelinjer hos Thorild," *Lunds universitets årsskrift*
(1913), n. f., avd. 1, bd. 9, n:r 5.
Lamm, Martin, *Upplysningstidens romantik: Den mystiskt sentimentala
strömningen i svenska litteraturen*, I–II. Stockholm, 1918–1920.
Nilsson, Albert, *Thorild*. Stockholm, 1915. Originally published in
1896.
———, "Thorild ännu en gång," *Edda: Nordisk tidskrift för litteratur-
forskning*, XV (1921), pp. 1 ff., 212 ff.
Till Thorilds minne (uppsatser af Wrangel, Forsvall, Borelius, Liljekrantz
och Karitz), *Lunds universitets årsskrift* (1908), n. f., avd. 1, bd. 40,
n:r 1.

A CRITIQUE OF THE CRITICS *(selections)*
1791

Criticism in its highest meaning is justice dispensed in the
world of genius.

Such a conception immediately raises it far above these wild
incursions in literature worthy only of Cossacks and Kalmucks
who seek merely what might be robbed and ravaged, and above
the low, rude mockery which ought to belong only to the Hotten-
tots. And yet, one of these is what most criticism has always
been!

To criticize in the world of genius is, then, to mete out justice;
to be a critic in a large and high sense is to be *just*. This is the
only divine thing belonging to mortals, for everything else that is
great shines and dazzles like a flare but is extinguished much
sooner than the foolish astonishment it creates.

But this word *just* is a very special word, because it means
steeped in justice and therefore necessarily demands that the laws
according to which one is to judge must be known.

If, peradventure, you, my dear sir, have never known these laws, you have a great and complete excuse, because in our literature as well as in that of all countries criticism without them has been and is a *darkness visible*, a clear barbarism.

You know how the great French geniuses eternally tear each other asunder, eternally so curse as if honor were the possession of none and the peace in which it should be enjoyed were not sacred; how among them to display some little talent or virtue is as dangerous as it is to display a jewel or the least amount of gold on an unsafe highway; how Voltaire said of himself that he was forced through a purgatory of derision every week; and Rousseau's holy life—was it not a long martyrdom under the cannibals of literature whose arch-cannibal was just this same Voltaire!

In England they are so much wilder as they are stronger.

And with us, my dear sir, is there anything so Kalmuckian and so Hottentotish, so fierce and so low, that it has not been tried? I ask you who are such a profound expert! This torch that was to illuminate the way for geniuses toward honor, has it not been thrown into their faces, singed the eyebrows and burnt the faces of those who might have made the world happy with expressions of divine truth, of the beauty of nature, or at least of some charm of humanity, and burned them so terribly that they afterwards have looked as if they had barely escaped from the pyre?

You, my dear sir, love literature. Tell me, do you not think that the curse of these spectacles still rests upon some bald pate that might have been covered with laurels though never so blessed—no, whose laurels from this field the thunderbolts of revenge have ravaged or will ravage?

And, truly, the heavy sighs of pain and the anxiety caused by the shame and suffering of the scourging for no crime—are they likely to bring amusement, to bring satisfaction, to anyone under heaven?

Yes, they do in literature and in all the genteel cliques literature has created!

Weakness itself, which in nature is always sacred because it is weak and calls for mercy, *res sacra miser*—weakness itself, *for* whose protection everything just and noble, all large-mindedness, all heroism exist and *without* whose protection half of God's own glory would vanish—weakness, has it not always been abandoned to every bully's puny power, always been offered as a plaything for the ferocity of the critics?

If that is not barbarism, then one can no longer speak of a difference between the customs of Kamchatka and those of Paris, and the deserts of Africa then would teem with the most wonderful of geniuses!

As I am convinced that it is from these wild antics in literature, from this abomination among smug geniuses, that the people of our time have taken their mad desire to deceive, to lie and deride, which desire is the peculiarly vital mood of the time, I made an attempt once to drive the derision to its highest point in order to show in a single example the whole of its nefarious majesty, almost as if one were to ignite a forest in which numerous bandits dwell and so with a single wise outrage put an end to all malicious outrages, with one single cruelty put an end to all cruelties.

The real strength of calumny does not lie, however, in certain outbursts of the fury of a few, but in the general wildness, in the barbarism which yet hides as with a nebula, the natural laws of justice.

I shall therefore attempt to formulate these laws, applying them first to literary criticism; afterwards they may be extended in application to common life.

A FUNDAMENTAL TRUTH. The only eternal basis for common justice of which all laws are the mere results is, like everything true and everything great, clear and simple—it is this: *To take everything for what it is*.

This simple and divine law of reality demands, however, more than one would think; it demands, not the small, foolish, flighty imagination which is now called quick wit, but *understanding*, and not the small, animated feeling which is now found so sweet, but a solid and high *integrity*.

THE FIRST LAW. The first and greatest error in reality is to take a thing as one's own which is not so at all; or, applied to our present topic, to regard as *belles-lettres* writing which does not belong to that category.

Therefore the first result to issue from our eternal, basic truth, the first law in justice, is: *To know what one is to judge*.

This, my dear sir, is just as necessary in the realm of literature as it is for a civic judge to know the boundaries of the district over which his authority extends.

The thing is this: everything that is uttered is not of literary quality. But in our new, quite half-human communities there are many tender, important, even stirring and exalted moments when speeches are made, yea, according to the finer nature of humanity—must be made: such as the hallowing of a departed friend's remains; the showing of reverence for the king; the observing of holidays and celebrations in a circumscribed world, and so forth. Now, as that noble and innocent fate may befall even the wealthiest speechmaker, that he does not have as many amanuenses as he has friends who wish to read and to own his speech, he has it printed. If this speech, my dear sir, spoken or printed, can make of him an author, then must the least important matter under the sun that is spoken or printed do likewise; and of this follows that all that breathe are authors, except the dumb animals.

And should a small, tyrannical pedant be allowed blindly to decree this for the fine reason that he might freely exercise his petty Tartarian authority upon everything that in its simplicity and innocence is most weak!

No, my dear sir, you do not want to do that. I appeal freely to your attention that as everything true and beautiful is taught to mankind it is inconspicuously disseminated, and that certain degrees of all fine arts have already descended from the masters to everyone who has enjoyed good breeding. So also with literature. To speak something courteously, to write something beautiful, to compose a little verse is now customary. And to frighten good and lovable people from the fortunate freedom of possessing and enjoying these small delights through a petty critical violence, like a literary terrorist, is so ridiculous an undertaking and so shameless that it is like a puny autocracy, as inopportune, and, according to our customs, as foolish as a proclamation decreeing that now "none who is not a dancing master may dance, none who is not a courtier may make a civil call or hold a reception, and none who is not a bishop may speak the name of God." It is pure insanity, sir; for the daintiest little maiden smiles and knows well enough that one may strike one's clavichord or draw one's embroidery designs just as one pleases without offending Gluck with the one or Raphael with the other.

But I understand: the truly divine lies in the printer's ink! Because, my dear reader, you may babble wittily, tenderly, sub-

limely, in verse and prose as much as you please and readily
show it to thousands—but don't you dare to sprinkle it with
this holy slush (even if you pay for it as conscientiously as an
angel); because then comes the terrible bad man with the hellish
torch of criticism and shouts out that your innocent letters are
not worthy of seeing the light of day, that your poor paper ought
to be burned—burned—burned, and perhaps you yourself ought
to be thrown in among the flames.

I have often thought, sir, that even a quite insignificant critic
truly considers himself a Pluto, book printing his Tartarus, his
taste, his whim, and his petty opinion Minos, Aeacus, and
Rhadamantus, his pride his Proserpina, his derision and his
mockeries Cerberus and the Furies, and that one must really
quake before him as with the death anguish for the eternal flames
before one can reach the River Lethe and one's corner in the
Elysian fields.

I am certain that you will immediately find this tyranny as
petty and as mean as it is fantastic; that you will anon consider
it either a wildness of heart or a stupidity of reason; that you
will find it impossible to contend that one's printer's ink and
paper can in itself be any more condemnable than one's writing
fluid and paper, or both any more than one's speech and thought;
and, finally, that when one judges on such a plane it must be
because of a puny barbaric ignorance of what it is one is to
judge.

This, my dear sir, is it: what one is to judge is not everything
that is written, not everything that is printed. Because the
greater part of this does not belong to literature but to the
common, pleasant procedure of life and its large, free movements. No civic judge in the world dares try the quite ridiculous
attempt of judging in his district everything that occurs, everything that happens everywhere. What the critic is to judge, sir,
is only—only—that which rightly comes before the judgment seat
of literature, namely, that which purely and publicly offers
itself for the battle and the honors of genius. Then, but only
then, arise in the whole power and splendor of your wisdom!

About everything else you should speak well or keep silent
because of that great, clear circumstance that it is none of your
business.

It is a wild imagination to think that everything that people
think, speak, express with ink, colors, or printer's ink is done to

challenge the test of strong heads. Quite the contrary: most of it is done for the purpose of bringing a small, passing delight to common life, of finding and enjoying something beautiful, of calming or stimulating a tender or happy feeling—a reason so good and often so sweet that the mere breathing of an acrid opinion upon it is mean and low.

"But are we not to discipline, scourge, devastate, exterminate the bad?" My dear sir, may God protect your own self! When you say the *bad* you mean the *weak*, and that is often lovable, always innocent. And—I speak now to your soul—would it not be reason enough for us to forgive weakness, yes, to hold it in esteem because it provides us with the divine thought and the sweet feeling of our own eminence? Alas, what would become of this eminence if it were not for weakness and the weak ones? But do not deceive yourself in your Tamerlanean heat. Weakness, sir, often ascends to the highest charms even though it still be weakness in comparison to a higher power. Don't you see what havoc you perpetrate? And I ask, what—*what*—god holds his shield over your own head?

This burning desire to chastise and exterminate the bad—that is, the weaker—is, I say, a madness when you consider that the bad, the weaker, ascends even up to God's own throne, that the cherubs and the seraphs are not so perfect but that the most exalted of all the world's critics could quite readily adjudge them harsh singers and fools in wit. And again, when you recall the disposition of great minds, how they thunder against violence, pitch their strength only against the strong, but smile in protective, divine mildness upon the weak, then you find that this burning desire to chastise and exterminate the bad, the weaker, is nothing but the desire of a wretch to be terrible, the great wit of a fool, and the heroism of a coward.

Should, however, the intention really be pure and all this critical cruelty be only the fire of love for the good which consumes that which is not good, then it is truly the love of a Japanese emperor who rules his dear people through the divine sanction of virtue, blissfully bestowed, but through threatening the terrors of hell upon the slightest error, by which the people become the blind slaves of law instead of wise and good citizens.

In literature—in order that you may see the similarity—no more than in any other fine art, no new beauty ever arose through a fear of errors, but through a happy fascination of beauty; and as soon as a greater beauty appears the lesser one fades without the least aid of fear or cruelty. Such is the mild order of nature which you will also recognize in all other spheres of beauty and good fortune in common life.

This is to say, my dear sir: it is only that charm which the new beauties of genius produce which elevates literature, and not at all any terrifying pedagogical power. Tyranny never revivifies anything. Tyranny is nothing but pedantry in power; if one does not persist in despising it, it serves only to inflict death or madness.

Now, sir, consider well—because this subject is as important for us as all of life's pleasant things—consider well if criticism among us has been anything but the cruel cowards' triumph over the weak, anything but a rule of the literary horde where one wretch has never enjoyed himself more than when he could be the other's tyrant, anything but the holiday of witty scoundrels.

But this is enough. It is clearly seen that not everything that is spoken or printed, but the really literary, that which purely and publicly presents itself for the battle and honors of genius, is what the critics must judge. And because all legislation should be definite, I add that the matter to be judged is everything that is written for a prize, for academies, and for no other reason than the honor of learning literature. But the moment someone says: This I have done without any consideration for the great honor of genius and only for the gratification of my friends!—then that product is, were it even the weakest of vanities, sacred under the protection of the common laws. About all such products you must, in true and noble criticism, speak well or keep silent, unless it should please you merely to quote some passages. However, do it honorably, and remember that it is not criticism.

But this boundary between what one may criticize and what one may not is, like all boundaries, in certain places and at certain times somewhat obscure. I am therefore going to bind the furies of criticism with a double chain, with the strength of two laws of eternal justice, to indicate how that which is to be judged must be judged.

SECOND LAW. That which finally is with right and reason in the realm of genius to be judged must be judged according to the true order of nature, and *to judge everything according to its degree and its kind* is the second law in our literary legislation.

Right at this moment, my dear sir, your active genius will discern what an immense and ridiculous confusion the insanity of forgetting this law must produce. You see that if you would judge your little lamp in the measure of the sun, and the sun in the measure of your little lamp; the rose in the measure of the oak, and the oak in the measure of the rose; the spark according to the lightning, and thunder according to your lute; the strong according to the fair, the fair according to strength; and, in all, the great genius according to the small and foolish— then finally your soul would become a whirlpool of contradictions, and you would see for yourself no other hope than that of throwing yourself headlong into the abyss of that selfsame confusion your own brain had created.

O, sir, what is a man without laws? But—these laws must be made by nature and not by literary Lilliputians.

There is great delight in seeing things in all clearness. In connection with our first law we cited an example; let us use it once more. An ordinary judge must first know where in the kingdom he is to judge, that is, over what district his jurisdiction extends; next, within his district he must know who are legally indicted and what the indictment is. But in the first place the case must have a designation indicating its degree and kind, a rubric, as definite as possible. For what would you, sir, with all your genius say if you saw him in the pomp of his power and in the glow of his justice proclaiming judgment with dignified gravity—upon Paul as if he were Peter, in a murder case as if it were a slander suit?

But I insist, sir, with full seriousness that in literature, with us as little as in any country, the critics have never yet quite known this great and clear law: to judge everything according to its degree and its kind.

Innumerable cruelties have through this barbaric ignorance been heaped upon the purest merits; and beauties which thousands could have worshiped and blessed in sweet happiness have been wildly condemned and crushed.

Because, my dear sir, everything is not made for everybody. But all souls should be allowed to live and should be comforted. A son weeps for his father at his grave, and he is not to be condemned because he does not have in his behavior the tragical sublimity of a Monvel. A peasant girl finds such great delight in a love song that she considers it an almost too beautiful gift from her sweetheart. The greatest impression of the beauty of literature, the greatest in the world in degree as in reach, is made upon the populace through ballads. And I, dear sir, can myself solemnly assure you that I have never found in the world's great poetry that intrinsic pathos I once found in *Reimund and Melusina*,[1] the exalted epic I found in *Olger Dansk*,[2] the touching morality I found in *Carsus and Moderus*,[3] the poetic, pleasing rapture I felt through *The Blue Bird*.[4]

Honestly! If I had not felt in my life all this in its small, poor simplicity both beautiful and holy, half of my soul would have been blind and cold, and I should never have felt the divinely exalted passion for the protection of the weak, this passion, sir, which is the only human in man and which shall sometime everywhere on earth overthrow tyranny.

The sun revivifies the smallest creature, the humblest flower; and the sun is the symbol of genius. Yet, why this pomp of imagination? Isn't the whole world composed of the weak? Are not you, am not I, small, poor, weak, in need of protection? And this greater for which we shrink in fear, is not that the same? Blessed be the strength of eternity; it could crush everything, but does all for the protection of everyone's life. Upward to this higher power I cast my eyes and find there that soft feeling for the weak which together with its divine exaltation is so beautiful that compared with the bliss of possessing it I count as insignificant and paltry the honor of sitting like a splendid but cold fool upon the throne of the whole world. Therefore, he who thoughtlessly tramples upon the weak is in my eyes nature's extremest scoundrel; and, therefore, my contempt for a tyrant is unbounded, though my hate may feel a limit.

But let us descend from this greater and more general to that which is nearer to us. And as it may well be that you with your

[1] Collection of medieval tales, legends, and metrical romances which were popular in Sweden in the eighteenth century, drawn in part from classical sources.

[2] *Olger Danske* (i.e., Holger the Dane) is an ancient popular ballad, known at an early period in the British Isles and on the Continent.

[3] Mainly a compilation of tales about Apollonius of Tyre. Both this and *Reimund and Melusina* came into vogue in Sweden through France.

[4] A medieval romance; the Swedish version of the eighteenth century is undoubtedly a translation from the French *L'Oiseau bleu*. The point Thorild makes in his essay is that these products of the people (because the romances as well as the ballad belong to folk literature) have something of an appeal which the polished literature, produced by authors according to "the rules," often lacks. (Translator's note.)

fine and rare genius have more imagination than reason I will use illustrations.

A mayor in his small town—with all due respect—might walk from one end of his realm to the other clad in his nightrobe, his nightcap, and slippers, smoking his pipe with familiar dignity, and not an eye would be offended, not a soul be vexed. No, on the contrary, it would seem as if his cap were a crown of government, as if his nightrobe were his mantle of righteousness, and the smoke from his pipe the dust of a Thor. So high, so splendid is this in its degree. Would you drag this man, such as he is, upon the stage of the world's great theater and from top to toe judge him as if he were the master of ceremonies in a reception of the Order of the Seraphim?

You upon your Shetland pony covered with gold and flowers and a resplendent Alexander on his Bucephalus proceeding together to the monstrous pomp of a circus cannot make a rule for an honest man from the country who upon his nag falters in bewilderment through the streets of Stockholm in search of his lodgings. Thus, sir, a poor shepherd on the hillside plays his flute without thereby wanting to snatch the lyre from Apollo's hand; and a bard in Skara[5] inspired at a festival occasion clasps his lyre without having any thought of crushing yours, which, I freely admit, you often play divinely.

It is clear that in these cases everything should be judged according to its degree and its kind. The people say as wisely as tenderly that "each bird sings with his own throat," and even you are undoubtedly happy to creep beneath the protection of this simple proverb. Quite a few share with you that happiness. And what would happen if one were at liberty to judge *My Amusements*[6] in accordance with Milton or Ariosto, and a poor little prologue in accordance with Shakespeare or Homer?

The measure for every beauty lies within its own degree and its kind. The law by which to judge is exactly that measure, and it must therefore thence be received. A peasant girl can be very sweet, but she is not made for the salon or the court. He who makes an address in verse in Skara intends thereby to please not Stockholm, not Paris or Rome, but Skara. When you, with the fanatical despotism of your criticism, summon him to the higher plane of literature, his beauties are lost and his errors

[5]Small country town near Stockholm, representing the typical small town.
[6]Poem by J. H. Kellgren, the poet-critic to whom the essay is addressed.

become monsters. On the contrary, in Skara his beauties remain beauties, and they counterbalance his errors. Only in that
place ought he be judged. Or, if you are too much in love with
your critical autocracy, you must—and it cannot offend your
highness since Our Lord himself descended even lower—you
must justly place your genius, as it were, in the center of Skara.
That, in all honesty, I consider, however, to be an incursion.
For if Skara according to God's, nature's, and the king's mild
laws may freely have its own poets, why should not Skara be
allowed the liberty of having its own critics?

Let us not hear another word about the necessity of a general
discipline in literature. Even that ought to come in the true
order of nature. One does not begin a reform in the church
with the sexton but with the bishop; the chaplain's foolishness
is excusable, the prelate's never. What king among us would
start his reform of customs and laws in the slums? Or what
philosopher would attempt to launch his new epoch in the world
of thought with a thundering against the weakest souls of the
masses? No, according to nature, improvements always begin
with the greater and the better. Thereafter the best works
downward influencing the lower orders of humanity through
the divinity of goodness and truth, just as the great heat and
light of the sun reach even the smallest particle you see glittering
in the dust.

When this true and beautiful law, "to judge everything according to its degree and its kind," has become generally understood you will no more see in criticism these high fools daring,
as individual autocrats or united in petty principalities, blindly
to condemn the strong because it is not weak or sweet enough,
the important because it is not light, the solemn because it is
not smiling, or the reverse. They shall not dare, with the mean
intention of scoffing, to call that which is made expressly for the
purpose of appealing to people's hearts and understanding a
"declamation"; to condemn as "against the rules" that which
is made intentionally in spite of the rules in order to find something greater *beyond the reach of art—that critics dare not mend*, as
Pope has it. And in general they shall no longer crown their
literary stupidity with this holy judgment of confusion—that the
great and the new have not the pretty, well-known delights, and
the pretty, well-known delights have nothing of the great and
the new!

THE THIRD LAW. The third law will surely, my dear sir, make you as surprised with its simplicity as it will make all critical tyranny afraid of its great consequences. It may be formulated thus: *Nothing is made for the sake of its faults, but for the sake of its merits*, nothing for the sake of its flatness, but for its value; nothing for the sake of its blots, but for its beauty. It is a truth concerning all degrees and kinds, genera and species, in the world of genius that should always be remembered.

That great statement rests upon this foundation: man starts with *nothing*. The first question on earth, concerning the necessary and useful as well as the merely pleasing, is therefore not about doing something *perfectly*, but about doing *something*. And about the product the only natural question is not how good it *might be* according to imagination or to high models, but how good it *is*. For what a thing *might be* lies in your thought and not in the thing itself. It is true that a thing gets, through the thought of the higher which it might be, a lesser worth, but it is its *own worth*. . . .

This doctrine belongs to another and higher place. Let us again, sir, come down to our own. When an insignificant mortal begins to write an insignificant piece—verse, lecture, book—his intention is surely that of doing something particularly true and beautiful, something pleasant, high, and worthy of the little world for which it is meant. You ought to see in him a little god, full of fire and seriousness, ready to call out his *Let there be*, already bidding chaos to cease, calling upon light to spread itself thereover, arranging the hidden splendors of his work, and finally, as if smiling in eternal happiness, finding it all good.

Do you believe, or can anyone believe, that this mortal means to do something remarkably flat and ugly and not the opposite: something which, in his intention and for his world, is remarkably great and beneficent? Whence has then, my dear sir, a critic that notable madness of taking a man's work in exactly the opposite meaning, to look only for errors for the sake of which it was not made; only at the flat and ugly which he strove with all his might to avoid? It is impossible for any mortal in his own sphere, desiring to make something beautiful, to produce something ugly. Even a madman, though he is in a world of wild hallucinations, does not make something small when he wishes to make something great. Haqvin Bager [7] wished to write naïvely

---

[7]Bager, Bjugg, and Hallberg were minor Swedish poetasters of the period.

and at the same time strongly; and he did. Bjugg has sought the majestic and important, and he has found it in both an original and perfect way to such an extent that I doubt if all the world's geniuses together could make a single Bjugg. Many orators in our country have pursued the genuine and the quaint with such fortune that none can read them without the most stirring interest.

"But all this is unfortunate!" you shout. Tell me then, at least, in what way and in what sense. For these blunders are much more noteworthy, greater, more important for both our enlightenment and our amusement than many virtues. Thus Haqvin Bager's verse and Hallberg's illustrations are of more value than the greater portion of all verse and lithographs produced in this century; and Bjugg's production, remarkable for poetic art and human ingenuity, is something far higher and therefore more worthy of immortality than perhaps half of Dalin's [8] octavos and than all the quarto tomes of Mrs. Nordenflycht's thought-phantasies, just as, sir, there was more that was noble in *The German Baron* than in a thousand cowards, and as Don Quixote, in his highness of mind, was so far above Cervantes, who created him, that that wit undoubtedly never could have composed his narrative had he not taken from the knightly stories all the romance and greatness of heart that the imagination of the time possessed.

Now it is quite common to see, sir, that the masses in their crude but true understanding know more of nature than all its petty critics; for they immediately, both for the sake of learning, wise reflection, and for mere vivid enjoyment, give more attention to the one German baron than the whole guard in all its pomp; and the world even to this day is more interested in Don Quixote than in a thousand chieftains with whose worth they are nevertheless acquainted.

The masses, the populace, are right, my dear sir, in their respect for the unusual even when it is most blundering. For besides the novel enjoyment of seeing the unusual there is something more important. The unusual was the only thing which first gave to mankind life and strength. The great heresies,

[8] Olof von Dalin (1708–1763) was the leading poet of the "Enlightenment" period. He published *The Swedish Argus* (Dec. 1732–Dec. 1734) in imitation of the *Spectator*. Hedvig Charlotta Nordenflycht (1718–1763) was the first woman writer to gain a national reputation in Sweden.

through their awakening of soul and mind, brought forth great truths; the great tyrannies, through their igniting of fire in hard hearts of slaves, brought forth divine laws and liberty. . . .

Large faults, my dear sir, spring up when large merits are sought; when that statement is made you will see how much large errors deserve your respect. To err is natural for all mortals, because all of us start with nothing and rise through degrees of weakness; flaws are found in everything on earth. Errors approaching the monstrous, ridiculousness approaching madness, are found in Homer and—in Shakespeare, who is far greater than Homer. But notice, sir, that "error in greatness," in the fate of all time, is something that concerns us a great deal, it may be in heroic deeds, in love, in the fall of mighty and wise empires, in the overthrow of religions and doctrines, in high endeavors of all kinds. And a quite good attempt in poetry, a quite good hodgepodge in prose, a quite good apocalypse in wisdom, a fool's demonstration, bombasts, prophecies, monstrosities, provide for us rarer, greater, and more animated amusements than nearly all that has been flawlessly composed or spoken in many centuries. Not the humor concocted by a petty, ill-dispositioned fool of the arts, but the great humor nature now and then produces has that naïve, genuine, and original art that gives us festivals of laughter. Bjugg's poem is a monstrosity; it is in every way as remarkable as the red mist that hovered over Europe a few summers ago, or as every prodigious meteor; it is as rich in the odd and the humorous as anything many master works have ever given the Swedes for which no gold can pay; and if you cherish the gloomy in anything, this poem, if not a chaos of human genius, if not so stirring as the sight of a destroyed world, as the ruins of Rome or Palmyra, as chasms of the Alps, has at least something of the same terrible high drama of the misfortune of genius as a Messina razed by an earthquake.

You should notice, sir, that justice is nothing but a pure and manly understanding, and, if the ancient world went too far when it considered a lunatic holy, it is nevertheless true today that if the innocent and small faults of mankind deserve pity, the innocent and great faults deserve respect.

JOHANN WOLFGANG von GOETHE
(1749–1832)

o◯ooo◯o

SAINTE-BEUVE, HIMSELF ONE OF THE MOST GIFTED CRITICS of his age, declared Goethe to be "the greatest of all modern critics, the greatest critic of all times." Matthew Arnold referred to him as "that great and supreme critic"; James Russell Lowell as "the most widely receptive of all critics." These opinions are typical of the praise that writers and scholars for a century and a half have showered upon Goethe's critical utterances. But when one begins searching for a sample of Goethe's criticism to include in an anthology, it is difficult to find; for Goethe was not a critic in the sense that Sainte-Beuve, Brunetière, or Arnold were, but as any great poet and thinker must inevitably be. Thus his literary criticism is imbedded in his poetry (note the classico-romantic symbolism in the second part of *Faust*), his autobiographical *Dichtung und Wahrheit*, and his other prose works.

Wilhelm Meister contains long passages of Shakespearean interpretation and almost a complete dramaturgy. Indeed, an early draft of the work was called *Wilhelm Meisters theatralische Sendung*. But instead of remaining a mere vehicle for the author's opinions on theatrical art, the book became an allegory of young Goethe's philosophy of life. As such it is a landmark in literary—but not critical—history, for it shaped the European novel for three or four decades and did much to bring about the romantic epoch which the mature Goethe so heartily disliked.

And here we have the secret of Goethe's reputation as a literary critic. He planted the seed which flowered for generations. He changed the course of literary history, not once but several times. In an age of change, he himself was not least changeable. The most influential founder of the "Sturm und Drang" school, he turned Hellenic; then, still denouncing romanticism, he spent much of his later life writing romantic ballads with Schiller. But perhaps, after all, his Hellenism was most significant. It is true that in Rome he followed in the footsteps of Winckelmann and, consequently, saw only the antique—a characteristic phase of the romantic movement. Yet his classicism was uncongenial to the Schlegels, whose organ, the *Athenaeum*, was founding the romantic school in Germany around 1798—the year Wordsworth and Coleridge were publishing the first edition of *Lyrical Ballads*. In 1805 Goethe was still defending classicism in art, as witnessed by his *Winckelmann und sein Jahrhundert*. But the second part of *Faust* (1827) was accepted as romantic, and apparently the author had attempted to reach a compromise between the two antagonistic schools.

Thus even the casual sayings of a man with such a remarkable literary career as this would be, if not formal literary criticism, at least unusually enlightening to both student and critic of literary history and theory. That this was true with Goethe, his *Conversations with Eckermann* amply demonstrate. We have, consequently, chosen selections from this interesting document.

BIBLIOGRAPHY

TEXT

Eckermann, J. P., *Gespräche mit Goethe in der letzten Jahren seines Lebens.* 3 vols. Leipzig, 1876.

Werke, Hrsg., H. Düntzer. 5 vols. Stuttgart und Leipzig, 1882–1915.

TRANSLATIONS

Conversations of Goethe with Eckermann and Soret, tr. by John Oxenford. London, 1850. Several subsequent editions.

Eckermann's Conversations with Goethe, tr. by S. M. Fuller (Marchesa Ossoli), new ed. Boston, 1852.

Goethe's Conversations with Eckermann, tr. by John Oxenford, with a preface by Eckermann and an introduction by Wallace Wood. London, 1901.

Goethe's Literary Essays, arr. and ed. by J. E. Spingarn [using John Oxenford translation], with a foreword by Viscount Haldane. New York, 1921.

CRITICISM

Baldensperger, Fernand, *Goethe en France*—étude de littérature comparée. 2d. ed. rev. Paris, 1920.

Brandes, Georg Morris Cohen, *Wolfgang Goethe,* authorized translation from the Danish by Allen W. Porterfield. New York, 1925.

Carlyle, Thomas, *Essays on Goethe,* with an introduction by Henry Morley. London, 1905.

Cassirer, Ernst, *Goethe und die geschichtliche Welt.* Berlin, 1932.

Croce, Benedetto, *Goethe,* with an introduction by Douglas Ainslie. New York, 1923.

Goethe Centenary Lectures, in *Rice Institute Pamphlets*, XIX, no. 2, (April, 1932), pp. 61–88. (Contents: "Goethe and Philosophy," by Radoslav Andrea Tsanoff. "Goethe and Literary Criticism," by Alan Dugold McKillop. "The Correspondence and Conversations of Goethe," by Marcel Morand. "Goethe and Science," by Asa Crawford Chandler. "Goethe and Shakespeare," by Stockton Axson. "Goethe, Sage and Poet," by Heinrich Neye.)

Grueningen, J. P. von, "Goethe in American Periodicals—1860–1900," *Publications of the Modern Language Association*, L (1935), 1155–1164.

Hutton, Richard, "Goethe and His Influence," in *Literary Essays*. London, 1908.

Jessen, Myra Richards, *Goethe als Kritiken der Lyrik;* Beiträge zu seiner Aesthetik und seiner Theorie. Bryn Mawr, Pa., 1932. (A Ph. D. thesis.)

Landgraf, Hugo, *Goethe und seine ausländischen Besucher*. München, 1932.

Mitchell, McBurney. "Goethe's Theory of the Novelle, 1785–1827." *Publications of the Modern Language Association*, XXX (1915), 215–236.

Pritzel, H. F. *Goethe und Amerika*. 1912.

Riemann, Robert, *Goethes Romantechnik*. Leipzig, 1902.

Santayana, George, *Three Philosophical Poets: Lucretius, Dante, and Goethe*. Cambridge, 1910.

Sommerfeld, Martin, *Goethe in Umwelt und Folgezeit;* gesammelte Studien. Leiden, 1935.

Thomas, Calvin, *Goethe*. New York, 1917.

Wahr, Frederick Burkhart, *Emerson and Goethe*. Ann Arbor, Michigan, 1915. (A Ph. D. thesis.)

CONVERSATIONS WITH ECKERMANN (*selections*)[1]

1827–1830

[The Universality of Poetry]

[January 31, 1827] I am more and more convinced that poetry is the universal possession of mankind, revealing itself everywhere, and at all times, in hundreds and hundreds of men. One makes it a little better than another, and swims on the surface a little longer than another—that is all. Herr von Matthisson must not think he is the man, nor must I think that I am the

---

[1]The conversations took place between 1822 and 1832. Published by J. P. Eckermann, *Gespräche mit Goethe in der letzten Jahren seines Lebens*, 1836–1848. Translated by John Oxenford, 1850. In order to save space we have followed J. E. Spingarn's example (*Goethe's Literary Essays* [New York, 1921], pp. 81–88) of arranging the conversation under topic headings, omitting quotation marks and connecting conversational tags. But, unlike Spingarn, we have indicated dates for purposes of identification.

man; but each must say to himself that the gift of poetry is by no means so very rare, and that nobody need think very much of himself because he has written a good poem.

But, really, we Germans are very likely to fall too easily into this pedantic conceit when we do not look beyond the narrow circle which surrounds us. I therefore like to look about me in foreign nations, and advise everyone to do the same. National literature is now rather an unmeaning term; the epoch of World Literature is at hand, and everyone must strive to hasten its approach. But, while we thus value what is foreign, we must not bind ourselves to anything in particular and regard it as a model. We must not give this value to the Chinese, or the Servian, or Calderon, or the Nibelungen; but if we really want a pattern, we must always return to the ancient Greeks, in whose works the beauty of mankind is constantly represented. All the rest we must look at only historically, appropriating to ourselves what is good, so far as it goes.

[Poetry and Patriotism][2]

[March 14, 1830] To write military songs, and sit in a room! That would have suited me! To have written them in the bivouac, when the horses at the enemy's outposts are heard neighing at night, would have been well enough; however, that was not my life and not my business, but that of Theodor Körner. His war songs suit him perfectly. But to me, who am not of a warlike nature, and who have no warlike sense, war songs would have been a mask which would have fitted my face very badly.

I have never affected anything in my poetry. I have never uttered anything which I have not experienced, and which has not urged me to production. I have only composed love songs when I have loved. How could I write songs of hatred without hating! And, between ourselves, I did not hate the French, although I thanked God that we were free from them. How could I, to whom culture and barbarism are alone of importance, hate a nation which is among the most cultivated of the earth, and to which I owe so great a part of my own culture?

Altogether, national hatred is something peculiar. You will always find it strongest and most violent where there is the

---

[2]"Goethe had been reproached 'for not taking up arms in the German War of Liberation, or at least co-operating as a poet' " (Spingarn's note in *Goethe's Literary Essays*).

lowest degree of culture. But there is a degree where it vanishes altogether, and where one stands to a certain extent *above* nations, and feels the weal or woe of a neighboring people as if it had happened to one's own. This degree of culture was conformable to my nature, and I had become strengthened in it long before I had reached my sixtieth year.

[March 1832] It is better for us moderns to say with Napoleon, "Politics are Destiny." But let us beware of saying, with our latest literati, that politics are poetry, or a suitable subject for the poet. The English poet Thomson wrote a very good poem on the Seasons, but a very bad one on Liberty, and that not from want of poetry in the poet, but from want of poetry in the subject.

If a poet would work politically, he must give himself up to a party; and so soon as he does that he is lost as a poet; he must bid farewell to his free spirit, his unbiased view, and draw over his ears the cap of bigotry and blind hatred.

The poet, as a man and citizen, will love his native land; but the native land of his poetic powers and poetic action is the good, noble, and beautiful, which is confined to no particular province or country, and which he seizes upon and forms wherever he finds it. Therein is he like the eagle, who hovers with free gaze over whole countries, and to whom it is of no consequence whether the hare on which he pounces is running in Prussia or in Saxony.

And, then, what is meant by love of one's country? what is meant by patriotic deeds? If the poet has employed a life in battling with pernicious prejudices, in setting aside narrow views, in enlightening the minds, purifying the tastes, ennobling the feelings and thoughts of his countrymen, what better could he have done? how could he have acted more patriotically?

[Poetry and History]

[January 31, 1827] Manzoni wants nothing except to know what a good poet is and what rights belong to him as such. He has too much respect for history and on this account always adds explanations to his pieces, in which he shows how faithful he has been to detail. Now, though his facts may be historical, his characters are not so, any more than my Thoas and Iphigenia.[3] No poet has ever known the historical characters which he has

---

[3]Characters in Goethe's tragedy, *Iphigenie auf Tauris* (1787).

painted; if he had, he could scarcely have made use of them. The poet must know what effects he wishes to produce and regulate the nature of his characters accordingly. If I had tried to make Egmont[4] as history represents him, the father of a dozen children, his light-minded proceedings would have appeared very absurd. I needed an Egmont more in harmony with his own actions and my poetic views; and this is, as Clara says, *my* Egmont.

What would be the use of poets if they only repeated the record of the historian? The poet must go further and give us, if possible, something higher and better. All the characters of Sophocles bear something of that great poet's lofty soul; and it is the same with the characters of Shakespeare. This is as it ought to be. Nay, Shakespeare goes farther and makes his Romans Englishmen; and there, too, he is right; for otherwise his nation would not have understood him.

Here again the Greeks were so great that they regarded fidelity to historic facts less than the treatment of them by the poet. We have a fine example in Philoctetes,[5] which subject has been treated by all three of the great tragic poets, and lastly and best by Sophocles. This poet's excellent play has, fortunately, come down to us entire, while of the *Philoctetes* of Aeschylus and Euripides only fragments have been found, although sufficient to show how they have managed the subject. If time permitted, I would restore these pieces as I did the *Phaëthon* of Euripides; it would be to me no unpleasant or useless task.

In this subject the problem was very simple, namely, to bring Philoctetes, with his bow, from the island of Lemnos. But the manner of doing this was the business of the poet, and here each could show the power of his invention, and one could excel another. Ulysses must fetch him; but shall he be recognized by Philoctetes or not? and if not, how shall he be disguised? Shall Ulysses go alone, or shall he have companions, and who shall they be? In Aeschylus the companion is unknown; in Euripides, it is Diomed; in Sophocles, the son of Achilles. Then, in what situation is Philoctetes to be found? Shall the island be inhabited or not? and, if inhabited, shall any sympathetic soul

---

[4]Chief character in Goethe's tragedy, *Egmont* (1788).

[5]Greek archer who slew one of the suitors of Helen of Troy, according to one legend it was Paris; dramatized by Euripides, Aeschylus, and Sophocles.

have taken compassion on him or not? And so with a hundred other things which are all at the discretion of the poet and in the selection and omission of which one may show his superiority in wisdom to another. This is the important point, and the poets of today should do like the ancients. They should not be always asking whether a subject has been used before, and look to south and north for unheard-of adventures which are often barbarous enough and merely make an impression as incidents. But to make something of a simple subject by a masterly treatment requires intellect and great talent, and these we do not find.

[Originality]

[December 16, 1828] The Germans cannot cease to be Philistines. They are now squabbling about some verses, which are printed both in Schiller's works and mine, and fancy it is important to ascertain which really belong to Schiller and which to me; as if anything could be gained by such investigation—as if the existence of such things were not enough. Friends like Schiller and myself, intimate for years, with the same interests, in habits of daily intercourse, and under reciprocal obligations, live so completely in one another that it is hardly possible to decide to which of the two the particular thoughts belong.

We have made many distichs together; sometimes I gave the thought, and Schiller made the verse; sometimes the contrary was the case; sometimes he made one line, and I the other. What matters the mine and thine? One must be a thorough Philistine, indeed, to attach the slightest importance to the solution of such questions. . . .

We are indeed born with faculties; but we owe our development to a thousand influences of the great world, from which we appropriate to ourselves what we can, and what is suitable to us. I owe much to the Greeks and French; I am infinitely indebted to Shakespeare, Sterne, and Goldsmith; but in saying this I do not exhaust the sources of my culture; that would be an endless as well as an unnecessary task. We might as well question a strong man about the oxen, sheep, and swine which he has eaten and which have given him strength. What is important is to have a soul which loves truth and receives it wherever it finds it.

Besides, the world is now so old, so many eminent men have lived and thought for thousands of years, that there is little new to be discovered or expressed. Even my theory of colors is not entirely new. Plato, Leonardo da Vinci, and many other excellent men have before me found and expressed the same thing in a detached form: my merit is that I have found it also, that I have said it again, and that I have striven to bring the truth once more into a confused world.

The truth must be repeated over and over again, because error is repeatedly preached among us, not only by individuals but by the masses. In periodicals and cyclopedias, in schools and universities, everywhere, in fact, error prevails, and is quite easy in the feeling that it has a decided majority on its side.

[May 12, 1825] People are always talking about originality; but what do they mean? As soon as we are born, the world begins to work upon us, and this goes on to the end. And, after all, what can we call our own except energy, strength, and will? If I could give an account of all that I owe to great predecessors and contemporaries, there would be but a small balance in my favor.

However, the time of life in which we are subjected to a new and important personal influence is, by no means, a matter of indifference. That Lessing, Winckelmann, and Kant were older than I, and that the first two acted upon my youth, the latter on my advanced age—this circumstance was for me very important. Again, that Schiller was so much younger than I, and engaged in his freshest strivings just as I began to be weary of the world—just, too, as the brothers von Humboldt and Schlegel were beginning their career under my eye—was of the greatest importance. I derived from it unspeakable advantages.

[April 15, 1829] What seduces young people is this. We live in a time in which so much culture is diffused that it has communicated itself, as it were, to the atmosphere which a young man breathes. Poetical and philosophic thoughts live and move within him, he has sucked them in with his very breath, but he thinks they are his own property and utters them as such. But after he has restored to the time what he has received from it, he remains poor. He is like a fountain which plays for a while with the water with which it is supplied, but which ceases to flow as soon as the liquid treasure is exhausted.

[Feb. 14, 1830] The critic of *Le Temps* has not been so wise. He presumes to point out to the poet the way he should go. This is a great fault; for one cannot thus make him better. After all, there is nothing more foolish than to say to a poet: "You should have done this in this way—and that in that." I speak from long experience. One can never make anything of a poet but what his nature intended him to be. If you force him to be another, you will destroy him. Now, the gentlemen of the *Globe*, as I said before, act very wisely. They print a long list of all the commonplaces which M. Arnault has picked up from every hole and corner; and by doing this they very cleverly point out the rock which the author has to avoid in future. It is almost impossible, in the present day, to find a situation which is thoroughly new. It is merely the manner of looking at it, and the art of treating and representing it, which can be new, and one must be the more cautious of every imitation.

[The Subject Matter of Poetry]

[September 18, 1823] The world is so great and rich, and life so full of variety, that you can never want occasions for poems. But they must all be occasional poems; that is to say, reality must give both impulse and material for their production. A particular case becomes universal and poetic by the very circumstance that it is treated by a poet. All my poems are occasional poems, suggested by real life, and having therein a firm foundation. I attach no value to poems snatched out of the air.

Let no one say that reality wants poetical interest; for in this the poet proves his vocation, that he has the art to win from a common subject an interesting side. Reality must give the motive, the points to be expressed, the kernel, as I may say; but to work out of it a beautiful, animated whole belongs to the poet. You know Fürnstein, called the Poet of Nature; he has written the prettiest poem possible on the cultivation of hops. I have now proposed to him to make songs for the different crafts of workingmen, particularly a weaver's song, and I am sure he will do it well, for he has lived among such people from his youth; he understands the subject thoroughly, and is therefore master of his material. That is exactly the advantage of small works; you need only choose those subjects of which you are master. With a great poem, this cannot be: no part can be evaded; all which belongs to the animation of the whole, and is interwoven into the plan, must be represented with precision. In youth, however, the knowledge of things is only one-sided.

A great work requires many-sidedness, and on that rock the young author splits. . . .

[Nov. 24, 1824] The majority of our young poets have no fault but this, that their subjectivity is not important, and that they cannot find matter in the objective. At best, they only find a material which is similar to themselves, which corresponds to their own subjectivity; but as for taking the material on its own account, merely because it is poetical, even when it is repugnant to their subjectivity, such a thing is never thought of.

Our German aestheticians are always talking about poetical and unpoetical objects, and in one respect they are not quite wrong, yet at bottom no real object is unpoetical if the poet knows how to use it properly.

[The Influence of Environment]

[May 3, 1827] . . . If a talent is to be speedily and happily developed, the great point is that a great deal of intellect and sound culture should be current in a nation.

We admire the tragedies of the ancient Greeks; but, to take a correct view of the case, we ought rather to admire the period and the nation in which their production was possible than the individual authors; for though these pieces differ a little from each other, and one of these poets appears somewhat greater and more finished than the other, still, taking all things together, only one decided character runs through the whole.

This is the character of grandeur, fitness, soundness, human perfection, elevated wisdom, sublime thought, clear, concrete vision, and whatever other qualities one might enumerate. But when we find all these qualities not only in the dramatic works that have come down to us, but also in lyrical and epic works, in the philosophers, the orators, and the historians, and in an equally high degree in the works of plastic art that have come down to us, we must feel convinced that such qualities did not merely belong to individuals, but were the current property of the nation and the whole period.

Now, take up Burns. How is he great except through the circumstance that the old songs of his predecessors lived in the mouth of the people—that they were, so to speak, sung at his cradle; that as a boy he grew up amongst them, and the high excellence of these models so pervaded him that he had therein a living basis on which he could proceed further? Again, why is he great but from this, that his own songs at once found susceptible ears amongst his compatriots; that, sung by reapers and sheaf binders, they at once greeted him in the field; and that his boon companions sang them to welcome him at the alehouse? Something was certainly to be done in this way.

On the other hand, what a pitiful figure is made by us Germans! Of our old songs—no less important than those of Scotland—how many lived among the people in the days of my youth? Herder and his successors first began to collect them and rescue them from oblivion; then they were at least printed in the libraries. Then, more lately, what songs have not Bürger[6] and Voss[7] composed! Who can say that they are more insignificant or less popular than those of the excellent Burns? but which of them so lives among us that it greets us from the mouth of the people? They are written and printed, and they remain in the libraries, quite in accordance with the general fate of German poets. Of my own songs, how many live? Perhaps one or another of them may be sung by a pretty girl at the piano; but among the people, properly so called, they have no sound. With what sensations must I remember the time when passages from Tasso were sung to me by Italian fishermen!

We Germans are of yesterday. We have indeed been properly cultivated for a century; but a few centuries more must still elapse before so much mind and elevated culture will become universal amongst our people that they will appreciate beauty like the Greeks, that they will be inspired by a beautiful song, and that it will be said of them "it is long since they were barbarians."

[Classic and Romantic]

[April 2, 1829] A new expression occurs to me which does not ill define the state of the case. I call the classic *healthy*, the romantic *sickly*. In this sense, the *Nibelungenlied* is as classic as the *Iliad*, for both are vigorous and healthy. Most modern productions are romantic, not because they are new, but because they are weak, morbid, and sickly; and the antique is classic, not because it is old, but because it is strong, fresh, joyous, and healthy. If we distinguish "classic" and "romantic" by these qualities, it will be easy to see our way clearly.

[6]Gottfried August Bürger (1747–1794), author of poems and ballads.
[7]Johann Heinrich Voss (1751–1826), minor German poet, composer of songs, idyls, and translations.

[April 5, 1829] Goethe also told me about a tragedy by a young poet. It is a pathological work; a superfluity of sap is bestowed on some parts which do not require it, and drawn out of those which stand in need of it. The subject was good, but the scenes which I expected were not there; while others, which I did not expect, were elaborated with assiduity and love. This is what I call pathological, or "romantic," if you would rather speak according to our new theory.

[Dec. 16, 1829] The French now begin to think justly of these matters. Both classic and romantic, say they, are equally good. The only point is to use these forms with judgment, and to be capable of excellence. You can be absurd in both, and then one is as worthless as the other. This, I think, is rational enough, and may content us for a while.

[March 21, 1830] The idea of the distinction between classical and romantic poetry, which is now spread over the whole world and occasions so many quarrels and divisions, came originally from Schiller and myself. I laid down the maxim of objective treatment in poetry, and would allow no other; but Schiller, who worked quite in the subjective way, deemed his own fashion the right one, and to defend himself against me, wrote the treatise upon *Naïve and Sentimental Poetry*. He proved to me that I myself, against my will, was romantic, and that my *Iphigenia*, through the predominance of sentiment, was by no means so classical and so much in the antique spirit as some people supposed.

The Schlegels took up this idea, and carried it further, so that it has now been diffused over the whole world; and everyone talks about classicism and romanticism—of which nobody thought fifty years ago.

[Shakespeare]

[December 25, 1825] But we cannot talk about Shakespeare; everything is inadequate. I have touched upon the subject in my *Wilhelm Meister*,[8] but that is not saying much. He is not a theatrical poet;[9] he never thought of the stage; it was far too

---

[8] Cf. Bk. III, chap. XI; Bk. IV, chaps. III and XIII; Bk. V, chap. IV ff.

[9] Most of the nineteenth-century Shakespeare critics regarded him as a poet rather than a dramatist, whose works could be better understood in the private study than on the public stage. This attitude also caused many romantic poets to write "closet drama," not intended for the stage at all.

narrow for his great mind: nay, the whole visible world was too narrow.[10]

He is even too rich and too powerful. A productive nature ought not to read more than one of his dramas in a year if it would not be wrecked entirely. I did well to get rid of him by writing *Goetz* and *Egmont*, and Byron did well by not having too much respect and admiration for him, but going his own way. How many excellent Germans have been ruined by him and Calderon!

Shakespeare gives us golden apples in silver dishes. We get, indeed, the silver dishes by studying his works; but, fortunately, we have only potatoes to put into them.

Macbeth is Shakespeare's best acting play, the one in which he shows most understanding with respect to the stage. But would you see his mind unfettered, read *Troilus and Cressida*,[11] where he treats the materials of the *Iliad* in his own fashion.

[The French Romanticists]

[March 14, 1830] Extremes are never to be avoided in any revolution. In a political one, nothing is generally desired in the beginning but the abolition of abuses; but, before people are aware, they are deep in bloodshed and horror. Thus the French, in their present literary revolution, desired nothing at first but a freer form; however, they will not stop there, but will reject the traditional contents together with the form. They begin to declare the representation of noble sentiments and deeds as tedious and attempt to treat of all sorts of abominations. Instead of the beautiful subjects from Grecian mythology, there are devils, witches, and vampires; and the lofty heroes of antiquity must give place to jugglers and galley slaves. This is piquant! This is effective! But after the public has once tasted this highly seasoned food and has become accustomed to it, it will always long for more, and that stronger. A young man of talent, who would produce an effect and be acknowledged, and who is great enough to go his own way, must accommodate himself to the taste of the day—nay, must seek to outdo his predecessors in the horrible and frightful. But in this chase after outward means of effect, all profound study, and all gradual and thorough development of

---

[10]For a fuller discussion of Shakespeare as "World-Spirit," see Goethe's essay, "Shakespeare ad Infinitum" (1813–1816).

[11]Cf. Goethe's essay on "Troilus and Cressida" (1824).

the talent and the man from within is entirely neglected. And this is the greatest injury which can befall a talent, although literature in general will gain by this tendency of the moment.

The extremes and excrescences which I have described will gradually disappear; but this great advantage will finally remain; besides a freer form, richer and more diversified subjects will have been attained, and no object of the broadest world and the most manifold life will be any longer excluded as unpoetical. I compare the present literary epoch to a state of violent fever, which is not in itself good and desirable, but of which improved health is the happy consequence. That abomination which now often constitutes the whole subject of a poetical work will in future only appear as a useful expedient; aye, the pure and the noble, which is now abandoned for the moment, will soon be resought with additional ardor. . . .

FRIEDRICH von SCHILLER

(1759–1805)

o◯oo◯o

IN THE ARCHAIC FEUDAL SOCIETY of eighteenth-century Germany the power of the nobility was almost unlimited. Hence it was possible not only for Duke Karl Eugen to force Schiller to attend a military school but also to compel him to study first law and then medicine, after which he was pressed into service in the duke's army as a military physician, a vocation extremely uncongenial to a brilliant young man with literary inclinations. The tempestuous nature of Schiller's early dramas, particularly *The Robbers*, no doubt reflects the author's rebellion and helped him to become the poet of freedom. Fortunately the young dramatist was soon able to escape from the duke's tyranny.

Schiller's great reputation is based on his success in drama, history, and lyric poetry, especially the ballad, but even at the military academy he was deeply interested in philosophy and aesthetics. His master's dissertation on *Philosophie der Physiologie* has been almost entirely lost, but the main ideas were doubtless repeated in the work *On the Connection between the Animal and the Spiritual Nature of Man*.[1] The thesis is that the universe is a divine work of art and that man's destiny is enlightenment and perfection. At this period in his life Schiller believed that artists learn to imitate the works of nature, music softens the savage breast, beauty ennobles morals and taste, and art leads man to science and to virtue.[2] Poetic lore and medical information are combined in his theory of morality and art. Mental pleasure is dependent upon physical well-being, and the good and the beautiful are almost analogous. The notion of the organic unity of all nature and the supremacy of spirit over body results in a curious Neoplatonic[3] doctrine: "By an admirable law of supreme wisdom every noble and generous passion beautifies the body, while those that are mean and detestable distort it into animal forms."[4] Such ideas led Schiller in the Preface

---

[1]See *Sämmtliche Schriften* (Hrsg. Karl Goedeke, 17 vols. in 15. Stuttgart, 1867–1876), I, 75–76.

[2]*Ibid.*, I, 156.

[3]For the expression of this doctrine in English poetry see Spenser's *Amoretti*.

[4]*Schriften*, I, 170.

of *The Robbers* to modify the "imitation of nature" theory to an accept-
ance of a more neoclassic theory of improved nature. In general,
Schiller's early philosophy is in the spirit of German Enlightenment
(*Aufklärungs-philosophie*), and he was influenced not only by Leibnitz and
Wolff but also Shaftesbury and the Scottish school.

In his essays on dramatic art Schiller regards the stage as a moral
institution.[5] And he now enlarges the function of art to include relaxation and purely aesthetic pleasure as well as contemplation and moral
improvement. In his essays on the aesthetics of tragedy,[6] however, he
no longer regards the pursuit of pleasure as desirable in itself but only
incidental. Most important is that "the pleasure we find in the
beautiful, pathetic, and sublime strengthens our moral sentiments."
(Some of Schiller's comments on the philosophy of tragedy are found
in our selection *On the Pathetic*.)

The Philosophical Letters purport to be a correspondence between
Schiller and Körner, who introduced Schiller to Kantian philosophy.[7]
The main idea in these is the relativity and limitation of human knowledge.[8] One letter to Körner, written December, 1792, contains the famous definition of Beauty as "freedom-in-the-appearance" (*Freiheit in der
Erscheinung*). The *Letters on the Aesthetical Education of Man* (1793–1795)
are memorable for the exposition of Schiller's theory of art as a form of
play (cf. Letter XV), a contribution of great importance in the history of
aesthetics. Wilm summarizes Schiller's philosophical position as follows:

> In the philosophy of art, his theory of the aesthetic state as one
> in which the various powers of man's nature come into spon-
> taneous and balanced play, his definition of beauty as freedom-
> in-the-appearance, his ethical concept of the beautiful soul (*die
> schöne Seele*), in which the harsh opposition between inclination
> and duty is resolved, and man is at peace with himself, his theory
> of the function of art in moral culture,—these and other charac-
> teristic ideas have assured Schiller an honorable place in the
> history of modern philosophy.[9]

But important as Schiller was poetically and philosophically, he was
only indirectly a literary critic. In a letter to Goethe he indicated his
own weakness:

[5]See "Über das gegenwärtige deutsche Theater" (1782) and "Die Schaubühne
als moralische Anstalt betrachtet" (1784), *Schriften*, II, 340–348; III, 509–524.
    [6]Schiller lectured on the subject at Jena in 1790 but the essays on the aesthetics
of tragedy were written in 1791–1792.
    [7]For Körner's influence on Schiller, see Josiah Royce's article in *Journal of
Speculative Philosophy*, XII, 379.   [8]Cf. *Schriften*, IV, 36–37.
    [9]Emil Carl Wilm, *The Philosophy of Schiller in Its Historical Relation* (Boston, 1912),
p. 157.

My understanding works more in a symbolizing method, and thus I hover, as a hybrid, between ideas and perceptions, between law and feeling, between a technical mind and genius. . . . the poetic mind generally got the better of me when I ought to have philosophized, and my philosophical mind when I wished to poetize.[10]

It was partly this tendency in Schiller which led Saintsbury to declare that he was not "a great critic, or even a good one. He could spin out of his interior more criticism, and of a better quality, than most men could. But he was excessively deficient in Love—that first and greatest fulfilling of the law of the true critic."[11] Nevertheless, Schiller will long be remembered for a few ideas which have profoundly influenced philosophical thinking on literary art.[12]

BIBLIOGRAPHY

TEXT

Sämmtliche Schriften. Hrsg. Karl Goedeke. 17 vols. in 15. Stuttgart, 1867–1876.

TRANSLATIONS

Aesthetical and Philosophical Essays, tr. from the German. New York, 1895.

Correspondence between Schiller and Goethe from 1794–1805, tr. by L. Dora Schmitz. London, 1877. Volume I covers 1794–1797.

Correspondence between Schiller and Goethe from 1794–1805, tr. from the third edition of the German notes. 2 vols. London, 1877–1879. (Bohn's Standard Library.)

Works, tr. from the German. 7 vols. London, 1889. (Bohn's Standard Library.)

CRITICISM

Basch, Victor, *La Poétique de Schiller*, essai d'esthétique littéraire. 2d. ed. Paris, 1911.

Bolze, Wilhelm, *Schillers philosophische Begründung der Aesthetik der Tragödie.* Leipzig, 1913.

Bornhausen, Karl, *Schiller, Goethe und das deutsche Menscheitsideal.* Leipzig, 1920.

[10]Letter VII.

[11]George Saintsbury, *History of Criticism* (Edinburgh, 1904), III, 383.

[12]One of these is no doubt "On Naïve and Sentimental Poetry," in which Schiller tried to work out a critical principle explaining the difference between his poetry and Goethe's. This essay called forth Friedrich Schlegel's reply in "Essays on the Study of Greek Poetry" (1797), *Works*, XII, 388. The question concerning the subjectivity and objectivity of these two German poets has never been settled.

Carlyle, Thomas, *The Life of Friedrich Schiller*, comprehending an examination of his works. 2d. ed. London, 1845.

Carter, A. L. *Parallel Themes and Their Treatment in Schiller and Shaftesbury*. Philadelphia, 1919.

Clark, R. T., Jr., "Union of the Arts in 'Die Braut von Messina,' " *Publications of the Modern Language Association*, LII (1937), 1135–1146.

Eggli, Edmond, *Schiller et le romantisme français*. 2 vols. Paris, 1927.

Headstrom, B. R., "Aesthetic Writings of Schiller," *Open Court*, XLIII (1929), 235–243.

Heine, G., *Das Verhältnis der Aesthetik zu Ethik bei Schiller*. Leipzig, 1894.

Kühnemann, Eugen, *Kants und Schillers Begründung der Aesthetik*. Munich, 1895.

Lotze, H., *Geschichte der Aesthetik in Deutschland*. Munich, 1868.

Meier, H., *Welchen Werth haben Schillers Schriften über die ästhetische Erziehung des Menschen*. Schleiz, 1879–1880.

Montargis, F., *L'Esthetique de Schiller*. Paris, 1892.

Phillipson, R., *Die ästhetische Erziehung ein Beitrag zur Lehre Kants, Schillers und Herbarts*. Magdeburg, 1890.

Rose, E., "The Function of Poetry according to Schiller," *Modern Language Forum*, XX (1938), 1936 ff.

Sommer, R., *Grundzüge einer Geschichte der deutschen Psychologie und Aesthetik von Wolff—Baumgarten bis Kant—Schiller*. Wurzburg, 1892.

Stahl, E. L., "The Genesis of Schiller's Theory of Tragedy," *German Studies*. Oxford, 1938.

Titsworth, Paul Emerson, "The Attitude of Goethe and Schiller toward the French Classic Drama," *Journal of English and Germanic Philology*, XI (1912), no. 4, 509–569.

Wilm, Emil Carl, *The Philosophy of Schiller in Its Historical Relations*. Boston, 1912.

Zimmermann, R., *Aesthetik*. Erster Theil. Vienna, 1858.

ON THE PATHETIC (*selections*)[1]

1793

The depicting of suffering, in the shape of simple suffering, is never the end of art, but it is of the greatest importance as a means of attaining its end. The highest aim of art is to represent the supersensuous, and this is effected in particular by tragic art, because it represents by sensible marks the moral man, maintaining himself in a state of passion, independently of the laws of nature. The principle of freedom in man becomes conscious of itself only by the resistance it offers to the violence of the feel-

---

[1]*Aesthetical and Philosophical Essays*, tr. [anon.] from the German (New York, 1895).

ings. Now the resistance can only be measured by the strength of the attack. In order, therefore, that the intelligence may reveal itself in man as a force independent of nature, it is necessary that nature should have first displayed all her power before our eyes. The *sensuous* being must be profoundly and strongly *affected*, *passion* must be in play, that the *reasonable* being may be able to testify his independence and manifest himself in *action*.

It is impossible to know if the empire which man has over his affections is the effect of a moral force till we have acquired the certainty that it is not an effect of insensibility. There is no merit in mastering the feelings which only lightly and transitorily skim over the surface of the soul. But to resist a tempest which stirs up the whole of sensuous nature, and to preserve in it the freedom of the soul, a faculty of resistance is required infinitely superior to the act of natural force. Accordingly it will not be possible to represent moral freedom, except by expressing passion, or suffering nature, with the greatest vividness; and the hero of tragedy must first have justified his claim to be a sensuous being before aspiring to our homage as a reasonable being, and making us believe in his strength of mind.

Therefore the *pathetic* is the first condition required most strictly in a tragic author, and he is allowed to carry his description of suffering as far as possible, without prejudice to the *highest end of his art*, that is, without moral freedom being oppressed by it. He must give in some sort to his hero, as to his reader, their full *load* of suffering, without which the question will always be put whether the resistance opposed to suffering is an act of the soul, something *positive*, or whether it is not rather a purely *negative* thing, a simple deficiency.

The latter case is offered in the purer French tragedy, where it is very rare, or perhaps unexampled, for the author to place before the reader suffering nature, and where generally, on the contrary, it is only the poet who warms up and declaims, or the comedian who struts about on stilts. The icy tone of declamation extinguishes all nature here, and the French tragedians, with their superstitious worship of *decorum*, make it quite impossible for them to paint human nature truly. Decorum, wherever it is, even in its proper place, always falsifies the expression of nature, and yet this expression is rigorously required by art. In a French tragedy, it is difficult for us to believe that the hero ever suffers, for he explains the state of his soul, as the coolest man would do, and always thinking of the effect he is making on others, he never lets nature pour forth freely. The kings, the princesses, and the heroes of Corneille or Voltaire never forget their *rank* even in the most violent excess of passion; and they part with their *humanity* much sooner than with their *dignity*. They are like those kings and emperors of our old picture books who go to bed with their crowns on.

What a difference from the Greeks and those of the moderns who have been inspired with their spirit in poetry! Never does the Greek poet blush at nature; he leaves to the sensuous all its rights, and yet he is quite certain never to be subdued by it. He has too much depth and too much rectitude in his mind not to distinguish the accidental, which is the principal point with false taste, from the really necessary; but all that is not humanity itself is accidental in man. The Greek artist who has to represent a Laocoön, a Niobe, and a Philoctetes, does not care for the king, the princes, or the king's son; he keeps to the *man*. Accordingly the skillful statuary sets aside the drapery, and shows us nude figures, though he knows quite well it is not so in real life. This is because drapery is to him an accidental thing, and because the necessary ought never to be sacrificed to the accidental. It is also because, if decency and physical necessities have their laws, these laws are not those of art. The statuary ought to show us, and wishes to show us, the *man* himself; drapery conceals him, therefore he sets that aside, and with reason.

The Greek sculptor rejects drapery as a useless and embarrassing load, to make way for *human nature;* and in like manner the Greek poet emancipates the human personages he brings forward from the equally useless constraint of decorum and all those icy laws of propriety which put nothing but what is artificial in man, and conceal nature in it. Take Homer and the tragedians; suffering nature speaks the language of truth and ingenuousness in their pages, and in a way to penetrate to the depths of our hearts. All the passions play their part freely, nor do the rules of propriety compress any feeling with the Greeks. The heroes are just as much under the influence of suffering as other men, and what makes them heroes is the very fact that they feel suffering strongly and deeply, without suffering overcoming them. They love life as ardently as others; but they are not so ruled by this feeling as to be unable to give up life when the duties of honor or humanity call on them to do so. Philoctetes filled the Greek stage with his lamentations; Hercules himself, when in fury, does not keep under his grief. Iphigenia, on the point of being sacrificed, confesses with a touching ingenuousness that she grieves to part with the light of the sun. Never does the Greek place his glory in being insensible or indifferent to suffering, but rather in *supporting* it, though feeling it in its fullness. The very gods of the Greeks must pay their tribute to nature, when the poet wishes to make the approximate to humanity. Mars, when wounded, roars like ten thousand men together, and Venus, scratched by an iron lance, mounts again to Olympus, weeping, and cursing all battles.

This lively susceptibility on the score of suffering, this warm, ingenuous nature, showing itself uncovered and in all truth in the monuments of Greek art, and filling us with such deep and lively emotions—this is a model presented for the imitation of all artists; it is a law which Greek genius has laid down for the fine arts. It is always and eternally nature which has the first rights over man; she ought never to be fettered, because man, before being anything else, is a sensuous creature. After the rights of nature come those of *reason*, because man is a rational, sensuous being, a moral person, and because it is a duty for this person not to let himself be ruled by nature, but to rule her. It is only after satisfaction has been given in the *first place* to *nature*, and after reason in the *second place* has made its rights acknowledged, that it is permitted for decorum in the third place to make good its claims, to impose on man, in the expression of his moral feelings, and of his sensations, considerations towards society, and to show in it the social being, the civilized man. The first law of the tragic art was to represent suffering nature. The second law is to represent the resistance of morality opposed to suffering.

Affection, as affection, is an unimportant thing; and the portraiture of affection, considered in itself, would be without any aesthetic value; for, I repeat it, nothing that only interests sensuous nature is worthy of being represented by art. Thus not only the affections that do nothing but enervate and soften man, but in general all affections, even those that are exalted, ecstatic, whatever may be their nature, are beneath the dignity of tragic art.

The soft emotions, only producing tenderness, are of the nature of the *agreeable*, with which the fine arts are not concerned. They only caress the senses, while relaxing and creating languidness, and only relate to external nature, not at all to the inner nature of man. A good number of our romances and of our tragedies, particularly those that bear the name of dramas—a sort of compromise between tragedy and comedy—a good number also of those highly appreciated family portraits belong to this class. The only effect of these works is to empty the lachrymal duct, and soothe the overflowing feelings; but the mind comes back from them empty, and the moral being, the noblest part of our nature, gathers no new strength whatever from them. "It is thus," says Kant, "that many persons feel themselves *edified* by a sermon that has nothing *edifying* in it." It seems also that modern music only aims at interesting the sensuous, and in this it flatters the taste of the day, which seeks to be agreeably tickled, but not to be startled, nor strongly moved and elevated. Accordingly we see music prefer all that is *tender;* and whatever be the noise in a concert room, silence is immediately restored, and everyone is all ears directly a sentimental passage is performed. Then an expression of sensibility common to animalism shows itself commonly on all faces; the eyes are swimming with intoxication, the open mouth is all desire, a voluptuous trembling takes hold of the entire body, the breath is quick and full, in short, all the symptoms of intoxication appear. This is an evident proof that the senses swim in delight, but that the mind or the principle of freedom in man has become a prey to the violence of the sensuous impression. Real taste, that of noble and manly minds, rejects all these emotions as unworthy of art, because they only please the *senses*, with which art has nothing in common.

But, on the other hand, real taste excludes all extreme affections, which only put sensuousness to the *torture*, without giving the mind any compensation. These affections oppress moral liberty by *pain*, as the others by voluptuousness; consequently they can excite aversion, and not the emotion that would alone be worthy of art. Art ought to charm the mind and give satisfaction to the feeling of moral freedom. This man who is a prey to his pain is to me simply a tortured animate being, and not a man tried by suffering. For a moral resistance to painful affections is already required of man—a resistance which can alone allow the principle of moral freedom, the intelligence, to make itself known in it.

If it is so, the poets and the artists are poor adepts in their art when they seek to reach the pathetic only by the sensuous force of affection and by representing suffering in the most vivid manner. They forget that suffering in itself can never be the last end of imitation, nor the immediate source of the pleasure we experience in tragedy. The pathetic only has aesthetic value in so far as it is sublime. Now, effects that only allow us to infer a purely sensuous cause, and that are founded only on the affection experienced by the faculty of sense, are never sublime, whatever energy they may display, for everything sublime proceeds *exclusively* from the reason.

I imply by passion the affections of pleasure as well as the painful affections, and to represent passion only, without coupling with it the expression of the supersensuous faculty which resists it, is to fall into what is properly called *vulgarity;* and the opposite is called *nobility*. Vulgarity and nobility are two ideas which, wherever they are applied, have more or less relation with the supersensuous share a man takes in a work. There is nothing noble but what has its source in the reason; all that issues from sensuousness alone is *vulgar* or *common*. We say of man that he acts in a *vulgar* manner when he is satisfied with obeying the suggestions of his sensuous instinct; that he acts suitably when he only obeys his instinct in conformity with the laws; that he acts *nobly* when he obeys reason only, without having regard to his instincts. We say of a physiognomy that it is *common* when it does not show any trace of the spiritual man, the intelligence; we say it has expression when it is the mind which has determined its features, and that it is noble when a pure spirit has determined them. If an architectural work is in question, we qualify it as *common* if it aims at nothing but a physical end; we name it noble if, independently of all physical aim, we find in it at the same time the expression of a conception.

Accordingly, I repeat it, correct taste disallows all painting of the affections, however energetic, which rests satisfied with expressing physical suffering and the physical resistance opposed to it by the subject, without making visible at the same time the superior principle of the nature of man, the presence of a supersensuous faculty. It does this in virtue of the principle developed farther back, namely, that it is not suffering in itself, but only the resistance opposed to suffering that is pathetic and deserving of being represented. It is for this reason that all the absolutely extreme degrees of the affections are forbidden to the artist as well as to the poet. All of these, in fact, oppress the force that resists from within; or rather, all betray of themselves, and without any necessity of other symptoms, the oppression of this force, because no affection can reach this last degree of intensity as long as the intelligence in man makes any resistance.

Then another question presents itself. How is this principle of resistance, this supersensuous force, manifested in the phenomenon of the affections? Only in one way, by mastering or, more commonly, by combating affection. I say *affection*, for sensuousness can also fight, but this combat of sensuousness is not carried on with the affection, but with the *cause* that produces it; a contest which has no moral character, but is all physical, the same combat that the earthworm, trodden under foot, and the wounded bull engage in, without thereby exciting the pathetic. When suffering man seeks to give an expression to his feelings, to remove his enemy, to shelter the suffering limb, he does all this in common with the animals, and instinct alone takes the initiative here without the will being applied to. Therefore, this is not an act that emanates from the man himself, nor does it show him as an intelligence. Sensuous nature will always fight the enemy that makes it suffer, but it will never fight against itself.

On the other hand, the contest with affection is a contest with sensuousness, and consequently presupposes something that is distinct from sensuous nature. Man can defend himself with the help of common sense and his muscular strength against the object that makes him suffer; against suffering itself he has no other arms than those of reason.

These ideas must present themselves to the eye in the portraiture of the affections, or be awakened by this portraiture in order that the pathetic may exist. But it is impossible to represent ideas, in the proper sense of the word, and positively, as nothing corresponds to pure ideas in the world of sense. But they can be always represented negatively and in an indirect way if the sensuous phenomenon by which they are manifested has some character of which you would seek in vain the conditions in *physical nature*. All phenomena of which the ultimate principle cannot be derived from the world of sense are an indirect representation of the upper-sensuous element.

And how does one succeed in representing something that is above nature without having recourse to supernatural means?

What can this phenomenon be which is accomplished by natural forces—otherwise it would not be a phenonenon—and yet which cannot be derived from physical causes without a contradiction? This is the problem; how can the artist solve it?

It must be remembered that the phenomena observable in a man in a state of passion are of two kinds. They are either phenomena connected simply with animal nature, and which, therefore, only obey the physical law, without the will being able to master them, or the independent force in him being able to exercise an immediate influence over them. It is the instinct which immediately produces these phenomena, and they obey blindly the laws of instinct. To this kind belong, for example, the organs of the circulation of the blood, of respiration, and all the surface of the skin. But, moreover, the other organs, and those subject to the will, do not always await the decision of the will; and often instinct itself sets them immediately in play, especially when the physical state is threatened with pain or with danger. Thus, the movements of my arm depend, it is true, on my will; but if I place my hand, without knowing it, on a burning body, the movement by which I draw it back is certainly not a voluntary act, but a purely instinctive phenomenon. Nay more, speech is assuredly subject to the empire of the will, and yet instinct can also dispose of this organ according to its whim, and even of the mind, without consulting beforehand the will, directly a sharp pain, or even an energetic affection, takes us by surprise. Take the most impassible stoic and make him see suddenly something very wonderful, or a terrible and unexpected object. Fancy him, for example, present when a man slips and falls to the bottom of an abyss. A shout, a resounding cry, and not only inarticulate, but a distinct word will escape his lips, and nature will have acted in him before the will: a certain proof that there are in man phenomena which cannot be referred to his person as an intelligence, but only to his instinct as a natural force.

But there is also in man a *second* order of phenomena which are subject to the influence and empire of the will, or which may be considered at all events as being of such a kind that will might *always have prevented* them, consequently phenomena for which the *person* and not instinct is responsible. It is the office of instinct to watch with a blind zeal over the interests of the senses; but it is the office of the *person* to hold instinct in proper bounds, out of respect for the moral law. Instinct in itself does not hold account of any law; but the person ought to watch that instinct may not infringe in any way on the decrees of reason. It is therefore evident that it is not for instinct alone to determine unconditionally all the phenomena that take place in man in the state of affection, and that on the contrary the will of man can place limits to instinct. When instinct only determines all phenomena in man, there is nothing more that can recall the *person;* there is only a physical creature before you, and consequently an animal; for every physical creature subject to the sway of instinct is nothing else. Therefore, if you wish to represent the person itself, you must propose to yourself in man certain phenomena that have been determined in opposition to instinct, or at least that have not been determined by instinct. That they have not been determined by instinct is sufficient to refer them to a higher source, the moment we see that instinct would no doubt have determined them in another way if its force had not been broken by some obstacle.

We are now in a position to point out in what way the supersensuous element, the moral and independent force of man, his Ego in short, can be represented in the phenomena of the affections. I understand that this is possible if the parts which only obey physical nature, those where will either disposes nothing at all, or only under certain circumstances, betray the presence of suffering; and if those, on the contrary, that escape the blind sway of instinct, that only obey physical nature, show no trace, or only a very feeble trace, of suffering, and consequently appear to have a certain degree of freedom. Now this want of harmony between the features imprinted on animal nature in virtue of the laws of physical necessity, and those determined with the spiritual and independent faculty of man, is precisely the point by which that supersensuous principle is discovered in man capable of placing limits to the effects produced by physical nature, and therefore distinct from the latter. The purely animal part of man obeys the physical law, and consequently may show itself oppressed by the affection. It is, therefore, in this part that all the strength of passion shows itself, and it answers in some degree as a measure to estimate the resistance—that is to say, of the energy of the moral faculty in man—which can only be judged according to the force of the attack. Thus in proportion as the affection manifests itself with decision and violence in the field of *animal nature*, without being able to exercise the same power in the field of *human nature*, so in proportion the latter makes itself manifestly known—in the same proportion the moral independence of man shows itself gloriously: the portraiture becomes pathetic and the pathetic sublime. . . .

Man is already a sublime object, but only in the aesthetic sense, when the *state* in which he is gives us an idea of his human destination, even though we might not find this destination realized in his *person*. He only becomes sublime to us in a moral point of view, when he acts, moreover, as a person, in manner conformable with this destination; if our respect bears not only on his moral faculty, but on the use he makes of this faculty; if dignity, in his case, is due not only to his moral aptitude, but to the real morality of his conduct. It is quite a different thing to direct our judgment and attention to the moral faculty generally, and to the possibility of a will absolutely free, and to be directing it to the use of this faculty, and to the reality of this absolute freedom of willing. . . .

MADAME de STAËL

(1766–1817)

o◯oo◯o

Madame de Staël was probably the most famous and influential woman of her age, playing a conspicuous role in society, literature, and politics. She was the daughter of Jacques Necker, renowned minister of finance under Louis XVI; married the baron of Staël-Holstein, Swedish minister to France, from whom she separated eleven years later; was for ten years exiled from France for her political opposition to Napoleon and, as traveler and writer, became one of the most widely known *émigrés* of the period; met, in 1804, the first year of her exile, A. W. Schlegel, who was separated from his wife, and lived and traveled with him as his mistress. Meanwhile she found time to write *Corinne* (1807), an aesthetic romance, or as she called it, "a picturesque tour concluded in the form of a novel," and *De l'Allemagne*, finally published, after having been banned by the censor in France, in 1813.

Madame de Staël's first publication under her own name was *Lettres sur les écrits et le caractère de Jean-Jacques Rousseau* (1788). Her great admiration for Rousseau influenced her whole intellectual life. *De la littérature* (1800) is a sociological and historical study, attempting to establish the intimate relationship between literature and society. Although this theory of the sociology of literature is frequently regarded as a modern idea, especially in the writings of such "sociological critics" as V. F. Calverton and Granville Hicks, it is actually, as Professor Guérard says, "hoary with age."[1] Herder popularized this point of view in his *Ideen*,[2] and later Taine gave it a more cogent form in his *Introduction to the History of English Literature*.[3]

[1] For a lively discussion of this point see Albert Guérard, "The Background of Literature: Race, Environment and Time," Pt. 1 in *Literature and Society* (Boston, 1935).

[2] J. G. Herder, *Ideen zur Philosophie der Geschichte der Menschheit* (1784–1791).

[3] See pp. 481–493. The idea is, of course, tied up with the rise of the historical point of view in literary criticism, which began in the Renaissance. A few examples of some French critics who contributed to the concept are: Saint-Évremond (whose essays were translated into English in 1685–1686) "Concerning Ancient and Modern Tragedy," "Concerning English Comedy," "Observations on the Taste and Discernment of the French," etc. Fontenelle, *Digressions sur les anciens et les modernes*

In "Of Literature in the Age of Louis XIV," Madame de Staël expresses her purpose in words which many of our present-day literary historians (such as Parrington) might well take as their text:

> The object of the present work is to examine what is the influence of Religion, of Manners, and of Laws upon Literature; and reciprocally how far Literature may affect Laws, Manners, and Religion. On the art of composition and the principles of taste there are extant, in the French tongue, treatises[4] the most accurate and complete: but, methinks, sufficient pains have not been taken to analyze the moral and political causes which modify and mark the character of Literature.[5]

Madame de Staël's most famous work is *De l'Allemagne* (1810), in which she completely renounced neoclassicism as an artificial transplantation. Romanticism she regarded as indigenous and national, though not the same in all countries, for each nation has its own peculiarities—and she was not narrowly patriotic, for, along with Goethe, Schiller, and Nietzsche, she regarded herself as a world citizen. French literature, she thought, needed foreign blood, and she desired to wed the Latin and Teutonic genius, to join French form and love of symmetry with the originality and strength of the Northern literatures.

BIBLIOGRAPHY

TEXT

De l'Allemagne. Paris, 1810; London (a reprint), 1813.
De la littérature considérée dans ses rapports avec les institutions sociales. 2d. ed. 2 vols. Paris, 1801.
De l'influence des passions sur le bonheur des individus et des nations. Paris, 1813.
Lettres sur les écrits et le caractère de J. J. Rousseau. Paris, 1814.

(1688), insisted that diversity of climate invalidates the rules and makes a relative criticism necessary. Abbé du Bas, *Réflexions critiques sur la poésie et sur la peinture* (1719; translated 1748), worked out a theory of climate to explain the progression and retrogression of humanity. Of course the historians (and philosophers of history) also influenced the literary critics, such as Lenglet du Fresnoy, in his *Méthode pour étudier l'histoire* (1713); Montesquieu in his *Considérations sur les causes de la grandeur et de la décadence des Romains* (1734); Turgot, in *Discours sur les progrès successifs de l'esprit humain* (1750); and Voltaire, in his *Essai sur l'histoire générale et sur les mœurs et l'esprit des nations depuis Charlemagne jusqu'à nos jours* (1755). In 1765 Voltaire used the phrase "la philosophie de l'histoire," but Herder was the first to use it in the modern sense. Montesquieu, in *L'Esprit des lois* (1748), pointed out the relation between laws and temperature, soil and food. In England Lord Bolingbroke, in *Letters on the Study and Use of History* (1752), studied history for its influence on conduct and insisted that the reader must get the historical point of view. David Hume and Edward Gibbon also made their contributions.

[4] The works of Voltaire, Marmontel, and Laharpe.
[5] *A Treatise on Ancient and Modern Literature* (London, 1803), II, pp. 48–49.

TRANSLATIONS

Germany, tr. [anon.]. London, 1813.

The Influence of Literature upon Society, tr. from the French, to which is Prefixed a Memoir of the Life and Writings of the Author. Boston, 1835.

CRITICISM

Blennerhassett, Charlotte Julia (von Leyden), *Madame de Staël, Her Friends and Her Influence in Politics and Literature*, tr. by J. E. Gordon Cumming. 3 vols. London, 1889.

Gibelin, Jean, *L'Esthétique de Schelling et l'Allemagne de Madame de Staël*. Paris, 1934.

Henning, Ian Allan, *L'Allemagne de Mme de Staël et la polémique romantique; première fortune de l'ouvrage en France et en Allemagne (1814–1830)*. Paris, 1929.

Jaeck, Emma Gertrude, *Madame de Staël and the Spread of German Literature*. New York, 1915.

Larg, David Glass, *Madame de Staël, la seconde vie (1800–1807)*. Paris, 1928.

——, *Madame de Staël, La vie dans l'œuvre (1766–1800); essai de biographie morale et intellectuelle*. Paris, 1924.

Sainte-Beuve, Charles Augustin, "Madame de Staël," in *Portraits of Celebrated Women*, tr. by H. W. Preston. Boston, 1868.

Whitford, Robert Calvin, *Madame de Staël's Literary Reputation in England*. University of Illinois, Urbana, 1918.

THE RELATION OF LITERATURE TO SOCIAL INSTITUTIONS *(selections)*[1]

1800

Chapter XIV

Concerning English Comic Interpretation

There are many types of comic interpretation distinguishable in the literature of all countries; and nothing is better adapted to make the characteristics of a nation intelligible than the nature of the light pleasantry most generally adopted by its writers. People are serious when alone; they are gay with others, especially in their writings; and they can excite laughter only by ideas that are so familiar to listeners that the meaning strikes at the first instant without the least effort of attention.

A comic interpretation cannot dispense with national acclaim so easily as a philosophic work, since it is subject, like everything

[1]Translated by Helena Brawley Watts, here published for the first time.

else pertaining to the mind, to the judgment of universal good taste. Great subtlety is necessary to account for the causes of comic effect; but it is none the less true that general agreement must be obtained as to what constitutes masterpieces of this kind as well as for other kinds of composition.

The comedy which owes its being to the inspiration of taste and genius, the comedy produced by combinations of wit, and the comedy which the English call humor have almost no connection with one another. And in none of these divisions is comedy of character included, because a great number of examples prove that it has nothing to do with the ability to write in a comic vein. Witty comedy may be produced easily by all men who are intelligent, but genuine comedy can only be inspired by the genius of one man and the good taste of several others.

In one of the following chapters, I shall discuss the reasons why the French alone were able to attain that perfection of taste, elegance, and quick penetration into the human heart which have produced the best works of Molière. Now let us attempt to discover why the characteristics of the English are opposed to the true genius of comedy.

Most Englishmen, engrossed by business, seek pleasure merely as a relaxation; and in the same fashion that fatigue in exciting hunger renders the appetite less difficult to please, so continual labor, mental or physical, disposes the mind to be content with any kind of diversion. Their domestic life, the severity of their religious beliefs, their serious occupations, and their dull climate make the English particularly susceptible to boredom; and for this reason the more delicate amusements of comedy are not enough for them. They require a strong shock to rouse them from their apathy, and their authors either partake of the taste of the spectators or themselves conform to it.

Exact observation of character is required to compose a good comedy. In order for a comic genius to develop he must live a great deal in society and attach great importance to success in society; he himself must understand and through a multitude of interests come into contact with the vanity which gives rise to all that is ridiculous as well as to all the combinations of self-love. The English generally live in retirement with their own families, or gather in public assemblies for the discussion of national affairs. The intermediate state called society scarcely exists among them; nevertheless, it is in this frivolous interval of life that refinement and taste are formed. . . .

The English have no comic author comparable to Molière; if they possessed one, they would not be able to appreciate all of his fine points. In such plays as *L'Avare*, *Tartufe*, *Le Misanthrope*, which represent human nature as it is in all countries, there are many instances of delicate wit and shades of vanity and conceit which the English not only would not notice but which they would not in the least understand, however natural these touches might be. They would not recognize themselves in such a play, however naturally they were portrayed; they do not realize that they might be so minutely described. Their strong passions and important occupations have made them consider life more generally.

There is to be found in Congreve a great deal of amusing and subtle wit, but there is not one natural sentiment. By a singular contradiction, the more simplicity and purity there is in the private manners of the English, the more they exaggerate the picture of vice in their comedies. The indecency of Congreve's plays would never have been tolerated in the French theater; there are many ingenious ideas in the dialogue but the morals which they represent were taken from some of the worst kind of French novels, which never in the smallest degree portrayed the morals of the French.

Nothing can resemble the English less than their comedies. One would think that, wishing to be gay, they had thought it necessary to depart as far as possible from their natural character; or that their respect for the sentiments which constitute the happiness of their domestic life was so profound that such feelings were held too sacred to admit their representation on the stage.

Congreve and many of his imitators heaped up all sorts of immoralities without verisimilitude. These plays are of no consequence to a nation such as the English, who amuse themselves with them as they would with tales of fantastic images in a world which is not their own.[2] But in France comedy in portraying manners as they are can influence customs to a large extent, and for this reason it is more important to impose severe restrictions on the art of comedy.

In English comedies, truly English characters are seldom found; perhaps in England, as in Rome, the dignity of a free

[2]See Lamb's "On the Artificial Comedy of the Last Century," below, pp. 291–295.

people opposes the representation of their own customs upon the stage; but the French willingly amuse themselves with their own foibles. Shakespeare and a few others represented some popular characters, such as Falstaff, Pistol, etc., but they are so overdrawn as to exclude almost entirely every natural resemblance. The people of all nations are amused with vulgar jokes; but it is only in France that the most biting comedy is at the same time the most delicate.

Mr. Sheridan is the author of some comedies in which the most brilliant and original wit appears in almost every scene; however, one exceptional author changes nothing in the general consideration of English comedies; and it is still necessary to distinguish between the elevation of wit and the genuine comic talent whose greatest exponent is Molière. An author of any country who is capable of conceiving a great number of ideas is sure of acquiring the art of opposing them in a striking manner. But antitheses alone do not constitute eloquence, contrasts are not the only secrets of humor; and there is in the comic writings of certain French authors something at once more natural and more inexplicable. The thought may be analyzed, but the effect is not produced by thought alone; it is a sort of dynamic force communicated by the general intelligence of the nation.

Comic spirit and eloquence are only connected in so far as involuntary inspiration carries the writer or the speaker to any degree of perfection in the one or the other. The spirit of those who surround you develops in you the power of persuasion or of pleasantry much better than reflection and study can do. Sensations are more definitely provoked by external causes, and all talents that depend immediately upon sensations require an impulse given by others. Sprightliness and eloquence are not the simple results of combinations of wit; the trend of the author's thought must be changed by the emotion which creates one or the other in order to obtain successful use of talent in these two types. But the disposition generally common to the English does not arouse their writers to any species of gaiety.

Swift, in *Gulliver's Travels* and the *Tale of a Tub*, like Voltaire in his philosophical works, draws some of his happiest witticisms from the opposition which exists between accepted errors and proscribed truths, between institutions and the nature of things. The illusions, the allegories, all the fictions of the intellect and all the disguises which it assumes are so many combinations from which gaiety must be produced; in all such types of style the efforts of thought go a great way, although they can never attain to the pliancy and the easiness of custom or the un-expected felicity of spontaneous impressions.

Nevertheless, there is in some of the writings of the English a sort of gaiety which has all the characteristics of originality and naturalness. To express this same gaiety which arises from the constitution almost as much as from the intellect, the English language has created a word, humor. It is entirely dependent upon the climate and the national habits of thought and cannot be imitated where the same causes do not exist. Certain works of Fielding and Swift, *Peregrine Pickle*, *Roderick Random*, and more especially the works of Sterne give a complete idea of the style called humor.

There is a moroseness, I could almost say a sadness, in this sort of comic writing. The writer who makes you laugh does not feel the smallest degree of the pleasure he causes. You may easily perceive that he wrote in a somber mood, and that he would be almost irritated with you for being amused. But as praise is sometimes the more agreeable for being given under a rough form, so the gaiety of comedy may receive additional strength from the gravity of its author. The English very seldom admit upon their stage this style of wit which they call humor, for its effect would in no sense be theatrical.

There is a degree of misanthropy even in the joking of the English and a varying degree of sociability in that of the French; the one should be read in solitude; the other is most striking amid a number of auditors. English comic writing almost always leads to a philosophical or moral end, while that of the French often has no aim but pleasure. . . .

Chapter XV

Concerning English Imagination in Poetry and Novels

The invention of incidents and the faculty of feeling and painting nature are talents which are absolutely distinct. One belongs more particularly to the literature of the South and the other to that of the North. I have, I think, developed the different causes; what remains to be examined is the particular character of the English poetic imagination.

The English have invented no new subjects for poetry as Tasso and Ariosto did; they have no romances founded upon marvelous incidents and supernatural events like the Arabian and Persian tales. There remained to them from the Nordic religion only a few images, not a brilliant and varied mythology like that of the Greeks. Their poets, however, have an inexhaustible fund of those sentiments and ideas which arise from the spectacle of nature. Invention of supernatural events has its end, the marvelous at best is limited in its combinations, and is capable only in a slight degree of that progress which is the property of moral truth in whose category it belongs. When poets attempt to dress philosophical and impassioned sentiments in imaginary colors, they enter, in a measure, that path along which enlightened men constantly advance unless they are stopped by ignorance or tyranny.

The English separated from the continent, *semotos orbe Britannos*, have had but little association at any period with the history and customs of their neighbors. In every type of literature they have a character peculiar to themselves; their poetry resembles neither that of the French nor that of the Germans. But they have not attained the degree of invention in fable and poetical incident which is the principal glory of Greek and Italian literature. The English observe nature and know how to depict it, but they are not creators. Their superiority consists in the talent of expressing in vivid fashion what they see and feel; they have the art of relating philosophical reflections closely allied to the sensations produced by the beauties of nature. The aspect of the sky and the earth, at all hours of the day and night, awakens in our minds innumerable thoughts; the man who gives himself up to ideas inspired by nature experiences a series of the purest and noblest impressions, always analogous to the great moral and religious ideas which unite man and the future.

In the Renaissance many of the English poets swerved from their national pattern to imitate the style of the Italians. I have already cited Waller and Cowley among this group; I will add Donne, Chaucer, and others. The English, however, have been less successful in this borrowed style than any other people; they are quite deficient in the graceful ease so essential to light writing; they lack that facile quickness and ease which are acquired only by being constantly in the society of men whose sole aim is pleasure.

There are many faults of taste in a poem by Pope, *The Rape of the Lock*, which was particularly intended to be a model of grace. There is nothing in the world that can be more tedious than Spenser's *Faerie Queene*. *Hudibras*, although on an intellectual plane, is filled with pleasantry which is drawn out to the point of satiety. Gay's *Fables* are witty but unnatural. Nor can any of the fugitive pieces of the English, their burlesques, and so forth, be compared with the writings of Voltaire, Ariosto, or La Fontaine. But is it not enough to know how to speak the language of profound passions? Is it necessary to attach a great deal of importance to all the rest?

How sublime are the meditations of the English! How fruitful in those sentiments which are developed by solitude! What profound philosophy is to be found in the *Essay on Man!* Is it possible to elevate the mind and the imagination to a greater eminence than it is in *Paradise Lost?* The merit of this work is not in the poetic invention; the subject is almost entirely taken from the book of Genesis; the allegory which the author has introduced is in many places to be censured by taste. We may often see that the poet is restrained and directed by his submission to orthodoxy. But what made Milton one of the greatest poets in the world is the imposing grandeur of the characters he has drawn. His work is always remarkable for its thought; for this poetry which has been so much admired was inspired by Milton's need to make the pictured images in his verse equal his mental conception of them. In order to make his intellectual ideas understood the poet had recourse to the most terrible pictures that can strike the imagination. Before he gave form to Satan, he conceived him as lacking physical being; he represented the fallen angel's moral nature before he gave him the outward symbol of a gigantic figure and described the horrors of the place which he inhabited. With what art he conducts him through the delightful paths of youth, nature, and innocence! It is not the happiness of animated enjoyment; it is tranquillity which Milton contrasts with crime. The opposition is made still greater in the distress of Adam and Eve, in which the elementary differences of the character and the destiny of the two sexes are painted as philosophy and imagination ought to characterize them.

Gray's *Elegy Written in a Country Churchyard*, the *Ode on a Distant Prospect of Eton College*, and Goldsmith's *Deserted Village* are filled with the noble melancholy which constitutes the majesty of sensible philosophy. Where can more poetical enthusiasm be found than in Dryden's *Alexander's Feast, or the Power of Music?* What passion exists in Pope's *Eloïsa to Abelard!* Can there be a more charming picture of love in marriage than the termination of Thomson's first ode in *The Seasons?*

What deep and awful meditations are there in Young's *Night Thoughts,* where man, deprived of that happy illusion which leads us to feel an interest in the present as well as in centuries to come, is described as reflecting upon the progress and termination of his existence. Young judges human life as if he did not belong to it; his thoughts rise above personal being to make for themselves an imperceptible place in the immensity of creation:

> What is the world? a grave;
> Where is the dust that has not been alive? . . .
> What is life? a war,
> Eternal war with woe. . . .[3]

This gloomy imagination, though most apparent in Young, nevertheless colors English poetry in general. The English works in verse frequently contain more ideas than the works in prose. If we find monotony in Ossian because of his images which have little variety in themselves, since they are not interspersed with reflections which interest the mind, we cannot make the same complaint of the English poets in general; they never fatigue when they give way to their philosophical sadness; it accords perfectly with the nature of our being and with our destiny. Nothing is able to arouse a more agreeable sensation than to re-enter by reading the habitual course of the poet's reflections; and if one wishes to recall the particular passages which one likes in the literature of any language, it will be seen that almost all of them have the same characteristics of elevation and melancholy.

It may be asked why the English, who are so happy in their government and in their customs and manners, should have imaginations so much more melancholy than those of the French. The answer is, liberty and virtue, the greatest results of human reason, require a species of meditation which naturally conducts the mind to serious objects. . . .

The English language, although it is not so harmonious or

[3]Night IX; quotation not exact.

pleasing to the ear as the languages of the South, has, in the energy of its sound, a very great advantage in poetry. Every word that is strongly accented has an effect upon the soul because it seems to come from a vivid impression. The French language excludes from poetry a large group of simple terms which are really noble in English because of the manner in which they are pronounced. I shall offer one example. At the moment Macbeth is seating himself at the festive table, he sees the place destined for him filled by the shade of Banquo whom he has just had assassinated, and exclaims several times, "The table is full !"[4] with such terrible fright that all the spectators shudder. If these same words were to be repeated in French, "La table est remplie," the greatest actor in the world could not make the audience forget their common connotation; the French pronunciation does not admit of that accent which ennobles every word by giving it life, and which makes all sounds tragic because they imitate the trouble of the soul and make it shared. . . .

Nevertheless the English poets often abuse the facilities which their language and the genius of their nation grants them. They exaggerate images; they make ideas too subtle; they exhaust what they express; and taste does not warn them to stop. But in a large measure this will be forgiven them because of the sincerity of their emotions. We judge the faults of their writings as those of nature and not as those of art.

There is one species of works of the imagination in which the English are pre-eminent; that is, in novels without marvelous events, without historical allusions, without allegories, founded solely upon the invention of characters and the events of private life. Up until now love has been the subject of these novels. The situation of women in England is the principal cause of the inexhaustible abundance of these writings. . . .

The novels of the English, like all their other writings, are spun out to a great length; because these novels are written to be read by those who have adopted the style of life which is described in them, those who live a retired life in the country in the bosom of their families, in the midst of the leisure afforded by the regular occupations and domestic affections. If it is possible for the French to bear all of the useless details which are heaped up in their writings, it is only because of the curiosity which is inspired by foreign customs. The French never tolerate

---

[4]*Macbeth*, III, iv, 46. The line is not repeated in the printed text of the play.

anything of a similar nature in their own works; this length, as
it were, makes interest lag. But English writers have a method
of exciting interest by a series of just, moral observations which
bear upon the noticeable tendencies of life. In all things the
English use care either to depict what they see, or to discover
what they are searching for.

Tom Jones cannot be considered simply as a novel; the abundance of philosophical ideas, the contrast of natural qualities
and of social hypocrisy are introduced into the action with
infinite art; and love, as I have said elsewhere, is only an accessory
to such subjects.

But Richardson, who stands in the first rank—and following
his writings are an infinity of novels, most of which are the
productions of feminine pens—gives a perfect idea of this sort
of writing which is indescribably interesting.

The old French romances are filled with adventures of chivalry
which do not in the least recall the events of life. Rousseau's
La Nouvelle Héloise is an eloquent and impassioned work, but it
characterizes the genius of only one man and not the customs
of a nation. All the other French novels that we admire are
imitations of the English; the subjects are not the same, but the
manner of treating them and the general character of this type
of invention belong exclusively to the English novelists. They
first ventured to imagine that the pictures of private affections
were sufficient to interest the mind and the heart of man; that
neither elevation of character, nor importance of rank, nor the
marvelous in events were necessary to captivate the imagination.
They thought that the power of love was sufficient to keep alive
the situation without wearying the attention. In short, it was
the English who first composed works of morality under the
forms of novels in which obscure virtues and destinies might
find motives for exaltation and create for themselves a sort of
heroism. . . .

AUGUST WILHELM von SCHLEGEL
1767–1845

o◯oo◯o

AUGUST WILHELM VON SCHLEGEL and his younger brother, Friedrich, are often regarded as the founders of the romantic school in Germany. Though this generalization is not strictly true, their combined critical writings did establish a philosophical foundation for the romantic movement. August Wilhelm contributed to Schiller's *Horen* and the *Musen-almanach*, and together the brothers edited the *Athenaeum*, a short-lived journal which might almost be called the official organ of the romantic school in Germany.

August Wilhelm is perhaps most famous, however, for his brilliant translation of Shakespeare into German, and his no less brilliant Shakespearean criticism, which so closely resembles Coleridge's lectures on the same subject that Coleridge was (though unjustly) accused of plagiarism. A. W. Schlegel also successfully translated Calderon and Spanish and Portuguese lyrics. Later he occupied himself with oriental studies, and edited the *Bhagavad-Gîta* with a Latin translation.

The older Schlegel's personal and professional life was as varied as his literary and scholarly achievements. After beginning the study of theology at the University of Göttingen, he shifted to philology. As a professor at the University of Jena he lectured on aesthetics and, with Friedrich, belonged to the circle of Tieck and Novalis. After his wife divorced him, he went to Berlin, engaged in a "Battle-of-the-Books" dispute with Kotzebue, a conservative critic, and published his *Spanish Theatre*. In 1805 he began a liaison with the French exile, Madame de Staël, which lasted until her death in 1817. He is said to have profoundly influenced her *De l'Allemagne*. In 1807 he attacked French classicism in *Comparaison entre la Phèdre de Racine et celle d'Euripide*, written in his own brilliant French. This work naturally aroused great opposition in France. In 1808 his Lectures on *Dramatic Art and Literature*, delivered in Vienna, won him great fame. In Sweden with Madame de Staël, whose liberal ideas had made her life unsafe in most European countries, A. W. Schlegel was ennobled by the crown prince—hence the "von" which he added to his name. After Madame de Staël's death, he accepted a professorship at the University of Bonn, but delivered his lectures on *Theory and History of Fine Art* in Berlin in 1827. The following year he found it necessary to defend himself against the charge of Catholic leanings which some of his lectures had aroused. The following selections from *A Course of Lectures on Dramatic Art and Literature*, translated by John Black and revised by the Reverend A. J. W. Morrison (London, 1846), illustrate August Wilhelm Schlegel's "universality of mind," his dramatic theories, his attack on the "rules," and his literary nationalism—an important aspect of the romantic movement in Europe and America.

BIBLIOGRAPHY

TEXT

Athenäum, eine Zeitschrift, von A. W. Schlegel and Friedrich Schlegel, neue Hrsg. von Fritz Baader. Berlin, 1905.
Briefwechsel mit Schiller und Goethe, Herausgabe von Joseph Körner und Ernst Wieneke. Leipzig, 1926.
Geschichte der deutschen Sprache und Poesie, Vorlesungen, gehalten an der Universität Bonn seit dem Wintersemester 1818–1819, Herausgabe von Joseph Körner. Berlin, 1913.
Kritische Schriften. 2 vols. Berlin, 1828.
Ludwig Tieck und die Brüder Schlegel; Briefe mit Einleitung und Anmerkungen herausgegeben von H. Lüdeke. Frankfort am Main, 1930.
Sämmtliche Werke, herausgegeben von Eduard Böcking. 12 vols. Leipzig, 1846–1847.
Vorlesungen über dramatische Kunst und Literatur. Kritische Ausgabe . . . von Giovanni Vittorio Amoretti. Leipzig, 1923.

TRANSLATIONS

A Course of Lectures on Dramatic Art and Literature, tr. by John Black. London, 1815.
——, revised by A. J. W. Morrison. London, 1846.

CRITICISM

Alt, Carl Hermann, *Schiller und die Brüder Schlegel*. Weimar, 1904.
Brandt, Otto Lampertus, *August Wilhelm Schlegel, der Romantiker und die Politik*. Berlin, 1919.
Körner, Josef, *Romantiker und Klassiker; die Brüder Schlegel in ihren Beziehungen zu Schiller und Goethe*. Berlin, 1924.
Helmholtz, Anna Augusta, *The Indebtedness of Samuel Taylor Coleridge to August Wilhelm von Schlegel*. University of Wisconsin, Madison, 1907.
Pichtos, Nicolaus M., *Die Aesthetik August Wilhelm von Schlegel in ihrer geschichtlichen Entwickelung*. Berlin, 1894.

LECTURES ON DRAMATIC ART AND LITERA-
TURE ANCIENT AND MODERN (*selections*)[1]

1808

Spirit of True Criticism[2]

. . . The history of the fine arts informs us what has been,
and the theory teaches what ought to be accomplished by them.
But without some intermediate and connecting link both would
remain independent and separate from one another and, each
by itself, inadequate and defective. This connecting link is
furnished by criticism, which both elucidates the history of the
arts and makes the theory fruitful. The comparing together,
and judging of the existing productions of the human mind,
necessarily throws light upon the conditions which are indispensable to the creation of original and masterly works of art.

Ordinarily, indeed, men entertain a very erroneous notion of
criticism, and understand by it nothing more than a certain
shrewdness in detecting and exposing the faults of a work of art.
As I have devoted the greater part of my life to this pursuit, I
may be excused if, by way of preface, I seek to lay before my
auditors my own ideas of the true genius of criticism.

We see numbers of men, and even whole nations, so fettered
by the conventions of education and habits of life that, even in
the appreciation of the fine arts, they cannot shake them off.
Nothing to them appears natural, appropriate, or beautiful,
which is alien to their own language, manners, and social relations. With this exclusive mode of seeing and feeling, it is no
doubt possible to attain, by means of cultivation, to great nicety
of discrimination within the narrow circle to which it limits and
circumscribes them. But no man can be a true critic or connois-
seur without universality of mind, without that flexibility which
enables him, by renouncing all personal predilections and
blind habits, to adapt himself to the peculiarities of other ages
and nations—to feel them, as it were, from their proper central
point, and, what ennobles human nature, to recognize and duly
appreciate whatever is beautiful and grand under the external
accessories which were necessary to its embodying, even though
occasionally they may seem to disguise and distort it. There is

[1]Translated by John Black and "revised according to the latest German edition"
by A. J. W. Morrison (London [Bohn's Library], 1846).
[2]From Lecture I.

no monopoly of poetry for particular ages and nations; and consequently that despotism in taste, which would seek to invest with universal authority the rules which at first, perhaps, were but arbitrarily advanced, is but a vain and empty pretension. Poetry, taken in its widest acceptation as the power of creating what is beautiful and representing it to the eye or the ear, is a universal gift of heaven, being shared to a certain extent even by those whom we call barbarians and savages. Internal excellence is alone decisive, and where this exists, we must not allow ourselves to be repelled by the external appearance. Everything must be traced up to the root of human nature: if it has sprung from thence, it has an undoubted worth of its own; but if, without possessing a living germ, it is merely externally attached thereto, it will never thrive nor acquire a proper growth. Many productions which appear at first sight dazzling phenomena in the province of the fine arts, and which as a whole have been honored with the appellation of works of a golden age, resemble the mimic gardens of children: impatient to witness the work of their hands, they break off here and there branches and flowers, and plant them in the earth; everything at first assumes a noble appearance: the childish gardener struts proudly up and down among his showy beds till the rootless plants begin to droop and hang their withered leaves and blossoms, and nothing soon remains but the bare twigs, while the dark forest, on which no art or care was ever bestowed, and which towered up towards heaven long before human remembrance, bears every blast unshaken and fills the solitary beholder with religious awe. . . .

Definition of the Drama[3]

. . . What is dramatic? To many the answer will seem very easy: where various persons are introduced conversing together, and the poet does not speak in his own person. This is, however, merely the first external foundation of the form, and that is dialogue. But the characters may express thoughts and sentiments without operating any change on each other, and so leave the minds of both in exactly the same state in which they were at the commencement; in such a case, however interesting the conversation may be, it cannot be said to possess a dramatic interest. I shall make this clear by alluding to a more tranquil

[3]From Lecture II.

species of dialogue, not adapted for the stage, the philosophic. When, in Plato, Socrates asks the conceited sophist Hippias what is the meaning of the beautiful, the latter is at once ready with a superficial answer, but is afterwards compelled by the ironical objections of Socrates to give up his former definition, and to grope about him for other ideas, till, ashamed at last and irritated at the superiority of the sage who has convicted him of his ignorance, he is forced to quit the field: this dialogue is not merely philosophically instructive, but arrests the attention like a drama in miniature. And justly, therefore, has this lively movement in the thoughts, this stretch of expectation for the issue, in a word, the dramatic cast of the dialogues of Plato, been always celebrated.

From this we may conceive wherein consists the great charm of dramatic poetry. Action is the true enjoyment of life, nay, life itself. Mere passive enjoyments may lull us into a state of listless complacency, but even then, if possessed of the least internal activity, we cannot avoid being soon wearied. The great bulk of mankind merely from their situation in life, or from their incapacity for extraordinary exertions, are confined within a narrow circle of insignificant operations. Their days flow on in succession under the sleepy rule of custom, their life advances by an insensible progress, and the bursting torrent of the first passions of youth soon settles into a stagnant marsh. From the discontent which this occasions they are compelled to have recourse to all sorts of diversions, which uniformly consist in a species of occupation that may be renounced at pleasure, and though a struggle with difficulties, yet with difficulties that are easily surmounted. But of all diversions the theater is undoubtedly the most entertaining. Here we may see others act even when we cannot act to any great purpose ourselves. The highest object of human activity is man, and in the drama we see men, measuring their powers with each other, as intellectual and moral beings, either as friends or foes, influencing each other by their opinions, sentiments, and passions, and decisively determining their reciprocal relations and circumstances. The art of the poet consists in separating from the fable whatever does not essentially belong to it, whatever, in the daily necessities of real life and the petty occupations to which they give rise, interrupts the progress of important actions, and concentrating within a narrow space a number of events calculated to attract the minds of the hearers and to fill them with attention and expectation. In this manner he gives us a renovated picture of life; a compendium of whatever is moving and progressive in human existence. . . .

Source of Pleasure Derived from Tragedy[4]

. . . Inward liberty and external necessity are two poles of the tragic world. It is only by contrast with its opposite that each of these ideas is brought into full manifestation. As the feeling of an internal power of self-determination elevates the man above the unlimited dominion of impulse and the instincts of nature, in a word, absolves him from nature's guardianship, so the necessity, which alongside of her he must recognize, is no mere natural necessity, but one lying beyond the world of sense in the abyss of infinitude; consequently, it exhibits itself as the unfathomable power of destiny. Hence this power extends also to the world of gods: for the Grecian gods are mere powers of nature; and although immeasurably higher than mortal man, yet, compared with infinitude, they are on an equal footing with himself. In Homer and in the tragedians, the gods are introduced in a manner altogether different. In the former their appearance is arbitrary and accidental, and communicate to the epic poem no higher interest than the charm of the wonderful. But in tragedy the gods either come forward as the servants of destiny, and mediate executors of its decrees; or else approve themselves godlike only by asserting their liberty of action, and entering upon the same struggles with fate which man himself has to encounter.

This is the essence of the tragical in the sense of the ancients. We are accustomed to give to all terrible or sorrowful events the appellation of tragic, and it is certain that such events are selected in preference by tragedy, though a melancholy conclusion is by no means indispensably necessary; and several ancient tragedies, viz., the *Eumenides*, *Philoctetes*, and in some degree also the *Oedipus Colonus*, without mentioning many of the pieces of Euripides, have a happy and cheerful termination.

But why does tragedy select subjects so awfully repugnant to the wishes and wants of our sensuous nature? This question has often been asked, and seldom satisfactorily answered. Some have said that the pleasure of such representations arises from

[4]From Lecture v.

the comparison we make between the calmness and tranquillity of our own situation, and the storms and perplexities to which the victims of passion are exposed. But when we take a warm interest in the persons of a tragedy, we cease to think of ourselves; and when this is not the case, it is the best of all proofs that we take but a feeble interest in the exhibited story, and that the tragedy has failed in its effect. Others again have had recourse to a supposed feeling for moral improvement, which is gratified by the view of poetical justice in the reward of the good and the punishment of the wicked. But he for whom the aspect of such dreadful examples could really be wholesome must be conscious of a base feeling of depression very far removed from genuine morality, and would experience humiliation rather than elevation of mind. Besides, poetical justice is by no means indispensable to a good tragedy; it may end with the suffering of the just and the triumph of the wicked, if only the balance be preserved in the spectator's own consciousness by the prospect of futurity. Little does it mend the matter to say with Aristotle that the object of tragedy is to purify the passions by pity and terror. In the first place commentators have never been able to agree as to the meaning of this proposition, and have had recourse to the most forced explanations of it. Look, for instance, into the *Dramaturgie* of Lessing. Lessing gives a new explanation of his own, and fancies he has found in Aristotle a poetical Euclid. But mathematical demonstrations are liable to no misconception, and geometrical evidence may well be supposed inapplicable to the theory of the fine arts. Supposing, however, that tragedy does operate this moral cure in us, still she does so by the painful feelings of terror and compassion: and it remains to be proved how it is that we take a pleasure in subjecting ourselves to such an operation.

Others have been pleased to say that we are attracted to theatrical representations from the want of some violent agitation to rouse us out of the torpor of our everyday life. Such a craving does exist; I have already acknowledged the existence of this want, when speaking of the attractions of the drama; but to it we must equally attribute the fights of wild beasts among the Romans, nay, even the combats of the gladiators. But must we, less indurated, and more inclined to tender feelings, require demigods and heroes to descend, like so many desperate gladiators, into the bloody arena of the tragic stage, in order to agitate our nerves by the spectacle of their sufferings? No: it is not the sight of suffering which constitutes the charm of a tragedy, or even of the games of the circus, or of the fight of wild beasts. In the latter we see a display of activity, strength, and courage; splendid qualities these, and related to the mental and moral powers of man. The satisfaction, therefore, which we derive from the representation, in a good tragedy, of powerful situations and overwhelming sorrows, must be ascribed either to the feeling of the dignity of human nature excited in us by such grand instances of it as are therein displayed, or to the trace of a higher order of things impressed on the apparently irregular course of events and mysteriously revealed in them, or perhaps to both these causes conjointly.

The true reason, therefore, why tragedy need not shun even the harshest subject is that a spiritual and invisible power can only be measured by the opposition which it encounters from some external force capable of being appreciated by the senses. The moral freedom of man, therefore, can only be displayed in a conflict with his sensuous impulses: so long as no higher call summons it to action, it is either actually dormant within him, or appears to slumber, since otherwise it does but mechanically fulfill its part as a mere power of nature. It is only amidst difficulties and struggles that the moral part of man's nature avouches itself. If, therefore, we must explain the distinctive aim of tragedy by way of theory, we would give it thus: that to establish the claims of the mind to a divine origin, its earthly existence must be disregarded as vain and insignificant, all sorrows endured and all difficulties overcome. . . .

The Chorus [5]

. . . I come now to another peculiarity which distinguishes the tragedy of the ancients from ours, I mean the Chorus. We must consider it as a personified reflection on the action which is going on; the incorporation into the representation itself of the sentiments of the poet, as the spokesman of the whole human race. This is its general poetical character; and that is all that here concerns us, and that character is by no means affected by the circumstance that the Chorus had a local origin in the feasts of Bacchus, and that, moreover, it always retained among the Greeks a peculiar national signification; publicity being . . .

[5]From Lecture v.

according to their republican notions, essential to the complete-ness of every important transaction. If in their compositions they reverted to the heroic ages, in which monarchical polity was yet in force, they nevertheless gave a certain republican cast to the families of their heroes, by carrying on the action in presence either of the elders of the people, or of other persons who represented some correspondent rank or position in the social body. This publicity does not, it is true, quite correspond with Homer's picture of the manners of the heroic age; but both costume and mythology were handled by dramatic poetry with the same spirit of independence and conscious liberty.

These thoughts, then, and these modes of feeling led to the introduction of the Chorus, which, in order not to interfere with the appearance of reality which the whole ought to possess, must adjust itself to the ever-varying requisitions of the exhibited stories. Whatever it might be and do in each particular piece, it represented in general, first the common mind of the nation, and then the general sympathy of all mankind. In a word, the Chorus is the ideal spectator.[6] It mitigates the impression of a heart-rending or moving story, while it conveys to the actual spectator a lyrical and musical expression of his own emotions, and elevates him to the region of contemplation. . . .

The Unities [7]

. . . Voltaire wishes to derive the Unity of Place and Time from the Unity of Action, but his reasoning is shallow in the extreme. "For the same reason," he says, "the Unity of Place is essential, because no one action can go on in several places at once." But still, as we have already seen, several persons necessarily take part in the one principal action, since it consists of a plurality of subordinate actions, and what should hinder these from pro-ceeding in different places at the same time? Is not the same war frequently carried on simultaneously in Europe and India; and must not the historian recount alike in his narrative the events which take place on both these scenes?

"The Unity of Time," he adds, "is naturally connected with the two first. If the poet represents a conspiracy, and extends the action to fourteen days, he must account to me for all that takes place in these fourteen days." Yes, for all that belongs to the matter in hand; all the rest, being extraneous to it, he passes

[6]Cf. Nietzsche, below, p. 521.   [7]From Lecture XVII.

over in silence, as every good storyteller would, and no person ever thinks of the omission. "If, therefore, he places before me the events of fourteen days, this gives at least fourteen different actions, however small they may be." No doubt, if the poet were so unskillful as to wind off the fourteen days one after another with visible precision, if day and night are just so often to come and go, and the characters to go to bed and to get up again just so many times. But the clever poet thrusts into the background all the intervals which are connected with no perceptible progress in the action, and in his picture annihilates all the pauses of absolute standstill, and contrives, though with a rapid touch, to convey an accurate idea of the period supposed to have elapsed. But why is the privilege of adopting a much wider space between the two extremes of the piece than the material time of the representation important to the dramatist, and even indispensable to him in many subjects? The example of a conspiracy given by Voltaire comes in here very opportunely.

A conspiracy plotted and executed in two hours is, in the first place, an incredible thing. Moreover, with reference to the characters of the personages of the piece, such a plot is very different from one in which the conceived purpose, however dangerous, is silently persevered in by all the parties for a considerable time. Though the poet does not admit this lapse of time into his exhibition immediately, in the midst of the characters, as in a mirror, he gives us as it were a perspective view of it. In this sort of perspective Shakespeare is the greatest master I know: a single word frequently opens to view an almost interminable vista of antecedent states of mind. Confined within the narrow limits of time, the poet is in many subjects obliged to mutilate the action by beginning close to the last decisive stroke, or else he is under the necessity of unsuitably hurrying on its progress: on either supposition he must reduce within petty dimensions the grand picture of a strong purpose, which is no momentary ebullition, but a firm resolve undauntedly maintained in the midst of all external vicissitudes till the time is ripe for its execution. It is no longer what Shakespeare has so often painted, and what he has described in the following lines:—

> Between the acting of a dreadful thing,
> And the first motion, all the interim is
> Like a phantasma, or a hideous dream:
> The genius, and the mortal instruments,

> And then in council; and the state of man,
> Like to a little kingdom, suffers then
> The nature of an insurrection.[8]

But why are the Greek and romantic poets so different in their practice with respect to place and time? The spirit of our criticism will not allow us to follow the practice of many critics, who so summarily pronounce the latter to be barbarians. On the contrary, we conceive that they lived in very cultivated times and were themselves highly cultivated men. As to the ancients, besides the structure of their stage, which, as we have already said, led naturally to the seeming continuity of time and the absence of change of scene, their observance of this practice was also favored by the nature of the materials on which the Grecian dramatist had to work. These materials were mythology, and, consequently, a fiction which, under the handling of preceding poets, had collected into continuous and perspicuous masses what in reality was detached and scattered about in various ways. Moreover, the heroic age which they painted was at once extremely simple in its manners, and marvelous in its incidents; and hence everything of itself went straight to the mark of a tragic resolution.

But the principal cause of the difference lies in the plastic spirit of the antique and the picturesque spirit of the romantic poetry. Sculpture directs our attention exclusively to the group which it sets before us; it divests it as far as possible from all external accompaniments, and, where they cannot be dispensed with, it indicates them as slightly as possible. Painting, on the other hand, delights in exhibiting, along with the principal figures, all the details of the surrounding locality and all secondary circumstances, and to open a prospect into a boundless distance in the background; and light and shade with perspective are its peculiar charms. Hence the dramatic, and especially the tragic, art of the ancients annihilates in some measure the external circumstances of space and time; while, by their changes, the romantic drama adorns its more varied pictures. Or, to express myself in other terms, the principle of the antique poetry is ideal; that of the romantic is mystical: the former subjects space and time to the internal free-agency of the mind; the latter honors these incomprehensible essences as supernatural powers, in which there is somewhat of indwelling divinity.

[8] *Julius Caesar*, ii, i, 63–69.

National Drama[9]

. . . In comedy, Lessing has already pointed out the difficulty of introducing national manners which are not provincial, inasmuch as with us the tone of social life is not modeled after a common central standard. If we wish pure comedies, I would strongly recommend the use of rhyme; with the more artificial form they might, perhaps, gradually assume also a peculiarity of substance.

To me, however, it appears that this is not the most urgent want: let us first bring to perfection the serious and higher species, in a manner worthy of the German character. Now, here, it appears to me that our taste inclines altogether to the romantic. What most attracts the multitude in our half-sentimental, half-humorous dramas, which one moment transport us to Peru and the next to Kamchatka and soon after into the times of chivalry, while the sentiments are all modern and lachrymose, is invariably a certain sprinkling of the romantic, which we recognize even in the most insipid magical operas. The true significance of this species was lost with us before it was properly found; the fancy has passed with the inventors of such chimeras, and the views of the plays are sometimes wiser than those of their authors. In a hundred playbills the name "romantic" is profaned by being lavished on rude and monstrous abortions; let us, therefore, be permitted to elevate it, by criticism and history, again to its true import. We have lately endeavored in many ways to revive the remains of our old national poetry. These may afford the poet a foundation for the wonderful festival play; but the most dignified species of the romantic is the historical.

In this field the most glorious laurels may yet be reaped by dramatic poets who are willing to emulate Goethe and Schiller. Only let our historical drama be in reality and thoroughly national; let it not attach itself to the life and adventures of single knights and petty princes who exercised no influence on the fortunes of the whole nation. Let it, at the same time, be truly historical, drawn from a profound knowledge, and transporting us back to the great olden time. In this mirror let the poet enable us to see, while we take deep shame to ourselves for what we are, what the Germans were in former times, and what they must be

[9]From Lecture xxx.

again. Let him impress it strongly on our hearts, that, if we do not consider the lessons of history better than we have hitherto done, we Germans—we, formerly the greatest and most illustrious nation of Europe, whose freely elected prince was willingly acknowledged the head of all Christendom—are in danger of disappearing altogether from the list of independent nations. The higher ranks, by their predilection for foreign manners, by their fondness for exotic literature, which, transplanted from its natural climate into hothouses, can only yield a miserable fruit, have long alienated themselves from the body of the people; still longer even, for three centuries at least, has internal dissension wasted our noblest energies in civil wars, whose ruinous consequences are now first beginning to disclose themselves. May all who have an opportunity of influencing the public mind exert themselves to extinguish at last the old misunderstandings, and to rally, as round a consecrated banner, all the well-disposed objects of reverence, which, unfortunately, have been too long deserted, but by faithful attachment to which our forefathers acquired so much happiness and renown, and to let them feel their indestructible unity as Germans! What a glorious picture is furnished by our history, from the most remote times, the wars with the Romans, down to the establishment of the German Empire! Then the chivalrous and brilliant era of the House of Hohenstaufen! and lastly, of greater political importance and more nearly concerning ourselves, the House of Hapsburg, with its many princes and heroes. What a field for a poet who, like Shakespeare, could discern the poetical aspect of the great events of the world! But, alas, so little interest do we Germans take in events truly important to our nation, that its greatest achievements still lack even a fitting historical record.

FRIEDRICH von SCHLEGEL

(1772–1829)

oᴑooᴑo

FRIEDRICH VON SCHLEGEL'S LIFE AND IDEAS parallel in many respects the career of his brother, August Wilhelm (172 f.). Like him
he studied and interpreted world literature from Greece and India
to his contemporary Germany; like other critics of his age, he profoundly admired the Greeks, but his hellenism was romantic; and
his contributions to the *Athenaeum*, edited by himself and his brother,
helped to found the romantic school. But Friedrich was at the same
time more brilliant and less stable than his illustrious brother. His
erotic novel *Lucinde*, based on the doctrine of complete moral freedom,
shocked his generation; and later his mysticism carried him and his
wife, Dorothea, the daughter of Mendelssohn, into the Catholic
church.

The mature views of Friedrich Schlegel are expressed in his *Lectures
on the History of Literature, Ancient and Modern*, which, however, is not a
history in the ordinary sense. As he says, it is not "replete with quotations and biographical notices."[1] It is a philosophical interpretation of
"the intellectual life of a nation," as seen, of course, through his own
romantic eyes. After outlining his platform in the opening lecture,
the "Influence of Literature on the Mode of Life and the Moral
Dignity of Nations," he traces the literary spirit through Greece,
Rome, the Germanic and Romance nations, down to contemporary
Germany.

Friedrich Schlegel clearly anticipates the later sociological interpretation of literature, as illustrated in the selection on Homer—see p. 188 ff.
Some of his assertions sound almost modern. But he shows his kinship
with Schiller and Lessing in his theory of nationality in literature, for
this nationalism does not exclude a tolerantly cosmopolitan view.[2] Like
the other romanticists, he deprecates the neoclassic subserviency to rules,
particularly the French enslavement to the classical "unities"; he
searches for the indigenous rules and unities of each age and country.
Shakespeare, for example, has his own unity:

---

[1]See 1815 Preface.   [2]Cf. Longfellow's similar views in *Kavanagh.*

In the works of Shakespeare a whole world is unfolded. Whosoever has comprehended this, and been penetrated with the spirit of his poetry will hardly allow the seeming want of form, or, rather, the form peculiar to his mighty genius, nor even the criticism of those who have misconceived the poet's meaning,[3] to disturb his admiration; as he progresses he will, rather, approve the form as both sufficient and excellent in itself, and in harmonious conformity with the spirit and essence of his art.[4]

In the history of German Romanticism the Schlegel brothers exerted great influence, for through their critical writings they contributed to the major developments of the movement: especially, the cult of medievalism, the spiritual and mystical doctrines, and the romantic theories of style and diction. But Friedrich's greatest single achievement was his history of European literature in his famous *Lectures*, though today the work is more interesting for its critical ideas than its historiography.

BIBLIOGRAPHY

TEXT

The Aesthetic and Miscellaneous Works, tr. by E. J. Millington. London, 1849.
Lectures on the History of Literature, Ancient and Modern. Edinburgh, 1841.
———, ed. by John Frost. Philadelphia, 1867.
———, "now first completely translated." London, 1859.

CRITICISM

Enders, Carl Friedrich, *Friedrich Schlegel; die Quellen seines Wesens und Werdens*. Leipzig, 1913.
Galaboff, Konstentin S., *Die Stellung Friedrich Schlegels und der anderen deutschen Romantiker zu Goethes "Wilhelm Meister" im Lichte des Wilhelm Meisters*. Göttingen, 1917.
Grønbech, Vilhelm Peter, *Friedrich Schlegel i Årene 1791–1808*. København, 1935.
Horwitz, Hugo, *Das Ich-problem der Romantik;* Die historiches Stellung Friedrich Schlegels innerhalb der modernen Geistesgeschichte. München, 1916.
Schlagdenhauffen, Alfred, *Frédéric Schlegel et son groupe;* la doctrine de l'Athenaeum (1798–1800). Paris, 1934.
Scholl, John William, *Friedrich Schlegel and Goethe, 1790–1802;* a study in early German Romanticism. Baltimore, 1906.

[3]He has in mind the critical tradition from Ben Jonson to Voltaire.
[4]In Lecture XII.

LECTURES ON THE HISTORY OF LITERATURE (*selections*)[1]

1815

National Literature[2]

. . . If literature be considered as the quintessence of the most distinguished and peculiar productions by which the spirit of an age and the character of a nation express themselves, in short, as the features in which the genius of an age or the character of a nation is unmistakably expressed, it must be admitted that an artistic and highly finished literature is undoubtedly one of the greatest advantages any nation can possess. But if an equal degree of literary excellence is demanded of all countries—irrespective of general development or any other distinctions soever—and in its absence censure is pronounced in terms of indiscriminate obloquy, such a requirement can accord neither with justice nor the operation of natural laws. Everywhere, in particulars as in generals, in small things equally with great, inventive fullness is destined to precede the perfection of finished art, legend anticipates history, poetry is the forerunner of criticism. Given a nation unendowed with poetic stores that date from some time prior to the period of regular artistic culture, and it may safely be asserted of the same that it will never attain to any nationality of character or vitality of genius. Poetic wealth like this, unaccompanied however by really great advances in literature or science, was possessed by the Greeks during the whole extent of time ranging from the Trojan adventures to the days of Solon and Pericles, and to this circumstance their intellect is chiefly indebted for its distinguishing excellence and brilliancy. In corresponding proportions the Middle Ages served in lieu of such a poetic pre-existence to modern Europe; their creative fancy few will dare to question. The beautifully silent process of growth necessarily precedes the appearance of the blossom, whilst the blossom, in its turn, reveals its graces before the matured charms of fruit are displayed. As in individuals, growth is the poetic bud of life, so in the career of nations there are moments of sudden development and intellectual expansion. With this universal springtime of poetry in the history of western nations, the age

---

[1]"Now first completely translated" (London, 1859). Preface signed by Henry G. Bohn; translation likely by him. [2]From Lecture VII.

of the Crusades, of chivalry, and love songs may be fittingly compared. . . .

The Homeric Poems[3]

. . . The relish with which the ancient Greeks appreciated the Homeric poems was materially enhanced by patriotic associations, whilst we are interested in them chiefly as vivid and beautiful representations of heroic life. They are free from the charge of narrow views or adulatory panegyrics exclusively bestowed on a particular lineage—a charge such as may be justly preferred against the old songs of Arabia or those of Ossian. Breathing the spirit of purest freedom, their representations of the phenomena of nature and of the varieties of human character evince a sensibility pure and universal. A whole world opens out before us as we read them, a world of living and moving imagery. The two prominent figures, Achilles and Ulysses, seem to start from the canvas into warm life; yet they are but characters and ideas so general as to be found repeated in nearly all Greek hero legends, though never again sketched with so masterly a hand or so exquisitely finished. Achilles, a hero destined to exhaust all the delights of mortality whilst still in the bloom and pride of youthful vigor, doomed moreover to be cut off by tragic fate in the prime of his days, is the loftier conception of the two; an echo of this chord may be found in the character of many a hero in the legends of various lands, next in beauty to the Grecian, perhaps, those of our own northern clime. The legendary traditions of heroic times, among the sprightliest nations, are overshadowed by elegiac sensibilities, plaints full of tenderness, and sometimes shrouded in somber grief. As if the transition from an age of glorious freedom and heroism had impressed succeeding generations with a feeling of dreary confinement, or the bard would transfer to the fictions of those times exclusively reminiscences of some pristine state of bliss, deep-seated in the bosom of the whole human family. A less magnificent, but still richly attractive form of poetic heroism is presented in the person of Ulysses, the roving, traveled hero, discreet, and experienced as brave, fitted to undergo danger and encounter adventures of every sort. Ample scope is thus afforded for portraying in easy flowing style the rare sights and products of foreign lands. In energy and pathos the epics of the north, in brilliant coloring

[3]From Lecture I.

those of the east, as far as our acquaintance extends, may compare with, if they do not surpass, the Homeric poems. But the peculiar distinction of the latter is the amount of living truth and clearness blended in harmonious unison with an almost infantile simplicity and affluent fancy. The narrative, whilst entering into minute detail with all the garrulousness of age, never grows tiresome, owing to the extreme freshness and grace of imagery ever and anon dexterously shifted. Character, passion, and dialogue are unfolded with dramatic skill, and individual circumstances described with almost historical fidelity. From this last quality, which completely distinguishes Homer from all other—even Grecian—bards, he possibly derives his name. Homeros signifies a surety or witness: and on account of his truthful accuracy, as a minstrel of the heroic time, he richly deserves this appellation. To us he is, indeed, *Homeros*, a surety as well as a witness of the epic ages in their genuine state. As for the other meaning, relative to his blindness, also involved in the word, it is clearly conjectural, forming part of a tissue of inventions respecting the life of one wholly unknown to us in his person, and it is undeserving of a moment's consideration. Without the direct testimony of Milton it would be sufficiently apparent from internal evidence in his poems that he saw only with the eye of the spirit and tasted not the exhilarating joyousness of sunlight. A melancholy haze broods over the page of Ossian, and it may reasonably be inferred that the gloom of night shaded the minstrel's brow. But whoever would ascribe the composition of the *Iliad* and *Odyssey*, the most lucid and transparent of all the poems of antiquity, to a blind bard must, before pronouncing such a verdict, determine to shut his own eyes to every kind of proof and argument.

In whatever century the Homeric poems originated, they transport us into times when the heroic element was fast approaching dissolution, or had just expired. Two worlds appear to meet in them: the wondrous past, which seemed to be never far removed from the poet's gaze, whilst occasionally it stood vividly before him; and the present breathing world in the midst of which he lived and moved. This blending of the present and past, by means of which the one was beautiful, the other rendered more intensely real, endows those poems with charms peculiarly their own.

At first kings and heroic races held sway throughout all Greece.

It is still so in the Homeric world. Soon after, regal dignity was nearly everywhere abolished: each city of any importance, each independent group, became a republic. On the establishment of this new political system, the various relations of life gradually grew more prosaic in character. Legends dealing with the older heroic time naturally became more and more foreign to the tastes of successive generations, and doubtless it was in a great measure owing to the changes in civil polity that Homer fell into a temporary oblivion, from which Solon and Pisistratus eventually rescued him.

On comparing Homer's works with Indian, Persian, or northern, old-Germanic heroic and mythological songs, there are two properties which serve as emphatic distinctions of the former. First, the harmonious evenness of a serene contemplation of life, as also of representation generally, which, together with remarkable clear-sightedness, are characteristic features of Greek intellect. And then the rich dramatic development of individual circumstances and objects depicted in these poems in connection with a skillfully interwoven series of choice episodes. This, again, while it is not a necessary ingredient in the structure of epic poesy, is a faculty inherent in the spirit of Grecian art. Intimately allied with these qualities is the decided prominence of the rhetorical element, one in which the innate skill of the Greeks was peculiarly fitted to shine. Marked by idiomatic traits delightfully reflected from life's own mirror, and affording a prospective vista of the dawn of young republicanism, this rhetoric is totally unlike the meretricious ornaments of later poetry. These features, in various degrees of difference, serve to identify Homer in contradistinction to all other rhapsodists of the Ionic school, and the whole body of Greek epic poets—of whom Hesiod may be cited as an exemplar—and confer on him an individuality easily recognized, though in many particulars of epic treatment the lesser heroic and mythological bards resemble both each other and Homer. A chaotic legendary confusion, often of gigantic proportions, is treated of by Hesiod in a style which the ancients termed *moderate*, inasmuch as it never assumed the form of wild and savage strength or soared into empyrean heights of fancy. The Homeric fullness of dramatic development is wanting: but, regarded simply as a delineation of manners, there may be found in Hesiod's works abundant traces of a growing republican spirit destined altogether to supplant the old heroic life. . . .

The Poet Aeschylus [4]

. . . Aeschylus is a poet of a very different kind [compared to Pindar] and animated by feelings altogether dissimilar. The warlike spirit of the soldier, inspired by Liberty herself, which breathes through his works is probably a reflection of the sentiment prevalent in haughty Athens during the great struggle. As a creative poet he had still to contend with a form that was only beginning to be molded: that great tragic form, peculiar to the Greeks, which Aeschylus was the first to conceive and cast without being enabled to perfect it. He excelled in delineating the terrible and tragic passions. With the depth of the poet, he combined the severe earnestness of the profound thinker. To this last term he had indeed the justest claims; the very charge that has been brought against him of betraying the mysteries or secret doctrines of the Eleusinian society in his poems proves his anxious longings after truth. From his genius, Greek mythology took a configuration altogether new. He does not only represent isolated tragic events—one uniformly tragic view of life, generally, pervades his whole works. The downfall of the older gods and Titans, and how their lofty lineage was displaced by a younger, more cunning, and less worthy race, is the oft-repeated story of his plaints: the original elevation and grandeur of nature and of man degenerating, in process of time, into imbecility and meanness. Yet, here and there, as in his Prometheus, he depicts giant strength rising superior to decay from amidst the crumbling fabric of a tottering world. There is in this a more than poetical sublimity.

. . . Aeschylus stands in perpetual conflict between ancient chaos and the idea of law and harmony; on this very account, the first of really tragic poets is of such significant import to the consideration of the whole of Grecian poetry. On rightly comprehending all the aspirations and ruling ideas it embodies, we shall find the older form of poesy placed midway between the savage innate strength and depth of original paganism and the later rational progress of civilization, between the first and second ages of the world, forcibly indicating a period of transition from the one to the other. Divided between Titanic power of will, the element of primeval times, with the recollections of which fancy was yet stored, and the idea of law and order as the principle of

[4]From Lecture I.

harmonious feeling. This discordance of the ancient world is most distinctly visible in Aeschylus. Next to the desire after harmony, to which I have alluded, the memories of a Titanic past, flowing from traditionary song, occupy the foremost place in ancient poesy: whilst the modern, Christian poet, having no actual source of legendary inspiration, fixes his gaze on the future rather than the past, as far as it can be attained by a presentiment of the divine in symbolical representations. . . .

Legitimate Subjects of Poetry[5]

. . . It were a false canon of criticism to maintain that the present is necessarily more unfit for poetic delineation simply because it is intrinsically of more ordinary and ignoble elements than the past. That which is mean doubtless strikes us with greater significancy and force when present to our gaze and close at hand; in the background of memory nobler shapes stand out in full relief, and thus hide much that is insignificant or unsightly. But it is competent for a true poet to overcome difficulties of this nature; it is his very province to shed a refulgence over the ordinary events of daily life, and to invest them with a higher importance, a deeper meaning. It were in vain, however, to gainsay the confining shackles of the present, or ignore the restraint it puts upon the fancy; if this latter be unnecessarily or immoderately restricted, it will indemnify itself by a greater licence in regard to language and description.

To express my views on this point in the shortest and clearest manner, I would repeat my previous remarks in reference to religious and Christian subjects of representation. The invisible world, the Deity, and pure spirits cannot be directly presented to us; nature and human beings are the legitimate and immediate themes of poetry. But that higher and spiritual world may be embodied in our earthly material, and its glories indistinctly shadowed forth. In like manner, indirect representation is most appropriate to the description of present reality. The choicest bloom of young life, and the highest ecstasy of passion, the rich fullness of an enlightened survey of the world, may all be easily transported into the traditionary past, whether longer or shorter, of a nation; they gain there an incomparably wider field, and appear in a purer light. Homer, the oldest poet of the past known to us, also exhibits the present in the liveliest and

[5]From Lecture XII.

freshest manner. The true poet embodies his own age and, in some measure, himself in his delineation of previous times. The following appears to me to be the correct and true relation of poetry to time. The proper business of poetry seems to be a representation of the eternal, the ever-important, and universally beautiful; but this is impracticable without a veil. A material basis is required; and this is found in her own peculiar sphere, that of legendary or national reminiscences. In her representation of these she transfers the rich treasures of the present—in so far as they admit of poetic treatment—and since she explains the enigma of existence and the intricacies of life as far as they are capable of solution, whilst prefiguring the bright glory of all things in her magic mirror, she reflects the luster of the future, the dawning streaks of approaching spring. Thus harmoniously blending all times and seasons, the past, the present, and the future, she proves herself to be the truthful representation of the eternal, or of perfected time. In a strictly philosophic sense the eternal is no nonentity, no mere negation of time, but rather its entire undivided fullness, in which all its elements are not torn asunder but intimately blended, a condition in which past love blooms anew in the unfading reality of an abiding remembrance, and the life of the present carries in it the germs of future hope and of continually increasing splendor. . . .

Dramatic Art [6]

. . . In the first and lowest scale of drama . . . I place those pieces in which we are presented with only the visible surface of life,—mere fleeting sketches of the world's panorama. And though all the keys of tragic passion were sounded from the highest to the lowest, though social refinement were correctly portrayed in comedy; yet, so long as the whole is confined to external appearances alone, a mere pleasing perspective for the eye to dwell upon or an impulse of pathos to thrill the heart, this would still be their inferior position. The second place in the scale of dramatic art is due to effective representations of human passion where the deeper shades and springs of action are portrayed—a delineation of characteristics, not individual, but general, of the world and of life, in manifold variety, their inconsistencies and their perplexing intricacies—in a word, a picture of man and his existence, recognized as an enigma and

[6]From Lecture xii.

treated as such. Did the aim of dramatic art purely consist of these important significant characteristics, not only would Shakespeare be entitled to rank as the first dramatist in the world, but there could scarcely be found a single poet, ancient or modern, worthy for a moment to be compared to him. But I conceive that the stage has yet another and a loftier aim. Instead of merely describing the enigma of existence, it should also *solve* it—extricate life from the tangled confusion of the present, and conduct it through the crisis of development to its final issue. Its penetrating glance thus extends to the realms of futurity, where every hidden thing becomes exposed to view, and the most complicated web is unraveled; raising the mortal veil, it permits us to scan the secrets of an invisible world, reflected from the mirror of a seer's fancy; it shows the soul how the inner life is formed by outward conflict, which results in the decisive victory of the immortal over the mortal. This altogether differs from what is commonly called the catastrophe in a tragedy. Many dramatic works are entirely deficient in this final solution as here indicated, or, if they allude to it at all, they do so simply in external form, without the slightest reference to the inner essence or spirit. This reminds me of Dante's three worlds, and the graphic force with which he introduces to our notice a series of living natures; first, the lowest abyss of perdition, then an intermediate state of suffering cheered by hope, till he brings us to the highest elevation of glory. All this may be applied to the drama—a circumstance which would entitle Dante to rank in a certain sense as a dramatic poet, save only that he presents us with a long series of catastrophes without sufficient explanation of previous phases of development. On the principle of that threefold solution of human destiny, three modes of lofty serious dramatic art may be enumerated, referring to the hidden spirit and the ultimate goal of life. In one of these the hero falls hopeless; in another the whole closes with a mixed satisfaction and reconciliation, still partially painful; in a third, a new life and the glorification of the inner man arise out of death and suffering. In illustration of the first of these species, involving heroic unmitigated ruin, I will only cite, among a host of modern examples, Wallenstein, Macbeth, and the Faust of the popular story. The dramatic art of the ancients inclines with decided partiality to this altogether tragical catastrophe, which accorded well with their belief in a terrible predestinating fate. The excellence of this form is perhaps enhanced by the hero's ruin seeming to depend not so much on the arbitrary decrees of fate as on his own voluntary and gradual approach to destruction, in the full exercise of free will, as in the above-named tragedies. . . .

Shakespeare[7]

. . . Shakespeare evidently regarded the stage of which he was so distinguished a master only as a prosaic application of his [poetic] art, a faithful sketch of life for the multitude, at the best a condescension of his powers. How little he who sounded all the depths of varied passion, who drew human nature as it is and with his magic pencil fixed each expression of its changing lineaments, the noblest and the coarsest, was himself rude or savage, is testified by the extreme tenderness that breathes over those idyllic effusions [i.e., his non-dramatic poetry]. Small is the number of those who are touched by this mild softness, just because it is so exquisite and so deep; but to a just comprehension of his dramas these lyrics are indispensable. They show us that, in his dramatic works, he seldom represents the reflection of himself, of what he felt and was, but the world as it stood clearly before him, though separated by a wide interval from himself and his deep tenderness of soul. Accordingly, the images presented to our view are thoroughly faithful, devoid of flattery or embellishment. If intelligence and penetrating depth of observation, as far as they are necessary to the characterizing of life, were the first of poetic qualities, hardly any other poet could enter into competition with him. Others have sought to transport us, for a moment, to an ideal condition of humanity: he presents us with a picture of man, in the depths of his fall and moral disorganization, with all his doings and sufferings, his thoughts and desires, with a painful minuteness. In this respect he may almost be called a satirist; and well might the complicated enigma of existence and of man's degradation, as set forth by him, produce a deeper and more lasting impression than is made by a host of splenetic caricaturists who are called satiric poets. But throughout his works there is radiant reminiscence of man's pristine dignity and elevation, from which immorality and meanness are an abnormal apostasy; and on every occasion this reminiscence, united to the poet's own nobility of soul and

[7]From Lecture xii.

tender feeling, beams forth in patriotic enthusiasm, sublime philanthropy, and glowing love.

Yet even the youthful fervor of love in his Romeo is a mere inspiration of death; Hamlet's skeptical views of life invest him with a strange mysteriousness; whilst in Lear, pain and grief reach the climax of madness. Hence this poet, externally so calm, so collected, so serene, and throughout controlled by reason, who appears as if he did nothing without a settled purpose, is inwardly the most dolorous and tragic of all ancient or modern dramatists. . . .

Conclusion[8]

. . . The intellectual problem of the age, to be worked out according to the bent of the German mind, is a full recognition of the eternal Word, valid for all time and reflected throughout the entirety of temporal science and art, this idea being in close affinity with the reunion and reconciliation of faith as well as of knowledge . . . This reunion of knowledge, which we cannot as yet designate by any other term than that of Christian philosophy, is not to be contrived after the fashion of a system or a sect, but must grow as the living tree from the root of revelation acknowledged as divine. Universal history and mythology, the empire of language and of physics, poetry and art, are but scattered rays of this one luminary of the highest knowledge. When this luminary bursts forth in the glory of meridian splendor, the glimmering torch of pantheism will recede into the shade before the awful presence of regained truth and a divine positive. Then, too, reflecting inquirers of every kind will more correctly estimate the real progress of the times, thoroughly distinct from that which the world calls the spirit of the age. Distinguished faculties will no longer continue in a state of dreamy existence, where they have slumbered for years, or start from chimerical reveries as though they had been unconscious of the lapse of one or two generations. The domains of high art likewise may be expected to be invigorated by a new breath of life, the false phantasmagoria of distorted tragedy giving place to the exalted poetry of truth, which, instead of describing with limited play of imagination the legend of any single age or race, shall hymn the story of eternal love and the mysteries of the soul veiled in the allegories of a world of spirits. Upon the whole, that luminary's

[8]From Lecture XVI.

rays are not to be confined to individual regions of mental culture; endowments and talents the most varied will have to contribute to the regeneration and growth, to the complete development of the tree of life. Just as the glory of the Creator is promoted throughout the vast realms of creation by the several graduated agencies of nature, respectively ministering and co-operating, disporting in childish glee, seeking and loving, or illumining; so in the little world of man, created after the image of the whole, the same fourfold degree of inferior and superior natures is clearly visible in its spiritual center, the department of intellectual life and action.

WILLIAM WORDSWORTH

(1770–1850)

∘◯∘∘◯∘

WORDSWORTH WAS NOT A CRITIC at all in the usual sense of the term, as Coleridge and Arnold were, yet his famous "Preface" to the second edition of *Lyrical Ballads* (1800) is probably the most widely known landmark in English literary history. Less famous, but also important, are his "Essay, Supplementary to the Preface" and his still less renowned "Preface" of 1815.

To some extent the importance of the Preface to *Lyrical Ballads* is due to the date of publication, for it conveniently marks the birth of the romantic movement in England. Wordsworth did not produce the movement but was produced by it. His Preface, however, may be regarded as a manifesto of the new age, and its influence is by no means dead even today. The essay was intended primarily as a defense of the contents of *Lyrical Ballads* and should not be considered as a program for all Wordsworth's literary production. Nevertheless, the doctrines are fairly consistent with the critical ideas of the new age and were the forerunners of Walt Whitman's 1855 "Preface,"[1] and even the "Credo" of the imagists (1915).[2]

In 1800 Wordsworth rejected the personification and "poetic diction" of neoclassicism, denounced morbid and sensational German romanticism, and turned to the simple, sane, and healthy life of the common people—the English farmer and peasant. Thus he attempted to restore the native idiom and the tone of the spoken voice to poetry. This step has been regarded as democratic and romantic, but it was also a step toward realism.

Wordsworth's theory of composition undoubtedly owes much to Locke, Hartley, and other eighteenth-century empiricists.[3] First he experiences (mainly from contact with external nature), then he

---

[1]Cf. p. 339.

[2]Two of their six points were: "To use the language of common speech . . ." and "To create new rhythms. . . ." Preface in *Some Imagist Poets, An Anthology* (Boston, 1915).

[3]See Arthur Beatty, *William Wordsworth: His Doctrine and Art in Their Historical Relations* (University of Wisconsin [Madison, 1927], second edition), pp. 124–126, *passim.*

"recollects" in tranquillity, and his soul divines the inner meaning of the experiences.

The logical inconsistencies of Wordsworth's doctrines have been pointed out by Coleridge in Chapter XIV of his *Biographia Literaria*.[4]

BIBLIOGRAPHY

TEXT

Literary Criticism, ed. by Nowell C. Smith. London, 1906.
Lyrical Ballads, a reprint, ed. with introd. by H. Littledale. Oxford, 1911.
Prose Works, ed. by William Knight. 2 vols. London and New York, 1896.

CRITICISM

Arnold, Matthew, *Essays in Criticism*. Second Series. London and New York, 1888.

Bagehot, Walter, "Wordsworth, Tennyson, and Browning," *National Review*, November, 1864; reprinted in *Literary Studies*. 3 vols. London, 1878–1879; 1895.

Barstow, Marjorie L., *Wordsworth's Theory of Poetic Diction:* A Study of the Historical and Personal Background of the Lyrical Ballads. Yale University Press, 1917.

Beach, Joseph W., "Expostulation and Reply," *Publications of the Modern Language Association*, XL (1925), 346 ff. Rebuttal of Barry Cerf's article—see below.

Beatty, Arthur, *William Wordsworth: His Doctrine and Art in Their Historical Relations*. University of Wisconsin Press, 1922; rev. ed., 1927. Shows the influence especially of Hartley. See, below, Rader's criticism of Beatty.

Campbell, O. J., and Mueschke, Paul, " 'The Borderers' as a Document in the History of Wordsworth's Aesthetic Development," *Modern Philology*, XXIII, 465 ff.

——, " 'Guilt and Sorrow': a Study in the Genesis of Wordsworth's Aesthetic," *Modern Philology*, XXIII, 293 ff.

Cerf, Barry, "Wordsworth's Gospel of Nature," *Publications of the Modern Language Association*, XXXVII (1922), 615 ff. By a disciple of More and Babbitt; reply by Beach—see above.

[4]Cf. p. 224 ff. As a result of the looseness of Wordsworth's critical terms, the scholars and critics have had difficulty in deciding whether under the term *language* Wordsworth meant to include only *vocabulary* or *style* in general. See Marjorie L. Barstow, *Wordsworth's Theory of Poetic Diction* (New Haven, 1917); and Thomas M. Raysor, "Coleridge's Criticism of Wordsworth," *Publications of the Modern Language Association*, LIV (1939), 496–510. Both the Cambridge and Oxford editors of *Biographia Literaria* (George Sampson and J. Shawcross) think that by "poetic diction" Wordsworth meant vocabulary, but Professor Raysor argues that Wordsworth meant to include style. This interpretation strengthens Coleridge's criticism of Wordsworth.

Garrod, H. W., *Wordsworth: Lectures and Essays.* Oxford University Press, 1923; 2d ed., 1927.

Gingerich, S. F., "Wordsworth," in *Essays in the Romantic Poets.* New York, 1924.

Herzberg, Max J., "Wordsworth and German Literature," *Publications of the Modern Language Association,* XL (1925), 302 ff.

Huxley, Aldous, *Holy Face and Other Essays.* London, 1929.

Knowlton, E. C., "Wordsworth and Hugh Blair," *Philological Quarterly,* VI (1927), 244 ff.

Lucas, F. L., *The Decline and Fall of the Romantic Ideal.* New York, 1936.

Newton, Annabel, *Wordsworth in Early American Criticism, 1824-1860.* University of Chicago Press, 1928.

Rader, Melvin, "The Transcendentalism of William Wordsworth," *Modern Philology,* XXVI (1928), 169 ff.

Raleigh, Sir Walter, *Wordsworth.* London, 1903.

Snider, Evelyn, *The Change in Wordsworth's Thought in 1805.* University of North Carolina, Chapel Hill, 1929. (A Ph. D. Thesis.)

Stallknecht, N. P., "Wordsworth and Philosophy: Suggestions Concerning the Source of the Poet's Doctrines and the Nature of His Mystical Experience," *Publications of The Modern Language Association,* XLIV (1929), 1116 ff.

Stephen, Leslie, "Wordsworth's Ethics," in *Hours in a Library.* Third Series. London, 1879.

Thompson, Frank T., "Emerson's Theory and Practice of Poetry," *Publications of the Modern Language Association,* XLIII (1928), 1170 ff. Treats Wordsworth's influence.

Thorpe, C. D., "Imagination, Coleridge versus Wordsworth," *Philological Quarterly,* XVIII (1939), 1-18.

Weaver, Bennett, "Wordsworth's Prelude: the Poetic Function of Memory," *Studies in Philology,* XXXIV (1937), 552-563.

PREFACE TO *LYRICAL BALLADS* (*selections*)[1]

1800

. . . The principal object, then, proposed in these poems[2] was to choose incidents and situations from common life, and to relate or describe them, throughout, as far as was possible in a selection of language really used by men, and, at the same time, to throw over them a certain coloring of imagination, whereby ordinary things should be presented to the mind in an unusual aspect; and, further, and above all, to make these incidents and situa-

---

[1]Published in the second edition of *Lyrical Ballads* (1800). Printed here complete except for introductory paragraphs.

[2]I.e., *Lyrical Ballads,* first edition, 1798.

tions interesting by tracing in them, truly though not ostenta-
tiously, the primary laws of our nature: chiefly, as far as regards
the manner in which we associate ideas in a state of excitement.
Humble and rustic life was generally chosen, because, in that
condition, the essential passions of the heart find a better soil in
which they can attain their maturity, are less under restraint,
and speak a plainer and more emphatic language; because in
that condition of life our elementary feelings coexist in a state of
greater simplicity, and, consequently, may be more accurately
contemplated, and more forcibly communicated; because the
manners of rural life germinate from those elementary feelings,
and, from the necessary character of rural occupations, are more
easily comprehended, and are more durable; and, lastly, because
in that condition the passions of men are incorporated with the
beautiful and permanent forms of nature. The language, too, of
these men has been adopted (purified indeed from what appear
to be its real defects, from all lasting and rational causes of dislike or disgust) because such men hourly communicate with the
best objects from which the best part of language is originally
derived; and because, from their rank in society and the sameness
and narrow circle of their intercourse, being less under the influence of social vanity, they convey their feelings and notions in
simple and unelaborated expressions. Accordingly, such a language, arising out of repeated experience and regular feelings, is
a more permanent, and a far more philosophical language, than
that which is frequently substituted for it by poets, who think
that they are conferring honor upon themselves and their art, in
proportion as they separate themselves from the sympathies of
men, and indulge in arbitrary and capricious habits of expression,
in order to furnish food for fickle tastes, and fickle appetites, of
their own creation.[3]

I cannot, however, be insensible to the present outcry against
the triviality and meanness, both of thought and language, which
some of my contemporaries have occasionally introduced into
their metrical compositions; and I acknowledge that this defect,
where it exists, is more dishonorable to the writer's own character
than false refinement or arbitrary innovation, though I should
contend at the same time that it is far less pernicious in the sum

---

[3]"It is worth while here to observe that the affecting parts of Chaucer are almost
always expressed in language pure and universally intelligible even to this day."
(Wordsworth's note.)

of its consequences. From such verses the poems in these volumes will be found distinguished at least by one mark of difference, that each of them has a worthy *purpose*. Not that I always began to write with a distinct purpose formally conceived; but habits of meditation have, I trust, so prompted and regulated my feelings that my descriptions of such objects as strongly excite those feelings will be found to carry along with them a *purpose*. If this opinion be erroneous, I can have little right to the name of a poet. For all good poetry is the spontaneous overflow of powerful feelings: and though this be true, poems to which any value can be attached were never produced on any variety of subjects but by a man who, being possessed of more than usual organic sensibility, had also thought long and deeply. For our continued influxes of feeling are modified and directed by our thoughts, which are indeed the representatives of all our past feelings; and, as by contemplating the relation of these general representatives to each other, we discover what is really important to men, so, by the repetition and continuance of this act, our feelings will be connected with important subjects, till at length, if we be originally possessed of much sensibility, such habits of mind will be produced that, by obeying blindly and mechanically the impulses of those habits, we shall describe objects and utter sentiments of such a nature and in such connection with each other that the understanding of the reader must necessarily be in some degree enlightened, and his affections strengthened and purified.

It has been said that each of these poems has a purpose. Another circumstance must be mentioned which distinguishes these poems from the popular poetry of the day; it is this, that the feeling therein developed gives importance to the action and situation, and not the action and situation to the feeling.

A sense of false modesty shall not prevent me from asserting that the reader's attention is pointed to this mark of distinction far less for the sake of these particular poems than from the general importance of the subject. The subject is indeed important! For the human mind is capable of being excited without the application of gross and violent stimulants; and he must have a very faint perception of its beauty and dignity who does not know this, and who does not further know that one being is elevated above another in proportion as he possesses this capability. It has therefore appeared to me, that to endeavor to produce or enlarge this capability is one of the best services in which, at any period, a writer can be engaged; but this service, excellent at all times, is especially so at the present day. For a multitude of causes, unknown to former times, are now acting with a combined force to blunt the discriminating powers of the mind, and, unfitting it for all voluntary exertion, to reduce it to a state of almost savage torpor. The most effective of these causes are the great national events which are daily taking place, and the increasing accumulation of men in cities, where the uniformity of their occupations produces a craving for extraordinary incident, which the rapid communication of intelligence hourly gratifies. To this tendency of life and manners the literature and theatrical exhibitions of the country have conformed themselves. The invaluable works of our elder writers, I had almost said the works of Shakespeare and Milton, are driven into neglect by frantic novels,[4] sickly and stupid German tragedies,[5] and deluges of idle and extravagant stories in verse.[6]— When I think upon this degrading thirst after outrageous stimulation, I am almost ashamed to have spoken of the feeble endeavor made in these volumes to counteract it; and, reflecting upon the magnitude of the general evil, I should be oppressed with no dishonorable melancholy had I not a deep impression of certain inherent and indestructible qualities of the human mind, and likewise of certain powers in the great and permanent objects that act upon it, which are equally inherent and indestructible; and were there not added to this impression a belief that the time is approaching when the evil will be systematically opposed, by men of greater powers, and with far more distinguished success.

Having dwelt thus long on the subject and aim of these poems, I shall request the reader's permission to apprise him of a few circumstances relating to their *style*, in order, among other reasons, that he may not censure me for not having performed what I never attempted. The reader will find that personifications of abstract ideas rarely occur in these volumes; and are utterly rejected as an ordinary device to elevate the style and raise it above prose. My purpose was to imitate, and, as far as possible, to adopt the very language of men; and assuredly such

[4]The "frantic novels" were probably the "Gothic romances," such as Mrs. Radcliffe's *Mysteries of Udolpho*.
[5]Perhaps early plays of Schiller and Goethe. August Kotzebue's *Misanthropy and Repentance* (1790), known in England as *The Stranger*, has also been suggested.
[6]Probably such poems as Gifford's *Maeviad* (1795), Landor's *Gebir* (1798), etc.

personifications do not make any natural or regular part of that language. They are, indeed, a figure of speech occasionally prompted by passion, and I have made use of them as such; but have endeavored utterly to reject them as a mechanical device of style, or as a family language which writers in meter seem to lay claim to by prescription. I have wished to keep the reader in the company of flesh and blood, persuaded that by so doing I shall interest him. Others who pursue a different track will interest him likewise; I do not interfere with their claim, but wish to prefer a claim of my own. There will also be found in these volumes little of what is usually called poetic diction;[7] as much pains has been taken to avoid it as is ordinarily taken to produce it; this has been done for the reason already alleged, to bring my language near to the language of men; and further, because the pleasure which I have proposed to myself to impart is of a kind very different from that which is supposed by many persons to be the proper object of poetry. Without being culpably particular, I do not know how to give my reader a more exact notion of the style in which it was my wish and intention to write, than by informing him that I have at all times endeavored to look steadily at my subject; consequently, there is I hope in these poems little falsehood of description, and my ideas are expressed in language fitted to their respective importance. Something must have been gained by this practice, as it is friendly to one property of all good poetry, namely, good sense: but it has necessarily cut me off from a large portion of phrases and figures of speech which from father to son have long been regarded as the common inheritance of poets. I have also thought it expedient to restrict myself still further, having abstained from the use of many expressions, in themselves proper and beautiful, but which have been foolishly repeated by bad poets till such feelings of disgust are connected with them as it is scarcely possible by any art of association to overpower.

If in a poem there should be found a series of lines, or even a single line, in which the language, though naturally arranged, and according to the strict laws of meter, does not differ from that of prose, there is a numerous class of critics who, when they stumble upon these prosaisms, as they call them, imagine that they have made a notable discovery, and exult over the

[7]In the Appendix to *Lyrical Ballads* Wordsworth has more to say about "poetic diction."

poet as over a man ignorant of his own profession. Now these men would establish a canon of criticism which the reader will conclude he must utterly reject if he wishes to be pleased with these volumes. And it would be a most easy task to prove to him that, not only the language of a large portion of every good poem, even of the most elevated character, must necessarily, except with reference to the meter, in no respect differ from that of good prose, but likewise that some of the most interesting parts of the best poems will be found to be strictly the language of prose when prose is well written. The truth of this assertion might be demonstrated by innumerable passages from almost all the poetical writings, even of Milton himself. To illustrate the subject in a general manner, I will here adduce a short composition of Gray, who was at the head of those who, by their reasonings, have attempted to widen the space of separation betwixt prose and metrical composition, and was more than any other man curiously elaborate in the structure of his own poetic diction.

> In vain to me the smiling mornings shine,
> And reddening Phoebus lifts his golden fire:
> The birds in vain their amorous descant join,
> Or cheerful fields resume their green attire.
> These ears, alas! for other notes repine;
> *A different object do these eyes require;*
> *My lonely anguish melts no heart but mine;*
> *And in my breast the imperfect joys expire;*
> Yet morning smiles the busy race to cheer,
> And new-born pleasure brings to happier men;
> The fields to all their wonted tribute bear;
> To warm their little loves the birds complain.
> *I fruitless mourn to him that cannot hear,*
> *And weep the more because I weep in vain.*[8]

It will easily be perceived that the only part of this sonnet which is of any value is the lines printed in italics; it is equally obvious that, except in the rhyme, and in the use of the single word "fruitless" for fruitlessly, which is so far a defect, the language of these lines does in no respect differ from that of prose.

By the foregoing quotation it has been shown that the language of prose may yet be well adapted to poetry; and it was

---

[8] "Sonnet on the Death of Richard West," written 1742.

previously asserted that a large portion of the language of every good poem can in no respect differ from that of good prose. We will go further. It may be safely affirmed that there neither is, nor can be, any *essential* difference between the language of prose and metrical composition. We are fond of tracing the resemblance between poetry and painting, and, accordingly, we call them sisters: but where shall we find bonds of connection sufficiently strict to typify the affinity betwixt metrical and prose composition? They both speak by and to the same organs; the bodies in which both of them are clothed may be said to be of the same substance, their affections are kindred, and almost identical, not necessarily differing even in degree; poetry [9] sheds no tears "such as angels weep," but natural and human tears; she can boast of no celestial ichor that distinguishes her vital juices from those of prose; the same human blood circulates through the veins of them both.

If it be affirmed that rhyme and metrical arrangement of themselves constitute a distinction which overturns what has just been said on the strict affinity of metrical language with that of prose, and paves the way for other artificial distinctions which the mind voluntarily admits, I answer that the language of such poetry as is here recommended is, as far as is possible, a selection of the language really spoken by men; that this selection, wherever it is made with true taste and feeling, will of itself form a distinction far greater than would at first be imagined, and will entirely separate the composition from the vulgarity and meanness of ordinary life; and, if meter be superadded thereto, I believe that a dissimilitude will be produced altogether sufficient for the gratification of a rational mind. What other distinction would we have? Whence is it to come? And where is it to exist? Not, surely, where the poet speaks through the mouths of his characters: it cannot be necessary here, either for elevation of style, or any of its supposed ornaments: for, if the poet's subject be judiciously chosen, it will naturally, and upon fit

[9] "I here use the word 'poetry' (though against my own judgment) as opposed to the word prose, and synonymous with metrical composition. But much confusion has been introduced into criticism by this contradistinction of poetry and prose, instead of the more philosophical one of poetry and matter of fact, or science. The only strict antithesis to prose is meter; nor is this, in truth, a *strict* antithesis, because lines and passages of meter so naturally occur in writing prose, that it would be scarcely possible to avoid them, even were it desirable." (Wordsworth's note.)

occasion, lead him to passions the language of which, if selected truly and judiciously, must necessarily be dignified and variegated, and alive with metaphors and figures. I forbear to speak of an incongruity which would shock the intelligent reader, should the poet interweave any foreign splendor of his own with that which the passion naturally suggests: it is sufficient to say that such addition is unnecessary. And, surely, it is more probable that those passages, which with propriety abound with metaphors and figures, will have their due effect, if, upon other occasions where the passions are of a milder character, the style also be subdued and temperate.

But, as the pleasure which I hope to give by the poems now presented to the reader must depend entirely on just notions upon this subject, and, as it is in itself of high importance to our taste and moral feelings, I cannot content myself with these detached remarks. And if, in what I am about to say, it shall appear to some that my labor is unnecessary, and that I am like a man fighting a battle without enemies, such persons may be reminded that, whatever be the language outwardly holden by men, a practical faith in the opinions which I am wishing to establish is almost unknown. If my conclusions are admitted, and carried as far as they must be carried if admitted at all, our judgments concerning the works of the greatest poets, both ancient and modern, will be far different from what they are at present, both when we praise, and when we censure: and our moral feelings influencing and influenced by these judgments will, I believe, be corrected and purified.

Taking up the subject, then, upon general grounds, let me ask, what is meant by the word poet? What is a poet?[10] To whom does he address himself? And what language is to be expected from him?—He is a man speaking to men: a man, it is true, endowed with more lively sensibility, more enthusiasm and tenderness, who has a greater knowledge of human nature and a more comprehensive soul than are supposed to be common among mankind; a man pleased with his own passions and volitions, and who rejoices more than other men in the spirit of life that is in him; delighting to contemplate similar volitions and passions as manifested in the goings-on of the universe, and habitually impelled to create them where he does not find them. To these qualities he has added a disposition to be affected

[10]Cf. Wordsworth's poem, "If Thou Indeed Derive Thy Light from Heaven."

more than other men by absent things as if they were present; an ability of conjuring up in himself passions, which are indeed far from being the same as those produced by real events, yet (especially in those parts of the general sympathy which are pleasing and delightful) do more nearly resemble the passions produced by real events than anything which, from the motions of their own minds merely, other men are accustomed to feel in themselves:—whence, and from practice, he has acquired a greater readiness and power in expressing what he thinks and feels, and especially those thoughts and feelings which, by his own choice, or from the structure of his own mind, arise in him without immediate external excitement.

But whatever portion of this faculty we may suppose even the greatest poet to possess, there cannot be a doubt that the language which it will suggest to him must often, in liveliness and truth, fall short of that which is uttered by men in real life, under the actual pressure of those passions, certain shadows of which the poet thus produces, or feels to be produced, in himself.

However exalted a notion we would wish to cherish of the character of a poet, it is obvious that, while he describes and imitates passions, his employment is in some degree mechanical, compared with the freedom and power of real and substantial action and suffering. So that it will be the wish of the poet to bring his feelings near to those of the persons whose feelings he describes, nay, for short spaces of time, perhaps, to let himself slip into an entire delusion, and even confound and identify his own feelings with theirs; modifying only the language which is thus suggested to him by a consideration that he describes for a particular purpose, that of giving pleasure. Here, then, he will apply the principle of selection which has been already insisted upon. He will depend upon this for removing what would otherwise be painful or disgusting in the passion; he will feel that there is no necessity to trick out or to elevate nature: and, the more industriously he applies this principle, the deeper will be his faith that no words which *his* fancy or imagination can suggest will be to be compared with those which are the emanations of reality and truth.

But it may be said by those who do not object to the general spirit of these remarks that, as it is impossible for the poet to produce upon all occasions language as exquisitely fitted for the passion as that which the real passion itself suggests, it is proper

that he should consider himself as in the situation of a translator
who does not scruple to substitute excellencies of another kind
for those which are unattainable by him, and endeavors occasionally to surpass his original in order to make some amends for
the general inferiority to which he feels that he must submit.
But this would be to encourage idleness and unmanly despair.
Further, it is the language of men who speak of what they do not
understand; who talk of poetry as of a matter of amusement
and idle pleasure; who will converse with us as gravely about a
taste for poetry,[11] as they express it, as if it were a thing as indifferent as a taste for ropedancing, or Frontiniac or Sherry.
Aristotle, I have been told, has said that poetry is the most
philosophic of all writing:[12] it is so: its object is truth, not individual and local, but general and operative; not standing upon
external testimony, but carried alive into the heart by passion;
truth which is its own testimony, which gives competence and
confidence to the tribunal to which it appeals, and receives
them from the same tribunal. Poetry is the image of man and
nature. The obstacles which stand in the way of the fidelity of
the biographer and historian, and of their consequent utility,
are incalculably greater than those which are to be encountered
by the poet who comprehends the dignity of his art. The poet
writes under one restriction only, namely, the necessity of giving
immediate pleasure to a human being possessed of that information which may be expected from him, not as a lawyer, a physician, a mariner, an astronomer, or a natural philosopher, but as
a man. Except this one restriction, there is no object standing
between the poet and the image of things; between this, and
the biographer and historian, there are a thousand.

Nor let this necessity of producing immediate pleasure be
considered as a degradation of the poet's art. It is far otherwise.
It is an acknowledgment of the beauty of the universe, an
acknowledgment the more sincere because not formal, but
indirect; it is a task light and easy to him who looks at the world
in the spirit of love: further, it is a homage paid to the native

---

[11]Cf. "Essay Supplementary to the Preface": *Taste* "is a metaphor taken from a
passive sense of the human body, and transferred to things which are in their essence
not passive,—to intellectual acts and operations . . . The profound and universal
in thought and imagination,—or, in ordinary language, the pathetic and the sublime,—are neither of them, accurately speaking, objects of a faculty which could
ever without a sinking in the spirit of nations have been designated by the metaphor
taste."   [12]Aristotle's *Poetics*, chap. IX.

and naked dignity of man, to the grand elementary principle of pleasure, by which he knows, and feels, and lives, and moves. We have no sympathy but what is propagated by pleasure: I would not be misunderstood; but wherever we sympathize with pain, it will be found that the sympathy is produced and carried on by subtle combinations with pleasure. We have no knowledge, that is, no general principles drawn from the contemplation of particular facts, but what has been built up by pleasure, and exists in us by pleasure alone. The man of science, the chemist and mathematician, whatever difficulties and disgusts they may have had to struggle with, know and feel this. However painful may be the objects with which the anatomist's knowledge is connected, he feels that his knowledge is pleasure; and where he has no pleasure he has no knowledge. What then does the poet? He considers man and the objects that surround him as acting and re-acting upon each other, so as to produce an infinite complexity of pain and pleasure; he considers man in his own nature and in his ordinary life as contemplating this with a certain quantity of immediate knowledge, with certain convictions, intuitions, and deductions which from habit acquire the quality of intuitions; he considers him as looking upon this complex scene of ideas and sensations, and finding everywhere objects that immediately excite in him sympathies which, from the necessities of his nature, are accompanied by an overbalance of enjoyment.

To this knowledge which all men carry about with them, and to these sympathies in which, without any other discipline than that of our daily life, we are fitted to take delight, the poet principally directs his attention. He considers man and nature as essentially adapted to each other, and the mind of man as naturally the mirror of the fairest and most interesting properties of nature. And thus the poet, prompted by this feeling of pleasure, which accompanies him through the whole course of his studies, converses with general nature, with affections akin to those which, through labor and length of time, the man of science has raised up in himself, by conversing with those particular parts of nature which are the objects of his studies. The knowledge both of the poet and the man of science is pleasure; but the knowledge of the one cleaves to us as a necessary part of our existence, our natural and unalienable inheritance; the other is a personal and individual acquisition, slow to come to us, and by no habitual and direct sympathy connecting us with our fellow-beings. The man of science seeks truth as a remote and unknown benefactor; he cherishes and loves it in his solitude: the poet, singing a song in which all human beings join with him, rejoices in the presence of truth as our visible friend and hourly companion. Poetry is the breath and finer spirit of all knowledge; it is the impassioned expression which is in the countenance of all science. Emphatically may it be said of the poet, as Shakespeare hath said of man, "that he looks before and after."[13] He is the rock of defense for human nature; an upholder and preserver, carrying everywhere with him relationship and love. In spite of difference of soil and climate, of language and manners, of laws and customs: in spite of things silently gone out of mind, and things violently destroyed, the poet binds together by passion and knowledge the vast empire of human society as it is spread over the whole earth, and over all time. The objects of the poet's thoughts are everywhere; though the eyes and senses of man are, it is true, his favorite guides, yet he will follow wheresoever he can find an atmosphere of sensation in which to move his wings. Poetry is the first and last of all knowledge—it is as immortal as the heart of man. If the labors of men of science should ever create any material revolution, direct or indirect, in our condition, and in the impressions which we habitually receive, the poet will sleep then no more than at present; he will be ready to follow the steps of the man of science, not only in those general indirect effects, but he will be at his side, carrying sensation into the midst of the objects of the science itself. The remotest discoveries of the chemist, the botanist, or mineralogist will be as proper objects of the poet's art as any upon which it can be employed if the time should ever come when these things shall be familiar to us, and the relations under which they are contemplated by the followers of these respective sciences shall be manifestly and palpably material to us as enjoying and suffering beings. If the time should ever come when what is now called science, thus familiarized to men, shall be ready to put on, as it were, a form of flesh and blood, the poet will lend his divine spirit to aid the transfiguration, and will welcome the being thus produced as a dear and genuine inmate of the household of man. It is not, then, to be supposed that anyone who holds that sublime notion

[13]*Hamlet*, IV, iv, 37.

of poetry which I have attempted to convey will break in upon the sanctity and truth of his pictures by transitory and accidental ornaments, and endeavor to excite admiration of himself by arts, the necessity of which must manifestly depend upon the assumed meanness of his subject.

What has been thus far said applies to poetry in general; but especially to those parts of composition where the poet speaks through the mouths of his characters; and upon this point it appears to authorize the conclusion that there are few persons of good sense who would not allow that the dramatic parts of composition are defective in proportion as they deviate from the real language of nature, and are colored by a diction of the poet's own, either peculiar to him as an individual poet or belonging simply to poets in general; to a body of men who, from the circumstance of their compositions being in meter, it is expected will employ a particular language.

It is not, then, in the dramatic parts of composition that we look for this distinction of language; but still it may be proper and necessary where the poet speaks to us in his own person and character. To this I answer by referring the reader to the description before given of a poet. Among the qualities there enumerated as principally conducing to form a poet is implied nothing differing in kind from other men, but only in degree. The sum of what was said is, that the poet is chiefly distinguished from other men by a greater promptness to think and feel without immediate external excitement, and a greater power in expressing such thoughts and feelings as are produced in him in that manner. But these passions and thoughts and feelings are the general passions and thoughts and feelings of men. And with what are they connected? Undoubtedly with our moral sentiments and animal sensations, and with the causes which excite these; with the operations of the elements and the appearances of the visible universe; with storm and sunshine, with the revolutions of the seasons, with cold and heat, with loss of friends and kindred, with injuries and resentments, gratitude and hope, with fear and sorrow. These, and the like, are the sensations and objects which the poet describes, as they are the sensations of other men, and the objects which interest them. The poet thinks and feels in the spirit of human passions. How, then, can his language differ in any material degree from that of all other men who feel vividly and see clearly? It might be *proved* that it is impossible. But supposing that this were not the case, the poet might then be allowed to use a peculiar language when expressing his feelings for his own gratification, or that of men like himself. But poets do not write for poets alone, but for men. Unless therefore we are advocates for that admiration which subsists upon ignorance, and that pleasure which arises from hearing what we do not understand, the poet must descend from this supposed height; and, in order to excite rational sympathy, he must express himself as other men express themselves. To this it may be added that, while he is only selecting from the real language of men, or, which amounts to the same thing, composing accurately in the spirit of such selection, he is treading upon safe ground, and we know what we are to expect from him. Our feelings are the same with respect to meter; for, as it may be proper to remind the reader, the distinction of meter is regular and uniform, and not, like that which is produced by what is usually called POETIC DICTION, arbitrary, and subject to infinite caprices upon which no calculation whatever can be made. In the one case, the reader is utterly at the mercy of the poet, respecting what imagery or diction he may choose to connect with the passion; whereas, in the other, the meter obeys certain laws to which the poet and reader both willingly submit because they are certain, and because no interference is made by them with the passion, but such as the concurring testimony of ages has shown to heighten and improve the pleasure which coexists with it.

It will now be proper to answer an obvious question, namely, Why, professing these opinions, have I written in verse? To this, in addition to such answer as is included in what has been already said, I reply, in the first place: Because, however I may have restricted myself, there is still left open to me what confessedly constitutes the most valuable object of all writing, whether in prose or verse; the great and universal passions of men, the most general and interesting of their occupations, and the entire world of nature before me—to supply endless combinations of forms and imagery. Now, supposing for a moment that whatever is interesting in these objects may be as vividly described in prose, why should I be condemned for attempting to superadd to such description the charm which, by the consent of all nations, is acknowledged to exist in metrical language? To this, by such as are yet unconvinced, it may be answered that a very small part of the pleasure given by poetry depends upon the meter, and that it is injudicious to write in meter, unless it be accompanied with the other artificial distinctions of style with which meter is usually accompanied, and that, by such deviation, more will be lost from the shock which will thereby be given to the reader's associations than will be counterbalanced by any pleasure which he can derive from the general power of numbers. In answer to those who still contend for the necessity of accompanying meter with certain appropriate colors of style in order to the accomplishment of its appropriate end, and who also, in my opinion, greatly underrate the power of meter in itself, it might, perhaps, as far as relates to these volumes, have been almost sufficient to observe that poems are extant, written upon more humble subjects, and in a still more naked and simple style, which have continued to give pleasure from generation to generation. Now, if nakedness and simplicity be a defect, the fact here mentioned affords a strong presumption that poems somewhat less naked and simple are capable of affording pleasure at the present day; and, what I wished *chiefly* to attempt, at present, was to justify myself for having written under the impression of this belief.

But various causes might be pointed out why, when the style is manly, and the subject of some importance, words metrically arranged will long continue to impart such a pleasure to mankind as he who proves the extent of that pleasure will be desirous to impart. The end of poetry is to produce excitement in coexistence with an overbalance of pleasure; but, by the supposition, excitement is an unusual and irregular state of the mind; ideas and feelings do not, in that state, succeed each other in accustomed order. If the words, however, by which this excitement is produced be in themselves powerful, or the images and feelings have an undue proportion of pain connected with them, there is some danger that the excitement may be carried beyond its proper bounds. Now the co-presence of something regular, something to which the mind has been accustomed in various moods and in a less excited state, cannot but have great efficacy in tempering and restraining the passion by an intertexture of ordinary feeling, and of feeling not strictly and necessarily connected with the passion. This is unquestionably true; and hence, though the opinion will at first appear paradoxical, from the tendency of meter to divest language, in a certain degree, of its reality, and thus to throw a sort of half-consciousness of un-substantial existence over the whole composition, there can be little doubt but that more pathetic situations and sentiments, that is, those which have a greater proportion of pain connected with them, may be endured in metrical composition, especially in rhyme, than in prose. The meter of the old ballads is very artless; yet they contain many passages which would illustrate this opinion; and, I hope, if the following poems be attentively perused, similar instances will be found in them. This opinion may be further illustrated by appealing to the reader's own experience of the reluctance with which he comes to the re-perusal of the distressful parts of *Clarissa Harlowe*,[14] or the *Gamester*,[15] while Shakespeare's writings, in the most pathetic scenes, never act upon us, as pathetic, beyond the bounds of pleasure—an effect which, in a much greater degree than might at first be imagined, is to be ascribed to small, but continual and regular impulses of pleasurable surprise from the metrical arrangement.—On the other hand (what it must be allowed will much more frequently happen) if the poet's words should be incommensurate with the passion, and inadequate to raise the reader to a height of desirable excitement, then (unless the poet's choice of his meter has been grossly injudicious) in the feelings of pleasure which the reader has been accustomed to connect with meter in general, and in the feeling, whether cheer-ful or melancholy, which he has been accustomed to connect with that particular movement of meter, there will be found something which will greatly contribute to impart passion to the words, and to effect the complex end which the poet pro-poses to himself.[16]

If I had undertaken a SYSTEMATIC defense of the theory here maintained, it would have been my duty to develop the various causes upon which the pleasure received from metrical language depends. Among the chief of these causes is to be reckoned a principle which must be well known to those who have made

[14]*Clarissa, or the History of a Young Lady* (1848), tragic novel by Samuel Richardson.
[15]*The Gamester* (1753), a domestic tragedy by Edward Moore.
[16]"With the theory of meter as relieving tragic pain, compare a remark of Goethe's in a letter to Schiller (May 5, 1798), at the time when he was composing *Faust:* 'Certain tragic scenes were written in prose, but they are quite intolerable com-pared with the others, through their naturalness and strength. I am trying, there-fore, to put them into rhyme, for then the idea is seen as if through a veil, and the direct impression of the tremendous material is softened'" (note by Alden in his *Critical Essays of the Early Nineteenth Century* [New York, 1921], p. 19).

any of the arts the object of accurate reflection; namely, the pleasure which the mind derives from the perception of similitude in dissimilitude. This principle is the great spring of the activity of our minds, and their chief feeder. From this principle the direction of the sexual appetite, and all the passions connected with it, take their origin: it is the life of our ordinary conversation; and upon the accuracy with which similitude in dissimilitude, and dissimilitude in similitude are perceived, depend our taste and our moral feelings. It would not be a useless employment to apply this principle to the consideration of meter, and to show that meter is hence enabled to afford much pleasure, and to point out in what manner that pleasure is produced. But my limits will not permit me to enter upon this subject, and I must content myself with a general summary.

I have said that poetry is the spontaneous overflow of powerful feelings: it takes its origin from emotion recollected in tranquillity: the emotion is contemplated till, by a species of reaction, the tranquillity gradually disappears, and an emotion, kindred to that which was before the subject of contemplation, is gradually produced, and does itself actually exist in the mind. In this mood successful composition generally begins, and in a mood similar to this it is carried on; but the emotion, of whatever kind, and in whatever degree, from various causes, is qualified by various pleasures, so that in describing any passions whatsoever, which are voluntarily described, the mind will, upon the whole, be in a state of enjoyment. If nature be thus cautious to preserve in a state of enjoyment a being so employed, the poet ought to profit by the lesson held forth to him and ought especially to take care that, whatever passions he communicates to his reader, those passions, if his reader's mind be sound and vigorous, should always be accompanied with an overbalance of pleasure. Now the music of harmonious metrical language, the sense of difficulty overcome, and the blind association of pleasure which has been previously received from works of rhyme or meter of the same or similar construction, an indistinct perception perpetually renewed of language closely resembling that of real life, and yet, in the circumstance of meter, differing from it so widely—all these imperceptibly make up a complex feeling of delight which is of the most important use in tempering the painful feeling always found intermingled with powerful descriptions of the deeper passions. This effect is always pro-

duced in pathetic and impassioned poetry; while, in lighter composition, the ease and gracefulness with which the poet manages
his numbers are themselves confessedly a principal source of the
gratification of the reader. All that it is *necessary* to say, however,
upon this subject may be effected by affirming, what few persons
will deny, that, of two descriptions, either of passions, manners,
or characters, each of them equally well executed, the one in
prose and the other in verse, the verse will be read a hundred
times where the prose is read once.

Having thus explained a few of my reasons for writing in
verse, and why I have chosen subjects from common life, and
endeavored to bring my language near to the real language of
men, if I have been too minute in pleading my own cause, I
have at the same time been treating a subject of general interest;
and for this reason a few words shall be added with reference
solely to these particular poems, and to some defects which will
probably be found in them. I am sensible that my associations
must have sometimes been particular instead of general, and
that, consequently, giving to things a false importance, I may
have sometimes written upon unworthy subjects; but I am less
apprehensive on this account, than that my language may
frequently have suffered from those arbitrary connections of
feelings and ideas with particular words and phrases, from which
no man can altogether protect himself. Hence I have no doubt
that, in some instances, feelings, even of the ludicrous, may be
given to my readers by expressions which appeared to me tender
and pathetic. Such faulty expressions, were I convinced they
were faulty at present, and that they must necessarily continue
to be so, I would willingly take all reasonable pains to correct.
But it is dangerous to make these alterations on the simple
authority of a few individuals, or even of certain classes of men;
for where the understanding of an author is not convinced, or
his feelings altered, this cannot be done without great injury to
himself: for his own feelings are his stay and support; and, if he
set them aside in one instance, he may be induced to repeat this
act till his mind shall lose all confidence in itself, and become
utterly debilitated. To this it may be added that the critic
ought never to forget that he is himself exposed to the same
errors as the poet, and, perhaps, in a much greater degree: for
there can be no presumption in saying of most readers that it is
not probable they will be so well acquainted with the various

stages of meaning through which words have passed, or with the fickleness or stability of the relations of particular ideas to each other; and, above all, since they are so much less interested in the subject, they may decide lightly and carelessly.

Long as the reader has been detained, I hope he will permit me to caution him against a mode of false criticism which has been applied to poetry, in which the language closely resembles that of life and nature. Such verses have been triumphed over in parodies, of which Dr. Johnson's stanza is a fair specimen:—

> I put my hat upon my head
> And walked into the Strand,
> And there I met another man
> Whose hat was in his hand.[17]

Immediately under these lines let us place one of the most justly admired stanzas of the "Babes in the Wood."

> These pretty babes with hand in hand
> Went wandering up and down;
> But never more they saw the Man
> Approaching from the Town.[18]

In both these stanzas the words, and the order of the words, in no respect differ from the most unimpassioned conversation. There are words in both, for example, "the Strand," and "the Town," connected with none but the most familiar ideas; yet the one stanza we admit as admirable, and the other as a fair example of the superlatively contemptible. Whence arises this difference? Not from the meter, not from the language, not from the order of the words; but the *matter* expressed in Dr. Johnson's stanza is contemptible. The proper method of treating trivial and simple verses, to which Dr. Johnson's stanza would be a fair parallelism, is not to say, this is a bad kind of poetry, or, this is not poetry; but, this wants sense; it is neither interesting in itself, nor can *lead* to anything interesting; the images neither originate in that sane state of feeling which arises out of thought, nor can excite thought or feeling in the reader. This is the only sensible manner of dealing with such verses. Why trouble yourself about the species till you have previously decided upon the genus? Why take pains to prove that an ape is not a Newton, when it is self-evident that he is not a man?

---

[17]According to the Memoirs of Joseph Cradock, Dr. Johnson composed this stanza in imitation of "The Hermit of Warkworth," in Percy's *Reliques* (Alden).
[18]Cf. Addison's praise of this ballad in *Spectator*, no. 85.

One request I must make of my reader, which is, that in judging these poems he would decide by his own feelings genuinely, and not by reflection upon what will probably be the judgment of others. How common is it to hear a person say, I myself do not object to this style of composition, or this or that expression, but, to such and such classes of people it will appear mean or ludicrous! This mode of criticism, so destructive of all sound unadulterated judgment, is almost universal: let the reader then abide, independently, by his own feelings, and, if he finds himself affected, let him not suffer such conjectures to interfere with his pleasure.

If an author by any single composition has impressed us with respect for his talents, it is useful to consider this as affording a presumption that on other occasions where we have been displeased, he, nevertheless, may not have written ill or absurdly; and further, to give him so much credit for this one composition as may induce us to review what has displeased us with more care than we should otherwise have bestowed upon it. This is not only an act of justice, but, in our decisions upon poetry especially, may conduce, in a high degree, to the improvement of our own taste; for an *accurate* taste in poetry, and in all the other arts, as Sir Joshua Reynolds has observed,[19] is an *acquired* talent, which can only be produced by thought and a long-continued intercourse with the best models of composition. This is mentioned, not with so ridiculous a purpose as to prevent the most inexperienced reader from judging for himself (I have already said that I wish him to judge for himself), but merely to temper the rashness of decision, and to suggest that, if poetry be a subject on which much time has not been bestowed, the judgment may be erroneous; and that, in many cases, it necessarily will be so.

Nothing would, I know, have so effectually contributed to further the end which I have in view as to have shown of what kind the pleasure is and how that pleasure is produced, which is confessedly produced by metrical composition essentially different from that which I have here endeavored to recommend: for the reader will say that he has been pleased by such composition: and what more can be done for him? The power of any art is limited; and he will suspect that, if it be proposed to furnish him with new friends, that can be only upon condition of his abandoning

[19] *The Discourses of Sir Joshua Reynolds* (London, 1924), pp. 103–134.

his old friends. Besides, as I have said, the reader is himself conscious of the pleasure which he has received from such composition, composition to which he has peculiarly attached the endearing name of poetry; and all men feel an habitual gratitude, and something of an honorable bigotry for the objects which have long continued to please them: we not only wish to be pleased, but to be pleased in that particular way in which we have been accustomed to be pleased. There is in these feelings enough to resist a host of arguments; and I should be the less able to combat them successfully, as I am willing to allow that, in order entirely to enjoy the poetry which I am recommending, it would be necessary to give up much of what is ordinarily enjoyed. But, would my limits have permitted me to point out how this pleasure is produced, many obstacles might have been removed, and the reader assisted in perceiving that the powers of language are not so limited as he may suppose; and that it is possible for poetry to give other enjoyments, of a purer, more lasting, and more exquisite nature. This part of the subject has not been altogether neglected, but it has not been so much my present aim to prove that the interest excited by some other kinds of poetry is less vivid and less worthy of the nobler powers of the mind, as to offer reasons for presuming that, if my purpose were fulfilled, a species of poetry would be produced which is genuine poetry; in its nature well adapted to interest mankind permanently, and likewise important in the multiplicity and quality of its moral relations.

From what has been said, and from a perusal of the poems, the reader will be able clearly to perceive the object which I had in view: he will determine how far it has been attained; and, what is a much more important question, whether it be worth attaining: and upon the decision of these two questions will rest my claim to the approbation of the public.

SAMUEL TAYLOR COLERIDGE

(1772–1834)

o◯oo◯o

MANY SCHOLARS REGARD COLERIDGE as the greatest English critic, and
no one who has read his lectures on Shakespeare can deny his genius.
But he was more than a critic: he was a gifted poet and philosopher
as well. His eminence as a critic is due in no small degree to his philosophy. In youth he was influenced by sentimentalism and materialism
(Godwin's mechanistic philosophy), but as he grew older he swung
more in the direction of Plato and the seventeenth-century English
Platonists, though he remained an independent thinker all his life. He
was both subjective and objective. He believed in a rational universe,
"a complex objectification of divine energies, a glorious and fascinating
world, replete with symbols of eternal reality."[1]

Literature, Coleridge thought, should give a vision of life, revealed
by reason, but likewise apprehended by intuition. Poetry should be
ideal, representative, generic. Characters should "be clothed with *generic*
attributes, with the *common* attributes of the class; not with such as one
gifted individual might *possibly* possess."[2] He disagreed with Wordsworth's theory of the place of rustic life and diction in poetry. To him
language was the product of the *inner* as well as the *outer* life, "the product
of philosophers, not of clowns or shepherds."[3]

Shakespeare was Coleridge's supreme poet, the poet of universal
experience, not, as the eighteenth-century critics thought, a "natural
genius."[4] Far from being "a great dramatist by mere instinct," his
judgment was equal to his genius, and the "supposed irregularities
and extravagances of Shakespeare were the mere dreams of pedantry." For the classical unities violated, Coleridge found a superior
organic unity of tone, feeling, psychology, imagery and diction brilliantly successful in content.

[1]Ernest Bernbaum, *Guide through the Romantic Movement* (New York, 1937), p. 104.
[2]*Biographia Literaria*, chap. XVII.
[3]See p. 224. For a spirited defense of the Coleridge side of the dispute with
Wordsworth, see Thomas M. Raysor, "Coleridge's Criticism of Wordsworth,"
Publications of the Modern Language Association, LIV (June, 1939), 496–510.
[4]See *original genius* in the index.

"The *Biographia Literaria* is the greatest book of criticism in English," says Arthur Symons, "and," he adds, "one of the most annoying books in any language." Annoying because "the thought of Coleridge has to be pursued across stones, ditches, and morasses." [7] Everyone has heard of Coleridge's addiction to drugs and his erratic life. Perhaps his aberrations prevented him from ever achieving the continuity of thought or the physical application necessary for working out a complete philosophical system and writing it down. We cannot be sure he did not think it out, but the remains are unquestionably fragmentary. Few critics, however, have left us such glorious fragments.

Biographia Literaria was begun as a preface to a work to be called, "Autobiographia Literaria: Sketches of My Literary Life and Opinions," but the preface gradually expanded into two volumes. Coleridge wrote the work between 1815–1816. It was printed in 1817.

The sources of Coleridge's literary theories are still in dispute. He denied German influence, but he undoubtedly read the German romantics, and was perhaps unconsciously influenced by them. His lectures on Shakespeare contain many quotations from August Schlegel without quotation marks, but this oversight is said to be the fault of the editors; Coleridge used quotation marks in his manuscripts. At any rate Lessing, Schiller, Jean Paul Richter, and the Schlegels belonged to the same movement that developed Coleridge, and they should be studied in connection with him—likewise Kant, Schilling, and the English Platonists. Professor Bernbaum thinks the influence of Henry Mackenzie and Maurice Morgann on Coleridge has been insufficiently studied.[8]

Coleridge's own influence on other critics has been tremendous, not only on Lamb, Hazlitt, De Quincey, Leigh Hunt, Carlyle, and others in England, but on Edgar Allan Poe in America.[9]

BIBLIOGRAPHY

TEXT

Biographia Epistolaris, being the biographical supplement of Coleridge's *Biographia Literaria*, with additional letters, etc., ed. by A. Turnbull. 2 vols. London, 1911. (Bohn Standard Library.)

[7]Introduction to Everyman's Library edition of *Biographia Literaria* (New York, 1906), pp. x–xi.
[8]Bernbaum, *op. cit.*, p. 107.
[9]Cf. Margaret Alterton, *Origins of Poe's Critical Theory*, University of Iowa Humanistic Studies (1925), II, no. 3, and Floyd Stovall, "Poe's Debt to Coleridge," University of Texas *Studies in English*, X (1930), 70–127.

Biographia Literaria, or Biographical Sketches of My Literary Life and Opinions, reprinted from the original plates. London, 1905.
——, ed. with critical introduction by J. A. Symons. New York, 1908. (Everyman's Library.)
——, ed. with *Aesthetical Essays,* by J. Shawcross. 2 vols. Oxford, 1907.
——, Chaps. i–iv, xiv–xxii, ed. by George Sampson, with an introductory essay by Sir Arthur Quiller-Couch. New York, 1920.
Essays and Lectures on Shakespeare and Some Other Old Poets and Dramatists. London, 1907.
The Friend. 3rd. ed. London, 1837.
Letters of Coleridge, ed. by Ernest H. Coleridge. 2 vols. London, 1895.
Miscellanies, Aesthetic and Literary, collected and ed. by Andrew J. George. Boston, 1895.
On Logic and Learning; with Selections from the Unpublished Manuscripts, ed. by Alice D. Snyder. Yale University Press, 1929.
Coleridge's Shakespearean Criticism, ed. by Thomas M. Raysor. 2 vols. Harvard University Press, 1931.
"Some Marginalia on Shakespeare," by Thomas M. Raysor, *Publications of the Modern Language Association,* XLII (1927), 762–765.
"Unpublished Fragments on Aesthetics," collected by Thomas M. Raysor, *Studies in Philology,* XXII (1925), 529 ff.

CRITICISM

Babbitt, Irving, "Coleridge and Imagination," *Nineteenth Century and After,* CVI (September, 1929), 383 ff.
Brandes, Georg, "Naturalistic Romanticism," *Main Currents of Nineteenth Century Literature.* Vol. IV. New York, 1906. By a "naturalistic" critic.
Brandl, Alois, *Samuel Taylor Coleridge und die englische Romantik.* Berlin, 1886. English translation by Lady Eastlake. London, 1887.
——, "Coleridge père du romanticisme anglais; les années d'or du poète," *Mercure de France,* CXCVIII (September 15, 1927), 556–589.
Crossley, A. C., "Coleridge and Criticism," *Spectator,* CXLII (January 26, 1929), 115–116.
Greever, Garland, *A Wiltshire Parson and His Friends.* Boston, 1926. W. L. Bowles, who may have influenced the poets, was a friend of Coleridge and Wordsworth.
Hamilton, M. P., "Wordsworth's Relation to Coleridge's Osorio," *Studies in Philology,* XXXIV (1937), 429–437.
Howard, Claud, *Coleridge's Idealism; A Study of Its Relationship to Kant and to the Cambridge Platonists.* Boston, 1924.
Helmholtz, Anna A., *The Indebtedness of Samuel Taylor Coleridge to August Wilhelm von Schlegel.* University of Wisconsin Press, 1907.

Kennedy, Virginia Wadlow, *Samuel Taylor Coleridge;* a selected bibliography of the best available editions of his writings, biographies, and criticism of him and of references showing his relations with contemporaries. Baltimore, 1935.

Lucas, F. L., *The Decline and Fall of the Romantic Ideal.* New York, 1936, pp. 157–200.

Minto, William, *Literature of the Georgian Era.* New York, 1895, pp. 190 ff.

Morrill, Dorothy I., *German Influence on Coleridge's Dramatic Criticism,* 1921. (An unpublished Radcliffe dissertation.)

——, "Coleridge's Theory of Dramatic Illusion," *Modern Language Notes,* XLII (1927), 436 ff.

Muirhead, John Henry, *Coleridge as Philosopher.* London, 1930.

Raysor, Thomas M., "Coleridge's Criticism of Wordsworth," *Publications of the Modern Language Association,* LIV (1939), 496–510. Defense of Coleridge in his criticism of Wordsworth.

——, "The Study of Shakespeare's Characters in the Eighteenth Century," *Modern Language Notes,* XLII (1927), 495 ff.

Richards, I. A., *Coleridge on Imagination.* London, 1934.

Sanders, C. R., "Maurice as a Commentator on Coleridge," *Publications of the Modern Language Association,* LIII (1938), 230–243.

Sherwood, Margaret, *Coleridge's Imaginative Conception of the Imagination.* Wellesley, Mass., 1937.

Stallknecht, Newton P., "Doctrine of Coleridge's *Dejection* and Its Relation to Wordsworth's Philosophy," *Publications of the Modern Language Association,* XLIX (1934), 196–207.

Stephen, Leslie, "Coleridge," in *Hours in a Library.* Vol. IV. London, 1907.

Thorpe, C. D., "Imagination: Coleridge versus Wordsworth," *Philological Quarterly,* XVIII (January, 1939), 1–18.

WORDSWORTH'S THEORY OF DICTION[1]

1817

Examination of the tenets peculiar to Mr. Wordsworth—Rustic life (above all, low and rustic life) especially unfavorable to the formation of a human diction—The best parts of language the product of philosophers, not of clowns or shepherds—Poetry essentially ideal and generic—The language of Milton as much the language of real life, yea, incomparably more so than that of the cottager.

As far then as Mr. Wordsworth in his preface contended, and most ably contended, for a reformation in our poetic diction; as

[1] *Biographia Literaria* (1817), chap. XVII.

far as he has evinced the truth of passion, and the *dramatic* propriety of those figures and metaphors in the original poets,
which, stripped of their justifying reasons, and converted into
mere artifices of connection or ornament, constitute the characteristic falsity in the poetic style of the moderns; and as far as he
has, with equal acuteness and clearness, pointed out the process
by which this change was effected, and the resemblances between
that state into which the reader's mind is thrown by the pleasurable confusion of thought from an unaccustomed train of words
and images, and that state which is induced by the natural
language of impassioned feeling; he undertook a useful task,
and deserves all praise, both for the attempt and for the execution. The provocations to this remonstrance in behalf of truth
and nature were still of perpetual recurrence before and after
the publication of this preface. I cannot likewise but add that
the comparison of such poems of merit as have been given to
the public within the last ten or twelve years, with the majority
of those produced previously to the appearance of that preface,
leave no doubt on my mind, that Mr. Wordsworth is fully
justified in believing his efforts to have been by no means inef-
fectual. Not only in the verses of those who have professed their
admiration of his genius, but even of those who have distinguished
themselves by hostility to his theory, and depreciation of his
writings, are the impressions of his principles plainly visible. It
is possible that with these principles others may have been
blended which are not equally evident; and some which are
unsteady and subvertible from the narrowness or imperfection
of their basis. But it is more than possible that these errors of
defect or exaggeration, by kindling and feeding the controversy,
may have conduced not only to the wider propagation of the
accompanying truths, but that, by their frequent presentation
to the mind in an excited state, they may have won for them a
more permanent and practical result. A man will borrow a
part from his opponent the more easily if he feels himself
justified in continuing to reject a part. While there remain
important points in which he can still feel himself in the right,
in which he still finds firm footing for continued resistance, he
will gradually adopt those opinions which were the least remote
from his own convictions, as not less congruous with his own
theory than with that which he reprobates. In like manner with
a kind of instinctive prudence, he will abandon by little and

little his weakest posts, till at length he seems to forget that they had ever belonged to him, or affects to consider them at most as accidental and "petty annexments," the removal of which leaves the citadel unhurt and unendangered.

My own differences from certain supposed parts of Mr. Wordsworth's theory ground themselves on the assumption that his words had been rightly interpreted, as purporting that the proper diction for poetry in general consists altogether in a language taken, with due exceptions, from the mouths of men in real life, a language which actually constitutes the natural conversation of men under the influence of natural feelings. My objection is, first, that in any sense this rule is applicable only to certain classes of poetry; secondly, that even to these classes it is not applicable, except in such a sense as hath never by anyone (as far as I know or have read) been denied or doubted; and lastly, that as far as, and in that degree in which it is practicable, yet as a rule it is useless, if not injurious, and therefore either need not or ought not to be practiced. The poet informs his reader that he had generally chosen low and rustic life; but not *as* low and rustic, or in order to repeat that pleasure of doubtful moral effect which persons of elevated rank and of superior refinement oftentimes derive from a happy imitation of the rude, unpolished manners and discourse of their inferiors. For the pleasure so derived may be traced to three exciting causes. The first is the naturalness, in fact, of the things represented. The second is the apparent naturalness of the representation, as raised and qualified by an imperceptible infusion of the author's own knowledge and talent, which infusion does, indeed, constitute it an imitation as distinguished from a mere copy. The third cause may be found in the reader's conscious feeling of his superiority awakened by the contrast presented to him; even as for the same purpose the kings and great barons of yore retained sometimes actual clowns and fools, but more frequently shrewd and witty fellows in that character. These, however, were not Mr. Wordsworth's objects. *He* chose low and rustic life, "because in that condition the essential passions of the heart find a better soil, in which they can attain their maturity, are less under restraint, and speak a plainer and more emphatic language; because in that condition of life our elementary feelings coexist in a state of greater simplicity, and consequently may be more accurately contemplated, and more forcibly communicated; because the manners of rural life germinate from those elementary feelings, and, from the necessary character of rural occupations, are more easily comprehended, and are more durable; and lastly, because in that condition the passions of men are incorporated with the beautiful and permanent forms of nature." [2]

Now it is clear to me that in the most interesting of the poems, in which the author is more or less dramatic, as "The Brothers," "Michael," "Ruth," "The Mad Mother," and others, the persons introduced are by no means taken from low or rustic life in the common acceptation of those words; and it is not less clear that the sentiments and language, as far as they can be conceived to have been really transferred from the minds and conversation of such persons, are attributable to causes and circumstances not necessarily connected with "their occupations and abode." The thoughts, feelings, language, and manners of the shepherd farmers in the vales of Cumberland and Westmoreland, as far as they are actually adopted in those poems, may be accounted for from causes which will and do produce the same results in every state of life, whether in town or country. As the two principal I rank that INDEPENDENCE which raises a man above servitude or daily toil for the profit of others, yet not above the necessity of industry and a frugal simplicity of domestic life; and the accompanying unambitious, but solid and religious, EDUCATION, which has rendered few books familiar but the Bible and the liturgy or hymnbook. To this latter cause, indeed, which is so far accidental that it is the blessing of particular countries and a particular age, not the product of particular places or employments, the poet owes the show of probability, that his personages might really feel, think, and talk with any tolerable resemblance to his representation. It is an excellent remark of Dr. Henry More's that "a man of confined education, but of good parts, by constant reading of the Bible will naturally form a more winning and commanding rhetoric than those that are learned: the intermixture of tongues and of artificial phrases debasing *their* style." [3]

It is, moreover, to be considered that to the formation of healthy feelings and a reflecting mind, negations involve impediments not less formidable than sophistication and vicious intermixture. I am convinced that for the human soul to prosper

---

[2] See p. 201.   [3] *Enthusiasmus triumphatus* (1656), sect. 35.

in rustic life a certain vantage ground is prerequisite. It is not every man that is likely to be improved by a country life or by country labors. Education, or original sensibility, or both, must pre-exist, if the changes, forms, and incidents of nature are to prove a sufficient stimulant. And where these are not sufficient, the mind contracts and hardens by want of stimulants: and the man becomes selfish, sensual, gross, and hard-hearted. Let the management of the POOR LAWS in Liverpool, Manchester, or Bristol be compared with the ordinary dispensation of the poor rates in agricultural villages, where the farmers are the overseers and guardians of the poor. If my own experience have not been particularly unfortunate, as well as that of the many respectable country clergymen with whom I have conversed on the subject, the result would engender more than skepticism concerning the desirable influences of low and rustic life in and for itself. Whatever may be concluded on the other side, from the stronger local attachments and enterprising spirit of the Swiss and other mountaineers, applies to a particular mode of pastoral life, under forms of property that permit and beget manners truly republican, not to rustic life in general, or to the absence of artificial cultivation. On the contrary the mountaineers, whose manners have been so often eulogized, are in general better educated and greater readers than men of equal rank elsewhere. But where this is not the case, as among the peasantry of North Wales, the ancient mountains, with all their terrors and all their glories, are pictures to the blind, and music to the deaf.

I should not have entered so much into detail upon this passage, but here seems to be the point to which all the lines of difference converge as to their source and center. (I mean, as far as, and in whatever respect, my poetic creed *does* differ from the doctrines promulgated in this preface.) I adopt with full faith the principle of Aristotle that poetry, as poetry, is essentially ideal, that it avoids and excludes all accident,[4] that its apparent individualities of rank, character, or occupation must be representative of a class; and that the persons of poetry must be clothed with generic attributes, with the common attributes of the class: not with such as one gifted individual might possibly

---

[4]Aristotle also says (Butcher translation), "It is not the function of the poet to relate what has happened, but what may happen,—what is possible according to the law of probability or necessity."

possess, but such as from his situation it is most probable beforehand that he would possess. If my premises are right and my
deductions legitimate, it follows that there can be no poetic
medium between the swains of Theocritus and those of an
imaginary golden age.

The characters of the vicar and the shepherd-mariner in the
poem of "The Brothers," that of the shepherd of Green-head
Ghyll in the "Michael," have all the verisimilitude and representative quality that the purposes of poetry can require. They
are persons of a known and abiding class, and their manners and
sentiments the natural product of circumstances common to
the class. . . . On the other hand, in the poems which are
pitched at a lower note, as the "Harry Gill" and "The Idiot Boy,"
the feelings are those of human nature in general; though the poet
has judiciously laid the scene in the country in order to place himself in the vicinity of interesting images, without the necessity of
ascribing a sentimental perception of their beauty to the persons
of his drama. In "The Idiot Boy," indeed, the mother's character
is not so much a real and native product of a "situation where the
essential passions of the heart find a better soil, in which they can
attain their maturity and speak a plainer and more emphatic language," as it is an impersonation of an instinct abandoned by
judgment. Hence the two following charges seem to me not
wholly groundless: at least, they are the only plausible objections which I have heard to that fine poem. The one is, that
the author has not, in the poem itself, taken sufficient care to
preclude from the reader's fancy the disgusting images of ordinary morbid idiocy, which yet it was by no means his intention
to represent. He has even by the "burr, burr, burr," uncoun-
teracted by any preceding description of the boy's beauty,
assisted in recalling them. The other is, that the idiocy of the
boy is so evenly balanced by the folly of the mother, as to present
to the general reader rather a laughable burlesque on the blindness of anile dotage, than an analytic display of maternal affection in its ordinary workings.

In "The Thorn," the poet himself acknowledges in a note the
necessity of an introductory poem, in which he should have
portrayed the character of the person from whom the words of
the poem are supposed to proceed: a superstitious man mod-
erately imaginative, of slow faculties and deep feelings, "a
captain of a small trading vessel, for example, who, being past

the middle age of life, had retired upon an annuity, or small independent income, to some village or country town of which he was not a native, or in which he had not been accustomed to live. Such men having nothing to do become credulous and talkative from indolence." But in a poem, still more in a lyric poem—and the Nurse in Shakespeare's *Romeo and Juliet* alone prevents me from extending the remark even to dramatic poetry, if indeed even the Nurse can be deemed altogether a case in point—it is not possible to imitate truly a dull and garrulous discourser, without repeating the effects of dullness and garrulity. However this may be, I dare assert that the parts (and these form the far larger portion of the whole) which might as well or still better have proceeded from the poet's own imagination, and have been spoken in his own character, are those which have given, and which will continue to give, universal delight; . . . the five following stanzas, with the exception of the four admirable lines at the commencement of the fourteenth, are felt by many unprejudiced and unsophisticated hearts, as sudden and unpleasant sinkings from the height to which the poet had previously lifted them, and to which he again re-elevates both himself and his reader.

If then I am compelled to doubt the theory by which the choice of characters was to be directed, not only *a priori*, from grounds of reason, but both from the few instances in which the poet himself need be supposed to have been governed by it, and from the comparative inferiority of those instances; still more must I hesitate in my assent to the sentence which immediately follows the former citation; and which I can neither admit as particular fact, nor as general rule. "The language, too, of these men is adopted (purified indeed from what appear to be its real defects, from all lasting and rational causes of dislike or disgust) because such men hourly communicate with the best objects from which the best part of language is originally derived; and because, from their rank in society and the sameness and narrow circle of their intercourse, being less under the action of social vanity, they convey their feelings and notions in simple and unelaborated expressions." To this I reply: that a rustic's language, purified from all provincialism and grossness, and so far reconstructed as to be made consistent with the rules of grammar (which are in essence no other than the laws of universal logic, applied to psychological materials) will not differ from the language of any other man of common sense, however learned or refined he may be, except as far as the notions which the rustic has to convey are fewer and more indiscriminate. This will become still clearer if we add the consideration (equally important though less obvious) that the rustic, from the more imperfect development of his faculties and from the lower state of their cultivation, aims almost solely to convey insulated facts, either those of his scanty experience or his traditional belief; while the educated man chiefly seeks to discover and express those connections of things, or those relative bearings of fact to fact, from which some more or less general law is deducible. For facts are valuable to a wise man, chiefly as they lead to the discovery of the indwelling law, which is the true being of things, the sole solution of their modes of existence, and in the knowledge of which consists our dignity and our power.

As little can I agree with the assertion that from the objects with which the rustic hourly communicates the best part of language is formed. For first, if to communicate with an object implies such an acquaintance with it as renders it capable of being discriminately reflected on, the distinct knowledge of an uneducated rustic would furnish a very scanty vocabulary. The few things and modes of action requisite for his bodily conveniences would alone be individualized, while all the rest of nature would be expressed by a small number of confused general terms.   Secondly, I deny that the words and combinations of words derived from the objects with which the rustic is familiar, whether with distinct or confused knowledge, can be justly said to form the best part of language. It is more than probable that many classes of the brute creation possess discriminating sounds by which they can convey to each other notices of such objects as concern their food, shelter, or safety. Yet we hesitate to call the aggregate of such sounds a language, otherwise than metaphorically. The best part of human language, properly so called, is derived from reflection on the acts of the mind itself. It is formed by a voluntary appropriation of fixed symbols to internal acts, to processes and results of imagination, the greater part of which have no place in the consciousness of uneducated man; though in civilized society, by imitation and passive remembrance of what they hear from their religious instructors and other superiors, the most uneducated share in the harvest which they neither sowed nor reaped.

If the history of the phrases in hourly currency among our peasants were traced, a person not previously aware of the fact would be surprised at finding so large a number, which three or four centuries ago were the exclusive property of the universities and the schools, and at the commencement of the Reformation had been transferred from the school to the pulpit, and thus gradually passed into common life. The extreme difficulty, and often the impossibility, of finding words for the simplest moral and intellectual processes of the languages of uncivilized tribes has proved perhaps the weightiest obstacle to the progress of our most zealous and adroit missionaries. Yet these tribes are surrounded by the same nature as our peasants are, but in still more impressive forms; and they are, moreover, obliged to particularize many more of them. When, therefore, Mr. Wordsworth adds, "accordingly, such a language" (meaning, as before, the language of rustic life purified from provincialism) "arising out of repeated experience and regular feelings, is a more permanent, and a far more philosophical language, than that which is frequently substituted for it by poets, who think that they are conferring honor upon themselves and their art in proportion as they indulge in arbitrary and capricious habits of expression," it may be answered that the language which he has in view can be attributed to rustics with no greater right than the style of Hooker or Bacon to Tom Brown or Sir Roger L'Estrange. Doubtless, if what is peculiar to each were omitted in each, the result must needs be the same. Further, that the poet who uses an illogical diction or a style fitted to excite only the low and changeable pleasure of wonder by means of groundless novelty substitutes a language of folly and vanity, not for that of the rustic, but for that of good sense and natural feeling.

Here let me be permitted to remind the reader that the positions which I controvert are contained in the sentences—"a selection of the real language of men";—"the language of these men" (that is, men in low and rustic life) "I propose to myself to imitate, and, as far as is possible, to adopt the very language of men."—"Between the language of prose and that of metrical composition, there neither is, nor can be, any essential difference." It is against these exclusively that my opposition is directed.

I object, in the very first instance, to an equivocation in the use of the word "real." Every man's language varies, according to the extent of his knowledge, the activity of his faculties, and the depth or quickness of his feelings. Every man's language has, first, its individualities; secondly, the common properties of the class to which he belongs; and thirdly, words and phrases of universal use. The language of Hooker, Bacon, Bishop Taylor, and Burke differs from the common language of the learned class only by the superior number and novelty of the thoughts and relations which they had to convey. The language of Algernon Sidney [5] differs not at all from that which every well-educated gentleman would wish to write, and (with due allowances for the undeliberateness, and less connected train, of thinking natural and proper to conversation) such as he would wish to talk. Neither one nor the other differ half so much from the general language of cultivated society, as the language of Mr. Wordsworth's homeliest composition differs from that of a common peasant. For "real," therefore, we must substitute ordinary, or *lingua communis*. And this, we have proved, is no more to be found in the phraseology of low and rustic life than in that of any other class. Omit the peculiarities of each and the result of course must be common to all. And assuredly the omissions and changes to be made in the language of rustics, before it could be transferred to any species of poem, except the drama or other professed imitation, are at least as numerous and weighty as would be required in adapting to the same purpose the ordinary language of tradesmen and manufacturers. Not to mention that the language so highly extolled by Mr. Wordsworth varies in every county, nay in every village, according to the accidental character of the clergyman, the existence or non-existence of schools; or even, perhaps, as the exciseman, publican, and barber happen to be, or not to be, zealous politicians, and readers of the weekly newspaper *pro bono publico*. Anterior to cultivation the *lingua communis* of every country, as Dante has well observed, exists everywhere in parts, and nowhere as a whole.[6]

Neither is the case rendered at all more tenable by the addition of the words, *in a state of excitement*. For the nature of a man's words, where he is strongly affected by joy, grief, or anger, must necessarily depend on the number and quality of the general

[5]*Discourses concerning Government* (1698).
[6]Probable reference to *De vulgari eloquentia*, I, xvi, "in qualibet redolet civitate, nec cubat in ulla."

truths, conceptions and images, and of the words expressing them, with which his mind had been previously stored. For the property of passion is not to create; but to set in increased activity. At least, whatever new connections of thoughts or images, or (which is equally, if not more than equally, the appropriate effect of strong excitement) whatever generalizations of truth or experience the heat of passion may produce, yet the terms of their conveyance must have pre-existed in his former conversations, and are only collected and crowded together by the unusual stimulation. It is indeed very possible to adopt in a poem the unmeaning repetitions, habitual phrases, and other blank counters which an unfurnished or confused understanding interposes at short intervals, in order to keep hold of his subject, which is still slipping from him, and to give him time for recollection; or, in mere aid of vacancy, as in the scanty companies of a country stage the same player pops backwards and forwards, in order to prevent the appearance of empty spaces, in the procession of *Macbeth* or *Henry VIII*. But what assistance to the poet, or ornament to the poem, these can supply, I am at a loss to conjecture. Nothing assuredly can differ either in origin or in mode more widely from the apparent tautologies of intense and turbulent feeling, in which the passion is greater and of longer endurance than to be exhausted or satisfied by a single representation of the image or incident exciting it. Such repetitions I admit to be a beauty of the highest kind, as illustrated by Mr. Wordsworth himself from the song of Deborah. *At her feet he bowed, he fell, he lay down: at her feet he bowed, he fell: where he bowed, there he fell down dead.*[7]

SHAKESPEARE'S JUDGMENT EQUAL TO HIS GENIUS[1]

1818

. . . Shakespeare appears, from his *Venus and Adonis* and *Rape of Lucrece* alone, apart from all his great works, to have possessed all the conditions of the true poet. Let me now proceed to destroy, as far as may be in my power, the popular notion that he was a great dramatist by mere instinct, that he

[7] Judges 5, 27.
[1] Coleridge lectured on Shakespeare during the years 1808, 1810–1813, and 1818. The manuscripts were published in 1837–1839 in *Literary Remains*. The selection reprinted here seems to have been written in 1818.

grew immortal in his own despite, and sank below men of second or third-rate power when he attempted aught beside the drama—even as bees construct their cells and manufacture their honey to admirable perfection, but would in vain attempt to build a nest. Now this mode of reconciling a compelled sense of inferiority with a feeling of pride began in a few pedants, who, having read that Sophocles was the great model of tragedy, and Aristotle the infallible dictator of its rules, and finding that the *Lear*, *Hamlet*, *Othello* and other masterpieces were neither in imitation of Sophocles, nor in obedience to Aristotle—and not having (with one or two exceptions) the courage to affirm that the delight which their country received from generation to generation, in defiance of the alterations of circumstances and habits, was wholly groundless—took upon them, as a happy medium and refuge, to talk of Shakespeare as a sort of beautiful *lusus naturae*, a delightful monster—wild, indeed, and without taste or judgment, but like the inspired idiots so much venerated in the East, uttering, amid the strangest follies, the sublimest truths. In nine places out of ten in which I find his awful name mentioned, it is with some epithet of "wild," "irregular," "pure child of nature," and so forth. If all this be true, we must submit to it; though to a thinking mind it cannot but be painful to find any excellence, merely human, thrown out of all human analogy, and thereby leaving us neither rules for imitation, nor motives to imitate;—but if false, it is a dangerous falsehood;—for it affords a refuge to secret self-conceit—enables a vain man at once to escape his reader's indignation by general swoln pane-gyrics, and merely by his *ipse dixit* to treat as contemptible what he has not intellect enough to comprehend, or soul to feel, without assigning any reason, or referring his opinion to any demonstrative principle;—thus leaving Shakespeare as a sort of Grand Lama, adored indeed, and his very excrements prized as relics, but with no authority or real influence. I grieve that every late voluminous edition of his works would enable me to substantiate the present charge with a variety of facts, one tenth of which would of themselves exhaust the time allotted to me. Every critic who has or has not made a collection of black letter books—in itself a useful and respectable amusement— puts on the seven-league boots of self-opinion, and strides at once from an illustrator into a supreme judge, and blind and deaf, fills his three-ounce phial at the waters of Niagara, and determines positively the greatness of the cataract to be neither more nor less than his three-ounce phial has been able to receive.

I think this a very serious subject. It is my earnest desire— my passionate endeavor—to enforce at various times and by various arguments and instances the close and reciprocal connection of just taste with pure morality. Without that acquaintance with the heart of man, or that docility and childlike gladness to be made acquainted with it, which those only can have who dare look at their own hearts—and that with a steadiness which religion only has the power of reconciling with sincere humility;—without this, and the modesty produced by it, I am deeply convinced that no man, however wide his erudition, however patient his antiquarian researches, can possibly understand, or be worthy of understanding, the writings of Shakespeare.

Assuredly that criticism of Shakespeare will alone be genial which is reverential. The Englishman who without reverence, a proud and affectionate reverence, can utter the name of William Shakespeare stands disqualified for the office of critic. He wants one at least of the very senses, the language of which he is to employ, and will discourse at best but as a blind man, while the whole harmonious creation of light and shade with all its subtle interchange of deepening and dissolving colors rises in silence to the silent *fiat* of the uprising Apollo. However inferior in ability I may be to some who have followed me, I own I am proud that I was the first in time who publicly demonstrated, to the full extent of the position, that the supposed irregularity and extravagances of Shakespeare were the mere dreams of a pedantry that arraigned the eagle because it had not the dimensions of the swan. In all the successive courses of lectures delivered by me, since my first attempt at the Royal Institution, it has been, and it still remains, my object to prove that in all points from the most important to the most minute, the judgment of Shakespeare is commensurate with his genius,— nay, that his genius reveals itself in his judgment, as in its most exalted form. And the more gladly do I recur to this subject from the clear conviction that to judge aright and with distinct consciousness of the grounds of our judgment concerning the works of Shakespeare implies the power and the means of judging rightly of all other works of intellect, those of abstract science alone excepted.

It is a painful truth that not only individuals, but even whole nations, are ofttimes so enslaved to the habits of their education and immediate circumstances as not to judge disinterestedly even on those subjects, the very pleasure arising from which consists in its disinterestedness, namely, on subjects of taste and polite literature. Instead of deciding concerning their own modes and customs by any rule of reason, nothing appears rational, becoming, or beautiful to them but what coincides with the peculiarities of their education. In this narrow circle individuals may attain to exquisite discrimination, as the French critics have done in their own literature; but a true critic can no more be such without placing himself on some central point from which he may command the whole—that is, some general rule which, founded in reason, or the faculties common to all men, must therefore apply to each—than an astronomer can explain the movements of the solar system without taking his stand in the sun. And let me remark that this will not tend to produce despotism, but, on the contrary, true tolerance in the critic. He will, indeed, require, as the spirit and substance of a work, something true in human nature itself, and independent of all circumstances; but, in the mode of applying it, he will estimate genius and judgment according to the felicity with which the imperishable soul of intellect shall have adapted itself to the age, the place, and the existing manners. The error he will expose lies in reversing this, and holding up the mere circumstances as perpetual, to the utter neglect of the power which can alone animate them. For art cannot exist without, or apart from, nature; and what has man of his own to give to his fellow man, but his own thoughts and feelings, and his observations, so far as they are modified by his own thoughts or feelings?

Let me, then, once more submit this question to minds emancipated alike from national, or party, or sectarian prejudice:— Are the plays of Shakespeare works of rude uncultivated genius, in which the splendor of the parts compensates, if aught can compensate, for the barbarous shapelessness and irregularity of the whole?—Or is the form equally admirable with the matter, and the judgment of the great poet not less deserving our wonder than his genius?—Or, again, to repeat the question in other words:—Is Shakespeare a great dramatic poet on account only of those beauties and excellences which he possesses in common with the ancients, but with diminished claims to our love and honor to the full extent of his differences from them?—Or are these very differences additional proofs of poetic wisdom, at once results and symbols of living power as contrasted with lifeless mechanism—or free and rival originality as contra-distinguished from servile imitation, or, more accurately, a blind copying of effects, instead of a true imitation of the essential principles?—Imagine not that I am about to oppose genius to rules. No! the comparative value of these rules is the very cause to be tried. The spirit of poetry, like all other living powers, must of necessity circumscribe itself by rules, were it only to unite power with beauty. It must embody in order to reveal itself; but a living body is of necessity an organized one; and what is organization but the connection of parts in and for a whole, so that each part is at once end and means?—This is no discovery of criticism;—it is a necessity of the human mind; and all nations have felt and obeyed it, in the invention of meter and measured sounds, as the vehicle and *involucrum*[2] of poetry—itself a fellow-growth from the same life, even as the bark is to the tree!

No work of true genius dares want its appropriate form,[3] neither indeed is there any danger of this. As it must not, so genius cannot, be lawless; for it is even this that constitutes it genius—the power of acting creatively under laws of its own origination. How then comes it that not only single *Zoili*,[4] but whole nations have combined in unhesitating condemnation of our great dramatist, as a sort of African nature, rich in beautiful monsters—as a wild heath where islands of fertility look the greener from the surrounding waste, where the loveliest plants now shine out among unsightly weeds, and now are choked by their parasitic growth, so intertwined that we cannot disentangle the weed without snapping the flower?—In this statement I have had no reference to the vulgar abuse of Voltaire,[5] save as far as his charges are coincident with the decisions of Shakespeare's own commentators and (so they would tell you) almost idola-trous admirers. The true ground of the mistake lies in the con-founding mechanical regularity with organic form.[6] The form is

---

[2]Envelope.

[3]See the discussion of form in Schlegel's *Lectures on Dramatic Art and Literature* (Black's translation, London, 1861), Lecture XII.

[4]Zoilus was a Greek critic who attacked Homer.

[5]See Voltaire's "Dissertation before Semiramis." For an account of the attack, consult T. R. Lounsbury, *Shakespeare and Voltaire* (1902).

[6]The German romantic theory of "organic form" profoundly affected Emerson, Thoreau, and Whitman. Cf. Fred W. Lorch, "Thoreau and the Organic Principle in Poetry," *Publications of the Modern Language Association*, LIII (1938), 286–302.

mechanic, when on any given material we impress a pre-determined form, not necessarily arising out of the properties of the material;—as when to a mass of wet clay we give whatever shape we wish it to retain when hardened. The organic form, on the other hand, is innate; it shapes, as it develops, itself from within, and the fullness of its development is one and the same with the perfection of its outward form. Such as the life is, such is the form. Nature, the prime genial artist, inexhaustible in diverse powers, is equally inexhaustible in forms;—each exterior is the physiognomy of the being within—its true image reflected and thrown out from the concave mirror;—and even such is the appropriate excellence of her chosen poet, of our own Shakespeare—himself a nature humanized, a genial under-standing directing self-consciously a power and an implicit wisdom deeper even than our consciousness.

I greatly dislike beauties and selections in general; but as proof positive of his unrivaled excellence, I should like to try Shakespeare by this criterion. Make out your amplest catalogue of all the human faculties, as reason or the moral law, the will, the feeling of the coincidence of the two (a feeling *sui generis et demonstratio demonstrationum*) called the conscience, the under-standing or prudence, wit, fancy, imagination, judgment—and then of the objects on which these are to be employed, as the beauties, the terrors, and the seeming caprices of nature, the realities and the capabilities—that is, the actual and the ideal—of the human mind, conceived as an individual or as a social being, as in innocence or in guilt, in a play paradise, or in a war field of temptation; and then compare with Shakespeare under each of these heads all or any of the writers in prose and verse that have ever lived! Who that is competent to judge doubts the result?—And ask your own hearts—ask your own common sense—to conceive the possibility of this man being— I say, not the "drunken savage"[7] of that wretched sciolist whom Frenchmen, to their shame, have honored before their elder and better worthies—but the anomalous, the wild, the irregular genius of our daily criticism! What! are we to have miracles in sport?—Or, I speak reverently, does God choose idiots by whom to convey divine truths to man?

[7]Allusion to Voltaire's attack on *Hamlet* in the Preface to *Mérope:* "One would suppose this work to be the fruit of the imagination of a drunken savage."

ARTHUR SCHOPENHAUER

(1788–1860)

oʘoooʘo

INDUCED BY HIS FATHER to enter a business which he hated, later forbidden by his widowed mother ever to enter her house, and, finally,
unable for many years to gain academic recognition for his philosophical works while his rivals taught at prominent universities, it is not surprising that the brilliant but proud and independent Schopenhauer
should have evolved a philosophy of pessimism. But these facts should
not blind us to his contribution. As Parker says, "Schopenhauer carried
the philosophy of romanticism further than it had been carried before,"[1]
and the student of modern "Naturalism" (which is but a sort of inverted
romanticism) will be able to discover the roots of this movement in
Schopenhauer's theory of the "Will."

The World as Will and Idea rests on Kant's "idealism," the doctrine
that everything is "idea." The external world can be experienced only
through man's consciousness; therefore, the world he knows is idea.
Kant did, however, believe that there was something—though unknow-
able—behind the subjective phenomena, and this something he called
"thing-in-itself." Schopenhauer simplified the Kantian system by iden-
tifying the noumenon behind appearances as Will. The Will was included in Kant's philosophy, but to him it was intelligent, whereas
Schopenhauer's Will was blind and irrational. This theory of the Will
closely resembles Darwin's *will to survive*, Bergson's *élan vital*, and the
Freudian *id*. The fact that the Will drives nature on blindly and unin-
telligently makes Schopenhauer's philosophy utterly pessimistic. Life
has no purpose whatsoever to him, and desire leads only to pain. Good
and pleasure are only the absence of pain, hence negative.

This philosophical background is essential for a full understanding of
Schopenhauer's theory of art and literature, for it explains the two
values which he finds in art: first, as knowledge which is enjoyed for
itself, and, second, as a means of escape from the pain of desire. In
contemplating a work of art, the spectator may forget himself to the
extent of being freed from the painful hunger of his will.[2] This asceti-

---

[1] DeWitt H. Parker, Introduction to *Schopenhauer Selections* (New York, 1928), p. xviii.
[2] Parker, *op. cit.*, p. xxv, attacks Schopenhauer's logic.

cism was partly the result of Schopenhauer's oriental studies, especially of the Upanishads, and partly of his own neurotic disposition—but it surprisingly anticipates the recent theories of Richards and Ogden.[3]

Schopenhauer also held, along with Goethe, Schelling, and others of his age, a theory of the universality of art. "Only the true works of art, which are drawn directly from nature and life, have eternal youth and enduring power, like nature and life themselves. For they belong to no age, but to humanity. . . ."[4]

BIBLIOGRAPHY

TEXT

Sämmtliche Werke, Hrsg. von Julius Frauenstädt. 6 vols. Leipzig, 1873–1874.

TRANSLATIONS

The Art of Literature, a series of essays, sel. and tr., with a preface by T. Bailey Saunders. London, 1891.
The Basis of Morality, tr. with an introduction and notes by Arthur Brodrick Bullock. London, 1903.
Essays, tr. by T. Bailey Saunders. New York, 1936.
Schopenhauer Selections, ed. by DeWitt H. Parker. New York, 1928. (Modern Student's Library.)
The World as Will and Idea, tr. by R. B. Haldane and J. Kemp. 3 vols. London, 1883–1886.

CRITICISM

Garwood, Helen, *Thomas Hardy, an Illustration of the Philosophy of Schopenhauer*. Philadelphia, 1911.
Hight, George Ainslie, *The Unity of Will, Studies of an Irrationalist*. London, 1906.
Kanovitch, Abraham, *The Will to Beauty;* being a continuation of the philosophies of Arthur Schopenhauer and Friedrich Nietzsche. New York, 1922.
Knox, Israel, *The Aesthetic Theories of Kant, Hegel, and Schopenhauer*. Columbia University Press, 1936.
Korten, Hertha, *Thomas Hardy's Napoleondichtung, The Dynasts:* ihre Abhängigkeit von Schopenhauer, ihr Einfluss auf Gerhart Hauptmann. Bonn am Rhine, 1919.

[3]C. K. Ogden, I. A. Richards, and James Wood, *Foundations of Aesthetics* (London, 1922).
[4]*World as Will and Idea*, sect. 50. Cf. also p. 245, below, the superiority of literature over history, the particular *vs.* universal.

Krauss, Ingrid, *Studien über Schopenhauer und den Pessimismus in der deutchen Literatur des XIX. Jahrhunderts.* Bern, 1931.

Tengler, Richard, *Schopenhauer und die Romantik.* Berlin, 1923.

Tsanoff, R. A., *Schopenhauer's Criticism of Kant's Theory of Experience.* Cornell Studies in Philosophy, no. 9. New York, 1911.

——, "Aspects of Modern Pessimism," *Rice Institute Pamphlets,* no. 9, (1922), 185–295.

THE WORLD AS WILL AND IDEA (*selection*)[1]

1818

[Poetry]

[51] If now, with the exposition which has been given of art in general, we turn from plastic and pictorial art to poetry, we shall have no doubt that its aim also is the revelation of the Ideas, the grades of the objectification of will, and the communication of them to the hearer with the distinctness and vividness with which the poetical sense comprehends them. Ideas are essentially perceptible; if, therefore, in poetry only abstract conceptions are directly communicated through words, it is yet clearly the intention to make the hearer perceive the Ideas of life in the representatives of these conceptions, and this can only take place through the assistance of his own imagination. But in order to set the imagination to work for the accomplishment of this end, the abstract conceptions, which are the immediate material of poetry as of dry prose, must be so arranged that their spheres intersect each other in such a way that none of them can remain in its abstract universality; but, instead of it, a perceptible representative appears to the imagination; and this is always further modified by the words of the poet according to what his intention may be. As the chemist obtains solid precipitates by combining perfectly clear and transparent fluids, the poet understands how to precipitate, as it were, the concrete, the individual, the perceptible idea, out of the abstract and transparent universality of the concepts by the manner in which he combines them. For the Idea can only be known by perception; and knowledge of the Idea is the end of art. The skill of a master, in poetry as in chemistry, enables us always to obtain the precise precipitate we intended. This end is assisted by the numerous epithets in poetry, by means of which the

[1]Reprinted, by special permission, from *Schopenhauer Selections* (Charles Scribner's Sons, 1928).

universality of every concept is narrowed more and more till we reach the perceptible.

> Where gentle winds from the blue heavens sigh,
> There stand the myrtles still, the laurel high,

calls up before the imagination by means of a few concepts the whole delight of a southern clime.

Rhythm and rhyme are quite peculiar aids to poetry. I can give no other explanation of their incredibly powerful effect than that our faculties of perception have received from time, to which they are essentially bound, some quality on account of which we inwardly follow, and, as it were, consent to each regularly recurring sound. In this way rhythm and rhyme are partly a means of holding our attention, because we willingly follow the poem read, and partly they produce in us a blind consent to what is read prior to any judgment, and this gives the poem a certain emphatic power of convincing independent of all reasons.

From the general nature of the material, that is, the concepts, which poetry uses to communicate the Ideas, the extent of its province is very great. The whole of nature, the Ideas of all grades, can be represented by means of it, for it proceeds according to the Idea it has to impart, so that its representations are sometimes descriptive, sometimes narrative, and sometimes directly dramatic. If, in the representation of the lower grades of the objectivity of will, plastic and pictorial art generally surpass it, because lifeless nature, and even brute nature, reveals almost its whole being in a single well-chosen moment; man, on the contrary, so far as he does not express himself by the mere form and expression of his person, but through a series of actions and the accompanying thoughts and emotions, is the principal object of poetry, in which no other art can compete with it, for here the progress or movement which cannot be represented in plastic or pictorial art just suits its purpose.

The revelation of the Idea, which is the highest grade of the objectivity of will, the representation of man in the connected series of his efforts and actions, is thus the great problem of poetry. It is true that both experience and history teach us to know man; yet oftener men than man, i. e., they give us empirical notes of the behavior of men to each other, from which we may frame rules for our own conduct, oftener than they afford us deep glimpses of the inner nature of man. The latter function, however, is by no means entirely denied them; but as often as it is the nature of mankind itself that discloses itself to us in history or in our own experience, we have comprehended our experience, and the historian has comprehended history, with artistic eyes, poetically, i. e., according to the Idea, not the phenomenon, in its inner nature, not in its relations. Our own experience is the indispensable condition of understanding poetry as of understanding history; for it is, so to speak, the dictionary of the language that both speak. But history is related to poetry as portrait painting is related to historical painting; the one gives us the true in the individual, the other the true in the universal; the one has the truth of the phenomenon, and can therefore verify it from the phenomenal, the other has the truth of the Idea, which can be found in no particular phenomenon, but yet speaks to us from them all. The poet from deliberate choice represents significant characters in significant situations; the historian takes both as they come. Indeed, he must regard and select the circumstances and the persons, not with reference to their inward and true significance, which expresses the Idea, but according to the outward, apparent, and relatively important significance with regard to the connection and the consequences. He must consider nothing in and for itself in its essential character and expression, but must look at everything in its relations, in its connection, in its influence upon what follows, and especially upon its own age. Therefore he will not overlook an action of a king, though of little significance, and in itself quite common, because it has results and influence. And, on the other hand, actions of the highest significance of particular and very eminent individuals are not to be recorded by him if they have no consequences. For his treatment follows the principle of sufficient reason, and apprehends the phenomenon, of which this principle is the form. But the poet comprehends the Idea, the inner nature of man apart from all relations, outside all time, the adequate objectivity of the thing-in-itself, at its highest grade. Even in that method of treatment which is necessary for the historian, the inner nature and significance of the phenomena, the kernel of all these shells, can never be entirely lost. He who seeks for it, at any rate, may find it and recognize it. Yet that which is significant in itself, not in its relations, the real unfolding of the Idea, will be found far more accurately and distinctly in poetry than in history, and, therefore, however paradoxical it may sound, far more really genuine inner truth is to be attributed to poetry than to history. For the historian must accurately follow the particular event, according to life, as it develops itself in time in the manifold tangled chains of causes and effects. It is, however, impossible that he can have all the data for this; he cannot have seen all and discovered all. He is forsaken at every moment by the original of his picture, or a false one substitutes itself for it, and this so constantly that I think I may assume that in all history the false outweighs the true. The poet, on the contrary, has comprehended the Idea of man from some definite side which is to be represented; thus it is the nature of his own self that objectifies itself in it for him. His knowledge, as we explained above when speaking of sculpture, is half a priori; his ideal stands before his mind firm, distinct, brightly illuminated, and cannot forsake him; therefore he shows us, in the mirror of his mind, the Idea pure and distinct, and his delineation of it down to the minutest particular is true as life itself. The great ancient historians are, therefore, in those particulars in which their data fail them, for example, in the speeches of their heroes—poets; indeed their whole manner of handling their material approaches to the epic. But this gives their representations unity, and enables them to retain inner truth, even when outward truth was not accessible, or indeed was falsified. And as we compared history to portrait painting, in contradistinction to poetry, which corresponds to historical painting, we find that Winckelmann's maxim, that the portrait ought to be the ideal of the individual, was followed by the ancient historians, for they represent the individual in such a way as to bring out that side of the Idea of man which is expressed in it. Modern historians, on the contrary, with few exceptions, give us in general only "a dustbin and a lumber room, and at the most a chronicle of the principal political events." Therefore, whoever desires to know man in his inner nature, identical in all its phenomena and developments, to know him according to the Idea, will find that the works of the great, immortal poet present a far truer, more distinct picture than the historians can ever give. For even the best of the historians are, as poets, far from the first; and moreover their hands are tied. In this aspect the relation between the historian and the poet may be illustrated by the following comparison. The mere, pure historian, who works only according to data, is like a man who, without any knowledge of mathematics, has investigated the relations of certain figures which he has accidentally found, by measuring them; and the problem thus empirically solved is affected, of course, by all the errors of the drawn figure. The poet, on the other hand, is like the mathematician, who constructs these relations a priori in pure perception, and expresses them not as they actually are in the drawn figure, but as they are in the Idea, which the drawing is intended to render for the senses. Therefore Schiller says:

> What has never anywhere come to pass,
> That alone never grows old.

Indeed I must attribute greater value to biographies, and especially to autobiographies, in relation to the knowledge of the nature of man, than to history proper, at least as it is commonly handled. Partly because in the former the data can be collected more accurately and completely than in the latter; partly, because in history proper it is not so much men as nations and heroes that act, and the individuals who do appear seem so far off, surrounded with such pomp and circumstance, clothed in the stiff robes of state, or heavy, inflexible armor, that it is really hard through all this to recognize the human movements. On the other hand, the life of the individual when described with truth, in a narrow sphere, shows the conduct of men in all its forms and subtilties, the excellence, the virtue, and even holiness of a few, the perversity, meanness, and knavery of most, the dissolute profligacy of some. Besides, in the only aspect we are considering here, that of the inner significance of the phenomenal, it is quite the same whether the objects with which the action is concerned are, relatively considered, trifling or important, farmhouses or kingdoms: for all these things in themselves are without significance, and obtain it only in so far as the will is moved by them. The motive has significance only through its relation to the will, while the relation which it has as a thing to other things like itself does not concern us here. As a circle of one inch in diameter, and a circle of forty million miles in diameter, have precisely the same geometrical properties, so are the events and the history of a village and a kingdom essentially the same; and we may study and learn to know mankind as well in the one as in the other. It is also a mistake to suppose that autobiographies are full of deceit and dissimulation. On the contrary, lying (though always possible) is perhaps more difficult there than elsewhere. Dissimulation is easiest in mere conversation; indeed, though it may sound paradoxical, it is really more difficult even in a letter. For in the case of a letter the writer is alone, and looks into himself, and not out on the world, so that what is strange and distant does not easily approach him; and he has not the test of the impression made upon another before his eyes. But the receiver of the letter peruses it quietly in a mood unknown to the writer, reads it repeatedly and at different times, and thus easily finds out the concealed intention. We also get to know an author as a man most easily from his books, because all these circumstances act here still more strongly and permanently. And in an autobiography it is so difficult to dissimulate that perhaps there does not exist a single one that is not, as a whole, more true, than any history that ever was written. The man who writes his own life surveys it as a whole, the particular becomes small, the near becomes distant, the distant becomes near again, the motives that influenced him shrink; he seats himself at the confessional, and has done so of his own free will; the spirit of lying does not so easily take hold of him here, for there is also in every man an inclination to truth which has first to be overcome whenever he lies, and which here has taken up a specially strong position. The relation between biography and the history of nations may be made clear for perception by means of the following comparison: History shows us mankind as a view from a high mountain shows us nature; we see much at a time, wide stretches, great masses, but nothing is distinct nor recognizable in all the details of its own peculiar nature. On the other hand, the representation of the life of the individual shows us the man, as we see nature if we go about among her trees, plants, rocks, and waters. But in landscape painting in which the artist lets us look at nature with his eyes, the knowledge of the Ideas, and the condition of pure will-less knowing, which is demanded by these, is made much easier for us; and, in the same way, poetry is far superior both to history and biography in the representation of the Ideas which may be looked for in all three. For here also genius holds up to us the magic glass, in which all that is essential and significant appears before us collected and placed in the clearest light, and what is accidental and foreign is left out.

The representation of the Idea of man, which is the work of the poet, may be performed, so that what is represented is also the representer. This is the case in lyrical poetry, in songs, properly so called, in which the poet only perceives vividly his own state and describes it. Thus a certain subjectivity is essential to this kind of poetry from the nature of its object. Again, what is to be represented may be entirely different from him who represents it, as is the case in all other kinds of poetry, in which the poet more or less conceals himself behind his representation, and at last disappears altogether. In the ballad the poet still expresses to some extent his own state through the tone and proportion of the whole; therefore, though much more objective than the lyric, it has yet something subjective. This becomes less in the idyll, still less in the romantic poem, almost entirely disappears in the true epic, and even to the last vestige in the drama, which is the most objective and, in more than one respect, the completest and most difficult form of poetry. The lyrical form of poetry is consequently the easiest, and although art, as a whole, belongs only to the true man of genius, who so rarely appears, even a man who is not in general very remarkable may produce a beautiful song if, by actual strong excitement from without, some inspiration raises his mental powers; for all that is required for this is a lively perception of his own state at a moment of emotional excitement. This is proved by the existence of many single songs by individuals who have otherwise remained unknown; especially the German national songs, of which we have an exquisite collection in the *Wunderhorn;* and also by innumerable love songs and other songs of the people in all languages;—for to seize the mood of a moment and embody it in a song is the whole achievement of this kind of poetry. Yet in the lyrics of true poets the inner nature of all mankind is reflected, and all that millions of past, present, and future men have found, or will find, in the same situations, which are constantly recurring, finds its exact expression in them. And because these situations, by constant recurrence, are permanent as man himself and always call up the same sensations, the lyrical productions of genuine poets remain through thousands of years true, powerful, and fresh. But if the poet is always the universal man, then all that has ever moved a human heart, all that human nature in any situation has ever produced from itself, all that dwells and broods in any human breast—is his theme and his

material, and also all the rest of nature. Therefore the poet may
just as well sing of voluptuousness as of mysticism, be Anacreon[2]
or Angelus Silesius,[3] write tragedies or comedies, represent the
sublime or the common mind—according to humor or vocation. And no one has the right to prescribe to the poet what he
ought to be—noble and sublime, moral, pious, Christian, one
thing or another, still less to reproach him because he is one
thing and not another. He is the mirror of mankind, and brings
to its consciousness what it feels and does.

If we now consider more closely the nature of the lyric proper,
and select as examples exquisite and pure models, not those
that approach in any way to some other form of poetry, such
as the ballad, the elegy, the hymn, the epigram, etc., we
shall find that the peculiar nature of the lyric, in the narrowest
sense, is this: It is the subject of will, i.e., his own volition,
which the consciousness of the singer feels; often as a released
and satisfied desire (joy), but still oftener as a restricted desire
(grief), always as an emotion, a passion, a moved frame of mind.
Besides this, however, and along with it, by the sight of surrounding nature, the singer becomes conscious of himself as the
subject of pure, will-less knowing, whose unbroken blissful peace
now appears, in contrast to the stress of desire which is always
restricted and always needy. The feeling of this contrast, this
alternation, is really what the lyric as a whole expresses, and
what principally constitutes the lyrical state of mind. In it pure
knowing comes to us, as it were, to deliver us from desire and its
stain; we follow, but only for an instant; desire, the remembrance
of our own personal ends, tears us anew from peaceful contemplation; yet ever again the next beautiful surrounding in
which the pure will-less knowledge presents itself to us, allures
us away from desire. Therefore, in the lyric and the lyrical
mood, desire (the personal interest of the ends), and pure perception of the surroundings presented, are wonderfully mingled
with each other; connections between them are sought for and
imagined; the subjective disposition, the affection of the will,
imparts its own hue to the perceived surroundings, and con-
versely, the surroundings communicate the reflex of their color
to the will. The true lyric is the expression of the whole of this

[2] Greek lyric poet who sang chiefly of love and wine, born c. 563 B.C., died c. 478 B.C.
[3] Angelus Silesius (Johannes Scheffler, 1624–1677), a German philosophical poet,
author of *Cherubinischer Wandersmann* (1657).

mingled and divided state of mind. In order to make clear by examples this abstract analysis of a frame of mind that is very far from all abstraction, any of the immortal songs of Goethe may be taken. As specially adapted for this end I shall recommend only a few: "The Shepherd's Lament," "Welcome and Farewell," "To the Moon," "On the Lake," "Autumn"; also the songs in the *Wunderhorn* are excellent examples, particularly the one which begins, "O Bremen, I must now leave thee." As a comical and happy parody of the lyrical character a song of Voss strikes me as remarkable. It describes the feeling of a drunk plumber falling from a tower, who observes in passing that the clock on the tower is at half-past eleven, a remark which is quite foreign to his condition, and thus belongs to knowledge free from will. Whoever accepts the view that has been expressed of the lyrical frame of mind will also allow that it is the sensuous and poetical knowledge of the principle which I established in my essay on the Principle of Sufficient Reason, and have also referred to in this work, that the identity of the subject of knowing with that of willing may be called the miracle *par excellence*, so that the poetical effect of the lyric rests finally on the truth of that principle. In the course of life these two subjects, or, in popular language, head and heart, are ever becoming further apart; men are always separating more between their subjective feeling and their objective knowledge. In the child the two are still entirely blended together; it scarcely knows how to distinguish itself from its surroundings, it is at one with them. In the young man all perception chiefly affects feeling and mood, and even mingles with it, as Byron very beautifully expresses—

> I live not in myself, but I become
> Portion of that around me; and to me
> High mountains are a feeling . . .[4]

This is why the youth clings so closely to the perceptible and outward side of things; this is why he is only fit for lyrical poetry, and only the full-grown man is capable of the drama. The old man we can think of as at the most an epic poet, like Ossian, and Homer, for narration is characteristic of old age.

In the more objective kinds of poetry, especially in the romance, the epic, and the drama, the end, the revelation of the

[4]*Childe Harold's Pilgrimage*, iii, 680–682.

Idea of man, is principally attained by two means, by true and profound representation of significant characters, and by the invention of pregnant situations in which they disclose themselves. For as it is incumbent upon the chemist not only to exhibit the simple elements, pure and genuine, and their principal compounds, but also to expose them to the influence of such reagents as will clearly and strikingly bring out their peculiar qualities, so is it incumbent on the poet not only to present to us significant characters truly and faithfully as nature itself; but, in order that we may get to know them, he must place them in those situations in which their peculiar qualities will fully unfold themselves, and appear distinctly in sharp outline; situations which are therefore called significant. In real life, and in history, situations of this kind are rarely brought about by chance, and they stand alone, lost and concealed in the multitude of those which are insignificant. The complete significance of the situations ought to distinguish the romance, the epic, and the drama from real life as completely as the arrangement and selection of significant characters. In both, however, absolute truth is a necessary condition of their effect, and want of unity in the characters, contradiction either of themselves or of the nature of humanity in general, as well as impossibility, or very great improbability in the events, even in mere accessories, offend just as much in poetry as badly drawn figures, false perspective, or wrong lighting in painting. For both in poetry and painting we demand the faithful mirror of life, of man, of the world, only made more clear by the representation, and more significant by the arrangement. For there is only one end of all the arts, the representation of the Ideas; and their essential difference lies simply in the different grades of the objectification of will to which the Ideas that are to be represented belong. This also determines the material of the representation. Thus the arts which are most widely separated may yet throw light on each other. For example, in order to comprehend fully the Ideas of water it is not sufficient to see it in the quiet pond or in the evenly flowing stream; but these Ideas disclose themselves fully only when the water appears under all circumstances and exposed to all kinds of obstacles. The effects of the varied circumstances and obstacles give it the opportunity of fully exhibiting all its qualities. This is why we find it beautiful when it tumbles, rushes, and foams, or leaps into the air, or falls in a cataract of spray; or, lastly, if artificially confined, it springs up in a foun-tain. Thus showing itself different under different circum-stances, it yet always faithfully asserts its character; it is just as natural to it to sprout up as to lie in glassy stillness; it is as ready for the one as for the other as soon as the circumstances appear. Now, what the engineer achieves with the fluid matter of water, the architect achieves with the rigid matter of stone, and just this the epic or dramatic poet achieves with the Idea of man. Unfolding and rendering distinct the Idea expressing itself in the object of every art, the Idea of the will, which objectifies itself at each grade, is the common end of all the arts. The life of man, as it shows itself for the most part in the real world, is like the water, as it is generally seen in the pond and the river; but in the epic, the romance, the tragedy, selected characters are placed in those circumstances in which all their special qualities unfold themselves, the depths of the human heart are revealed, and become visible in extraordinary and very significant actions. Thus poetry objectifies the Idea of man, an Idea which has the peculiarity of expressing itself in highly individual characters.

Tragedy is to be regarded, and is recognized as the summit of poetical art, both on account of the greatness of its effect and the difficulty of its achievement. It is very significant for our whole system, and well worthy of observation, that the end of this highest poetical achievement is the representation of the terrible side of life. The unspeakable pain, the wail of humanity, the triumph of evil, the scornful mastery of chance, and the irretrievable fall of the just and innocent, is here presented to us; and in this lies a significant hint of the nature of the world and of existence. It is the strife of will with itself, which here, com-pletely unfolded at the highest grade of its objectivity, comes into fearful prominence. It becomes visible in the suffering of men, which is now introduced, partly through chance and error, which appear as the rulers of the world, personified as fate, on account of their insidiousness, which even reaches the appear-ance of design; partly it proceeds from man himself, through the self-mortifying efforts of a few, through the wickedness and perversity of most. It is one and the same will that lives and appears in them all, but whose phenomena fight against each other and destroy each other. In one individual it appears powerfully, in another more weakly; in one more subject to reason, and softened by the light of knowledge, in another less so, till at last, in some single case, this knowledge, purified and heightened by suffering itself, reaches the point at which the phenomenon, the veil of Maya, no longer deceives it. It sees through the form of the phenomenon, the principle of individuation. The egoism which rests on this perishes with it, so that now the *motives* that were so powerful before have lost their might, and instead of them the complete knowledge of the nature of the world, which has a *quieting* effect on the will, produces resignation, the surrender not merely of life, but of the very will to live. Thus we see in tragedies the noblest men, after long conflict and suffering, at last renounce the ends they have so keenly followed, and all the pleasures of life forever, or else freely and joyfully surrender life itself. So is it with the steadfast prince of Calderon; with Gretchen in *Faust;* with Hamlet, whom his friend Horatio would willingly follow, but is bade remain a while, and in this harsh world draw his breath in pain, to tell the story of Hamlet, and clear his memory; so also is it with the Maid of Orleans, the Bride of Messina; they all die purified by suffering, i.e., after the will to live which was formerly in them is dead. In the *Mohammed* of Voltaire this is actually expressed in the concluding words which the dying Palmira addresses to Mohammed: "The world is for tyrants: live!" On the other hand, the demand for so-called poetical justice rests on entire misconception of the nature of tragedy, and, indeed, of the nature of the world itself. It boldly appears in all its dullness in the criticisms which Dr. Samuel Johnson made on particular plays of Shakespeare, for he very naïvely laments its entire absence.[5] And its absence is certainly obvious, for in what has Ophelia, Desdemona, or Cordelia offended? But only the dull, optimistic, Protestant-rationalistic, or peculiarly Jewish view of life will make the demand for poetical justice, and find satisfaction in it. The true sense of tragedy is the deeper insight, that it is not his own individual sins that the hero atones for, but original sin, i.e., the crime of existence itself:

> Pues el delito mayor
> Del hombre es auer nacido;

> For the greatest crime of man
> Is that he was born;

as Calderon exactly expresses it.[6]

[5] See above, pp. 76–77.   [6] Segismundo in *Life Is a Dream*, ɪ, ii, 111–112.

I shall allow myself only one remark, more closely concerning the treatment of tragedy. The representation of a great misfortune is alone essential to tragedy. But the many different ways in which this is introduced by the poet may be brought under three specific conceptions. It may happen by means of a character of extraordinary wickedness, touching the utmost limits of possibility, who becomes the author of the misfortune; examples of this kind are Richard III, Iago in *Othello*, Shylock in *The Merchant of Venice*, Franz Moor, Phaedra of Euripides, Creon in the *Antigone*, etc., etc. Secondly, it may happen through blind fate, that is, chance and error; a true pattern of this kind is the *Oedipus Rex* of Sophocles, the *Trachiniae*[7] also; and in general most of the tragedies of the ancients belong to this class. Among modern tragedies, *Romeo and Juliet*, *Tancred* by Voltaire, and *The Bride of Messina*,[8] are examples. Lastly, the misfortune may be brought about by the mere position of the *dramatis personae* with regard to each other, through their relations; so that there is no need either for a tremendous error or an unheard-of accident, nor yet for a character whose wickedness reaches the limits of human possibility; but characters of ordinary morality, under circumstances such as often occur, are so situated with regard to each other that their position compels them, knowingly and with their eyes open, to do each other the greatest injury, without any one of them being entirely in the wrong. This last kind of tragedy seems to me far to surpass the other two, for it shows us the greatest misfortune, not as an exception, not as something occasioned by rare circumstances or monstrous characters, but as arising easily and of itself out of the actions and characters of men, indeed almost as essential to them, and thus brings it terribly near to us. In the other two kinds we may look on the prodigious fate and the horrible wickedness as terrible powers which certainly threaten us, but only from afar, which we may very well escape without taking refuge in renunciation. But in the last kind of tragedy we see that those powers which destroy happiness and life are such that their path to us also is open at every moment; we see the greatest sufferings brought about by entanglements that our fate might also partake of, and through actions that perhaps we also are

---

[7] The subject of Sophocles's tragedy, *The Trachinian Women*, or the *Trachiniae*, is the death of Hercules at Trachis.

[8] Play by Schiller, presented in 1803, combining classical and romantic elements.

capable of performing, and so could not complain of injustice; then shuddering we feel ourselves already in the midst of hell. This last kind of tragedy is also the most difficult of achievement; for the greatest effect has to be produced in it with the least use of means and causes of movement, merely through the position and distribution of the characters; therefore even in many of the best tragedies this difficulty is evaded. Yet one tragedy may be referred to as a perfect model of this kind, a tragedy which in other respects is far surpassed by more than one work of the same great master; it is *Clavigo*.[9] *Hamlet* belongs to a certain extent to this class, as far as the relation of Hamlet to Laertes and Ophelia is concerned. *Wallenstein* [10] has also this excellence. *Faust* belongs entirely to this class, if we regard the events connected with Gretchen and her brother as the principal action;[11] also the *Cid* of Corneille, only that it lacks the tragic conclusion, while on the contrary the analogous relation of Max to Thekla [12] has it.

[9]Tragedy by Goethe (1774).
[10]Perhaps Schiller's greatest drama, a trilogy, written and produced between 1791–1799.
[11]The fatal duel of Valentine, Gretchen's brother, with Faust and Gretchen's tragic death are events which occur in Part 1 of Goethe's masterpiece.
[12]Max Piccolomini and Thekla are the lovers in *Wallenstein*.

WILLIAM HAZLITT

(1778–1830)

o○○○○○

BORN A FEW YEARS before the French Revolution, William Hazlitt lived through the periods of English enthusiasm and reaction toward the revolutionary ideals, and as a consequence he became cynical about human nature, though he always supported liberal views and political reforms. He intended to enter the Unitarian ministry, but he found Hackney Theological College uncongenial, whereupon he retired to his father's parsonage, to read voraciously Bacon, Hobbes, Berkeley, Hume, Burke, Rousseau, and the major English novelists and essayists. In 1798, the year of the first edition of *Lyrical Ballads*, he met Coleridge and Wordsworth, a great experience which he recorded in "My First Acquaintance with Poets." At this period Hazlitt was mainly interested in philosophy, but in order to prepare himself for a useful vocation he apprenticed himself to his brother, John, who was famous throughout London for his miniatures. He studied and practiced painting for several years, but finally gave it up.

At about the age of forty, Hazlitt demonstrated his genius for the critical essay, first as a contributor to the *Edinburgh Review*. His bold and colorful style gained quick recognition. He was a master of allusion and paradox and a devotee of the romantic past.[1] Editors eagerly engaged his pen. But his democratic ideas caused the reactionary *Quarterly Review* and *Blackwood's Magazine* to stage against him one of the most slanderous and disgraceful attacks in literary history. The *Quarterly Review* condemned Hazlitt's first book, *The Round Table* (1817), as vulgar, silly, flat, ill-humored, and abusive.[2] So great was the influence of the *Quarterly* at that time that it ruined the sale of his *Characters of Shakespeare's Plays*, which was being widely read, by supposedly proving "that Mr. Hazlitt's knowledge of Shakespeare and the English language is on a par with the purity of his morals[3] and the depth of his understanding."[4] He was baited into vituperative retort and his disposition was probably irreparably damaged.

[1] Cf. "Why Distant Objects Please," in *Table Talk*. [2] *Quarterly Review*, April, 1817.
[3] Lockhart waged a long and bitter campaign against Hazlitt's moral character.
[4] *Quarterly Review*, January, 1818.

Despite Dr. Johnson's own impatience with judgments by rules,[5] the rationalistic-analytical method of the neoclassical age continued through much of the early nineteenth century, but the Longinian personal enthusiasm[6] was beginning to take hold. Hazlitt caught the spirit of A. W. Schlegel and of Coleridge, who probably influenced him, and wrote literary criticism with all the gusto and vigor of the best informal essayist. He described his aims as

> merely to read over a set of authors with the audience, as I would do with a friend, to point out a favorite passage, to explain an objection; or if a remark or a theory occurs, to state it in illustration of the subject, but neither to tire him nor puzzle myself with pedantical rules and pragmatical formulas of criticism that can do no good to anybody.[7]

This sounds dangerously like "impressionism," not to say "dilettantism," but Zeitlin thinks Hazlitt was merely expressing his "emancipation from arbitrary codes,"[8] and that the passage "was not equivalent to a declaration of anarchy." Rather he had "a catholic and many-sided sympathy." Deeply read but not pedantic or even academic, somewhat indifferent to technique though justly famous for his own style, Hazlitt was richly endowed with a poetic imagination and a natural critical faculty. As an interpreter of Shakespeare he is acknowledged by scholars and critics to be in a class with Schlegel, Coleridge, and Lamb.[9]

Four of Hazlitt's best critical works are *The Characters of Shakespeare's Plays* (1817); *Lectures on the English Poets* (1818), which contains the well-known exposition "On Poetry in General," a treatise comparable to Sidney's and Shelley's in its depth and illumination; *Lectures on the English Comic Writers* (1819), from which we reprint below the introductory essay, "On Wit and Humor"; and *Lectures on the Dramatic Literature of the Age of Elizabeth* (1821).

BIBLIOGRAPHY

TEXT

Characters of Shakespeare's Plays. New York, 1845.
Collected Works, ed. by A. R. Waller and Arnold Glover with an introduction by W. E. Henley. 12 vols. London, 1902–1904.

[5]"Life of Pope," in Johnson's *Lives* (Hill ed.), IV, 248.
[6]Cf. *On Literary Excellence*, Gilbert, *Literary Criticism: Plato to Dryden*, pp. 144–198.
[7]*Age of Elizabeth*, V, 301, in *Collected Works*.
[8]Jacob Zeitlin, *Hazlitt on English Literature* (New York, 1913), p. xli.
[9]See *ibid.*, p. lxxi, for a good summary of Hazlitt's influence on other critics, English and American.

Hazlitt on English Literature, an introduction to the appreciation of literature, ed. by Jacob Zeitlin. New York, 1913.

Lectures on the English Comic Writers. 3d. ed. Ed. by his son. New York, 1845.

Lectures on the English Poets, delivered at the Surrey institution. London, 1818.

BIOGRAPHY AND CRITICISM

Birrell, Augustine, *William Hazlitt.* London, 1902. (English Men of Letters.)

Chandler, Zilpha Emma, *An Analysis of the Stylistic Technique of Addison, Johnson, Hazlitt, and Pater.* University of Iowa Press, 1928.

Eckler, Eric A., "Materials for the Study of William Hazlitt as a Social Critic," [Abstract of thesis] University of Pittsburgh *Bulletin*, XXXIV (1937), 113–121.

Howe, P. P., *Life of William Hazlitt.* 2d. ed. New York, 1923.

Law, Marie Hamilton, *The English Familiar Essay in the Early Nineteenth Century;* the elements, old and new, which went into its making, as exemplified in the writings of Hunt, Hazlitt, and Lamb. (A Ph. D. thesis, privately printed.) Philadelphia, 1934.

Schneider, Elisabeth, *The Aesthetics of William Hazlitt;* a study of the philosophical basis of his criticism. University of Pennsylvania Press, 1933.

Zeitlin, Jacob, "William Hazlitt, an Appreciation of a Great Literary Journalist," *Saturday Review of Literature*, XI (1935), 417–418.

ON WIT AND HUMOR[1]

1819

Man is the only animal that laughs and weeps; for he is the only animal that is struck with the difference between what things are, and what they ought to be. We weep at what thwarts or exceeds our desires in serious matters: we laugh at what only disappoints our expectations in trifles. We shed tears from sympathy with real and necessary distress; as we burst into laughter from want of sympathy with that which is unreasonable and unnecessary, the absurdity of which provokes our spleen or mirth, rather than any serious reflections on it.

To explain the nature of laughter and tears is to account for the condition of human life; for it is in a manner compounded of these two! It is a tragedy or a comedy—sad or merry, as it happens. The crimes and misfortunes that are inseparable from

[1]Introduction to Lecture 1 of *English Comic Writers* (1819).

it shock and wound the mind when they once seize upon it, and when the pressure can no longer be borne, seek relief in tears: the follies and absurdities that men commit, or the odd accidents that befall them, afford us amusement from the very rejection of these false claims upon our sympathy and end in laughter. If everything that went wrong, if every vanity or weakness in another gave us a sensible pang, it would be hard indeed: but as long as the disagreeableness of the consequences of a sudden disaster is kept out of sight by the immediate oddity of the circumstances, and the absurdity or unaccountableness of a foolish action is the most striking thing in it, the ludicrous prevails over the pathetic, and we receive pleasure instead of pain from the farce of life which is played before us, and which discomposes our gravity as often as it fails to move our anger or our pity!

Tears may be considered as the natural and involuntary resource of the mind overcome by some sudden and violent emotion before it has had time to reconcile its feelings to the change of circumstances: while laughter may be defined to be the same sort of convulsive and involuntary movement, occasioned by mere surprise or contrast (in the absence of any more serious emotion), before it has time to reconcile its belief to contradictory appearances. If we hold a mask before our face and approach a child with this disguise on, it will at first, from the oddity and incongruity of the appearance, be inclined to laugh; if we go nearer to it, steadily, and without saying a word, it will begin to be alarmed and be half inclined to cry: if we suddenly take off the mask, it will recover from its fears and burst out a-laughing; but if, instead of presenting the old well-known countenance, we have concealed a satyr's head or some frightful caricature behind the first mask, the suddenness of the change will not in this case be a source of merriment to it, but will convert its surprise into an agony of consternation, and will make it scream out for help, even though it may be convinced that the whole is a trick at bottom.

The alternation of tears and laughter, in this little episode in common life, depends almost entirely on the greater or less degree of interest attached to the different changes of appearance. The mere suddenness of the transition, the mere balking our expectations and turning them abruptly into another channel, seems to give additional liveliness and gaiety to the animal spirits; but the instant the change is not only sudden, but threatens serious consequences or calls up the shape of danger, terror supersedes our disposition to mirth, and laughter gives place to tears. It is usual to play with infants, and make them laugh by clapping your hands suddenly before them; but, if you clap your hands too loud, or too near their sight, their countenances immediately change, and they hide them in the nurse's arms. Or suppose the same child grown up a little older comes to a place, expecting to meet a person it is particularly fond of, and does not find that person there, its countenance suddenly falls, its lips begin to quiver, its cheek turns pale, its eye glistens, and it vents its little sorrow (grown too big to be concealed) in a flood of tears. Again, if the child meets the same person unexpectedly after long absence, the same effect will be produced by an excess of joy, with different accompaniments; that is, the surprise and the emotion excited will make the blood come into his face, his eyes sparkle, his tongue falter or be mute; but in either case the tears will gush to his relief and lighten the pressure about his heart. On the other hand, if a child is playing at hide-and-seek or blindman's buff with persons it is ever so fond of, and either misses them where it had made sure of finding them or suddenly runs up against them where it had least expected it, the shock or additional impetus given to the imagination by the disappointment or the discovery, in a matter of this indifference, will only vent itself in a fit of laughter.[2] The transition here is not from one thing of importance to another, or from a state of indifference to a state of strong excitement, but merely from one impression to another that we did not at all expect and when we had expected just the contrary. The mind having been led to form a certain conclusion, and the result producing an immediate solution of continuity in the chain of our ideas, this alternate excitement and relaxation of the imagination, the object also striking upon the mind more vividly in its loose unsettled state, and before it has had time to recover and collect itself, causes that alternate excitement and relaxation, or irregular convulsive movement of the muscular and nervous system, which constitutes physical laughter. The *discontinuous* in our sensations produces a correspondent jar and discord in the

[2] A child that has hid itself out of the way in sport is under a great temptation to laugh at the unconsciousness of others as to its situation. A person concealed from assassins is in no danger of betraying his situation by laughing. (Hazlitt's note.)

frame. The steadiness of our faith and of our features begins to give way at the same time. We turn with an incredulous smile from a story that staggers our belief, and we are ready to split our sides with laughing at an extravagance that sets all common sense and serious concern at defiance.

To understand or define the ludicrous, we must first know what the serious is. Now the serious is the habitual stress which the mind lays upon the expectation of a given order of events, following one another with a certain regularity and weight of interest attached to them. When this stress is increased beyond its usual pitch of intensity so as to overstrain the feelings by the violent opposition of good to bad, or of objects to our desires, it becomes the pathetic or tragical. The ludicrous or comic is the unexpected loosening or relaxing this stress below its usual pitch of intensity, by such an abrupt transposition of the order of our ideas as, taking the mind unawares, throws it off its guard, startles it into a lively sense of pleasure, and leaves no time nor inclination for painful reflections.

The essence of the laughable then is the incongruous, the disconnecting one idea from another, or the jostling of one feeling against another. The first and most obvious cause of laughter is to be found in the simple succession of events, as in the sudden shifting of a disguise, or some unlooked-for accident, without any absurdity of character or situation. The accidental contradiction between our expectations and the event can hardly be said, however, to amount to the ludicrous: it is merely laughable. The ludicrous is where there is the same contradiction between the object and our expectations, heightened by some deformity or inconvenience, that is, by its being contrary to what is customary or desirable; as the ridiculous, which is the highest degree of the laughable, is that which is contrary not only to custom but to sense and reason, or is a voluntary departure from what we have a right to expect from those who are conscious of absurdity and propriety in words, looks, and actions.

Of these different kinds or degrees of the laughable, the first is the most shallow and short-lived; for the instant the immediate surprise of a thing's merely happening one way or another is over, there is nothing to throw us back upon our former expectation, and renew our wonder at the event a second time. The second sort, that is, the ludicrous arising out of the improbable or distressing, is more deep and lasting either because the painful catastrophe excites a greater curiosity or because the old impression, from its habitual hold on the imagination, still recurs mechanically so that it is longer before we can seriously make up our minds to the unaccountable deviation from it.   The third sort, or the ridiculous arising out of absurdity as well as improbability, that is, where the defect or weakness is of a man's own seeking, is the most refined of all, but not always so pleasant as the last because the same contempt and disapprobation which sharpens and subtilizes our sense of the impropriety, adds a severity to it inconsistent with perfect ease and enjoyment. This last species is properly the province of satire. The principle of contrast is, however, the same in all the stages, in the simply laughable, the ludicrous, the ridiculous; and the effect is only the more complete, the more durably and pointedly this principle operates.

To give some examples in these different kinds. We laugh, when children, at the sudden removing of a pasteboard mask; we laugh, when grown up, more gravely at the tearing off the mask of deceit. We laugh at absurdity; we laugh at deformity. We laugh at a bottlenose in a caricature; at a stuffed figure of an alderman in a pantomime; and at the tale of Slaukenbergius.[3] A giant standing by a dwarf makes a contemptible figure enough. Rosinante and Dapple[4] are laughable from contrast, as their masters from the same principle make two for a pair. We laugh at the dress of foreigners, and they at ours.   Three chimney sweepers, meeting three Chinese in Lincoln's-Inn Fields, they laughed at one another till they were ready to drop down. Country people laugh at a person because they never saw him before.   Anyone dressed in the height of the fashion, or quite out of it, is equally an object of ridicule. One rich source of the ludicrous is distress with which we cannot sympathize from its absurdity or insignificance. Women laugh at their lovers. We laugh at a damned author, in spite of our teeth, and though he may be our friend. "There is something in the misfortunes of our best friends that pleases us."[5] We laugh at people on the top of a stagecoach, or in it, if they seem in great extremity. It is hard to hinder children from laughing at a stammerer, at a Negro, at a drunken man, or even at a madman. We laugh at mischief. We laugh at what we do not believe. We say that an

---

[3] *Tristram Shandy*, Bk. IV.   [4] Respectively Don Quixote's mount and Sancho's ass.
[5] See La Rochefoucauld, *Reflections, or Sentences and Moral Maxims* (1665), XCIX.

argument, or an assertion that is very absurd, is quite ludicrous.
We laugh to show our satisfaction with ourselves, or our contempt for those about us, or to conceal our envy or our ignorance. We laugh at fools, and at those who pretend to be wise—
at extreme simplicity, awkwardness, hypocrisy, and affectation.
"They were talking of me," says Scrub, "for they laughed *con-
sumedly*." [6] Lord Foppington's insensibility to ridicule and airs of
ineffable self-conceit are no less admirable; [7] and Joseph Surface's [8]
cant maxims of morality, when once disarmed of their power to
do hurt, become sufficiently ludicrous. We laugh at that in
others which is a serious matter to ourselves; because our self-
love is stronger than our sympathy, sooner takes the alarm, and
instantly turns our heedless mirth into gravity, which only
enhances the jest to others. Someone is generally sure to be the
sufferer by a joke. What is sport to one, is death to another. It
is only very sensible or very honest people who laugh as freely
at their own absurdities as at those of their neighbors. In general
the contrary rule holds, and we only laugh at those misfortunes
in which we are spectators, not sharers. The injury, the disappointment, shame, and vexation that we feel put a stop to
our mirth; while the disasters that come home to us and excite
our repugnance and dismay are an amusing spectacle to others.
The greater resistance we make, and the greater the perplexity
into which we are thrown, the more lively and piquant is the
intellectual display of cross purposes to the bystanders. Our
humiliation is their triumph. We are occupied with the disagreeableness of the result instead of its oddity or unexpectedness. Others see only the conflict of motives and the sudden
alternation of events; we feel the pain as well, which more than
counterbalances the speculative entertainment we might receive
from the contemplation of our abstract situation.

You cannot force people to laugh; you cannot give a reason
why they should laugh; they must laugh of themselves, or not at
all. As we laugh from a spontaneous impulse, we laugh the
more at any restraint upon this impulse. We laugh at a thing
merely because we ought not. If we think we must not laugh,
this perverse impediment makes our temptation to laugh the
greater; for, by endeavoring to keep the obnoxious image out
of sight, it comes upon us more irresistibly and repeatedly; and

---

[6] Farquhar, *The Beaux' Stratagem*, III, i.   [7] Vanbrugh, *The Relapse*.
[8] The hypocritical brother in Sheridan's *School for Scandal*.

the inclination to indulge our mirth, the longer it is held back, collects its force and breaks out the more violently in peals of laughter. In like manner, anything we must not think of makes us laugh, by its coming upon us by stealth and unawares, and from the very efforts we make to exclude it. A secret, a loose word, a wanton jest, make people laugh. Aretino[9] laughed himself to death at hearing a lascivious story. Wickedness is often made a substitute for wit; and in most of our good old comedies, the intrigue of the plot and the double meaning of the dialogue go hand-in-hand, and keep up the ball with wonderful spirit between them. The consciousness, however it may arise, that there is something that we ought to look grave at, is almost always a signal for laughing outright: we can hardly keep our countenance at a sermon, a funeral, or a wedding. What an excellent old custom was that of throwing the stocking![10] What a deal of innocent mirth has been spoiled by the disuse of it! It is not an easy matter to preserve decorum in courts of justice. The smallest circumstance that interferes with the solemnity of the proceedings throws the whole place into an uproar of laughter. People at the point of death often say smart things. Sir Thomas More jested with his executioner.[11] Rabelais[12] and Wycherley both died with a bon mot in their mouths.

Misunderstandings (*mal-entendus*), where one person means one thing, and another is aiming at something else, are another great source of comic humor, on the same principle of ambiguity and contrast. There is a high-wrought instance of this in the dialogue between Aimwell and Gibbet, in the *Beaux' Stratagem*,[13] where Aimwell mistakes his companion for an officer in a marching regiment, and Gibbet takes it for granted that the gentleman is a highwayman. The alarm and consternation occasioned by someone saying to him in the course of common conversation, "I apprehend you," is the most ludicrous thing in that admirably natural and powerful performance, Mr. Emery's *Robert Tyke*.[14] Again, unconsciousness in the person

---

[9]Probably Pietro Aretino, improvident and profligate Italian blackmailer and satirist. While laughing, he fell from a stool and killed himself.

[10] On the wedding night, according to an old custom, the bride's stocking was thrown among the guests; the person hit by it was supposed to be the first one to be married. Cf. *OED*.

[11] See *Spectator*, no. 349.   [12] Cf. Bacon's *Apophthegms*, XLIII.

[13]Farquhar, *The Beaux' Stratagem* (1707), III, ii.

[14]In Thomas Morton's *School of Reform* (1805).

himself of what he is about, or of what others think of him, is also a great heightener of the sense of absurdity. It makes it come the fuller home upon us from his insensibility to it. His simplicity sets off the satire and gives it a finer edge. It is a more extreme case still where the person is aware of being the object of ridicule, and yet seems perfectly reconciled to it as a matter of course. So wit is often the more forcible and pointed for being dry and serious, for it then seems as if the speaker himself had no intention in it, and we were the first to find it out. Irony, as a species of wit, owes its force to the same principle. In such cases it is the contrast between the appearance and the reality, the suspense of belief and the seeming incongruity, that gives point to the ridicule, and makes it enter the deeper when the first impression is overcome. Excessive impudence, as in the *Liar*,[15] or excessive modesty, as in the hero of *She Stoops to Conquer;* or a mixture of the two, as in the *Busybody*,[16] are equally amusing. Lying is a species of wit and humor. To lay anything to a person's charge from which he is perfectly free shows spirit and invention; and the more incredible the effrontery, the greater is the joke.

There is nothing more powerfully humorous than what is called *keeping* in comic character, as we see it very finely exemplified in Sancho Panza and Don Quixote. The proverbial phlegm and the romantic gravity of these two celebrated persons may be regarded as the height of this kind of excellence. The deep feeling of character strengthens the sense of the ludicrous. Keeping in comic character is consistency in absurdity, a determined and laudable attachment to the incongruous and singular. The regularity completes the contradiction; for the number of instances of deviation from the right line, branching out in all directions, shows the inveteracy of the original bias to any extravagance or folly, the natural improbability, as it were, increasing every time with the multiplication of chances for a return to common sense, and in the end mounting up to an incredible and unaccountably ridiculous height, when we find our expectations as invariably baffled. The most curious problem of all is this truth of absurdity to itself. That reason and good sense should be consistent is not wonderful; but that caprice and whim and fantastical prejudice should be uniform and infallible in their results is the surprising thing. But while

[15]Samuel Foote, *The Liar* (1762).   [16]Susannah Centilivre, *The Busybody* (1709).

this characteristic clue to absurdity helps on the ridicule, it also softens and harmonizes its excesses; and the ludicrous is here blended with a certain beauty and decorum, from this very truth of habit and sentiment, or from the principle of similitude in dissimilitude. The devotion to nonsense, and enthusiasm about trifles, is highly affecting as a moral lesson; it is one of the striking weaknesses and greatest happinesses of our nature. That which excites so lively and lasting an interest in itself, even though it should not be wisdom, is not despicable in the sight of reason and humanity. We cannot suppress the smile on the lip; but the tear should also stand ready to start from the eye. The history of hobbyhorses is equally instructive and delightful; and, after the pair I have just alluded to, my Uncle Toby's [17] is one of the best and gentlest that "ever lifted leg!" [18] The inconveniences, odd accidents, falls, and bruises to which they expose their riders contribute their share to the amusement of the spectators; and the blows and wounds that the Knight of the Sorrowful Countenance received in his many perilous adventures have applied their healing influence to many a hurt mind. In what relates to the laughable, as it arises from unforeseen accidents or self-willed scrapes, the pain, the shame, the mortification, and utter helplessness of situation add to the joke, provided they are momentary or overwhelming only to the imagination of the sufferer. Malvolio's punishment and apprehensions are as comic, from our knowing that they are not real, [19] as Christopher Sly's drunken transformation and short-lived dream of happiness are for the like reason. [20] Parson Adams's fall into the tub at the 'Squire's, or his being discovered in bed with Mrs. Slipslop, [21] though pitiable, are laughable accidents; nor do we read with much gravity of the loss of his "Aeschylus," serious as it was to him at the time. A Scotch clergyman, as he was going to church, seeing a spruce conceited mechanic who was walking before him suddenly covered all over with dirt, either by falling into the kennel or by some other calamity befalling him, smiled and passed on; but afterwards seeing the same person, who had stopped to refit, seated directly facing him in the gallery, with a look of perfect satisfaction and com-

---

[17] Sterne, *Tristram Shandy*, Bk. I, chaps. XXIV–XXV.
[18] Burns's "Tam O'Shanter," l. 80.   [19] *Twelfth Night*, IV, ii.
[20] *The Taming of the Shrew*, Induction.
[21] See *Joseph Andrews*, Bk. III, chap. VII; Bk. IV, chap. XIV; and Bk. II, chap. XII.

posure as if nothing of the sort had happened to him, the idea of his late disaster and present self-complacency struck him so powerfully that, unable to resist the impulse, he flung himself back in the pulpit, and laughed till he could laugh no longer. I remember reading a story, in an odd number of the *European Magazine*, of an old gentleman who used to walk out every afternoon with a gold-headed cane in the fields opposite Baltimore House, which were then open, only with footpaths crossing them. He was frequently accosted by a beggar with a wooden leg, to whom he gave money, which only made him more importunate. One day, when he was more troublesome than usual, a well-dressed person happening to come up, and observing how saucy the fellow was, said to the gentleman, "Sir, if you will lend me your cane for a moment, I'll give him a good thrashing for his impertinence." The old gentleman, smiling at the proposal, handed him his cane, which the other no sooner was going to apply to the shoulders of the culprit, than he immediately whipped off his wooden leg and scampered off with great alacrity, and his chastiser after him as hard as he could go. The faster the one ran, the faster the other followed him, brandishing the cane, to the great astonishment of the gentleman who owned it, till having fairly crossed the fields, they suddenly turned a corner, and nothing more was seen of either of them.

In the way of mischievous adventure, and a wanton exhibition of ludicrous weakness in character, nothing is superior to the comic parts of the *Arabian Nights' Entertainments*. To take only the set of stories of the Little Hunchback who was choked with a bone, and the Barber of Bagdad and his seven brothers: there is that of the tailor who was persecuted by the miller's wife and who, after toiling all night in the mill, got nothing for his pains; of another who fell in love with a fine lady who pretended to return his passion and, inviting him to her house as the preliminary condition of her favor, had his eyebrows shaved, his clothes stripped off and, being turned loose into a winding gallery, he was to follow her and by overtaking obtain all his wishes, but after a turn or two stumbled on a trap door and fell plump into the street, to the great astonishment of the spectators and his own, shorn of his eyebrows, naked, and without a ray of hope left; that of the castle-building peddler who, in kicking his wife, the supposed daughter of an emperor, kicks down his basket of glass, the brittle foundation of his ideal wealth, his good fortune, and his arrogance; that, again, of the beggar who dined with the Barmecide, and feasted with him on the names of wines and dishes; and, last and best of all, the inimitable story of the Impertinent Barber himself, one of the seven, and worthy to be so—his pertinacious, incredible, teasing, deliberate, yet unmeaning folly, his wearing out the patience of the young gentleman whom he is sent for to shave, his preparations and his professions of speed, his taking out an astrolabe to measure the height of the sun while his razors are getting ready, his dancing the dance of Zimri and singing the song of Zamtout, his disappointing the young man of an assignation, following him to the place of rendezvous and alarming the master of the house in his anxiety for his safety, by which his unfortunate patron loses his hand in the affray: and this is felt as an awkward accident. The danger which the same loquacious person is afterwards in, of losing his head for want of saying who he was, because he would not forfeit his character of being "justly called the Silent," is a consummation of the jest, though, if it had really taken place, it would have been carrying the joke too far. There are a thousand instances of the same sort in the *Thousand and One Nights*, which are an inexhaustible mine of comic humor and invention, and which, from the manners of the East which they describe, carry the principle of callous indifference in a jest as far as it can go. The serious and marvelous stories in that work, which have been so much admired and so greedily read, appear to me monstrous and abortive fictions, like disjointed dreams dictated by a preternatural dread of arbitrary and despotic power, as the comic and familiar stories are rendered proportionably amusing and interesting from the same principle operating in a different direction and producing endless uncertainty and vicissitude and an heroic contempt for the untoward accidents and petty vexations of human life. It is the gaiety of despair, the mirth and laughter of a respite during pleasure from death. The strongest instances of effectual and harrowing imagination are in the story of Amine and her three sisters, whom she led by her side as a leash of hounds, and of the ghoul who nibbled grains of rice for her dinner, and preyed on human carcasses. In this condemnation of the serious parts of the *Arabian Nights*, I have nearly all the world, and in particular the author of the *Ancient Mariner*, against me, who must be allowed to be a judge of such matters, and who said, with a subtlety of philosophical conjecture which he alone possesses, "that if I did not like them, it was because I did not dream." On the other hand, I have Bishop Atterbury on my side, who, in a letter to Pope, fairly confesses that "he could not read them in his old age."

There is another source of comic humor which has been but little touched on or attended to by the critics—not the infliction of casual pain, but the pursuit of uncertain pleasure and idle gallantry. Half the business and gaiety of comedy turns upon this. Most of the adventures, difficulties, demurs, hairbreadth 'scapes, disguises, deceptions, blunders, disappointments, successes, excuses, all the dexterous maneuvers, artful innuendoes, assignations, billets-doux, *double entendres*, sly allusions, and elegant flattery have an eye to this—to the obtaining of those "favors secret, sweet, and precious,"[22] in which love and pleasure consist, and which when attained and the equivoque is at an end, the curtain drops and the play is over. All the attractions of a subject that can only be glanced at indirectly, that is a sort of forbidden ground to the imagination, except under severe restrictions which are constantly broken through; all the resources it supplies for intrigue and invention; the bashfulness of the clownish lover, his looks of alarm and petrified astonishment; the foppish affectation and easy confidence of the happy man; the dress, the airs, the languor, the scorn, and indifference of the fine lady; the bustle, pertness, loquaciousness, and tricks of the chambermaid; the impudence, lies, and roguery of the valet; the matchmaking and unmaking; the wisdom of the wise; the sayings of the witty, the folly of the fool; "the soldier's, scholar's, courtier's eye, tongue, sword, the glass of fashion and the mold of form,"[23] have all a view to this. It is the closet in *Bluebeard*. It is the life and soul of Wycherley, Congreve, Vanbrugh, and Farquhar's plays. It is the salt of comedy, without which it would be worthless and insipid. It makes Horner[24] decent, and Millamant[25] divine. It is the jest between Tattle and Miss Prue.[26] It is the bait with which Olivia, in the *Plain Dealer*, plays with honest Manly. It lurks at the bottom of the

---

[22] Burns, "Tam O'Shanter," l. 48.   [23] See *Hamlet*, III, i, 159; 161.
[24] Horner in Wycherley's *Country Wife*.
[25] Millamant in Congreve's *Way of the World*.
[26] Tattle and Miss Prue in Congreve's *Love for Love*.

catechism which Archer teaches Cherry,[27] and which she learns by heart. It gives the finishing grace to Mrs. Amlet's confession—"Though I'm old, I'm chaste."[28] Valentine and his Angelica[29] would be nothing without it; Miss Peggy[30] would not be worth a gallant; and Slender's "sweet Anne Page"[31] would be no more! "The age of comedy would be gone, and the glory of our playhouses extinguished forever."[32] Our old comedies would be invaluable, were it only for this, that they keep alive this sentiment, which still survives in all its fluttering grace and breathless palpitations on the stage.

Humor is the describing the ludicrous as it is in itself; wit is the exposing it, by comparing or contrasting it with something else. Humor is, as it were, the growth of nature and accident; wit is the product of art and fancy. Humor, as it is shown in books, is an imitation of the natural or acquired absurdities of mankind, or of the ludicrous in accident, situation, and character: wit is the illustrating and heightening the sense of that absurdity by some sudden and unexpected likeness or opposition of one thing to another, which sets off the quality we laugh at or despise in a still more contemptible or striking point of view. Wit, as distinguished from poetry, is the imagination or fancy inverted, and so applied to given objects as to make the little look less, the mean more light and worthless; or to divert our admiration or wean our affections from that which is lofty and impressive, instead of producing a more intense admiration and exalted passion, as poetry does. Wit may sometimes, indeed, be shown in compliments as well as satire, as in the common epigram—

> Accept a miracle, instead of wit:
> See two dull lines with Stanhope's pencil writ.[33]

But then the mode of paying it is playful and ironical, and contradicts itself in the very act of making its own performance an humble foil to another's. Wit hovers round the borders of

---

[27] Archer and Cherry in Farquhar's *Beaux' Stratagem*.
[28] Mrs. Amlet in Vanbrugh's *The Commander*, III, i.
[29] Valentine and Angelica in Congreve's *Love for Love*.
[30] Miss Peggy in Garrick's *Country Girl*.
[31] Slender and Anne Page, in *Merry Wives of Windsor*.
[32] Paraphrase from Burke's *Reflections on the French Revolution* (Paine ed.), p. 89.
[33] Spence, *Anecdotes* (1820), p. 378.

the light and trifling, whether in matters of pleasure or pain; for, as soon as it describes the serious seriously, it ceases to be wit, and passes into a different form. Wit is, in fact, the eloquence of indifference, or an ingenious and striking exposition of those evanescent and glancing impressions of objects which affect us more from surprise or contrast to the train of our ordinary and literal preconceptions, than from anything in the objects themselves exciting our necessary sympathy or lasting hatred. The favorite employment of wit is to add littleness to littleness, and heap contempt on insignificance by all the arts of petty and incessant warfare; or, if it ever affects to aggrandize and use the language of hyperbole, it is only to betray into derision by a fatal comparison, as in the mock-heroic; or, if it treats of serious passion, it must do it so as to lower the tone of intense and high-wrought sentiment by the introduction of burlesque and familiar circumstances. To give an instance or two. Butler, in his *Hudibras*, compares the change of night into day, to the change of color in a boiled lobster:

> The sun had long since, in the lap
> Of Thetis, taken out his nap;
> And, like a lobster boiled, the morn
> From black to red, began to turn:
> When Hudibras, whom thoughts and aching
> 'Twixt sleeping kept all night, and waking,
> Began to rub his drowsy eyes,
> And from his couch prepared to rise,
> Resolving to dispatch the deed
> He vowed to do with trusty speed.[34]

Compare this with the following stanzas in Spenser, treating of the same subject:

> By this the Northern waggoner had set
> His seven-fold team behind the stedfast star,
> That was in ocean waves yet never wet,
> But firm is fixed and sendeth light from far
> To all that in the wide deep wand'ring are:
> And cheerful Chanticleer with his note shrill,
> Had warned once that Phoebus' fiery car
> In haste was climbing up the eastern hill,
> Full envious that night so long his room did fill.[35]

[34]*Hudibras*, II, ii, 29–38.   [35]*The Faerie Queene*, I, ii, I.

At last the golden oriental gate
Of greatest heaven 'gan to open fair,
And Phoebus, fresh as bridegroom to his mate,
Came dancing forth, shaking his dewy hair,
And hurled his glist'ring beams through gloomy air:
Which when the wakeful elf perceived, straightway
He started up and did himself prepare
In sun-bright arms and battailous array,
For with that pagan proud he combat will that day.[36]

In this last passage, every image is brought forward that can give effect to our natural impression of the beauty, the splendor, and solemn grandeur of the rising sun; pleasure and power wait on every line and word; whereas, in the other, the only memorable thing is a grotesque and ludicrous illustration of the alteration which takes place from darkness to gorgeous light, and that brought from the lowest instance, and with associations that can only disturb and perplex the imagination in its conception of the real object it describes. There cannot be a more witty, and at the same time degrading comparison, than that in the same author, of the Bear turning round the polestar to a bear tied to a stake:

But now a sport more formidable
Had raked together village rabble;
'Twas an old way of recreating
Which learned butchers call bearbaiting,
A bold adventrous exercise
With ancient heroes in high prize,
For authors do affirm it came
From Isthmian or Nemaean game;
Others derive it from the Bear
That's fixed in northern hemisphere,
And round about his pole does make
A circle like a bear at stake,
That at the chain's end wheels about
And overturns the rabble rout.[37]

I need not multiply examples of this sort. Wit or ludicrous invention produces its effect oftenest by comparison, but not always. It frequently effects its purposes by unexpected and subtle distinctions. For instance, in the first kind, Mr. Sheridan's description of Mr. Addington's administration as the fag end of

[36] *Ibid.*, I, v, 2.   [37] *Hudibras*, I, i, 675–688.

Mr. Pitt's, who had remained so long on the treasury bench that, like Nicias in the fable, "he left the sitting part of the man behind him,"[38] is as fine an example of metaphorical wit as any on record. The same idea seems, however, to have been included in the old well-known nickname of the *Rump* Parliament. Almost as happy an instance of the other kind of wit, which consists in sudden retorts, in turns upon an idea, and diverting the train of your adversary's argument abruptly and adroitly into another channel, may be seen in the sarcastic reply of Porson,[39] who, hearing someone observe that "certain modern poets would be read and admired when Homer and Vergil were forgotten," made answer—"And not till then!" Sir Robert Walpole's definition of the gratitude of place-expectants, "that it is a lively sense of *future* favors,"[40] is no doubt wit, but it does not consist in the finding out any coincidence or likeness, but in suddenly transposing the order of time in the common account of this feeling, so as to make the professions of those who pretend to it correspond more with their practice. It is filling up a blank in the human heart with a word that explains its hollowness at once. Voltaire's saying, in answer to a stranger who was observing how tall his trees grew, "that they had nothing else to do,"[41] was a quaint mixture of wit and humor, making it out as if they really led a lazy, laborious life; but there was here neither allusion or metaphor. Again, that master stroke in *Hudibras* is sterling wit and profound satire, where speaking of certain religious hypocrites he says, that they

> Compound for sins they are inclined to,
> By damning those they have no mind to;[42]

but the wit consists in the truth of the character, and in the happy exposure of the ludicrous contradiction between the pretext and the practice; between their lenity towards their own vices, and their severity to those of others. The same principle of nice distinction must be allowed to prevail in those lines of the same author, where he is professing to expound the dreams of judicial astrology.

---

[38]Speech on the Definitive Treaty of Peace (May 14, 1794).

[39]Probably quoted from Byron's *English Bards and Scottish Revivals*.

[40]Hazlitt is the only authority for this quotation from Walpole. Cf. La Rochefoucauld, *Maxims*, CCXCVIII.

[41]Cf. *Works*, XII, 212.   [42]*Hudibras*, I, i, 215–216.

> There's but the twinkling of a star
> Betwixt a man of peace and war;
> A thief and justice, fool and knave,
> A huffing officer and a slave;
> A crafty lawyer and pickpocket,
> A great philosopher and a blockhead;
> A formal preacher and a player,
> A learned physician and manslayer.[43]

The finest piece of wit I know of, is in the lines of Pope on the Lord Mayor's show—

> Now night descending, the proud scene is o'er,
> But lives in Settle's numbers one day more.[44]

This is certainly as mortifying an inversion of the idea of poetical immortality as could be thought of; it fixes the *maximum* of littleness and insignificance: but it is not by likeness to anything else that it does this, but by literally taking the lowest possible duration of ephemeral reputation, marking it (as with a slider) on the scale of endless renown, and giving a rival credit for it as his loftiest praise. In a word, the shrewd separation or disentangling of ideas that seem the same, or where the secret contradiction is not sufficiently suspected and is of a ludicrous and whimsical nature, is wit just as much as the bringing together those that appear at first sight totally different. There is then no sufficient ground for admitting Mr. Locke's celebrated definition of wit, which he makes to consist in the finding out striking and unexpected resemblances in things so as to make pleasant pictures in the fancy, while judgment and reason, according to him, lie the clean contrary way, in separating and nicely distinguishing those wherein the smallest difference is to be found.[45]

---

[43]*Ibid.*, ii, iii, 957–964.   [44]*Dunciad*, i, 89–90.

[45]His words are: "If in having our ideas in the memory ready at hand consists quickness of parts, in this of having them unconfused and being able nicely to distinguish one thing from another where there is but the least difference consists in a great measure the exactness of judgment and clearness of reason which is to be observed in one man above another. And hence, perhaps, may be given some reason of that common observation that men who have a great deal of wit and prompt memories have not always the clearest judgment or deepest reason. For wit lying mostly in the assemblage of ideas and putting them together with quickness and variety, wherein can be found any resemblance or congruity, thereby to make up pleasant pictures and agreeable visions in the fancy; judgment, on the contrary, lies quite on the other side, in separating carefully one from another, ideas wherein can be found the least difference, thereby to avoid being misled by similitude and

On this definition Harris, the author of *Hermes*,[46] has very well observed that the demonstrating the equality of the three angles of a right-angled triangle to two right ones, would, upon the principle here stated, be a piece of wit instead of an act of the judgment or understanding, and Euclid's *Elements* a collection of epigrams. On the contrary it has appeared that the detection and exposure of difference, particularly where this implies nice and subtle observation, as in discriminating between pretense and practice, between appearance and reality, is common to wit and satire with judgment and reasoning, and certainly the comparing and connecting our ideas together is an essential part of reason and judgment, as well as of wit and fancy. Mere wit, as opposed to reason or argument, consists in striking out some casual and partial coincidence which has nothing to do, or at least implies no necessary connection with the nature of the things, which are forced into a seeming analogy by a play upon words, or some irrelevant conceit, as in puns, riddles, alliteration, etc. The jest, in all such cases, lies in the sort of mock-identity, or nominal resemblance, established by the intervention of the same words expressing different ideas, and countenancing as it were, by a fatality of language, the mischievous insinuation which the person who has the wit to take advantage of it wishes to convey. So when the disaffected French wits applied to the new order of the *Fleur du lys* the *double entendre* of *Compagnons d'Ulysse*, or companions of Ulysses, meaning the animal into which the fellow travelers of the hero of the *Odyssey*

by affinity to take one thing for another" "Essay," I, 143). This definition, such as it is, Mr. Locke took without acknowledgment from Hobbes, who says in his *Leviathan*, "This difference of quickness is caused by the difference of men's passions that love and dislike some one thing, some another, and therefore some men's thoughts run one way, some another, and are held to, and observe differently the things that pass through their imagination. And whereas in this succession of men's thoughts there is nothing to observe in the things they think on, but either in what they be like one another, or in what they be unlike, . . . those that observe their similitudes, in case they be such as are but rarely observed by others, are said to have a good wit, by which in this occasion is meant a good fancy. But they that observe their differences and dissimilitudes, which is called distinguishing and discerning and judging between thing and thing, in case such discerning be not easy are said to have a good judgment; and particularly in matter of conversation and business; wherein times, places, and persons are to be discerned, this virtue is called discretion. The former, that is, fancy, without the help of judgment, is not commended for a virtue; but the latter, which is judgment or discretion, is commended for itself, without the help of fancy" (*Leviathan* [1652], Pt. i, chap. viii).

[46]James Harris, *Hermes, or a Philosophical Inquiry concerning Universal Grammar* (1751).

were transformed, this was a shrewd and biting intimation of a
galling truth (if truth it were) by a fortuitous concourse of letters
of the alphabet, jumping in "a foregone conclusion," but there
was no proof of the thing, unless it was self-evident. And, indeed,
this may be considered as the best defense of the contested
maxim—That *ridicule is the test of truth;* viz., that it does not contain or attempt a formal proof of it, but owes its power of conviction to the bare suggestion of it, so that if the thing when once
hinted is not clear in itself, the satire fails of its effect and falls to
the ground. The sarcasm here glanced at the character of the
new or old French noblesse may not be well founded; but it is so
like truth, and "comes in such a questionable shape," backed
with the appearance of an identical proposition, that it would
require a long train of facts and labored arguments to do away
the impression, even if we were sure of the honesty and wisdom
of the person who undertook to refute it. A flippant jest is as
good a test of truth as a solid bribe; and there are serious sophistries,

> Soul-killing lies, and truths that work small good,[47]

as well as idle pleasantries. Of this we may be sure, that ridicule
fastens on the vulnerable points of a cause, and finds out the
weak sides of an argument; if those who resort to it sometimes
rely too much on its success, those who are chiefly annoyed by it
almost always are so with reason, and cannot be too much on
their guard against deserving it. Before we can laugh at a thing,
its absurdity must at least be open and palpable to common
apprehension. Ridicule is necessarily built on certain supposed
facts, whether true or false, and on their inconsistency with
certain acknowledged maxims, whether right or wrong. It is,
therefore, a fair test, if not of philosophical or abstract truth, at
least of what is truth according to public opinion and common
sense; for it can only expose to instantaneous contempt that
which is condemned by public opinion, and is hostile to the
common sense of mankind. Or to put it differently, it is the test
of the quantity of truth that there is in our favorite prejudices.
To show how nearly allied wit is thought to be to truth, it is not
unusual to say of any person—"Such a one is a man of sense, for
though he said nothing, he laughed in the right place." Alliteration comes in here under the head of a certain sort of verbal wit;

[47]Lamb, *John Woodvil*, ii, ii, 91.

or, by pointing the expression, sometimes points the sense. Mr. Grattan's wit or eloquence (I don't know by what name to call it) would be nothing without this accompaniment. Speaking of some ministers whom he did not like, he said, "Their only means of government are the guinea and the gallows." There can scarcely, it must be confessed, be a more effectual mode of political conversion than one of these applied to a man's friends, and the other to himself. The fine sarcasm of Junius on the effect of the supposed ingratitude of the Duke of Grafton at court—"The instance might be painful, but the principle would please"[48]—notwithstanding the profound insight into human nature it implies, would hardly pass for wit without the alliteration, as some poetry would hardly be acknowledged as such without the rhyme to clench it. A quotation or a hackneyed phrase dextrously turned or wrested to another purpose has often the effect of the liveliest wit. An idle fellow who had only fourpence left in the world, which had been put by to pay for the baking some meat for his dinner, went and laid it out to buy a new string for a guitar. An old acquaintance, on hearing this story, repeated those lines out of the "Allegro"—

> And ever against *eating* cares
> Lap me in soft Lydian airs.[49]

The reply of the author of the periodical paper called the *World* to a lady at church, who, seeing him look thoughtful, asked what he was thinking of—"The next World"—is a perversion of an established formula of language, something of the same kind. Rhymes are sometimes a species of wit, where there is an alternate combination and resolution or decomposition of the elements of sound, contrary to our usual division and classification of them in ordinary speech, not unlike the sudden separation and reunion of the component parts of the machinery in a pantomime. The author who excels infinitely the most in this way is the writer of *Hudibras*. He also excels in the invention of single words and names which have the effect of wit by sounding big, and meaning nothing:—"full of sound and fury, signifying nothing." But of the artifices of this author's burlesque style I shall have occasion to speak hereafter. It is not always easy to distinguish between the wit of words and that of things; "For thin partitions do their bounds divide." Some of the late

---

[48]Junius, Letter XLIX.   [49]"L'Allegro," 135–136.

Mr. Curran's [50] bons mots or *jeux d'esprit* might be said to owe their birth to this sort of equivocal generation, or were a happy mixture of verbal wit and a lively and picturesque fancy of legal acuteness in detecting the variable applications of words, and of a mind apt at perceiving the ludicrous in external objects. "Do you see anything ridiculous in this wig?" said one of his brother judges to him. "Nothing but the head" was the answer. Now here instantaneous advantage was taken of the slight technical ambiguity in the construction of language, and the matter-of-fact is flung into the scale as a thumping makeweight. After all, verbal and accidental strokes of wit, though the most surprising and laughable, are not the best and most lasting. That wit is the most refined and effectual which is founded on the detection of unexpected likeness or distinction in things, rather than in words. It is more severe and galling—that is, it is more unpardonable though less surprising, in proportion as the thought suggested is more complete and satisfactory from its being inherent in the nature of the things themselves. *Haeret lateri lethalis arundo.*[51] Truth makes the greatest libel; and it is that which barbs the darts of wit. The Duke of Buckingham's saying, "Laws are not, like women, the worse for being old," [52] is an instance of a harmless truism and the utmost malice of wit united. This is, perhaps, what has been meant by the distinction between true and false wit. Mr. Addison, indeed, goes so far as to make it the exclusive test of true wit that it will bear translation into another language[53]—that is to say, that it does not depend at all on the form of expression. But this is by no means the case. Swift would hardly have allowed of such a straitlaced theory to make havoc with his darling conundrums, though there is no one whose serious wit is more that of things, as opposed to a mere play either of words or fancy. I ought, I believe, to have noticed before, in speaking of the difference between wit and humor, that wit is often pretended absurdity, where the person overacts or exaggerates a certain part with a conscious design to expose it as if it were another person, as when Mandrake in the *Twin Rivals* says, "This glass is too big, carry it away, I'll drink out of the bottle." [54] On the contrary, when Sir

---

[50]Cf. "On the Conversation of Authors," in *The Plain Speaker.*
[51]*Aeneid*, IV, 73: "Fast in her side clings the deadly reed."
[52] Buckingham's Speech on the Dissolution of Parliament (1676).
[53]*Spectator*, no. 61.   [54]Farquhar, *Twin Rivals*, II, ii, 18–19.

Hugh Evans says, very innocently, " 'Od's plessed will, I will not be absence at the grace," [55] though there is here a great deal of humor, there is no wit. This kind of wit of the humorist, where the person makes a butt of himself and exhibits his own absurdities or foibles purposely in the most pointed and glaring lights, runs through the whole of the character of Falstaff and is, in truth, the principle on which it is founded. It is an irony directed against one's self. Wit is, in fact, a voluntary act of the mind or exercise of the invention, showing the absurd and ludicrous consciously, whether in ourselves or another. Cross-readings, where the blunders are designed, are wit; but, if anyone were to light upon them through ignorance or accident, they would be merely ludicrous.

It might be made an argument of the intrinsic superiority of poetry or imagination to wit, that the former does not admit of mere verbal combinations. Whenever they do occur, they are uniformly blemishes. It requires something more solid and substantial to raise admiration or passion. The general forms and aggregate masses of our ideas must be brought more into play to give weight and magnitude. Imagination may be said to be the finding out something similar in things generally alike, or with like feelings attached to them; while wit principally aims at finding out something that seems the same, or amounts to a momentary deception where you least expected it, namely, in things totally opposite. The reason why more slight and partial, or merely accidental and nominal resemblances serve the purposes of wit, and indeed characterize its essence as a distinct operation and faculty of the mind, is that the object of ludicrous poetry is naturally to let down and lessen; and it is easier to let down than to raise up; to weaken than to strengthen; to disconnect our sympathy from passion and power than to attach and rivet it to any object of grandeur or interest; to startle and shock our preconceptions by incongruous and equivocal combinations than to confirm, enforce, and expand them by powerful and lasting associations of ideas, or striking and true analogies. A slight cause is sufficient to produce a slight effect. To be indifferent or skeptical requires no effort; to be enthusiastic and in earnest requires a strong impulse and collective power. Wit and humor (comparatively speaking, or taking the extremes to judge of the gradations by) appeal to our indolence, our vanity,

[55] *Merry Wives of Windsor,* I, i, 276.

our weakness, and insensibility; serious and impassioned poetry appeals to our strength, our magnanimity, our virtue, and humanity. Anything is sufficient to heap contempt upon an object; even the bare suggestion of a mischievous allusion to what is improper dissolves the whole charm, and puts an end to our admiration of the sublime or beautiful. Reading the finest passage in Milton's *Paradise Lost* in a false tone will make it seem insipid and absurd. The caviling at, or invidiously pointing out, a few slips of the pen will embitter the pleasure or alter our opinion of a whole work and make us throw it down in disgust. The critics are aware of this vice and infirmity in our nature and play upon it with periodical success. The meanest weapons are strong enough for this kind of warfare, and the meanest hands can wield them. Spleen can subsist on any kind of food. The shadow of a doubt, the hint of an inconsistency, a word, a look, a syllable, will destroy our best-formed convictions. What puts this argument in as striking a point of view as anything is the nature of parody or burlesque, the secret of which lies merely in transposing or applying at a venture to anything, or to the lowest objects, that which is applicable only to certain given things or to the highest matters. "From the sublime to the ridiculous there is but one step."[56] The slightest want of unity of impression destroys the sublime; the detection of the smallest incongruity is an infallible ground to rest the ludicrous upon. But in serious poetry, which aims at riveting our affections, every blow must tell home. The missing a single time is fatal, and undoes the spell. We see how difficult it is to sustain a continued flight of impressive sentiment: how easy it must be then to travesty or burlesque it, to flounder into nonsense, and be witty by playing the fool. It is a common mistake, however, to suppose that parodies degrade, or imply a stigma on the subject; on the contrary, they in general imply something serious or sacred in the originals. Without this, they would be good for nothing, for the immediate contrast would be wanting, and with this they are sure to tell. The best parodies are, accordingly, the best and most striking things reversed. Witness the common travesties of Homer and Vergil. Mr. Canning's court parodies on Mr. Southey's popular odes [57] are also an instance in point

---

[56]Cf. Napoleon's "*Du sublime au ridicule il n'y a qu'un pas,*" the original of which is probably to be found in Paine's *Age of Reason*, Pt. II, note.

[57]In the *Anti-Jacobin* (1797-1798).

(I do not know which were the cleverest); and the best of the *Rejected Addresses* [58] is the parody on Crabbe, though I do not certainly think that Crabbe is the most ridiculous poet now living.

Lear and the Fool are the sublimest instance I know of passion and wit united, or of imagination unfolding the most tremendous sufferings, and of burlesque on passion playing with it, aiding and relieving its intensity by the most pointed, but familiar and indifferent illustrations of the same thing in different objects, and on a meaner scale. The Fool's reproaching Lear with "making his daughters his mothers," [59] his snatches of proverbs and old ballads, "The hedge sparrow fed the cuckoo so long that it had its head bit off by its young," and "Whoop jug, I know when the horse follows the cart," [60] are a running commentary of trite truisms, pointing out the extreme folly of the infatuated old monarch and in a manner reconciling us to its inevitable consequences.

Lastly, there is a wit of sense and observation, which consists in the acute illustration of good sense and practical wisdom, by means of some far-fetched conceit or quaint imagery. The matter is sense, but the form is wit. Thus the lines in Pope—

> 'Tis with our judgments as our watches, none
> Go just alike; yet each believes his own—[61]

are witty, rather than poetical; because the truth they convey is a mere dry observation on human life, without elevation or enthusiasm, and the illustration of it is of that quaint and familiar kind that is merely curious and fanciful. Cowley is an instance of the same kind in almost all his writings. Many of the jests and witticisms in the best comedies are moral aphorisms and rules for the conduct of life, sparkling with wit and fancy in the mode of expression. The ancient philosophers also abounded in the same kind of wit, in telling home truths in the most unexpected manner. In this sense Aesop was the greatest wit and moralist that ever lived. Ape and slave, he looked askance at human nature, and beheld its weaknesses and errors transferred to

[58]*Rejected Addresses*, written by James and Horace Smith. This parody by James Smith, published 1812.

[59]*King Lear*, I, iv, 188; text reads ". . . thou madest thy daughters thy mother."

[60]Correct quotation reads: "May not an ass know when the cart draws the horse? Whoop jug, I love thee" (*King Lear*, I, iv, 244–245).

[61]*Essay on Criticism*, ll. 9–10.

another species. Vice and virtue were to him as plain as any objects of sense. He saw in man a talking, absurd, obstinate, proud, angry animal; and clothed these abstractions with wings, or a beak, or tail, or claws, or long ears, as they appeared embodied in these hieroglyphics in the brute creation. His moral philosophy is natural history. He makes an ass bray wisdom, and a frog croak humanity. The store of moral truth, and the fund of invention in exhibiting it in eternal forms, palpable and intelligible, and delightful to children and grown persons, and to all ages and nations, are almost miraculous. The invention of a fable is to me the most enviable exertion of human genius: it is the discovering a truth to which there is no clue, and which, when once found out, can never be forgotten. I would rather have been the author of Aesop's *Fables*, than of Euclid's *Elements!* That popular entertainment, Punch and the Puppet Show, owes part of its irresistible and universal attraction to nearly the same principle of inspiring inanimate and mechanical agents with sense and consciousness. The drollery and wit of a piece of wood is doubly droll and farcical. Punch is not merry in himself, but "he is the cause of heartfelt mirth in other men." [62] The wires and pulleys that govern his motions are conductors to carry off the spleen, and all "that perilous stuff that weighs upon the heart." [63] If we see a number of people turning the corner of a street, ready to burst with secret satisfaction, and with their faces bathed in laughter, we know what is the matter—that they are just come from a puppet show. Who can see three little painted, patched-up figures, no bigger than one's thumb, strut, squeak and gibber, sing, dance, chatter, scold, knock one another about the head, give themselves airs of importance, and "imitate humanity most abominably," [64] without laughing immoderately? We overlook the farce and mummery of human life in little, and for nothing; and what is still better, it costs them who have to play in it nothing. We place the mirth, and glee, and triumph to our own account; and we know that the bangs and blows they have received go for nothing as soon as the showman puts them up in his box and marches off quietly with them, as jugglers of a less amusing description sometimes march off with the wrongs and rights of mankind in their pockets! —I have heard no bad judge of such matters say that "he liked a comedy better than a tragedy, a farce better than a comedy, a

[62]Cf. *Henry IV*, Pt. II, I, ii, 11.   [63]*Macbeth*, v, iii, 44.   [64]*Hamlet*, III, ii, 39.

pantomime better than a farce, but a puppet show best of all."
I look upon it, that he who invented puppet shows was a greater
benefactor to his species than he who invented operas!

I shall conclude this imperfect and desultory sketch of wit
and humor with Barrow's celebrated description of the same
subject. He says, "But first it may be demanded, what the thing
we speak of is, or what this facetiousness doth import; to which
question I might reply, as Democritus did to him that asked the
definition of a man—'*tis that which we all see and know;* and one
better apprehends what it is by acquaintance than I can inform
him by description. It is, indeed, a thing so versatile and multiform, appearing in so many shapes, so many postures, so many
garbs, so variously apprehended by several eyes and judgments,
that it seemeth no less hard to settle a clear and certain notice
thereof than to make a portrait of Proteus or to define the figure
of fleeting air. Sometimes it lieth in pat allusion to a known
story, or in seasonable application of a trivial saying, or in
forging an apposite tale; sometimes it playeth in words and
phrases, taking advantage from the ambiguity of their sense, or
the affinity of their sound; sometimes it is wrapped in a dress of
luminous expression; sometimes it lurketh under an odd similitude. Sometimes it is lodged in a sly question, in a smart answer,
in a quirkish reason, in a shrewd intimation, in cunningly diverting or cleverly restoring an objection; sometimes it is couched
in a bold scheme of speech, in a tart irony, in a lusty hyperbole,
in a startling metaphor, in a plausible reconciling of contradictions, or in acute nonsense; sometimes a scenical representation
of persons or things, a counterfeit speech, a mimical look or
gesture passeth for it; sometimes an affected simplicity, sometimes a presumptuous bluntness giveth it being; sometimes it
riseth only from a lucky hitting upon what is strange, sometimes
from a crafty wresting obvious matter to the purpose; often it
consisteth in one knows not what and springeth up one can
hardly tell how. Its ways are unaccountable and inexplicable,
being answerable to the numberless rovings of fancy and windings
of language. It is, in short, a manner of speaking out of the
simple and plain way (such as reason teacheth and knoweth
things by), which by a pretty surprising uncouthness in conceit
or expression doth affect and amuse the fancy, showing in it
some wonder and breathing some delight thereto. It raiseth
admiration, as signifying a nimble sagacity of apprehension, a

special felicity of invention, a vivacity of spirit, and reach of wit more than vulgar: it seeming to argue a rare quickness of parts that one can fetch in remote conceits applicable; a notable skill that he can dextrously accommodate them to a purpose before him, together with a lively briskness of humor, not apt to damp those sportful flashes of imagination. (Whence in Aristotle such persons are termed ἐπιδέξιοι, dextrous men and εὔτροποι, men of facile or versatile manners, who can easily turn themselves to all things, or turn all things to themselves.) It also procureth delight by gratifying curiosity with its rareness or semblance of difficulty (as monsters, not for their beauty but their rarity; as juggling tricks, not for their use but their abstruseness, are beheld with pleasure); by diverting the mind from its road of serious thoughts; by instilling gaiety and airiness of spirit; by provoking to such dispositions of spirit, in way of emulation or complaisance, and by seasoning matter, otherwise distasteful or insipid, with an unusual and thence grateful tang." [65]

I will only add by way of general caution that there is nothing more ridiculous than laughter without a cause, nor anything more troublesome than what are called laughing people. A professed laugher is as contemptible and tiresome a character as a professed wit: the one is always contriving something to laugh at, the other is always laughing at nothing. An excess of levity is as impertinent as an excess of gravity. A character of this sort is well personified by Spenser, in the Damsel of the Idle Lake—

—Who did assay
To laugh at shaking of the leavés light.[66]

Anyone must be mainly ignorant or thoughtless who is surprised at everything he sees, or wonderfully conceited who expects everything to conform to his standard of propriety. Clowns and idiots laugh on all occasions; and the common failing of wishing to be thought satirical often runs through whole families in country places, to the great annoyance of their neighbors. To be struck with incongruity in whatever comes before us does not argue great comprehension or refinement of perception, but rather a looseness and flippancy of mind and

[65]Barrow's *Works*, Sermon 14.
[66] Spenser, *Faerie Queene*, Bk. II, vi, 7:
Sometimes to do him laugh, she would assay
To laugh at shaking of the leaves light,

temper which prevents the individual from connecting any two ideas steadily or consistently together. It is owing to a natural crudity and precipitateness of the imagination which assimilates nothing properly to itself. People who are always laughing, at length laugh on the wrong side of their faces, for they cannot get others to laugh with them. In like manner, an affectation of wit by degrees hardens the heart and spoils good company and good manners. A perpetual succession of good things puts an end to common conversation. There is no answer to a jest, but another; and, even where the ball can be kept up in this way without ceasing, it tires the patience of the bystanders, and runs the speakers out of breath. Wit is the salt of conversation, not the food.

The four chief names for comic humor out of our own language are Aristophanes and Lucian among the ancients, Molière and Rabelais among the moderns. Of the two first I shall say, for I know, but little. I should have liked Aristophanes better if he had treated Socrates less scurvily, for he has treated him most scurvily both as to wit and argument. His *Plutus* and his *Birds* are striking instances, the one of dry humor, the other of airy fancy. Lucian is a writer who appears to deserve his full fame: he has the licentious and extravagant wit of Rabelais, but directed more uniformly to a purpose; and his comic productions are interspersed with beautiful and eloquent descriptions, full of sentiment, such as the exquisite account of the fable of the halcyon[67] put into the mouth of Socrates, and the heroic eulogy on Bacchus, which is conceived in the highest strain of glowing panegyric.

The two other authors I proposed to mention are modern, and French. Molière, however, in the spirit of his writings, is almost as much an English as a French author—quite a *barbare* in all in which he really excelled. He was unquestionably one of the greatest comic geniuses that ever lived: a man of infinite wit, gaiety, and invention—full of life, laughter, and whim. But it cannot be denied that his plays are in general mere farces, without scrupulous adherence to nature, refinement of character, or common probability. The plots of several of them could not be carried on for a moment without a perfect collusion between the parties to wink at contradictions, and act in defiance of the evidence of their senses. For instance, take the *Médecin malgré lui*

---

[67]Scholars do not any longer attribute this fable to Lucian.

(the "Mock Doctor"), in which a common woodcutter takes upon himself and is made successfully to support through a whole play, the character of a learned physician, without exciting the least suspicion; and yet, notwithstanding the absurdity of the plot, it is one of the most laughable and truly comic productions that can well be imagined. The rest of his lighter pieces, the *Bourgeois gentilhomme*, *Monsieur Pourceaugnac*, *George Dandin* (or *Barnaby Brittle*),[68] etc., are of the same description—gratuitous assumptions of character, and fanciful and outrageous caricatures of nature. He indulges at his peril in the utmost license of burlesque exaggeration, and gives a loose to the intoxication of his animal spirits. With respect to his two most labored comedies, the *Tartufe* and *Misanthrope*, I confess that I find them rather hard to get through: they have much of the improbability and extravagance of the others, united with the endless commonplace prosing of French declamation. What can exceed, for example, the absurdity of the Misanthrope, who leaves his mistress, after every proof of her attachment and constancy, for no other reason than that she will not submit to the *technical formality* of going to live with him in a wilderness? The characters, again, which Celimene gives of her female friends, near the opening of the play, are admirable satires (as good as Pope's characters of women), but not exactly in the spirit of comic dialogue. The strictures of Rousseau on this play, in his Letter to D'Alembert, are a fine specimen of the best philosophical criticism.[69] The same remarks apply in a greater degree to the *Tartufe*. The long speeches and reasonings in this play tire one almost to death: they may be very good logic, or rhetoric, or philosophy, or anything but comedy. If each of the parties had retained a special pleader to speak his sentiments, they could not have appeared more verbose or intricate. The improbability of the character of Orgon is wonderful. This play is in one point of view invaluable, as a lasting monument of the credulity of the French to all verbal professions of wisdom or virtue; and its existence can only be accounted for from that astonishing and tyrannical predominance which words exercise over things in the mind of every Frenchman. The *École des femmes*, from which Wycherley has borrowed his *Country Wife*, with the true spirit of original genius, is, in my judgment, the masterpiece of Molière.

[68] Play based on Molière's *George Dandin* (1791).
[69] "Lettre à M. d'Alembert," *Petits chefs-d'œuvre* (ed. Firmin-Didot), pp. 405 ff.

The set speeches in the original play, it is true, would not be borne on the English stage, nor indeed on the French, but that they are carried off by the verse. The *Critique de l'école des femmes*, the dialogue of which is prose, is written in a very different style. Among other things, this little piece contains an exquisite, and almost unanswerable defense of the superiority of comedy over tragedy.[70] Molière was to be excused for taking this side of the question.

A writer of some pretensions among ourselves has reproached the French with "an equal want of books and men."[71] There is a common French print, in which Molière is represented reading one of his plays in the presence of the celebrated Ninon de l'Enclos, to a circle of the wits and first men of his own time. Among these are the great Corneille; the tender, faultless Racine; Fontaine, the artless old man, unconscious of immortality; the accomplished St. Évremond; the Duke de la Rochefoucauld, the severe anatomizer of the human breast; Boileau, the flatterer of courts and judge of men! Were these men nothing? They have passed for men (and great ones) hitherto, and though the prejudice is an old one, I should hope it may still last our time.

Rabelais is another name that might have saved this unjust censure. The wise sayings and heroic deeds of Gargantua and Pantagruel ought not to be set down as nothing. I have already spoken my mind at large of this author;[72] but I cannot help thinking of him here, sitting in his easy chair, with an eye languid with excess of mirth, his lip quivering with a new-born conceit, and wiping his beard after a well-seasoned jest, with his pen held carelessly in his hand, his wine flagons, and his books of law, of school divinity, and physic, before him, which were his jest books, whence he drew endless stores of absurdity; laughing at the world and enjoying it by turns, and making the world laugh with him again, for the last three hundred years, at his teeming wit and its own prolific follies. Even to those who have never read his works, the name of Rabelais is a cordial to the spirits, and the mention of it cannot consist with gravity or spleen!

[70]*La Critique de l'école des femmes*, sc. vi.
[71]"Equally a want of books and men," Wordsworth, *Poems Dedicated to National Independence and Liberty*, p. xv.
[72]See *Lectures on the English Poets* (*Works*, ed. P. P. Howe), V, 111–113.

CHARLES LAMB

(1775–1834)

oᏅᎾ𝗈𝗈Ꮕᴑ

CHARLES LAMB WON IMMORTALITY as the author of *Essays of Elia*, which included such unsurpassable informal essays as his "Dissertation upon Roast Pig" and "Old China." Even the scholars do not always seem to remember that he wrote more about books and authors than any other subject, and second most about actors, a subject closely akin to literature. Also there is wide disagreement as to the value of his literary criticism. The late Professor Saintsbury was inclined to agree with Hazlitt that Lamb was capricious, dilettantish, and likely to "discern no beauties but what are concealed from superficial eyes, and overlook all that are obvious to the vulgar part of mankind." [1] But perhaps this is only a way of saying that Lamb never attempted systematic or exhaustive criticism. He regarded all his writings as the products of an amateur, and his criticisms are decidedly impromptu and private in nature. Nevertheless, there are undoubtedly many who agree with Mr. Blunden, Lamb's recent delightful biographer, when he declares that Lamb was "the most perceptive, bold and appropriate critic of Shakespeare and his contemporaries who had yet spoken; for not even Coleridge, lecturing in 1808 and again in 1810 and 1811, had presented the old drama with such fullness of reading and finished utterances." [2]

The candor, humanity, and humor of Lamb make it difficult to pigeonhole him. He hated sham and dullness of all kinds, whether in his friends or enemies, and on occasion his sincerity offended his friends Coleridge and Wordsworth—especially in his review of *Lyrical Ballads*. Though definitely belonging to the romantic movement, Lamb never renounced Pope, Prior, Shenstone, Swift, Defoe, and other great writers of their period. His greatest love was for the Elizabethans, though he was also fond of Burton and Sir Thomas Browne.

Lamb's theories of literature are implied rather than definitely stated. In general they are those of Wordsworth, Coleridge, Hazlitt, and Leigh Hunt, yet, as Blunden cautions, these critics did not bother to square

[1]George Saintsbury, *A History of Criticism* (New York, 1904), III, 238.
[2]Edmund Blunden, *Charles Lamb and His Contemporaries* (New York, 1933), p. 110.

their theories exactly with those of their neighbors, "but their main harmony was none the worse for that."[3] Lamb was concerned with the total impression; he was a personal and half-private judge. His method was chiefly that of catching the spirit of the authors under discussion and conveying it to his readers.

This sort of criticism, delightful as it is to read, is dangerous to comment upon. Take Lamb's charming essay "On Artificial Comedy," for example. The main thesis so offended the pompous Macaulay that he made a serious and almost impassioned reply,[4] and many a teacher has taken it seriously as an extenuation of the licentious Restoration comedy, but Brander Matthews has argued fairly convincingly that "he never meant seriously that the Restoration Comedies are sound and wholesome works, as refreshing in their austere morality as the Fathers." For "a humorist sees things as no one else does. He notes a tiny truth, and he likes it, and straightway he raises it to the nth, and, lo! it is a paradox."[5]

Brander Matthews also saw another paradox in Lamb's opinion "that the plays of Shakespeare are less calculated for performance on a stage than those of almost any other dramatist whatever," [6] and regarded it as simple-minded to take Lamb literally. "The light plays of Wycherley and of Farquhar did not offend Charles Lamb, and the wit delighted him. To him the comedies of Shakespeare lost somewhat of their range and elevation when seen across the footlights of the stage." [7] But to the average reader it will probably seem that Lamb was entirely serious in his firm belief that the great tragic heroes are too subtle to be completely recreated on the stage, and this belief was certainly taken seriously enough by his contemporaries and the later romantics who wrote their "closet dramas." But be that as it may, Lamb has remained for several generations one of the most exquisite revealers of hidden beauties and is at least one impressionistic critic who will undoubtedly continue to live.

It is believed by Mr. Blunden that many of Lamb's journalistic essays and occasional book reviews have never been collected, and no doubt only a small portion of his brilliant and clever literary and critical

---

[3]Blunden, op. cit., p. 95.

[4]See his "Comedy of the Restoration," which he wrote as a review of Leigh Hunt's edition of the Dramatic Works of Wycherley, Congreve, and Farquhar for the Edinburgh Review, July, 1841.

[5]The Dramatic Essays of Charles Lamb, ed. by Brander Matthews (New York, 1891), pp. 10–11.

[6]Lamb, "On the Tragedies of Shakespeare, Considered with Reference to Their Fitness for State Representation."   [7]Matthews, op. cit., p. 11.

opinions ever got recorded for posterity. But his published works, from *Specimens of the English Dramatic Poets* (1808) to the *Last Essays of Elia* (1833), are rich in observations on art and literature.

BIBLIOGRAPHY

TEXT

The Dramatic Essays of Charles Lamb, ed. with an introduction and notes by Brander Matthews. New York, 1891.

As Between Friends; Criticism of Themselves and One Another in the Letters of Coleridge, Wordsworth, and Lamb, ed. by Barbara Birkhoff. Harvard University Press, 1930.

Lamb's Criticism, a selection from the literary criticism of Charles Lamb, ed. with an introduction and short notes by E. M. W. Tillyard. London, 1923.

Letters, with a sketch of his life by T. N. Talfourd. 2 vols. London, 1837.

Letters of Charles Lamb, to Which Are Added Those of His Sister, Mary, ed. by E. V. Lucas. 3 vols. Yale University Press, 1935.

Life, Letters, and Writings of Charles Lamb, ed. by Percy Fitzgerald. 6 vols. London, 1875.

Selected Letters, ed. by G. T. Clapton. New York, 1925.

The Works of Charles and Mary Lamb, ed. by Thomas Hutchinson. 2 vols. Oxford University Press, 1924.

Works . . . ed. by William Macdonald. 12 vols. London, 1903.

Works of Charles and Mary Lamb, ed. by E. V. Lucas. 7 vols. London, 1903–1905.

BIOGRAPHY AND CRITICISM

Ainger, Alfred, *Charles Lamb*. New York, 1882. (English Men of Letters.)

Blunden, Edmund C., *Charles Lamb and His Contemporaries*. Cambridge University Press, 1933.

Derocquigny, Jules, *Charles Lamb, sa vie et son œuvre*. Lille, 1904.

Lucas, E. V., *Life of Charles Lamb*. 2 vols. 5th. ed. New York, 1921.

McDonald, Wilbert Lorne, "Charles Lamb, the Greatest of the Essayists," *Publications of the Modern Language Association*, XXXII (1917), 547–572.

May, James Lewis, *Charles Lamb, a Study*. London, 1934.

More, Paul Elmer, *Shelburne Essays*. Vols. II and IV. New York, 1904–1910.

Roe, F. W., *Charles Lamb and Shakespeare*. University of Wisconsin Press, 1916.

Williams, Orlo, *Charles Lamb*. London, 1934.

ON THE ARTIFICIAL COMEDY OF THE
LAST CENTURY (*selection*)[1]
1822

The artificial comedy, or comedy of manners, is quite extinct on our stage. Congreve and Farquhar show their heads once in seven years only, to be exploded and put down instantly. The times cannot bear them. Is it for a few wild speeches, an occasional license of dialogue? I think not altogether. The business of their dramatic characters will not stand the moral test. We screw everything up to that. Idle gallantry in a fiction, a dream, the passing pageant of an evening, startles us in the same way as the alarming indications of profligacy in a son or ward in real life should startle a parent or guardian. We have no such middle emotions as dramatic interests left. We see a stage libertine playing his loose pranks of two hours' duration, and of no after consequence, with the severe eyes which inspect real vices with their bearings upon two worlds. We are spectators to a plot or intrigue (not reducible in life to the point of strict morality), and take it all for truth. We substitute a real for a dramatic person, and judge him accordingly. We try him in our courts, from which there is no appeal to the *dramatis personae*, his peers. We have been spoiled with—not sentimental comedy—but a tyrant far more pernicious to our pleasures which has succeeded to it, the exclusive and all-devouring drama of common life; where the moral point is everything; where, instead of the fictitious half-believed personages of the stage (the phantoms of old comedy), we recognize ourselves, our brothers, aunts, kinsfolk, allies, patrons, enemies—the same as in life—with an interest in what is going on so hearty and substantial that we cannot afford our moral judgment, in its deepest and most vital results, to compromise or slumber for a moment. What is *there* transacting, by no modification is made to affect us in any other manner than the same events or characters would do in our relationships of life. We carry our fireside concerns to the theater with us. We do not go thither like our ancestors, to escape from the pressure of reality so much as to confirm our experience of it; to make assurance double, and take a bond of fate. We must live our toilsome lives twice over, as it was the mournful privilege

<hr>

[1]The second of three essays on "The Old Actors," published in the *London Magazine* (April, 1822)

of Ulysses to descend twice to the shades. All that neutral ground of character which stood between vice and virtue, or which in fact was indifferent to neither, where neither properly was called in question, that happy breathing-place from the burden of a perpetual moral questioning—the sanctuary and quiet Alsatia of hunted casuistry—is broken up and defranchised, as injurious to the interests of society. The privileges of the place are taken away by law. We dare not dally with images, or names, of wrong. We bark like foolish dogs at shadows. We dread infection from the scenic representation of disorder, and fear a painted pustule. In our anxiety that our morality should not take cold, we wrap it up in a great blanket surtout of precaution against the breeze and sunshine.

I confess for myself that (with no great delinquencies to answer for) I am glad for a season to take an airing beyond the diocese of the strict conscience—not to live always in the precincts of the law courts—but now and then, for a dream-while or so, to imagine a world with no meddling restrictions—to get into recesses, whither the hunter cannot follow me—

> —Secret shades
> Of woody Ida's inmost grove,
> While yet there was no fear of Jove.[2]

I come back to my cage and my restraint the fresher and more healthy for it. I wear my shackles more contentedly for having respired the breath of an imaginary freedom. I do not know how it is with others, but I feel the better always for the perusal of one of Congreve's—nay, why should I not add even of Wycherley's?—comedies. I am the gayer at least for it; and I could never connect those sports of a witty fancy in any shape with any result to be drawn from them to imitation in real life. They are a world of themselves almost as much as fairyland. Take one of their characters, male or female (with few exceptions they are alike), and place it in a modern play, and my virtuous indignation shall rise against the profligate wretch as warmly as the Catos of the pit could desire; because in a modern play I am to judge of the right and the wrong. The standard of *police* is the measure of *political justice*. The atmosphere will blight it; it cannot live here. It has got into a moral world, where it has no business, from which it must needs fall headlong; as dizzy and

---

[2]Milton, "Il Penseroso," ll. 28–30.

incapable of making a stand as a Swedenborgian bad spirit that
has wandered unawares into the sphere of one of his Good Men
or Angels.   But in its own world do we feel the creature is so
very bad?—The Fainalls, and the Mirabels,[3] the Dorimants[4]
and the Lady Touchwoods,[5] in their own sphere, do not offend
my moral sense; in fact, they do not appeal to it at all. They
seem engaged in their proper element. They break through no
laws of conscious restraints. They know of none. They have
got out of Christendom into the land—what shall I call it?—of
cuckoldry—the Utopia of gallantry, where pleasure is duty,
and the manners perfect freedom. It is altogether a speculative
scene of things, which has no reference whatever to the world
that is. No good person can be justly offended as a spectator,
because no good person suffers on the stage. Judged morally,
every character in these plays—the few exceptions only are
mistakes—is alike essentially vain and worthless. The great art
of Congreve is especially shown in this, that he has entirely
excluded from his scenes—some little generosities in the part of
Angelica[6] perhaps excepted—not only anything like a faultless
character, but any pretensions to goodness or good feelings
whatsoever. Whether he did this designedly, or instinctively,
the effect is as happy as the design (if design) was bold. I used
to wonder at the strange power which his *Way of the World* in
particular possesses of interesting you all along in the pursuits
of characters for whom you absolutely care nothing—for you
neither hate nor love his personages—and I think it is owing to
this very indifference for any that you endure the whole. He
has spread a privation of moral light, I will call it, rather than
by the ugly name of palpable darkness, over his creations; and
his shadows flit before you without distinction or preference.
Had he introduced a good character, a single gush of moral
feeling, a revulsion of the judgment to actual life and duties, the
impertinent Goshen would have only lighted to the discovery
of deformities, which now are none because we think them none.

Translated into real life, the characters of his and his friend
Wycherley's dramas, are profligates and strumpets—the business of their brief existence, the undivided pursuit of lawless

[3]Characters in Congreve's *Way of the World*.
[4]Character in Etherege's *Man of Mode*.
[5]Character in Congreve's *Double Dealer*.
[6]Character in Congreve's *Love for Love*.

gallantry. No other spring of action, or possible motive of conduct, is recognized; principles which, universally acted upon, must reduce this frame of things to a chaos. But we do them wrong in so translating them. No such effects are produced in *their* world. When we are among them, we are amongst a chaotic people. We are not to judge them by our usages. No reverend institutions are insulted by their proceedings—for they have none among them. No peace of families is violated— for no family ties exist among them. No purity of the marriage bed is stained—for none is supposed to have a being. No deep affections are disquieted, no holy wedlock bands are snapped asunder—for affection's depth and wedded faith are not of the growth of that soil. There is neither right nor wrong—gratitude or its opposite—claim or duty—paternity or sonship. Of what consequence is it to Virtue, or how is she at all concerned about it, whether Sir Simon or Dapperwit steal away Miss Martha; or who is the father of Lord Froth's or Sir Paul Pliant's children?[7]

The whole is a passing pageant, where we should sit as unconcerned at the issues, for life or death, as at the battle of the frogs and mice. But, like Don Quixote, we take part against the puppets, and quite as impertinently. We dare not contemplate an Atlantis,[8] a scheme, out of which our coxcombical moral sense is for a little transitory ease excluded. We have not the courage to imagine a state of things for which there is neither reward nor punishment. We cling to the painful necessities of shame and blame. We would indict our very dreams.

Amidst the mortifying circumstances attendant upon growing old, it is something to have seen the *School for Scandal* in its glory. This comedy grew out of Congreve and Wycherley, but gathered some allays of the sentimental comedy which followed theirs. It is impossible that it should be now *acted*, though it continues at long intervals to be announced in the bills. Its hero, when Palmer played it at least, was Joseph Surface. When I remember the gay boldness, the graceful solemn plausibility, the measured step, the insinuating voice—to express it in a word—the downright *acted* villainy of the part, so different from the pressure of conscious, actual wickedness—the hypocritical assumption of hypocrisy—which made Jack so deservedly a favorite in that character, I must needs conclude the present generation of playgoers more virtuous than myself, or more dense. I freely

[7]Characters in Wycherley's *Love in a Wood*.   [8]Bacon's utopianistic commonwealth.

confess that he divided the palm with me with his better brother; that, in fact, I liked him quite as well. Not but there are passages —like that, for instance where Joseph is made to refuse a pittance to a poor relation—incongruities which Sheridan was forced upon by the attempt to join the artificial with the sentimental comedy, either of which must destroy the other—but over these obstructions Jack's manner floated him so lightly that a refusal from him no more shocked you than the easy compliance of Charles gave you in reality any pleasure; you got over the paltry question as quickly as you could, to get back into the regions of pure comedy, where no cold moral reigns. The highly artificial manner of Palmer in this character counteracted every disagreeable impression which you might have received from the contrast, supposing them real, between the two brothers. You did not believe in Joseph with the same faith with which you believed in Charles. The latter was a pleasant reality, the former a no less pleasant poetical foil to it. The comedy, I have said, is incongruous—a mixture of Congreve with sentimental incompatibilities; the gaiety upon the whole is buoyant, but it required the consummate art of Palmer to reconcile the discordant elements.

A player with Jack's talents, if we had one now, would not dare to do the part in the same manner. He would instinctively avoid every turn which might tend to unrealize, and so to make the character fascinating. He must take his cue from his spectators, who would expect a bad man and good man as rigidly opposed to each other as the deathbeds of those geniuses are contrasted in the prints, which, I am sorry to say, have disappeared from the windows of my old friend Carrington Bowles, of St. Paul's Churchyard memory (an exhibition as venerable as the adjacent cathedral, and almost coeval) of the bad and good man at the hour of death; where the ghastly apprehensions of the former—and truly the grim phantom with his reality of a toasting fork is not to be despised—so finely contrast with the meek, complacent kissing of the rod, taking it in like honey and butter, with which the latter submits to the scythe of the gentle bleeder, Time, who wields his lancet with the apprehensive finger of a popular young ladies' surgeon. What flesh, like loving grass, would not covet to meet halfway the stroke of such a delicate mower?—John Palmer was twice an actor in this exquisite part. . . .

PERCY BYSSHE SHELLEY

(1792–1822)

oᒐooᒐo

SHELLEY's *Defense of Poetry* is recognized as one of the three or four greatest critical essays in the English language. Though it lacks the novelty of Wordsworth's *Preface*, or even of Young's *Conjectures*, its scope is as broad and its depth as profound as any criticism of its age. The central themes of this essay are the foundation and nature of poetry, the effects of poetry upon society (comprising two thirds of the total bulk), the inspiration of the poet, and the poet's influence for moral good. Some of the minor themes are almost equally important, such as poetry in relation to history, the poet's final rank (determined by a "jury of his peers impaneled from the selectest spirits of all time"), Romantic faith in the poet as prophet,[1] and the use of poetry in social and political revolution.

The immediate provocation of Shelley's *Defense* was Thomas Love Peacock's sneering attack on the uselessness of poetic art in *The Four Ages of Poetry;*[2] but, as Dr. White has pointed out, this essay is "thoroughly . . . a part of Shelley's life and thought,"[3] and it therefore reflects his literary sources and enunciates his whole philosophy of art and life. Shelley was reading the *Ion* when he received Peacock's *Four Ages,*[4] and it is obvious from internal evidence in the *Defense* that he had a copy of Sidney's *Defense of Poesie* near at hand when he wrote the reply.[5] Certainly his thought was influenced by both Plato and

---

[1]For interesting comments on this point, see Katherine Gilbert and Helmut Kuhn, *A History of Esthetics* (New York, 1939), p. 405.

[2]Edited with Introduction and notes by H. F. B. Brett-Smith, in Peacock's *Four Ages of Poetry*, Shelley's *Defence of Poetry*, and Browning's *Essay on Shelley* (Oxford, 1923).

[3]Newman Ivey White, *Shelley* (New York, 1940), II, 280.

[4]See letter to Peacock, February 15, 1821, printed by Roger Ingpen, ed., *The Letters of Percy Bysshe Shelley*, 2 vols. (London, 1914), II, 847.

[5]The *Defense* was written in 1821 and sent to Charles Ollier for publication, but it was not printed until 1840, when Mary Shelley brought out *Essays, Letters from Abroad, Translations and Fragments* (Edward Moxon, Dover Street, London). See Walter Peck, *Shelley; His Life and Work* (New York, 1927), II, 200. For the manuscript sources of the text see Lucas Verkoren, *A Study of Shelley's "Defense of Poetry"* (Amsterdam, [1937?]), 39–48; for the printed editions of the text, see *ibid.,* 48–63.

Sidney, and through Sidney he touched the stream of Renaissance tradition.[6] A number of Shelley's contemporaries had also written on poetic theory, and it is more than probable that he was familiar with their work.[7]

The Defense of Poetry begins with an analysis of the imagination of the poet. Poets are the possessors of "The quick Dreams, the passion winged ministers of thought,"[8] which bring them into close contact with the good. Imagination is "the principle of synthesis" which "has for its objects those forms which are common to universal nature and existence itself." Like all Romanticists, Shelley believes imagination to be superior to reason, but apparently he found difficulty in expressing his theory of the imagination, as the manuscript fragments published by Richard Garnett indicate;[9] and indeed he might, for a full explanation of his doctrine of imagination as "the power of association" would involve him in a theory of knowledge. Wordsworth's "powers requisite for the production of poetry"[10] Shelley attempted to blend in his one word, *imagination*, and to derive thereby a purer essence of the truth.[11]

It is the poet's imagination, then, through which he comes into contact with divine forces and is inspired to see and feel with greater power than ordinary men. This idea Shelley probably derived from Plato, for in a similar manner Socrates explains to Ion the function of the poet in society and the divine origin of his inspiration.[12] Even in attributing the source of his inspiration to "intellectual beauty"[13] Shelley indicates his debt to Plato, as likewise in his belief that the poet

[6]For a study of Shelley's indebtedness to Sidney, see A. S. Cook, ed., *Defense of Poetry* (Boston, 1890), Introduction and notes; the influence of Plato is stressed by Brett-Smith, *op. cit.;* and Verkoren, *op. cit.*, 67–108.

[7]Newman I. White, *The Best of Shelley* (New York, 1932), p. 512, lists Wordsworth, Coleridge, Hazlitt, Byron (letters to John Murray on Bowles and Pope).

[8]*Adonais*, IX.

[9]In one of these fragments, which Garnett thought formed "part of the original exordium of the 'Defence of Poetry' " imagination is called "mind combining the elements of thought itself. It has been termed the power of association; and on an accurate anatomy of the function of the mind, it would be difficult to assign any other origin to the mass of what we perceive and know than this power."

[10]These are: Observation and Description, Sensibility, Reflection, Imagination and Fancy, and Invention—Preface of 1815. This preface also contains a fuller description of Wordsworth's concept of the imagination.

[11]Coleridge seems to have had somewhat the same idea when he wrote: "I reflect with delight, how little a mere theory, though of his own workmanship, interferes with the processes of genuine imagination in a man of true poetic genius, who possesses, as Mr. Wordsworth, if ever man did, most assuredly does possess, 'The Vision and the Faculty divine' " (*Biographia Literaria*, chap. XVIII).

[12]*Ion*, pp. 533–534 (Jowett's translation). Cf. *Adonais*, LIV.

[13]Cf. "Hymn to Intellectual Beauty" and *Prometheus Unbound*, IV, 561–563, and compare Plato's *Symposium*, which Shelley translated.

sees more of the "deep truth" which is "imageless" than do other men.
The poet is the first chain linking mankind with the Divine. It is the
poet's mission, then, to stir into consciousness the imagination of mankind, thereby arousing man from a selfish consideration of himself.[14]
Thus does Shelley answer Peacock's accusation of the lack of utility
in poetry by asserting its high moral purpose—though he rejected
the Renaissance theory of didacticism.[15] And what nobler function
could the poet have than to awake and make free the mind and the
imagination of man?

BIBLIOGRAPHY

TEXT

An Apology for Poetry, with Browning's *Essay on Shelley*, ed. by L. Win-
stanley. Boston, 1911. (Belles Lettres edition.)
The Best of Shelley, ed. by Newman I. White, New York, 1932.
Complete Works in Verse and Prose; now first brought together with many
pieces not before published, ed. with preface, notes, and appendices
by H. Buxton Forman. 8 vols. London, 1876–1880; 1882.
A Defense of Poetry, ed. with introduction and notes by Albert S. Cook.
Boston, 1890.
Peacock's *Four Ages of Poetry*, Shelley's *Defence of Poetry*, Browning's
Essay on Shelley, ed. by H. F. B. Brett-Smith. Boston, 1921.
Shelley's Literary and Philosophical Criticism, ed. by John Shawcross. Lon-
don, 1909.

BIOGRAPHY AND CRITICISM

Campbell, Olwen Ward, *Shelley and the Unromantics.* New York, 1924.
Carpenter, Edward, and Barnefield, George, *The Psychology of the Poet
Shelley.* New York, 1925.

[14]In his Preface to the *Revolt of Islam* Shelley explains in some detail what he
hopes to accomplish. See also the fragment, "Speculations on Morals," in the
Complete Works of Percy Bysshe Shelley in Verse and Prose, ed. by H. Buxton Forman
(London, 1880), VI, 308.
[15]"The highest moral purpose aimed at in the highest species of the drama is the
teaching of the human heart, through its sympathies and antipathies, the knowledge
of itself; in proportion to the possession of which knowledge every human being is
wise, just, sincere, tolerant and kind" (Preface to *The Cenci*). In the Preface to
Prometheus Unbound Shelley calls "didactic poetry" his "abhorrence": "My purpose
has hitherto been simply to familiarize poetical readers with beautiful idealism of
moral excellence; aware that, until the mind can love, and admire, and trust, and
hope, and endure, reasoned principles of moral conduct are seeds cast upon the
highway of life which the unconscious passenger tramples into dust, although they
would bear the harvest of his happiness."

Croce, Benedetto, *The Defence of Poetry, Variations on the Theme of Shelley*, tr. by E. F. Carritt. The Philip Maurice Deneke Lecture delivered at Lady Margaret Hall, Oxford on the 17th of October 1933. Oxford, Clarendon Press, 1933.

Dodds, Mrs. Annie Edwards [Powell], *The Romantic Theory of Poetry, an Examination in the Light of Croce's Aesthetic*. New York, 1926.

Edmunds, Edward William, *Shelley and His Poetry*. New York, 1918.

Grabo, Carl Henry, *The Magic Plant: The Growth of Shelley's Thought*. University of North Carolina Press, [1936].

Peck, Walter Edwin, *Shelley, His Life and Work*. 2 vols. New York, 1927.

Solve, Melvin T., *Shelley: His Theory of Poetry*. University of Chicago Press, 1927.

Stokoe, Frank Woodyer, *German Influence in the English Romantic Period, 1788-1818*, with special reference to Scott, Shelley, and Byron. London, 1926.

Stovall, Floyd, *Desire and Restraint in Shelley*. Duke University Press, 1931.

Verkoren, Lucas. *A Study of Shelley's "Defense of Poetry"*; its origin, textual history, sources and significance. Amsterdam, [c. 1937].

White, Newman I., *Shelley*. 2 vols. New York, 1940.

A DEFENSE OF POETRY (*selections*)

1821

According to one mode of regarding those two classes of mental action which are called reason and imagination, the former may be considered as mind contemplating the relations borne by one thought to another, however produced; and the latter as mind acting upon those thoughts so as to color them with its own light, and composing from them, as from elements, other thoughts, each containing within itself the principle of its own integrity. The one is the τὸ ποιεῖν,[1] or the principle of synthesis, and has for its object those forms which are common to universal nature and existence itself; the other is the τὸ λογίζειν,[2] or principle of analysis, and its action regards the relations of things simply as relations; considering thoughts, not in their integral unity, but as the algebraical representations which conduct to certain general results. Reason is the enumeration of quantities already known; imagination is the perception of the value of those quantities, both separately and as a whole. Reason respects the differences, and imagination the similitudes of things. Reason is to the imagination as the instrument to

[1]Act of creating. [2]Act of reasoning; the form is grammatically incorrect.

the agent, as the body to the spirit, as the shadow to the substance.

Poetry, in a general sense, may be defined to be "the expression of the imagination"; and poetry is connate with the origin of man. Man is an instrument over which a series of external and internal impressions are driven, like the alternations of an ever-changing wind over an Aeolian lyre, which move it by their motion to ever-changing melody. But there is a principle within the human being, and perhaps within all sentient beings, which acts otherwise than in the lyre, and produces not melody alone, but harmony, by an internal adjustment of the sounds and motions thus excited to the impressions which excite them. It is as if the lyre could accommodate its chords to the motions of that which strikes them, in a determined proportion of sound; even as the musician can accommodate his voice to the sound of the lyre. A child at play by itself will express its delight by its voice and motions; and every inflection of tone and every gesture will bear exact relation to a corresponding antitype in the pleasurable impressions which awakened it; it will be the reflected image of that impression; and as the lyre trembles and sounds after the wind has died away, so the child seeks, by prolonging in its voice and motions the duration of the effect, to prolong also a consciousness of the cause. In relation to the objects which delight a child, these expressions are what poetry is to higher objects. The savage (for the savage is to ages what the child is to years) expresses the emotions produced in him by surrounding objects in a similar manner; and language and gesture, together with plastic or pictorial imitation, become the image of the combined effect of those objects, and his apprehension of them. Man in society, with all his passions and his pleasures, next becomes the object of the passions and pleasures of man; an additional class of emotions produces an augmented treasure of expression; and language, gesture, and the imitative arts become at once the representation and the medium, the pencil and the picture, the chisel and the statue, the chord and the harmony. The social sympathies, or those laws from which, as from its elements, society results, begin to develop themselves from the moment that two human beings coexist; the future is contained within the present, as the plant within the seed; and equality, diversity, unity, contrast, mutual dependence, become the prin-

ciples alone capable of affording the motives according to which
the will of a social being is determined to action, inasmuch as he
is social; and constitute pleasure in sensation, virtue in sentiment, beauty in art, truth in reasoning, and love in the intercourse of kind. Hence men, even in the infancy of society,
observe a certain order in their words and actions, distinct from
that of the objects and the impressions represented by them, all
expression being subject to the laws of that from which it proceeds. But let us dismiss those more general considerations
which might involve an inquiry into the principles of society
itself, and restrict our view to the manner in which the imagination is expressed upon its forms.

In the youth of the world, men dance and sing and imitate
natural objects, observing in these actions, as in all others, a
certain rhythm or order. And, although all men observe a
similar, they observe not the same order in the motions of the
dance, in the melody of the song, in the combinations of language, in the series of their imitations of natural objects. For
there is a certain order or rhythm belonging to each of these
classes of mimetic representation, from which the hearer and
the spectator receive an intenser and purer pleasure than from
any other: the sense of an approximation to this order has been
called taste by modern writers. Every man, in the infancy of art,
observes an order which approximates more or less closely to
that from which this highest delight results; but the diversity is
not sufficiently marked as that its gradations should be sensible,
except in those instances where the predominance of this faculty
of approximation to the beautiful (for so we may be permitted
to name the relation between this highest pleasure and its cause)
is very great. Those in whom it exists to excess are poets, in the
most universal sense of the word; and the pleasure resulting
from the manner in which they express the influence of society
or nature upon their own minds, communicates itself to others,
and gathers a sort of reduplication from the community. Their
language is vitally metaphorical; that is, it marks the before
unapprehended relations of things and perpetuates their apprehension, until words, which represent them, become, through
time, signs for portions or classes of thought instead of pictures
of integral thoughts; and then, if no new poets should arise to
create afresh the associations which have been thus disorganized,
language will be dead to all the nobler purposes of human inter-

course. These similitudes or relations are finely said by Lord Bacon to be "the same footsteps of nature impressed upon the various subjects of the world";[3] and he considers the faculty which perceives them as the storehouse of axioms common to all knowledge. In the infancy of society every author is necessarily a poet, because language itself is poetry; and to be a poet is to apprehend the true and the beautiful, in a word, the good which exists in the relation subsisting, first between existence and perception, and secondly between perception and expression. Every original language near to its source is in itself the chaos of a cyclic poem; the copiousness of lexicography and the distinctions of grammar are the works of a later age, and are merely the catalogue and the form of the creations of poetry.

But poets, or those who imagine and express this indestructible order, are not only the authors of language and of music, of the dance, and architecture, and statuary, and painting; they are the institutors of laws, and the founders of civil society, and the inventors of the arts of life, and the teachers who draw into a certain propinquity with the beautiful and the true that partial apprehension of the agencies of the invisible world which is called religion. Hence all original religions are allegorical, or susceptible of allegory, and, like Janus, have a double face of false and true. Poets, according to the circumstances of the age and nation in which they appeared, were called, in the earlier epochs of the world, legislators or prophets: a poet essentially comprises and unites both these characters.[4] For he not only beholds intensely the present as it is, and discovers those laws according to which present things ought to be ordered, but he beholds the future in the present, and his thoughts are the germs of the flower and the fruit of latest time. Not that I assert poets to be prophets in the gross sense of the word, or that they can foretell the form as surely as they foreknow the spirit of events: such is the pretense of superstition, which would make poetry an attribute of prophecy, rather than prophecy an attribute of poetry. A poet participates in the eternal, the infinite, and the one; as far as relates to his conceptions, time and place and

[3] *Advancement of Learning*, Bk. II: "The same footsteps of nature treading or printing upon several subjects or matters."

[4] Cf. Sidney's *Defense of Poesie:* "Among the Romans a poet was called *vates*, which is as much as a diviner, foreseer, or prophet . . ." Carlyle, Emerson, and Whitman had much to say about the poet as prophet; it was one of the fundamental critical concepts of the time.

number are not. The grammatical forms which express the moods of time, and the difference of persons, and the distinction of place, are convertible with respect to the highest poetry without injuring it as poetry; and the choruses of Aeschylus, and the book of Job, and Dante's *Paradise*, would afford, more than any other writings, examples of this fact, if the limits of this essay did not forbid citation. The creations of music, sculpture, and painting are illustrations still more decisive.

Language, color, form, and religious and civil habits of action are all the instruments and materials of poetry; they may be called poetry by that figure of speech which considers the effect as a synonym of the cause. But poetry in a more restricted sense expresses those arrangements of language, and especially metrical language, which are created by that imperial faculty whose throne is curtained within the invisible nature of man. And this springs from the nature itself of language, which is a more direct representation of the actions and passions of our internal being, and is susceptible of more various and delicate combinations, than color, form, or motion, and is more plastic and obedient to the control of that faculty of which it is the creation. For language is arbitrarily produced by the imagination, and has relation to thoughts alone; but all other materials, instruments, and conditions of art have relations among each other which limit and interpose between conception and expression. The former is as a mirror which reflects, the latter as a cloud which enfeebles, the light of which both are mediums of communication. Hence the fame of sculptors, painters, and musicians, although the intrinsic powers of the great masters of these arts may yield in no degree to that of those who have employed language as the hieroglyphic of their thoughts, has never equaled that of poets in the restricted sense of the term; as two performers of equal skill will produce unequal effects from a guitar and a harp. The fame of legislators and founders of religions, so long as their institutions last, alone seems to exceed that of poets in the restricted sense; but it can scarcely be a question, whether, if we deduct the celebrity which their flattery of the gross opinions of the vulgar usually conciliates, together with that which belonged to them in their higher character of poets, any excess will remain.

We have thus circumscribed the word *poetry* within the limits of that art which is the most familiar and the most perfect expression of the faculty itself. It is necessary, however, to make the circle still narrower, and to determine the distinction between measured and unmeasured language; for the popular division into prose and verse is inadmissible in accurate philosophy.

Sounds as well as thoughts have relation both between each other and towards that which they represent, and a perception of the order of those relations has always been found connected with a perception of the order of the relations of thoughts. Hence the language of poets has ever affected a sort of uniform and harmonious recurrence of sound, without which it were not poetry, and which is scarcely less indispensable to the communication of its influence than the words themselves without reference to that peculiar order. Hence the vanity of translation; it were as wise to cast a violet into a crucible that you might discover the formal principles of its color and odor, as to seek to transfuse from one language into another the creations of a poet. The plant must spring again from its seed, or it will bear no flower—and this is the burthen of the curse of Babel.

An observation of the regular mode of the recurrence of harmony in the language of poetical minds, together with its relation to music, produced meter, or a certain system of traditional forms of harmony and language. Yet it is by no means essential that a poet should accommodate his language to this traditional form, so that the harmony, which is its spirit, be observed. The practice is indeed convenient and popular, and to be preferred especially in such composition as includes much action; but every great poet must inevitably innovate upon the example of his predecessors in the exact structure of his peculiar versification. The distinction between poets and prose writers is a vulgar error. The distinction between philosophers and poets has been anticipated. Plato was essentially a poet—the truth and splendor of his imagery and the melody of his language are the most intense that it is possible to conceive. He rejected the harmony of the epic, dramatic, and lyrical forms because he sought to kindle a harmony in thoughts divested of shape and action, and he forbore to invent any regular plan of rhythm which would include, under determinate forms, the varied pauses of his style. Cicero sought to imitate the cadence of his periods, but with little success. Lord Bacon was a poet. His language has a sweet and majestic rhythm which satisfies

the sense, no less than the almost superhuman wisdom of his philosophy satisfies the intellect; it is a strain which distends, and then
bursts the circumference of the reader's mind, and pours itself
forth together with it into the universal element with which it
has perpetual sympathy.   All the authors of revolutions in
opinion are not only necessarily poets as they are inventors, nor
even as their words unveil the permanent analogy of things by
images which participate in the life of truth; but as their periods
are harmonious and rhythmical, and contain in themselves the
elements of verse, being the echo of the eternal music. Nor are
those supreme poets, who have employed traditional forms of
rhythm on account of the form and action of their subjects, less
capable of perceiving and teaching the truth of things than
those who have omitted that form. Shakespeare, Dante, and
Milton (to confine ourselves to modern writers) are philosophers
of the very loftiest power.

A poem is the very image of life expressed in its eternal truth.
There is this difference between a story and a poem, that a
story is a catalogue of detached facts, which have no other
connection than time, place, circumstance, cause, and effect;
the other is the creation of actions according to the unchangeable
forms of human nature, as existing in the mind of the Creator,
which is itself the image of all other minds.[5] The one is partial,
and applies only to a definite period of time, and a certain
combination of events which can never again recur; the other
is universal, and contains within itself the germ of a relation to
whatever motives or actions have place in the possible varieties
of human nature. Time, which destroys the beauty and the use
of the story of particular facts, stripped of the poetry which
should invest them, augments that of poetry, and forever develops
new and wonderful applications of the eternal truth which it
contains. Hence epitomes have been called the moths of just
history;[6] they eat out the poetry of it. A story of particular
facts is as a mirror which obscures and distorts that which should
be beautiful: poetry is a mirror which makes beautiful that which
is distorted.

The parts of a composition may be poetical, without the

[5]Cf. Sidney's *Defense of Poesie:* "The historian, wanting the precept, is so tied,
not to what should be but to what is, to the particular truth of things and not to
the general reason of things, that his example draweth no necessary consequence."
[6]Bacon's *Advancement of Learning*, Bk. II.

composition as a whole being a poem.[7] A single sentence may
be considered as a whole, though it may be found in the midst
of a series of unassimilated portions: a single word even may
be a spark of inextinguishable thought. And thus all the great
historians, Herodotus, Plutarch, Livy, were poets; and although
the plan of these writers, especially that of Livy, restrained them
from developing this faculty in its highest degree, they made
copious and ample amends for their subjection, by filling all the
interstices of their subjects with living images.

Having determined what is poetry, and who are poets, let us
proceed to estimate its effects upon society.

Poetry is ever accompanied with pleasure: all spirits on which
it falls open themselves to receive the wisdom which is mingled
with its delight. In the infancy of the world, neither poets themselves nor their auditors are fully aware of the excellence of
poetry: for it acts in a divine and unapprehended manner,
beyond and above consciousness; and it is reserved for future
generations to contemplate and measure the mighty cause and
effect in all the strength and splendor of their union. Even in
modern times, no living poet ever arrived at the fullness of his
fame; the jury which sits in judgment upon a poet, belonging as
he does to all time, must be composed of his peers: it must be
impaneled by Time from the selectest of the wise of many generations. A poet is a nightingale, who sits in darkness and sings to
cheer its own solitude with sweet sounds; his auditors are as men
entranced by the melody of an unseen musician, who feel that
they are moved and softened, yet know not whence or why.
The poems of Homer and his contemporaries were the delight
of infant Greece; they were the elements of that social system
which is the column upon which all succeeding civilization has
reposed. . . . Every epoch, under names more or less specious,
has deified its peculiar errors; Revenge is the naked idol of the
worship of a semibarbarous age; and Self-deceit is the veiled
image of unknown evil, before which luxury and satiety lie
prostrate. But a poet considers the vices of his contemporaries
as the temporary dress in which his creations must be arrayed,
and which cover without concealing the eternal proportions of

---

[7]Cf. Coleridge, *Biographia Literaria*, xiv; and John Henry Newman, "Poetry, with
Reference to Aristotle's 'Poetics' ": "Thus there is an apparent, but no real contradiction, in saying a poem may be but partially poetical." Poe perhaps borrowed
this idea from Coleridge. Cf. "The Poetical Principle," pp. 346–367, below.

their beauty. An epic or dramatic personage is understood to wear them around his soul, as he may the ancient armor or the modern uniform around his body; whilst it is easy to conceive a dress more graceful than either. The beauty of the internal nature cannot be so far concealed by its accidental vesture, but that the spirit of its form shall communicate itself to the very disguise, and indicate the shape it hides from the manner in which it is worn. A majestic form and graceful motions will express themselves through the most barbarous and tasteless costume. Few poets of the highest class have chosen to exhibit the beauty of their conceptions in its naked truth and splendor; and it is doubtful whether the alloy of costume, habit, etc., be not necessary to temper this planetary music for mortal ears.

The whole objection, however, of the immorality of poetry rests upon a misconception of the manner in which poetry acts to produce the moral improvement of man. Ethical science arranges the elements which poetry has created, and propounds schemes and proposes examples of civil and domestic life: nor is it for want of admirable doctrines that men hate, and despise, and censure, and deceive, and subjugate one another. But poetry acts in another and diviner manner. It awakens and enlarges the mind itself by rendering it the receptacle of a thousand unapprehended combinations of thought. Poetry lifts the veil from the hidden beauty of the world, and makes familiar objects be as if they were not familiar; it reproduces all that it represents, and the impersonations clothed in its Elysian light stand thenceforward in the minds of those who have once contemplated them, as memorials of that gentle and exalted content which extends itself over all thoughts and actions with which it coexists. The great secret of morals is love; or a going out of our own nature, and an identification of ourselves with the beautiful which exists in thought, action, or person, not our own. A man, to be greatly good, must imagine intensely and comprehensively; he must put himself in the place of another and of many others; the pains and pleasures of his species must become his own. The great instrument of moral good is the imagination; and poetry administers to the effect by acting upon the cause. Poetry enlarges the circumference of the imagination by replenishing it with thoughts of ever new delight, which have the power of attracting and assimilating to their own nature all other thoughts, and which form new intervals and interstices whose void forever craves fresh food. Poetry strengthens the faculty which is the organ of the moral nature of man, in the same manner as exercise strengthens a limb. A poet therefore would do ill to embody his own conceptions of right and wrong, which are usually those of his place and time, in his poetical creations, which participate in neither. By this assumption of the inferior office of interpreting the effect, in which perhaps after all he might acquit himself but imperfectly, he would resign a glory in a participation of the cause. There was little danger that Homer, or any of the eternal poets, should have so far misunderstood themselves as to have abdicated this throne of their widest dominion. Those in whom the poetical faculty, though great, is less intense, as Euripides, Lucan, Tasso, Spenser, have frequently affected a moral aim, and the effect of their poetry is diminished in exact proportion to the degree in which they compel us to advert to this purpose. . . .

But let us not be betrayed from a defense into a critical history of poetry and its influence on society. Be it enough to have pointed out the effects of poets, in the large and true sense of the word, upon their own and all succeeding times.

But poets have been challenged to resign the civic crown to reasoners and mechanists, on another plea. It is admitted that the exercise of the imagination is most delightful, but it is alleged that that of reason is more useful. Let us examine, as the grounds of this distinction, what is here meant by utility. Pleasure or good, in a general sense, is that which the consciousness of a sensitive and intelligent being seeks, and in which, when found, it acquiesces. There are two kinds of pleasure, one durable, universal, and permanent; the other transitory and particular. Utility may either express the means of producing the former or the latter. In the former sense, whatever strengthens and purifies the affections, enlarges the imagination, and adds spirit to sense is useful. But a narrower meaning may be assigned to the word utility, confining it to express that which banishes the importunity of the wants of our animal nature, the surrounding men with security of life, the dispersing the grosser delusions of superstition, and the conciliating such a degree of mutual forbearance among men as may consist with the motives of personal advantage.

Undoubtedly the promoters of utility, in this limited sense, have their appointed office in society. They follow the footsteps of poets, and copy the sketches of their creations into the book of common life. They make space and give time. Their exertions are of the highest value, so long as they confine their administration of the concerns of the inferior powers of our nature within the limits due to the superior ones. But whilst the skeptic destroys gross superstitions, let him spare to deface, as some of the French writers[8] have defaced, the eternal truths charactered upon the imaginations of men. Whilst the mechanist abridges, and the political economist combines labor, let them beware that their speculations, for want of correspondence with those first principles which belong to the imagination, do not tend, as they have in modern England, to exasperate at once the extremes of luxury and of want. They have exemplified the saying, "To him that hath, more shall be given; and from him that hath not, the little that he hath shall be taken away."[9] The rich have become richer, and the poor have become poorer; and the vessel of the state is driven between the Scylla and Charybdis of anarchy and despotism. Such are the effects which must ever flow from an unmitigated exercise of the calculating faculty.

It is difficult to define pleasure in its highest sense,[10] the definition involving a number of apparent paradoxes. For, from an inexplicable defect of harmony in the constitution of human nature, the pain of the inferior is frequently connected with the pleasures of the superior portions of our being. Sorrow, terror, anguish, despair itself, are often the chosen expressions of an approximation to the highest good. Our sympathy in tragic fiction depends on this principle; tragedy delights by affording a shadow of that pleasure which exists in pain. This is the source also of the melancholy which is inseparable from the sweetest melody. The pleasure that is in sorrow is sweeter than the pleasure of pleasure itself. And hence the saying, "It is better to go to the house of mourning than to the house of mirth."[11] Not that this highest species of pleasure is necessarily linked with pain. The delight of love and friendship, the ecstasy of the admiration of nature, the joy of the perception and still more of the creation of poetry, is often wholly unalloyed.

[8] Such as Voltaire's attack on Shakespeare; see p. 39, note 4.
[9] Matthew 25, 29 (paraphrase).
[10] Cf. Shelley's "To a Skylark" and Keats's "Ode to a Nightingale."
[11] Ecclesiastes 7, 2.

The production and assurance of pleasure in this highest sense is true utility. Those who produce and preserve this pleasure are poets or poetical philosophers.

The exertions of Locke, Hume, Gibbon, Voltaire, Rousseau, and their disciples in favor of oppressed and deluded humanity are entitled to the gratitude of mankind. Yet it is easy to calculate the degree of moral and intellectual improvement which the world would have exhibited, had they never lived. A little more nonsense would have been talked for a century or two, and perhaps a few more men, women, and children burnt as heretics. We might not at this moment have been congratulating each other on the abolition of the Inquisition in Spain. But it exceeds all imagination to conceive what would have been the moral condition of the world if neither Dante, Petrarch, Boccaccio, Chaucer, Shakespeare, Calderon, Lord Bacon, nor Milton had ever existed; if Raphael and Michelangelo had never been born; if the Hebrew poetry had never been translated; if a revival of the study of Greek literature had never taken place; if no monuments of ancient sculpture had been handed down to us; and if the poetry of the religion of the ancient world had been extinguished together with its belief. The human mind could never, except by the intervention of these excitements, have been awakened to the invention of the grosser sciences, and that application of analytical reasoning to the aberrations of society which it is now attempted to exalt over the direct expression of the inventive and creative faculty itself.

We have more moral, political, and historical wisdom than we know how to reduce into practice; we have more scientific and economical knowledge than can be accommodated to the just distribution of the produce which it multiplies. The poetry in these systems of thought is concealed by the accumulation of facts and calculating processes. There is no want of knowledge respecting what is wisest and best in morals, government, and political economy, or at least, what is wiser and better than what men now practice and endure. But we let "*I dare not* wait upon *I would*, like the poor cat in the adage."[12] We want the creative faculty to imagine that which we know; we want the generous impulse to act that which we imagine; we want the poetry of life: our calculations have outrun conception; we have eaten more than we can digest. The cultivation of those

[12]*Macbeth*, I, vii, 44–45.

sciences which have enlarged the limits of the empire of man over the external world has, for want of the poetical faculty, proportionally circumscribed those of the internal world; and man, having enslaved the elements, remains himself a slave. To what but a cultivation of the mechanical arts in a degree disproportioned to the presence of the creative faculty, which is the basis of all knowledge, is to be attributed the abuse of all invention for abridging and combining labor, to the exasperation of the inequality of mankind? From what other cause has it arisen that the discoveries which should have lightened, have added a weight to the curse imposed on Adam? Poetry, and the principle of Self, of which money is the visible incarnation, are the God and Mammon of the world.

The functions of the poetical faculty are twofold: by one it creates new materials of knowledge, and power, and pleasure; by the other it engenders in the mind a desire to reproduce and arrange them according to a certain rhythm and order which may be called the beautiful and the good. The cultivation of poetry is never more to be desired than at periods when, from an excess of the selfish and calculating principle, the accumulation of the materials of external life exceed the quantity of the power of assimilating them to the internal laws of human nature. The body has then become too unwieldy for that which animates it.

Poetry is indeed something divine. It is at once the center and circumference of knowledge; it is that which comprehends all science, and that to which all science must be referred. It is at the same time the root and blossom of all other systems of thought; it is that from which all spring, and that which adorns all; and that which, if blighted, denies the fruit and the seed, and withholds from the barren world the nourishment and the succession of the scions of the tree of life. It is the perfect and consummate surface and bloom of all things; it is as the odor and the color of the rose to the texture of the elements which compose it, as the form and splendor of unfaded beauty to the secrets of anatomy and corruption. What were virtue, love, patriotism, friendship—what were the scenery of this beautiful universe which we inhabit; what were our consolations on this side of the grave, and what were our aspirations beyond it—if poetry did not ascend to bring light and fire from those eternal regions where the owl-winged faculty of calculation dare not

ever soar? Poetry is not like reasoning, a power to be exerted
according to the determination of the will. A man cannot say,
"I will compose poetry." The greatest poet even cannot say it;
for the mind in creation is as a fading coal, which some invisible
influence, like an inconstant wind, awakens to transitory brightness; this power arises from within, like the color of a flower
which fades and changes as it is developed, and the conscious
portions of our natures are unprophetic either of its approach or
its departure. Could this influence be durable in its original
purity and force, it is impossible to predict the greatness of the
results; but when composition begins, inspiration is already on
the decline, and the most glorious poetry that has ever been
communicated to the world is probably a feeble shadow of the
original conceptions of the poet. I appeal to the greatest poets
of the present day whether it is not an error to assert that the
finest passages of poetry are produced by labor and study. The
toil and the delay recommended by critics can be justly interpreted to mean no more than a careful observation of the inspired moments, and an artificial connection of the spaces
between their suggestions by the intertexture of conventional
expressions—a necessity only imposed by the limitedness of the
poetical faculty itself; for Milton conceived the *Paradise Lost*
as a whole before he executed it in portions. We have his own
authority also for the muse having "dictated" to him the "unpremeditated song."[13] And let this be an answer to those who
would allege the fifty-six various readings of the first line of the
Orlando Furioso. Compositions so produced are to poetry what
mosaic is to painting. The instinct and intuition of the poetical
faculty is still more observable in the plastic and pictorial arts;
a great statue or picture grows under the power of the artist as a
child in the mother's womb; and the very mind which directs
the hands in formation is incapable of accounting to itself for
the origin, the gradations, or the media of the process.

Poetry is the record of the best and happiest moments of the
happiest and best minds. We are aware of evanescent visitations
of thought and feeling, sometimes associated with place or
person, sometimes regarding our own mind alone, and always
arising unforeseen and departing unbidden, but elevating and
delightful beyond all expression; so that even in the desire and
the regret they leave, there cannot but be pleasure, participating

[13]"Unpremeditated verse" (*Paradise Lost*, ix, 24).

as it does in the nature of its object. It is, as it were, the inter-penetration of a diviner nature through our own; but its foot-steps are like those of a wind over the sea, which the morning calm erases, and whose traces remain only as on the wrinkled sand which paves it. These and corresponding conditions of being are experienced principally by those of the most delicate sensibility and the most enlarged imagination; and the state of mind produced by them is at war with every base desire. The enthusiasm of virtue, love, patriotism, and friendship is essen-tially linked with such emotions; and, whilst they last, self appears as what it is, an atom to a universe. Poets are not only subject to these experiences as spirits of the most refined organi-zation, but they can color all that they combine with the evanes-cent hues of this ethereal world; a word, a trait in the represen-tation of a scene or a passion will touch the enchanted chord, and reanimate, in those who have ever experienced these emotions, the sleeping, the cold, the buried image of the past. Poetry thus makes immortal all that is best and most beautiful in the world; it arrests the vanishing apparitions which haunt the interlunations of life, and veiling them or in language or in form, sends them forth among mankind, bearing sweet news of kindred joy to those with whom their sisters abide—abide, because there is no portal of expression from the caverns of the spirit which they inhabit into the universe of things. Poetry redeems from decay the visitations of the divinity in man.

Poetry turns all things to loveliness; it exalts the beauty of that which is most beautiful, and it adds beauty to that which is most deformed; it marries exultation and horror, grief and pleasure, eternity and change; it subdues to union under its light yoke all irreconcilable things. It transmutes all that it touches, and every form moving within the radiance of its presence is changed by wondrous sympathy to an incarnation of the spirit which it breathes; its secret alchemy turns to potable gold the poisonous waters which flow from death through life; it strips the veil of familiarity from the world, and lays bare the naked and sleeping beauty which is the spirit of its forms.

All things exist as they are perceived: at least in relation to the percipient. "The mind is its own place, and in itself can make a heaven of hell, a hell of heaven."[14] But poetry defeats the curse which binds us to be subjected to the accident of surrounding

14 *Paradise Lost*, I, 254–255.

impressions. And whether it spreads its own figured curtain, or withdraws life's dark veil from before the scene of things, it equally creates for us a being within our being. It makes us the inhabitants of a world to which the familiar world is a chaos. It reproduces the common universe of which we are portions and percipients, and it purges from our inward sight the film of familiarity which obscures from us the wonder of our being. It compels us to feel that which we perceive, and to imagine that which we know. It creates anew the universe, after it has been annihilated in our minds by the recurrence of impressions blunted by reiteration. It justifies the bold and true words of Tasso: *Non merita nome di creatore, se non Iddio ed il Poeta.*[15]

A poet, as he is the author to others of the highest wisdom, pleasure, virtue, and glory, so he ought personally to be the happiest, the best, the wisest, and the most illustrious of men. As to his glory, let time be challenged to declare whether the fame of any other institutor of human life be comparable to that of a poet. That he is the wisest, the happiest, and the best, inasmuch as he is a poet, is equally incontrovertible: the greatest poets have been men of the most spotless virtue, of the most consummate prudence, and, if we would look into the interior of their lives, the most fortunate of men; and the exceptions, as they regard those who possessed the poetic faculty in a high yet inferior degree, will be found on consideration to confirm rather than destroy the rule. Let us for a moment stoop to the arbitration of popular breath, and usurping and uniting in our own persons the incompatible characters of accuser, witness, judge, and executioner, let us decide without trial, testimony, or form that certain motives of those who are "there sitting where we dare not soar," are reprehensible. Let us assume that Homer was a drunkard, that Vergil was a flatterer, that Horace was a coward, that Tasso was a madman, that Lord Bacon was a peculator, that Raphael was a libertine, that Spenser was a poet laureate.[16] It is inconsistent with this division of our subject to cite living poets, but posterity has done ample justice to the great names now referred to. Their errors have been weighed and found to have been dust in the balance; if their sins "were

---

[15]"None merits the name of creator except God and the Poet."

[16]"This contemptuous use of the title 'poet laureate' is due to Shelley's hatred of subserviency to courtly honors on the part of men of letters, and more particularly to the animosity existing between Southey, then poet laureate, and the poets of the radical group. The title is not accurately used of Spenser" (Alden).

as scarlet, they are now white as snow"; they have been washed in the blood of the mediator and redeemer, Time. Observe in what a ludicrous chaos the imputations of real or fictitious crime have been confused in the contemporary calumnies against poetry and poets;[17] consider how little is as it appears—or appears as it is; look to your own motives, and judge not, lest ye be judged.

Poetry, as has been said, differs in this respect from logic, that it is not subject to the control of the active powers of the mind, and that its birth and recurrence have no necessary connection with the consciousness or will. It is presumptuous to determine that these are the necessary conditions of all mental causation, when mental effects are experienced insusceptible of being referred to them. The frequent recurrence of the poetical power, it is obvious to suppose, may produce in the mind a habit of order and harmony correlative with its own nature and with its effects upon other minds. But in the intervals of inspiration, and they may be frequent without being durable, a poet becomes a man and is abandoned to the sudden reflux of the influences under which others habitually live. But as he is more delicately organized than other men and sensible to pain and pleasure, both his own and that of others, in a degree unknown to them, he will avoid the one and pursue the other with an ardor proportioned to this difference. And he renders himself obnoxious to calumny when he neglects to observe the circumstances under which these objects of universal pursuit and flight have disguised themselves in one another's garments.

But there is nothing necessarily evil in this error, and thus cruelty, envy, revenge, avarice, and the passions purely evil have never formed any portion of the popular imputations on the lives of poets.

I have thought it most favorable to the cause of truth to set down these remarks according to the order in which they were suggested to my mind by a consideration of the subject itself, instead of observing the formality of a polemical reply; but if the view which they contain be just, they will be found to involve a refutation of the arguers against poetry, so far at least as regards the first division of the subject. I can readily conjecture what should have moved the gall of some learned and

[17]An English court had deprived Shelley of his children because of his alleged atheism, and Lord Byron had been exiled by public opinion.

intelligent writers who quarrel with certain versifiers; I, like them, confess myself unwilling to be stunned by the *Theseids* of the hoarse Codri[18] of the day. Bavius and Maevius[19] undoubtedly are, as they ever were, insufferable persons. But it belongs to a philosophical critic to distinguish rather than confound.

The first part of these remarks has related to poetry in its elements and principles; and it has been shown, as well as the narrow limits assigned them would permit, that what is called poetry, in a restricted sense, has a common source with all other forms of order and of beauty according to which the materials of human life are susceptible of being arranged, and which is poetry in an universal sense.

The second part[20] will have for its object an application of these principles to the present state of the cultivation of poetry, and a defense of the attempt to idealize the modern forms of manners and opinions, and compel them into a subordination to the imaginative and creative faculty. For the literature of England, an energetic development of which has ever preceded or accompanied a great and free development of the national will, has arisen, as it were, from a new birth. In spite of the low-thoughted envy which would undervalue contemporary merit, our own will be a memorable age in intellectual achievements, and we live among such philosophers and poets as surpass beyond comparison any who have appeared since the last national struggle for civil and religious liberty. The most unfailing herald, companion, and follower of the awakening of a great people to work a beneficial change in opinion or institution is poetry. At such periods there is an accumulation of the power of communicating and receiving intense and impassioned conceptions respecting man and nature. The persons in whom this power resides may often, as far as regards many portions of their nature, have little apparent correspondence with that spirit of good of which they are the ministers. But even whilst they deny and abjure, they are yet compelled to serve the power which is seated on the throne of their own soul. It is impossible to read the compositions of the most celebrated writers of the present day without being startled with the electric

---

[18]"Am I never to retort, being so often bored by hoarse Codrus' *Theseid?*" (Juvenal, *Satires*, I, 1–2).
[19]Vergil hated Bavius and Maevius; see *Eclogues*, III, 90.
[20]I.e., the second part of this essay, never written.

life which burns within their words. They measure the circumference and sound the depths of human nature with a comprehensive and all-penetrating spirit, and they are themselves perhaps the most sincerely astonished at its manifestations; for it is less their spirit than the spirit of the age. Poets are the hierophants of an unapprehended inspiration; the mirrors of the gigantic shadows which futurity casts upon the present; the words which express what they understand not; the trumpets which sing to battle and feel not what they inspire; the influence which is moved not, but moves. Poets are the unacknowledged legislators of the world.

VICTOR MARIE HUGO

(1802–1885)

o⊙ooꙶo

VICTOR HUGO, one of the most spectacular personalities of the romantic movement, attracted public attention first as a child prodigy. It is said that he wrote a tragic drama when he was only fourteen, and he was given honorable mention by the French Academy when he was fifteen years old. He seems to have cleverly anticipated the dominance of romanticism and to have shrewdly made himself leader of the movement. Alfred de Vigny, Alexandre Dumas, *père*, and Casimir Delavigne were loyal henchmen, and for a time so was Sainte-Beuve, before he became a distinguished critic.

Every new literary movement is accompanied by a good deal of polemical writing by the leaders, and sometimes, as with Wordsworth's Preface to *Lyrical Ballads* and Whitman's equally famous Preface to *Leaves of Grass*, these writings make literary history and win for their authors the name of critic. It was so with Hugo. His criticism is to be found in his numerous prefaces, and these also enable us to trace the growth of his theories on art and life.

Hugo made his critical début in *Le Conservateur littéraire* between 1819 and 1821 with reactionary and neoclassical opinions. But a few years later, in the prefaces to the editions of his *Odes et ballades* (1822–1828), we perceive a transition to a conservative variety of romanticism. In the 1826 Preface he boldly made an outright attack upon classicism, followed in the succeeding year by the epoch-making Preface to *Cromwell*, which came to be regarded as the romantic manifesto for the drama and the battle cry of the movement. In this Preface Hugo attempts to announce a new criticism for a new era: "Behold, then, a new religion, a new society; upon this twofold foundation there must inevitably spring up a new poetry."[1] He defends the grotesque in art, renounces the unities, imitation, and rules, and predicts that the time will soon come when writers will be judged "not according to rules and species" but by "the special laws of their individual temperaments."[2]

---

[1] Walt Whitman states a similar belief in his 1855 Preface to *Leaves of Grass*.
[2] Cf. Thorild's "A Critique of the Critics," above, pp. 125 ff.

In his Preface to *Les Orientales* (1829) Hugo extends the new literary freedom to all art. In his Preface to *Hernani* (1830) he maintains "that literary liberty is the inevitable corollary of political and social liberty." After 1830 Hugo is concerned mainly with the theory of the drama, through which he desires to propagate liberty and democracy. As Professor Rew says, in *William Shakespeare* (1864) we have "a final proclamation of Hugo's theories on art and life."[3] He was thrilled by the majestic junction of beauty and utility in the greatest English dramatist.

In the Preface to *Cromwell*, reprinted below, it will be noticed that his chief illustrations and models are chosen from the Middle Ages and Shakespeare. Barrett H. Clark says that "Hugo's method is rather inspirational than logical, and his arguments are on the whole somewhat unsound."[4] But the same charge might be (and has been) made regarding all the great romantic manifestoes.

BIBLIOGRAPHY

TEXT

Œuvres complètes. 48 vols. Paris, 1880–1889.
Littérature et philosophie mêlées. 2 vols. Paris, 1876.
La Préface de Cromwell, ed. with introduction and notes by Maurice Souriau. Paris, 1897.
Préface de Cromwell and Hernani, ed. with introduction and notes by John R. Effinger, Jr. Chicago, 1900.

TRANSLATIONS

William Shakespeare, tr. by Melville B. Anderson. Chicago, 1887.
——. Authorized copyright. English translation. London, 1864.
Works; Vol. V, *Dramatic Works,* tr. by Frederick L. Slous and Mrs. Newton Crosland. New York, 1887.
——. London, 1916.

BIOGRAPHY AND CRITICISM

Berret, Paul, *Victor Hugo.* Paris, 1927.
Daudet, Léon, *Flambeaux.* Paris, 1929.
Davidson, A. F., *Victor Hugo, His Life and Works.* London, 1912.
Flutre, Fernand, *Victor Hugo.* Paris, 1929.
Gautier, Théophile, *Histoire du romantisme.* Paris, 1874.
Giese, William, *Victor Hugo, the Man and the Poet.* New York, 1926.

[3] I am greatly indebted to my colleague, Dr. Cecil L. Rew, for the examination of his doctor's thesis (unpublished, in University of Illinois Library) on *Literary Theories of the French Romanticists: A Study of Their Principal Critical Writings.* (G. W. A.)
[4] *European Theories of the Drama* (Cincinnati, 1918), p. 367.

Joussain, André, *L'Esthétique de Victor Hugo, le pittoresque dans le lyrisme et dans l'épopée; contribution à l'étude de la poétique romantique.* Paris, 1920.

Rossé, Charles Albert, *Les Théories littéraires de Victor Hugo* (*Essai de classification, d'analyse et de critique*). Paris, 1903.

Schenck, Eunice Morgan, *Le Part de Charles Nodier dans la formation des idées romantiques de Victor Hugo jusqu'à La préface de Cromwell.* Paris, 1914. Ph. D. thesis, Bryn Mawr College, *Monographs of Bryn Mawr College*, XVI.

Séché, Léon, *Le Cénacle de Joseph Delorme (1827–1830).* (*Documents inédits.*) Paris, 1912.

Swinburne, Algernon Charles, *Essays and Studies.* London, 1875.

——, *A Study of Victor Hugo.* London, 1886.

PREFACE TO CROMWELL (*selections*)[1]

1825

. . . Let us set out from a fact. The same type of civilization, or to use a more exact, although more extended expression, the same society, has not always inhabited the earth. The human race as a whole has grown, has developed, has matured, like one of ourselves. It was once a child, it was once a man; we are now looking on at its impressive old age. Before the epoch which modern society has dubbed "ancient," there was another epoch which the ancients called "fabulous," but which it would be more accurate to call "primitive." Behold then three great successive orders of things in civilization, from its origin down to our days. Now, as poetry is always superposed upon society, we propose to try to demonstrate, from the form of its society, what the character of the poetry must have been in those three great ages of the world—primitive times, ancient times, modern times.

In primitive times, when man awakes in a world that is newly created, poetry awakes with him. In the face of the marvelous things that dazzle and intoxicate him, his first speech is a hymn simply. He is still so close to God that all his meditations are ecstatic, all his dreams are visions. His bosom swells, he sings as he breathes. His lyre has but three strings—God, the soul, creation; but this threefold mystery envelops everything, this threefold idea embraces everything. The earth is still almost deserted. There are families but no nations; patriarchs, but no

[1] Reprinted from the translation by George Burnham Ives in the *Works of Victor Hugo* (1909) by the kind permission of the publishers, Little, Brown, and Company.

kings. Each race exists at its own pleasure; no property, no laws, no contentions, no wars. Everything belongs to each and all. Society is a community. Man is restrained in nought. He leads that nomadic pastoral life with which all civilizations begin, and which is so well adapted to solitary contemplation, to fanciful reverie. He follows every suggestion, he goes hither and thither, at random. His thought, like his life, resembles a cloud that changes its shape and its direction according to the wind that drives it. Such is the first man, such is the first poet. He is young, he is cynical. Prayer is his sole religion, the ode is his only form of poetry.

This ode, this poem of primitive times, is Genesis.

By slow degrees, however, this youth of the world passes away. All the spheres progress; the family becomes a tribe, the tribe becomes a nation . . . [the nations] overflow upon another; hence, the migrations of nations—voyages. Poetry reflects these momentous events; from ideas it proceeds to things. It sings of ages, of nations, of empires. It becomes epic, it gives birth to Homer. . . .

[Ancient] civilization can find its one expression only in the epic. The epic will assume diverse forms, but it will never lose its specific character. Pindar is more priestlike than patriarchal, more epic than lyrical. If the chroniclers, the necessary accompaniments of the second age of the world, set about collecting traditions and begin to reckon by centuries, they labor to no purpose—chronology cannot expel poesy; history remains an epic. Herodotus is a Homer.

But it is in the ancient tragedy, above all, that the epic breaks out at every turn. It mounts the Greek stage without losing aught, so to speak, of its immeasurable, gigantic proportions. Its characters are still heroes, demigods, gods; its themes are visions, oracles, fatality; its scenes are battles, funeral rites, catalogues. That which the rhapsodists formerly sang, the actors declaim—that is the whole difference.

There is something more. When the whole plot, the whole spectacle of the epic poem have passed to the stage, the Chorus takes all that remains. The Chorus annotates the tragedy, encourages the heroes, gives descriptions, summons and expels the daylight, rejoices, laments, sometimes furnishes the scenery, explains the moral bearing of the subject, flatters the listening assemblage. Now, what is the Chorus, this anomalous character standing between the spectacle and the spectator, if it be not the poet completing his epic?[2]

The theater of the ancients is like their dramas, huge, pontifical, epic. It is capable of holding thirty thousand spectators; the plays are given in the open air, in bright sunlight; the performances last all day. The actors disguise their voices, wear masks, increase their stature; they make themselves gigantic, like their roles. The stage is immense. It may represent at the same moment both the interior and the exterior of a temple, a palace, a camp, a city. Upon it, vast spectacles are displayed. There is—we cite only from memory—Prometheus on his mountain; there is Antigone, at the top of a tower, seeking her brother Polynices in the hostile army (*The Phoenicians*); there is Evadne hurling herself from a cliff into the flames where the body of Capaneus is burning (*The Suppliants* of Euripides); there is a ship sailing into port and landing fifty princesses with their retinues (*The Suppliants* of Aeschylus). Architecture, poetry, everything assumes a monumental character. In all antiquity there is nothing more solemn, more majestic. Its history and its religion are mingled on its stage. Its first actors are priests; its scenic performances are religious ceremonies, national festivals . . . tragedy simply re-echoes the epic. All the ancient tragic authors derive their plots from Homer. . . .

But the age of the epic draws near its end. . . . A spiritual religion, supplanting the material and external paganism, makes its way to the heart of the ancient society, kills it, and deposits, in that corpse of a decrepit civilization, the germ of modern civilization. This religion is complete, because it is true; between its dogma and its cult, it embraces a deep-rooted moral. And first of all, as a fundamental truth, it teaches man that he has two lives to live, one ephemeral, the other immortal; one on earth, the other in heaven. It shows him that he, like his destiny, is twofold: that there is in him an animal and an intellect, a body and a soul; in a word, that he is the point of intersection, the common link of the two chains of beings which embrace all creation—of the chain of material beings and the chain of incorporeal beings; the first starting from the rock to arrive at man, the second starting from man to end at God. . . .[3]

---

[2] Compare A. W. Schlegel, above, p. 179 f.

[3] The "Chain of Being" concept was well known in Hugo's day. For a history of the idea see Arthur O. Lovejoy, *The Great Chain of Being*, Harvard University Press, 1936.

Thus paganism, which molded all creations from the same clay, minimizes divinity and magnifies man. Homer's heroes are of almost the same stature as his gods. Ajax defies Jupiter, Achilles is the peer of Mars. Christianity on the contrary, as we have seen, draws a broad line of division between spirit and matter. It places an abyss between the soul and the body, an abyss between man and God.

At this point—to omit nothing from the sketch upon which we have ventured—we will call attention to the fact that, with Christianity, and by its means, there entered into the mind of the nations a new sentiment, unknown to the ancients and marvelously developed among moderns, a sentiment which is more than gravity and less than sadness—melancholy. In truth, might not the heart of man hitherto deadened by religions purely hierarchical and sacerdotal, awake and feel springing to life within it some unexpected faculty, under the breath of a religion that is human because it is divine, a religion which makes of the poor man's prayer, the rich man's wealth, a religion of equality, liberty, and charity? Might it not see all things in a new light, since the gospel had shown it the soul through the senses, eternity behind life?

Moreover, at that very moment the world was undergoing so complete a revolution that it was impossible there should not be a revolution in men's minds. . . . But the instant that Christian society became firmly established, the ancient continent was thrown into confusion. . . . Man, withdrawing within himself in the presence of these imposing vicissitudes, began to take pity upon mankind, to reflect upon the bitter disillusionments of life. Of this sentiment, which to Cato the heathen was despair, Christianity fashioned melancholy.

At the same time was born the spirit of scrutiny and curiosity. These great catastrophes were also great spectacles, impressive cataclysms. It was the North hurling itself upon the South; the Roman world changing shape; the last convulsive throes of a whole universe in the death agony. As soon as that world was dead, lo! clouds of rhetoricians, grammarians, sophists, swooped down like insects on its immense body. People saw them swarming and heard them buzzing in that seat of putrefaction. They vied with one another in scrutinizing, commenting, disputing. Each limb, each muscle, each fiber of the huge prostrate body was twisted and turned in every direction. Surely it must have been a keen satisfaction to those anatomists of the mind, to be able, at their debut, to make experiments on a large scale; to have a dead society to dissect, for their first "subject."

Thus we see melancholy and meditation, the demons of analysis and controversy, appear at the same moment, and, as it were, hand-in-hand. At one extremity of the era of transition is Longinus, at the other St. Augustine. We must beware of casting a disdainful eye upon that epoch wherein all that has since borne fruit was contained in germs; upon that epoch whose least eminent writers, if we may be pardoned a vulgar but expressive phrase, made fertilizer for the harvest that was to follow. The Middle Ages were grafted on the Lower Empire.

Behold, then, a new religion, a new society; upon this twofold foundation there must inevitably spring up a new poetry. . . . [Art] will set about doing as nature does, mingling in its creations—but without confounding them—darkness and light, the grotesque and the sublime; in other words, the body and the soul, the beast and the intellect; for the starting point of religion is always the starting point of poetry. All things are connected.

Thus, then, we see a principle unknown to the ancients, a new type, introduced in poetry; and as an additional element in anything modifies the whole of the thing, a new form of the art is developed. This type is the grotesque; its new form is comedy. . . . Not that it is strictly true that comedy and the grotesque were entirely unknown to the ancients. In fact, such a thing would be impossible. Nothing grows without a root; the germ of the second epoch always exists in the first. In the *Iliad* Thersites and Vulcan furnish comedy, one to the mortals, the other to the gods. There is too much nature and originality in the Greek tragedy for there not to be an occasional touch of comedy in it. . . . But one feels that this part of the art is still in its infancy. . . . Comedy is almost imperceptible in the great epic *ensemble* of ancient times. . . .

In the idea of men of modern times, however, the grotesque plays an enormous part. It is found everywhere; on the one hand it creates the abnormal and the horrible, on the other the comic and the burlesque. It fastens upon religion a thousand original superstitions, upon poetry a thousand picturesque fancies. It is the grotesque which scatters lavishly in air, water, earth, fire, those myriads of intermediary creatures which we find all alive in the popular traditions of the Middle Ages; it is

the grotesque which impels the ghastly antics of the witches'
revels, which gives Satan his horns, his cloven foot, and his bat's
wings. It is the grotesque, still the grotesque, which now casts
into the Christian hell the frightful faces which the severe genius
of Dante and Milton will evoke, and again peoples it with those
laughter-moving figures amid which Callot,[4] the burlesque
Michelangelo, will disport himself. If it passes from the world
of imagination to the real world, it unfolds an inexhaustible
supply of parodies of mankind. Creations of its fantasy are the
Scaramouches, Crispins, and Harlequins,[5] grinning silhouettes
of man, types altogether unknown to serious-minded antiquity,
although they originated in classic Italy. It is the grotesque,
lastly, which, coloring the same drama with the fancies
of the North and of the South in turn, exhibits Sganarelle[6]
capering about Don Juan and Mephistopheles crawling about
Faust.

And how free and open it is in its bearing! how boldly it
brings into relief all the strange forms which the preceding age
had timidly wrapped in swaddling clothes! Ancient poetry,
compelled to provide the lame Vulcan with companions, tried
to disguise their deformity by distributing it, so to speak, upon
gigantic proportions. Modern genius retains this myth of the
supernatural smiths, but gives it an entirely different character
and one which makes it even more striking; it changes the
giants to dwarfs and makes gnomes of the Cyclops. With like
originality, it substitutes for the somewhat commonplace
Lernaen Hydra[7] all the local dragons of our national legends—
the gargoyle of Rouen, the *gra-ouilli* of Metz, the *chair sallée* of
Troyes, the *drée* of Montlhéry, the *tarasque* of Tarascon—monsters of forms so diverse, whose outlandish names are an additional attribute. All these creations draw from their own nature
that energetic and significant expression before which antiquity
seems sometimes to have recoiled. Certain it is that the Greek

---

[4]Jacques Callot (1592–1635), French engraver.

[5]Scaramouch, properly a buffoon, later used colloquially for a ne'er-do-well stock
character in seventeenth-century Italian farce. Harlequin, in modern comedy, a
posturing, acrobatic character in parti-colored tights: now used generally to signify
a person who cuts amusing capers, not unlike a clown. Crispin, a clever and un-
scrupulous comic character of Italian origin.

[6]Sganarelle, a stock character in several of Molière's comedies; cf. his *Don Juan*
(1663).

[7]The capture of the Hydra of Lerna was one of the seven labors of Hercules.

Eumenides[8] are much less horrible, and consequently less *true*, than the witches in *Macbeth*. Pluto is not the devil.

In our opinion a most novel book might be written upon the employment of the grotesque in the arts. One might point out the powerful effects the moderns have obtained from that fruitful type, upon which narrow-minded criticism continues to wage war even in our own day. It may be that we shall be led by our subject to call attention in passing to some features of this vast picture. We will simply say here that, as a means of contrast with the sublime, the grotesque is, in our view, the richest source that nature can offer art. . . . And it would be true also to say that contact with the abnormal has imparted to the modern sublime a something purer, grander, more sublime, in short, than the beautiful of the ancients; and that is as it should be. . . .

It is interesting to study the first appearance and the progress of the grotesque in modern times. At first, it is an invasion, an irruption, an overflow, as of a torrent that has burst its banks. It rushes through the expiring Latin literature, imparts some coloring to Persius, Petronius, and Juvenal, and leaves behind it the *Golden Ass* of Apuleius. Thence it diffuses itself through the imaginations of the new nations that are remodeling Europe. It abounds in the work of the fabulists, the chroniclers, the romancists. We see it make its way from the South to the North. It disports itself in the dreams of the Teutonic nations, and at the same time vivifies with its breath the admirable Spanish *romanceros*, a veritable *Iliad* of the age of chivalry. For example, it is the grotesque which describes thus, in the *Roman de la Rose*, an august ceremonial, the election of a king:

> A long-shanked knave they chose, I wis,
> Of all their men the boniest.

More especially it imposes its characteristic qualities upon that wonderful architecture which, in the Middle Ages, takes the place of all the arts. It affixes its mark on the façades of cathedrals, frames its hells and purgatories in the ogive arches of great doorways, portrays them in brilliant hues on window

---

[8]Eumenides, ancient goddesses worshiped at the foot of the Areopagus in Athens and in other places. By and after Aeschylus they were identified with the Erinyes, or avenging deities, supposedy three in number, Alecto (unceasing anger), Tisiphone (avenger of murder) and Megaera (jealousy); according to some legends they had snakes for hair.

glass, exhibits its monsters, its bulldogs, its imps about capitals, along friezes, on the edges of roofs. It flaunts itself in numberless shapes on the wooden façades of houses, on the stone façades of chateaux, on the marble façades of palaces. From the arts it makes its way into the national manners, and while it stirs applause from the people for the *graciosos* of comedy, it gives to the kings, court jesters. Later, in the age of etiquette, it will show us Scarron [9] on the very edge of Louis the Fourteenth's bed. Meanwhile, it decorates coats of arms, and draws upon knights' shields the symbolic hieroglyphs of feudalism. From the manners, it makes its way into the laws; numberless strange customs attest its passage through the institutions of the Middle Ages. Just as it represented Thespis, [10] smeared with wine lees, leaping in her tomb, it dances with the Basoche [11] on the famous marble table which served at the same time as a stage for the popular farces and for the royal banquets. Finally, having made its way into the arts, the manners, and the laws, it enters even the Church. In every Catholic city we see it organizing some one of those curious ceremonies, those strange processions, wherein religion is attended by all varieties of superstition—the sublime attended by all the forms of the grotesque. To paint it in one stroke, so great is its vigor, its energy, its creative sap, at the dawn of letters, that it casts at the outset, upon the threshold of modern poetry, three burlesque Homers: Ariosto in Italy, Cervantes in Spain, Rabelais in France.

It would be mere surplusage to dwell further upon the influence of the grotesque in the third civilization. Everything tends to show its close creative alliance with the beautiful in the so-called "romantic" period. Even among the simplest popular legends there are none which do not somewhere, with an admirable instinct, solve this mystery of modern art. Antiquity could not have produced *Beauty and the Beast*. [12]

[9] A seventeenth-century French poet and writer of burlesques; husband of Madame de Maintenon.

[10] Thespis, Greek poet of the sixth century, B.C., reputed founder of tragedy, said to have introduced monologues and perhaps dialogues into the dithyrambic choruses.

[11] *Basoche*, a French guild of clerks instituted in the fourteenth century, from whom the legal representatives were recruited. They gave plays, and once a year the King of Basoches reviewed his subjects.

[12] *Beauty and the Beast*, a well-known fairy tale; the French version was by Madame Leprince de Beaumont (1757), which furnished Grétry the subject for his opera *Zémire and Azor*.

It is true that at the period at which we have arrived the predominance of the grotesque over the sublime in literature is clearly indicated. But it is a spasm of reaction, an eager thirst for novelty, which is but temporary; it is an initial wave which gradually recedes. The type of the beautiful will soon resume its rights and its role, which is not to exclude the other principle, but to prevail over it. . . . The time has come when the balance between the two principles is to be established. A man, a poet king, *poeta soverano*, as Dante calls Homer, is about to adjust everything. The two rival genii combine their flames, and thence issues Shakespeare.

We have now reached the poetic culmination of modern times. Shakespeare is the drama; and the drama, which with the same breath molds the grotesque and the sublime, the terrible and the absurd, tragedy and comedy—the drama is the distinguishing characteristic of the third epoch of poetry, of the literature of the present day.

Thus to sum up hurriedly the facts that we have noted thus far, poetry has three periods, each of which corresponds to an epoch of civilization;[13] the ode, the epic, and the drama. Primitive times are lyrical, ancient times epical, modern times dramatic. The ode sings of eternity, the epic imparts solemnity to history, the drama depicts life. The characteristic of the first poetry is ingenuousness, of the second, simplicity, of the third, truth. The rhapsodists mark the transition from the lyric to the epic poets, as do the romanticists that from the lyric to the dramatic poets. Historians appear in the second period, chroniclers and critics in the third. The characters of the ode are colossi—Adam, Cain, Noah; those of the epic are giants— Achilles, Atreus, Orestes; those of the drama are men—Hamlet, Macbeth, Othello. The ode lives upon the ideal, the epic upon the grandiose, the drama upon the real. Lastly, this threefold poetry flows from three great sources—the Bible, Homer, Shakespeare. . . .

In a word, civilization begins by singing of its dreams, then narrates its doings, and, lastly, sets about describing what it thinks. It is, let us say in passing, because of this last, that the drama, combining the most opposed qualities, may be at the same time full of profundity and full of relief, philosophical and picturesque.

[13]Cf. Friedrich Schlegel, above, pp. 187–188.

It would be logical to add here that everything in nature and in life passes through these three phases, the lyric, the epic, and the dramatic, because everything is born, acts, and dies. If it were not absurd to confound the fantastic conceits of the imagination with the stern deductions of the reasoning faculty, a poet might say that the rising of the sun, for example, is a hymn, noonday a brilliant epic, and sunset a gloomy drama wherein day and night, life and death, contend for mastery. But that would be poetry—folly, perhaps—and *what does it prove?* . . .

The drama is complete poetry. The ode and the epic contain it only in germ; it contains both of them in a state of high development, and epitomizes both. Surely, he who said: "The French have not the epic brain," said a true and clever thing; if he had said, "the moderns," the clever remark would have been profound. It is beyond question, however, that there is epic genius in that marvelous *Athalie*,[14] so exalted and so simple in its sublimity that the royal century was unable to comprehend it. It is certain, too, that the series of Shakespeare's chronicle dramas presents a grand epic aspect. But it is lyric poetry above all that befits the drama; it never embarrasses it, adapts itself to all its caprices, disports itself in all forms, sometimes sublime as in Ariel, sometimes grotesque as in Caliban. Our era being above all else dramatic is for that very reason eminently lyric. There is more than one connection between the beginning and the end; the sunset has some features of the sunrise; the old man becomes a child once more. But this second childhood is not like the first; it is as melancholy as the other is joyous. It is the same with lyric poetry. Dazzling, dreamy, at the dawn of civilization, it reappears, solemn and pensive, at its decline. The Bible opens joyously with Genesis and comes to a close with the threatening Apocalypse. The modern ode is still inspired but is no longer ignorant. It meditates more than it scrutinizes; its musing is melancholy. We see, by its painful labor, that the muse has taken the drama for her mate. . . .

The drama, then, is the goal to which everything in modern poetry leads. *Paradise Lost* is a drama before it is an epic. As we know, it first presented itself to the poet's imagination in the first of these forms, and as a drama it always remains in the reader's memory, so prominent is the old dramatic framework still beneath Milton's epic structure! When Dante had finished

[14]*Athalie*, by Racine (1690).

his terrible *Inferno,* when he had closed its doors and nought remained save to give his work a name, the unerring instinct of his genius showed him that that multiform poem was an emanation of the drama, not of the epic; and on the front of that gigantic monument, he wrote with his pen of bronze: *Divina Commedia.*

Thus we see that the only two poets of modern times who are of Shakespeare's stature follow him in unity of design. They coincide with him in imparting a dramatic tinge to all our poetry; like him, they blend the grotesque with the sublime; and, far from standing by themselves in the great literary *ensemble* that rests upon Shakespeare, Dante and Milton are, in some sort, the two supporting abutments of the edifice of which he is the central pillar, the buttresses of the arch of which he is the keystone. . . .

In the drama, as it may be conceived at least, if not executed, all things are connected and follow one another as in real life. The body plays its part no less than the mind; and men and events, set in motion by this twofold agent, pass across the stage, burlesque and terrible in turn, and sometimes both at once. Thus the judge will say: "Off with his head and let us go to dinner!" Thus the Roman senate will deliberate over Domitian's turbot. . . .

It is a striking fact that all these contrasts are met with in the poets themselves, taken as men. By dint of meditating upon existence, of laying stress upon its bitter irony, of pouring floods of sarcasm and raillery upon our infirmities, the very men who make us laugh so heartily become profoundly sad. These Democrituses are Heraclituses as well. Beaumarchais was surly, Molière gloomy, Shakespeare melancholy.

The fact is, then, that the grotesque is one of the supreme beauties of the drama. It is not simply an appropriate element of it, but is oftentimes a necessity . . . it will bring Romeo face to face with the apothecary, Macbeth with the witches, Hamlet with the gravediggers. Sometimes it may, without discord, as in the scene between King Lear and his jester, mingle its shrill voice with the most sublime, the most dismal, the dreamiest music of the soul.

That is what Shakespeare alone among all has succeeded in doing, in a fashion of his own, which it would be no less fruitless than impossible to imitate—Shakespeare, the god of the stage, in whom, as in a trinity, the three characteristic geniuses of our stage, Corneille, Molière, Beaumarchais, seem united.

We see how quickly the arbitrary distinction between the species of poetry vanishes before common sense and taste. No less easily one might demolish the alleged rule of the two unities. We say *two* and not *three* unities because unity of plot or of *ensemble*, the only true and well-founded one, was long ago removed from the sphere of discussion. . . .[15]

"But," someone will say, "this rule that you discard is borrowed from the Greek drama." Wherein, pray, do the Greek stage and drama resemble our stage and drama? Moreover, we have already shown that the vast extent of the ancient stage enabled it to include a whole locality so that the poet could, according to the exigencies of the plot, transport it at his pleasure from one part of the stage to another, which is practically equivalent to a change of stage setting. Curious contradiction! The Greek theater, restricted as it was to a national and religious object, was much more free than ours, whose only object is the enjoyment and, if you please, the instruction of the spectator. The reason is that the one obeys only the laws that are suited to it, while the other takes upon itself conditions of existence which are absolutely foreign to its essence. One is artistic, the other artificial. . . .

Unity of time rests on no firmer foundation than unity of place. A plot forcibly confined within twenty-four hours is as absurd as one confined within a peristyle. Every plot has its proper duration as well as its appropriate place . . . and then, if twenty-four hours can be comprised in two, it is a logical consequence that four hours may contain forty-eight. Thus Shakespeare's unity must be different from Corneille's. . . .

We imagine that someone may say: "There is something in too frequent changes of scene which confuses and fatigues the spectator, and which produces a bewildering effect on his attention; it may be, too, that manifold transitions from place to place, from one time to another time, demand explanations which repel the attention; one should also avoid leaving, in the midst of the plot, gaps which prevent the different parts of the drama from adhering closely to one another, and which, moreover, puzzle the spectator because he does not know what there may be in these gaps." But these are precisely the difficul-

[15]Cf. *unities* in the index.

ties which art has to meet. These are some of the obstacles peculiar to one subject or another, as to which it would be impossible to pass judgment once for all. It is for genius to overcome, not for treatises or poetry to evade them.

A final argument taken from the very bowels of the art would of itself suffice to show the absurdity of the rule of the two unities. It is the existence of the third unity, unity of plot—the only one that is universally admitted, because it results from a fact; neither the human eye nor the human mind can grasp more than one *ensemble* at one time. This one is as essential as the other two are useless. It is the one which fixes the viewpoint of the drama; now, by that very fact, it excludes the other two. There can no more be three unities in the drama than three horizons in a picture. . . . Unity of plot is the stage law of perspective. . . .

But still the same refrain is repeated, and will be, no doubt, for a long while to come: "Follow the rules! Copy the models! It was the rules that shaped the models." One moment! In that case there are two sorts of models: those which are made according to the rules; and prior to them, those according to which the rules were made. Now, in which of these two categories should genius seek a place for itself? Although it is always disagreeable to come in contact with pedants, is it not a thousand times better to give them lessons than to receive lessons from them? And then—copy! Is the reflection equal to the light? Is the satellite which travels unceasingly in the same circle equal to the central creative planet? With all his poetry Vergil is no more than the moon of Homer.

And whom are we to copy, I pray to know? The ancients? We have just shown that their stage has nothing in common with ours. Moreover, Voltaire, who will have none of Shakespeare, will have none of the Greeks either. Let him tell us why. "The Greeks ventured to produce scenes no less revolting to us. Hippolyte, crushed by his fall, counts his wounds and utters doleful cries. Philoctetes falls in his paroxysms of pain, black blood flows from his wound. Oedipus, covered with the blood that still drops from the sockets of the eyes he has torn out, complains bitterly of gods and men. We hear the shrieks of Clytemnestra, murdered by her own son, and Electra, on the stage, cries: 'Strike! spare her not! she did not spare our father!' Prometheus is fastened to a rock by nails driven through his stomach and his arms. The Furies reply to Clytemnestra's bleeding shade with inarticulate roars. Art was in its infancy in the time of Aeschylus, as it was in London in Shakespeare's time."

Whom shall we copy, then? The modern? What? Copy copies! God forbid!

"But," someone else will object, "according to your conception of the art, you seem to look for none but great poets, to count always upon genius." Art certainly does not count upon mediocrity. It prescribes no rules for it, it knows nothing of it; in fact, mediocrity has no existence so far as art is concerned; art supplies wings, not crutches. Alas! D'Aubignac[16] followed rules, Campistron[17] copied models. What does it matter to art? It does not build its palaces for ants. It lets them make their anthill without taking the trouble to find out whether they have built their burlesque imitation of its palace upon its foundation. . . .

Let us then speak boldy. The time for it has come, and it would be strange if, in this age, liberty, like the light, should penetrate everywhere except to the one place where freedom is most natural—the domain of thought. Let us take the hammer to theories and poetic systems. Let us throw down the old plastering that conceals the façade of art. There are neither rules nor models; or, rather, there are no other rules than the general laws of nature, which soar above the whole field of art, and the special rules which result from the conditions appropriate to the subject of each composition. . . .

The poet—let us insist on this point—should take counsel therefore only of nature, truth, and inspiration which is itself both truth and nature. "Quando he," says Lope de Vega,

> *Quando he de escrivir una comedia,*
> *Encierro los preceptos con seis llaves.*[18]

To secure these precepts, "six keys" are none too many, in very truth. Let the poet beware especially of copying anything whatsoever—Shakespeare no more than Molière, Schiller no more than Corneille. If genuine talent could abdicate its own nature in this matter, and thus lay aside its original personality,

---

[16]François Hédelin D'Aubignac (1604–1676), minor French writer.
[17]Jean Galbert de Campistron (1656–1723), French dramatist.
[18]"When I have to write a comedy,
I lock up the rules with six keys."

to transform itself into another, it would lose everything by playing this role of its own double. It is as if a god should turn valet. We must draw our inspiration from the original sources. It is the same sap, distributed through the soil, that produces all the trees of the forest, so different in bearing power, in fruit, in foliage. . . .

But nature! nature and truth!—And here, in order to prove that, far from demolishing art, the new ideas aim only to reconstruct it more firmly and on a better foundation, let us try to point out the impassable limit which, in our opinion, separates reality according to art from reality according to nature. It is careless to confuse them as some ill-informed partisans of *romanticism* do. Truth in art cannot possibly be, as several writers have claimed, *absolute* reality. Art cannot produce the thing itself. Let us imagine, for example, one of those unreflecting promoters of absolute nature, of nature viewed apart from art, at the performance of a romantic play, say *Le Cid*. "What's that?" he will ask at the first word. "The Cid speaks in verse? It isn't natural to speak in verse"—"How would you have him speak, pray?"—"In prose." Very good. A moment later, "How's this!" he will continue, if he is consistent; "the Cid is speaking French!"—"Well?"—"Nature demands that he speak his own language; he can't speak anything but Spanish."

We shall fail entirely to understand, but again—very good. You imagine that this is all? By no means: before the tenth sentence in Castilian, he is certain to rise and ask if the Cid who is speaking is the real Cid, in flesh and blood. By what right does the actor, whose name is Pierre or Jacques, take the name of the Cid? That is *false*. There is no reason why he should not go on to demand that the sun should be substituted for the footlights, *real* trees and *real* houses for those deceitful wings. For, once started on that road, logic has you by the collar, and you cannot stop.

We must admit, therefore, or confess ourselves ridiculous, that the domains of art and nature are entirely distinct. Nature and art are two things—were it not so, one or the other would not exist. Art, in addition to its idealistic side, has a terrestrial, material side. Let it do what it will, it is shut in between grammar and prosody, between Vaugelas [19] and Richelet. [20] For its more

[19] Claude Favre de Vaugelas (1585–1650), French grammarian and man of letters.
[20] Pierre Cesar Richelet (1631–1698), French grammarian.

capricious creations, it has formulae, methods of execution, a complete apparatus to set in motion. For genius there are delicate instruments, for mediocrity, tools.

It seems to us that someone has already said that the drama is a mirror wherein nature is reflected. But if it be an ordinary mirror, a smooth and polished surface, it will give only a dull image of objects with no relief—faithful, but colorless; everyone knows that color and light are lost in a simple reflection. The drama, therefore, must be a concentrating mirror, which, instead of weakening, concentrates and condenses the colored rays, which makes of a mere gleam a light, and of a light a flame. Then only is the drama acknowledged by art.

The stage is an optical point. Everything that exists in the world—in history, in life, in man—should be and can be reflected therein, but under the magic wand of art. Art turns the leaves of the ages, of nature, studies chronicles, strives to reproduce actual facts (especially in respect to manners and peculiarities, which are much less exposed to doubt and contradiction than are concrete facts), restores what the chroniclers have lopped off, harmonizes what they have collected, divines and supplies their omissions, fills their gaps with imaginary scenes which have the color of the time, groups what they have left scattered about, sets in motion anew the threads of Providence which work the human marionettes, clothes the whole with a form at once poetical and natural, and imparts to it that vitality of truth and brilliancy which gives birth to illusion, that prestige of reality which arouses the enthusiasm of the spectator, and of the poet first of all, for the poet is sincere. Thus the aim of art is almost divine: to bring to life again if it is writing history, to create if it is writing poetry. . . .

It will readily be imagined that, for a work of this kind, if the poet must *choose* (and he must), he should choose, not the *beautiful*, but the *characteristic*. Not that it is advisable to "make local color," as they say today; that is, to add as an afterthought a few discordant touches here and there to a work that is at best utterly conventional and false. The local color should not be on the surface of the drama, but in its substance, in the very heart of the work, whence it spreads of itself, naturally, evenly, and so to speak, into every corner of the drama, as the sap ascends from the root to the tree's topmost leaf. The drama should be thoroughly impregnated with this color of the time, which should be, in some sort, in the air, so that one detects it only on entering the theater, and that on going forth one finds oneself in a different period and atmosphere. It requires some study, some labor, to attain this end; so much the better. It is well that the avenues of art should be obstructed by those brambles from which everybody recoils except those of powerful will. Besides, it is this very study, fostered by an ardent inspiration, which will ensure the drama against a vice that kills it—the *commonplace*. To be commonplace is the failing of shortsighted, short-breathed poets. In this tableau of the stage, each figure must be held down to its most prominent, most individual, most precisely defined characteristic. Even the vulgar and the trivial should have an accent of their own. Like God, the true poet is present in every part of his work at once. Genius resembles the die which stamps the king's effigy on copper and golden coins alike.

We do not hesitate—and this will demonstrate once more to honest men how far we are from seeking to discredit the art— we do not hesitate to consider verse as one of the means best adapted to protect the drama from the scourge we have just mentioned, as one of the most powerful dams against the irrup- tion of the commonplace, which, like democracy, is always flowing between full banks in men's minds. And at this point we beg the younger literary generation, already so rich in men and in works, to allow us to point out an error into which it seems to have fallen—an error too fully justified, indeed, by the extraordinary aberrations of the old school. The new century is at that growing age at which one can readily set oneself right. . . .

If we were entitled to say what, in our opinion, the style of dramatic poetry should be, we would declare for a free, out- spoken, sincere verse, which dares say everything without prudery, expresses its meaning without seeking for words; which passes naturally from comedy to tragedy, from the sublime to the grotesque; by turns practical and poetical, both artistic and inspired, profound and impulsive, of wide range and true; verse which is apt opportunely to displace the caesura, in order to disguise the monotony of the Alexandrines; more inclined to the *enjambement* that lengthens the line, than to the inversion of phrases that confuses the sense; faithful to rhyme, that enslaved queen, that supreme charm of our poetry, that creator of our meter; verse that is inexhaustible in the verity of its turns of thought, unfathomable in its secrets of composition and of grace; assuming, like Proteus,[21] a thousand forms without changing its type and character; avoiding long speeches; taking delight in dialogue; always hiding behind the characters of the drama; intent, before everything, on being in its place, and when it falls to its lot to be *beautiful*, being so only by chance, as it were, in spite of itself and unconsciously; lyric, epic, dramatic, at need; capable of running through the whole gamut of poetry, of skipping from high notes to low, from the most exalted to the most trivial ideas, from the most extravagant to the most solemn, from the most superficial to the most abstract, without ever passing beyond the limits of a spoken scene; in a word, such verse as a man would write whom a fairy had endowed with Corneille's mind and Molière's brain. It seems to us that such verse would be *as fine as prose*. . . .

One feels that prose, which is necessarily more timid, obliged to wean the drama from anything like epic or lyric poetry, reduced to dialogue and to matter-of-fact . . . has much narrower wings. And then, too, it is much more easy of access; mediocrity is at its ease in prose; and for the sake of a few works of distinction such as have appeared of late, the art would very soon be overloaded with abortions and embryos. Another faction of the reformers incline to drama written in both prose and verse, as Shakespeare composed it. This method has its advantages. There might, however, be some incongruity in the transitions from one form to the other; and when a tissue is homogeneous it is much stouter. However, whether the drama should be written in prose is only a secondary question. The rank of a work is certain to be fixed, not according to its form, but according to its intrinsic value. In questions of this sort, there is only one solution. There is but one weight that can turn the scale in the balance of art—that is, genius.

Meanwhile, the first, the indispensable merit of a dramatic writer, whether he write in prose or verse, is correctness. Not a mere superficial correctness, the merit or defect of the descriptive school, which makes Lhomond [22] and Restaut [23] the two wings of its Pegasus; but that intimate deep-rooted, deliberate correct-

---

[21] A sea god who had the power of changing his form at will.
[22] Charles François Lhomond (1727–1794), classical grammarian.
[23] Pierre Restaut (1696–1765), French grammarian.

ness, which is permeated with the genius of a language, which has sounded its roots and searched its etymology; always unfettered, because it is sure of its footing, and always more in harmony with the logic of the language. Our Lady Grammar leads the other in leading strings; the other holds grammar in leash. It can venture anything, can create or invent its style; it has a right to do so. For, whatever certain men may have said who did not think what they were saying, and among whom we must place, notably, him who writes these lines, the French tongue is not *fixed* and never will be. A language does not become fixed. The human intellect is always on the march, or, if you prefer, in movement, and languages with it. Things are made so. When the body changes, how could the coat not change? The French of the nineteenth century can no more be the French of the eighteenth century than the latter is the French of the seventeenth, or the French of the seventeenth is that of the sixteenth. Montaigne's is not Rabelais's, Pascal's is not Montaigne's, Montesquieu's is not Pascal's. Each of the four languages, taken by itself, is admirable because it is original. Every age has its own ideas; it must have also words adapted to those ideas. Languages are like the sea; they move to and fro incessantly. . . . In vain, therefore, should we seek to petrify the mobile physiognomy of our idiom in a fixed form. In vain do our literary Joshuas cry out to the language to stand still; languages and the sun do not stand still. The day when they become *fixed*, they are dead.—That is why the French of a certain contemporary school is a dead language. . . .

Taste is the common sense of genius. This is what will soon be demonstrated by another school of criticism, powerful, outspoken, well-informed—a school of the century which is beginning to put forth vigorous shoots under the dead and withered branches of the old school. This youthful criticism, as serious as the other is frivolous, as learned as the other is ignorant, has already established organs that are listened to, and one is sometimes surprised to find, even in the least important sheets, excellent articles emanating from it. Joining hands with all that is fearless and superior in letters, it will deliver us from two scourges: tottering *classicism* and false *romanticism*. . . .

We are approaching, then, the moment when we shall see the new criticism prevail, firmly established upon a broad and deep foundation. People generally will understand that writers should be judged, not according to rules and species, which are contrary to nature and art, but according to the immutable principles of the art of composition, and the special laws of their individual temperaments. The sound judgment of all men will be ashamed of the criticism which broke Pierre Corneille on the wheel, gagged Jean Racine, and ridiculously rehabilitated John Milton only by virtue of the epic code of Père le Bossu.[24] People will consent to place themselves at the author's stand-point, to view the subject with his eyes, in order to judge a work intelligently. They will lay aside—and it is M. de Chateaubriand who speaks—"the paltry criticism of defects for the noble and fruitful criticism of beauties." It is time that all acute minds should grasp the thread that frequently connects what we, following our special whim, call "defects" with what we call "beauty." Defects—at all events those which we call by that name—are often inborn, necessary, inevitable conditions of good qualities.

[24]René le Bossu (1631–1680), wrote *Traité du poème épique*, the leading doctrine of which was that the subject should be chosen before the characters and that the action should be arranged without reference to the characters.

EDGAR ALLAN POE

(1809–1849)

o◯ooo◯o

PRIOR TO POE, with few exceptions, American criticism had tended toward provincialism. This was true especially in its tendency to judge literature on the basis of its nationalism and its moralism. And it was against these two prevalent bases of criticism that Poe reacted in his militant crusade to judge literature squarely by the universal laws of art alone, although he saw beauty in "all noble thoughts . . . and holy impulses" (see *post*, p. 366). As an editor he said his "leading object" in his critical magazine would be

> to assert in precept and to maintain in practice, the rights, while in effect it demonstrates the advantages, of an absolutely independent criticism;—a criticism self-sustained; guiding itself only by the purest rules of Art; analysing and urging these rules as it applies them; holding itself aloof from all personal bias; acknowledging no fear save that of outraging the right; . . . It will endeavor to support the general interests of the republic of letters, without reference to particular regions—regarding the world at large as the true audience of the author."[1] Criticism is not, we think, an essay, nor a sermon, nor an oration, nor a chapter in history, nor a philosophical speculation, nor a prose poem, nor an art-novel, nor a dialogue. . . . Following the highest authority, we would wish, in a word, to limit criticism to comment upon *Art*. A book is written—and it is only as the book that we subject it to review. With the opinions of the work itself, the critic has really nothing to do. It is his part simply to decide upon *the mode* in which these opinions are brought to bear.[2]

[1] The passage occurs in Poe's prospectus for the *Penn Magazine*, quoted in Woodberry's *Life of Edgar Allan Poe* (1909), I, 274. For Poe's discussion of, and general aversion to literary nationalism, see his "Nationality in American literature" in *Marginalia;* the opening pages of his essay on *The Culprit Fay and Other Poems;* and "Exordium," *Complete Works* (ed. Harrison, hereafter referred to as *Works*), XI, 1–8. On the vogue of the doctrine he attacked, see B. T. Spencer, "A National Literature, 1837–1855," *American Literature*, VIII, 125–169 (May, 1936).

[2] From "Exordium" (*Graham's Magazine*, January, 1842), which is perhaps the best elaboration of his critical position.

Thus Poe sought a type of criticism which might be called aesthetically judicial, as distinguished from criticism which seeks to explain a work by its historical origins or to appreciate it by re-living its author's vision sympathetically. His criticism is essentially deductive, involving the application of aesthetic theories and principles to specific works. In aesthetic theory, however, Poe combined certain elements of the eighteenth and nineteenth centuries. Undoubtedly his emphasis on rationality and form and unity in literature is akin to the earlier century.[3] He said that "man's chief idiosyncrasy" was *reason* and that any "action *without* reason" represented "his *un*natural state." [4] His great interest in exact verse technique, in choice of the right word, and in form are all interests of good neoclassicists. He is akin to the later eighteenth century in his interest in melancholy,[5] graveyardism (cf. "Berenice"), and Gothic horror as aesthetic materials, but he added to these a nineteenth-century psychological interest. His greatest debt to the eighteenth century, however, is his desire, especially in *Eureka*, to take the symmetrical unity of the Universe, defined in the scientific theories of Newton, as his literary model. The "supremeness of symmetry" in the Universe, he says, is its "poetical essence" and makes it "the most sublime of poems." [6] Yet Poe doubtless learned certain of his main critical ideas from Germans such as A. W. Schlegel and principally from Coleridge[7] (in part a medium for German ideas). Poe's mind shows considerable growth. His early preference for a wild or Gothic imagination unrestrained by reason gradually gave way to an ideal involving the balanced interpenetration of imagination and reason akin to the ideal of Coleridge.[8] Like Coleridge, Poe came to distinguish sharply between Fancy, as capricious, and Imagination as "a lesser degree of the creative power in God" [9] who manifests himself in

[3] See evidence cited, especially in regard to the principle of "unity (or totality) of interest" in Prescott's excellent introduction to *The Critical Writings of Poe*, pp. xxx–xxxiii. On the subject of Poe's probable sources, see, in bibliography following, the studies by Campbell, Alterton, Pritchard, Cobb, and Alterton and Craig.

[4] *Works*, XVI, 6–7.

[5] His doctrine that melancholy is inseparable from beauty may have been suggested also by A. W. Schlegel.

[6] *Works*, XVI, 302. This central ideal of unity (see *Works*, ed. by Stedman and Woodberry, VIII, 126; *Works*, ed. by Harrison, XI, 106; XIV, 196, 267; XVII, 266 especially) has been brilliantly related to his interest in Newtonian science in the introduction to *Poe* (1935), pp. xiii–cxviii, by Alterton and Craig.

[7] See Stovall's "Poe's Debt to Coleridge," especially pp. 80–119, where the points made here are elaborated in the light of full evidence. On p. 83 Stovall summarizes Poe's theory of poetry; see also the summary in H. H. Clark's *Major American Poets* (New York, 1936), pp. 844–846.

[8] This development has been traced through four periods by Alterton and Craig.

[9] *Works*, VIII, 283 (in review of Halleck and Drake, 1836).

the unity and harmony of immutable law. In an imaginative work, "the main conception springs . . . from . . . the moral sentiments . . . of the ideal."[10] He rejected realistic literature because there remains "still a thirst unquenchable."

> This burning thirst belongs to the *immortal* essence of man's nature. It is equally a consequence and an indication of his perennial life. It is the desire of the moth for the star. . . . Inspired with a prescient ecstasy of the beauty beyond the grave, it struggles by multiform novelty of combination among the things and thoughts of Time, to anticipate some portion of that loveliness whose very elements, perhaps, appertain solely to Eternity.[11]

Like Coleridge, Poe insisted that "in excessive *generalization* lies one of the leading errors" of criticism, especially in America; he urged that universal aesthetic principles should be given "particular and methodical application"[12] to specific passages of the literature criticized. Like Coleridge, Poe held that the immediate object of poetry is pleasure, and not truth, that beauty is the sole province of the poem, although the muse is "not forbidden to depict—but to reason and preach of virtue."[13] And, like Coleridge in part, Poe regarded music as an essential element in poetry,[14] and he wrote his "Rationale of Verse"[15] on the "timer's" theory that the technique of music and poetry in achieving

[10]*Ibid.*, X, 65 (in review of Moore, 1840). In discussing poetry, Poe emphasizes the fact that "imagination is its soul." He defines "the poetic principle" as "strictly and simply, the human aspiration for supernal beauty," the manifestation of the principle being "always found in *an elevating excitement of the soul*—quite independent of that passion which is the intoxication of the heart—or of that truth which is the satisfaction of the reason" (*Works*, XIV, 290). N. Foerster (*American Criticism*, pp. 39 ff.) argues that actually Poe's indefinite ideality is not spiritual but sensuous, divorced from the moral imagination. "His vision oscillated not between the earthly and the supernal, but between the infernal and the Arcadian," the latter involving "roseate harmonies of sensuous longing posing as spirituality" (*ibid.*, p. 50).

[11]See Alterton and Craig, pp. 345–346.

[12]*Works*, XI, 133 (in review of Dawes, 1842).

[13]*Ibid.*, XI, 71 (in review of Longfellow, 1842). For Poe's further discussion of the question of the didactic, see *Works* (ed. Harrison), VII, xxxvii, xliii; IX, 305; X, 141; XI, 67–68; 79, 84, 244–254; XII, 33–34; XIII, 131; and Stovall's study of "Al Aaraaf." Although in contrast to the moralists it is perhaps proper to call Poe essentially an aesthete, it should be noted that he does not object to the aesthetic use of virtue. At the end of the "The Poetic Principle" he finds beauty in "all noble thoughts . . . in all holy impulses."

[14]*Works*, XI, 74 (in review of Longfellow, 1842). (See Coleridge parallels in Stovall's study, *op. cit.*, pp. 87–88.)

[15]So great an authority on its subject as George Saintsbury (*History of Literary Criticism*, III, 635) regards Poe's "Rationale of Verse" as "one of the best things ever written on English prosody and quite astonishingly original." See full analysis in Gay W. Allen's *American Prosody*, pp. 57 ff.

harmony are essentially the same, thus foreshadowing Lanier's *Science of English Verse*. "The perception of pleasure in the quality of *sounds* is the principle of music," while verse is "an inferior and less capable music."[16] Poe is unique among earlier American critics in his meticulous attention to versification.

He is usually regarded as one of the early masters of the short story in the sense that he formalized its technique, especially in his review of Hawthorne's *Twice-Told Tales*. In the short story he sought "the immense force derivable from totality" of effect, to be attained by hitting the reader on the same nerve from the "very initial sentence" to the end. He sought compression and focus: "In the whole composition there should not be one word written of which the tendency, direct or indirect, is not to the one pre-established design." He sought verisimilitude, especially in his tales dealing with the psychology of the fear of fear and tales of ratiocination such as "The Gold Bug" and "Murders in the Rue Morgue." And he sought finality and a conclusive winding up of the interest aroused in the beginning.

In putting his principles into critical practice, Poe was naturally influenced by the fact that he was obliged to work as a journalist,[17] as well as by his own peculiar aristocratic temperament. He liked to attract attention by something sensational; witness his very title, "Longfellow and Other Plagiarists"! He had to deal not with the timeless masters (which the academic Lowell had leisure to treat) but with his own timely contemporaries, many of whom turned out to be ephemeral. Just as in political and social matters Poe was an aristocrat scornful of humanitarian tenderness, so in critical matters his cold, logical, and somewhat haughty temperament led him to scorn warm appreciation and to carry out his harsh doctrine that "in pointing out frankly the errors of a work, we do nearly all that is critically necessary in displaying its merits."[18] "In general," he said, "we should not be overscrupulous about niceties of phrase, when the matter in hand is a dunce to be gibbeted. Speak out—or the person may not understand you. Is he to be hung? Then hang him by all means; but make no bow where you mean no obeisance . . ." Thus Poe's actual critical practice is somewhat unique (or was before H. L. Mencken!) in its destructive

---

[16] *Works*, XIV, 219–220.

[17] For discussion see P. H. Boynton, "Poe and Journalism," *English Journal*, XXI, 345–352 (May, 1932); F. L. Pattee, *The Development of the American Short Story* (New York, 1923), especially pp. 130–134; and H. S. Canby, *Classic Americans* (New York, 1931), pp. 263–307. In *Marginalia* Poe said, "The whole tendency of the age is magazine-ward."

[18] *Works*, XI, 42 (in review of Dickens, 1842).

"tomahawk" manner, and it naturally aroused bitter antagonism. He was not only an absolutist in his allegiance to aesthetic principles, but he had a diabolical way of minutely analyzing chapter and verse to prove and illustrate the way in which an author violated them. In his own day he doubtless seemed unduly concerned with art and unduly meticulous and harsh in enforcing his judgments; but perhaps his concern with aesthetics and with craftsmanship and his fearlessness in defending them were exactly what were most needed in an age prone to let its judgment of literary art be confused with irrelevant political and moralistic biases.

BIBLIOGRAPHY

TEXT

The Complete Works of Edgar Allan Poe, ed. by J. A. Harrison. 17 vols. New York, 1902. (The Virginia edition; by all odds the best edition.)

Edgar Allan Poe Letters Till Now Unpublished, in the Valentine Museum, Richmond, Virginia, ed. by Mary Newton Stanard. Philadelphia, 1925. With introduction and commentary.

Last Letters of Edgar Allan Poe to Sarah Helen Whitman, ed. by J. A. Harrison. New York, 1909.

The Poems of Edgar Allan Poe, ed. by Killis Campbell. Boston, 1917. Contains scholarly notes of great value.

Selections from the Critical Writings of Edgar Allan Poe, ed. with introduction, by F. C. Prescott. New York, 1909.

The Works of Edgar Allan Poe, ed. by J. H. Ingram, 4 vols. Edinburgh, 1874–1875, 1880, etc.

The Works of Edgar Allan Poe, ed. by E. C. Stedman and G. E. Woodberry. 10 vols. Chicago, 1894–1895, New York, 1914.

The Works of the Late Edgar Allan Poe, ed. by R. W. Griswold. 4 vols. New York, 1850–1856, 1858, etc.

The Works of Edgar Allan Poe, ed. by R. H. Stoddard. 6 vols. New York, 1884, 1894.

Woodberry, G. E., ed., "The Poe-Chivers Papers," *Century Magazine*, XLIII, 435–447 (January, 1903), 545–558 (February, 1903).

BIBLIOGRAPHY

Cambridge History of American Literature, II, 452–468. An excellent bibliography, but includes items only to 1918.

Campbell, Killis, "The Poe Canon," in *The Mind of Poe*. Cambridge, 1933, pp. 187–238. Also "Gleanings in the Bibliography of Poe," *Modern Language Notes*, XXXII, 267–272; and "Recent Books about Poe," *Studies in Philology*, XXIV, 474–479.

Engel, C. E., "L'État des travaux sur Poe en France," *Modern Philology*, XXIX, 482–485.

Heartman, C. F., and Rede, Kenneth, *A Census of First Editions and Source Materials of Edgar Allan Poe in American Collections*. 2 vols. Metuchen, New Jersey, 1932. Vol. I includes "A Bibliographical Checklist of First Editions"; Vol. II, "Edgar Allan Poe's Contributions to Annuals and Periodicals."

Robertson, J. W., *A Bibliography of the Writings of Edgar A. Poe*, 2 vols. San Francisco, 1934. Chronological list, 1827–1850. The latest bibliography, including many rare items. David Randall's review, *Publishers' Weekly*, CXXV, 1540–1543 (April 21, 1934) is valuable for the inaccuracies it corrects in Robertson.

BIOGRAPHY AND CRITICISM

Allen, Gay W., "Edgar Allan Poe," in *American Prosody*. New York, 1935, pp. 56–90.

Allen, Hervey, *Israfel: The Life and Times of Edgar Allan Poe*. 2 vols. New York, 1926. Rev. ed. in one volume, 1934. The most elaborate biography.

Alterton, Margaret, *Origins of Poe's Critical Theory*, University of Iowa Humanistic Studies (1925), II, no. 3.

Alterton, Margaret, and Craig, Hardin, *Edgar Allan Poe*. New York, 1935. (American Writers Series.)

Baldwin, Summerfield, "The Aesthetic Theory of Edgar Poe," *Sewanee Review*, XXVI, 210–221 (April–June, 1918).

Belden, H. M., "Observation and Imagination in Coleridge and Poe: a Contrast," in *In Honor of the Ninetieth Birthday of Charles Frederick Johnson*. Hartford, Connecticut, 1928.

Brownell, W. C., "Poe," in *American Prose Masters*. New York, 1909, pp. 207–267.

Campbell, Killis, *The Mind of Poe, and Other Studies*. Harvard University Press, 1933.

——, *The Poems of Edgar Allan Poe*. Boston, 1917. Introduction and detailed commentary on each of the poems.

——, ed., *Poe's Short Stories*. New York, 1927.

Canby, H. S., "Poe," in *Classic Americans*. New York, 1931, pp. 263–307.

De Mille, George E., "Poe," in *Literary Criticism in America*. New York, 1931, pp. 86–117.

Foerster, Norman, "Poe," in *American Criticism*. Boston, 1928, pp. 1–51.

Harrison, J. A., *Life and Letters of Edgar Allan Poe*. 2 vols. New York, 1903.

Jackson, D. K., *Poe and the Southern Literary Messenger*. Richmond, 1934.

More, P. E., "The Origins of Hawthorne and Poe," in *Shelburne Essays*. First Series. New York, 1904, pp. 51–70.

Pope-Hennessy, Una, *Edgar Allan Poe (1809–1849): A Critical Biography.* London, 1934.

Pritchard, J. P., "Aristotle's *Poetics* and Certain American Critics," *Classical Weekly*, XXVII, 81–85 (1934).

Stedman, E. C., *Poets of America.* Boston, 1885, pp. 225–272.

Stovall, Floyd, "An Interpretation of Poe's 'Al Aaraaf,' " University of Texas *Studies in English*, IX (1929), 106–133. Furnishes a mass of evidence to support Woodberry's view that Coleridge was "the guiding genius of Poe's entire intellectual life"; pp. 80–114 deal with poetic and critical theory.

Werner, W. L., "Poe's Theories and Practices in Poetic Technique," *American Literature*, II, 157–165 (May, 1930).

Wilson, J. S., "Poe's Philosophy of Composition," *North American Review*, CCXXIII, 675–684.

——, *Tales of Edgar Allan Poe.* New York, 1927, pp. v–xxi.

Wilt, Napier, "Poe's Attitude toward His Tales," *Modern Philology*, XXV, 101–105 (August, 1927).

Woodberry, G. E., *Edgar Allan Poe.* Boston, 1885. (American Men of Letters Series.)

——, *The Life of Edgar Allan Poe, Personal and Literary, with His Chief Correspondence with Men of Letters.* 2 vols. Boston, 1909. Generally regarded as the best literary biography of Poe.

THE POETIC PRINCIPLE

1848

In speaking of the Poetic Principle, I have no design to be either thorough or profound. While discussing, very much at random, the essentiality of what we call poetry, my principal purpose will be to cite for consideration, some few of those minor English or American poems which best suit my own taste, or which, upon my own fancy, have left the most definite impression. By "minor poems" I mean, of course, poems of little length. And here, in the beginning, permit me to say a few words in regard to a somewhat peculiar principle which, whether rightfully or wrongfully, has always had its influence in my own critical estimate of the poem. I hold that a long poem does not exist. I maintain that the phrase, " a long poem," is simply a flat contradiction in terms.

I need scarcely observe that a poem deserves its title only inasmuch as it excites, by elevating the soul. The value of the poem is in the ratio of this elevating excitement. But all excitements are, through a psychal necessity, transient. That degree of excitement which would entitle a poem to be so called at all, cannot be sustained throughout a composition of any great length. After the lapse of half an hour, at the very utmost, it flags—fails—a revulsion ensues—and then the poem is, in effect, and in fact, no longer such.

There are, no doubt, many who have found difficulty in reconciling the critical dictum that the *Paradise Lost* is to be devoutly admired throughout, with the absolute impossibility of maintaining for it, during perusal, the amount of enthusiasm which that critical dictum would demand. This great work, in fact, is to be regarded as poetical, only when, losing sight of that vital requisite in all works of art, unity, we view it merely as a series of minor poems. If, to preserve its unity—its totality of effect or impression—we read it (as would be necessary) at a single sitting, the result is but a constant alternation of excitement and depression. After a passage of what we feel to be true poetry, there follows, inevitably, a passage of platitude which no critical pre-judgment can force us to admire; but if, upon completing the work, we read it again; omitting the first book— that is to say, commencing with the second—we shall be surprised at now finding that admirable which we before condemned—that damnable which we had previously so much admired. It follows from all this that the ultimate, aggregate, or absolute effect of even the best epic under the sun is a nullity: —and this is precisely the fact.

In regard to the *Iliad*, we have, if not positive proof, at least very good reason, for believing it intended as a series of lyrics; but, granting the epic intention, I can say only that the work is based in an imperfect sense of art. The modern epic is, of the supposititious ancient model, but an inconsiderate and blind-fold imitation. But the day of these artistic anomalies is over. If, at any time, any very long poem *were* popular in reality, which I doubt, it is at least clear that no very long poem will ever be popular again.

That the extent of a poetical work is, *ceteris paribus*, the measure of its merit seems undoubtedly, when we thus state it, a proposition sufficiently absurd—yet we are indebted for it to the Quarterly Reviews. Surely there can be nothing in mere *size*, abstractly considered—there can be nothing in mere *bulk*, so far as a volume is concerned, which has so continuously elicited admiration from these saturnine pamphlets! A mountain, to be sure, by the mere sentiment of physical magnitude which it conveys *does* impress us with a sense of the sublime—but no man is impressed after *this* fashion by the material grandeur of even the *Columbiad*. Even the Quarterlies have not instructed us to be so impressed by it. *As yet*, they have not *insisted* on our estimating Lamartine by the cubic foot, or Pollok by the pound— but what else are we to *infer* from their continual prating about "sustained effort"? If, by "sustained effort," any little gentleman has accomplished an epic, let us frankly commend him for the effort—if this indeed be a thing commendable—but let us forbear praising the epic on the effort's account. It is to be hoped that common sense, in the time to come, will prefer deciding upon a work of art, rather by the impression it makes, by the effect it produces, than by the time it took to impress the effect or by the amount of "sustained effort" which had been found necessary in effecting the impression. The fact is, that perseverance is one thing, and genius quite another—nor can all the Quarterlies in Christendom confound them. By-and-by, this proposition, with many which I have been just urging, will be received as self-evident. In the meantime, by being generally condemned as falsities, they will not be essentially damaged as truths.

On the other hand, it is clear that a poem may be improperly brief. Undue brevity degenerates into mere epigrammatism. A *very* short poem, while now and then producing a brilliant or vivid, never produces a profound or enduring effect. There must be the steady pressing down of the stamp upon the wax. De Béranger has wrought innumerable things, pungent and spirit-stirring; but, in general, they have been too imponderous to stamp themselves deeply into the public attention; and thus, as so many feathers of fancy, have been blown aloft only to be whistled down the wind.

A remarkable instance of the effect of undue brevity in depressing a poem—in keeping it out of the popular view—is afforded by the following exquisite little serenade:

> I arise from dreams of thee
>   In the first sweet sleep of night,
> When the winds are breathing low,
>   And the stars are shining bright;
> I arise from dreams of thee,
>   And a spirit in my feet
> Has led me—who knows how?—
>   To thy chamber window, sweet!

The wandering airs, they faint
  On the dark, the silent stream—
The champak odors fail
  Like sweet thoughts in a dream;
The nightingale's complaint,
  It dies upon her heart,
As I must die on thine,
  O, beloved as thou art!

O, lift me from the grass!
  I die, I faint, I fail!
Let thy love in kisses rain
  On my lips and eyelids pale.
My cheek is cold and white, alas!
  My heart beats loud and fast:
Oh! press it close to thine again,
  Where it will break at last!

Very few, perhaps, are familiar with these lines—yet no less a poet than Shelley is their author. Their warm, yet delicate and ethereal imagination will be appreciated by all—but by none so thoroughly as by him who has himself arisen from sweet dreams of one beloved to bathe in the aromatic air of a southern midsummer night.

One of the finest poems by Willis—the very best, in my opinion, which he has ever written—has, no doubt, through this same defect of undue brevity, been kept back from its proper position, not less in the critical than in the popular view.

The shadows lay along Broadway,
  'Twas near the twilight-tide—
And slowly there a lady fair
  Was walking in her pride.
Alone walked she; but, viewlessly,
  Walked spirits at her side.

Peace charmed the street beneath her feet,
  And Honor charmed the air;
And all astir looked kind on her,
  And called her good as fair—
For all God ever gave to her
  She kept with chary care.

She kept with care her beauties rare
  From lovers warm and true—

For her heart was cold to all but gold,
  And the rich came not to woo—
But honored well are charms to sell,
  If priests the selling do.

Now walking there was one more fair—
  A slight girl, lily-pale;
And she had unseen company
  To make the spirit quail—
'Twixt Want and Scorn she walked forlorn,
  And nothing could avail.

No mercy now can clear her brow
  For this world's peace to pray;
For, as love's wild prayer dissolved in air,
  Her woman's heart gave way!—
But the sin forgiven by Christ in Heaven
  By man is cursed alway!

In this composition we find it difficult to recognize the Willis who has written so many mere "verses of society." The lines are not only richly ideal, but full of energy; while they breathe an earnestness—an evident sincerity of sentiment—for which we look in vain throughout all the other works of this author.

While the epic mania—while the idea that, to merit in poetry, prolixity is indispensable—has for some years past been gradually dying out of the public mind, by mere dint of its own absurdity—we find it succeeded by a heresy too palpably false to be long tolerated, but one which, in the brief period it has already endured, may be said to have accomplished more in the corruption of our poetical literature than all its other enemies combined. I allude to the heresy of the *didactic*. It has been assumed, tacitly and avowedly, directly and indirectly, that the ultimate object of all poetry is truth. Every poem, it is said, should inculcate a moral; and by this moral is the poetical merit of the work to be adjudged. We Americans especially have patronized this happy idea; and we Bostonians, very especially, have developed it in full. We have taken it into our heads that to write a poem simply for the poem's sake, and to acknowledge such to have been our design, would be to confess ourselves radically wanting in the true poetic dignity and force:—but the simple fact is that, would we but permit ourselves to look into our own souls, we should immediately there discover that under the sun there neither exists nor *can* exist any work more thor-

oughly dignified—more supremely noble than this very poem—
this poem *per se*—this poem which is a poem and nothing more—
this poem written solely for the poem's sake.

With as deep a reverence for the true as ever inspired the
bosom of man, I would, nevertheless, limit in some measure its
modes of inculcation. I would limit to enforce them. I would
not enfeeble them by dissipation. The demands of truth are
severe. She has no sympathy with the myrtles. All *that* which is
so indispensable in song, is precisely all *that* with which *she* has
nothing whatever to do. It is but making her a flaunting paradox
to wreathe her in gems and flowers. In enforcing a truth, we
need severity rather than efflorescence of language. We must
be simple, precise, terse. We must be cool, calm, unimpassioned.
In a word, we must be in that mood which, as nearly as possible,
is the exact converse of the poetical. *He* must be blind, indeed,
who does not perceive the radical and chasmal differences
between the truthful and the poetical modes of inculcation.
He must be theory-mad beyond redemption who, in spite of
these differences, shall still persist in attempting to reconcile the
obstinate oils and waters of poetry and truth.

Dividing the world of mind into its three most obvious distinctions, we have the pure intellect, taste, and the moral sense.
I place taste in the middle, because it is just this position which,
in the mind, it occupies. It holds intimate relations with either
extreme; but from the moral sense is separated by so faint a
difference that Aristotle has not hesitated to place some of its
operations among the virtues themselves. Nevertheless, we find
the *offices* of the trio marked with a sufficient distinction. Just
as the intellect concerns itself with truth, so taste informs us of
the beautiful while the moral sense is regardful of duty. Of this
latter, while conscience teaches the obligation, and reason the
expediency, taste contents herself with displaying the charms:—
waging war upon vice solely on the ground of her deformity—
her disproportion, her animosity to the fitting, to the appropriate,
to the harmonious—in a word, to beauty.

An immortal instinct, deep within the spirit of man, is thus,
plainly, a sense of the beautiful. This it is which administers to
his delight in the manifold forms, and sounds, and odors, and
sentiments amid which he exists. And just as the lily is repeated
in the lake, or the eyes of Amaryllis in the mirror, so is the mere
oral or written repetition of these forms, and sounds, and colors,

and odors, and sentiments a duplicate source of delight. But this mere repetition is not poetry. He who shall simply sing, with however glowing enthusiasm, or with however vivid a truth of description, of the sights, and sounds, and odors, and colors, and sentiments which greet *him* in common with all mankind—he, I say, has yet failed to prove his divine title. There is still a something in the distance which he has been unable to attain. We have still a thirst unquenchable, to allay which he has not shown us the crystal springs. This thirst belongs to the immortality of man. It is at once a consequence and an indication of his perennial existence. It is the desire of the moth for the star. It is no mere appreciation of the beauty before us—but a wild effort to reach the beauty above. Inspired by an ecstatic prescience of the glories beyond the grave, we struggle, by multiform combinations among the things and thoughts of time, to attain a portion of that loveliness whose very elements, perhaps, appertain to eternity alone. And thus when by poetry—or when by music, the most entrancing of the poetic moods—we find ourselves melted into tears—we weep then—not as the Abbate Gravina supposes—through excess of pleasure, but through a certain, petulant, impatient sorrow at our inability to grasp *now*, wholly, here on earth, at once and forever, those divine and rapturous joys, of which *through* the poem, or *through* the music, we attain to but brief and indeterminate glimpses.

The struggle to apprehend the supernal loveliness—this struggle, on the part of souls fittingly constituted—has given to the world all *that* which it (the world) has ever been enabled at once to understand and *to feel* as poetic.

The poetic sentiment, of course, may develop itself in various modes—in painting, in sculpture, in architecture, in the dance— very especially in music—and very peculiarly, and with a wide field, in the composition of the landscape garden. Our present theme, however, has regard only to its manifestation in words. And here let me speak briefly on the topic of rhythm. Contenting myself with the certainty that music in its various modes of meter, rhythm, and rhyme is of so vast a moment in poetry as never to be wisely rejected—is so vitally important an adjunct, that he is simply silly who declines its assistance—I will not now pause to maintain its absolute essentiality. It is in music, perhaps, that the soul most nearly attains the great end for which, when inspired by the poetic sentiment, it struggles—the creation of supernal beauty. It *may* be, indeed, that here this sublime end is, now and then, attained *in fact*. We are often made to feel, with a shivering delight, that from an earthly harp are stricken notes which *cannot* have been unfamiliar to the angels. And thus there can be little doubt that in the union of poetry with music in its popular sense we shall find the widest field for the poetic development. The old bards and minne-singers had advantages which we do not possess—and Thomas Moore, singing his own songs, was, in the most legitimate manner, perfecting them as poems.

To recapitulate, then:—I would define, in brief, the poetry of words as *the rhythmical creation of beauty*. Its sole arbiter is taste. With the intellect or with the conscience, it has only collateral relations. Unless incidentally, it has no concern whatever either with duty or with truth.

A few words, however, in explanation. *That* pleasure which is at once the most pure, the most elevating, and the most in-tense is derived, I maintain, from the contemplation of the beautiful. In the contemplation of beauty we alone find it possible to attain that pleasurable elevation or excitement *of the soul* which we recognize as the poetic sentiment, and which is so easily distinguished from truth, which is the satis-faction of the reason, or from passion, which is the excitement of the heart. I make beauty, therefore—using the word as inclusive of the sublime—I make beauty the province of the poem, simply because it is an obvious rule of art that effects should be made to spring as directly as possible from their causes:—no one as yet having been weak enough to deny that the peculiar elevation in question is at least *most readily* attain-able in the poem. It by no means follows, however, that the incitements of passion, or the precepts of duty, or even the lessons of truth may not be introduced into a poem, and with advantage; for they may subserve, incidentally, in various ways, the general purposes of the work:—but the true artist will always contrive to tone them down in proper subjection to that *beauty* which is the atmosphere and the real essence of the poem.

I cannot better introduce the few poems which I shall present for your consideration than by the citation of the Proem to Mr. Longfellow's "Waif":

The day is done, and the darkness
　　Falls from the wings of Night,
As a feather is wafted downward
　　From an eagle in his flight.

I see the lights of the village
　　Gleam through the rain and the mist,
And a feeling of sadness comes o'er me,
　　That my soul cannot resist;

A feeling of sadness and longing,
　　That is not akin to pain,
And resembles sorrow only
　　As the mist resembles the rain.

Come, read to me some poem,
　　Some simple and heartfelt lay,
That shall soothe this restless feeling,
　　And banish the thoughts of day.

Not from the grand old masters,
　　Not from the bards sublime,
Whose distant footsteps echo
　　Through the corridors of Time.

For, like strains of martial music,
　　Their mighty thoughts suggest
Life's endless toil and endeavor;
　　And tonight I long for rest.

Read from some humbler poet,
　　Whose songs gushed from his heart,
As showers from the clouds of summer,
　　Or tears from the eyelids start;

Who through long days of labor,
　　And nights devoid of ease,
Still heard in his soul the music
　　Of wonderful melodies.

Such songs have power to quiet
　　The restless pulse of care,
And come like the benediction
　　That follows after prayer.

Then read from the treasured volume
　　The poem of thy choice,
And lend to the rhyme of the poet
　　The beauty of thy voice.

> And the night shall be filled with music,
>   And the cares that infest the day
> Shall fold their tents, like the Arabs,
>   And as silently steal away.

With no great range of imagination, these lines have been justly admired for their delicacy of expression. Some of the images are very effective. Nothing can be better than—

> ————The bards sublime,
>   Whose distant footsteps echo
> Down the corridors of Time.

The idea of the last quatrain is also very effective. The poem, on the whole, however, is chiefly to be admired for the graceful *insouciance* of its meter, so well in accordance with the character of the sentiments, and especially for the *ease* of the general manner. This "ease," or naturalness, in a literary style, it has long been the fashion to regard as ease in appearance alone— as a point of really difficult attainment. But not so:—a natural manner is difficult only to him who should never meddle with it —to the unnatural. It is but the result of writing with the understanding, or with the instinct, that *the tone*, in composition, should always be that which the mass of mankind would adopt—and must perpetually vary, of course, with the occasion. The author who, after the fashion of the *North American Review*, should be, upon *all* occasions, merely "quiet," must necessarily upon *many* occasions, be simply silly, or stupid; and has no more right to be considered "easy," or "natural," than a Cockney exquisite, or than the sleeping beauty in the wax-works.

Among the minor poems of Bryant, none has so much impressed me as the one which he entitles "June." I quote only a portion of it:

> There, through the long, long summer hours,
>   The golden light should lie,
> And thick young herbs and groups of flowers
>   Stand in their beauty by.
> The oriole should build and tell
> His love-tale, close beside my cell;
>   The idle butterfly
> Should rest him there, and there be heard
> The housewife-bee and hummingbird.

And what if cheerful shouts at noon
   Come, from the village sent,
Or songs of maids, beneath the moon,
   With fairy laughter blent?
And what if, in the evening light,
Betrothèd lovers walk in sight
   Of my low monument?
I would the lovely scene around
Might know no sadder sight nor sound.

I know, I know I should not see
   The season's glorious show,
Nor would its brightness shine for me,
   Nor its wild music flow;
But if, around my place of sleep,
The friends I love should come to weep,
   They might not haste to go.
Soft airs, and song, and light, and bloom
Should keep them lingering by my tomb.

These to their softened hearts should bear
   The thought of what has been,
And speak of one who cannot share
   The gladness of the scene;
Whose part, in all the pomp that fills
The circuit of the summer hills,
   Is—that his grave is green;
And deeply would their hearts rejoice
To hear again his living voice.

The rhythmical flow, here, is even voluptuous—nothing could be more melodious. The poem has always affected me in a remarkable manner. The intense melancholy which seems to well up, perforce, to the surface of all the poet's cheerful sayings about his grave, we find thrilling us to the soul—while there is the truest poetic elevation in the thrill. The impression left is one of a pleasurable sadness. And if, in the remaining compositions which I shall introduce to you, there be more or less of a similar tone always apparent, let me remind you that (how or why we know not) this certain taint of sadness is inseparably connected with all the higher manifestations of true beauty. It is, nevertheless,

A feeling of sadness and longing
   That is not akin to pain,

And resembles sorrow only
As the mist resembles the rain.

The taint of which I speak is clearly perceptible even in a poem so full of brilliancy and spirit as the "Health" of Edward Coate Pinckney:

I fill this cup to one made up
Of loveliness alone,
A woman, of her gentle sex
The seeming paragon;
To whom the better elements
And kindly stars have given
A form so fair, that, like the air,
'Tis less of earth than heaven.

Her every tone is music's own,
Like those of morning birds,
And something more than melody
Dwells ever in her words;
The coinage of her heart are they,
And from her lips each flows
As one may see the burdened bee
Forth issue from the rose.

Affections are as thoughts to her,
The measures of her hours;
Her feelings have the fragrancy,
The freshness of young flowers;
And lovely passions, changing oft,
So fill her, she appears
The image of themselves by turns,—
The idol of past years!

Of her bright face one glance will trace
A picture on the brain,
And of her voice in echoing hearts
A sound must long remain;
But memory, such as mine of her,
So very much endears,
When death is nigh, my latest sigh
Will not be life's but hers.

I fill this cup to one made up
Of loveliness alone,
A woman, of her gentle sex
The seeming paragon—

> Her health! and would on earth there stood
>   Some more of such a frame,
> That life might be all poetry,
>   And weariness a name.

It was the misfortune of Mr. Pinckney to have been born too far south. Had he been a New Englander, it is probable that he would have been ranked as the first of American lyrists, by that magnanimous cabal which has so long controlled the destinies of American letters, in conducting the thing called the *North American Review*. The poem just cited is especially beautiful; but the poetic elevation which it induces, we must refer chiefly to our sympathy in the poet's enthusiasm. We pardon his hyperboles for the evident earnestness with which they are uttered.

It was by no means my design, however, to expatiate upon the *merits* of what I should read you. These will necessarily speak for themselves. Boccalini, in his *Advertisements from Parnassus*, tells us that Zoilus once presented Apollo a very caustic criticism upon a very admirable book:—whereupon the god asked him for the beauties of the work. He replied that he only busied himself about the errors. On hearing this, Apollo, handing him a sack of unwinnowed wheat, bade him pick out *all the chaff* for his reward.

Now this fable answers very well as a hit at the critics—but I am by no means sure that the god was in the right. I am by no means certain that the true limits of the critical duty are not grossly misunderstood. Excellence, in a poem especially, may be considered in the light of an axiom, which need only be properly *put*, to become self-evident. It is *not* excellence if it require to be demonstrated as such:—and thus, to point out too particularly the merits of a work of art, is to admit that they are *not* merits altogether.

Among the "melodies" of Thomas Moore is one whose distinguished character as a poem proper, seems to have been singularly left out of view. I allude to his lines beginning— "Come rest in this bosom." The intense energy of their expression is not surpassed by anything in Byron. There are two of the lines in which a sentiment is conveyed that embodies the *all in all* of the divine passion of love—a sentiment which, perhaps, has found its echo in more, and in more passionate, human hearts than any other single sentiment ever embodied in words:

Come, rest in this bosom, my own stricken deer,
Though the herd have fled from thee, thy home is still here;
Here still is the smile, that no cloud can o'ercast,
And a heart and a hand all thy own to the last.

Oh! what was love made for, if 't is not the same
Through joy and through torment, through glory and shame?
I know not, I ask not, if guilt 's in that heart,
I but know that I love thee, whatever thou art.

Thou hast called me thy angel in moments of bliss,
And thy angel I'll be, 'mid the horrors of this,—
Through the furnace, unshrinking, thy steps to pursue,
And shield thee, and save thee,—or perish there too!

It has been the fashion, of late days, to deny Moore imagination, while granting him fancy—a distinction originating with Coleridge—than whom no man more fully comprehended the great powers of Moore. The fact is, that the fancy of this poet so far predominates over all his other faculties, and over the fancy of all other men, as to have induced, very naturally, the idea that he is fanciful *only*. But never was there a greater mistake. Never was a grosser wrong done the fame of a true poet. In the compass of the English language I can call to mind no poem more profoundly—more weirdly *imaginative*, in the best sense, than the lines commencing—"I would I were by that dim lake"—which are the composition of Thomas Moore. I regret that I am unable to remember them.

One of the noblest—and, speaking of fancy, one of the most singularly fanciful of modern poets, was Thomas Hood. His "Fair Ines" had always, for me, an inexpressible charm:

O saw ye not fair Ines?
　She's gone into the West,
To dazzle when the sun is down,
　And rob the world of rest:
She took our daylight with her,
　The smiles that we love best,
With morning blushes on her cheek,
　And pearls upon her breast.

O turn again, fair Ines,
　Before the fall of night,
For fear the Moon should shine alone,
　And stars unrivaled bright;

And blessed will the lover be
　　That walks beneath their light,
And breathes the love against thy cheek
　　I dare not even write!

Would I had been, fair Ines,
　　That gallant cavalier,
Who rode so gaily by thy side,
　　And whispered thee so near!
Were there no bonny dames at home,
　　Or no true lovers here,
That he should cross the seas to win
　　The dearest of the dear?

I saw thee, lovely Ines,
　　Descend along the shore,
With bands of noble gentlemen,
　　And banners waved before;
And gentle youth and maidens gay,
　　And snowy plumes they wore;
It would have been a beauteous dream,
　　If it had been no more!

Alas, alas, fair Ines,
　　She went away with song,
With music waiting on her steps,
　　And shoutings of the throng;
But some were sad, and felt no mirth,
　　But only music's wrong,
In sounds that sang Farewell, Farewell,
　　To her you've loved so long.

Farewell, farewell, fair Ines,
　　That vessel never bore
So fair a lady on its deck,
　　Nor danced so light before,—
Alas for pleasure on the sea,
　　And sorrow on the shore!
The smile that blest one lover's heart
　　Has broken many more!

"The Haunted House," by the same author, is one of the truest poems ever written—one of the *truest*—one of the most unexceptionable—one of the most thoroughly artistic, both in its theme and in its execution. It is, moreover, powerfully ideal—imaginative. I regret that its length renders it unsuitable for the purposes of this lecture. In place of it, permit me to offer the universally appreciated "Bridge of Sighs."

> One more Unfortunate,
> Weary of breath,
> Rashly importunate,
> Gone to her death!
>
> Take her up tenderly,
> Lift her with care;
> Fashioned so slenderly,
> Young, and so fair!
>
> Look at her garments
> Clinging like cerements;
> Whilst the wave constantly
> Drips from her clothing;
> Take her up instantly,
> Loving, not loathing.
>
> Touch her not scornfully;
> Think of her mournfully,
> Gently and humanly;
> Not of the stains of her,
> All that remains of her
> Now is pure womanly.
>
> Make no deep scrutiny
> Into her mutiny
> Rash and undutiful;
> Past all dishonor,
> Death has left on her
> Only the beautiful.
>
> Still, for all slips of hers,
> One of Eve's family—
> Wipe those poor lips of hers
> Oozing so clammily.
> Loop up her tresses
> Escaped from the comb,
> Her fair auburn tresses;
> Whilst wonderment guesses
> Where was her home?
>
> Who was her father?
> Who was her mother?
> Had she a sister?
> Had she a brother?

Or was there a dearer one
Still, and a nearer one
Yet, than all other?

Alas! for the rarity
Of Christian charity
Under the sun!
Oh! it was pitiful!
Near a whole city full,
Home she had none.

Sisterly, brotherly,
Fatherly, motherly
Feelings had changed:
Love, by harsh evidence,
Thrown from its eminence;
Even God's providence
Seeming estranged.

Where the lamps quiver
So far in the river,
With many a light
From window and casement,
From garret to basement,
She stood, with amazement,
Houseless by night.

The bleak wind of March
Made her tremble and shiver;
But not the dark arch,
Or the black flowing river:
Mad from life's history,
Glad to death's mystery,
Swift to be hurled—
Anywhere, anywhere
Out of the world!

In she plunged boldly,
No matter how coldly
The rough river ran,—
Over the brink of it,
Picture it—think of it,
Dissolute man!
Lave in it, drink of it
Then, if you can!

Take her up tenderly,
Lift her with care;

Fashioned so slenderly,
Young, and so fair!

Ere her limbs frigidly
Stiffen too rigidly,
Decently,—kindly,—
Smooth, and compose them,
And her eyes, close them,
Staring so blindly!

Dreadfully staring
Through muddy impurity,
As when with the daring
Last look of despairing
Fixed on futurity.

Perishing gloomily,
Spurred by contumely,
Cold inhumanity,
Burning insanity,
Into her rest.
Cross her hands humbly,
As if praying dumbly,
Over her breast!
Owning her weakness,
Her evil behavior,
And leaving, with meekness,
Her sins to her Savior!

The vigor of this poem is no less remarkable than its pathos.
The versification, although carrying the fanciful to the very
verge of the fantastic, is nevertheless admirably adapted to the
wild insanity which is the thesis of the poem.

Among the minor poems of Lord Byron is one which has
never received from the critics the praise which it undoubtedly
deserves:

Though the day of my destiny's over,
    And the star of my fate hath declined,
Thy soft heart refused to discover
    The faults which so many could find;
Though thy soul with my grief was acquainted,
    It shrunk not to share it with me,
And the love which my spirit hath painted
    It never hath found but in *thee*.

Then when nature around me is smiling,
   The last smile which answers to mine,
I do not believe it beguiling,
   Because it reminds me of thine;
And when winds are at war with the ocean,
   As the breasts I believed in with me,
If their billows excite an emotion,
   It is that they bear me from *thee*.

Though the rock of my last hope is shivered,
   And its fragments are sunk in the wave,
Though I feel that my soul is delivered
   To pain—it shall not be its slave.
There is many a pang to pursue me:
   They may crush, but they shall not contemn—
They may torture, but shall not subdue me—
   'T is of *thee* that I think—not of them.

Though human, thou didst not deceive me,
   Though woman, thou didst not forsake,
Though loved, thou forborest to grieve me,
   Though slandered, thou never couldst shake,—
Though trusted, thou didst not disclaim me,
   Though parted, it was not to fly,
Though watchful, 't was not to defame me,
   Nor mute, that the world might belie.

Yet I blame not the world, nor despise it,
   Nor the war of the many with one—
If my soul was not fitted to prize it,
   'T was folly not sooner to shun:
And if dearly that error hath cost me,
   And more than I once could foresee,
I have found that whatever it lost me,
   It could not deprive me of *thee*.

From the wreck of the past, which hath perished,
   Thus much I at least may recall,
It hath taught me that which I most cherished,
   Deserved to be dearest of all:
In the desert a fountain is springing,
   In the wide waste there still is a tree,
And a bird in the solitude singing,
   Which speaks to my spirit of *thee*.

Although the rhythm here is one of the most difficult, the versification could scarcely be improved. No nobler *theme* ever en-

gaged the pen of poet. It is the soul-elevating idea that no man
can consider himself entitled to complain of Fate while, in his
adversity, he still retains the unwavering love of woman.

From Alfred Tennyson—although in perfect sincerity I regard
him as the noblest poet that ever lived—I have left myself time
to cite only a very brief specimen. I call him, and *think* him the
noblest of poets—*not* because the impressions he produces are,
at *all* times, the most profound—*not* because the poetical excitement which he induces is, at *all* times, the most intense—but
because it *is*, at all times, the most ethereal—in other words,
the most elevating and the most pure. No poet is so little of the
earth, earthy. What I am about to read is from his last long
poem, *The Princess:*

> Tears, idle tears, I know not what they mean,
> Tears from the depth of some divine despair
> Rise in the heart, and gather to the eyes,
> In looking on the happy autumn-fields,
> And thinking of the days that are no more.
>
> Fresh as the first beam glittering on a sail
> That brings our friends up from the underworld,
> Sad as the last which reddens over one
> That sinks with all we love below the verge;
> So sad, so fresh, the days that are no more.
>
> Ah, sad and strange as in dark summer dawns
> The earliest pipe of half-awakened birds
> To dying ears, when unto dying eyes
> The casement slowly grows a glimmering square;
> So sad, so strange, the days that are no more.
>
> Dear as remembered kisses after death,
> And sweet as those by hopeless fancy feigned
> On lips that are for others; deep as love,
> Deep as first love, and wild with all regret;
> O Death in Life, the days that are no more!

Thus, although in a very cursory and imperfect manner, I
have endeavored to convey to you my conception of the Poetic
Principle. It has been my purpose to suggest that, while this
principle itself is strictly and simply the human aspiration for
supernal beauty, the manifestation of the principle is always
found in *an elevating excitement of the soul*—quite independent of
that passion which is the intoxication of the heart—or of that

truth which is the satisfaction of the reason. For, in regard to passion, alas! its tendency is to degrade, rather than to elevate the soul. Love, on the contrary—love—the true, the divine Eros—the Uranian, as distinguished from the Dionaean Venus—is unquestionably the purest and truest of all poetical themes. And in regard to truth—if, to be sure, through the attainment of a truth, we are led to perceive a harmony where none was apparent before, we experience, at once, the true poetical effect—but this effect is referable to the harmony alone, and not in the least degree to the truth which merely served to render the harmony manifest.

We shall reach, however, more immediately a distinct conception of what the true poetry is, by mere reference to a few of the simple elements which induce in the poet himself the true poetical effect. He recognizes the ambrosia which nourishes his soul, in the bright orbs that shine in heaven—in the volutes of the flower—in the clustering of low shrubberies—in the waving of the grain-fields—in the slanting of tall, eastern trees—in the blue distance of mountains—in the grouping of clouds—in the twinkling of half-hidden brooks—in the gleaming of silver rivers—in the repose of sequestered lakes—in the star-mirroring depths of lonely wells. He perceives it in the songs of birds—in the harp of Aeolus—in the sighing of the night wind—in the repining voice of the forest—in the surf that complains to the shore—in the fresh breath of the woods—in the scent of the violet—in the voluptuous perfume of the hyacinth—in the suggestive odor that comes to him, at eventide, from far-distant, undiscovered islands, over dim oceans, illimitable and unexplored. He owns it in all noble thoughts—in all unworldly motives—in all holy impulses—in all chivalrous, generous, and self-sacrificing deeds. He feels it in the beauty of woman—in the grace of her step—in the luster of her eye—in the melody of her voice—in her soft laughter—in her sigh—in the harmony of the rustling of her robes. He deeply feels it in her winning endearments—in her burning enthusiasms—in her gentle charities—in her meek and devotional endurances—but above all—ah, far above all—he kneels to it—he worships it in the faith, in the purity, in the strength, in the altogether divine majesty—of her *love*.

Let me conclude—by the recitation of yet another brief poem—one very different in character from any that I have before quoted. It is by Motherwell, and is called "The Song of the Cavalier." With our modern and altogether rational ideas of the absurdity and impiety of warfare, we are not precisely in that frame of mind best adapted to sympathize with the sentiments, and thus to appreciate the real excellence of the poem. To do this fully, we must identify ourselves, in fancy, with the soul of the old cavalier.

> Then mounte! then mounte, brave gallants, all,
>   And don your helmes amaine:
> Death's couriers, Fame and Honor, call
>   Us to the field againe.
> No shrewish teares shall fill our eye
>   When the sword-hilt's in our hand,—
> Heart-whole we'll part, and no whit sighe
>   For the fayrest of the land;
> Let piping swaine, and craven wight,
>   Thus weepe and puling crye,
> Our business is like men to fight,
>   And hero-like to die!

RALPH WALDO EMERSON

(1803–1882)

∘◯∘∘◯∘

WHILE POE SOUGHT A BEAUTY which tended in practice to be essentially divorced from virtue, a beauty to be arrived at mainly by mechanical means and attention to form, Emerson believed that the highest "beauty is the mark God sets upon virtue,"[1] that it is inseparable from the good life, and that since "expression is organic," form will take care of itself as the spontaneous by-product of the inspired idea. While Poe loathed generalized criticism and delighted in analyzing prosodic details and parts, Emerson practiced his theory that "criticism is an art when it does not stop at the words of the poet, but looks at the order of his thoughts and the essential quality of his mind. Then the critic is poet. 'Tis a question not of talents but of tone; and not particular merits, but the mood of mind into which one and another can bring us."[2] Both Poe and Emerson, however, were influenced by Coleridge[3] and his idealistic concept of poetry and the poetic imagination. Yet Emerson was more deeply rooted in the whole idealistic tradition which stretches from his master Plato[4] through the German transcendentalist Immanuel Kant whom Emerson praised as having provided "the best analysis of the mind."[5] Thus Emerson adopted as the basis of much of his criticism the idealistic distinctions between the law-abiding imagination and the capricious fancy, between inspired genius and prosaic talent, between intuitive reason and the logical understanding. Poetry is to be judged by its approach to architypes or ideals which exist not in the real world but in the highest imaginations of men, just as scientists discover immutable and universal laws of sensuous phenomena by examining them in the light of abstract hypotheses generated intuitively within their own

---

[1] Emerson's *Works* (Centenary edition), I, 19. For further evidence of his belief in "an interchangeable truth, beauty, and goodness, each wholly interfused in the other," see *ibid.*, III, 6–7; XII, 330; I, 354–355; VII, 48; X, 55; *Journals*, III, 35, 200.

[2] *Works*, XII, 305. This is the conclusion of Emerson's essay "Art and Criticism."

[3] For full discussion see F. T. Thompson, "Emerson's Indebtedness to Coleridge," *Studies in Philology*, XXIII, 55–76 (January, 1926).

[4] See Emerson's great tribute in his essay on Plato in *Representative Men;* his profound debt to Plato has been ably analyzed in J. S. Harrison's *Teachers of Emerson* (New York, 1910).　　　　　　　　　　　　　　　　　　　　　　　　　[5] *Works*, X, 328.

minds. Painting and poetry, Emerson says, appeal "to the vaticinating reason, and ask whether the object be agreeable to the pre-existent harmonies."[6] "Herein," he says, "is the legitimation of criticism, in the mind's faith that the poems are a corrupt version of some text in nature with which they ought to be made to tally."[7] "Truth and goodness subsist forevermore . . . What is this immortal demand for more, which belongs to our constitution? this enormous ideal? There is no such critic and beggar as this terrible Soul. No historical person begins to content us."[8]

Emerson attacked mere antiquarianism and the abject worship of books unrelated to the reader's own ethical life. But in the scholar's idle times, when he was visited by no direct inspiration of his own, he thought that books "well used" were "the best of things."[9] For books represent the past, tradition, one of our three teachers, the others being nature and action; and past, present, and future are "triple blossoms from one root."[10] He concludes his essay on "History" with the conviction that history, tradition embodied in books, should be read and written in the light of the faith that in all ages "the Mind is One,"[11] that men at their best have all been inspired by and in harmony with the "animated law" and the "beneficent tendency" which is the "Over-Soul."[12] Since the genius of past writers is nothing idiosyncratic but simply "a larger imbibing of the *common* heart,"[13] in a "creative reading" the "great poet makes *us* feel our own wealth" and enables *us* to be "born into the great, the universal mind."[14] Emerson said that his transcendental age was distinguished by "the enlargement and independency of the individual," and that "in literature the effect appeared in the decided tendency of criticism."[15] "There is something of poverty in our criticism. We assume that there are few great men, all the rest are little . . . We should know how to praise Socrates, or Plato, or St. John, without impoverishing us. In good hours we do not find Shakespeare or Homer over-great . . . Tis the good reader that makes the good book . . . The light by which we see in this world comes out from the soul of the observer."[16] Just as to Emerson God is revealed directly, without mediator or advocate, whenever anyone has a psychological impulse to do anything good, to approach even afar off what generations of men have agreed to call God-like, so whenever anyone imaginatively enters into the spirit of a great book he becomes akin to

[6]*Journals*, IV, 102–103.   [7]*Works*, III, 25.   [8]*Ibid.*, VII, 307.
[9]*Ibid.*, I, 89. See also Emerson's essay "Books."   [10]*Ibid.*, IX, 115.
[11]*Ibid.*, II, 38.   [12]*Works*, IX, 315; IV, 186.   [13]*Ibid.*, II, 288.
[14]*Ibid.*, II, 289; 296.   [15]*Ibid.*, X, 327–328.   [16]*Ibid.*, VII, 296.

its author and partakes of his inspiration. " 'Every scripture is to be interpreted by the same spirit which gave it forth,'—is the fundamental law of criticism. A life in harmony with Nature, the love of truth and of virtue, will purge the eyes to understand her text."[17] We must see the "most famous books [as] parts of a pre-established harmony, fatal, unalterable."[18] "Criticism should not be querulous and wasting, all knife and root-puller, but guiding, instructive, inspiring, a south wind, not an east wind."[19] In urging such an appreciative entering into books, Emerson was thinking, of course, only of the great books which he habitually read. He thought "the human mind would be a gainer if all the secondary writers were lost,—say, in England, all but Shakespeare, Milton, and Bacon . . . Never read any book that is not a year old . . . Never read any but famed books . . . Be sure then to read no mean books."[20] In most novels he found "no power, no furtherance. 'Tis only confectionery."

However, Emerson thought there were sufficient materials in the America of his day to serve as the basis of a great literature. He upbraided his contemporaries because they hesitated to chant their "own times and social circumstance. . . . Our log-rolling, our stumps and . . . politics . . . Oregon and Texas, are yet unsung. Yet America is a poem in our eyes; its ample geography dazzles the imagination, and it will not wait long for meters."[21] But just as the fact, the falling apple, was interpreted by Newton to reveal the law of gravity which is universal, so Emerson would have the fact, the American scene, used as the symbol of the unseen, the universal "spiritual laws."[22] Just as to the master artist, Michelangelo, in every block of marble no matter how shapeless and unattractive there is a lovely apparition which the shaping imagination can call forth, so to Emerson the "invariable mark of wisdom is to see the miraculous in the common," our material surroundings; for to him the imagination is "defined to be the use which the Reason makes of the material world"[23] in which "every natural fact is a symbol of some spiritual fact."[24]

Such are the general criteria Emerson uses in his criticism. In practice, Emerson takes high ground, and seldom if ever drops to the dis-

[17]*Ibid.*, I, 35.   [18]*Journals*, V, 398–399.   [19]*Journals*, VII, 291.

[20]*Works*, VII, 194–196 (in his essay "Books"). But see Flanagan in bibliography.

[21]*Ibid.*, III, 37–38. The third part of the essay "The Poet" is devoted to the demand for a literature which will take its start from the American scene. It will be recalled that at first Emerson praised Whitman's *Leaves of Grass*.

[22]Cf. *Works*, I, 25–35 (the chapter called "Language" in *Nature*). For full discussion see E. G. Sutcliffe, Emerson's *Theories of Literary Expression*, chap. III, "The Fact and the Symbol," pp. 27–106.

[23]*Works*, I, 52.

[24]*Ibid.*, I, 26.

cussion of formal minutiae which interested Poe. He usually begins a critical essay with a brief biography, and then proceeds to a general exposition of the writer's broad contributions, especially his ethical ideas, and concludes by a discussion of the extent to which he used variety, the life of the senses, to enlighten us regarding the One, the life of the spirit. The rare beauty of his style, and his optimistic inspirationalism do much to give his criticism a peculiar "lift" and memorable charm.

BIBLIOGRAPHY

TEXT

Complete Works of Ralph Waldo Emerson. Centenary edition. 12 vols. Boston, 1903–1904. Edited by Emerson's son, with a valuable bibliographical introduction and detailed notes. The standard edition.

A Correspondence between John Sterling and Ralph Waldo Emerson, ed. by E. W. Emerson. Boston, 1897.

The Correspondence of Thomas Carlyle and Ralph Waldo Emerson, 1834–1872, ed. by C. E. Norton. Rev. ed. 2 vols. Boston, 1888.

Emerson-Clough Letters, ed. by H. F. Lowry and R. L. Rusk. Cleveland, 1934. Sixteen hitherto unpublished letters by Emerson.

Emerson's Journals, ed. by Edward Emerson and Waldo Emerson Forbes. 10 vols. Boston, 1909–1914.

"The Emerson-Thoreau Correspondence," ed. by F. B. Sanborn, *Atlantic Monthly,* LXIX, 577–596, 736–753 (May and June, 1892).

The Heart of Emerson's Journals, ed. by Bliss Perry. Boston, 1926.

Letters, ed. by R. L. Rusk. 6 vols. Columbia University Press, 1939. The definitive edition of hitherto uncollected letters.

Letters from Ralph Waldo Emerson to a Friend [Samuel Gray Ward], ed. by C. E. Norton. Boston, 1899.

Uncollected Lectures of Ralph Waldo Emerson, ed. by C. L. F. Godhes. New York, 1932.

Uncollected Writings, Essays, Addresses, Poems, Reviews and Letters by Ralph Waldo Emerson, ed. by C. C. Bigelow. New York, 1912.

BIBLIOGRAPHY

Cooke, G. W., *A Bibliography of Ralph Waldo Emerson.* Boston, 1908. Exhaustive up to its date. Pp. 205–309 list studies about Emerson.

Steeves, H. R., *The Cambridge History of American Literature.* New York, 1917. I, 551–566. "It includes in particular all the publications of importance which have appeared [up to 1917] since Mr. Cooke's volume."

BIOGRAPHY AND CRITICISM

Allen, Gay W., *American Prosody.* New York, 1935, pp. 91–121.

Arnold, Matthew, "Emerson," in *Discourses in America.* London, 1885, pp. 138–207.

De Mille, G. E., *Literary Criticism in America*. New York, 1931, pp. 118–132.

Flanagan, J. T., "Emerson as a Critic of Fiction," *Philological Quarterly*, XV, 30–45 (January, 1936).

Foerster, Norman, "Emerson," in *American Criticism*. Boston, 1928, pp. 52–110.

Goddard, H. C., *Studies in New England Transcendentalism*. New York, 1908. The standard study of the subject.

——, "Transcendentalism," in *The Cambridge History of American Literature*, I, 326–348, with bibliography, pp. 546–551.

Gohdes, C. L. F., *The Periodicals of American Transcendentalism*. Durham, North Carolina, 1931.

Gorely, Jean, "Emerson's Theory of Poetry," *Poetry Review*, XXII, 263–273 (July–August, 1931).

Gray, H. D., *Emerson: A Statement of New England Transcendentalism as Expressed in the Philosophy of its Chief Exponent*. Stanford University Press, 1917.

Harrison, J. S., *The Teachers of Emerson*. New York, 1910. Emerson's profound debt to dualistic Platonism and Neo-Platonism with some reference to Bacon and Coleridge.

Jorgenson, C. E., "Emerson's Paradise under the Shadow of Swords," *Philological Quarterly*, XI, 274–292 (July, 1932).

MacRea, Donald, "Emerson and the Arts," *The Art Bulletin*, XX, 78–95 (1938). (Based on a doctoral dissertation.)

Michaud, Régis, *L'Esthétique d'Emerson*. Paris, 1927.

Moore, J. B., "Emerson on Wordsworth," *Publications of the Modern Language Association*, XLI, 179–192 (March, 1926).

Perry, Bliss, *Emerson Today*. Princeton, 1931.

——, *The Praise of Folly*. Boston, 1923, pp. 81–113.

Pettigrew, R. C., "Emerson and Milton," *American Literature*, III, 45–59 (March, 1931).

Stenberg, J. J., "Emerson and Oral Discourse," in *Studies in Rhetoric and Public Speaking in Honor of James Albert Winans by Pupils and Colleagues*. New York, 1925, pp. 153–180.

Sutcliffe, E. G., *Emerson's Theories of Literary Expression*. University of Illinois Studies in Language and Literature (1923), VIII, no. 1.

Thompson, F. T., "Emerson and Carlyle," *Studies in Philology*, XXIV, 438–453 (July, 1927).

——, "Emerson's Indebtedness to Coleridge," *Studies in Philology*, XXIII, 55–76 (January, 1926).

——, "Emerson's Theory and Practice of Poetry," *Publications of the Modern Language Association*, XLIII, 1170–1184 (December, 1928).

Ustick, W. L., "Emerson's Debt to Montaigne," *Washington University Studies*, Humanistic Series (1921), IX, 4th series, no. 2, 245–262.

THE POET
1844

A moody child and wildly wise
Pursued the game with joyful eyes,
Which chose, like meteors, their way,
And rived the dark with private ray:
They overleapt the horizon's edge,
Searched with Apollo's privilege;
Through man, and woman, and sea, and star
Saw the dance of nature forward far;
Through worlds, and races, and terms, and times
Saw musical order, and pairing rhymes.

Olympian bards who sung
Divine ideas below,
Which always find us young,
And always keep us so.

Those who are esteemed umpires of taste are often persons who have acquired some knowledge of admired pictures or sculptures, and have an inclination for whatever is elegant; but if you inquire whether they are beautiful souls, and whether their own acts are like fair pictures, you learn that they are selfish and sensual. Their cultivation is local, as if you should rub a log of dry wood in one spot to produce fire, all the rest remaining cold. Their knowledge of the fine arts is some study of rules and particulars, or some limited judgment of color or form, which is exercised for amusement or for show. It is a proof of the shallowness of the doctrine of beauty as it lies in the minds of our amateurs that men seem to have lost the perception of the instant dependence of form upon soul. There is no doctrine of forms in our philosophy. We were put into our bodies, as fire is put into a pan to be carried about; but there is no accurate adjustment between the spirit and the organ, much less is the latter the germination of the former. So in regard to other forms, the intellectual men do not believe in any essential dependence of the material world on thought and volition. Theologians think it a pretty air castle to talk of the spiritual meaning of a ship or a cloud, of a city or a contract, but they prefer to come again to the solid ground of historical evidence; and even the poets are contented with a civil and conformed manner of living, and to write poems from the fancy, at a safe distance from their own experience. But the highest minds of the world have never ceased to explore the double meaning, or shall I say the quadruple or the centuple or much more manifold meaning, of every sensuous fact; Orpheus, Empedocles, Heraclitus, Plato, Plutarch, Dante, Swedenborg, and the masters of sculpture, picture, and poetry. For we are not pans and barrows, nor even porters of the fire and torchbearers, but children of the fire, made of it, and only the same divinity transmuted and at two or three removes, when we know least about it. And this hidden truth, that the fountains whence all this river of Time and its creatures floweth are intrinsically ideal and beautiful, draws us to the consideration of the nature and functions of the poet, or the man of beauty; to the means and materials he uses, and to the general aspect of the art in the present time.

The breadth of the problem is great, for the poet is representative. He stands among partial men for the complete man, and apprises us not of his wealth, but of the common wealth. The young man reveres men of genius, because, to speak truly, they are more himself than he is. They receive of the soul as he also receives, but they more. Nature enhances her beauty, to the eye of loving men, from their belief that the poet is beholding her shows at the same time. He is isolated among his contemporaries by truth and by his art, but with this consolation in his pursuits, that they will draw all men sooner or later. For all men live by truth and stand in need of expression. In love, in art, in avarice, in politics, in labor, in games, we study to utter our painful secret. The man is only half himself, the other half is his expression.

Notwithstanding this necessity to be published, adequate expression is rare. I know not how it is that we need an interpreter, but the great majority of men seem to be minors, who have not yet come into possession of their own, or mutes, who cannot report the conversation they have had with nature. There is no man who does not anticipate a supersensual utility in the sun and stars, earth and water. These stand and wait to render him a peculiar service. But there is some obstruction or some excess of phlegm in our constitution, which does not suffer them to yield the due effect. Too feeble fall the impressions of nature on us to make us artists. Every touch should thrill. Every man should be so much an artist that he could report in conversation what had befallen him. Yet, in our experience, the rays or appulses have sufficient force to arrive at the senses, but not enough to reach the quick and compel the reproduction of themselves in speech. The poet is the person in whom these powers are in balance, the man without impediment, who sees and handles that which others dream of, traverses the whole scale of experience, and is representative of man, in virtue of being the largest power to receive and to impart.

For the universe has three children, born at one time, which reappear under different names, in every system of thought, whether they be called cause, operation, and effect; or, more poetically, Jove, Pluto, Neptune; or, theologically, the Father, the Spirit, and the Son; but which we will call here the Knower, the Doer, and the Sayer. These stand respectively for the love of truth, for the love of good, and for the love of beauty. These three are equal. Each is that which he is, essentially, so that he cannot be surmounted or analyzed, and each of these three has the power of the others latent in him and his own, patent.

The poet is the sayer, the namer, and represents beauty. He is a sovereign, and stands on the center. For the world is not painted or adorned, but is from the beginning beautiful; and God has not made some beautiful things, but beauty is the creator of the universe. Therefore the poet is not any permissive potentate, but is emperor in his own right. Criticism is infested with a cant of materialism, which assumes that manual skill and activity is the first merit of all men, and disparages such as say and do not, overlooking the fact that some men, namely poets, are natural sayers, sent into the world to the end of expression, and confounds them with those whose province is action but who quit it to imitate the sayers. But Homer's words are as costly and admirable to Homer as Agamemnon's victories are to Agamemnon. The poet does not wait for the hero or the sage, but, as they act and think primarily, so he writes primarily what will and must be spoken, reckoning the others, though primaries also, yet, in respect to him, secondaries and servants; as sitters or models in the studio of a painter, or as assistants who bring building materials to an architect.

For poetry was all written before time was, and whenever we are so finely organized that we can penetrate into that region where the air is music, we hear those primal warblings and attempt to write them down, but we lose ever and anon a word or a verse and substitute something of our own, and thus miswrite the poem. The men of more delicate ear write down these cadences more faithfully, and these transcripts, though imperfect, become the songs of the nations. For nature is as truly beautiful as it is good, or as it is reasonable, and must as much appear as it must be done, or be known. Words and deeds are quite indifferent modes of the divine energy. Words are also actions, and actions are a kind of words.

The sign and credentials of the poet are that he announces that which no man foretold. He is the true and only doctor; he knows and tells; he is the only teller of news, for he was present and privy to the appearance which he describes. He is a beholder of ideas and an utterer of the necessary and causal. For we do not speak now of men of poetical talents, or of industry and skill in meter, but of the true poet. I took part in a conversation the other day concerning a recent writer of lyrics, a man of subtle mind, whose head appeared to be a music box of delicate tunes and rhythms, and whose skill and command of language we could not sufficiently praise. But when the question arose whether he was not only a lyrist but a poet, we were obliged to confess that he is plainly a contemporary, not an eternal man. He does not stand out of our low limitations, like a Chimborazo under the line, running up from a torrid base through all the climates of the globe, with belts of the herbage of every latitude on its high and mottled sides; but this genius is the landscape-garden of a modern house, adorned with fountains and statues, with well-bred men and women standing and sitting in the walks and terraces. We hear, through all the varied music, the ground-tone of conventional life. Our poets are men of talents who sing, and not the children of music. The argument is secondary, the finish of the verses is primary.

For it is not meters, but a meter-making argument that makes a poem—a thought so passionate and alive that like the spirit of a plant or an animal it has an architecture of its own, and adorns nature with a new thing. The thought and the form are equal in the order of time, but in the order of genesis the thought is prior to the form. The poet has a new thought; he has a whole new experience to unfold; he will tell us how it was with him, and all men will be the richer in his fortune. For the experience of each new age requires a new confession, and the world seems always waiting for its poet. I remember when I was young how much I was moved one morning by tidings that

genius had appeared in a youth who sat near me at table. He
had left his work and gone rambling none knew whither, and
had written hundreds of lines, but could not tell whether that
which was in him was therein told; he could tell nothing but
that all was changed,—man, beast, heaven, earth, and sea.
How gladly we listened! how credulous! Society seemed to be
compromised. We sat in the aurora of a sunrise which was
to put out all the stars. Boston seemed to be at twice the distance
it had the night before, or was much farther than that. Rome—
what was Rome? Plutarch and Shakespeare were in the yellow
leaf, and Homer no more should be heard of. It is much to
know that poetry has been written this very day, under this
very roof, by your side. What! that wonderful spirit has not
expired! These stony moments are still sparkling and animated!
I had fancied that the oracles were all silent, and nature had
spent her fires; and behold! all night, from every pore, these
fine auroras have been streaming. Everyone has some interest
in the advent of the poet, and no one knows how much it may
concern him. We know that the secret of the world is profound,
but who or what shall be our interpreter, we know not. A
mountain ramble, a new style of face, a new person, may put
the key into our hands. Of course the value of genius to us is in
the veracity of its report. Talent may frolic and juggle; genius
realizes and adds. Mankind, in good earnest, have availed so
far in understanding themselves and their work, that the
foremost watchman on the peak announces his news. It
is the truest word ever spoken, and the phrase will be the
fittest, most musical, and the unerring voice of the world for
that time.

All that we call sacred history attests that the birth of a poet
is the principal event in chronology. Man, never so often
deceived, still watches for the arrival of a brother who can hold
him steady to a truth until he has made it his own. With what
joy I begin to read a poem, which I confide in as an inspiration!
And now my chains are to be broken; I shall mount above these
clouds and opaque airs in which I live—opaque, though they
seem transparent—and from the heaven of truth I shall see and
comprehend my relations. That will reconcile me to life and
renovate nature, to see trifles animated by a tendency, and to
know what I am doing. Life will no more be a noise; now I
shall see men and women, and know the signs by which they

may be discerned from fools and satans. This day shall be better than my birthday: then I became an animal; now I am invited into the science of the real. Such is the hope, but the fruition is postponed. Oftener it falls that this winged man, who will carry me into the heaven, whirls me into mists, then leaps and frisks about with me as it were from cloud to cloud, still affirming that he is bound heavenward; and I, being myself a novice, am slow in perceiving that he does not know the way into the heavens, and is merely bent that I should admire his skill to rise like a fowl or a flying fish, a little way from the ground or the water; but the all-piercing, all-feeding, and ocular air of heaven that man shall never inhabit. I tumble down again soon into my old nooks, and lead the life of exaggerations as before, and have lost my faith in the possibility of any guide who can lead me thither where I would be.

But, leaving these victims of vanity, let us, with new hope, observe how nature, by worthier impulses, has insured the poet's fidelity to his office of announcement and affirming, namely by the beauty of things, which becomes a new and higher beauty when expressed. Nature offers all her creatures to him as a picture language. Being used as a type, a second wonderful value appears in the object, far better than its old value; as the carpenter's stretched cord, if you hold your ear close enough, is musical in the breeze. "Things more excellent than every image," says Jamblichus, "are expressed through images." Things admit of being used as symbols because nature is a symbol, in the whole, and in every part. Every line we can draw in the sand has expression; and there is no body without its spirit or genius. All form is an effect of character; all condition, of the quality of the life; all harmony, of health; and for this reason a perception of beauty should be sympathetic, or proper only to the good. The beautiful rests on the foundations of the necessary. The soul makes the body, as the wise Spenser teaches:—

> So every spirit, as it is more pure,
> And hath in it the more of heavenly light,
> So it the fairer body doth procure
> To habit in, and it more fairly dight,
> With cheerful grace and amiable sight.
> For, of the soul, the body form doth take,
> For soul is form, and doth the body make.

Here we find ourselves suddenly not in a critical speculation but in a holy place, and should go very warily and reverently. We stand before the secret of the world, there where being passes into appearance and unity into variety.

The universe is the externization of the soul. Wherever the life is, that bursts into appearance around it. Our science is sensual, and therefore superficial. The earth and the heavenly bodies, physics and chemistry, we sensually treat, as if they were self-existent; but these are the retinue of that being we have. "The mighty heaven," said Proclus, "exhibits, in its trans-figurations, clear images of the splendor of intellectual per-ceptions; being moved in conjunction with the unapparent periods of intellectual natures." Therefore science always goes abreast with the just elevation of the man, keeping step with religion and metaphysics; or the state of science is an index of our self-knowledge. Since everything in nature answers to a moral power, if any phenomenon remains brute and dark it is because the corresponding faculty in the observer is not yet active.

No wonder then, if these waters be so deep, that we hover over them with a religious regard. The beauty of the fable proves the importance of the sense; to the poet, and to all others; or, if you please, every man is so far a poet as to be susceptible of these enchantments of nature; for all men have the thoughts whereof the universe is the celebration. I find that the fascination resides in the symbol. Who loves nature? Who does not? Is it only poets, and men of leisure and cultivation, who live with her? No; but also hunters, farmers, grooms, and butchers, though they express their affection in their choice of life and not in their choice of words. The writer wonders what the coachman or the hunter values in riding, in horses and dogs. It is not superficial qualities. When you talk with him, he holds these at as slight a rate as you. His worship is sympathetic; he has no definitions, but he is commanded in nature by the living power which he feels to be there present. No imitation or playing of these things would content him; he loves the earnest of the north wind, of rain, of stone and wood and iron. A beauty not ex-plicable is dearer than a beauty which we can see to the end of. It is nature the symbol, nature certifying the supernatural, body overflowed by life which he worships with coarse but sincere rites.

The inwardness and mystery of this attachment drive men of every class to the use of emblems. The schools of poets and philosophers are not more intoxicated with their symbols than the populace with theirs. In our political parties, compute the power of badges and emblems. See the great ball which they roll from Baltimore to Bunker Hill! In the political processions, Lowell goes in a loom, and Lynn in a shoe, and Salem in a ship. Witness the cider barrel, the log cabin, the hickory stick, the palmetto, and all the cognizances of party. See the power of national emblems. Some stars, lilies, leopards, a crescent, a lion, an eagle, or other figure which came into credit God knows how, on an old rag of bunting, blowing in the wind on a fort at the ends of the earth, shall make the blood tingle under the rudest or the most conventional exterior. The people fancy they hate poetry, and they are all poets and mystics!

Beyond this universality of the symbolic language, we are apprised of the divineness of this superior use of things, whereby the world is a temple whose walls are covered with emblems, pictures, and commandments of the Deity—in this, that there is no fact in nature which does not carry the whole sense of nature; and the distinctions which we make in events, and in affairs, of low and high, honest and base, disappear when nature is used as a symbol. Thought makes everything fit for use. The vocabulary of an omniscient man would embrace words and images excluded from polite conversation. What would be base, or even obscene, to the obscene, becomes illustrious, spoken in a new connection of thought. The piety of the Hebrew prophets purges their grossness. The circumcision is an example of the power of poetry to raise the low and offensive. Small and mean things serve as well as great symbols. The meaner the type by which a law is expressed, the more pungent it is, and the more lasting in the memories of men; just as we choose the smallest box or case in which any needful utensil can be carried. Bare lists of words are found suggestive to an imaginative and excited mind; as it is related of Lord Chatham that he was accustomed to read in Bailey's *Dictionary* when he was preparing to speak in Parliament. The poorest experience is rich enough for all the purposes of expressing thought. Why covet a knowledge of new facts? Day and night, house and garden, a few books, a few actions, serve us as well as would all trades and all spectacles. We are far from having exhausted the significance of

the few symbols we use. We can come to use them yet with a
terrible simplicity. It does not need that a poem should be long.
Every word was once a poem. Every new relation is a new word.
Also we use defects and deformities to a sacred purpose, so
expressing our sense that the evils of the world are such only
to the evil eye. In the old mythology, mythologists observe,
defects are ascribed to divine natures, as lameness to Vulcan,
blindness to Cupid, and the like—to signify exuberances.

For as it is dislocation and detachment from the life of God
that makes things ugly, the poet, who re-attaches things to
nature and the Whole—re-attaching even artificial things, and
violations of nature, to nature, by a deeper insight—disposes
very easily of the most disagreeable facts. Readers of poetry see
the factory village and the railway, and fancy that the poetry
of the landscape is broken up by these; for these works of art are
not yet consecrated in their reading; but the poet sees them fall
within the great Order not less than the beehive or the spider's
geometrical web. Nature adopts them very fast into her vital
circles, and the gliding train of cars she loves like her own.
Besides, in a centered mind, it signifies nothing how many
mechanical inventions you exhibit. Though you add millions,
and never so surprising, the fact of mechanics has not gained a
grain's weight. The spiritual fact remains unalterable by many or
by few particulars; as no mountain is of any appreciable height
to break the curve of the sphere. A shrewd country boy goes
to the city for the first time, and the complacent citizen is not
satisfied with his little wonder. It is not that he does not see all
the fine houses and know that he never saw such before, but he
disposes of them as easily as the poet finds place for the railway.
The chief value of the new fact is to enhance the great and
constant fact of Life, which can dwarf any and every circumstance, and to which the belt of wampum and the commerce
of America are alike.

The world being thus put under the mind for verb and noun,
the poet is he who can articulate it. For, though life is great,
and fascinates, and absorbs, and though all men are intelligent
of the symbols through which it is named, yet they cannot
originally use them. We are symbols and inhabit symbols;
workmen, work, and tools, words and things, birth and death,
all are emblems; but we sympathize with the symbols, and being
infatuated with the economical uses of things, we do not know

that they are thoughts. The poet, by an ulterior intellectual perception, gives them a power which makes their old use forgotten, and puts eyes and a tongue into every dumb and inanimate object. He perceives the independence of the thought on the symbol, the stability of the thought, the accidency and fugacity of the symbol. As the eyes of Lyncaeus were said to see through the earth, so the poet turns the world to glass, and shows us all things in their right series and procession. For through that better perception he stands one step nearer to things and sees the flowing or metamorphosis, perceives that thought is multiform, that within the form of every creature is a force impelling it to ascend into a higher form, and, following with his eyes the life, uses the forms which express that life and so his speech flows with the flowing of nature. All the facts of the animal economy, sex, nutriment, gestation, birth, growth, are symbols of the passage of the world into the soul of man, to suffer there a change and reappear a new and higher fact. He uses forms according to the life, and not according to the form. This is true science. The poet alone knows astronomy, chemistry, vegetation, and animation, for he does not stop at these facts, but employs them as signs. He knows why the plain or meadow of space was strown with these flowers we call suns and moons and stars; why the great deep is adorned with animals, with men, and gods; for in every word he speaks he rides on them as the horses of thought.

By virtue of this science the poet is the namer, or language maker, naming things sometimes after their appearance, sometimes after their essence, and giving to every one its own name and not another's, thereby rejoicing the intellect, which delights in detachment or boundary. The poets made all the words, and therefore language is the archives of history, and, if we must say it, a sort of tomb of the muses. For though the origin of most of our words is forgotten, each word was at first a stroke of genius, and obtained currency because for the moment it symbolized the world to the first speaker and to the hearer. The etymologist finds the deadest word to have been once a brilliant picture. Language is fossil poetry. As the limestone of the continent consists of infinite masses of the shells of animalcules, so language is made up of images or tropes, which now, in their secondary use, have long ceased to remind us of their poetic origin. But the poet names the thing because he sees it, or comes one step nearer to it than any other. This expression or naming is not art, but a second nature, grown out of the first, as a leaf out of a tree. What we call nature is a certain self-regulated motion or change; and nature does all things by her own hands, and does not leave another to baptize her but baptizes herself; and this through the metamorphosis again. I remember that a certain poet described it to me thus:—

Genius is the activity which repairs the decays of things, whether wholly or partly of a material and finite kind. Nature, through all her kingdoms, insures herself. Nobody cares for planting the poor fungus; so she shakes down from the gills of one agaric countless spores, any one of which, being preserved, transmits new billions of spores tomorrow or next day. The new agaric of this hour has a chance which the old one had not. This atom of seed is thrown into a new place, not subject to the accidents which destroyed its parent two rods off. She makes a man; and having brought him to ripe age, she will no longer run the risk of losing this wonder at a blow, but she detaches from him a new self, that the kind may be safe from accidents to which the individual is exposed. So when the soul of the poet has come to ripeness of thought, she detaches and sends away from it its poems or songs—a fearless, sleepless, deathless progeny, which is not exposed to the accidents of the weary kingdom of time; a fearless, vivacious offspring, clad with wings (such was the virtue of the soul out of which they came), which carry them fast and far, and infix them irrecoverably into the hearts of men. These wings are the beauty of the poet's soul. The songs, thus flying immortal from their mortal parent, are pursued by clamorous flights of censures, which swarm in far greater numbers and threaten to devour them; but these last are not winged. At the end of a very short leap they fall plump down and rot, having received from the souls out of which they came no beautiful wings. But the melodies of the poet ascend and leap and pierce into the deeps of infinite time.

So far the bard taught me, using his freer speech. But nature has a higher end, in the production of new individuals, than security, namely *ascension*, or the passage of the soul into higher forms. I knew in my younger days the sculptor who made the statue of the youth which stands in the public garden. He was, as I remember, unable to tell directly what made him happy or unhappy, but by wonderful indirections he could tell. He rose one day, according to his habit, before the dawn, and saw the morning break, grand as the eternity out of which it came, and for many days after, he strove to express this tranquillity, and lo! his chisel had fashioned out of marble the form of a beautiful youth, Phosphorus, whose aspect is such that it is said all persons who look on it become silent. The poet also resigns himself to his mood, and that thought which agitated him is expressed, but *alter idem*, in a manner totally new. The expression is organic, or the new type which things themselves take when liberated. As, in the sun, objects paint their images on the retina of the eye, so they, sharing the aspiration of the whole universe, tend to paint a far more delicate copy of their essence in his mind. Like the metamorphosis of things into higher organic forms is their change into melodies. Over everything stands its daemon or soul, and, as the form of the thing is reflected by the eye, so the soul of the thing is reflected by a melody. The sea, the mountain ridge, Niagara, and every flower bed, pre-exist, or super-exist, in pre-cantations, which sail like odors in the air, and when any man goes by with an ear sufficiently fine, he overhears them and endeavors to write down the notes without diluting or depraving them. And herein is the legitimation of criticism, in the mind's faith that the poems are a corrupt version of some text in nature with which they ought to be made to tally. A rhyme in one of our sonnets should not be less pleasing than the iterated nodes of a seashell, or the resembling difference of a group of flowers. The pairing of the birds is an idyl, not tedious as our idyls are; a tempest is a rough ode, without falsehood or rant; a summer, with its harvest sown, reaped, and stored, is an epic song, subordinating how many admirably executed parts. Why should not the symmetry and truth that modulate these glide into our spirits, and we participate the invention of nature?

This insight, which expresses itself by what is called imagination, is a very high sort of seeing, which does not come by study, but by the intellect being where and what it sees; by sharing the path or circuit of things through forms, and so making them translucid to others. The path of things is silent. Will they suffer a speaker to go with them? A spy they will not suffer; a lover, a poet, is the transcendency of their own nature—him they will suffer. The condition of true naming, on the poet's part, is his resigning himself to the divine *aura* which breathes through forms, and accompanying that.

It is a secret which every intellectual man quickly learns, that beyond the energy of his possessed and conscious intellect, he is capable of a new energy (as of an intellect doubled on itself), by abandonment to the nature of things; that beside his privacy of power as an individual man, there is a great public power on which he can draw, by unlocking, at all risks, his human doors, and suffering the ethereal tides to roll and circulate through him; then he is caught up into the life of the universe, his speech is thunder, his thought is law, and his words are universally intelligible as the plants and animals. The poet knows that he speaks adequately then only when he speaks somewhat wildly, or "with the flower of the mind"; not with the intellect used as an organ, but with the intellect released from all service and suffered to take its direction from its celestial life; or as the ancients were wont to express themselves, not with intellect alone but with the intellect inebriated by nectar. As the traveler who has lost his way throws his reins on his horse's neck and trusts to the instinct of the animal to find his road, so must we do with the divine animal who carries us through this world. For if in any manner we can stimulate this instinct, new passages are opened for us into nature; the mind flows into and through things hardest and highest, and the metamorphosis is possible.

This is the reason why bards love wine, mead, narcotics, coffee, tea, opium, the fumes of sandalwood and tobacco, or whatever other procurers of animal exhilaration. All men avail themselves of such means as they can, to add this extraordinary power to their normal powers; and to this end they prize conversation, music, pictures, sculpture, dancing, theaters, traveling, war, mobs, fires, gaming, politics, or love, or science, or animal intoxication,—which are several coarser or finer *quasi*-mechanical substitutes for the true nectar, which is the ravishment of the intellect by coming nearer to the fact. These are auxiliaries to the centrifugal tendency of a man, to his passage out into free space, and they help him to escape the custody of that body in which he is pent up, and of that jail yard of individual relations in which he is enclosed. Hence a great number of such as were professionally expressers of beauty, as painters, poets, musicians, and actors, have been more than others wont

to lead a life of pleasure and indulgence; all but the few who
received the true nectar; and, as it was a spurious mode of
attaining freedom, as it was an emancipation not into the
heavens but into the freedom of baser places, they were punished
for that advantage they won, by a dissipation and deterioration.
But never can any advantage be taken of nature by a trick.
The spirit of the world, the great calm presence of the Creator,
comes not forth to the sorceries of opium or of wine. The sublime vision comes to the pure and simple soul in a clean and
chaste body. That is not an inspiration, which we owe to
narcotics, but some counterfeit excitement and fury. Milton says
that the lyric poet may drink wine and live generously, but
the epic poet, he who shall sing of the gods and their descent
unto men, must drink water out of a wooden bowl. For poetry
is not "Devil's wine," but God's wine. It is with this as it is with
toys. We fill the hands and nurseries of our children with all
manner of dolls, drums, and horses; withdrawing their eyes from
the plain face and sufficing objects of nature, the sun and moon,
the animals, the water and stones, which should be their toys.
So the poet's habit of living should be set on a key so low that
the common influences should delight him. His cheerfulness
should be the gift of the sunlight; the air should suffice for his
inspiration, and he should be tipsy with water. That spirit
which suffices quiet hearts, which seems to come forth to such
from every dry knoll of sere grass, from every pine stump and
half-imbedded stone on which the dull March sun shines, comes
forth to the poor and hungry, and such as are of simple taste.
If thou fill thy brain with Boston and New York, with fashion
and covetousness, and wilt stimulate thy jaded senses with wine
and French coffee, thou shalt find no radiance of wisdom in the
lonely waste of the pine woods.

If the imagination intoxicates the poet, it is not inactive in
other men. The metamorphosis excites in the beholder an
emotion of joy. The use of symbols has a certain power of
emancipation and exhilaration for all men. We seem to be
touched by a wand which makes us dance and run about happily,
like children. We are like persons who come out of a cave or
cellar into the open air. This is the effect on us of tropes, fables,
oracles, and all poetic forms. Poets are thus liberating gods.
Men have really got a new sense, and found within their world
another world, or nest of worlds; for, the metamorphosis once

seen, we divine that it does not stop. I will not now consider
how much this makes the charm of algebra and the mathematics, which also have their tropes, but it is felt in every definition;
as when Aristotle defines *space* to be an immovable vessel in
which things are contained;—or when Plato defines a *line* to be
a flowing point; or *figure* to be a bound of solid; and many the
like. What a joyful sense of freedom we have when Vitruvius
announces the old opinion of artists that no architect can build
any house well who does not know something of anatomy.
When Socrates, in Charmides, tells us that the soul is cured of
its maladies by certain incantations, and that these incantations are beautiful reasons, from which temperance is generated
in souls; when Plato calls the world an animal, and Timaeus
affirms that the plants also are animals; or affirms a man to be a
heavenly tree, growing with his root, which is his head, upward;
and, as George Chapman, following him, writes—

> So in our tree of man, whose nervie root
> Springs in his top;—

when Orpheus speaks of hoariness as "that white flower which
marks extreme old age"; when Proclus calls the universe the
statue of the intellect; when Chaucer, in his praise of "gentilesse,"
compares good blood in mean condition to fire, which, though
carried to the darkest house betwixt this and the mount of
Caucasus, will yet hold its natural office and burn as bright as if
twenty thousand men did it behold; when John saw, in the
Apocalypse, the ruin of the world through evil, and the stars
fall from heaven, as the fig tree casteth her untimely fruit; when
Aesop reports the whole catalogue of common daily relations
through the masquerade of birds and beasts;—we take the cheerful
hint of the immortality of our essence and its versatile habit and
escapes, as when the gypsies say of themselves, "it is in vain to
hang them, they cannot die."

The poets are thus liberating gods. The ancient British bards
had for the title of their order, "Those who are free throughout
the world." They are free, and they make free. An imaginative
book renders us much more service at first, by stimulating us
through its tropes, than afterward when we arrive at the precise
sense of the author. I think nothing is of any value in books
excepting the transcendental and extraordinary. If a man is
inflamed and carried away by his thought, to that degree that

he forgets the authors and the public and heeds only this one dream which holds him like an insanity, let me read his paper, and you may have all the arguments and histories and criticism. All the value which attaches to Pythagoras, Paracelsus, Cornelius Agrippa, Cardan, Kepler, Swedenborg, Schelling, Oken, or any other who introduces questionable facts into his cosmogony, as angels, devils, magic, astrology, palmistry, mesmerism, and so on, is the certificate we have of departure from routine, and that here is a new witness. That also is the best success in conversation, the magic of liberty, which puts the world like a ball in our hands. How cheap even the liberty then seems; how mean to study, when an emotion communicates to the intellect the power to sap and upheave nature: how great the perspective! nations, times, systems, enter and disappear like threads in tapestry of large figure and many colors; dream delivers us to dream, and while the drunkenness lasts we will sell our bed, our philosophy, our religion, in our opulence.

There is good reason why we should prize this liberation. The fate of the poor shepherd, who, blinded and lost in the snowstorm, perishes in a drift within a few feet of his cottage door, is an emblem of the state of man. On the brink of the waters of life and truth, we are miserably dying. The inaccessibleness of every thought but that we are in, is wonderful. What if you come near to it; you are as remote when you are nearest as when you are farthest. Every thought is also a prison; every heaven is also a prison. Therefore we love the poet, the inventor, who in any form, whether in an ode or in an action or in looks and behavior, has yielded us a new thought. He unlocks our chains and admits us to a new scene.

This emancipation is dear to all men, and the power to impart it, as it must come from greater depth and scope of thought, is a measure of intellect. Therefore all books of the imagination endure, all which ascend to that truth that the writer sees nature beneath him, and uses it as his exponent. Every verse or sentence possessing this virtue will take care of its own immortality. The religions of the world are the ejaculations of a few imaginative men.

But the quality of the imagination is to flow, and not to freeze. The poet did not stop at the color or the form, but read their meaning; neither may he rest in this meaning, but he makes the same objects exponents of his new thought. Here is the difference betwixt the poet and the mystic, that the last nails a symbol to one sense, which was a true sense for a moment, but soon becomes old and false. For all symbols are fluxional; all language is vehicular and transitive, and is good, as ferries and horses are, for conveyance, not as farms and houses are, for homestead. Mysticism consists in the mistake of an accidental and individual symbol for an universal one. The morning-redness happens to be the favorite meteor to the eyes of Jacob Behmen, and comes to stand to him for truth and faith; and, he believes, should stand for the same realities to every reader. But the first reader prefers as naturally the symbol of a mother and child, or a gardener and his bulb, or a jeweler polishing a gem. Either of these, or of a myriad more, are equally good to the person to whom they are significant. Only they must be held lightly, and be very willingly translated into the equivalent terms which others use. And the mystic must be steadily told,— All that you say is just as true without the tedious use of that symbol as with it. Let us have a little algebra, instead of this trite rhetoric—universal signs, instead of these village symbols— and we shall both be gainers. The history of hierarchies seems to show that all religious error consisted in making the symbol too stark and solid, and was at last nothing but an excess of the organ of language.

Swedenborg, of all men in the recent ages, stands eminently for the translator of nature into thought. I do not know the man in history to whom things stood so uniformly for words. Before him the metamorphosis continually plays. Everything on which his eye rests obeys the impulses of moral nature. The figs become grapes whilst he eats them. When some of his angels affirmed a truth, the laurel twig which they held blossomed in their hands. The noise which at a distance appeared like gnashing and thumping, on coming nearer was found to be the voice of disputants. The men in one of his visions, seen in heavenly light, appeared like dragons and seemed in darkness; but to each other they appeared as men, and when the light from heaven shone into their cabin, they complained of the darkness and were compelled to shut the window that they might see.

There was this perception in him which makes the poet or seer an object of awe and terror, namely that the same man or society of men may wear one aspect to themselves and their com-

panions, and a different aspect to higher intelligences. Certain
priests, whom he describes as conversing very learnedly together,
appeared to the children, who were at some distance, like dead
horses; and many the like misappearances. And instantly the
mind inquires whether these fishes under the bridge, yonder
oxen in the pasture, those dogs in the yard, are immutably
fishes, oxen, and dogs, or only so appear to me, and perchance
to themselves appear upright men; and whether I appear as a
man to all eyes. The Brahmins and Pythagoras propounded the
same question, and if any poet has witnessed the transformation
he doubtless found it in harmony with various experiences. We
have all seen changes as considerable in wheat and caterpillars.
He is the poet and shall draw us with love and terror, who sees
through the flowing vest the firm nature, and can declare it.

I look in vain for the poet whom I describe. We do not with
sufficient plainness or sufficient profoundness address ourselves
to life, nor dare we chant our own times and social circumstance.
If we filled the day with bravery, we should not shrink from
celebrating it. Time and nature yield us many gifts, but not
yet the timely man, the new religion, the reconciler, whom all
things await. Dante's praise is that he dared to write his autobiography in colossal cipher, or into universality. We have yet
had no genius in America, with tyrannous eye, which knew
the value of our incomparable materials, and saw, in the barbarism and materialism of the times, another carnival of the
same gods whose picture he so much admires in Homer; then
in the Middle Age; then in Calvinism. Banks and tariffs, the
newspaper and caucus, Methodism and Unitarianism, are flat
and dull to dull people, but rest on the same foundations of
wonder as the town of Troy, and the temple of Delphi, and are
as swiftly passing away. Our logrolling, our stumps and their
politics, our fisheries, our Negroes and Indians, our boats and
our repudiations, the wrath of rogues and the pusillanimity of
honest men, the northern trade, the southern planting, the
western clearing, Oregon and Texas, are yet unsung. Yet
America is a poem in our eyes; its ample geography dazzles the
imagination, and it will not wait long for meters. If I have not
found that excellent combination of gifts in my countrymen
which I seek, neither could I aid myself to fix the idea of the
poet by reading now and then in Chalmers's collection of five
centuries of English poets. These are wits more than poets,

though there have been poets among them. But when we adhere
to the ideal of the poet, we have our difficulties even with Milton
and Homer. Milton is too literary, and Homer too literal and
historical.

But I am not wise enough for a national criticism, and must
use the old largeness a little longer, to discharge my errand
from the muse to the poet concerning his art.

Art is the path of the creator to his work. The paths or
methods are ideal and eternal, though few men ever see them;
not the artist himself for years, or for a lifetime, unless he come
into the conditions. The painter, the sculptor, the composer,
the epic rhapsodist, the orator, all partake one desire, namely to
express themselves symmetrically and abundantly, not dwarfishly
and fragmentarily. They found or put themselves in certain
conditions, as, the painter and sculptor before some impressive
human figures; the orator into the assembly of the people; and
the others in such scenes as each has found exciting to his intellect; and each presently feels the new desire. He hears a voice,
he sees a beckoning. Then he is apprised, with wonder, what
herds of daemons hem him in. He can no more rest; he says,
with the old painter, "By God it is in me and must go forth of
me." He pursues a beauty, half seen, which flies before him.
The poet pours out verses in every solitude. Most of the things
he says are conventional, no doubt; but by and by he says something which is original and beautiful. That charms him. He would
say nothing else but such things. In our way of talking we say,
"That is yours, this is mine"; but the poet knows well that it is
not his; that it is as strange and beautiful to him as to you; he
would fain hear the like eloquence at length. Once having
tasted this immortal ichor, he cannot have enough of it, and as
an admirable creative power exists in these intellections, it is of
the last importance that these things get spoken. What a little of
all we know is said! What drops of all the sea of our science are
baled up! and by what accident it is that these are exposed,
when so many secrets sleep in nature! Hence the necessity of
speech and song; hence these throbs and heart beatings in the
orator, at the door of the assembly, to the end namely that
thought may be ejaculated as Logos, or Word.

Doubt not, O poet, but persist. Say, "It is in me, and shall
out." Stand there, balked and dumb, stuttering and stam-
mering, hissed and hooted, stand and strive, until at last rage

draw out of thee that *dream*-power which every night shows thee is thine own; a power transcending all limit and privacy, and by virtue of which a man is the conductor of the whole river of electricity. Nothing walks, or creeps, or grows, or exists, which must not in turn arise and walk before him as exponent of his meaning. Comes he to that power, his genius is no longer exhaustible. All the creatures by pairs and by tribes pour into his mind as into a Noah's ark, to come forth again to people a new world. This is like the stock of air for our respiration or for the combustion of our fireplace; not a measure of gallons, but the entire atmosphere if wanted. And therefore the rich poets, as Homer, Chaucer, Shakespeare, and Raphael, have obviously no limits to their works except the limits of their lifetime, and resemble a mirror carried through the street, ready to render an image of every created thing.

O poet! a new nobility is conferred in groves and pastures, and not in castles by the sword blade any longer. The conditions are hard, but equal. Thou shalt leave the world, and know the muse only. Thou shalt not know any longer the times, customs, graces, politics, or opinions of men, but shalt take all from the muse. For the time of towns is tolled from the world by funereal chimes, but in nature the universal hours are counted by succeeding tribes of animals and plants, and by growth of joy on joy. God wills also that thou abdicate a manifold and duplex life, and that thou be content that others speak for thee. Others shall be thy gentlemen, and shall represent all courtesy and worldly life for thee; others shall do the great and resounding actions also. Thou shalt lie close hid with nature, and canst not be afforded to the Capitol or the Exchange. The world is full of renunciations and apprenticeships, and this is thine; thou must pass for a fool and a churl for a long season. This is the screen and sheath in which Pan has protected his well-beloved flower, and thou shalt be known only to thine own, and they shall console thee with tenderest love. And thou shalt not be able to rehearse the names of thy friends in thy verse, for an old shame before the holy ideal. And this is the reward; that the ideal shall be real to thee, and the impressions of the actual world shall fall like summer rain, copious, but not troublesome to thy invulnerable essence. Thou shalt have the whole land for thy park and manor, the sea for thy bath and navigation, without tax and without envy; the woods and the rivers thou shalt own, and thou shalt possess that wherein others are only tenants and boarders. Thou true landlord! sea lord! air lord! Wherever snow falls or water flows or birds fly, wherever day and night meet in twilight, wherever the blue heaven is hung by clouds or sown with stars, wherever are forms with transparent boundaries, wherever are outlets into celestial space, wherever is danger, and awe, and love,—there is beauty, plenteous as rain, shed for thee, and though thou shouldst walk the world over, thou shalt not be able to find a condition inopportune or ignoble.

WALT WHITMAN

(1819–1892)

o◯oo◯o

ALTHOUGH WHITMAN WAS HIMSELF in debt to Homer, Shakespeare, and the Bible, he wrote *Democratic Vistas*, as he said, to announce "a native-expression spirit . . . for these States, self-contained, different from others, more expansive, more rich and free," turning its "vision toward the future, more than toward the past," inspiring itself "with science . . . and the principles of its own democratic spirit only." As he summed up the matter in "A Backward Glance o'er Traveled Roads": "Modern science and democracy seemed to be throwing out their challenge to poetry to put them in its statements in contradistinction to the songs and myths of the past." He would express, then, his "own physical, emotional, moral, intellectual, and aesthetic personality, in the midst of, and tallying [with], the momentous spirit and facts of its immediate days, and of current America," since "in estimating first-class song, a sufficient nationality . . . is often, if not always, the first element."[1] Tainelike, he is proud that the "*Leaves* could not possibly have emerged or been fashioned or completed, from . . . any other land than democratic America . . ." And in the essay on *American National Literature* (1891) he indicates his devotion to a literature which avoids imaginative selection in the interest of the ideal and the universal, which seeks to be a "mirror" to social history: "First to me comes an almost indescribably august form, the People, with varied typical shapes and attitudes—then the divine mirror, Literature."

[1]Herder, as Professor Kind has shown, developed the eighteenth-century cult of "original genius" on a nationalistic scale. And Whitman concludes "A Backward Glance" by emphasizing "what Herder taught the young Goethe, that really great poetry is always the result of a national spirit." He admired Taine (*Critic*, Dec. 3, 1881, p. 331), who saw literature as the inevitable result of time and place and race. It is amusing, considering the popular notion that Whitman is exclusively American in his ideas, to find him concluding a long summary of Hegel's ideas with the conviction that this German gives us "the most thoroughly *American points of view* I know. In my opinion the above [progressive] formulas of Hegel are an essential and crowning justification of New World democracy . . ." ("Carlyle from American Points of View," in *Specimen Days*). See also Mr. Boatright's study of "Whitman and Hegel," in bibliography following. And of course Whitman must have seen himself as the answer to his master Emerson's plea (in the third part of his essay "The Poet") for a poet to celebrate America.

In considering Whitman's application of his nationalistic theories to specific authors, the nature of his equipment and medium prepares us for the brief and fragmentary character of his critical essays. Unlike Lowell, Whitman was not a professor preparing extensive and rounded essays for an academic audience; he was primarily a journalist and conversationalist. He is, of course, of considerable historical significance as a literary theorist in urging new ideals which he and others embodied in literary art. But, like most critics who single one thing out of the full circumference of things which makes for good literature, Whitman's actual criticism often involves misplaced emphasis. He did not entirely ignore art and form and beauty, but his remarks on such matters are usually obvious and trite, and they are strikingly subordinated to an attempt to ascertain the author's attitude toward democracy.[2]

Since before the nineteenth century few European writers strove to write in praise of American democracy, one can easily foretell Whitman's verdict in the light of his peculiarly narrow criteria. Thus Shakespeare is the "tally of feudalism" and his works are "incarnated, uncompromising feudalism, in literature";[3] he and his fellows are "poisonous to the idea of the pride and dignity of the common people, the life blood of democracy."[4] However, since democracy has not yet found a comparable poetic statesman, he concluded, in "A Backward Glance," that the feudalistic Shakespeare still "holds the proud distinction of being the loftiest of the singers life has yet given voice to." Whitman's attitude toward Scott is apparent in the title of his essay, "The Anti-Democratic Bearing of Scott's Novels." Like Shakespeare and Tennyson, Scott is the incarnation of "principles of caste which we Americans have come on earth to destroy."[5] The essay on Tennyson is more appreciative and expressionistic than most of Whitman's essays; he slights what he calls Tennyson's "non-democracy" because "The course of progressive politics [democracy] is so certain and resistless . . . that we can well afford the warning calls, threats . . . of such voices as Carlyle's and Tennyson's."[6] He finds the latter's ideal of woman "a false one—at any rate for

<hr>

[2]Whitman himself recognized his own limitations—"I am," he said, "a hell of a critic." Horace Traubel, *With Whitman in Camden*, I, 56.

[3]"British Literature," *Complete Writings* (New York, 1902), in 10 vols., V, 274. (Henceforth all references are to this edition unless otherwise indicated.)

[4]"Democratic Vistas," *Works*, V, 90. For full evidence confirming this view of Shakespeare, see studies listed in the following bibliography by Furness and Johnson.

[5]"Poetry Today in America," *Works*, V, 209.

[6]"A Word about Tennyson," *Prose Works* (published by McKay), p. 402.

America." Of Tennyson's "Locksley Hall Sixty Years After" he says, "A cynical vein of denunciation of democratic opinions and aspirations runs throughout the poem." This Whitman sees as "a legitimate consequence of the tone and convictions of the earlier standards."[7]

In 1846 young Whitman imagined the Carlyle of *Heroes* a democrat in the sense that "he is quick to champion the downtrodden, and earnest in his wrath at tyranny." But after Carlyle's death and Froude's memoirs appeared, he concluded that in Carlyle's work "the great masses of humanity stand for nothing." "All that is comprehended under the terms republicanism and democracy were distasteful to him from the first, and as he grew older they became hateful and contemptible."[8] On the other hand, Whitman praised Burns as representative of the "middle classes everywhere" and as making poetry out of "work-a-day agricultural labor and life." But "Burns is not at all great for New World study" chiefly because he has "little spirituality."[9]

In Whitman's old age, especially in *Poetry Today in America*, he came to temper his nationalism with internationalism and a desire for a universality of spirit. He saw the glory of America "in a vaster, saner, more surrounding comradeship, uniting closer and closer not only the American States, but all nations, and all humanity. That O poets! is not that a theme worth chanting, striving for?"[10] But in *Years of the Modern* "the solidarity of races" is sought by this exponent of love by means of having European aristocracies "broken" and kings "removed." In the poem "Rise O Days from Your Fathomless Deeps" he is "fully satisfied" to see "warlike America rise" and democracy "strike with vengeful stroke." His prophecy in *Passage to India* that science, by inventions furthering communication, will do away with conflicting nationalisms does not seem to have come true—yet, at least. In *Democratic Vistas* (1871), admitting that "New World democracy . . . is, so far, an almost complete failure in its social aspects, and in really grand religious, moral, literary, and aesthetic results," Whitman said that "we have peremptorily to dismiss every pretensive production, however fine its aesthetic or intellectual points which violates or ignores, or even does not celebrate, the divine idea of All." This sounds re-

[7]*Ibid.*, pp. 401–402.
[8]"Carlyle from American Points of View," *Works*, IV, 314.
[9]"Robert Burns as Poet and Person," *Works*, VI, 128 ff.
[10]See also "The Bible as Poetry," where he says it "has united this diverse world" and has been "the principal factor in cohering the nations, eras, and paradoxes of the globe, by giving them a common platform of two or three great ideas . . ." (*Prose Works*, published by McKay, p. 381). He here praises the great poets of the ancient past for their "blending of individuality with universality."

ligious. But whereas most men have meant by "divine" something godlike toward which centuries of men have striven as toward perfection, we recall that Whitman regarded himself as more perfect than any of the gods worshiped to date.[11] Hence, to criticize literature on the basis of its being godlike, appears to mean its being Whitman-like. The reader must decide for himself whether this criterion suggests the moral elevation the divine implies to most people. However, no one can question the fact that historically Whitman has been a very powerful seminal influence on criticism.

BIBLIOGRAPHY

TEXT

In Re Walt Whitman, ed. by his literary executors, Horace L. Traubel, Richard Maurice Bucke, and Thomas B. Harned. Philadelphia, 1893. Includes three early reviews of *Leaves of Grass* written by Whitman himself and published anonymously.

The Complete Writings of Walt Whitman, issued under the editorial supervision of his literary executors, Richard Maurice Bucke, Thomas B. Harned, and Horace L. Traubel. With additional bibliographical and critical material by Oscar Lovell Triggs. 10 vols. New York, 1902. The standard edition.

Leaves of Grass, including "Sands at Seventy." 1st Annex, "Good-Bye My Fancy"; 2d Annex, "A Backward Glance O'er Travel'd Roads." Philadelphia, 1891–1892.

Leaves of Grass, Inclusive edition, ed. by Emory Holloway. Garden City, New York, 1924.

The Letters of Anne Gilchrist and Walt Whitman, ed. with an introduction by Thomas B. Harned. Garden City, New York, 1918.

The Uncollected Poetry and Prose of Walt Whitman, ed. with an introduction by Emory Holloway. 2 vols. Garden City, New York, 1921.

Walt Whitman's Workshop, a coll. of unpublished mss.; ed. with an introduction and notes by Clifton J. Furness. Harvard University Press, 1928.

BIBLIOGRAPHY

Allen, Gay W., "Walt Whitman Bibliography, 1918–1934," *Bulletin of Bibliography Pamphlets*, no. 30. Boston, 1935. Brings the lists in the *Cambridge History of American Literature* nearly up to date.

[11]*Song of Myself*, sect. 48: ". . . nothing, not God, is greater to one than one's self is . . ."; "I hear and behold God in every object . . ."; "I see God . . . in my own face in the glass." In sect. 41 he accepts "the rough deific sketches [the gods of earlier religions] to fill out better in myself."

Holloway, Emory, in the *Cambridge History of American Literature*. New York, 1918, II, 551–581. The most extensive basic bibliography, including poetry and prose published in periodicals.

Shay, Frank, *The Bibliography of Walt Whitman*. New York, 1920. Excellent up to its date. Does not include works about Whitman.

BIOGRAPHY, INTERPRETATION, CRITICISM

Allen, Gay W., *American Prosody*. New York, 1935, pp. 217–243.

Arvin, Newton, *Whitman*. New York, 1938. A socialist view.

Campbell, Killis, "The Evolution of Whitman as an Artist," *American Literature*, VI, 254–263 (November, 1934).

Canby, H. S., *Classic Americans*. New York, 1931, pp. 308–351.

Catel, Jean, *Rythme et langage dans l'édition des "Leaves of Grass," 1855*. Montpellier, 1930.

——, *Walt Whitman: la naissance du poète*. Paris, 1929.

De Sélincourt, Basil, *Walt Whitman: a Critical Study*. London, 1914.

Dowden, Edward, "The Poetry of Democracy: Walt Whitman," in *Studies in Literature, 1789–1877*. London, 1892. First printed in the *Westminster Review*, July, 1871.

Foerster, Norman, "Whitman," in *American Criticism*. Boston, 1928, pp. 157–222. Valuable.

Furness, C. J., "Walt Whitman's Estimate of Shakespeare," *Harvard Studies and Notes in Philology and Literature*, XV, 1–33 (1932).

Gohdes, C. L. F., "Whitman and Emerson," *Sewanee Review*, XXXVII, 79–93 (January, 1929).

Gummere, F. B., "Whitman and Taine," in *Democracy and Poetry*. Boston, 1911, pp. 96–148.

Holloway, Emory, *Whitman: an Interpretation in Narrative*. New York, 1926.

——, "Whitman as Critic of America," *Studies in Philology*, XX, 345–369 (July, 1923).

Johnson, M. O., *Walt Whitman as a Critic of Literature*, in Studies in Language, Literature, and Criticism, no. 16. University of Nebraska, 1938.

Lowell, Amy, "Walt Whitman and the New Poetry," *Yale Review*, XVI, 502–519 (April, 1927).

Pound, Louise, "Walt Whitman and the Classics," *Southwest Review*, X, 75–83 (January, 1925).

Sherman, S. P., "Walt Whitman," in *Americans*. New York, 1922, pp. 153–185.

Speake, Marian R., *Contemporary American Criticism of Walt Whitman, 1855–92*. [1926.] An unpublished dissertation available at the Library of the University of Iowa.

Stovall, Floyd, "Introduction" and "Bibliography," in *Walt Whitman*. New York, 1934, pp. xi–lxiii. (American Writers Series.)

Stovall, Floyd, "Main Drifts in Whitman's Poetry," *American Literature*, IV, 3–21 (March, 1932).
Traubel, Horace, *With Walt Whitman in Camden.* 3 vols. New York, 1906–1914.

PREFACE TO *LEAVES OF GRASS*[1]

1855; 1882

America does not repel the past or what the past has produced under its forms or amid other politics or the idea of castes or the old religions—accepts the lesson with calmness—is not impatient because the slough still sticks to opinions and manners in literature while the life which served its requirements has passed into the new life of the new forms—perceives that the corpse is slowly borne from the eating and sleeping rooms of the house—perceives that it waits a little while in the door—that it was fittest for its days—that its action has descended to the stalwart and well-shaped heir who approaches—and that he shall be fittest for his days.

The Americans of all nations at any time upon the earth have probably the fullest poetical nature. The United States themselves are essentially the greatest poem. In the history of the earth hitherto, the largest and most stirring appear tame and orderly to their ampler largeness and stir. Here at last is something in the doings of man that corresponds with the broadcast doings of the day and night. Here is action untied from strings, necessarily blind to particulars and details, magnificently moving in masses. Here is the hospitality which forever indicates heroes. Here the performance, disdaining the trivial, unapproached in the tremendous audacity of its crowds and groupings, and the push of its perspective, spreads with crampless and flowing breadth, and showers its prolific and spendid extravagance. One sees it must indeed own the riches of the summer and winter, and need never be bankrupt while corn grows from the ground, or the orchards drop apples, or the bays contain fish, or men beget children upon women.

Other states indicate themselves in their deputies—but the genius of the United States is not best or most in its executives or

---

[1]This text of the preface is that of the revision of 1882. The original preface to *Leaves of Grass* (1855), not afterward reprinted by Whitman, was much longer, more rhapsodic, and more eccentrically punctuated than is the version given here.

legislatures, nor in its ambassadors or authors, or colleges or churches or parlors, nor even in its newspapers or inventors—but always most in the common people, south, north, west, east, in all its States, through all its mighty amplitude. The largeness of the nation, however, were monstrous without a corresponding largeness and generosity of the spirit of the citizen. Not swarming states, nor streets and steamships, nor prosperous business, nor farms, nor capital, nor learning, may suffice for the ideal of man—nor suffice the poet. No reminiscences may suffice either. A live nation can always cut a deep mark, and can have the best authority the cheapest—namely, from its own soul. This is the sum of the profitable uses of individuals or states, and of present action and grandeur, and of the subjects of poets. (As if it were necessary to trot back generation after generation to the eastern records! As if the beauty and sacredness of the demonstrable must fall behind that of the mythical! As if men do not make their mark out of any times! As if the opening of the western continent by discovery, and what has transpired in North and South America, were less than the small theater of the antique, or the aimless sleepwalking of the Middle Ages!) The pride of the United States leaves the wealth and finesse of the cities, and all returns of commerce and agriculture, and all the magnitude of geography or shows of exterior victory, to enjoy the sight and realization of full-sized men or one full-sized man unconquerable and simple.

The American poets are to enclose old and new, for America is the race of races. The expression of the American poet is to be transcendent and new. It is to be indirect, and not direct or descriptive or epic. Its quality goes through these to much more. Let the age and wars of other nations be chanted, and their eras and characters be illustrated, and that finish the verse. Not so the great psalm of the republic. Here the theme is creative and has vista. Whatever stagnates in the flat of custom or obedience or legislation, the great poet never stagnates. Obedience does not master him, he masters it. High up out of reach he stands turning a concentrated light—he turns the pivot with his finger—he baffles the swiftest runners as he stands, and easily overtakes and envelops them. The time straying toward infidelity and confections and persiflage he withholds by steady faith. Faith is the antiseptic of the soul—it pervades the common people and preserves them—they never give up believing and expecting and

trusting. There is that indescribable freshness and unconsciousness about an illiterate person that humbles and mocks the power
of the noblest expressive genius. The poet sees for a certainty
how one not a great artist may be just as sacred and perfect as
the greatest artist.

The power to destroy or remold is freely used by the greatest
poet, but seldom the power of attack. What is past is past. If he
does not expose superior models, and prove himself by every
step he takes, he is not what is wanted. The presence of the great
poet conquers—not parleying, or struggling, or any prepared
attempts. Now he has passed that way, see after him! There is
not left any vestige of despair, or misanthropy, or cunning,
or exclusiveness, or the ignominy of a nativity or color, or delusion of hell or the necessity of hell—and no man thenceforward
shall be degraded for ignorance or weakness or sin. The greatest
poet hardly knows pettiness or triviality. If he breathes into
anything that was before thought small, it dilates with the
grandeur and life of the universe. He is a seer—he is individual—
he is complete in himself—the others are as good as he, only he
sees it and they do not. He is not one of the chorus—he does not
stop for any regulation—he is the president of regulation. What
the eyesight does to the rest, he does to the rest. Who knows
the curious mystery of the eyesight? The other senses corroborate
themselves, but this is removed from any proof but its own, and
foreruns the identities of the spiritual world. A single glance of it
mocks all the investigations of man, and all the instruments and
books of the earth, and all reasoning. What is marvelous? what
is unlikely? what is impossible or baseless or vague—after you
have once just opened the space of a peach-pit, and given audience to far and near, and to the sunset, and had all things enter
with electric swiftness, softly and duly, without confusion or
jostling or jam?

The land and sea, the animals, fishes, and birds, the sky of
heaven and the orbs, the forests, mountains and rivers, are not
small themes—but folks expect of the poet to indicate more than
the beauty and dignity which always attach to dumb real objects
—they expect him to indicate the path between reality and their
souls. Men and women perceive the beauty well enough—probably as well as he. The passionate tenacity of hunters, woodmen,
early risers, cultivators of gardens and orchards and fields, the
love of healthy women for the manly form, seafaring persons,

drivers of horses, the passion for light and the open air, all is an old varied sign of the unfailing perception of beauty, and of a residence of the poetic in outdoor people. They can never be assisted by poets to perceive—some may, but they never can. The poetic quality is not marshaled in rhyme or uniformity, or abstract addresses to things, nor in melancholy complaints or good precepts, but is the life of these and much else, and is in the soul. The profit of rhyme is that it drops seeds of a sweeter and more luxuriant rhyme, and of uniformity that it conveys itself into its own roots in the ground out of sight. The rhyme and uniformity of perfect poems show the free growth of metrical laws, and bud from them as unerringly and loosely as lilacs and roses on a bush, and take shapes as compact as the shapes of chestnuts and oranges, and melons and pears, and shed the perfume impalpable to form. The fluency and ornaments of the finest poems or music or orations or recitations are not independent but dependent. All beauty comes from beautiful blood and a beautiful brain. If the greatnesses are in conjunction in a man or woman, it is enough—the fact will prevail through the universe; but the gaggery and gilt of a million years will not prevail. Who troubles himself about his ornaments or fluency is lost. This is what you shall do: Love the earth and sun and the animals, despise riches, give alms to everyone that asks, stand up for the stupid and crazy, devote your income and labor to others, hate tyrants, argue not concerning God, have patience and indulgence toward the people, take off your hat to nothing known or unknown, or to any man or number of men—go freely with powerful uneducated persons, and with the young, and with the mothers of families—re-examine all you have been told in school or church or in any book, and dismiss whatever insults your own soul; and your very flesh shall be a great poem and have the richest fluency, not only in its words, but in the silent lines of its lips and face, and between the lashes of your eyes, and in every motion and joint of your body. The poet shall not spend his time in unneeded work. He shall know that the ground is already plowed and manured; others may not know it, but he shall. He shall go directly to the creation. His trust shall master the trust of everything he touches—and shall master all attachment.

The known universe has one complete lover, and that is the greatest poet. He consumes an eternal passion, and is indifferent which chance happens, and which possible contingency of fortune or misfortune, and persuades daily and hourly his delicious pay. What balks or breaks others is fuel for his burning progress to contact and amorous joy. Other proportions of the reception of pleasure dwindle to nothing to his proportions. All expected from heaven or from the highest, he is rapport with in the sight of the daybreak, or the scenes of the winter woods, or the presence of children playing, or with his arm round the neck of a man or woman. His love above all love has leisure and expanse —he leaves room ahead of himself. He is no irresolute or suspicious lover—he is sure—he scorns intervals. His experience and the showers and thrills are not for nothing. Nothing can jar him—suffering and darkness cannot—death and fear cannot. To him complaint and jealousy and envy are corpses buried and rotten in the earth—he saw them buried. The sea is not surer of the shore, or the shore of the sea, than he is of the fruition of his love, and of all perfection and beauty.

The fruition of beauty is no chance of miss or hit—it is as inevitable as life—it is exact and plumb as gravitation. From the eyesight proceeds another eyesight, and from the hearing proceeds another hearing, and from the voice proceeds another voice, eternally curious of the harmony of things with man. These understand the law of perfection in masses and floods— that it is profuse and impartial—that there is not a minute of the light or dark, nor an acre of the earth and sea, without it— nor any direction of the sky, nor any trade or employment, nor any turn of events. This is the reason that about the proper expression of beauty there is precision and balance. One part does not need to be thrust above another. The best singer is not the one who has the most lithe and powerful organ. The pleasure of poems is not in them that take the handsomest measure and sound.

Without effort and without exposing in the least how it is done, the greatest poet brings the spirit of any or all events and passions and scenes and persons, some more and some less, to bear on your individual character as you hear or read. To do this well is to compete with the laws that pursue and follow Time. What is the purpose must surely be there—and the clue of it must be there—and the faintest indication is the indication of the best, and then becomes the clearest indication. Past and present and future are not disjoined but joined. The greatest poet forms the consistence of what is to be, from what has been and is. He drags the dead out of their coffins and stands them again on their feet. He says to the past, Rise and walk before me that I may realize you. He learns the lesson—he places himself where the future becomes present. The greatest poet does not only dazzle his rays over character and scenes and passions—he finally ascends and finishes all—he exhibits the pinnacles that no man can tell what they are for, or what is beyond—he glows a moment on the extremest verge. He is most wonderful in his last half-hidden smile or frown; by that flash of the moment of parting the one that sees it shall be encouraged or terrified afterwards for many years. The greatest poet does not moralize or make applications of morals—he knows the soul. The soul has that measureless pride which consists in never acknowledging any lessons or deductions but its own. But it has sympathy as measureless as its pride, and the one balances the other, and neither can stretch too far while it stretches in company with the other. The inmost secrets of art sleep with the twain. The greatest poet has lain close betwixt both, and they are vital in his style and thoughts.

The art of art, the glory of expression and the sunshine of the light of letters, is simplicity. Nothing is better than simplicity—nothing can make up for excess, or for the lack of definiteness. To carry on the heave of impulse and pierce intellectual depths and give all subjects their articulations are powers neither common nor very uncommon. But to speak in literature with the perfect rectitude and insouciance of the movements of animals, and the unimpeachableness of the sentiment of trees in the woods and grass by the roadside, is the flawless triumph of art. If you have looked on him who has achieved it, you have looked on one of the masters of the artists of all nations and times. You shall not contemplate the flight of the gray gull over the bay, or the mettlesome action of the blood horse, or the tall leaning of sunflowers on their stalk, or the appearance of the sun journeying through heaven, or the appearance of the moon afterward, with any more satisfaction than you shall contemplate him. The great poet has less a marked style, and is more the channel of thoughts and things without increase or diminution, and is the free channel of himself. He swears to his art, I will not be meddlesome, I will not have in my writing any elegance, or effect, or originality, to hang in the way between me and the rest like curtains. I will have nothing hang in the way, not the richest curtains. What I tell I tell for precisely what it is. Let who may exalt or startle or fascinate or soothe, I will have purposes as health or heat or snow has, and be as regardless of observation. What I experience or portray shall go from my composition without a shred of my composition. You shall stand by my side and look in the mirror with me.

The old red blood and stainless gentility of great poets will be proved by their unconstraint. A heroic person walks at his ease through and out of that custom or precedent or authority that suits him not. Of the traits of the brotherhood of first-class writers, savants, musicians, inventors, and artists, nothing is finer than silent defiance advancing from new free forms. In the need of poems, philosophy, politics, mechanism, science, behavior, the craft of art, an appropriate native grand opera, shipcraft, or any craft, he is greatest forever and ever who contributes the greatest original practical example. The cleanest expression is that which finds no sphere worthy of itself, and makes one.

The messages of great poems to each man and woman are, Come to us on equal terms, only then can you understand us. We are no better than you, what we inclose you inclose, what we enjoy you may enjoy. Did you suppose there could be only one Supreme? We affirm there can be unnumbered Supremes, and that one does not countervail another any more than one eyesight countervails another—and that men can be good or grand only of the consciousness of their supremacy within them. What do you think is the grandeur of storms and dismemberments, and the deadliest battles and wrecks, and the wildest fury of the elements, and the power of the sea, and the motion of nature, and the throes of human desires, and dignity and hate and love? It is that something in the soul which says, Rage on, whirl on, I tread master here and everywhere—Master of the spasms of the sky and of the shatter of the sea, Master of nature and passion and death and of all terror and all pain.

The American bards shall be marked for generosity and affection, and for encouraging competitors. They shall be kosmos, without monopoly or secrecy, glad to pass anything to anyone— hungry for equals night and day. They shall not be careful of riches and privilege—they shall be riches and privilege—they shall perceive who the most affluent man is. The most affluent man is he that confronts all the shows he sees by equivalents out of the stronger wealth of himself. The American bard shall delineate no class of persons, nor one or two out of the strata of interests, nor love most nor truth most, nor the soul most, nor the body most—and not be for the Eastern States more than the Western, or the Northern States more than the Southern.

Exact science and its practical movements are no checks on the greatest poet, but always his encouragement and support. The outset and remembrance are there—there the arms that lifted him first, and braced him best—there he returns after all his goings and comings. The sailor and traveler—the anatomist, chemist, astronomer, geologist, phrenologist, spiritualist, mathematician, historian, and lexicographer are not poets, but they are the lawgivers of poets, and their construction underlies the structure of every perfect poem. No matter what rises or is uttered, they sent the seed of the conception of it— of them and by them stand the visible proofs of souls. If there shall be love and content between the father and the son, and if the greatness of the son is the exuding of the greatness of the father, there shall be love between the poet and the man of demonstrable science. In the beauty of poems are henceforth the tuft and final applause of science.

Great is the faith of the flush of knowledge, and of the investigation of the depths of qualities and things. Cleaving and circling here swells the soul of the poet, yet is president of itself always. The depths are fathomless, and therefore calm. The innocence and nakedness are resumed—they are neither modest nor immodest. The whole theory of the supernatural, and all that was twined with it or educed out of it, departs as a dream. What has ever happened—what happens, and whatever may or shall happen, the vital laws inclose all. They are sufficient for any case and for all cases—none to be hurried or retarded—any special miracle of affairs or persons inadmissible in the vast clear scheme where every motion and every spear of grass, and the frames and spirits of men and women and all that concerns them, are unspeakably perfect miracles, all referring to all, and each distinct and in its place. It is also not consistent with the reality of the soul to admit that there is anything in the known universe more divine than men and women.

Men and women, and the earth and all upon it, are simply to be taken as they are, and the investigation of their past and present and future shall be unintermitted, and shall be done with perfect candor. Upon this basis philosophy speculates, ever looking toward the poet, ever regarding the eternal tendencies of all toward happiness, never inconsistent with what is clear to the senses and to the soul. For the eternal tendencies of all toward happiness make the only point of sane philosophy. Whatever comprehends less than that—whatever is less than the laws of light and of astronomical motion—or less than the laws that follow the thief, the liar, the glutton, and the drunkard, through this life and doubtless afterward—or less than vast stretches of time, or the slow formation of density, or the patient upheaving of strata—is of no account. Whatever would put God in a poem or system of philosophy as contending against some being or influence, is also of no account. Sanity and ensemble characterize the great master—spoilt in one principle, all is spoilt. The great master has nothing to do with miracles. He sees health for himself in being one of the mass—he sees the hiatus in singular eminence. To the perfect shape comes common ground. To be under the general law is great, for that is to correspond with it. The master knows that he is unspeakably great, and that all are unspeakably great—that nothing, for instance, is greater than to conceive children, and bring them up well—that to *be* is just as great as to perceive or tell.

In the make of the great masters the idea of political liberty is indispensable. Liberty takes the adherence of heroes wherever men and women exist—but never takes any adherence or welcome from the rest more than from poets. They are the voice and exposition of liberty. They out of ages are worthy the grand idea—to them it is confided and they must sustain it. Nothing has precedence of it and nothing can warp or degrade it.

As the attributes of the poets of the kosmos concenter in the real body, and in the pleasure of things, they possess the superiority of genuineness over all fiction and romance. As they emit themselves, facts are showered over with light—the daylight is lit with more volatile light—the deep between the setting and rising sun goes deeper many fold. Each precise object or condition or combination or process exhibits a beauty—the multiplication table its—old age its—the carpenter's trade its—the grand opera its—the huge-hulled clean-shaped New York clipper at sea under steam or full sail gleams with unmatched beauty—the American circles and large harmonies of government gleam with theirs—and the commonest definite intentions and actions with theirs. The poets of the kosmos advance through all interpositions and coverings and turmoils and stratagems to first principles. They are of use—they dissolve poverty from its need, and riches from its conceit. You large proprietor, they say, shall not realize or perceive more than anyone else. The owner of the library is not he who holds a legal title to it, having bought and paid for it. Anyone and everyone is owner of the library (indeed he or she alone is owner) who can read the same through all the varieties of tongues and subjects and styles, and in whom they enter with ease, and make supple and powerful and rich and large.

These American States, strong and healthy and accomplished, shall receive no pleasure from violations of natural models, and must not permit them. In paintings or moldings or carvings in mineral or wood, or in the illustrations of books or newspapers, or in the patterns of woven stuffs, or anything to beautify rooms or furniture or costumes, or to put upon cornices or monuments, or on the prows or sterns of ships, or to put anywhere before the human eye indoors or out, that which distorts honest shapes, or which creates unearthly beings or places or contingencies, is a nuisance and revolt. Of the human form especially, it is so great it must never be made ridiculous. Of ornaments to a work nothing outré can be allowed—but those ornaments can be allowed that conform to the perfect facts of the open air, and that flow out of the nature of the work, and come irrepressibly from it, and are necessary to the completion of the work. Most works are most beautiful without ornament. Exaggerations will be revenged in human physiology. Clean and vigorous children are jetted and conceived only in those communities where the models of natural forms are public every day. Great genius and the people of these States must never be demeaned to romances. As soon as histories are properly told, no more need of romances.

The great poets are to be known by the absence in them of tricks, and by the justification of perfect personal candor. All faults may be forgiven of him who has perfect candor. Henceforth let no man of us lie, for we have seen that openness wins the inner and outer world, and that there is no single exception, and that never since our earth gathered itself in a mass have deceit or subterfuge or prevarication attracted its smallest

particle or the faintest tinge of a shade—and that through the
enveloping wealth and rank of a state, or the whole republic of
states, a sneak or sly person shall be discovered and despised—
and that the soul has never been once fooled and never can be
fooled—and thrift without the loving nod of the soul is only a
fetid puff—and there never grew up in any of the continents of
the globe, nor upon any planet or satellite, nor in that condition
which precedes the birth of babes, nor at any time during the
changes of life, nor in any stretch of abeyance or action of vitality,
nor in any process of formation or reformation anywhere, a being
whose instinct hated the truth.

Extreme caution or prudence, the soundest organic health,
large hope and comparison and fondness for women and children, large alimentiveness and destructiveness and causality,
with a perfect sense of the oneness of nature, and the propriety
of the same spirit applied to human affairs, are called up of the
float of the brain of the world to be parts of the greatest poet
from his birth out of his mother's womb, and from her birth
out of her mother's. Caution seldom goes far enough. It has
been thought that the prudent citizen was the citizen who
applied himself to solid gains, and did well for himself and for
his family, and completed a lawful life without debt or crime.
The greatest poet sees and admits these economies as he sees
the economies of food and sleep, but has higher notions of prudence than to think he gives much when he gives a few slight
attentions at the latch of the gate. The premises of the prudence
of life are not the hospitality of it, or the ripeness and harvest of
it. Beyond the independence of a little sum laid aside for
burial-money, and of a few clapboards around and shingles
overhead on a lot of American soil owned, and the easy dollars
that supply the year's plain clothing and meals, the melancholy
prudence of the abandonment of such a great being as a man is
to the toss and pallor of years of money-making with all their
scorching days and icy nights, and all their stifling deceits and
underhanded dodgings, or infinitesimals of parlors, or shameless
stuffing while others starve, and all the loss of the bloom and
odor of the earth, and of the flowers and atmosphere, and of
the sea, and of the true taste of the women and men you pass
or have to do with in youth or middle age, and the issuing sickness and desperate revolt at the close of a life without elevation
or naïveté (even if you have achieved a secure 10,000 a year, or

election to Congress or the governorship), and the ghastly chatter of a death without serenity or majesty, is the great fraud upon modern civilization and forethought, blotching the surface and system which civilization undeniably drafts, and moistening with tears the immense features it spreads and spreads with such velocity before the reached kisses of the soul.

Ever the right explanation remains to be made about prudence. The prudence of the mere wealth and respectability of the most esteemed life appears too faint for the eye to observe at all, when little and large alike drop quietly aside at the thought of the prudence suitable for immortality. What is the wisdom that fills the thinness of a year, or seventy or eighty years—to the wisdom spaced out by ages, and coming back at a certain time with strong reinforcements and rich presents, and the clear faces of wedding guests as far as you can look in every direction running gaily toward you? Only the soul is of itself— all else has reference to what ensues. All that a person does or thinks is of consequence. Nor can the push of charity or personal force ever be anything else than the profoundest reason, whether it brings arguments to hand or no. No specification is necessary —to add or subtract or divide is in vain. Little or big, learned or unlearned, white or black, legal or illegal, sick or well, from the first inspiration down the windpipe to the last expiration out of it, all that a male or female does that is vigorous and benevolent and clean is so much sure profit to him or her in the unshakable order of the universe, and through the whole scope of it forever. The prudence of the greatest poet answers at last the craving and glut of the soul, puts off nothing, permits no letup for its own case or any case, has no particular sabbath or judgment day, divides not the living from the dead or the righteous from the unrighteous, is satisfied with the present, matches every thought or act by its correlative, and knows no possible forgiveness or deputed atonement.

The direct trial of him who would be the greatest poet is today. If he does not flood himself with the immediate age as with vast oceanic tides—if he be not himself the age transfigured, and if to him is not opened the eternity which gives similitude to all periods and locations and processes, and animate and inanimate forms, and which is the bond of time, and rises up from its inconceivable vagueness and infiniteness in the swimming shapes of today, and is held by the ductile anchors of life, and makes the present spot the passage from what was to what shall be, and commits itself to the representation of this wave of an hour, and this one of the sixty beautiful children of the wave —let him merge in the general run, and wait his development.

Still the final test of poems, or any character or work, remains. The prescient poet projects himself centuries ahead, and judges performer or performance after the changes of time. Does it live through them? Does it still hold on untired? Will the same style, and the direction of genius to similar points, be satisfactory now? Have the marches of tens and hundreds and thousands of years made willing detours to the right hand and the left hand for his sake? Is he beloved long and long after he is buried? Does the young man think often of him? and the young woman think often of him? and do the middle-aged and the old think of him?

A great poem is for ages and ages in common, and for all degrees and complexions, and all departments and sects, and for a woman as much as a man, and a man as much as a woman. A great poem is no finish to a man or woman, but rather a beginning. Has anyone fancied he could sit at last under some due authority, and rest satisfied with explanations, and realize and be content and full? To no such terminus does the greatest poet bring—he brings neither cessation nor sheltered fatness and ease. The touch of him, like nature, tells in action. Whom he takes he takes with firm sure grasp into live regions previously unattained—thenceforward is no rest—they see the space and ineffable sheen that turn the old spots and lights into dead vacuums. Now there shall be a man cohered out of tumult and chaos—the elder encourages the younger and shows him how—they two shall launch off fearlessly together till the new world fits an orbit for itself and looks unabashed on the lesser orbits of the stars, and sweeps through the ceaseless rings, and shall never be quiet again.

There will soon be no more priests. Their work is done. A new order shall arise, and they shall be the priests of man, and every man shall be his own priest. They shall find their inspiration in real objects today, symptoms of the past and future. They shall not deign to defend immortality or God, or the perfection of things, or liberty, or the exquisite beauty and reality of the soul. They shall arise in America, and be responded to from the remainder of the earth.

The English language befriends the grand American expression—it is brawny enough, and limber and full enough. On the tough stock of a race who through all change of circumstances was never without the idea of political liberty, which is the animus of all liberty, it has attracted the terms of daintier and gayer and subtler and more elegant tongues. It is the powerful language of resistance—it is the dialect of common sense. It is the speech of the proud and melancholy races, and of all who aspire. It is the chosen tongue to express growth, faith, self-esteem, freedom, justice, equality, friendliness, amplitude, prudence, decision, and courage. It is the medium that shall well-nigh express the inexpressible.

No great literature, nor any like style of behavior or oratory, or social intercourse or household arrangements, or public institutions, or the treatment by bosses of employed people, nor executive detail, or detail of the army and navy, nor spirit of legislation or courts, or police or tuition or architecture, or songs or amusements, can long elude the jealous and passionate instinct of American standards. Whether or no the sign appears from the mouths of the people, it throbs a live interrogation in every freeman's and freewoman's heart, after that which passes by, or this built to remain. Is it uniform with my country? Are its disposals without ignominious distinctions? Is it for the ever-growing communes of brothers and lovers, large, well-united, proud, beyond the old models, generous beyond all models? Is it something grown fresh out of the fields, or drawn from the sea for use to me today here? I know that what answers for me, an American, in Texas, Ohio, Canada, must answer for any individual or nation that serves for a part of my materials. Does this answer? Is it for the nursing of the young of the republic? Does it solve readily with the sweet milk of the nipples of the breasts of the Mother of Many Children?

America prepares with composure and good will for the visitors that have sent word. It is not intellect that is to be their warrant and welcome. The talented, the artist, the ingenious, the editor, the statesman, the erudite, are not unappreciated— they fall in their place and do their work. The soul of the nation also does its work. It rejects none, it permits all. Only toward the like of itself will it advance half-way. An individual is as superb as a nation when he has the qualities which make a superb nation. The soul of the largest and wealthiest and proud-est nation may well go half-way to meet that of its poets.

JAMES RUSSELL LOWELL

(1819—1891)

o◯oo◯o

As A CRITIC LOWELL had much of the ethical and imaginative idealism of Emerson, whose influence[1] he gratefully acknowledged; but he also had a much deeper knowledge, a more comprehensive range, and he was more concerned with strictly literary matters such as the history of language, style, and form. All things considered, Lowell is our greatest American critic,[2] and in certain respects he is nearly the equal of the English Arnold.

In recent years, however, Lowell's reputation has suffered, partly through certain misunderstandings on the part of hasty readers who do not know his work as a whole. Much of the confusion and inconsistency with which Lowell is sometimes charged can be clarified if one reads his work chronologically and attends, as one must in the case of Wordsworth, to the *growth*[3] of Lowell's mind; within his successive periods his literary theories have a very considerable unity and consistency. Thus up to 1850 he urged an anti-traditional literature of didacticism[4] devoted to furthering social reforms such as abolition of slavery; from 1850 to 1867 the war to preserve a united nation, in conjunction with British hostility toward the North, helped to make him urge an indigenous and nationalistic literature;[5] and from 1867 on, as professor of comparative literature and as ambassador to Spain and England, his growing

---

[1]Lowell's *Writings* (Elmwood edition), II, 392.

[2]N. Foerster (*American Criticism*, p. 111 and p. 149) assembles evidence to show that "Lowell's creed is almost the unwritten constitution of the republic of letters."

[3]The growth of Lowell's mind has been examined in H. H. Clark's "Lowell—Humanitarian, Nationalist, or Humanist?" *Studies in Philology*, XXVII, 411–441 (July, 1930), and also in more detail in the forthcoming Introduction to *Lowell* by N. Foerster and H. H. Clark in the American Writers Series.

[4]See his preface to *The Pioneer* (1843), his "Ode" of 1842, "L'Envoi" of 1843, and *Round Table*, pp. 28 ff.

[5]See *Lectures on Some English Poets* (given in 1855), pp. 63, 92, 167; preface to the *Biglow Papers* (1862); his reviews of Holland's *Bitter-Sweet*, *Atlantic* (May, 1859), and of Whittier, *Function of the Poet and Other Essays*, pp. 129; 132; 137; his praise of Cooper's Leatherstocking, *Round Table*, p. 221; and his essay on "A Great Public Character," *Writings*, II, 3, 11–12. All references are to the Elmwood edition unless otherwise indicated.

knowledge of the literatures of other lands and ages led him to advocate a literature which, if rooted in local soil, is devoted to those unchanging aspects of the human spirit which are universal.[6] In fact, his
mutations in literary ideals enabled Lowell to father at different times
very different tendencies and enabled him to touch the history of
American literary taste at most points on its circumference.   Again,
many modern readers, accustomed to the orderly method of scientific
treatises, have censured Lowell's critical essays as being diffuse and disjointed and without the steady march of an ordered argument.   It may
be, however, that this weakness has been his strength in getting what
he has to say so widely read and in forming American literary taste.
Bliss Perry, himself a continuator of the Lowell tradition, explains the
zest with which Lowell is read by the fact that his criticisms belong to
"the whole tradition of the English bookish essay" which "has always
welcomed copious, well-informed, enthusiastic, disorderly, and affectionate talk about books.   It demands gusto rather than strict method,
discursiveness rather than concision, abundance of matter rather than
mere neatness of design."[7]   And finally, those who charge Lowell with
being a bookish aristocratic Brahmin who sought refuge from America
in the great European masters of past ages and who contributed nothing
to the crusade for a fresh and indigenous American literature forget his
Biglow Papers, glorifying rustic common sense, and their epoch-making
preface attacking a bookish literature and language and urging a completely indigenous and native literature, in dialect, deeply rooted in
the soil.   If, after Lowell, American taste turned, with Mark Twain and
Howells, toward realism and a racy indigenousness sensitive to vernacu-
lar expression, we must remember that it was Lowell himself, whose
vast popularity as the author of the *Biglow Papers* and the founder of
the *Atlantic Monthly*[8] (in 1857), did much to initiate this realistic tendency and to give it the sanction of his high professorial authority.   He

    [6]See his essay on Percival, 1867 (*Writings*, II, 113–117), his review of Piatt (*Func-
tion of the Poet*, etc., pp. 141–145); *Writings*, III, 77, 234; II, 194; IV, 227–228; III,
252–253; he also came to think that dialect was less important than saying something
universally important clearly—see the Riverside edition of the *Works*, III, 304, 328;
VII, 42, 131, 158, 216–217, 277; and R. P. Nye, "Lowell and American Speech,"
Philological Quarterly, XVII (1939), 249–256.
    [7]Bliss Perry, *The Praise of Folly and Other Papers* (Boston, 1923), p. 145.
    [8]F. L. Pattee (*Century Readings in the American Short Story* [New York, 1927], p. 117)
says that "Lowell preferred native themes and native tangs and actuality in our
native fiction, and knowing this the younger writers for the *Atlantic* unconsciously
began to write more naturally and spontaneously."   F. L. Mott (*A History of American Magazines* [Harvard University Press, 1938], II, 173, 501) says that Lowell "went
counter to the general honeyed stickiness" then current and "made his magazine
a great force for the more realistic, vital fiction."

eagerly sought for the *Atlantic* realistic stories, and he discovered and published such pioneers of realism as Harriet Prescott Spofford, Rose Terry Cooke, and Rebecca Harding Davis, whose "Life in the Iron Mills" seems ultra-realistic even to an age accustomed to Sherwood Anderson and Dreiser.

On the other hand, after 1867, Lowell's critical essays, rich in appreciation, did much to introduce to the American people the great artists and thinkers of the European past; as a liberal transcending his age and nation, sensitive to excellence in whatever race or place or time, Lowell did much to liberalize the narrow taste of a frontier people who, in their ignorance of or contempt for what they regarded as a "feudal" European past, were starving themselves aesthetically. In his later period, in which most of his full-length critical essays were written, he insisted that literature "must be judged . . . absolutely, with reference, that is, to the highest standard, and not relatively to the fashions and opportunities of the age in which he lived."[9] This standard he derived from the headwaters of the Greek critical tradition. The stamp of the Greeks, he says, "is upon all the allowed measures and weights of aesthetic criticism. . . . The model is not there to be copied merely, but that the study of it may lead us insensibly to the same processes of thought by which its purity of outline and harmony of parts were attained, and enable us to feel that strength is consistent with repose, that multiplicity is not abundance, that grace is but a more refined form of power, and that a thought is none the less profound that the limpidity of its expression allows us to measure it at a glance. To be possessed with this conviction gives us at least a determinate point of view, and enables us to appeal a case of taste to a court of final judicature, whose decisions are guided by immutable principles."[10] With the Greeks, Lowell placed great emphasis on organic and harmonized form. "Spenser," he says, "in the enthusiasm of his new Platonism, tells us that '*Soul* is form, and doth the body make,' and no doubt this is true of the highest artistic genius. Form without soul . . . is a lifeless thing . . . For the soul is not only that which gives form, but that which gives life, the mysterious and pervasive essence always in itself beautiful, not always so in the shapes which it informs, but even then full of infinite suggestion. In literature it is what we call genius, an insoluble

[9]*Writings*, V, 167 (essay on Dante, 1872); III, 247.
[10]*Ibid.*, III, 252–253, essay on "Shakespeare Once More," (1868). For full discussion regarding Lowell's relation to the classicists, see studies listed in the following bibliography by Pritchard and Foerster.

ingredient which kindles, lights, inspires, and transmits impulsion to other minds, wakens energies in them hitherto latent, and makes them startlingly aware that they too may be parts of the controlling purpose of the world."[11] Form Lowell defines as "the artistic sense of decorum controlling the co-ordination of parts and insuring their harmonious subservience to a common end," and style he defines as "a lower form of the same faculty . . . which has to do with the perfection of the parts themselves, and whose triumph it is to produce the greatest effect with the least possible expenditure of material."[12] Lowell's critical heritage from the Greeks, however, was reinforced and given a modern color by his admiration for the critical principles of Coleridge and, partly through him, of the Germans. Coleridge he regarded as "a main influence" in teaching the modern mind "to recognize in the imagination an important factor not only in the happiness but in the destiny of man. In criticism he was, indeed, a teacher and interpreter whose service was incalculable. He owed much to Lessing, something to Schiller, and more to the younger Schlegel, but he owed most to his own sympathetic and penetrative imagination."[13] Lowell also thought that Carlyle, who at one period was "the first in insight of English critics," showed "the influence of his master, Goethe, the most widely receptive of critics."[14] Lowell's own debt to Goethe[15] is considerable; it will be recalled that he took Goethe's three questions all critics should answer as the guide for his essay on Shakespeare, an essay which has many parallels to Goethe's own analysis of Shakespeare.

BIBLIOGRAPHY

TEXT

The Complete Writings. 16 vols. Elmwood edition. Boston, 1904. Includes Norton's *Letters* (3 vols.), and Scudder's *Life* (2 vols.).

Early Prose Writings, with a prefatory note by Dr. Hale . . . and an introduction by Walter Littlefield. London, 1902.

The Function of the Poet and Other Essays . . . collected and edited by Albert Mordell. Boston, 1920. Early essays and reviews throwing important light on the growth of Lowell's mind.

Lectures on the English Poets. Cleveland, 1897. The Rowfant Club here reprints from the Boston *Daily Advertiser* the Lowell Institute lectures given by Lowell in 1855.

---

[11]*Writings*, VII, 317 (in his address on "The Study of Modern Languages," which he gave as the president of the Modern Language Association in 1889).
[12]*Ibid.*, VII, 320.   [13]*Ibid.*, VII, 84–85 (1885).   [14]*Ibid.*, II, 62–63 (1866).
[15]See Wurfl's study, listed in the following bibliography.

The Round Table. Boston, 1913. A title given by an anonymous editor to a collection of nine of Lowell's reviews not included in his collected works.

BIBLIOGRAPHY

Cooke, G. W., *A Bibliography of James Russell Lowell.* Boston, 1906.
Chamberlain, J. C., and Livingston, L. S., *First Editions of the Writings of James Russell Lowell.* New York, 1914.

BIOGRAPHY AND CRITICISM

Allen, Gay W., "Lowell," in *American Prosody.* New York, 1934, pp. 244-270.
Clark, H. H., "Lowell's Criticism of Romantic Literature," *Publications of the Modern Language Association,* XLI, 209-228 (March, 1926).
——, "Lowell—Humanitarian, Nationalist, or Humanist?" *Studies in Philology,* XXVII, 411-441 (July, 1930).
De Mille, George E., "Lowell," in *Literary Criticism in America.* New York, 1931, pp. 49-85.
Foerster, Norman, "Lowell," in *Nature in American Literature.* New York, 1923, pp. 143-175.
——, "Lowell," in *American Criticism.* Boston, 1928, pp. 111-156.
Lange, Alexis F., "James Russell Lowell as a Critic," *California University Chronicle,* VIII, 352-364 (1906).
Lockwood, Ferris, "Mr. Lowell on Art-Principles," *Scribner's Magazine,* XV, 186-189 (February, 1894).
Palmer, Ray, "James Russell Lowell and Modern Literary Criticism," *International Review,* IV, 264-281 (March, 1877). A review of Lowell's *Among My Books,* both series.
Parrington, V. L., "Lowell, Cambridge Brahmin," in *The Romantic Revolution in America.* New York, 1927, pp. 460-472.
Parsons, E. S., "Lowell's Conception of Poetry," *Colorado College Publications,* Language Series, II, no. 20, 67-84 (1908).
Perry, Bliss, "Lowell," in *The Praise of Folly and Other Papers.* Boston, 1923, pp. 130-150. An appreciative essay.
Pettigrew, R. C., "Lowell's Criticism of Milton," *American Literature,* III, 457-464 (January, 1932).
Pollak, Gustav, "Lowell," in *The International Perspective in Criticism: Goethe, Grillparzer, Sainte-Beuve, Lowell.* New York, 1914, pp. 58-83.
Pritchard, J. P., "Lowell's Debt to Horace's *Ars Poetica*," *American Literature,* III, 259-276 (November, 1931).
——, "Aristotle's *Poetics* and Certain American Literary Critics," *Classical Weekly,* XXVII, 81-85; 89-93; 97-99 (1934). The critics are Poe, Lowell, and Stedman. Lowell is treated in the issue for January 15, 1934, pp. 89-93.
Reilly, J. J., *James Russell Lowell as a Critic.* New York, 1915.

Robertson, J. M., "Lowell as a Critic," *North American Review,* CCIX, 246–262 (February, 1919).

Thorndike, A. H., "Lowell," in *The Cambridge History of American Literature.* New York, 1918, II, 245–257.

Warren, Austin, "Lowell on Thoreau," *Studies in Philology,* XXVII, 442–461 (July, 1930).

Watson, William, "Lowell as a Critic," in *Excursions in Criticism.* London, 1893, pp. 87–96.

Wendell, Barrett, "Mr. Lowell as a Teacher," in *Stelligeri.* New York, 1893, pp. 205–217.

Wurfl, George, "Lowell's Debt to Goethe," *Pennsylvania State College Studies,* I, no. 2, pp. 1–89.

THE FUNCTION OF THE POET[1]
1855[2]

Whether, as some philosophers assume, we possess only the fragments of a great cycle of knowledge in whose center stood the primeval man in friendly relation with the powers of the universe, and build our hovels out of the ruins of our ancestral palace; or whether, according to the development theory of others, we are rising gradually, and have come up out of an atom instead of descending from an Adam, so that the proudest pedigree might run up to a barnacle or a zoophyte at last, are questions that will keep for a good many centuries yet. Confining myself to what little we can learn from history, we find tribes rising slowly out of barbarism to a higher or lower point of culture and civility, and everywhere the poet also is found, under one name or other, changing in certain outward respects, but essentially the same.

And however far we go back, we shall find this also—that the poet and the priest were united originally in the same person; which means that the poet was he who was conscious of the world of spirit as well as that of sense, and was the ambassador of the gods to men. This was his highest function, and hence his name of "seer." He was the discoverer and declarer of the perennial beneath the deciduous. His were the *epea pteroenta,* the true

---

[1] "This was the concluding lecture in the course which Lowell read before the Lowell Institute in the winter of 1855. Doubtless Lowell never printed it because, as his genius matured, he felt that its assertions were too absolute, and that its style bore too many marks of haste in composition, and was too rhetorical for an essay to be read in print" (Charles Eliot Norton).

[2] Date of composition; not published until 1894.

"winged words" that could fly down the unexplored future and carry the names of ancestral heroes, of the brave and wise and good. It was thus that the poet could reward virtue and, by and by, as society grew more complex, could burn in the brand of shame. This is Homer's character of Demodocus, in the eighth book of the *Odyssey*, "whom the Muse loved and gave the good and ill"—the gift of conferring good or evil immortality. The first histories were in verse; and, sung as they were at feasts and gatherings of the people, they awoke in men the desire of fame, which is the first promoter of courage and self-trust, because it teaches men by degrees to appeal from the present to the future. We may fancy what the influence of the early epics was when they were recited to men who claimed the heroes celebrated in them for their ancestors, by what Bouchardon, the sculptor, said, only two centuries ago: "When I read Homer, I feel as if I were twenty feet high." Nor have poets lost their power over the future in modern times. Dante lifts up by the hair the face of some petty traitor, the Smith or Brown of some provincial Italian town, lets the fire of his Inferno glare upon it for a moment, and it is printed forever on the memory of mankind. The historians may iron out the shoulders of Richard the Third as smooth as they can, they will never get over the wrench that Shakespeare gave them.

The peculiarity of almost all early literature is that it seems to have a double meaning, that, underneath its natural, we find ourselves continually seeing or suspecting a supernatural meaning. In the older epics the characters seem to be half typical and only half historical. Thus did the early poets endeavor to make realities out of appearances; for, except a few typical men in whom certain ideas get embodied, the generations of mankind are mere apparitions who come out of the dark for a purposeless moment, and re-enter the dark again after they have performed the nothing they came for.

Gradually, however, the poet as the "seer" became secondary to the "maker." His office became that of entertainer rather than teacher. But always something of the old tradition was kept alive. And if he has now come to be looked upon merely as the best expresser, the gift of seeing is implied as necessarily antecedent to that, and of seeing very deep, too. If any man would seem to have written without any conscious moral, that man is Shakespeare. But that must be a dull sense, indeed, which does not see through his tragic—yes, and his comic—masks awful eyes that flame with something intenser and deeper than a mere scenic meaning—a meaning out of the great deep that is behind and beyond all human and merely personal character. Nor was Shakespeare himself unconscious of his place as a teacher and profound moralist: witness that sonnet in which he bewails his having neglected sometimes the errand that was laid upon him:

> Alas, 'tis true I have gone here and there,
> And made myself a motley to the view,
> Gored mine own thoughts, sold cheap what is
>   most dear,
> Made old offenses of affections new;
> Most true it is that I have looked on truth
> Askance and strangely;

the application of which is made clear by the next sonnet, in which he distinctly alludes to his profession.

There is this unmistakable stamp on all the great poets—that, however in little things they may fall below themselves, whenever there comes a great and noble thing to say, they say it greatly and nobly, and bear themselves most easily in the royalties of thought and language. There is not a mature play of Shakespeare's in which great ideas do not jut up in mountainous permanence, marking forever the boundary of provinces of thought, and known afar to many kindreds of men.

And it is for this kind of sight, which we call insight, and not for any faculty of observation and description, that we value the poet. It is in proportion as he has this that he is an adequate expresser, and not a juggler with words. It is by means of this that for every generation of man he plays the part of "namer." Before him, as before Adam, the creation passes to be named anew: first the material world; then the world of passions and emotions; then the world of ideas. But whenever a great imagination comes, however it may delight itself with imaging the outward beauty of things, however it may seem to flow thoughtlessly away in music like a brook, yet the shadow of heaven lies also in its depth beneath the shadow of earth. Continually the visible universe suggests the invisible. We are forever feeling this in Shakespeare. His imagination went down to the very bases of things, and while his characters are the most natural that poet ever created, they are also perfectly ideal, and are more truly the personifications of abstract thoughts and passions than those of any allegorical writer whatever.

Even in what seems so purely a picturesque poem as the *Iliad*, we feel something of this. Beholding as Homer did, from the tower of contemplation, the eternal mutability and nothing permanent but change, he must look underneath the show for the reality. Great captains and conquerors came forth out of the eternal silence, entered it again with their trampling hosts, and shoutings, and trumpet blasts, and were as utterly gone as those echoes of their deeds which he sang, and which faded with the last sound of his voice and the last tremble of his lyre. History relating outward events alone was an unmeaning gossip, with the world for a village. This life could only become other than phantasmagoric, could only become real, as it stood related to something that was higher and permanent. Hence the idea of Fate, of a higher power unseen—that shadow, as of an eagle circling to its swoop, which flits stealthily and swiftly across the windy plains of Troy. In the *Odyssey* we find pure allegory.

Now, under all these names—praiser, seer, soothsayer—we find the same idea lurking. The poet is he who can best see and best say what is ideal—what belongs to the world of soul and of beauty. Whether he celebrate the brave and good man, or the gods, or the beautiful as it appears in man or nature, something of a religious character still clings to him; he is the revealer of Deity. He may be unconscious of his mission; he may be false to it; but in proportion as he is a great poet, he rises to the level of it the more often. He does not always directly rebuke what is bad and base, but indirectly by making us feel what delight there is in the good and fair. If he besiege evil, it is with such beautiful engines of war (as Plutarch tells us of Demetrius) that the besieged themselves are charmed with them. Whoever reads the great poets cannot but be made better by it, for they always introduce him to a higher society, to a greater style of manners and of thinking. Whoever learns to love what is beautiful is made incapable of the low and mean and bad. If Plato excludes the poets from his Republic, it is expressly on the ground that they speak unworthy things of the gods; that is, that they have lost the secret of their art, and use artificial types instead of speaking the true universal language of imagination. He who translates the divine into the vulgar, the spiritual into the sensual, is the reverse of a poet.

The poet, under whatever name, always stands for the same thing—imagination. And imagination in its highest form gives him the power, as it were, of assuming the consciousness of whatever he speaks about, whether man or beast, or rock or tree. It is the ring of Canace, which whoso has on understands the language of all created things. And as regards expression, it seems to enable the poet to condense the whole of himself into a single word. Therefore, when a great poet has said a thing, it is finally and utterly expressed, and has as many meanings as there are men who read his verse. A great poet is something more than an interpreter between man and nature; he is also an interpreter between man and his own nature. It is he who gives us those key words, the possession of which makes us masters of all the unsuspected treasure-caverns of thought, and feeling, and beauty which open under the dusty path of our daily life.

And it is not merely a dry lexicon that he compiles,—a thing which enables us to translate from one dead dialect into another as dead,—but all his verse is instinct with music, and his words open windows on every side to pictures of scenery and life. The difference between the dry fact and the poem is as great as that between reading the shipping news and seeing the actual coming and going of the crowd of stately ships,—"the city on the inconstant billows dancing,"—as there is between ten minutes of happiness and ten minutes by the clock. Everybody remembers the story of the little Montague who was stolen and sold to the chimney sweep: how he could dimly remember lying in a beautiful chamber; how he carried with him in all his drudgery the vision of a fair, sad mother's face that sought him everywhere in vain; how he threw himself one day, all sooty as he was from his toil, on a rich bed and fell asleep, and how a kind person woke him, questioned him, pieced together his broken recollections for him, and so at last made the visions of the beautiful chamber and the fair, sad countenance real to him again. It seems to me that the offices that the poet does for us are typified in this nursery-tale. We all of us have our vague reminiscences of the stately home of our childhood,—for we are all of us poets and geniuses in our youth, while earth is all new to us, and the chalice of every buttercup is brimming with the wine of poesy,—and we all remember the beautiful, motherly countenance which nature bent over us there. But somehow we all get stolen away thence; life becomes to us a sooty taskmaster, and we crawl through dark passages without end—till suddenly the word of some poet redeems us, makes us know who we are.

and of helpless orphans makes us the heirs to a great estate. It is to our true relations with the two great worlds of outward and inward nature that the poet reintroduces us.

But the imagination has a deeper use than merely to give poets a power of expression. It is the everlasting preserver of the world from blank materialism. It forever puts matter in the wrong, and compels it to show its title to existence. Wordsworth tells us that in his youth he was sometimes obliged to touch the walls to find if they were visionary or no, and such experiences are not uncommon with persons who converse much with their own thoughts. Dr. Johnson said that to kick one's foot against a stone was a sufficient confutation of Berkeley, and poor old Pyrrho has passed into a proverb because, denying the objectivity of matter, he was run over by a cart and killed. But all that he affirmed was that to the soul the cart was no more real than its own imaginative reproduction of it, and perhaps the shade of the philosopher ran up to the first of his deriders who crossed the Styx with a triumphant "I told you so! The cart did not run over *me*, for here I am without a bone broken."

And, in another sense also, do those poets who deal with human character, as all the greater do, continually suggest to us the purely phantasmal nature of life except as it is related to the world of ideas. For are not their personages more real than most of those in history? Is not Lear more authentic and permanent than Lord Raglan? Their realm is a purely spiritual one in which space and time and costume are nothing. What matters it that Shakespeare puts a seaport in Bohemia, and knew less geography than Tommy who goes to the district school? He understood eternal boundaries, such as are laid down on no chart, and are not defined by such transitory affairs as mountain chains, rivers, and seas.

No great movement of the human mind takes place without the concurrent beat of those two wings, the imagination and the understanding. It is by the understanding that we are enabled to make the most of this world, and to use the collected material of experience in its condensed form of practical wisdom; and it is the imagination which forever beckons toward that other world which is always future, and makes us discontented with this. The one rests upon experience; the other leans forward and listens after the *in*experienced, and shapes the features of that future with which it is forever in travail. The imagination might be defined as the common sense of the invisible world, as the understanding is of the visible; and as those are the finest individual characters in which the two moderate and rectify each other, so those are the finest eras where the same may be said of society. In the voyage of life, not only do we depend on the needle, true to its earthly instincts, but upon observation of the fixed stars, those beacons lighted upon the eternal promontories of heaven above the stirs and shiftings of our lower system.

But it seems to be thought that we have come upon the earth too late, that there has been a feast of imagination formerly, and all that is left for us is to steal the scraps. We hear that there is no poetry in railroads and steamboats and telegraphs, and especially none in Brother Jonathan. If this be true, so much the worse for him. But because *he* is a materialist shall there be no more poets? When we have said that we live in a materialistic age we have said something which meant more than we intended. If we say it in the way of blame, we have said a foolish thing, for probably one age is as good as another, and, at any rate, the worst is good enough company for us. The age of Shakespeare was richer than our own, only because it was lucky enough to have such a pair of eyes as his to see it, and such a gift of speech as his to report it. And so there is always room and occasion for the poet, who continues to be, just as he was in the early time, nothing more nor less than a "seer." He is always the man who is willing to take the age he lives in on trust, as the very best that ever was. Shakespeare did not sit down and cry for the water of Helicon to turn the wheels of his little private mill at the Bankside. He appears to have gone more quietly about his business than any other playwright in London, to have drawn off what water power he needed from the great prosy current of affairs that flows alike for all and in spite of all, to have ground for the public what grist they wanted, coarse or fine, and it seems a mere piece of luck that the smooth stream of his activity reflected with such ravishing clearness every changing mood of heaven and earth, every stick and stone, every dog and clown and courtier that stood upon its brink. It is a curious illustration of the friendly manner in which Shakespeare received everything that came along,—of what a *present* man he was,—that in the very same year that the mulberry tree was brought into England, he got one and planted it in his garden at Stratford.

It is perfectly true that this is a materialistic age, and for that very reason we want our poets all the more. We find that every generation contrives to catch its singing larks without the sky's falling. When the poet comes, he always turns out to be the man who discovers that the passing moment is the inspired one, and that the secret of poetry is not to have lived in Homer's day, or Dante's, but to be alive now. To be alive now, that is the great art and mystery. They are dead men who live in the past, and men yet unborn that live in the future. We are like Hans in Luck, forever exchanging the burdensome good we have for something else, till at last we come home empty-handed.

That pale-faced drudge of Time opposite me there, that weariless sexton whose callous hands bury our rosy hours in the irrevocable past, is even now reaching forward to a moment as rich in life, in character, and thought, as full of opportunity, as any since Adam. This little isthmus that we are now standing on is the point to which martyrs in their triumphant pain, prophets in their fervor, and poets in their ecstasy, looked forward as the golden future, as the land too good for them to behold with mortal eyes; it is the point toward which the faint-hearted and desponding hereafter will look back as the priceless past when there was still some good and virtue and opportunity left in the world.

The people who feel their own age prosaic are those who see only its costume. And that is what makes it prosaic—that we have not faith enough in ourselves to think our own clothes good enough to be presented to posterity in. The artists fancy that the court dress of posterity is that of Van Dyck's time, or Caesar's. I have seen the model of a statue of Sir Robert Peel,—a statesman whose merit consisted in yielding gracefully to the present,—in which the sculptor had done his best to travesty the real man into a make-believe Roman. At the period when England produced its greatest poets, we find exactly the reverse of this, and we are thankful that the man who made the monument of Lord Bacon had genius to copy every button of his dress, everything down to the rosettes on his shoes, and then to write under his statue, "Thus sat Francis Bacon"—not "Cneius Pompeius"—"Viscount Verulam." Those men had faith even in their own shoestrings.

After all, how is our poor scapegoat of a nineteenth century to blame? Why, for not being the seventeenth, to be sure! It is always raining opportunity, but it seems it was only the men two hundred years ago who were intelligent enough not to hold their cups bottom-up. We are like beggars who think if a piece of gold drop into their palm it must be counterfeit, and would rather change it for the smooth-worn piece of familiar copper. And so, as we stand in our mendicancy by the wayside, Time tosses carefully the great golden today into our hats, and we turn it over grumblingly and suspiciously, and are pleasantly surprised at finding that we can exchange it for beef and potatoes. Till Dante's time the Italian poets thought no language good enough to put their nothings into but Latin,—and indeed a dead tongue was the best for dead thoughts,—but Dante found the common speech of Florence, in which men bargained and scolded and made love, good enough for him, and out of the world around him made a poem such as no Roman ever sang.

In our day, it is said despairingly, the understanding reigns triumphant: it is the age of common sense. If this be so, the wisest way would be to accept it manfully. But, after all, what is the meaning of it? Looking at the matter superficially, one would say that a striking difference between our science and that of the world's gray fathers is that there is every day less and less of the element of wonder in it. What they saw written in light upon the great arch of heaven and, by a magnificent reach of sympathy of which we are incapable, associated with the fall of monarchs and the fate of man, is for us only a professor, a piece of chalk, and a blackboard. The solemn and unapproachable skies we have vulgarized; we have peeped and botanized among the flowers of light, pulled off every petal, fumbled in every calyx, and reduced them to the bare stem of order and class. The stars can no longer maintain their divine reserves, but whenever there is a conjunction and congress of planets, every enterprising newspaper sends thither its special reporter with his telescope. Over those arcana of life where once a mysterious presence brooded, we behold scientific explorers skipping like so many incarnate notes of interrogation. We pry into the counsels of the great powers of nature, we keep our ears at the keyhole, and know everything that is going to happen. There is no longer any sacred inaccessibility, no longer any enchanting unexpectedness, and life turns to prose the moment there is nothing unattainable. It needs no more a voice out of the unknown proclaiming "Great Pan is dead!" We have found his tombstone, deciphered the arrowheaded inscription upon it, know his age to a day, and that he died universally regretted.

Formerly science was poetry. A mythology which broods over us in our cradle, which mingles with the lullaby of the nurse, which peoples the day with the possibility of divine encounters, and night with intimation of demonic ambushes, is something quite other, as the material for thought and poetry, from one that we take down from our bookshelves, as sapless as the shelf it stood on, as remote from all present sympathy with man or nature as a town history with its genealogies of Mr. Nobody's great-grandparents.

We have utilized everything. The Egyptians found a hint of the solar system in the concentric circles of the onion, and revered it as a symbol, while we respect it as a condiment in cookery, and can pass through all Weathersfield without a thought of the stars. Our world is a museum of natural history; that of our forefathers was a museum of supernatural history. And the rapidity with which the change has been going on is almost startling, when we consider that so modern and historical a personage as Queen Elizabeth was reigning at the time of the death of Dr. John Faustus, out of whose story the Teutonic imagination built up a mythus that may be set beside that of Prometheus.

Science, looked at scientifically, is bare and bleak enough. On those sublime heights the air is too thin for the lungs, and blinds the eyes. It is much better living down in the valleys, where one cannot see farther than the next farmhouse. Faith was never found in the bottom of a crucible, nor peace arrived at by analysis or synthesis. But all this is because science has become too grimly intellectual, has divorced itself from the moral and imaginative part of man. Our results are not arrived at in that spirit which led Kepler (who had his theory-traps set all along the tracks of the stars to catch a discovery) to say, "In my opinion the occasions of new discoveries have been no less wonderful than the discoveries themselves."

But we are led back continually to the fact that science cannot, if it would, disengage itself from human nature and from imagination. No two men have ever argued together without at least agreeing in this, that something more than proof is required to produce conviction, and that a logic which is capable of grinding the stubbornest facts to powder (as every man's *own* logic always is) is powerless against so delicate a structure as the brain. Do what we will, we cannot contrive to bring together the yawning edges of proof and belief, to weld them into one. When Thor strikes Skrymir with his terrible hammer, the giant asks if a leaf has fallen. I need not appeal to the Thors of argument in the pulpit, the senate, and the mass meeting, if they have not sometimes found the popular giant as provokingly insensible. The $\sqrt{-x}$ is nothing in comparison with the chance-caught smell of a single flower which by the magic of association re-creates for us the unquestioning day of childhood. Demonstration may lead to the very gate of heaven, but there she makes us a civil bow, and leaves us to make our way back again to Faith, who has the key. That science which is of the intellect alone steps with indifferent foot upon the dead body of Belief, if only she may reach higher or see farther.

But we cannot get rid of our wonder—we who have brought down the wild lightning, from writing fiery doom upon the walls of heaven, to be our errand boy and penny postman. Wonder is crude imagination; and it is necessary to us, for man shall not live by bread alone, and exact knowledge is not enough. Do we get nearer the truth or farther from it that we have got a gas or an imponderable fluid instead of a spirit? We go on exorcising one thing after another, but what boots it? The evasive genius flits into something else, and defies us. The powers of the outer and inner world form hand in hand a magnetic circle for whose connection man is necessary. It is the imagination that takes his hand and clasps it with that other stretched to him in the dark, and for which he was vainly groping. It is that which renews the mystery in nature, makes it wonderful and beautiful again, and out of the gases of the man of science remakes the old spirit. But we seem to have created too many wonders to be capable of wondering any longer; as Coleridge said, when asked if he believed in ghosts, that he had seen too many of them. But nature all the more imperatively demands it, and science can at best but scotch it, not kill it. In this day of newspapers and electric telegraphs, in which common sense and ridicule can magnetize a whole continent between dinner and tea, we say that such a phenomenon as Mahomet were impossible, and behold Joe Smith and the State of Deseret! Turning over the yellow leaves of the same copy of Webster on *Witchcraft* which Cotton Mather studied, I thought, "Well, that goblin is laid at last!"—and while I mused the tables were turning, and the chairs beating the devil's tattoo all over Christendom. I have a neighbor who dug down through tough strata of clay to a spring pointed out by a witch-hazel rod in the hands of a seventh son's seventh son, and the water is the sweeter to him for the wonder that is mixed with it. After all, it seems that our scientific gas, be it never so brilliant, is not equal to the dingy old Aladdin's lamp.

It is impossible for men to live in the world without poetry of some sort or other. If they cannot get the best they will get some substitute for it, and thus seem to verify Saint Augustine's slur that it is wine of devils. The mind bound down too closely to what is practical either becomes inert, or revenges itself by rushing into the savage wilderness of "isms." The insincerity of our civilization has disgusted some persons so much that they have sought refuge in Indian wigwams and found refreshment in taking a scalp now and then. Nature insists above all things upon balance. She contrives to maintain a harmony between the material and spiritual, nor allows the cerebrum an expansion at the cost of the cerebellum. If the character, for example, run on one side into religious enthusiasm, it is not unlikely to develop on the other a counterpoise of worldly prudence. Thus the Shaker and the Moravian are noted for thrift, and mystics are not always the worst managers. Through all changes of condition and experience man continues to be a citizen of the world of idea as well as the world of fact, and the tax gatherers of both are punctual.

And these antitheses which we meet with in individual character we cannot help seeing on the larger stage of the world also, a moral accompanying a material development. History, the great satirist, brings together Alexander and the blower of peas to hint to us that the tube of the one and the sword of the other were equally transitory; but meanwhile Aristotle was conquering kingdoms out of the unknown, and establishing a dynasty of thought from whose hand the scepter has not yet passed. So there are Charles V and Luther; the expansion of trade resulting from the Spanish and Portuguese discoveries and the Elizabethan literature; the Puritans seeking spiritual El Dorados while so much valor and thought were spent in finding mineral ones. It seems to be the purpose of God that a certain amount of genius shall go to each generation, particular quantities being represented by individuals, and while no *one* is complete in himself, all collectively make up a whole ideal figure of a man. Nature is not like certain varieties of the apple that cannot bear two years in succession. It is only that her expansions are uniform in all directions, that in every age she completes her circle, and like a tree adds a ring to her growth be it thinner or thicker.

Every man is conscious that he leads two lives, the one trivial and ordinary, the other sacred and recluse; the one which he carries to the dinner table and to his daily work, which grows old with his body and dies with it, the other that which is made up of the few inspiring moments of his higher aspiration and attainment, and in which his youth survives for him, his dreams, his unquenchable longings for something nobler than success. It is this life which the poets nourish for him, and sustain with their immortalizing nectar. Through them he feels once more the white innocence of his youth. His faith in something nobler than gold and iron and cotton comes back to him, not as an upbraiding ghost that wrings its pale hands and is gone, but beautiful and inspiring as a first love that recognizes nothing in him that is not high and noble. The poets are nature's perpetual pleaders, and protest with us against what is worldly. Out of their own undying youth they speak to ours. "Wretched is the man," says Goethe, "who has learned to despise the dreams of his youth!" It is from this misery that the imagination and the poets, who are its spokesmen, rescue us. The world goes to church, kneels to the eternal Purity, and then contrives to sneer at innocence and ignorance of evil by calling it green. Let every man thank God for what little there may be left in him of his vernal sweetness. Let him thank God if he have still the capacity for feeling an unmarketable enthusiasm, for that will make him worthy of the society of the noble dead, of the companionship of the poets. And let him love the poets for keeping youth young, woman womanly, and beauty beautiful.

There is as much poetry as ever in the world if we only knew how to find it out; and as much imagination, perhaps, only that it takes a more prosaic direction. Every man who meets with misfortune, who is stripped of material prosperity, finds that he has a little outlying mountain-farm of imagination, which did not appear in the schedule of his effects, on which his spirit is able to keep itself alive, though he never thought of it while he was fortunate. Job turns out to be a great poet as soon as his flocks and herds are taken away from him.

There is no reason why our continent should not sing as well

as the rest. We have had the practical forced upon us by our
position. We have had a whole hemisphere to clear up and put
to rights. And we are descended from men who were hardened
and stiffened by a downright wrestle with necessity. There was
no chance for poetry among the Puritans. And yet if any people
have a right to imagination, it should be the descendants of
these very Puritans. They had enough of it, or they could never
have conceived the great epic they did, whose books are States,
and which is written on this continent from Maine to California.

But there seems to be another reason why we should not
become a poetical people. Formerly the poet embodied the
hopes and desires of men in visible types. He gave them the
shoes of swiftness, the cap of invisibility, and the purse of Fortu-
natus. These were once stories for grown men, and not for the
nursery as now. We are apt ignorantly to wonder how our
forefathers could find satisfaction in fiction the absurdity of
which any of our primary-school children could demonstrate.
But we forget that the world's gray fathers were children themselves, and that in their little world, with its circle of the black
unknown all about it, the imagination was as active as it is with
people in the dark. Look at a child's toys, and we shall understand the matter well enough. Imagination is the fairy god-
mother (every child has one still), at the wave of whose wand
sticks become heroes, the closet in which she has been shut fifty
times for being naughty is turned into a palace, and a bit of
lath acquires all the potency of Excalibur.

But nowadays it is the understanding itself that has turned
poet. In her railroads she has given us the shoes of swiftness.
Fine-Ear herself could not hear so far as she who in her magnetic
telegraph can listen in Boston and hear what is going on in New
Orleans. And what need of Aladdin's lamp when a man can
build a palace with a patent pill? The office of the poet seems
to be reversed, and he must give back these miracles of the
understanding to poetry again, and find out what there is
imaginative in steam and iron and telegraph wires. After all,
there is as much poetry in the iron horses that eat fire as in
those of Diomed that fed on men. If you cut an apple across
you may trace in it the lines of the blossom that the bee hum-
med around in May, and so the soul of poetry survives in things
prosaic. Borrowing money on a bond does not seem the most
promising subject in the world, but Shakespeare found the

Merchant of Venice in it. Themes of song are waiting everywhere for the right man to sing them, like those enchanted swords which no one can pull out of the rock till the hero comes, and he finds no more trouble than in plucking a violet.

John Quincy Adams, making a speech at New Bedford, many years ago, reckoned the number of whaleships (if I remember rightly) that sailed out of that port, and, comparing it with some former period, took it as a type of American success. But, alas! it is with quite other oil that those far-shining lamps of a nation's true glory which burn forever must be filled. It is not by any amount of material splendor or prosperity, but only by moral greatness, by ideas, by works of imagination, that a race can conquer the future. No voice comes to us from the once mighty Assyria but the hoot of the owl that nests amid her crumbling palaces. Of Carthage, whose merchant fleets once furled their sails in every port of the known world, nothing is left but the deeds of Hannibal. She lies dead on the shore of her once subject sea, and the wind of the desert only flings its handfuls of burial-sand upon her corpse. A fog can blot Holland or Switzerland out of existence. But how large is the space occupied in the maps of the soul by little Athens and powerless Italy! They were great by the soul, and their vital force is as indestructible as the soul.

Till America has learned to love art, not as an amusement, not as the mere ornament of her cities, not as a superstition of what is *comme il faut* for a great nation, but for its humanizing and ennobling energy, for its power of making men better by arousing in them a perception of their own instincts for what is beautiful, and therefore sacred and religious, and an eternal rebuke of the base and worldly, she will not have succeeded in that high sense which alone makes a nation out of a people, and raises it from a dead name to a living power. Were our little mother island sunk beneath the sea, or, worse, were she conquered by Scythian barbarians, yet Shakespeare would be an immortal England, and would conquer countries, when the bones of her last sailor had kept their ghastly watch for ages in unhallowed ooze beside the quenched thunders of her navy.

Old Purchas in his *Pilgrims* tells of a sacred caste in India who, when they go out into the street, cry out, "Poo! Poo!" to warn all the world out of their way lest they should be defiled by something unclean. And it is just so that the understanding in its pride of success thinks to pooh-pooh all that it considers impractical and visionary. But whatever of life there is in man, except what comes of beef and pudding, is in the visionary and unpractical, and if it be not encouraged to find its activity or its solace in the production or enjoyment of art and beauty, if it be bewildered or thwarted by an outward profession of faith covering up a practical unbelief in anything higher and holier than the world of sense, it will find vent in such wretched holes and corners as table tippings and mediums who sell news from heaven at a quarter of a dollar the item. Imagination cannot be banished out of the world. She may be made a kitchen drudge, a Cinderella, but there are powers that watch over her. When her two proud sisters, the intellect and understanding, think her crouching over her ashes, she startles and charms by her splendid apparition, and Prince Soul will put up with no other bride.

The practical is a very good thing in its way—if it only be not another name for the worldly. To be absorbed in it is to eat of that insane root which the soldiers of Antonius found in their retreat from Parthia—which whoso tasted kept gathering sticks and stones as if they were some great matter till he died.

One is forced to listen, now and then, to a kind of talk which makes him feel as if this were the after-dinner time of the world, and mankind were doomed hereafter forever to that kind of contented materialism which comes to good stomachs with the nuts and raisins. The dozy old world has nothing to do now but stretch its legs under the mahogany, talk about stocks, and get rid of the hours as well as it can till bedtime. The centuries before us have drained the goblet of wisdom and beauty, and all we have left is to cast horoscopes in the dregs. But divine beauty, and the love of it, will never be without apostles and messengers on earth, till Time flings his hourglass into the abyss as having no need to turn it longer to number the indistinguishable ages of Annihilation. It was a favorite speculation with the learned men of the sixteenth century that they had come upon the old age and decrepit second childhood of creation, and while they maundered, the soul of Shakespeare was just coming out of the eternal freshness of Deity, "trailing" such "clouds of glory" as would beggar a Platonic year of sunsets.

No; morning and the dewy prime are born into the earth again with every child. It is our fault if drought and dust usurp the noon. Every age says to her poets, like the mistress to her lover, "Tell me what I am like"; and, in proportion as it brings forth anything worth seeing, has need of seers and will have them. Our time is not an unpoetical one. We are in our heroic age, still face to face with the shaggy forces of unsubdued nature, and we have our Theseuses and Perseuses, though they may be named Israel Putnam and Daniel Boone. It is nothing against us that we are a commercial people. Athens was a trading community; Dante and Titian were the growth of great marts, and England was already commercial when she produced Shakespeare.

This lesson I learn from the past: that grace and goodness, the fair, the noble, and the true, will never cease out of the world till the God from whom they emanate ceases out of it; that they manifest themselves in an eternal continuity of change to every generation of men, as new duties and occasions arise; that the sacred duty and noble office of the poet is to reveal and justify them to men; that so long as the soul endures, endures also the theme of new and unexampled song; that while there is grace in grace, love in love, and beauty in beauty, God will still send poets to find them and bear witness of them, and to hang their ideal portraitures in the gallery of memory. God with us is forever the mystical name of the hour that is passing. The lives of the great poets teach us that they were the men of their generation who felt most deeply the meaning of the present.

VISSARION BELINSKI

(1811–1848)

∘◯∘∘◯∘

VISSARION BELINSKI IS WITHOUT A DOUBT one of the important critical figures of the nineteenth century. In the field of Russian literature, his significance, surely, can no longer be challenged; even though a Dostoevski, a Turgenev, and others, after having hailed his talent, were later led to endeavor to belittle it, chiefly as a reaction to the critic's ever-growing "socialness," which was to lead him in the end to a complete acceptance of socialism. The social quality of Belinski's thinking is evident in the excerpts here given from the essay, "On the General Signification of the Term Literature," which gives his view of literature as "the property of all society," states his theory of its organic-historic continuity, its dialectical cause-and-effect relationships, and, above all, his conception of "a general, humane, universal literature," which is akin to Goethe's *Weltliteratur*, as well as to that "world literature" of which Marx and Engels speak in the *Communist Manifesto*.[1]

It is by no means surprising, if a "rediscovery" of Belinski is now in progress in the Soviet Union, with his works being reprinted in large editions, and with statues being erected in his honor in Moscow and Leningrad, by order of the Central Executive Committee of the U.S.S.R. (Lenin had praised his famous Letter to Gogol; while the hostile reaction of the intelligentsia following the revolution of 1905, due in good part to the influence of Dostoevski, had stamped him as a writer of the Left.) To the literary historian, Belinski is of interest as exhibiting, in the province of criticism, the essential continuity of the young Soviet literature of today with that of the century preceding. In this respect, the "fierce Vissarion," as Goncharov termed him, may be said to share honors with the aesthetician, Chernishevski, who, in his criticism of Platonic idealism, practically identified art with life, vitality, joy of living, etc., with man as the center of reference. Both Belinski and Chernishevski, it may be noted, represent the post-Hegelian Feuerbach influence, and both may accordingly be looked upon as transi-

---

[1] ". . . from the numerous national and local literatures there arises a world literature," etc.

tional figures, from the point of view of the new literature with its Marxist background; but, all in all, it is probably Belinski who affords us the earliest and best example that we have of a literary criticism of true social depth. (It may be instructive to compare his thought with that of a Taine, a Buckle, or the eighteenth-century Diderot.)

However, what is likely to interest, especially, the student of general literature—or of "comparative criticism," if we may make use of Fidelino de Figueiredo's term—in connection with Belinski's work is the manifestation that is to be found in it of the influence of the Hegelian philosophy upon literary criticism, along with reminiscences of Schelling. In the extracts that follow, numerous reflections of Hegel's "world soul," "over-soul," the "idea," etc., will be discoverable; and what is Belinski's interpretation of Hamlet, if not his own reading of the philosopher's "alienation" and "reconciliation"? As Plakhanov has pointed out, Belinski took his Hegel from the preface to the *Philosophy of Law*. This led him for a time to an absolute "truce with reality," against which he later violently revolted, having come to see his previous acceptance of reality, including the horrors of the czarist régime, as the result of "fever or madness."[2] He then went on to the Utopian socialism of Saint-Simon and Fourier and to a Feuerbachian materialism.

For the purposes of the present anthology, it has seemed that the earlier Belinski would be of significance—particularly, if one keeps in mind what was happening in France and Germany in the 1830's. Meanwhile, it is rather astonishing that a critic of his stature could remain so practically unknown to the world of western culture and ideas. As a practicing critic, he had no little to do with the early reputations of Dostoevski, Lermontov, Turgenev, Goncharov, Koltsov, and many others. He is, distinctly, a turning point in Russian literature.

BIBLIOGRAPHY

TEXT

Sbornik istoriko-literaturnych statei V. G. Belinski po novi russokoi literature. Sost. V. Pokrovski. Moskva, 1898.

Sochineniya. Moskva [n.d.].

Sochineniya. Moskva, 1860–1893.

Sochinniya: v chetirekh tomakh: s portretom avtora so smika V. Basnetsova i izbrannimi picmami Belinskavo: so spravochnim ukazatelem soch. Belinskavo: izdaniey 4-e. Kiev-Peterburg-Odessa, 1910.

[2] See an article by A. Starchakov, "Belinski Has Triumphed," *International Literature*, no. 8 (1936), pp. 89–94.

CRITICISM

Lerner, N. O., *Belinski*. Berlin, 1922.
Pypin, Aleksandr Nikolaevich. *Belinski ego zhizni perepiska.* Izdanie
    vtorae s dopolneniyami i primiechaniyami.   Knigoizdatelstvo
    "Kolos." St. Petersburg, 1908.
Shchukin, Stephan Efimovich, *V. G. Belinski i sotsializm.* Moskva, 1929.
Starchakov, A., "Belinski Has Triumphed," *International Literature*,
    no. 8 (1936), pp. 89–94.

ON THE GENERAL SIGNIFICATION
OF THE TERM LITERATURE (*selections*)[1]

1834–1840

Literature is the last and highest expression of the thought of a
people, manifested in words. An organic continuity of development is the thing that gives literature its character, and which
at the same time distinguishes it from mere oral and written
tradition.   If the literary production bears the stamp of an
essential worth, it is for the reason that it is not, and cannot be,
an affair of chance, wholly unrelated to the productions that
have preceded it; the latter have at least a light to shed upon it;
while it in turn gives rise to other literary manifestations, or in
any event exerts upon them a direct or indirect influence.
It follows that contemporary French literature, and the same
would apply to the German, cannot be properly understood
and evaluated without a knowledge of the French literature of
the seventeenth century, which calls for an acquaintance with
the age of Louis XIV. And just as a general familiarity with the
literature of the Middle Ages is requisite to a comprehension of
the French from the sixteenth century on, so one must know
something of the Greek and Roman classics if one is to make a
study of any of the European literatures, from the Renaissance
down to the present time.

In each sphere of development of the human intellect we find
a series of organically related facts, each of which is continuously
giving rise to others. As a consequence, in addition to the
literature of this or that people, there is yet another general,
humane, universal literature, one possessing a history of its own.
The subject of that history is the evolution of human conscious-

---

[1]Translated especially for this volume by Samuel Putnam, who also wrote the
preceding introduction.

ness in the realm of the word. A literature without a history, that is to say, without its own inner, organic, and vital links, is not a literature; it is no more than tradition, oral or written. Tradition, it is true, of either sort, may have a history; the question is, what kind? Such a history is nothing other than a general catalogue, more or less, of those works which have been preserved in the memory of a people or handed down in writing— a catalogue that requires explanations and learned commentaries. But a catalogue may serve merely as the material of history; it cannot in itself be history.

The era of literature with all modern peoples properly begins with the invention of printing. As a result, the concept of literature, whether we will it or not, is bound up with that of the printing press. Up to that time, as a matter of fact, the literary production of Europe bears the fragmentary, fortuitous character of oral traditions set down in writing. Italy alone provides an exception; it was the most civilized of European countries while France was still deeply immersed in the night of ignorance and barbarism. As early as the thirteenth and fourteenth centuries, Italy could point to a Dante, a Petrarch, and a Boccaccio; but it was not until the sixteenth century that France produced a Rabelais and a Montaigne, along with such comparatively minor figures as a Ronsard and a Regnier—its first great poet, Corneille, was to come the century following. Even in the Middle Ages, we meet with certain outstanding figures who in intellectual strength are far in advance of their time. Such a one was Abelard, in twelfth-century France. Individuals of this sort, however, leave little impress; their forceful thinking, while it may be treasured for a number of centuries following their death, is like a flash of lightning in the surrounding dark. Down to the beginning of the sixteenth century, scientific thought, like necromancy, brigandage, and smuggling, was a thing to be kept shrouded in darkness, and intellectual compositions in manuscript form were secretively passed from one initiate to another. In a word, what we have here is written tradition, not literature. It was only in Italy that tradition in a barbarous age took on the form of literature; or at least we may say that in Italy poetry already is literature at a time when in other European countries it is still in the stage of oral and written tradition.

In the realm of oral tradition there is no outstanding name, for the reason that the author here is the entire people. No one

knows who it is has put together the simple, naïve songs in which
is so glowingly and artlessly reflected the outward and inner
life of a young race or tribe. In a period of racial childhood, the
people are not concerned with the names of their poets, nor are
the poets themselves concerned with handing down their names
to posterity. In such ages, poetry is not a set task, but an instinctive urge: man poetizes without realizing that he is a poet. A
song is handed down from father to son, from generation to
generation; and in the course of time, it undergoes certain
changes. One person shortens it, another expands it; one works
it over, and one combines it with another song, or adds another
by way of supplement. Thus out of songs there come poems,
to whose authorship the people alone may lay claim. From this
it should be clear as to why it is that tradition, when it turns its
attention to poetic compositions, does not trouble to pass on
the names of those who have created them, and we accordingly
are left in ignorance as to who the author of the *Nibelungenlied*
was, and other poems of that kind.

Literature is something else again. Its creator is no longer the
people, but an individual, giving intellectual expression to one
side of the popular mind. With literature, personality comes
into its own, and literary eras are always marked by the names
of individuals. Literature carves out for itself a distinct and
independent province, the essential rights of which are recognized by all society. It none the less relies always upon the public,
and receives its justification in the verdict of society. It lives, not
in the light of a solitary lamp, of hermit or intellectual, but in
the bright and open light of day. It draws its support, not from
a small circle of the élite, a little secret society of the enlightened
few, but from the people as a whole, or at any rate, from the
favored social classes. Literature is the property of all society,
which itself is reflected there, in conscious and refined form, with
all those things of which it is the immediate source; for it is here
that society discovers its true life, elevated to the ideal and the
plane of consciousness. Whence it is, in those periods and eras
commonly known as literary, the historical development of a
people is to be found mirrored in its literature; and if literature
has a light to throw on political history, history in turn performs
the same service for letters. The history of eighteenth-century
France is pre-eminently set forth in the literature of the age. . . .

We have said that literature is the consciousness of a people, giving historic expression in verbal form to its wit and fancy. Only that which is capable of organic development can have a history, only that which takes as its point of departure the embryonic seed to be found in the national soul (or substance) of a people and which, setting out from that which has gone before, leads on to that which is to follow. An organic development is possible only with that which holds its own seedlike content, containing within itself the potential life and form of the plant that is to be and endowed with a corresponding vitality which, the necessary conditions of soil, atmosphere, sun, and humidity being given, proceeds to fulfill its function by changing the seed into the stalk and the stalk into the trunk, with leafy branches, blossoms, and fruit. Accordingly, only those peoples are to be found possessing a literature whose national development affords expression to that of humankind, and whose world-destiny has conferred upon them the role of leaders of humanity in the great drama of universal history.

And so it is, among the nations of antiquity, the Greeks and Romans alone possessed a literature of so high a significance that it has not been lost, but has come down as a priceless heritage to our own times to aid in the development of a social, intellectual, and literary life for the peoples of the modern world. The reason for this is the wealth of content, the substantial life-giving seed that lay in the Greek intellect. Wrapped in this seed was the fructifying idea out of which the entire history, and with it the literature, of the race was to evolve. The idea in question was one which, in its Hellenic form, embraced the whole of humanity; and as a consequence, Greek literature, having served the Greeks, did not die with them, but became the common property of the nations with whom it continues to be an expression of man.

Roman literature does not possess so high an artistic significance as the Greek; the best and greatest production of the Romans was the Justinian Code, fruit of the historic evolvement of Roman life. Nevertheless, the seed in the national soul, coming to maturity in the "eternal city," civilizing the ancient world, and giving a fresh direction to modern civilization, holds so great a world-wide historic and humane significance that, by reason of it, Latin literature, poetic and historical, growing so to speak on the grave of Roman life, is esteemed almost as highly as is Greek literature.

It may be said, then, that the more fructifying the substantial idea in the life of a people, the greater the extent to which a people succeeds in giving expression in its own life to the life of all humanity, and the greater the influence which it exerts upon the destiny of mankind, the higher and more important does the literature of that people thereby become, and the more nearly does it fall within the meaning of literature in the broadest sense. On the other hand, in the degree to which the intellectual life of a people fails to serve as a source for other peoples, the more distinct a nation's destiny is from that of mankind at large, the less organic significance does its literature possess. It follows that those nations with no literature of any significance greatly outnumber the ones that have a literature of some importance to the world. . . .

The possession of a universal-historical significance indicates merely a higher degree of worth on the part of a literature, but is not in itself an indispensable attribute.[2] There may be a literature even without such a significance, yet organically evolved and possessing a history of its own. A literature of this sort is a good deal more important to the nation producing it than it is to other nations. A universal-historic significance, on the other hand, confers upon literature a general interest, makes it known to other peoples; whereas the sphere of influence and the visible importance of a literature lacking such a significance is limited by the confines of the nationality to which it gives expression. Such literatures are the Swedish, Dutch, Polish, and Bohemian. These literatures may boast of a number of notably gifted writers, but the interest of the outside world is restricted to the few, and does not extend to the collective production. . . . Meanwhile, there are in these countries numerous other writers, equally gifted and worthy of note, whose fame and influence has not spread abroad, but whose importance is purely local or national. They render a very great service, it may be, to their native tongue, its literature, and to their native land, but not to mankind at large; and for this reason, they are only known and appreciated by their countrymen; the rest of the world has neither the inclination to make their acquaintance nor the means of doing so.

But if a literature is to be, for the nation that produces it,

---

[2]Belinski here modifies the absolute statement he has previously made. The text has been followed in each instance. (Translator's note.)

an expression of that nation's consciousness and intellectual life, it is necessary that it be closely bound up with the national history and capable of shedding light upon the latter; it is necessary that it have its own history and organic development. If these conditions are not fulfilled, however large a number of books may be published in a language, it merely goes to show that, with the people in question, the art of printing flourishes; it does not show that there is a literature there. Similarly, the presence of a number of outstanding writers of talent simply shows that there are in the country individuals with the urge to create and to publish books; once again, it does not indicate a literature. Above all, the state of the book trade is not to be taken as an indication; for this only points to the fact that there are a number of literate inhabitants who must have something to read, even though it be but to while away time or for amusement's sake, or due, perhaps, to an ignorance of foreign languages, or to a special fondness for the native product. Such purely superficial indications as these cannot serve to establish the presence of a literature among any people.

It is true enough that, without books, without writers, without readers, no kind of literature would be possible; just as it would be impossible to have a theater without a stage, plays, actors, and an audience. It takes, however, something more to produce a real literature; it is the spirit of a people, expressive of its history, that does that. In order to have a literature, a nation must live, not merely on the practical, but on the moral and spiritual plane as well, contributing through its national life to the development of some side of the universal spirit of man.

SHAKESPEARE'S *HAMLET* (*selection*)

c. 1835

Hamlet! I wonder if you get the full, deep meaning of the word: human life, mankind, you, I, each and every one of us, now in a tragic and now in a comic, but always a pity-inspiring, melancholy aspect. For Hamlet is the most brilliant jewel in the resplendent diadem of the Prince of Dramatic Poets, crowned by all mankind and without a rival before or after—Hamlet. Shakespeare on the Moscow stage! . . .

Who is there who is not familiar, if only by hearsay, with the name of Shakespeare, one of those names which are known to all the world, and which have become the property of the race? It would doubtless be going too far to say that, as a pure poet, Shakespeare towers above all others; but as a dramatist, there is none other who may rightfully occupy a place beside him. Possessing the gift of creation in the highest degree, one of the world's great intellects, his genius was endowed with an objectivity which makes of him the superlative dramatist that he is, capable of seeing things as they are, apart from his own personality, of entering into them and living their life.

For Shakespeare there is neither good nor bad; there exists only life, which he calmly observes and sets down in his creations, being carried away by none of its manifestations and giving undue importance to none. If his villains appear as their own executioners, this is not out of any desire for our edification, nor is it due to a hatred of evil; it is because that is the way things are in reality, in accordance with the perduring law of human reason, which has it that he who, of his own free will, becomes an outcast from the world of light and love, the same shall dwell in the stifling, tortured atmosphere of hatred and of darkness. And if the upright individual, even in his sufferings, finds a point of support that is somewhere beyond happiness,[1] this once again is not for the sake of edification, nor does it represent an attachment to the good; it is the way things have always been; for the law of reason would have it that love and light are man's native air, which he freely and joyously breathes in, even beneath the crushing burden of fate. At the same time, this objectivity is not to be explained by a lack of passion; without passion there can be no poetry, and Shakespeare is a great poet. He does not sacrifice reality to a preconceived idea; but his sorrow-laden, at times deeply suffering gaze as he looks out over the world of men shows the price that he has paid for the truth behind his figurative creations.

There are two kinds of people: one kind vegetates; the other kind lives. For the former, life is a sleep; and if the couch be a warm and downy one, that is all they ask. For the latter— people in the true sense of the word—life is an exploit, the fulfilment of which with the favor of circumstance constitutes happiness; but there must be, and is, a happiness to be found

---

[1]Cf. Carlyle, *Sartor Resartus*, chap. IX: "There is in man a HIGHER than Love of Happiness: he can do without Happiness, and instead thereof find Blessedness!" (Translator's note.)

under conditions of self-accepted suffering and privation, but only when man, having slain his ego in an inner contemplation of, or communion with, life in the absolute, thereby finds himself once more. Such a soul-searching means many struggles, many sufferings; and to it many are called but few are chosen.

With every man the age of infancy is marked by an unconscious harmony of the soul with nature, as a result of which life is a happy affair, though he is not aware that he is happy. Childhood is followed by youth, as a transition to manhood; and this is always a period of dissolution, disharmony, and consequent false steps. Man is now no longer satisfied with a natural consciousness and simple feelings; he wants to know; but if he is to attain to a satisfying knowledge, it must be through a myriad of errors: he must wrestle with himself, and he must fall. Such is the immutable law, for mankind and for man.

This period comes on in two ways. It may come of itself, as the result of a deep, rich inner life, demanding to know the wherefore of it all—in which case, we have a Faust. In other cases, it is hastened by external circumstances, although these circumstances are not the cause, which lies, rather, in the soul of man—and then we have a Hamlet. The laws of life may be few in number, but in their working they display an infinite variety. Hamlet's dissolution is symbolized by his weakness of will in the presence of a moral obligation. This is the idea behind Shakespeare's gigantic creation, one first put into words by Goethe in his *Wilhelm Meister*, and since become an oft-repeated commonplace. Hamlet, however, emerges from the struggle by mastering his will; hence, this weakness cannot be the basic idea, after all, but merely the outward expression of another, more universal and more profound,—the idea of dissolution as the result of doubt, which in turn is the consequence of having outgrown the stage of the child's unconscious communion with nature. . . .

Hamlet brings before us the whole of that individual, real and living world which is its own; and observe how simple, usual, and natural a world it is, for all its unaccustomed grandeur. Is not human history, the story of mankind, likewise an exalted and unusual tale, with all its simplicity and accustomed naturalness?

Here we have a young man, son of a great king and heir to his throne, who, carried away by a thirst for knowledge, dwells in a dull and tedious foreign land, which yet is neither dull nor foreign to him, for the reason that in it he finds that of which he is in search: a life of learning, an inner life. He is by nature pensive and inclined to melancholy, as are all those whose lives are wrapped up in themselves. He is an ardent, well-bred youth; whatever is evil fills him with a fiery indignation, while he is rendered happy by all that is good. His love for his father borders on idolatry; it is no empty form with him, since what he loves is that greatness and nobility for which his soul yearns. He has friends, comrades in the quest of the ideal, rather than fellow roisterers and companions in debauchery. Lastly, he is in love with a maiden; and this love it is that gives him faith in life and a joy in living. We do not know whether he would have been a great ruler, destined to mark an epoch in the life of his people; but we do know that ruling to him would have meant to make all dependent upon him happy and to do all the good that lay in his power.

However, a Hamlet such as the one we have depicted is no more than an agglomerate of noble qualities, out of which it is necessary to fashion something that is individual and real; he is merely a refined spirit, and not as yet a real, flesh and blood being. He for a time is happy and content with life so long as reality has not fled his vision; for he has yet to learn that the noble is that which is, and not that which, in accordance with his own personal, subjective way of looking at things, ought to be. He is, in other words, in a state of moral childhood, which must inevitably be followed by collapse. Such is the common, unavoidable lot of the ordinary run of mortals; to find a way out of this discord and to achieve a spiritual harmony by the path of inner struggle and contemplation is a fate reserved for the select few.

And then, of a sudden, this fine spirit, this pensive dreamer of ours receives word of his beloved father's death. Mourning for his father he accepts as a solemn duty on the part of all those nearest of kin to the late monarch. But what does he find? He finds that his mother, the woman whom his father had so passionately and so tenderly loved,

> That he might not beteem the winds of heaven
> Visit her face too roughly

—he finds that this woman not only has failed to mourn her husband as she should; she has not even troubled to keep up appearances by observing the proprieties, but has gone with unseemly haste from her consort's tomb to the bridal altar— and with the dead man's own brother, her brother-in-law, bringing him as a dowry the throne of a kingdom!

Then it is Hamlet begins to perceive that his dreams of life and life itself are not one and the same thing, and that one of the two must be false. In his eyes, it is life that has lied, not his dreams. And what happens to our noble-souled young man as, from the mouth of his father's ghost, he hears the fearful tale of the fratricide, with a hint as to terrible secrets beyond the tomb, along with a covenant of vengeance? He at once casts from him good and evil, and curses out life! His mother is a weak, guilty creature; his mother is a woman; and womankind there-fore is damned in his regard. He tramples into the mire the noble emotion of love, and speaks to Ophelia such words as no woman should hear, above all, from a lover. He offers her such insults as no woman could forgive in a man, however much she might love him.

His trust in things was Hamlet's very life; and now, this trust has been slain, or in any event, rudely shaken. Why? Because he has glimpsed the world of mankind, not as he would like to behold it, but as it is in very deed. Next to this trust which is no more, love was his life; and he now forswears it because he has a contempt for all women. Again, why? Because his mother inspires him with contempt; as though her unworthiness were sufficient to render contemptible the sex as a whole. Add to this the fact that Hamlet utterly fails to distinguish between royal dignity and human worth, demanding of those about him not genuflections, but love and warmth of feeling, while seeing in them only cunning, servile courtiers—bearing this in mind, his disillusionment is not so hard to understand.

But to lose one's faith in people as a result of some bitter experience is not equivalent to an irrevocable loss of everything; such a disillusioning would seem to be due, rather, to a temporary exasperation, which, while it may be more or less prolonged, cannot constitute the permanent soul state of a great-minded individual. To lose faith in one's self, on the other hand, to discover that one's judgment is at absolute variance with life —that is a terrible thing; that is really to lose faith. And this was the state in which Hamlet found himself. Having heard his father's voice from the tomb, having listened to the covenant of vengeance, he is convinced that the exaction of this vengeance is his sovereign duty. In the first surging transport of emotion, he swears by heaven and earth to fly to his revenge as he would to a love tryst—and the next moment he realizes that he is impotent when it comes to doing his duty and carrying out his vow.

What is the source of this impotence? It comes from the fact that Hamlet was born to love people and to render them happy, and not to punish and cast them down; nor is he endowed with that type of mind which is able to combine love with hatred, and from one and the same pair of lips to utter, now words of graciousness, and now the syllables of ire and retribution. This is what to us appears as weakness. It is a weakness that would have no meaning, had it been selected by so great a genius as Shakespeare as the basic idea of one of his finest creations; and if such were the case, would it have taken so firm a hold of mankind's imagination? Objectivity cannot be the sole virtue of a work of art; underlying it there must be a profound idea. Human weakness is not an abstraction; but it does not take in the whole of man's spiritual life, and hence is not suited to serve as a subject for artistic creation on the part of one of the world's greatest writers.

It is not to be forgotten that Hamlet is the protagonist of the drama, through whom the author expresses his thought and in whom, accordingly, the interest centers. Is there any special pleasure to be had from the spectacle of human weakness? If this were true, what would become of that all-encompassing life view of Shakespeare's? Or why is it the play arouses in the mind of reader or spectator so deep a feeling of calmness and reconciliation? It might be expected to arouse despair and to inspire in us an aversion to life, like the monstrous productions of the immature geniuses of the young French literature. But this is not what happens! Hamlet, it is true, displays weakness of will; but it is necessary to understand the meaning of this weakness. It is the result of the transition from the child's unthinking self-harmony and joy to that period of discord and strife which inevitably marks the passage to manhood and a conscious, satisfying adjustment with the world.

In the life of the spirit, there is nothing that is contradictory, and discord and struggle hold their own warrant of egress; or, otherwise, man would be a pitiable creature indeed. The greater an individual's elevation of soul, the more terrible is his downfall; and, by the same token, the more impressive will be his victory over his own finiteness, the deeper and holier will be his joy. Let us see what it was that impelled Hamlet to so terrifying a state of discord, so torturing a self-struggle. The failure of life's reality to correspond with the ideal, that is it. Hence comes the inevitable weakness and indecision. What, then, is it that brings about spiritual harmony? The answer is very simple: "It was destined so to be." It is within himself that Hamlet finds the necessary strength and resolution. He resolves to kill his uncle, and would have killed him at the first, had not another crime presented itself upon the moment. He forgives Laertes his own death, and cries, "I am dead, Horatio." Then, exacting a promise from his friend to make known the truth and save his name from obloquy, he dies. His death for the spectator is accompanied by the strains of mournful music; for the passing of this soul, purified by contemplation of life in the absolute, brings an involuntary sorrow, but a sweetly solemn one; since the spectator in his own soul now perceives that there is in life nothing of the fortuitous or the arbitrary, but only that which has to be; and he is as a result reconciled with the world of things as they are, the world of reality.

JOHN RUSKIN

(1819–1900)

o◯oo◯o

JOHN RUSKIN WAS THE SON of a wealthy London wine merchant and a dour, puritanical Scotch mother. From his father he received excellent instruction in the appreciation of art and literature and from his mother a thorough knowledge of the Bible and an uncompromising moral conscience. From youth to old age his favorite authors, whom he had read aloud to his parents, were Homer, Dante, Shakespeare, and some of the principal English classics. According to Professor Roe, he was also a disciple of Carlyle.[1]

Ruskin made no special pretensions to being a literary critic. His first articles were published in an architectural magazine and his first book, Volume One of *Modern Painters* (1843), was a defense of Turner. His *Seven Lamps of Architecture* (1849) and *Stones of Venice* (1851–1853) deal with art in general. The year 1860, however, marked the end of his writings primarily on art; during the last forty years of his life he was concerned almost exclusively with social, industrial, educational, ethical, and religious questions, and his socialistic experiments. He even regretted that he had wasted so many of his earlier years in writing books on art.

But almost all Ruskin's fifty volumes have some bearing on literary theory. His most fundamental doctrine, which he advanced in *Modern Painters* and *Seven Lamps of Architecture*, was that architecture and painting are the expression of national life (religion, morality, social customs, etc.), and this theory led him to draw many illustrations from literature—so many, in fact, that a sizable body of strictly literary criticism is contained in Ruskin's published works. Even his letters to laboring men, *Fors Clavigera* (1871–1884), and his autobiography, *Praeterita* (1885–1889), are sprinkled with discussions of authors and books.

As early as the second volume of *Modern Painters* (1846) Ruskin had worked out a complete aesthetics, leaning heavily upon Plato and Plotinus and continuing the doctrines of Coleridge. Beauty he regarded

---

[1] See Frederick William Roe, *Social Philosophy of Carlyle and Ruskin* (New York, 1921).

as an emanation from the Infinite and a disclosure of it. Like Plato, every natural object was to him a symbol or a reflection of an "idea" in the spiritual realm. This belief, no less than with Carlyle[2] and Emerson,[3] was part of Ruskin's religion.

Ruskin's aesthetics includes two kinds of Beauty, "Typical Beauty" and "Vital Beauty," both expressing some aspect of divinity. "Typical Beauty" has six attributes, as follows: (1) Infinity—Divine Incomprehensibility—the feeling inspired by the sight of natural objects;[4] (2) Unity—Divine Comprehensiveness;[5] (3) Repose—Divine Permanence;[6] (4) Symmetry—Divine Justice;[7] (5) Purity—Divine Energy;[8] and (6) Moderation—Divine Government by law.[9] "Vital Beauty" is both relative and generic. Relative beauty, he argued, exists in organic creatures who give evidence of happiness.[10] Generic beauty exists when individuals of the same species perfectly fulfill their intended function, i.e., when the individual is the *ideal* representative of its genera.[11]

Like Coleridge again, Ruskin worked out an elaborate theory of the imagination, which he defined as follows: "Imagination is the result of a common and vital, but not therefore less divine spirit, of which some portion is given to all living creatures in such a manner as may be adapted to their rank in creation."[12] Imagination is a link between man and God.[13] And a work of art involves the creation of order and beauty out of the unselected raw materials of nature—it is not a transcript or mere imitation of nature.[14] But a work of art is not produced by merely selecting and rearranging; it is a genuine creation, though still true to nature, for the imperfect may be used as a foil to the perfect—cf. Caliban and Miranda. This is the "Imagination Associative."[15] The artist may also, from his inner experience, see in nature (e.g., a landscape) a single mood. This is the "Imagination Contemplative."[16] The "Imagination Penetrative," by intuition and intensity of effort, plunges to the heart of things and reveals their inner mystery.[17] Fancy, one important function of which is to recall images

---

[2]Cf. chapter on "Symbols" in *Sartor Resartus*.

[3]Cf. "Nature is the symbol of spirit," *Nature*, sect. 4; "Beauty" is also discussed in this same essay, sect. 3.   [4]*Modern Painters*, II, Pt. 1, chap. v.

[5]*Ibid.*, chap. vi.   [7]*Ibid.*, chap. viii.   [9]*Ibid.*, chap. x.   [11]*Ibid.*, chap. xiii.

[6]*Ibid.*, chap. vii.   [8]*Ibid.*, chap. ix.   [10]*Ibid.*, chap. xii.   [12]*Ibid.*, chap. i.

[13]It is interesting here to contrast Lanier, Ruskin's American disciple, on this idea. Lanier says "As a philosophic truth music does carry our emotions toward the Infinite" (*Music and Poetry*, p. 18).

[14]For discussions of the "imitation" theory see index.

[15]*Modern Painters*, II, sect. 2, chap. ii.

[16]*Ibid.*, chap. iv. But "The Pathetic Fallacy" seems to contradict this doctrine.

[17]*Ibid.*, chap. iii.

to the memory, sees the outside, Imagination the inside. Both are needed, but Imagination is the source of artistic genius. This in brief is an outline of the aesthetics founded in Neoplatonism and the philosophy of Coleridge, and carried still further by William Morris and his school, but it has had little influence on modern aesthetics.

Ruskin's most famous literary doctrine, however, is his "moralistic theory." He believes that "every great composition in the world, every great piece of painting or literature . . . is an assertion of moral law. . . ."[18] In fact, he would make morality the criterion of artistic merit, "*the fineness of the possible art is an index of the moral purity and majesty of the emotion it expresses.*"[19] Evil in literature cannot be tolerated: "The imaginative power always purifies; the want of it therefore as essentially defiles. . . ."[20] *Candide* is "gratuitous filth."[21] Gustave Doré's paintings are corrupt and show "national decrepitude."[22] Ruskin, therefore, makes a special application of the theories of Taine[23] and Madame de Staël[24] regarding the relationship between art and society.[25]

BIBLIOGRAPHY

TEXT

Lectures on Architecture and Painting, delivered at Edinburgh in November, 1853. London, 1854.

Lectures on Art, delivered before the University of Oxford in Hilary term, 1870. Oxford, 1870.

Mornings in Florence; being simple studies of Christian art for English travellers. New York, 1885.

Pre-Raphaelitism. London, 1851.

Selections from Ruskin as Literary Critic, ed. with introduction by A. H. R. Ball. New York, 1928.

The Unity of Art, delivered at the annual meeting of the Manchester School of Art, February 22, 1859. Manchester, 1859.

Works, ed. by E. T. Cook and Alexander Wedderburn. 39 vols. London, 1903–1912.

CRITICISM

Benson, A. C., *Ruskin; a study in personality.* London, 1911.

Collingwood, William Gershom, *Life and Work of John Ruskin.* 2 vols. Boston, 1893.

[18]*Fors Clavigera*, IV, Letter LXXXIII.   [19]*Lectures on Art*, par. 67.
[20]*Fors Clavigera*, II, Letter XXXIV. Compare Lanier, "Wherever there is contest as between artistic and moral beauty, unless the moral side prevail, all is lost" (*English Novel*, p. 282).
[21]*Fors Claveriga*, II, Letter XXXIV.   [22]*Ibid.*   [23]See pp. 481 ff.   [24]See pp. 162 ff.
[25]Cf. Henry Ladd, *The Victorian Morality of Art* (New York, 1932).

Cook, Edward Tyas, *Life of John Ruskin*. London, 1911.

Goedecke, Heinrich, *John Ruskin's Stil in der Entwicklung der englischen Prosa des XIX Jahrhunderts mit besonderer Berücksichtigung des Einflusses der Bibel*. Münster, 1916.

La Sizeranne, Robert de, *Ruskin and the Religion of Beauty*, tr. from the French by the Countess of Galloway. London, 1899.

Ladd, Henry A., *The Victorian Morality of Art*. New York, 1932.

Meynell, Mrs. Alice Christiana [Thompson], *John Ruskin*. Edinburgh, 1901.

Sieper, Ernst, *Das Evangelium der Schönheit in der englischen Literatur und Kunst des XIX Jahrhundert;* 30 Vorträge über die Verbreitung und Entwickelung der ästhetischen Kultur in England. Dortmund, [n.d.], pp. 184–330.

OF THE PATHETIC FALLACY (*selection*)[1]

1856

4. Now . . . we may go on at our ease to examine the point in question—namely, the difference between the ordinary, proper, and true appearances of things to us; and the extraordinary, or false appearances, when we are under the influence of emotion, or contemplative fancy; false appearances, I say, as being entirely unconnected with any real power of character in the object, and only imputed to it by us.

For instance—

> The spendthrift crocus, bursting through the mould
> Naked and shivering, with his cup of gold.[2]

This is very beautiful, and yet very untrue. The crocus is not a spendthrift, but a hardy plant; its yellow is not gold, but saffron. How is it that we enjoy so much the having it put into our heads that it is anything else than a plain crocus?

It is an important question. For, throughout our past reasonings about art, we have always found that nothing could be good, or useful, or ultimately pleasurable, which was untrue. But here is something pleasurable in written poetry which is nevertheless *un*true. And what is more, if we think over our favorite poetry, we shall find it full of this kind of fallacy, and that we like it all the more for being so.

5. It will appear also, on consideration of the matter, that this fallacy is of two principal kinds. Either, as in this case of the

---

[1]*Modern Painters*, III, Pt. IV.   [2]Oliver Wendell Holmes, *Astraea*.

crocus, it is the fallacy of willful fancy, which involves no real expectation that it will be believed; or else it is a fallacy caused by an excited state of the feelings, making us, for the time, more or less irrational. Of the cheating of the fancy we shall have to speak presently; but in this chapter, I want to examine the nature of the other error, that which the mind admits when affected strongly by emotion. Thus, for instance, in *Alton Locke*—

> They rowed her in across the rolling foam—
> The cruel, crawling foam.[3]

The foam is not cruel, neither does it crawl. The state of mind which attributes to it these characters of a living creature is one in which the reason is unhinged by grief. All violent feelings have the same effect. They produce in us a falseness in all our impressions of external things, which I would generally characterize as the "pathetic fallacy."

6. Now we are in the habit of considering this fallacy as eminently a character of poetical description, and the temper of mind in which we allow it as one eminently poetical, because passionate. But, I believe, if we look well into the matter, that we shall find the greatest poets do not often admit this kind of falseness— that it is only the second order of poets who much delight in it.[4]

---

[3]Charles Kingsley, *Alton Locke*.

[4]I admit two orders of poets, but no third; and by these two orders I mean the creative (Shakespeare, Homer, Dante), and reflective or perceptive (Wordsworth, Keats, Tennyson). But both of these must be *first*-rate in their range, though their range is different; and with poetry second-rate in *quality* no one ought to be allowed to trouble mankind. There is quite enough of the best,—much more than we can ever read or enjoy in the length of a life; and it is a literal wrong or sin in any person to encumber us with inferior work. I have no patience with apologies made by young pseudo poets, "that they believe there is *some* good in what they have written: that they hope to do better in time," etc. *Some* good! If there is not *all* good, there is no good. If they ever hope to do better, why do they trouble us now? Let them rather courageously burn all they have done, and wait for the better days. There are few men, ordinarily educated, who in moments of strong feelings could not strike out a poetical thought, and afterwards polish it so as to be presentable. But men of sense know better than so to waste their time; and those who sincerely love poetry, know the touch of the master's hand on the chords too well to fumble among them after him. Nay, more than this, all inferior poetry is an injury to the good, inasmuch as it takes away the freshness of rhymes, blunders upon and gives a wretched commonalty to good thoughts; and, in general, adds to the weight of human weariness in a most woeful and culpable manner. There are few thoughts likely to come across ordinary men, which have not already been expressed by greater men in the best possible way; and it is a wiser, more generous, more noble thing to remember and point out the perfect words, than to invent poorer ones, wherewith to encumber temporarily the world. (Ruskin's note.)

Thus, when Dante describes the spirits falling from the bank of Acheron "as dead leaves flutter from a bough,"[5] he gives the most perfect image possible of their utter lightness, feebleness, passiveness, and scattering agony of despair, without, however, for an instant losing his own clear perception that *these* are souls, and *those* are leaves; he makes no confusion of one with the other. But when Coleridge speaks of

> The one red leaf, the last of its clan,
> That dances as often as dance it can.[6]

he has a morbid, that is to say, a so far false, idea about the leaf; he fancies a life in it, and will, which there are not; confuses its powerlessness with choice, its fading death with merriment, and the wind that shakes it with music. Here, however, there is some beauty, even in the morbid passage; but take an instance in Homer and Pope. Without the knowledge of Ulysses, Elpenor, his youngest follower, has fallen from an upper chamber in the Circean palace, and has been left dead, unmissed by his leader, or companions, in the haste of their departure. They cross the sea to the Cimmerian land; and Ulysses summons the shades from Tartarus. The first which appears is that of the lost Elpenor. Ulysses, amazed, and in exactly the spirit of bitter and terrified lightness which is seen in Hamlet,[7] addresses the spirit with the simple startled words:—

> Elpenor! How camest thou under the shadowy darkness? Hast thou come faster on foot than I in my black ship?[8]

Which Pope renders thus:—

> O, say, what angry power Elpenor led
> To glide in shades, and wander with the dead?
> How could thy soul, by realms and seas disjoined,
> Outfly the nimble sail, and leave the lagging wind?

I sincerely hope the reader finds no pleasure here, either in the nimbleness of the sail, or the laziness of the wind! And yet how is it that these conceits are so painful now, when they have been pleasant to us in the other instances?

7. For a very simple reason. They are not a *pathetic* fallacy at all, for they are put into the mouth of the wrong passion—a pas-

---

[5]*Inferno*, III, 112.   [6]*Christabel*, Pt. I, 49–50.
[7]"Well said, old mole! can'st work i' the earth so fast?" (I, v, 162).
[8]*Odyssey*, XI, 56–57.

sion which never could possibly have spoken them—agonized curiosity. Ulysses wants to know the facts of the matter; and the very last thing his mind could do at the moment would be to pause, or suggest in any wise what was *not* a fact. The delay in the first three lines, and conceit in the last, jar upon us instantly, like the most frightful discord in music. No poet of true imaginative power could possibly have written the passage.[9]

Therefore, we see that the spirit of truth must guide us in some sort, even in our enjoyment of fallacy. Coleridge's fallacy has no discord in it, but Pope's has set our teeth on edge. Without farther questioning, I will endeavor to state the main bearings of this matter.

8. The temperament which admits the pathetic fallacy is, as I said above, that of a mind and body in some sort too weak to deal fully with what is before them or upon them; borne away, or overclouded, or overdazzled by emotion; and it is a more or less noble state, according to the force of the emotion which has induced it. For it is no credit to a man that he is not morbid or inaccurate in his perceptions, when he has no strength of feeling to warp them; and it is in general a sign of higher capacity and stand in the ranks of being, that the emotions should be strong enough to vanquish, partly, the intellect, and make it believe what they choose. But it is still a grander condition when the intellect also rises, till it is strong enough to assert its rule against, or together with, the utmost efforts of the passions; and the whole man stands in an iron glow, white hot, perhaps, but still strong, and in no wise evaporating; even if he melts, losing none of his weight.

So, then, we have the three ranks: the man who perceives rightly, because he does not feel, and to whom the primrose is very accurately the primrose, because he does not love it. Then, secondly, the man who perceives wrongly, because he feels, and

---

[9]It is worth while comparing the way a similar question is put by the exquisite sincerity of Keats [*Hyperion*, III]:

> He wept, and his bright tears
> Went trickling down the golden bow he held.
> Thus, with half-shut, suffused eyes, he stood;
> While from beneath some cumbrous boughs hard by,
> With solemn step, an awful goddess came.
> And there was purport in her looks for him,
> Which he with eager guess began to read:
> Perplexed the while, melodiously he said,
> "*How camest thou over the unfooted sea?*" (Ruskin's note.)

to whom the primrose is anything else than a primrose: a star, or a sun, or a fairy's shield, or a forsaken maiden. And then, lastly, there is the man who perceives rightly in spite of his feelings, and to whom the primrose is forever nothing else than itself—a little flower apprehended in the very plain and leafy fact of it, whatever and how many soever the associations and passions may be that crowd around it. And, in general, these three classes may be rated in comparative order, as the men who are not poets at all, and the poets of the second order, and the poets of the first; only however great a man may be, there are always some subjects which *ought* to throw him off his balance; some, by which his poor human capacity of thought should be conquered, and brought into the inaccurate and vague state of perception, so that the language of the highest inspiration becomes broken, obscure, and wild in metaphor, resembling that of the weaker man, overborne by weaker things.

9. And thus, in full, there are four classes: the men who feel nothing, and therefore see truly; the men who feel strongly, think weakly, and see untruly (second order of poets); the men who feel strongly, think strongly, and see truly (first order of poets); and the men who, strong as human creatures can be, are yet submitted to influences stronger than they, and see in a sort untruly, because what they see is inconceivably above them. This last is the usual condition of prophetic inspiration.

10. I separate these classes, in order that their character may be clearly understood; but of course they are united each to the other by imperceptible transitions, and the same mind, according to the influences to which it is subjected, passes at different times into the various states. Still, the difference between the great and less mean is, on the whole, chiefly in this point of *alterability*. That is to say, the one knows too much, and perceives and feels too much of the past and future, and of all things beside and around that which immediately affects him, to be in any wise shaken by it. His mind is made up; his thoughts have an accustomed current; his ways are steadfast; it is not this or that new sight which will at once unbalance him. He is tender to impression at the surface, like a rock with deep moss upon it; but there is too much mass of him to be moved. The smaller man, with the same degree of sensibility, is at once carried off his feet; he wants to do something he did not want to do before; he views all the universe in a new light through his tears; he is gay

or enthusiastic, melancholy or passionate, as things come and go to him. Therefore the high creative poet might even be thought, to a great extent, impassive (as shallow people think Dante stern), receiving indeed all feelings to the full, but having a great center of reflection and knowledge in which he stands serene, and watches the feeling, as it were, from far off.

Dante, in his most intense moods, has entire command of himself, and can look around calmly, at all moments, for the image or the word that will best tell what he sees to the upper or lower world. But Keats and Tennyson, and the poets of the second order, are generally themselves subdued by the feelings under which they write, or, at least, write as choosing to be so; and therefore admit certain expressions and modes of thought which are in some sort diseased or false.

11. Now so long as we see that the *feeling* is true, we pardon, or are even pleased by, the confessed fallacy of sight which it induces: we are pleased, for instance, with those lines of Kingsley's above quoted, not because they fallaciously describe foam, but because they faithfully describe sorrow. But the moment the mind of the speaker becomes cold, that moment every such expression becomes untrue, as being forever untrue in the external facts. And there is no greater baseness in literature than the habit of using these metaphorical expressions in cool blood. An inspired writer, in full impetuosity of passion, may speak wisely and truly of "raging waves of the sea foaming out their own shame";[10] but it is only the basest writer who cannot speak of the sea without talking of "raging waves," "remorseless floods," "ravenous billows," etc.; and it is one of the signs of the highest power in a writer to check all such habits of thought, and to keep his eyes fixed firmly on the *pure fact*, out of which if any feeling comes to him or his reader, he knows it must be a true one.

To keep to the waves, I forget who it is who represents a man in despair, desiring that his body may be cast into the sea,

> *Whose changing mound, and foam that passed away,*
> Might mock the eyes that questioned where I lay.[11]

Observe, there is not a single false, or even overcharged, expression. "Mound" of the sea wave is perfectly simple and true; "changing" is as familiar as may be; "foam that passed away,"

[10]Jude 13.   [11]Authorship unknown.

strictly literal; and the whole line descriptive of the reality with a degree of accuracy which I know not any other verse, in the range of poetry, that altogether equals. For most people have not a distinct idea of the clumsiness and massiveness of a large wave. The word "wave" is used too generally of ripples and breakers, and bendings in light drapery or grass: it does not by itself convey a perfect image. But the word "mound" is heavy, large, dark, definite; there is no mistaking the kind of wave meant, nor missing the sight of it. Then the term "changing" has a peculiar force also. Most people think of waves as rising and falling. But if they look at the sea carefully, they will perceive that the waves do not rise and fall. They change. Change both place and form, but they do not fall; one wave goes on, and on, and still on; now lower, now higher, now tossing its mane like a horse, now building itself together like a wall, now shaking, now steady, but still the same wave, till at last it seems struck by something and changes, one knows not how, becomes another wave.

The close of the line insists on this image, and paints it still more perfectly—"foam that passed away." Not merely melting, disappearing, but passing on, out of sight, on the career of the wave. Then, having put the absolute ocean fact as far as he may before our eyes, the poet leaves us to feel about it as we may, and to trace for ourselves the opposite fact—the image of the green mounds that do not change, and the white and written stones that do not pass away; and thence to follow out also the associated images of the calm life with the quiet grave, and the despairing life with the fading foam:

Let no man move his bones.

As for Samaria, her king is cut off like the foam upon the water.[12]

But nothing of this is actually told or pointed out, and the expressions, as they stand, are perfectly severe and accurate, utterly uninfluenced by the firmly governed emotion of the writer. Even the word "mock" is hardly an exception, as it may stand merely for "deceive" or "defeat," without implying any impersonation of the waves.

12. It may be well, perhaps, to give one or two more instances to show the peculiar dignity possessed by all passages which thus limit their expression to the pure fact, and leave the hearer to gather what he can from it. Here is a notable one from the *Iliad*.

[12] II Kings 23, 18; Hosea 10, 7.

Helen, looking from the Scaean gate of Troy over the Grecian host, and telling Priam the names of its captains, says at last:

> I see all the other dark-eyed Greeks; but two I cannot see,— Castor and Pollux,—whom one mother bore with me. Have they not followed from fair Lacedaemon, or have they indeed come in their sea-wandering ships, but now will not enter into the battle of men, fearing the shame and the scorn that is in Me?

Then Homer:

> So she spoke. But them, already, the life-giving earth possessed, there in Lacedaemon, in the dear fatherland.[13]

Note, here, the high poetical truth carried to the extreme. The poet has to speak of the earth in sadness, but he will not let that sadness affect or change his thoughts of it. No; though Castor and Pollux be dead, yet the earth is our mother still, fruitful, life-giving. These are the facts of the thing. I see nothing else than these. Make what you will of them. . . .

14. Now in this there is the exact type of the consummate poetical temperament. For, be it clearly and constantly remembered, that the greatness of a poet depends upon the two faculties, acuteness of feeling, and command of it. A poet is great, first in proportion to the strength of his passion, and then, that strength being granted, in proportion to his government of it; there being, however, always a point beyond which it would be inhuman and monstrous if he pushed this government, and, therefore, a point at which all feverish and wild fancy becomes just and true. Thus the destruction of the kingdom of Assyria cannot be contemplated firmly by a prophet of Israel. The fact is too great, too wonderful. It overthrows him, dashes him into a confused element of dreams. All the world is, to his stunned thought, full of strange voices. "Yea, the fir trees rejoice at thee, and the cedars of Lebanon, saying, 'Since thou art gone down to the grave, no feller is come up against us.' "[14] So, still more, the thought of the presence of Deity cannot be borne without this great astonishment. "The mountains and the hills shall break forth before you into singing, and all the trees of the field shall clap their hands."[15]

15. But by how much this feeling is noble when it is justified by the strength of its cause, by so much it is ignoble when there

---

[13]*Iliad*, III, 243.   [14]Isaiah 14, 8.   [15]*Ibid.*, 55, 12.

is not cause enough for it; and beyond all other ignobleness in the mere affectation of it, in hardness of heart. Simply bad writing may almost always, as above noticed, be known by its adoption of these fanciful metaphorical expressions, as a sort of current coin; yet there is even a worse, at least a more harmful, condition of writing than this, in which such expressions are not ignorantly and feelinglessly caught up, but, by some master, skillful in handling, yet insincere, deliberately wrought out with chill and studied fancy; as if we should try to make an old lava stream look red-hot again, by covering it with dead leaves, or white-hot, with hoarfrost.

When Young is lost in veneration, as he dwells on the character of a truly good and holy man, he permits himself for a moment to be overborne by the feeling so far as to exclaim:

> Where shall I find him? angels, tell me where.
> You know him; he is near you; point him out.
> Shall I see glories beaming from his brow,
> Or trace his footsteps by the rising flowers?[16]

This emotion has a worthy cause, and is thus true and right. But now hear the cold-hearted Pope say to a shepherd girl:

> Where'er you walk, cool gales shall fan the glade;
> Trees, where you sit, shall crowd into a shade;
> Your praise the birds shall chant in every grove,
> And winds shall waft it to the powers above.
> But would you sing, and rival Orpheus' strain,
> The wondering forests soon should dance again;
> The moving mountains hear the powerful call,
> And headlong streams hang, listening, in their fall.[17]

This is not, nor could it for a moment be mistaken for, the language of passion. It is simple falsehood, uttered by hypocrisy; definite absurdity, rooted in affectation, and coldly asserted in the teeth of nature and fact. Passion will indeed go far in deceiving itself; but it must be a strong passion, not the simple wish of a lover to tempt his mistress to sing. Compare a very closely parallel passage in Wordsworth,[18] in which the lover has lost his mistress:

> Three years had Barbara in her grave been laid,
> When thus his moan he made:—

---

[16]*Night Thoughts*, II, 345.   [17]"Pastorals: Summer, or Alexis."
[18]The piece beginning "'Tis said that some have died for love . . ."

"Oh move, thou cottage, from behind yon oak,
   Or let the ancient tree uprooted lie,
That in some other way yon smoke
   May mount into the sky.
If still behind yon pinetree's ragged bough,
   Headlong, the waterfall must come,
   Oh, let it, then, be dumb—
Be anything, sweet stream, but that which thou art now."

Here is a cottage to be moved, if not a mountain, and a water-fall to be silent, if it is not to hang listening: but with what different relation to the mind that contemplates them! Here, in the extremity of its agony, the soul cries out wildly for relief, which at the same moment it partly knows to be impossible, but partly believes possible, in a vague impression that a miracle *might* be wrought to give relief even to a less sore distress—that nature is kind, and God is kind, and that grief is strong: it knows not well what *is* possible to such grief. To silence a stream, to move a cottage wall—one might think it could do as much as that!

16. I believe these instances are enough to illustrate the main point I insist upon respecting the pathetic fallacy—that so far as it *is* a fallacy, it is always the sign of a morbid state of mind, and comparatively of a weak one. Even in the most inspired prophet it is a sign of the incapacity of his human sight or thought to bear what has been revealed to it. In ordinary poetry, if it is found in the thoughts of the poet himself, it is at once a sign of his belonging to the inferior school; if in the thoughts of the characters imagined by him, it is right or wrong according to the genuineness of the emotion from which it springs; always, however, implying necessarily *some* degree of weakness in the character.

THE RELATION OF ART TO MORALS *(selections)*[1]

1870

. . . And now I pass to the arts with which I have special concern, in which, though the facts are exactly the same, I shall have more difficulty in proving my assertion,[2] because very few

---

[1]Extract from *The Relation of Art to Morals*, a work which Ruskin wrote while he was Slade professor of art at Oxford. The selection given here provides a convenient recapitulation of the opinions on art and morals expressed earlier in *Modern Painters* and *Stones of Venice*.

[2]That is, as he has said above, "the enforcing of the religious sentiments of men, the perfecting of their ethical state, and the doing them material service."

of us are as cognizant of the merit of painting as we are of that of language; and I can only show you whence that merit springs, after having thoroughly shown you in what it consists. But in the meantime, I have simply to tell you that the manual arts are as accurate exponents of ethical state as other modes of expression; first, with absolute precision, of that of the workman,[3] and then with precision, disguised by many distorting influences, of that of the nation to which it belongs.

And, first, they are a perfect exponent of the mind of the workman: but, being so, remember, if the mind be great or complex, the art is not an easy book to read; for we must ourselves possess all the mental characters of which we are to read the signs. No man can read the evidence of labor who is not himself laborious, for he does not know what the work cost: nor can he read the evidence of true passion if he is not passionate; nor of gentleness if he is not gentle: and the most subtle signs of fault and weakness of character he can only judge by having had the same faults to fight with. I myself, for instance, know impatient work, and tired work, better than most critics, because I am myself always impatient, and often tired: so also, the patient and indefatigable touch of a mighty master becomes more wonderful to me than to others. Yet, wonderful in no mean measure it will be to you all, when I make it manifest;—and as soon as we begin our real work, and you have learned what it is to draw a true line, I shall be able to make manifest to you—and undisputably so—that the day's work of a man like Mantegna[4] or Paul Veronese[5] consists of an unfaltering, uninterrupted succession of movements of the hand more precise than those of the finest fencer: the pencil leaving one point and arriving at another, not only with unerring precision at the extremity of the line, but with an unerring and yet varied course—sometimes over spaces a foot or more in extent—yet a course so determined everywhere that either of these men could, and Veronese often does, draw a finished profile, or any other portion of the contour of the face with one line, not afterwards changed. Try, first, to realize to yourselves the muscular precision of that action, and the intellectual strain of it; for the movement of a fencer is perfect in practiced monotony; but the movement of the hand of a great painter

---

[3]By *workman* he means *artist*.
[4]Andrea Mantegna (1431–1506), Italian painter and engraver.
[5]Paul Veronese (1528–1588), painter of the Venetian school.

is at every instant governed by direct and new intention. Then imagine that muscular firmness and subtlety, and the instantaneously selective and ordinant energy of the brain, sustained all day long, not only without fatigue, but with a visible joy in the exertion, like that which an eagle seems to take in the wave of his wings, and this all life long, and through long life, not only without failure of power, but with visible increase of it, until the actually organic changes of old age. And then consider, so far as you know anything of physiology, what sort of an ethical state of body and mind that means!—ethic through ages past! what fineness of race there must be to get it, what exquisite balance and symmetry of the vital powers! And then, finally, determine for yourselves whether a manhood like that is consistent with any viciousness of soul, with any mean anxiety, any gnawing lust, any wretchedness of spite or remorse, any consciousness of rebellion against law of God or man, or any actual, though unconscious violation of even the least law to which obedience is essential for the glory of life, and the pleasing of its Giver.

It is, of course, true that many of the strong masters had deep faults of character, but their faults always show in their work. It is true that some could not govern their passions; if so, they died young, or they painted ill when old. But the greater part of our misapprehension in the whole matter is from our not having well known who the great painters were, and taking delight in the petty skill that was bred in the fumes of the taverns of the North,[6] instead of theirs who breathed empyreal air, sons of the morning, under the woods of Assisi and the crags of Cadore.[7]

It is true, however, also, as I have pointed out long ago, that the strong masters fall into two great divisions, one leading simple and natural lives, the other restrained in a Puritanism of the worship of beauty; and these two manners of life you may recognize in a moment by their work. Generally the naturalists are the strongest; but there are two of the Puritans, whose work if I can succeed in making clearly understandable to you during my three years here,[8] it is all I need care to do. But of these two Puritans one I cannot name to you, and the other I at present

---

[6] A slur on Dutch art.
[7] Towns in Italy, indicating Ruskin's preference for Italian art.
[8] At Oxford University, where he was then Slade professor of art.

will not. One I cannot, for no one knows his name, except the
baptismal one, Bernard, or "dear little Bernard"—Bernardino,
called from his birthplace (Luino, on the Lago Maggiore),
Bernard of Luino. The other [9] is a Venetian, of whom many of
you probably have never heard, and of whom, through me, you
shall not hear, until I have tried to get some picture by him over
to England. . . .

Finally, you must remember that great obscurity has been
brought upon the truth in this matter by the want of integrity
and simplicity in our modern life. I mean integrity in the Latin
sense, wholeness. Everything is broken up, and mingled in
confusion, both in our habits and thoughts; besides being in
great part imitative: so that you not only cannot tell what a man
is, but sometimes you cannot tell whether he *is* at all!—whether
you have indeed to do with a spirit, or only with an echo. And
thus the same inconsistencies appear now, between the work of
artists of merit and their personal characters, as those which you
find continually disappointing expectation in the lives of men of
modern literary power;—the same conditions of society having
obscured or misdirected the best qualities of the imagination,
both in our literature and art. Thus there is no serious question
with any of us as to the personal character of Dante and Giotto, [10]
of Shakespeare and Holbein;[11] but we pause timidly in the
attempt to analyze the moral laws of the art skill in recent poets,
novelists, and painters.

Let me assure you once for all, that as you grow older, if you
enable yourselves to distinguish by the truth of your own lives,
what is true in those of other men, you will gradually perceive
that all good has its origin in good, never in evil; that the fact
of either literature or painting being truly fine of their kind,
whatever their mistaken aim, or partial error, is proof of their
noble origin: and that, if there is indeed sterling value in the
thing done, it has come of a sterling worth in the soul that did it,
however alloyed or defiled by conditions of sin which are sometimes more appalling or more strange than those which all may
detect in their own hearts, because they are part of a personality
altogether larger than ours, and as far beyond our judgment in

---

[9]Reference to Vittore Carpaccio (*c.* 1450–*c.* 1522). Did Ruskin not know that
the National Gallery, London, had purchased one of his pictures in 1865?
[10] Giotto (1276?–1337?), Florentine painter and architect.
[11]Hans Holbein (*c.* 1460–1524), German painter.

its darkness as beyond our following in its light. And it is sufficient warning against what some might dread as the probable
effect of such a conviction on your own minds, namely, that
you might permit yourselves in the weaknesses which you imagined to be allied to genius, when they took the form of personal
temptations;—it is surely, I say, sufficient warning against so
mean a folly to discern, as you may with little pains, that, of all
human existences, the lives of men of that distorted and tainted
nobility of intellect are probably the most miserable.

I pass to the second, and for us the more practically important
question, What is the effect of noble art upon other men; what
has it done for national morality in time past: and what effect
is the extended knowledge or possession of it likely to have upon
us now? And here we are at once met by the facts, which are as
gloomy as indisputable, that while many peasant populations,
among whom scarcely the rudest practice of art has ever been
attempted, have lived in comparative innocence, honor, and
happiness, the worst foulness and cruelty of savage tribes have
been frequently associated with fine ingenuities of decorative
design; also, that no people has ever attained the higher stages
of art skill, except at a period of its civilization which was sullied
by frequent, violent, and even monstrous crime; and, lastly,
that the attaining of perfection in art power, has been hitherto,
in every nation, the accurate signal of the beginning of its
ruin.

Respecting which phenomena, observe first, that although
good never springs out of evil, it is developed to its highest by
contention with evil. There are some groups of peasantry, in faraway nooks of Christian countries, who are nearly as innocent
as lambs; but the morality which gives power to art is the
morality of men, not of cattle.

Secondly, the virtues of the inhabitants of many country
districts are apparent, not real; their lives are indeed artless,
but not innocent; and it is only the monotony of circumstances and the absence of temptation which prevent the exhibition of evil passions not less real because often dormant
nor less foul because shown only in petty faults or inactive
malignities.

But you will observe also that *absolute* artlessness to men in
any kind of moral health is impossible; they have always, at least,
the art by which they live—agriculture or seamanship; and in

these industries, skillfully practiced, you will find the law of their moral training; while, whatever the adversity of circumstances, every rightly minded peasantry, such as that of Sweden, Denmark, Bavaria, or Switzerland, has associated with its needful industry a quite studied school of pleasurable art in dress; and generally also in song and simple domestic architecture.

Again, I need not repeat to you here what I endeavored to explain in the first lecture in the book I called *The Two Paths*,[12] respecting the arts of savage races: but I may now note briefly that such arts are the result of an intellectual activity which has found no room to expand and which the tyranny of nature or of man has condemned to disease through arrested growth. And where neither Christianity nor any other religion conveying some moral help has reached, the animal energy of such races necessarily flames into ghastly conditions of evil, and the grotesque or frightful forms assumed by their art are precisely indicative of their distorted moral nature.

But the truly great nations nearly always begin from a race possessing this imaginative power; and for some time their progress is very slow and their state not one of innocence but of feverish and faultful animal energy. This is gradually subdued and exalted into bright human life; the art instinct purifying itself with the rest of the nature until social perfectness is nearly reached; and then comes the period when conscience and intellect are so highly developed that new forms of error begin in the inability to fulfill the demands of the one or to answer the doubts of the other. Then the wholeness of the people is lost; all kinds of hypocrisies and oppositions of science develop themselves; their faith is questioned on one side, and compromised with on the other; wealth commonly increases at the same period to a destructive extent; luxury follows; and the ruin of the nation is then certain: while the arts all this time are simply, as I said at first, the exponents of each phase of its moral state, and no more control it in its political career than the gleam of the firefly guides its oscillation. It is true that their most splendid results are usually obtained in the swiftness of the power which is hurrying to the precipice; but to lay the charge of the catastrophe to the art by which it is illumined is to find a cause for the cataract in the hues of its iris. It is true that the colossal vices belonging to periods of great national wealth (for wealth,

[12]Lectures delivered in 1858–1859; published 1859.

you will find, is the real root of all evil)[13] can turn every good gift and skill of nature or of man to evil purpose. If, in such times, fair pictures have been misused, how much more fair realities? And if Miranda is immoral to Caliban, is that Miranda's fault? . . .

[13]Cf. I Timothy 6, 10.

CHARLES AUGUSTIN SAINTE-BEUVE

(1804–1869)

o◯ooo◯o

SAINTE-BEUVE'S HIGH RANK among the great critics of all time is universally admitted. Professor Harper believed him to be "the most serviceable literary critic France has known,"[1] and the late eminent critic and historian, George Saintsbury, declared that, "We shall certainly look in vain anywhere for such an example [of criticism] in quality and quantity combined as is presented by the *Causeries du lundi* and the *Nouveaux lundis*."[2] Yet despite his reputation as a critic, Sainte-Beuve founded no school, advanced no new theories, was little concerned with aesthetics. The fact that he was a journalist most of his life may explain in part why he had a "morbid aversion to conclusions,"[3] but his inherent skepticism prevented him from ever accepting any dogma for more than a fleeting moment, and his active participation in the literary life of France from 1826 to 1869 carried him through several stages of youthful romanticism to middle-age conservatism in literary taste.

After studying medicine for three years and becoming interested in the influence of material upon mental phenomena, Sainte-Beuve found congenial employment with the *Globe*, a liberal journal begun in 1824 by M. Dubois, one of Sainte-Beuve's professors at the Collège Charlemagne. His review of Hugo's *Odes and Ballads* led to his being taken into *Le Cenacle*, "a kind of Mutual Admiration Society for poets, painters, and sculptors in Paris, who had, each of them, according to his own story, a masterpiece in preparation or conception, and all of them together a monopoly of French genius."[4]

Under *Le Cenacle* influence Sainte-Beuve wrote his first critical treatise,[5] on French poetry of the sixteenth century, in which he attempted to show that Molière, Racine, Corneille, and Boileau were preceded by great poets. But Sainte-Beuve had been experimenting in poetry before he joined the Hugo circle, and the autobiographical *Life, Poems, and Thoughts of Joseph Delorme* (1829) was perhaps influenced

---

[1]George McLean Harper, *Masters of French Literature* (New York, 1901), p. 9.
[2]George Saintsbury, *History of Criticism* (Edinburgh, 1904), III, 318.
[3]William Matthews, Introduction to *Monday-Chats* (Chicago, 1877), p. lii.
[4]*Ibid.*, xviii.   [5]Published serially in the *Globe*, 1827; book form, July, 1828.

most by *Werther*, *René*, and *Childe Harold*. He was interested at the time in the English Lake school, but Delorme is more "Sturm und Drang" than Wordsworthian. *Consolations* (1830) is in the same romantic style but contains more religious mysticism. *Volupté* (1834), an immature novel, and *Book of Love*, "a small collection of verses recording his passion for Madame Hugo and designed to implicate her,"[6] were artistic failures. With *August Thoughts* (1837), written on the Wordsworthian theory that common experiences are the proper subjects for poetry, Sainte-Beuve gave up the attempt to achieve success as a creative writer and for the remainder of his life confined his talent to literary criticism, his natural province.

When the *Revue de Paris* was founded in 1829, Sainte-Beuve began his brilliant career as a critic. In 1830, after the July Revolution, he returned to the *Globe*, now an organ of Saint-Simonianism. The following year the *Revue des deux mondes* was founded, and Sainte-Beuve contributed to it for thirty-seven years. The decade of 1830–1840 was a period of transformation, by the end of which Sainte-Beuve had settled into his thirty-year creed of rationalism. This period includes the renowned *Causeries du lundi*, begun in the *Constitutionnel* and continued in the *Moniteur* until within a few months of his death. In all he published over forty volumes of literary, biographical, and historical essays.

Much has been said and written about Sainte-Beuve's forsaking romanticism and his betrayal of his old friends, but *classic* and *romantic* and the literary schools probably never had much meaning for him. As a critic he was always, like Emerson, concerned with the man behind the book. "Sainte-Beuve's criticism thus becomes largely a kind of biography centered in psychologic portraiture."[7] In 1829 he declared that "there are in poetry no good and no bad subjects, there are only good and bad poets."[8] In 1861 he stated that, "The foremost superiority of a critic is to recognize the advent of a power, the dawning of a Genius."[9] Though he admired Taine's method, Sainte-Beuve believed that

> something still eludes him, the most vital part of man eludes him, which is the reason why out of twenty men, or a hundred, or a thousand, apparently subject to almost the same intrinsic or external conditions, not one resembles the other, and there is one among them all who excels through originality.[10]

[6]Harper, *op. cit.*, p. 118.
[7]William Frederic Giese, *Sainte-Beuve, A Literary Portrait* (University of Wisconsin Studies in Language and Literature, no. 31, 1931), p. 215.
[8]Preface to *Les Orientales*.   [9]*Chateaubriand et son groupe littéraire*, I, 267.
[10]Review of Taine's *History of English Literature*, *Nouveaux lundis*, VIII.

In Sainte-Beuve's "temple of taste" there is room for all sorts of literary artists—for anyone "who has enriched the human mind."[11] Furthermore,

> Sainte-Beuve says that in writing on a given author he, as it were, pays him a visit, is his guest, and observes all the courtesies and amenities that this relation implies. The author entertains his critic *chez lui*. The resultant criticism is conversable, sympathetic, generously open to impressions—it is the criticism of comprehension [as opposed to the criticism of judgment, of a Boileau or a Johnson].[12]

Sainte-Beuve's literary criticism was admired by such literary minds as Goethe, Matthew Arnold, and the late Irving Babbitt, but his influence has perhaps been greater among the "psychographers"[13] than the literary critics themselves. In fact, Sainte-Beuve was the first "psycographer," a "naturalist of souls."

BIBLIOGRAPHY

TEXT

Cahiers de Sainte-Beuve: suivis de quelques pages de littérature antique. Paris, 1876.

Causeries du lundi. 15 vols. Paris, 1851-1862.

Chateaubriand et son groupe littéraire sous l'empire. 2 vols. Paris, 1861.

Correspondance de Sainte-Beuve. 3 vols. Paris, 1877–1878.

Correspondance générale; recueillie, classée et annotée par Jean Bonnerot. Paris, 1935.

Nouveaux lundis. 5th ed. 13 vols. Paris, 1879–1884.

Nouvelle correspondance. Paris, 1880.

Portraits contemporains. 5 vols. Paris, 1869–1871.

Portraits littéraires. 3 vols. Paris, 1862–1864.

Port-Royal. 2nd. ed. 5 vols. Paris, 1849–1859.

TRANSLATIONS

Essays, tr. with an introduction by Elizabeth Lee. London, [1892].

Monday-Chats, sel. and tr. from *Causeries du lundi,* with an introduction by William Matthews. Chicago, 1877.

Portraits of the Seventeenth century, Historic and Literary, tr. by Katharine P. Wormeley. New York, 1925.

[11]"What is a Classic," *Causeries du lundi,* III, 49–50.   [12]Giese, *op. cit.,* p. 192.

[13]A psychographer is a psychological biographer; the term was first used by Gamaliel Bradford with reference to himself. The present-day American critic and literary historian, Van Wyck Brooks, perhaps also owes something to Sainte-Beuve.

Portraits of the Eighteenth century, Historic and Literary, tr. by Katharine P. Wormeley, with a critical introduction by Edmond Scherer. New York, 1925.

Selected Essays, with introduction, bibliography, and notes, ed. by John R. Effinger, Jr. Boston, 1895.

Seven of the Causeries du lundi, ed. with notes and introduction by George McLean Harper. New York, 1897.

BIOGRAPHY AND CRITICISM

Arnold, Matthew, "Sainte-Beuve," *Essays in Criticism.* Third series. Boston, 1910.

——, "Sainte-Beuve," *Encyclopaedia Britannica,* 11th ed., XXIII.

Austin, Alfred, "Sainte-Beuve's Critical Method," *Cornhill Magazine,* XXXVIII (1878), pp. 24–35.

Babbitt, Irving, "Impressionist versus Judicial Criticism," *Publications of the Modern Language Association,* n.s. XIV, no. 3 (1906), pp. 687–705.

——, *Masters of Modern French Criticism.* Boston, 1912.

Bellesort, André, *Sainte-Beuve et le dix-neuvième siècle.* Paris, 1927.

Brown, E. K., "Arnold and the Eighteenth Century," *University of Toronto Quarterly,* IX (1940), pp. 202–213.

Brunetière, Ferdinand, *L'Évolution des genres: la critique.* Paris, 1890.

——, "Sainte-Beuve," *Living Age,* CCXLV (1905), pp. 513–522.

——, "Sainte-Beuve," *Monthly Review,* XIX (1905), pp. 125–140.

Caumont, A., *La critique littéraire de Sainte-Beuve.* Frankfort a.M., 1887.

Choisy, Louis Frederic, *Sainte-Beuve: l'homme et le poète.* Paris, 1921.

Dowden, Edward, *New Studies in Literature.* Boston, 1895.

Faguet, Emil, *Politiques et moralistes du XIXᵉ siècle.* Third series. 3 vols. Paris, 1891–1899.

France, Anatole, Preface to *Poésies complètes de Sainte-Beuve.* Paris, 1879.

Giese, William Frederic, *Sainte-Beuve, a Literary Portrait.* University of Wisconsin Studies in Language and Literature (1931), no. 31.

Giraud, V., *Sainte-Beuve critique. Table alphabétique et analytique des "Premiers lundis," "Nouveaux lundis," et "Portraits contemporains," avec une étude sur Sainte-Beuve et son œuvre.* Paris, 1902.

Guérard, A. L., *French Prophets of Yesterday.* London and New York, 1913.

Harper, G. M., *Masters of French Literature.* New York, 1901.

——, *Charles-Augustin Sainte-Beuve.* Philadelphia, 1909.

James, Henry, "Sainte-Beuve," *North American Review,* CXXX (1880), pp. 51–68.

MacClintock, Lander, *Sainte-Beuve's Critical Theory and Practice after 1849.* University of Chicago, 1920. (A Ph. D. thesis.)

Michaut, Gustave Marie, *Sainte-Beuve.* Paris, 1921.

Michaut, Gustave Marie, *Sainte-Beuve avant les lundis; essai sur la formation de son esprit et de sa méthode*. Fribourg, 1903.
More, Paul Elmer, *Shelburne Essays*. Third series. New York, 1906.
Saintsbury, George, *A History of Criticism*. Edinburgh, 1904.
Séché, Léon, *Études d'histoire romantique: Sainte-Beuve*. Paris, 1904.
Scherer, E., *Études critiques sur la littérature contemporaine*. Vol. IV. Paris, 1863–1895.

A LITERARY TRADITION (*selections*)[1]

1858

. . . I, that am a critic, may be allowed to invoke the example of the greatest of critics, Goethe—him of whom we may say that he is not only tradition but that he is all traditions united. Which, from a literary point of view, predominates in him? The classical element. In him I can see the Greek temple even on the shores of Tauris. He wrote *Werther*, but it is *Werther* written by one who carries his Homer into the fields, and who will find him again even when his hero has lost him. It is thus that he has preserved his lordly serenity; no one dwells in the clouds less than he; he enlarges Parnassus, he makes stages in it, he peoples it at every station, at every summit, at every angle of its rocks; he makes it like, perhaps even too like, that pinnacled rather than rounded hill, Montserrat in Catalonia, but he does not destroy it. Without that taste for Greece which chastens and tethers his universal indifference, or, if you prefer, his universal curiosity, Goethe might have lost himself in the indefinite, the indeterminate. So many summits are familiar to him, that if Olympus were not his summit by predilection, where would he go? or rather, where would he not go? he, the most openminded of men, and the most advanced in the direction of the East? His transformations, his pilgrimages in the pursuit of the various forms of beauty, would have had no end, but he came back, he settled down, he knew the point of view from which to contemplate the universe that it might appear in its most beautiful light. As for himself, whenever we wish to form an image of the critical spirit at its highest pitch of intelligence and of considered understanding, we figure him to ourselves as an attentive and watchful spectator,

[1] A lecture delivered at the opening of the session of the *École Normale*, April 12, 1858; given, as the author tells us, to illustrate the difference between the duties of a professor and those of a critic. The business of the latter is to discover new talent; that of the former, to maintain a good tradition of taste. (Translator's note.)
The translation is by A. J. Butler.

curious from afar off, on the lookout for every discovery, for all that goes by, for every sail on the horizon—but from the heights of his Sunium.

He it was, the author of *Werther* and of *Faust*, one who knew what he was talking about, who so justly said: "By classic I understand sound, and by romantic sickly." But as the classic, and even the romantic, form part of tradition, if we are to consider it in its entire series, and in the full extent of the past, I must pause at this saying of Goethe's, and I should like, in your presence to try to explain it to myself. Well, then, the classic, in its most general character and in its widest definition, comprises all literatures in a healthy and happily flourishing condition, literatures in full accord and in harmony with their period, with their social surroundings, with the principles and powers which direct society, satisfied with themselves. Let us be quite clear, I mean satisfied to belong to their nation, to their age, to the government under which they come to birth and flourish (joy of intellect, it has been said, is the mark of strength of intellect; that is no less true for literatures than for individuals), those literatures which are and feel themselves to be at home, in their proper road, not out of their proper class, not agitating, not having for their principle discomfort, which has never been a principle of beauty. I am not the person to speak evil of romantic literatures, I keep within the terms of Goethe and of historical explanation. People are not born when they wish to be, they cannot choose their moment for hatching out, they cannot, especially in youth, avoid the general currents which are passing in the air, and which blow dryness or moisture, fever or health; and there are similar currents for the soul. That feeling of fundamental contentment, in which there is, before all things, hope, into which discouragement does not enter, where you may say that there is a period before you which will outlast you, which is stronger than you, a period which will protect and judge, where you have a fine field for a career, for an honorable and glorious development in the full light of day— that is what gives the first foundation upon which afterwards arise, like palaces and temples in regular order, harmoniously constructed and regular works.

When you live in a perpetual instability of public affairs, when you see society change often before your eyes, you are tempted to disbelieve in literary immortality, and consequently

to grant yourself every license. Now it falls to nobody's lot to
give himself this feeling of security and of a steady and durable
period, one must breathe it in with the air in the hours of youth.
Romantic literatures, which are above all things matters of
sudden assault and of adventure, have their merits, their exploits,
their brilliantly played parts, but outside of established rules.
They perch themselves astride of two or three periods, never
getting fairly into the saddle on a single one, uneasy, inquiring,
eccentric by nature, either much in advance or much in arrear,
in other respects willful and wandering.

Classical literature never complains, never groans, never
feels ennui. Sometimes, in company with sorrow, and by way of
sorrow, one may outstrip it, but beauty is more tranquil.

The classic, I repeat, possesses among its other characteristics that of loving its own country, its own times, of seeing
nothing more desirable or more beautiful. It is legitimately
for and of these. Its motto should be "Activity with tranquillity." That is true of the age of Pericles, of the age of Augustus,
no less than of the reign of Louis XIV. Let us hear the great
poets and the orators of those periods speak under their fair sky,
as it were under their dome of blue, their hymns of praise still
resound in our ears: they carried the art of applause very far.
Romanticism, like Hamlet, has homesickness, it seeks for what
it has not, seeks it even beyond the clouds; it dreams, it sees in
visions. In the nineteenth century it adores the Middle Ages;
in the eighteenth, it was already revolutionary with Rousseau.
In Goethe's sense of the word, there are romanticists of various
times. Chrysostom's young friend Stagirius, or Augustine in
his youth, were of this kind, Renés[2] before their time; sick men,
but they were sick men who might be healed, and Christianity
healed them by exorcising the demon. Hamlet, Werther,
Childe Harold, the true Renés, are sick men of the kind who
sing and suffer, who enjoy their malady—romantics more or
less in a dilettante way; they are sick for sickness' sake.

Oh! if one day in our fair fatherland, in our capital which
grows daily in magnificence, which is for us so fine a representative of the country, we felt ourselves happy, honestly happy
of belonging to it; if, above all, young souls, touched by a kind
of inspiration, caught by that praiseworthy and salutary contentment which does not engender a childish pride but only adds

[2]The sentimental hero of Chateaubriand's novel by the same name.

emulation to life, could feel themselves happy to live in an age, under a social system, which allows or favors all the finer developments of humanity; if they would not from the outset put themselves in an attitude of revolt, of opposition or fault-finding, of bitterness, of regrets or of hopes too late or premature; if they would consent to spread out and to direct all their powers in the wide field open before them, then the balance would be restored between talent and its surroundings, between men of parts and the social system; we should find ourselves again in unison, strife and moral sickness would cease, and literature would again of itself become classical, both in grandeur of line and in what is essential, its fundamental basis. It is not that people would have more talent or more knowledge, but more order, more harmony, more proportion, a noble aim, and simpler means and more courage to arrive at it; we should perhaps begin again to have works that would last.

It is here no mission, no claim of ours to produce such; we have above all to preserve them. What is the best and surest manner of maintaining tradition? In the first place it is to possess it complete, not to concentrate and crowd it upon certain points too close together, not to exaggerate it here and overlook it there. There is no need to tell you these things, since the models are familiar and present to you, from the first beginnings, and in different literatures, and your minds are furnished with true standards of comparison in every kind. Others have set up the pillars on the foundation of yourselves, you have the patterns of true beauty. He who can see Plato, Sophocles, Demosthenes, face to face, is under no temptation to grant too much, even to the most illustrious of the moderns. That is the weak point of those who only possess one language and one literature. Frederick the Great granted everything to Voltaire, even to Voltaire as a poet, and adjudged to him all the crowns, merely because he had no sufficient standard of comparison. Through overnarrowing of tradition, through making it too cut and dried, many of those who at the beginning of this century claimed the exclusive title of classics were, in the strife of that time, those who could least do so.

As each age renews itself, portions of recent tradition which are believed well based crumble into ruin after a certain fashion, and the only result is that the indestructible marble rock appears all the more in its true solidity.

In order to maintain tradition, it is not always sufficient to attach it firmly to its most lofty and most august monuments; it is necessary to verify it and to check it incessantly at the points nearest to us, even to rejuvenate it, and to keep it in perpetual relation with what is living. Here we touch a somewhat delicate question. It is no business of mine to introduce into the curriculum too recent names, to go out of my way to judge the works of the present day, to confuse functions and parts. A professor is not a critic. The critic, if he does his duty (and where are such critics at the present day?) is a sentinel always awake, always on the lookout; but he does not only cry "Who goes there?" he gives help; far from resembling a pirate, or delighting in shipwrecks, he sometimes, like the coasting pilot, goes to the help of those whom the tempest overtakes as they enter or leave port. The professor's obligations are smaller, or, I should say, different. He is bound to more reserve and more dignity. He must not go far from the sacred places which it is his part to show and to tend. Still, he cannot entirely escape all knowledge of novelties, of arrivals and approaches, announced with all pomp, of sails which are signaled from time to time on the horizon as those of invincible armadas. He must know them, at least the chief of them. He must have his opinion. In a word, he must keep his eye on the neighboring shore, and never go to sleep.

To go to sleep on tradition is a danger with which we are little threatened. We are no longer in the days when, if you were born in a capital, you never left it. We have seen classics who have grown feeble in the second generation, who have become sedentary and homekeeping. They have acted like the son of Charles V, of all emperors the most traveled, that Philip II who never stirred from his Escurial. Nobody nowadays has any right to rest so quiet, even in the best established admirations. One thing or another is constantly moving as we watch it, and there open, as in our old cities, long, new vistas which change the most familiar views. Instruction is bound, whether it will or not, to take fresh bearings, to reconsider in these things. There are ways also in which it can renew itself, in which it can modify the manner in which it does service to taste, and defends tradition. I will take our seventeenth century, for example.

Criticism and erudition are guided by the historical spirit, have devoted themselves for some years past to a great work which has its value, and the importance and undoubted utility of which I should be far from depreciating. There has come a taste for original sources. People have wished to make a closer acquaintance with everything by the aid of papers and documents at first hand, and, as far as possible, unpublished. . . .

Their papers have been examined, their autograph letters, the first editions of their works, the evidence of their surroundings, the journals of the secretaries who knew them best, and in this way notions have been formed of them somewhat different and certainly more precise than could be obtained from the mere reading of their published works. . . .

Not a day passes without someone announcing a discovery; everyone wishes to make it his own, everyone boasts of it, and puffs his wares unchecked. Disproportionate importance and literary value are attributed to works hitherto unknown. People are proud of "finds," merely curious (when they are that), which cost no thought, no effort of the mind, but merely the trouble of going and picking them up. One would say that the era of the scholiasts and commentators was reopening and beginning anew; a man gets no less honor and consideration for this, nay, more, than if he had attempted a fine novel, a fine poem, or tried the ways of true invention, the lofty roads of thought. . . .

Let us maintain the degrees of art, the stages of intelligence. Let us encourage all industrious research, but let us in everything leave the master's place to talent, to careful thought, to judgment, to reason, to taste. . . .

The best way not only of appreciating but of getting others to appreciate fine works is to have no predilection, to give one's self full liberty every time one reads them or speaks them, to forget, if possible, that one has possessed them for a long time, and to begin upon them again as if one had only today made their acquaintance. Thus, steeped again in its source, one's opinion, even if it may sometimes remain inferior to what one had previously formed, at any rate recovers life and freshness. The man of taste, even though he be not destined to teach and have his full leisure, ought for his own sake, it seems to me, to return every four or five years upon the best of his old admirations, to verify them, to put them to the question again as though they were new—that is to say, to reawaken and refresh them even at the risk of seeing them now and then somewhat deranged; the important point is that they should be living. . . .

I have often remarked that when two good intellects pass totally different judgments on the same author we may safely wager that it is because they are not, in fact, fixing their thoughts for the moment on the same object, on the same works of the author in question, on the same passages of his works; that it is because they have not the whole of him before their eyes, that they are not for the moment taking him in entirely. A closer attention, a wider knowledge, will bring together differing judgments and restore them to harmony. But even in the regular graduated circle of lawful admiration a certain latitude must be allowed to the diversity of tastes, minds, and ages. . . .

HIPPOLYTE ADOLPHE TAINE

(1828–1893)

oꙨooꙨo

TAINE'S THEORY concerning the relationship between the writer and his environment may profitably be used to examine his own life and writings. Born and educated during the anti-romantic reaction in France (1820–1850), during the period of Comtean positivism in science and the beginnings of a materialistic psychology, it is hardly surprising that Taine should have become a sociological historian of letters and a forerunner of naturalism.

The troubled times in which he lived gave Taine a varied experience in both life and letters. After serving for a short while as professor at Toulon, then at Nevers, he was removed in 1852 by politicians. He took his doctor's degree in 1853, after writing two dissertations, *De personis Platonicis* and an essay on La Fontaine's fables. In 1855 his essay on Livy was crowned by the French Academy. In 1864 he became professor of the history of art and aesthetics at the École des Beaux Arts, but was again removed by politicians. Meanwhile he had published his great work, *Histoire de la littérature anglaise* (1864), which he had hoped would effect his election to the French Academy, but he had so many bitter enemies that he was not elected until 1878.

By the middle of the nineteenth century it was obvious that the great ambitions of the French Revolutionists had failed of achievement. Taine decided that only parties and personalities, not political conduct, had changed. Human nature appalled him. His consequent pessimism, positivism, and "hard-boiled" realism remind us of the American writers of the post-World-War generation, and the intellectual temper of the times was probably somewhat similar, for Taine's followers were such men as Zola, Bourget, and Maupassant, who in turn profoundly influenced Frank Norris, Hamlin Garland, Theodore Dreiser, and other "realists" in America.

And just as Zola was trying to find a "scientific" way to write novels, so Taine was trying in the spirit of science to explain each writer in terms of his heredity and environment. Literature, he decided, was like fossils imprinted by a once-living organism in sand before it had hardened into stone. Like the geologist and the biologist, the literary historian and critic should collect his artifacts and then try to reconstruct and understand the past age. Consequently, he was not interested in permanent artistic values and moral standards; in fact, they had no meaning to him except as specimens of their age, race, and environment.

Taine has been accused of not following his own theory, but few critical theories of the nineteenth century have had a deeper and more lasting influence on twentieth-century literature and criticism than Taine's, as expressed in his famous Introduction to his *History of English Literature.*

BIBLIOGRAPHY

TEXT

Derniers essais de critique et d'histoire. Paris, 1894.
Essais de critique et d'histoire. 2nd ed. Paris, 1866.
Essai sur les fables de La Fontaine. Paris, 1853.
De l'idéal dans l'art. Paris, 1867.
Introduction à l'histoire de la littérature anglaise, ed., with an Essay on Taine, by Irving Babbitt. Boston, 1898.
Nouveaux essais de critique et d'histoire. Paris, 1865.

TRANSLATIONS

History of English Literature, tr. by H. van Laun with a preface by the author. New York, 1871. Other editions in 1878, 1885, 1904, etc.
The Ideal in Art, tr. by John Durand. New York, 1869.
Lectures on Art, tr. by John Durand. New York, 1877.

CRITICISM

Babbitt, Irving, *Masters of Modern French Criticism.* Boston, 1912.
Bazalellotti, Giacomo, *La Philosophie de H. Taine,* traduit de l'italien par Auguste Dietrich. Paris, 1900.
Bourget, Paul, *Essais de psychologie contemporaine.* 2 vols. 5th ed. Paris, 1889. Vol. I, Baudelaire, Renan, Flaubert, Taine, Stendhal.
Brunetière, Ferdinand, *L'Évolution des genres dans l'histoire de la littérature.* Paris, 1890. Tome I, Introduction, L'évolution de la critique depuis la renaissance jusqu'à nos jours.
Chevrillon, André, *Taine; formation de sa pensée.* Paris, 1932.
Gibaudan, René, *Les Idées sociales de Taine.* Paris, 1928.
Gummere, Francis Barton, *Democracy and Poetry.* Boston, 1911.
Hennequin, Émile, *La Critique scientifique.* 3 éd. Paris, 1894.
Monod, Gabriel Jacques Jean, *Les Maîtres de l'histoire: Renan, Taine, Michelet.* Paris, 1896.

Planche, Gustave, "Le Panthéisme et l'histoire à propos des 'Essais de critique de M. Taine,'" *Revue des deux mondes*, CXII (1857), 667–691.

Roe, Frederick Charles, *Taine et L'Angleterre*. Paris, 1923.

Sainte-Beuve, Charles Augustin, *Causeries du lundi*. Paris, 1857, XIII, pp. 249–267, 268–274; XV, pp. 54 ff.

——, *Nouveaux lundis*. Paris, 1885, VIII, pp. 66–137.

Sherer, Edmond, *Mélanges de critiques religieuses*. Paris, 1858.

Zeitlin, Julius, "Taine und die Kultur-Geschichte," *Philosophische Studien*, XX (1902), 670–712.

[RACE, SURROUNDINGS, AND EPOCH][1]

1864

History has been transformed, within a hundred years in Germany, within sixty years in France, and that by the study of their literatures.

It was perceived that a literary work is not a mere individual play of imagination, the isolated caprice of an excited brain, but a transcript of contemporary manners, a manifestation of a certain kind of mind. It was concluded that we might recover, from the monuments of literature, a knowledge of the manner in which men thought and felt centuries ago. The attempt was made, and it succeeded.

Pondering on these modes of feeling and thought, men decided that they were facts of the highest kind. They saw that these facts bore reference to the most important occurrences, that they explained and were explained by them, that it was necessary thenceforth to give them a rank, and a most important rank, in history. This rank they have received, and from that moment history has undergone a complete change: in its subject matter, its system, its machinery, the appreciation of laws and of causes. It is this change, such as it is and must be, that we shall here endeavor to exhibit.

I

What is your first remark on turning over the great, stiff leaves of a folio, the yellow sheets of a manuscript—a poem, a code of laws, a confession of faith? This, you say, did not come into existence all alone. It is but a mold, like a fossil shell,

---

[1] Extracts from Taine's Introduction to his *History of English Literature* (1864), translated by H. van Laun (Edinburgh, 1873).

an imprint, like one of those shapes embossed in stone by an animal which lived and perished. Under the shell there was an animal, and behind the document there was a man. Why do you study the shell, except to bring before you the animal? So you study the document only to know the man. The shell and the document are lifeless wrecks, valuable only as a clue to the entire and living existence. We must get hold of this existence, endeavor to re-create it. It is a mistake to study the document as if it were isolated. This were to treat things like a simple scholar, to fall into the error of the bibliomaniac. Neither mythology nor languages exist in themselves; but only men, who arrange words and imagery according to the necessities of their organs and the original bent of their intellects. A dogma is nothing in itself; look at the people who have made it—a portrait, for instance, of the sixteenth century, say the stern powerful face of an English archbishop or martyr. Nothing exists except through some individual man; it is this individual with whom we must become acquainted. When we have established the parentage of dogmas, or the classification of poems, or the progress of constitutions, or the transformation of idioms, we have only cleared the soil: genuine history is brought into existence only when the historian begins to unravel, across the lapse of time, the living man, toiling, impassioned, entrenched in his customs, with his voice and features, his gestures and his dress, distinct and complete as he from whom we have just parted in the street. Let us endeavor, then, to annihilate as far as possible this great interval of time, which prevents us from seeing man with our eyes, with the eyes of our head. . . . Let us make the past present: in order to judge of a thing, it must be before us; there is no experience in respect of what is absent. Doubtless this reconstruction is always incomplete; it can produce only incomplete judgments; but that we cannot help. It is better to have an imperfect knowledge than none at all; and there is no other means of acquainting ourselves approximately with the events of other days, than to *see* approximately the men of other days.

This is the first step in history; it was made in Europe at the revival of imagination, toward the close of the last century, by Lessing and Walter Scott; a little later in France, by Chateaubriand, Augustin Thierry, Michelet, and others. And now for the second step.

II

When you consider with your eyes the visible man, what do you look for? The man invisible. The words which enter your ears, the gestures, the motions of his head, the clothes he wears, visible acts and deeds of every kind, are expressions merely; somewhat is revealed beneath them, and that is a soul. An inner man is concealed beneath the outer man; the second does but reveal the first. You look at his house, furniture, dress; and that in order to discover in them the marks of his habits and tastes, the degree of his refinement or rusticity, his extravagance or his economy, his stupidity or his acuteness. You listen to his conversation, and you note the inflections of his voice, the changes in his attitudes; and that in order to judge of his vivacity, his self-forgetfulness or his gaiety, his energy or his constraint. You consider his writings, his artistic productions, his business transactions or political ventures; and that in order to measure the scope and limits of his intelligence, his inventiveness, his coolness, to find out the order, the character, the general force of his ideas, the mode in which he thinks and resolves. All these externals are but avenues converging towards a center; you enter them simply in order to reach that center; and that center is the genuine man, I mean that mass of faculties and feelings which are the inner man. We have reached a new world, which is infinite, because every action which we see involves an infinite association of reasonings, emotions, sensations new and old, which have served to bring it to light, and which, like great rocks deep-seated in the ground, find in it their end and their level. This underworld is a new subject matter, proper to the historian. If his critical education is sufficient, he can lay bare, under every detail of architecture, every stroke in a picture, every phrase in a writing, the special sensation whence detail, stroke, or phrase had issue; he is present at the drama which was enacted in the soul of artist or writer; the choice of a word, the brevity or length of a sentence, the nature of a metaphor, the accent of a verse, the development of an argument—everything is a symbol to him; while his eyes read the text, his soul and mind pursue the continuous development and the ever-changing succession of the emotions and conceptions out of which the text has sprung: in short, he works out its psychology. . . .

This is the second step; we are in a fair way to its completion.

It is the fit work of the contemporary critic. No one has done it so justly and grandly as Sainte-Beuve: in this respect we are all his pupils; his method has revolutionized, in our days, in books, and even in newspapers, every kind of literary, of philosophical and religious criticism. From it we must set out in order to begin the further development. I have more than once endeavored to indicate this development; there is here, in my mind, a new path open to history, and I will try to describe it more in detail.

III

When you have observed and noted in man one, two, three, then a multitude of sensations, does this suffice, or does your knowledge appear complete? Is psychology only a series of observations? No; here as elsewhere we must search out the causes after we have collected the facts. No matter if the facts be physical or moral, they all have their causes; there is a cause for ambition, for courage, for truth, as there is for digestion, for muscular movement, for animal heat. Vice and virtue are products, like vitriol and sugar; and every complex phenomenon arises from other more simple phenomena on which it hangs. Let us then seek the simple phenomena for moral qualities; as we seek them for physical qualities; and let us take the first fact that presents itself: for example, religious music, that of a Protestant church. There is an inner cause which has turned the spirit of the faithful toward these grave and monotonous melodies, a cause broader than its effect; I mean the general idea of the true, external worship which man owes to God. It is this which has modeled the architecture of Protestant places of worship, thrown down the statues, removed the pictures, destroyed the ornaments, curtailed the ceremonies, shut up the worshipers in high pews which prevent them from seeing anything, and regulated the thousand details of decoration, posture, and general externals. This again comes from another more general cause, the idea of human conduct in all its comprehensiveness, internal and external, prayers, actions, duties of every kind which man owes to God; it is this which has enthroned the doctrine of grace, lowered the status of the clergy, transformed the sacraments, suppressed various practices, and changed religion from a discipline to a morality. This second idea in its turn depends upon a third still more general, that of moral perfection, such as is met with in the perfect God, the unerring judge, the stern watcher of souls, before whom every soul is sinful, worthy of punishment, incapable of virtue or salvation, except by the power of conscience which He calls forth, and the renewal of heart which He produces. That is the master idea, which consists in erecting duty into an absolute king of human life, and in prostrating all ideal models before a moral model. Here we track the root of man; for to explain this conception it is necessary to consider the race itself. . . .

IV

There is, then, a system in human sentiments and ideas; and this system has for its motive power certain general traits, certain characteristics of the intellect and the heart common to men of one race, age, or country. As in mineralogy the crystals, however diverse, spring from certain simple physical forms, so in history, civilizations, however diverse, are derived from certain simple spiritual forms. The former are explained by a primitive geometrical element, as the latter are by a primitive psychological element. In order to master the classification of mineralogical systems, we must first consider a regular and general solid, its sides and angles, and observe in this the numberless transformations of which it is capable. So, if you would realize the system of historical varieties, consider first a human soul generally, with its two or three fundamental faculties, and in this compendium you will perceive the principal forms which it can present. After all, this kind of ideal picture, geometrical as well as psychological, is not very complex, and we speedily see the limits of the outline in which civilizations, like crystals, are constrained to exist.

What is really the mental structure of man? Images or representations of things which float within him, exist for a time, are effaced, and return again after he has been looking upon a tree, an animal, any visible object. This is the subject matter, the development whereof is double, either speculative or practical, according as the representations resolve themselves into a *general conception* or an *active resolution*. Here we have the whole of man in an abridgment; and in this limited circle human diversities meet, sometimes in the womb of the primordial matter, sometimes in the twofold primordial development. However minute in their elements, they are enormous in the aggregate, and the

least alteration in the factors produces vast alteration in the
result. According as the representation is clear and as it were
punched out or confused and faintly defined, according as it
embraces a great or small number of the characteristics of the
object, according as it is violent and accompanied by impulses
or quiet and surrounded by calm, all the operations and processes of the human machine are transformed. So, again, according as the ulterior development of the representation
varies, the whole human development varies. If the general
conception in which it results is a mere dry notation (in Chinese
fashion), language becomes a sort of algebra, religion and
poetry dwindle, philosophy is reduced to a kind of moral and
practical common sense, science to a collection of utilitarian
formulas, classifications, mnemonics, and the whole intellect
takes a positive bent. If, on the contrary, the general representation in which the conception results is a poetical and figurative
creation, a living symbol, as among the Aryan races, language
becomes a sort of delicately shaded and colored epic poem,
in which every word is a person, poetry and religion assume a
magnificent and inexhaustible grandeur, metaphysics are
widely and subtly developed without regard to positive applications; the whole intellect, in spite of the inevitable deviations
and shortcomings of its effort, is smitten with the beautiful and
the sublime and conceives an ideal capable by its nobleness and
its harmony of rallying round it the tenderness and enthusiasm
of the human race. If, again, the general conception in which
the representation results is poetical but not graduated; if man
arrives at it not by an uninterrupted gradation, but by a quick
intuition; if the original operation is not a regular development,
but a violent explosion—then, as with the Semitic races, metaphysics are absent, religion conceives God only as a king solitary
and devouring, science cannot grow, the intellect is too rigid
and unbending to reproduce the delicate operations of nature,
poetry can give birth only to vehement and grandiose exclama-
tions, language cannot unfold the web of argument and of eloquence, man is reduced to a lyric enthusiasm, an unchecked
passion, a fanatical and limited action. In this interval between
the particular representation and the universal conception are
found the germs of the greatest human differences. Some races,
as the classical, pass from the first to the second by a graduated
scale of ideas, regularly arranged, and general by degrees;

others, as the Germanic, traverse the same ground by leaps, without uniformity, after vague and prolonged groping. Some, like the Romans and English, halt at the first steps; others, like the Hindoos and Germans, mount to the last. . . .

V

Three different sources contribute to produce this elementary moral state—RACE, SURROUNDINGS, and EPOCH. What we call the race are the innate and hereditary dispositions which man brings with him into the world and which, as a rule, are united with the marked differences in the temperament and structure of the body. They vary with various peoples. There is a natural variety of men, as of oxen and horses, some brave and intelligent, some timid and dependent, some capable of superior conceptions and creations, some reduced to rudimentary ideas and inventions, some more specially fitted to special works, and gifted more richly with particular instincts, as we meet with species of dogs better favored than others—these for coursing, those for fighting, those for hunting, these again for house dogs or shepherds' dogs. We have here a distinct force—so distinct that amidst the vast deviations which the other two motive forces produce in him, one can recognize it still; and a race, like the old Aryans, scattered from the Ganges as far as the Hebrides, settled in every clime, and every stage of civilization, transformed by thirty centuries of revolutions, nevertheless manifests in its languages, religions, literatures, philosophies, the community of blood and of intellect which to this day binds its off-shoots together. Different as they are, their parentage is not obliterated; barbarism, culture and grafting, differences of sky and soil, fortunes good and bad, have labored in vain: the great marks of the original model have remained, and we find again the two or three principal lineaments of the primitive stamp underneath the secondary imprints which time has laid upon them. There is nothing astonishing in this extraordinary tenacity. Although the vastness of the distance lets us but half perceive—and by a doubtful light—the origin of species,[2] the events of history sufficiently illumine the events anterior to history, to explain the almost immovable steadfastness of the primordial marks. When we meet with them, fifteen, twenty, thirty centuries before our era, in an Aryan, an Egyptian, a Chinese, they

[2]Darwin, *The Origin of Species;* Prosper Lucas, *De L'hérédité.*

represent the work of a great many ages, perhaps of several myriads of centuries. For as soon as an animal begins to exist, it has to reconcile itself with its surroundings; it breathes and renews itself, is differently affected according to the variations in air, food, temperature. Different climate and situation bring it various needs and, consequently, a different course of activity; and this, again, a different set of habits; and still again, a different set of aptitudes and instincts. Man, forced to accommodate himself to circumstances, contracts a temperament and a character corresponding to them; and his character, like his temperament, is so much more stable, as the external impression is made upon him by more numerous repetitions, and is transmitted to his progeny by a more ancient descent. So that at any moment we may consider the character of a people as an abridgment of all its preceding actions and sensations; that is, as a quantity and as a weight, not infinite,[3] since everything in nature is finite, but disproportioned to the rest, and almost impossible to lift, since every moment of an almost infinite past has contributed to increase it, and because, in order to raise the scale, one must place in the opposite scale a still greater number of actions and sensations. Such is the first and richest source of these master faculties from which historical events take their rise; and one sees at the outset that, if it be powerful, it is because this is no simple spring but a kind of lake, a deep reservoir wherein other springs have, for a multitude of centuries, discharged their several streams.

Having thus outlined the interior structure of a race, we must consider the surroundings in which it exists. For man is not alone in the world; nature surrounds him, and his fellow men surround him; accidental and secondary tendencies overlay his primitive tendencies, and physical or social circumstances disturb or confirm the character committed to their charge. Sometimes the climate has had its effect. Though we can follow but obscurely the Aryan peoples from their common fatherland to their final settlements, we can yet assert that the profound differences which are manifest between the German races on the one side, and the Greek and Latin on the other, arise for the most part from the difference between the countries in which they are settled: some in cold moist lands, deep in rugged marshy forests or on the shores of a wild ocean, beset by melan-

---

[3]Spinoza, *Ethics*, Pt. IV, axiom.

choly or violent sensations, prone to drunkenness and gluttony, bent on a fighting, blood-spilling life; others, again, within the loveliest landscapes, on a bright and pleasant seacoast, enticed to navigation and commerce, exempt from gross cravings of the stomach, inclined from the beginning to social ways, to a settled organization of the state, to feelings and dispositions such as develop the art of oratory, the talent for enjoyment, the inventions of science, letters, arts. . . . These are the most efficacious of the visible causes which mold the primitive man: they are to nations what education, career, condition, abode, are to individuals; and they seem to comprehend everything, since they comprehend all external powers which mold human matter, and by which the external acts on the internal.

There is yet a third rank of causes; for, with the forces within and without, there is the work which they have already produced together, and this work itself contributes to produce that which follows. Beside the permanent impulse and the given surroundings, there is the acquired momentum. When the national character and surrounding circumstances operate, it is not upon a *tabula rasa*, but on a ground on which marks are already impressed. According as one takes the ground at one moment or another, the imprint is different; and this is the cause that the total effect is different. Consider, for instance, two epochs of a literature or art—French tragedy under Corneille and under Voltaire, the Greek drama under Aeschylus and under Euripides, Italian painting under da Vinci and under Guido. Truly, at either of these two extreme points the general idea has not changed; it is always the same human type which is its subject of representation or painting; the mold of verse, the structure of the drama, the form of body has endured. . . . Thus it is with a people as with a plant; the same sap, under the same temperature, and in the same soil, produces, at different steps of its progressive development, different formations, buds, flowers, fruits, seed-vessels, in such a manner that the one which follows must always be preceded by the former, and must spring up from its death. And if now you consider no longer a brief epoch, as our own time, but one of those wide intervals which embrace one or more centuries, like the Middle Ages, or our last classic age, the conclusion will be similar. A certain dominant idea has had sway; men, for two, for five hundred years, have taken to themselves a certain ideal model of man: in the Middle Ages, the knight and the monk; in our classic age, the courtier, the man who speaks well. This creative and universal idea is displayed over the whole field of action and thought; and, after covering the world with its involuntarily systematic works, it has faded, it has died away, and lo, a new idea springs up, destined to a like domination, and as manifold creations. And here remember that the second depends in part upon the first, and that the first, uniting its effect with those of national genius and surrounding circumstances, imposes on each new creation its bent and direction. The great historical currents are formed after this law—the long dominations of one intellectual pattern, or a master idea, such as the period of spontaneous creations called the Renaissance, or the period of oratorical models called the Classical Age, or the series of mystical systems called the Alexandrian and Christian eras, or the series of mythological efflorescences which we meet with in the infancy of the German people, of the Indian, and the Greek. Here as elsewhere we have but a mechanical problem; the total effect is a result, depending entirely on the magnitude and direction of the producing causes. The only difference which separates these moral problems from physical ones is that the magnitude and direction cannot be valued or computed in the first as in the second. . . . So much we can say with confidence that the unknown creations towards which the current of the centuries conducts us will be raised up and regulated altogether by the three primordial forces; that if these forces could be measured and computed, we might deduce from them as from a formula the characteristics of future civilization; and that if, in spite of the evident crudeness of our notations, and the fundamental inexactness of our measures, we try now to form some idea of our general destiny, it is upon an examination of these forces that we must base our prophecy. For, in enumerating them, we traverse the complete circle of the agencies; and when we have considered, RACE, SURROUNDINGS, and EPOCH, which are the internal mainsprings, the external pressure, and the acquired momentum, we have exhausted not only the whole of the actual causes, but also the whole of the possible causes of motion.

VI

It remains for us to examine how these causes, when applied to a nation or an age, produce their results. As a spring, rising

from a height and flowing downwards spreads its streams according to the depth of the descent, stage after stage, until it reaches
the lowest level of the soil, so the disposition of intellect or soul
impressed on a people by race, circumstances, or epoch, spreads
in different proportions and by regular descents, down the diverse orders of facts which make up its civilization.[4] If we arrange
the map of a country, starting from the watershed, we find that
below this common point the streams are divided into five or six
principal basins, then each of these into several secondary basins,
and so on, until the whole country with its thousand details is
included in the ramifications of this network. So, if we arrange
the psychological map of the events and sensations of a human
civilization, we find first of all five or six well-defined provinces—
religion, art, philosophy, the state, the family, the industries. . . .
If now we examine and compare these diverse groups of facts,
we find first of all that they are made up of parts, and that all
have parts in common. Let us take first the three chief works
of human intelligence—religion, art, philosophy. What is a
philosophy but a conception of nature and its primordial causes,
under the form of abstractions and formulas? What is there at
the bottom of a religion or of an art but a conception of this
same nature and of these same causes under form of symbols
more or less precise, and personages more or less marked; with
this difference, that in the first we believe that they exist, in the
second we believe that they do not exist? Let the reader consider
a few of the great creations of the intelligence in India, Scandi-
navia, Persia, Rome, Greece, and he will see that, throughout,
art is a kind of philosophy made sensible, religion a poem taken
for true, philosophy an art and a religion dried up, and reduced
to simple ideas. There is therefore, at the core of each of these
three groups, a common element, the conception of the world
and its principles; and if they differ among themselves, it is because each combines with the common, a distinct element: now the
power of abstraction, again the power to personify and to believe,
and finally the power to personify and not to believe. . . .

VIII

History now attempts, or rather is very near attempting, this
method of research. The question propounded nowadays is of

---

[4]For this scale of co-ordinate effects, consult Renan, *Langues sémitiques*, chap. I;
Mommsen, *Comparison between the Greek and Roman Civilizations*, 3rd. ed., I, chap. II;
Tocqueville, *Conséquences de la démocratie en Amérique*, III.

this kind. Given a literature, philosophy, society, art, group of arts, what is the moral condition which produced it? what the conditions of race, epoch, circumstance, the most fitted to produce this moral condition? There is a distinct moral condition for each of these formations, and for each of their branches; one for art in general, one for each kind of art—for architecture, painting, sculpture, music, poetry; each has its special germ in the wide field of human psychology; each has its law, and it is by virtue of this law that we see it raised, by chance, as it seems, wholly alone, amid the miscarriage of its neighbors, like painting in Flanders and Holland in the seventeenth century, poetry in England in the sixteenth, music in Germany in the eighteenth. At this moment, and in these countries, the conditions have been fulfilled for one art, not for others, and a single branch has budded in the general barrenness. History must search nowadays for these rules of human growth; with the special psychology of each special formation it must occupy itself; the finished picture of these characteristic conditions it must now labor to compose. No task is more delicate or more difficult; Montesquieu tried it, but in his time history was too new to admit of his success; they had not yet even a suspicion of the road necessary to be traveled, and hardly now do we begin to catch sight of it. Just as in its elements astronomy is a mechanical and physiology a chemical problem, so history in its elements is a psychological problem. There is a particular system of inner impressions and operations which makes an artist, a believer, a musician, a painter, a man in a nomadic or social state; and of each the birth and growth, the energy, the connection of ideas and emotions are different: each has his moral history and his special structure, with some governing disposition and some dominant feature. To explain each, it would be necessary to write a chapter of psychological analysis, and barely yet has such a method been rudely sketched. One man alone, Stendhal, with a peculiar bent of mind and a strange education, has undertaken it, and to this day the majority of readers find his books paradoxical and obscure: his talent and his ideas were premature; his admirable divinations were not understood, any more than his profound sayings thrown out cursorily, or the astonishing precision of his system and of his logic. It was not perceived that, under the exterior of a conversationalist and a man of the world, he explained the most complicated of esoteric mechanisms; that he laid his finger on

the mainsprings; that he introduced into the history of the heart
scientific processes, the art of notation, decomposition, deduction; that he first marked the fundamental causes of nationality,
climate, temperament; in short, that he treated sentiments as
they should be treated—in the manner of the naturalist, and of
the natural philosopher, who classifies and weighs forces. . . .
In his writings, in Sainte-Beuve, in the German critics, the
reader will see all the wealth that may be drawn from a literary
work: when the work is rich, and people know how to interpret
it, we find there the psychology of a soul, frequently of an age,
now and then of a race. In this light, a great poem, a fine novel,
the confessions of a superior man, are more instructive than a
heap of historians with their histories. I would give fifty volumes
of charters and a hundred volumes of state papers for the memoirs of Cellini, the epistles of St. Paul, the table talk of Luther,
or the comedies of Aristophanes. In this consists the importance
of literary works: they are instructive because they are beautiful;
their utility grows with their perfection; and if they furnish
documents it is because they are monuments. The more a book
brings sentiments into light, the more it is a work of literature;
for the proper office of literature is to make sentiments visible.
The more a book represents important sentiments, the higher is
its place in literature; for it is by representing the mode of being
of a whole nation and a whole age that a writer rallies round
him the sympathies of an entire age and of an entire nation.
That is why, amid the writings which set before our eyes the
sentiments of preceding generations, a literature, and notably a
grand literature, is incomparably the best. It resembles those
admirable apparatuses of extraordinary sensibility by which
physicians disentangle and measure the most recondite and
delicate changes of a body. Constitutions, religions, do not
approach it in importance; the articles of a code of laws and of a
creed only show us the spirit roughly and without delicacy. If
there are any writings in which politics and dogma are full of
life, it is in the eloquent discourses of the pulpit and the tribune,
memoirs, unrestrained confessions; and all this belongs to literature: so that, in addition to itself, it has all the advantage of
other works. It is then chiefly by the study of literatures that
one may construct a moral history, and advance toward the
knowledge of psychological laws, from which events spring. . . .

MATTHEW ARNOLD

(1822–1888)

o◯oo◯o

MATTHEW ARNOLD WAS THE SON of Dr. Thomas Arnold, the famous headmaster of Rugby, and was educated at Winchester, Rugby, and Balliol College, Oxford. Though not a distinguished student, he won the Newdigate poetry prize and became a fellow of Oriel College. In 1851 he was appointed inspector of schools, and, with a ten-year interruption (1857–1867) while he was professor of poetry at Oxford, he continued in educational work until the year of his death. Two of these biographical facts are of special importance to Arnold's literary criticism: his classical education and his lifelong connection with pedagogy, for the one led him to a classical philosophy of literature and the other undoubtedly influenced him to tie up this philosophy with his social, religious, and educational doctrines.

Arnold laid the foundation of his critical theories in 1853 in the Preface to the second edition of his poems. Here he plainly reveals his predilection for Greek literature and classical standards. He thinks the subject is everything, the manner of treatment secondary, though the right subject will result in the "grand style," and he tries to preserve the "wholesome regulative laws of poetry." After he became professor of poetry at Oxford, and forsook poetry for criticism, Arnold elaborated these ideas into a doctrine strikingly similar in many ways to the "New Humanism" of the American critics, Irving Babbitt and Paul Elmer More. Like them, he believed in moderation, restraint, and the standards of the greatest writers and thinkers of the past. The personal and impressionistic judgment of the romantics was displeasing to him. One of his favorite phrases was that literature is "a criticism of life." "We have to turn to poetry to interpret life for us, to console us, to sustain us."

As a classicist and humanist, Arnold believed in an absolute. His constant thesis was that criticism should search out and propagate the *best* that had been thought and said in the world. Those familiar phrases of his, repeated over and over again in his writings, show as nothing else could his faith in absolutes: "see life steadily and see it whole," cultivate "the complete man," "a disinterested endeavor to learn and propagate the best." He defined culture (in *Culture and*

Anarchy) as "a study of perfection," whose function was to "make reason and the will of God prevail." But what is the "best," "perfection," and "the will of God"? For such pragmatical and relativistic questions Arnold would have had only scorn, for he felt sure of his own ground, but of course he could only answer in such generalities as "sweetness and light."

By the recurrent word "disinterestedness" Arnold apparently meant that the critic should hold himself independent of political parties, schools, and cliques—avoid propaganda and a prejudicial view. Certainly Arnold did not believe in indifference to social problems, for he conceived the primary function of literature to be the liberalizing and humanizing of life. Thus in education he championed the study of the humanities (as in his classic lecture on "Literature and Science"), and debated with Thomas Huxley the increasing emphasis upon science.

Though in disposition an aristocrat to his very finger tips, Arnold hated class antagonism. He knew that in his day the aristocrats had lost their strength and that the survivors were aesthetically "barbarians" (*Culture and Anarchy*). He was keenly aware that the middle class, most of whom were "Philistines," were in power for the time being, but he prophesied the rise of the "populace" (i.e., the proletariat). In order to prevent a further vulgarization of society, however, he fought for an educational system that would prepare for a classless and more humanized society. "Culture," he said in *Culture and Anarchy*, "seeks to do away with classes . . . inequality materializes our upper class, vulgarizes our middle class, brutalizes our lower class." He even advocated a sort of State Socialism.

In his later years Arnold wrote *Literature and Dogma* (1873), in which he attempted to liberalize religion; *Mixed Essays* (1879); and the second series of *Essays in Criticism* (1888). His most outstanding critical volumes remain *On Translating Homer* (1861), the first series of *Essays in Criticism* (1865), and *On the Study of Celtic Literature* (1867).

BIBLIOGRAPHY

TEXT

Culture and Anarchy, an essay in political and social criticism; and *Friendship's Garland* . . . New York, 1883.
Discourses in America, with notes by F. R. Tomlinson. New York, 1924.
Essays in Criticism. First and second series complete. Home library. New York, 1902.
Essays in Criticism, with an introduction by E. J. O'Brien. Third series. Boston, 1910.

CRITICISM

Dawson, William Harbutt, *Matthew Arnold and His Relation to the Thought of Our Time.* New York, 1904.

Elias, Otto, *Matthew Arnolds politische Grundanschauungen.* Leipzig, 1931.

Garrod, Heathcote William, *Poetry and the Criticism of Life.* Harvard University Press, 1931.

Harvey, Charles H., *Matthew Arnold, a Critic of the Victorian Period.* London, 1931.

James, Henry, *Views and Reviews* . . . introduction by LeRoy Phillips. Boston, 1908.

Kelman, John, *Prophets of Yesterday and Their Message for Today.* Harvard University Press, 1924.

Kelso, Alexander P., *Matthew Arnold on Continental Life and Literature.* Oxford, 1914. (The Matthew Arnold Memorial prize essay, 1913.)

Orrick, James Bentley, *Matthew Arnold and Goethe.* London, 1928.

Renwanz, Johannes, *Matthew Arnold und Deutschland.* Griefswald, 1927.

Sells, Iris Esther [Robertson], *Matthew Arnold and France.* New York, 1935.

Shafer, Robert, *Christianity and Naturalism;* essays in criticism. Second series. Yale University Press, 1926.

Sherman, Stuart Pratt, *Matthew Arnold, How to Know Him.* Indianapolis, 1917.

THE FUNCTION OF CRITICISM AT THE PRESENT TIME (*selection*)[1]

1864

. . . It is of the last importance that English criticism should clearly discern what rule for its course, in order to avail itself of the field now opening to it and to produce fruit for the future, it ought to take. The rule may be summed up in one word—*disinterestedness.* And how is criticism to show disinterestedness? By keeping aloof from what is called "the practical view of things"; by resolutely following the law of its own nature, which is to be a free play of the mind on all subjects which it touches. By steadily refusing to lend itself to any of those ulterior, political, practical considerations about ideas, which plenty of people will be sure to attach to them, which perhaps ought often to be attached to them, which in this country at any rate are certain to be attached to them quite sufficiently, but which criticism has

[1]Originally published in the *National Review*, November, 1864. This early essay contains the fundamental ideas on which Arnold constructed his whole critical theory.

really nothing to do with. Its business is, as I have said, simply
to know the best that is known and thought in the world, and by
in its turn making this known, to create a current of true and
fresh ideas. Its business is to do this with inflexible honesty, with
due ability; but its business is to do no more, and to leave alone
all questions of practical consequences and applications, questions which will never fail to have due prominence given to
them. Else criticism, besides being really false to its own nature,
merely continues in the old rut which it has hitherto followed in
this country, and will certainly miss the chance now given to it.
For what is at present the bane of criticism in this country? It
is that practical considerations cling to it and stifle it. It sub-
serves interests not its own. Our organs of criticism are organs of
men and parties having practical ends to serve, and with them
those practical ends are the first thing and the play of mind the
second; so much play of mind as is compatible with the prosecu-
tion of those practical ends is all that is wanted. An organ like
the *Revue des deux mondes*, having for its main function to understand and utter the best that is known and thought in the world,
existing, it may be said, as just an organ for a free play of the
mind, we have not. But we have the *Edinburgh Review*, existing
as an organ of the old Whigs, and for as much play of the mind
as may suit its being that; we have the *Quarterly Review*, existing
as an organ of the Tories, and for as much play of mind as may
suit its being that; we have the *British Quarterly Review*, existing as
an organ of the political Dissenters, and for as much play of
mind as may suit its being that; we have the *Times*, existing as an
organ of the common, satisfied, well-to-do Englishman, and for
as much play of mind as may suit its being that. And so on
through all the various fractions, political and religious, of our
society; every fraction has, as such, its organ of criticism, but the
notion of combining all fractions in the common pleasure of a
free disinterested play of mind meets with no favor. Directly this
play of mind wants to have more scope, and to forget the pressure
of practical considerations a little, it is checked, it is made to feel
the chain. We saw this the other day in the extinction, so much
to be regretted, of the *Home and Foreign Review*.[2] Perhaps in no
organ of criticism in this country was there so much knowledge,
so much play of mind; but these could not save it. The *Dublin
Review* subordinates play of mind to the practical business of Eng-

2Published 1862–1864.

lish and Irish Catholicism, and lives. It must needs be that men should act in sects and parties, that each of these sects and parties should have its organ, and should make this organ subserve the interests of its action; but it would be well, too, that there should be a criticism, not the minister of these interests, not their enemy, but absolutely and entirely independent of them. No other criticism will ever attain any real authority or make any real way towards its end—the creating a current of true and fresh ideas.

It is because criticism has so little kept in the pure intellectual sphere, has so little detached itself from practice, has been so directly polemical and controversial, that it has so ill accomplished, in this country, its best spiritual work; which is to keep man from a self-satisfaction which is retarding and vulgarizing, to lead him towards perfection, by making his mind dwell upon what is excellent in itself, and the absolute beauty and fitness of things. A polemical practical criticism makes men blind even to the ideal imperfection of their practice, makes them willingly assert its ideal perfection, in order the better to secure it against attack; and clearly this is narrowing and baneful for them. If they were reassured on the practical side, speculative considerations of ideal perfection they might be brought to entertain, and their spiritual horizon would thus gradually widen. Sir Charles Adderley[3] says to the Warwickshire farmers:

"Talk of the improvement of breed! Why, the race we ourselves represent, the men and women, the old Anglo-Saxon race, are the best breed in the whole world. . . . The absence of a too enervating climate, too unclouded skies, and a too luxurious nature, has produced so vigorous a race of people, and has rendered us so superior to all the world."

Mr. Roebuck[4] says to the Sheffield cutlers:

"I look around me and ask what is the state of England? Is not property safe? Is not every man able to say what he likes? Can you not walk from one end of England to the other in perfect security? I ask you whether, the world over or in past history, there is anything like it? Nothing. I pray that our unrivaled happiness may last."

Now obviously there is a peril for poor human nature in words and thoughts of such exuberant self-satisfaction, until we find ourselves safe in the streets of the Celestial City.

[3]A Conservative Member of Parliament, later Lord Norton.
[4]Member of Parliament, for Sheffield, a radical and Benthamite.

Das wenige verschwindet leicht dem Blicke
Der vorwärts sieht, wie viel noch übrig bleibt—[5]

says Goethe; "the little that is done seems nothing when we look
forward and see how much we have yet to do." Clearly this is a
better line of reflection for weak humanity, so long as it remains
on this earthly field of labor and trial.

But neither Sir Charles Adderley nor Mr. Roebuck is by nature
inaccessible to considerations of this sort. They only lose sight of
them owing to the controversial life we all lead, and the practical
form which all speculation takes with us. They have in view opponents whose aim is not ideal, but practical; and in their zeal to
uphold their own practice against these innovators, they go so far
as even to attribute to this practice an ideal perfection. Somebody has been wanting to introduce a six-pound franchise, or to
abolish church rates, or to collect agricultural statistics by force,
or to diminish local self-government. How natural, in reply to
such proposals, very likely improper or ill-timed, to go a little
beyond the mark and to say stoutly, "Such a race of people as we
stand, so superior to all the world! The old Anglo-Saxon race,
the best breed in the whole world! I pray that our unrivaled happiness may last! I ask you whether, the world over or in past
history, there is anything like it?" And so long as criticism answers this dithyramb by insisting that the old Anglo-Saxon race
would be still more superior to all others if it had no church rates,
or that our unrivaled happiness would last yet longer with a six-
pound franchise, so long will the strain, "The best breed in the
whole world!" swell louder and louder, everything ideal and refining will be lost out of sight, and both the assailed and their
critics will remain in a sphere, to say the truth, perfectly un-
vital, a sphere in which spiritual progression is impossible. But
let criticism leave church rates and the franchise alone, and in
the most candid spirit, without a single lurking thought of practical innovation, confront with our dithyramb this paragraph on
which I stumbled in a newspaper immediately after reading
Mr. Roebuck:

"A shocking child murder has just been committed at Notting-
ham. A girl named Wragg left the workhouse there on Saturday
morning with her young illegitimate child. The child was soon
afterwards found dead on Mapperly Hills, having been strangled.
Wragg is in custody."

[5]*Iphigenie auf Tauris*, I, ii.

Nothing but that; but, in juxtaposition with the absolute eulogies of Sir Charles Adderley and Mr. Roebuck, how eloquent, how suggestive are those few lines! "Our old Anglo-Saxon breed, the best in the whole world!"—how much that is harsh and ill-favored there is in this best! *Wragg!* If we are to talk of ideal perfection, of "the best in the whole world," has anyone reflected what a touch of grossness in our race, what an original short-coming in the more delicate spiritual perceptions, is shown by the natural growth amongst us of such hideous names—Higginbot-tom, Stiggins, Bugg! In Ionia and Attica they were luckier in this respect than "the best race in the world"; by the Ilissus there was no Wragg, poor thing! And "our unrivaled happiness"—what an element of grimness, bareness, and hideousness mixes with it and blurs it; the workhouse, the dismal Mapperly Hills—how dismal those who have seen them will remember—the gloom, the smoke, the cold, the strangled illegitimate child! "I ask you whether, the world over or in past history, there is any-thing like it?" Perhaps not, one is inclined to answer; but at any rate, in that case, the world is very much to be pitied. And the final touch—short, bleak and inhuman: *Wragg is in custody.* The sex lost in the confusion of our unrivaled happiness; or (shall I say?) the superfluous Christian name lopped off by the straight-forward vigor of our old Anglo-Saxon breed! There is profit for the spirit in such contrasts as this; criticism serves the cause of perfection by establishing them. By eluding sterile conflict, by refusing to remain in the sphere where alone narrow and relative conceptions have any worth and validity, criticism may dimin-ish its momentary importance, but only in this way has it a chance of gaining admittance for those wider and more perfect conceptions to which all its duty is really owed. Mr. Roebuck will have a poor opinion of an adversary who replies to his de-fiant songs of triumph only by murmuring under his breath, *Wragg is in custody;* but in no other way will these songs of triumph be induced gradually to moderate themselves, to get rid of what in them is excessive and offensive, and to fall into a softer and truer key.

It will be said that it is a very subtle and indirect action which I am thus prescribing for criticism, and that, by embracing in this manner the Indian virtue of detachment and abandoning the sphere of practical life, it condemns itself to a slow and ob-scure work. Slow and obscure it may be, but it is the only proper work of criticism. The mass of mankind will never have any ardent zeal for seeing things as they are; very inadequate ideas will always satisfy them. On these inadequate ideas reposes, and must repose, the general practice of the world. That is as much as saying that whoever sets himself to see things as they are will find himself one of a very small circle; but it is only by this small circle resolutely doing its own work that adequate ideas will ever get current at all. The rush and roar of practical life will always have a dizzying and attracting effect upon the most collected spectator, and tend to draw him into its vortex; most of all will this be the case where that life is so powerful as it is in England. But it is only by remaining collected, and refusing to lend himself to the point of view of the practical man, that the critic can do the practical man any service; and it is only by the greatest sincerity in pursuing his own course, and by at last convincing even the practical man of his sincerity, that he can escape misunderstandings which perpetually threaten him.

For the practical man is not apt for fine distinctions, and yet in these distinctions truth and the highest culture greatly find their account. But it is not easy to lead a practical man—unless you reassure him as to your practical intentions, you have no chance of leading him—to see that a thing which he has always been used to look at from one side only, which he greatly values, and which, looked at from that side, quite deserves, perhaps, all the prizing and admiring which he bestows upon it—that this thing, looked at from another side, may appear much less beneficent and beautiful, and yet retain all its claims to our practical allegiance. Where shall we find language innocent enough, how shall we make the spotless purity of our intentions evident enough, to enable us to say to the political Englishman that the British Constitution itself, which, seen from the practical side, looks such a magnificent organ of progress and virtue, seen from the speculative side—with its compromises, its love of facts, its horror of theory, its studied avoidance of clear thoughts—that, seen from this side, our august Constitution sometimes looks—forgive me, shade of Lord Somers![6]—a colossal machine for the manufacture of Philistines? How is Cobbett[7] to say this and not be misunderstood, blackened as he is with the smoke of a lifelong conflict in the field of political practice? how is Mr. Carlyle to

[6]An eighteenth-century statesman, noted as a defender of the Constitution.
[7]William Cobbett (1762–1835), English political writer.

say it and not be misunderstood, after his furious raid into this field with his *Latter-Day Pamphlets?* how is Mr. Ruskin, after his pugnacious political economy? I say, the critic must keep out of the region of immediate practice in the political, social, humanitarian sphere, if he wants to make a beginning for that more free speculative treatment of things, which may perhaps one day make its benefits felt even in this sphere, but in a natural and thence irresistible manner.

Do what he will, however, the critic will still remain exposed to frequent misunderstandings, and nowhere so much as in this country. For here people are particularly indisposed even to comprehend that without this free disinterested treatment of things truth and the highest culture are out of the question. So immersed are they in practical life, so accustomed to take all their notions from this life and its processes, that they are apt to think that truth and culture themselves can be reached by the processes of this life, and that it is an impertinent singularity to think of reaching them in any other. "We are all *terrae filii*,"[8] cries their eloquent advocate; "all Philistines together. Away with the notion of proceeding by any other course than the course dear to the Philistines; let us have a social movement, let us organize and combine a party to pursue truth and new thought, let us call it *the liberal party*, and let us all stick to each other, and back each other up. Let us have no nonsense about independent criticism, and intellectual delicacy, and the few and the many. Don't let us trouble ourselves about foreign thought; we shall invent the whole thing for ourselves as we go along. If one of us speaks well, applaud him; if one of us speaks ill, applaud him too; we are all in the same movement, we are all liberals, we are all in pursuit of truth." In this way the pursuit of truth becomes really a social, practical, pleasurable affair, almost requiring a chairman, a secretary, and advertisements; with the excitement of an occasional scandal, with a little resistance to give the happy sense of difficulty overcome; but, in general, plenty of bustle and very little thought. To act is so easy, as Goethe says; to think is so hard! It is true that the critic has many temptations to go with the stream, to make one of the party movement, one of these *terrae filii;* it seems ungracious to refuse to be a *terrae filius*, when so many excellent people are; but the critic's duty is to refuse, or, if resistance is vain, at least to cry with Obermann:[9] *Périssons en résistant.* . . .

<hr />

[8] Children of Earth.   [9] The hero of a work by Senancour (1804).

THE STUDY OF POETRY (*selections*)[1]
1880

"The future of poetry is immense, because in poetry, where
it is worthy of its high destinies, our race, as time goes on, will
find an ever surer and surer stay. There is not a creed which is
not shaken, not an accredited dogma which is not shown to be
questionable, not a received tradition which does not threaten
to dissolve. Our religion has materialized itself in the fact, in
the supposed fact; it has attached its emotion to the fact, and
now the fact is failing it. But for poetry the idea is everything;
the rest is a world of illusion, of divine illusion. Poetry attaches
its emotion to the idea; the idea *is* the fact. The strongest part
of our religion today is its unconscious poetry." [2]

Let me be permitted to quote these words of my own, as
uttering the thought which should, in my opinion, go with us
and govern us in all our study of poetry. In the present work
it is the course of one great contributory stream to the world-
river of poetry that we are invited to follow. We are here invited to trace the stream of English poetry. But whether we
set ourselves, as here, to follow only one of the several streams
that make the mighty river of poetry, or whether we seek to
know them all, our governing thought should be the same. We
should conceive of poetry worthily, and more highly than it
has been the custom to conceive of it. We should conceive of it
as capable of higher uses, and called to higher destinies, than
those which in general men have assigned to it hitherto. More
and more mankind will discover that we have to turn to poetry
to interpret life for us, to console us, to sustain us. Without
poetry, our science will appear incomplete; and most of what
now passes with us for religion and philosophy will be replaced
by poetry. Science, I say, will appear incomplete without it.
For finely and truly does Wordsworth call poetry "the impassioned expression which is in the countenance of all science";
and what is a countenance without its expression? Again,
Wordsworth finely and truly calls poetry "the breath and finer
spirit of all knowledge": our religion, parading evidences such
as those on which the popular mind relies now; our philosophy,

[1]Arnold contributed this essay as a general introduction to T. H. Ward's edition
of *English Poets* (1880). It is famous for the doctrine of poetic "touchstones" as a
guide to taste.

[2]Quoted from Arnold's Introduction to *The Hundred Greatest Men*.

pluming itself on its reasonings about causation and finite and infinite being; what are they but the shadows and dreams and false shows of knowledge? The day will come when we shall wonder at ourselves for having trusted to them, for having taken them seriously; and the more we perceive their hollowness, the more we shall prize "the breath and finer spirit of knowledge" offered to us by poetry.

But if we conceive thus highly of the destinies of poetry, we must also set our standard for poetry high, since poetry, to be capable of fulfilling such high destinies, must be poetry of a high order of excellence. We must accustom ourselves to a high standard and to a strict judgment. Sainte-Beuve relates that Napoleon one day said, when somebody was spoken of in his presence as a charlatan: "Charlatan as much as you please; but where is there *not* charlatanism?"—"Yes," answers Sainte-Beuve, "in politics, in the art of governing mankind, that is perhaps true. But in the order of thought, in art, the glory, the eternal honor is that charlatanism shall find no entrance; herein lies the inviolableness of that noble portion of man's being." It is admirably said, and let us hold fast to it. In poetry, which is thought and art in one, it is the glory, the eternal honor, that charlatanism shall find no entrance; that this noble sphere be kept inviolate and inviolable. Charlatanism is for confusing or obliterating the distinctions between excellent and inferior, sound and unsound or only half-sound, true and untrue or only half-true. It is charlatanism, conscious or unconscious, whenever we confuse or obliterate these. And in poetry, more than anywhere else, it is unpermissible to confuse or obliterate them. For in poetry the distinction between excellent and inferior, sound and unsound or only half-sound, true and untrue or only half-true, is of paramount importance. It is of paramount importance because of the high destinies of poetry. In poetry, as a criticism of life under the conditions fixed for such a criticism by the laws of poetic truth and poetic beauty, the spirit of our race will find, we have said, as time goes on and as other helps fail, its consolation and stay. But the consolation and stay will be of power in proportion to the power of the criticism of life. And the criticism of life will be of power in proportion as the poetry conveying it is excellent rather than inferior, sound rather than unsound or half-sound, true rather than untrue or half-true.

The best poetry is what we want; the best poetry will be found to have a power of forming, sustaining, and delighting us as nothing else can. A clearer, deeper sense of the best in poetry, and of the strength and joy to be drawn from it, is the most precious benefit which we can gather from a poetical collection such as the present. And yet in the very nature and conduct of such a collection there is inevitably something which tends to obscure in us the consciousness of what our benefit should be and to distract us from the pursuit of it. We should therefore steadily set it before our minds at the outset and should compel ourselves to revert constantly to the thought of it as we proceed.

Yes; constantly in reading poetry, a sense for the best, the really excellent, and of the strength and joy to be drawn from it should be present in our minds and should govern our estimate of what we read. But this real estimate, the only true one, is liable to be superseded, if we are not watchful, by two other kinds of estimate, the historic estimate and the personal estimate, both of which are fallacious. A poet or a poem may count to us historically, they may count to us on grounds personal to ourselves, and they may count to us really. They may count to us historically. The course of development of a nation's language, thought, and poetry is profoundly interesting; and by regarding a poet's work as a stage in this course of development we may easily bring ourselves to make it of more importance as poetry than in itself it really is, we may come to use a language of quite exaggerated praise in criticizing it; in short, to overrate it. So arises in our poetic judgments the fallacy caused by the estimate which we may call historic. Then, again, a poet or a poem may count to us on grounds personal to ourselves. Our personal affinities, likings, and circumstances have great power to sway our estimate of this or that poet's work and to make us attach more importance to it as poetry than in itself it really possesses, because to us it is, or has been, of high importance. Here also we overrate the object of our interest, and apply to it a language of praise which is quite exaggerated. And thus we get the source of a second fallacy in our poetic judgments—the fallacy caused by an estimate which we may call personal.

Both fallacies are natural. It is evident how naturally the study of the history and development of a poetry may incline a man to pause over reputations and works once conspicuous but now obscure, and to quarrel with a careless public for skipping, in obedience to mere tradition and habit, from one famous name or work in its national poetry to another, ignorant of what it misses, and of the reason for keeping what it keeps, and of the whole process of growth in its poetry. The French have become diligent students of their own early poetry, which they long neglected; the study makes many of them dissatisfied with their so-called classical poetry, the court tragedy of the seventeenth century, a poetry which Pellisson[3] long ago reproached with its want of the true poetic stamp, with its *politesse stérile et rampante*,[4] but which nevertheless has reigned in France as absolutely as if it had been the perfection of classical poetry indeed. The dissatisfaction is natural; yet a lively and accomplished critic, M. Charles d'Héricault, the editor of Clément Marot,[5] goes too far when he says that "the cloud of glory playing round a classic is a mist as dangerous to the future of a literature as it is intolerable for the purposes of history." "It hinders," he goes on, "it hinders us from seeing more than one single point, the culminating and exceptional point, the summary, fictitious and arbitrary, of a thought and of a work. It substitutes a halo for a physiognomy, it puts a statue where there was once a man, and, hiding from us all trace of the labor, the attempts, the weaknesses, the failures, it claims not study but veneration; it does not show us how the thing is done, it imposes upon us a model. Above all, for the historian this creation of classic personages is inadmissible; for it withdraws the poet from his time, from his proper life, it breaks historical relationships, it blinds criticism by conventional admiration, and renders the investigation of literary origins unacceptable. It gives us a human personage no longer, but a God seated immovable amidst His perfect work, like Jupiter on Olympus; and hardly will it be possible for the young student, to whom such work is exhibited at such a distance from him, to believe that it did not issue ready made from that divine head."

All this is brilliantly and tellingly said, but we must plead for a distinction. Everything depends on the reality of a poet's classic character. If he is a dubious classic, let us sift him; if he

---

[3] Paul Pellisson (1624–1693), poet of the time of Louis XIV.
[4] "Barren and cringing civility."
[5] French poet (1467–1544), famous for his epigrams and familiar verse.

is a false classic, let us explode him. But if he is a real classic, if his work belongs to the class of the very best (for this is the true and right meaning of the word *classic, classical*), then the great thing for us is to feel and enjoy his work as deeply as ever we can, and to appreciate the wide difference between it and all work which has not the same high character. This is what is salutary, this is what is formative; this is the great benefit to be got from the study of poetry. Everything which interferes with it, which hinders it, is injurious. True, we must read our classic with open eyes and not with eyes blinded with superstition; we must perceive when his work comes short, when it drops out of the class of the very best, and we must rate it, in such cases, at its proper value. But the use of this negative criticism is not in itself, it is entirely in its enabling us to have a clearer sense and a deeper enjoyment of what is truly excellent. To trace the labor, the attempts, the weaknesses, the failures of a genuine classic, to acquaint one's self with his time and his life and his historical relationships, is mere literary dilettantism unless it has that clear sense and deeper enjoyment for its end. It may be said that the more we know about a classic the better we shall enjoy him; and, if we lived as long as Methuselah and had all of us heads of perfect clearness and wills of perfect steadfastness, this might be true in fact as it is plausible in theory. But the case here is much the same as the case with the Greek and Latin studies of our schoolboys. The elaborate philological groundwork which we require them to lay is in theory an admirable preparation for appreciating the Greek and Latin authors worthily. The more thoroughly we lay the groundwork, the better we shall be able, it may be said, to enjoy the authors. True, if time were not so short, and schoolboys' wits not so soon tired and their power of attention exhausted; only, as it is, the elaborate philological preparation goes on, but the authors are little known and less enjoyed. So with the investigator of "historic origins" in poetry. He ought to enjoy the true classic all the better for his investigations; he often is distracted from the enjoyment of the best, and with the less good he overbusies himself, and is prone to overrate it in proportion to the trouble which it has cost him. . . .

Indeed there can be no more useful help for discovering what poetry belongs to the class of the truly excellent, and can therefore do us most good, than to have always in one's mind lines and expressions of the great masters, and to apply them as a touchstone to other poetry. Of course we are not to require this other poetry to resemble them; it may be very dissimilar. But if we have any tact we shall find them, when we have lodged them well in our minds, an infallible touchstone for detecting the presence or absence of high poetic quality, and also the degree of this quality, in all other poetry which we may place beside them. Short passages, even single lines, will serve our turn quite sufficiently. Take the two lines which I have just quoted from Homer, the poet's comment on Helen's mention of her brothers;[6]—or take his

$$\text{Ἀ δειλώ, τί σφῶϊ δόμεν Πηλῆϊ ἄνακτι}$$
$$\text{θνητῷ; ὑμεῖς δ᾿ ἐστὸν ἀγήρω τ᾿ ἀθανάτω τε.}$$
$$\text{ἦ ἵνα δυστήνοισι μετ᾿ ἀνδράσιν ἄλγε᾿ ἔχητον;}[7]$$

the address of Zeus to the horses of Peleus;—or take finally his

$$\text{Καὶ σέ, γέρον; τὸ πρὶν μὲν ἀκούομεν ὄλβιον εἶναι.}[8]$$

the words of Achilles to Priam, a suppliant before him. Take that incomparable line and a half of Dante, Ugolino's tremendous words—

> Io no piangeva; sì dentro impietrai.
> Piangevan elli . . .[9]

take the lovely words of Beatrice to Vergil—

> Io son fatta da Dio, sua mercè, tale,
> Che la vostra miseria non mi tange,
> Nè fiamma d'esto incendio non m'assale . . .[10]

take the simple, but perfect, single line—

> In la sua volontade è nostra pace.[11]

[6] "So said she; they long since in Earth's soft arms were reposing,
    There, in their own dear land, their fatherland, Lacedaemon."
(*Iliad*, III, 243–244; translated by Dr. Hawtrey. This and the following five notes are Arnold's.)
[7] "Ah, unhappy pair, why gave we you to King Peleus, to a mortal? but ye are without old age, and immortal. Was it that with men born to misery ye might have sorrow?" (*Iliad*, XVII, 443–445).
[8] "Nay, and thou too, old man, in former days wast, as we hear, happy" (*Iliad*, XXIV, 543).
[9] "I wailed not, so of stone grew I within; *they* wailed" (*Inferno*, XXXIII, 39–40).
[10] "Of such sort hath God, thanked be His mercy, made me, that your misery toucheth me not, neither doth the flame of this fire strike me" (*Inferno*, II, 91–93).
[11] "In His will is our peace" (*Paradiso*, III, 85).

Take of Shakespeare a line or two of Henry the Fourth's expostulation with sleep—

>   Wilt thou upon the high and giddy mast
>   Seal up the ship-boy's eyes, and rock his brains
>   In cradle of the rude imperious surge . . .[12]

and take, as well, Hamlet's dying request to Horatio—

>   If thou didst ever hold me in thy heart,
>   Absent thee from felicity awhile,
>   And in this harsh world draw thy breath in pain
>   To tell my story . . .[13]

Take of Milton that Miltonic passage—

>   Darkened so, yet shone
>   Above them all the archangel; but his face
>   Deep scars of thunder had intrenched, and care
>   Sat on his faded cheek . . .[14]

add two such lines as—

>   And courage never to submit or yield
>   And what is else not to be overcome . . .[15]

and finish with the exquisite close to the loss of Proserpine, the loss

>   . . . which cost Ceres all that pain
>   To seek her through the world.[16]

These few lines, if we have tact and can use them, are enough even of themselves to keep clear and sound our judgments about poetry, to save us from fallacious estimates of it, to conduct us to a real estimate.

The specimens I have quoted differ widely from one another, but they have in common this: the possession of the very highest poetical quality. If we are thoroughly penetrated by their power, we shall find that we have acquired a sense enabling us, whatever poetry may be laid before us, to feel the degree in which a high poetical quality is present or wanting there. Critics give themselves great labor to draw out what in the abstract constitutes the characters of a high quality of poetry. It is much better simply to have recourse to concrete examples; —to take specimens of poetry of the high, the very highest

---

[12]*Henry IV*, Pt. ii, iii, i, 18–20.   [13]*Hamlet*, v, ii, 357–360.
[14]*Paradise Lost*, i, 599–602.   [15]*Ibid.*, i, 108–109.   [16]*Ibid.*, iv, 271–272.

quality, and to say: The characters of a high quality of poetry
are what is expressed *there*. They are far better recognized by
being felt in the verse of the master than by being perused in
the prose of the critic. Nevertheless if we are urgently pressed
to give some critical account of them, we may safely, perhaps,
venture on laying down, not indeed how and why the characters
arise, but where and in what they arise. They are in the matter
and substance of the poetry, and they are in its manner and
style. Both of these, the substance and matter on the one hand,
the style and manner on the other, have a mark, an accent, of
high beauty, worth, and power. But if we are asked to define
this mark and accent in the abstract, our answer must be: No,
for we should thereby be darkening the question, not clearing it.
The mark and accent are as given by the substance and matter
of that poetry, by the style and manner of that poetry, and of all
other poetry which is akin to it in quality.

Only one thing we may add as to the substance and matter
of poetry, guiding ourselves by Aristotle's profound observation that the superiority of poetry over history consists in its
possessing a higher truth and a higher seriousness ($\phi\iota\lambda\omicron\sigma o$-
$\phi\dot{\omega}\tau\epsilon\rho o\nu\ \kappa\alpha\dot{\iota}\ \sigma\pi o\upsilon\delta\alpha\iota\acute{o}\tau\epsilon\rho o\nu$). Let us add, therefore, to what we
have said, this: that the substance and matter of the best
poetry acquire their special character from possessing, in an
eminent degree, truth and seriousness. We may add yet further, what is in itself evident, that to the style and manner of
the best poetry their special character, their accent, is given
by their diction, and, even yet more, by their movement. And
though we distinguish between the two characters, the two
accents, of superiority, yet they are nevertheless vitally connected one with the other. The superior character of truth and
seriousness, in the matter and substance of the best poetry, is
inseparable from the superiority of diction and movement
marking its style and manner. The two superiorities are closely
related and are in steadfast proportion one to the other. So
far as high poetic truth and seriousness are wanting to a poet's
matter and substance, so far also, we may be sure, will a high
poetic stamp of diction and movement be wanting to his style
and manner. In proportion as this high stamp of diction and
movement, again, is absent from a poet's style and manner, we
shall find, also, that high poetic truth and seriousness are absent from his substance and matter. . . .

FRIEDRICH WILHELM NIETZSCHE

(1844–1900)

oᘒoooᘒo

THOUGH THE VERY NAME OF FRIEDRICH NIETZSCHE, the antichrist German egoist who finally died a madman, is anathema to a multitude of American people, few writers of the nineteenth century have more profoundly influenced—or it may be more luckily anticipated—the intellectual temper of the twentieth century, with its capitalistic "will to power," its moral disillusionment, and its pessimistic literature. Nietzsche is in the blood of the Frank Norrises, the D. H. Lawrences, the H. L. Menckens, the George Bernard Shaws, and nearly all the anti-humanistic critics.

A mystic[1] and an opponent of rationalism and science, Nietzsche has, paradoxically, become associated with the Bismarck "blood-and-iron" philosophy, but as Havelock Ellis has remarked, "Nietzsche was of the tribe of the great cosmopolitan Germans of the eighteenth century. He was not patriotic, he had loathing rather than admiration for Germanism, France was for him the great home of culture, and he desired to be a good European rather than a good German."[2] These fundamental contradictions in Nietzsche's life, thought, and reputation make it almost foolhardy to attempt a brief explanation of his philosophy and aesthetics. Indeed, as Kennedy has shown,[3] Nietzsche passed through several distinct periods of development—and final degeneration.

The Birth of Tragedy from the Spirit of Music (usually referred to as *The Birth of Tragedy*) was written at the time when Nietzsche still expected through Wagner a Dionysiac rebirth of tragic art; but after Wagner wrote *Parzifal*, Nietzsche renounced him as too German and too Christian—the latter he could never forgive his former idol. In his autobiography, *Ecce Homo*, Nietzsche claims that he really meant himself when he used Wagner's name in *The Birth of Tragedy*. But his essential philosophy was unchanged, for in the autobiography he

---

[1] In *Ecce Homo* Nietzsche claims that he is not a mystic, but certainly his writings—especially *Thus Spake Zarathustra*—are extraordinarily mystical in style.

[2] Havelock Ellis, *Affirmations* (Boston, 1915), p. xi. Cf. *Ecce Homo* (Modern Library edition, 1927), pp. 32 ff.

[3] J. M. Kennedy, *The Quintessence of Nietzsche* (New York, 1910), pp. 120 ff.

seemed to think, as Knight says,[4] that "the Greeks got rid of pessimism" by means of the Dionysiac "will to life." And it is not difficult to reconcile this view with Zarathustra's teachings of the "superman" and the perfectibility of man through self-assertion.

The well-known modern anthropologist, Miss Ruth Benedict, has explained Nietzsche's terms "Dionysian" and "Apollonian" in this illuminating manner:

> The basic contrast between the Pueblos and the other [aboriginal] cultures of North America is the contrast that is named and described by Nietzsche in his studies of Greek tragedy. He discusses two diametrically opposed ways of arriving at the values of existence. The Dionysian pursues them through "the annihilation of the ordinary bounds and limits of existence"; he seeks to attain in his most valued moments escape from the boundaries imposed upon him by his five senses, to break through into another order of experience. The desire of the Dionysian, in personal experience or in ritual, is to press through it toward a certain psychological state, to achieve excess. The closest analogy to the emotions he seeks is drunkenness, and he values the illuminations of frenzy. With Blake, he believes "the path of excess leads to the palace of wisdom." The Apollonian distrusts all this, and has often little idea of the nature of such experiences. He finds means to outlaw them from his conscious life. He "knows but one law, measure in the Hellenic sense." He keeps the middle of the road, stays within the known map, does not meddle with disruptive psychological states. In Nietzsche's fine phrase, even in the exaltation of the dance he "remains what he is, and retains his civic name."[5]

The following selections from Clifton Fadiman's brilliant translation of *The Birth of Tragedy* contain the core of Nietzsche's doctrine, with a brief insight into his theory of the disintegration of Greek tragedy through Socratic rationalism and intellectual (i.e., decadent) Euripidean comedy.

BIBLIOGRAPHY

TEXT

Werke. 15 vols. Leipzig, 1904–1907.

[4] A. H. J. Knight, *Some Aspects of the Life and Works of Nietzsche* (Cambridge, England, 1933), p. 75. Knight says (p. 75, footnote) that both Nietzsche and the Greeks were pessimistic.

[5] Ruth Benedict, *Patterns of Culture* (Boston and New York, 1934), pp. 78–79; quoted by special permission of Houghton Mifflin Company.

TRANSLATIONS

Complete Works, authorized English translation, ed. by Oscar Levy.
18 vols. Edinburgh, 1909–1914. Vol. I, *The Birth of Tragedy*, tr.
by William A. Haussmann.
Ecce Homo and *The Birth of Tragedy*, tr. by Clifton Fadiman. New
York, [1927].

CRITICISM

Bluhm, Heinz, "Nietzsche's Early Views on Literary Studies," *Monat-shefte fur die Unterricht*, XXVII, 259–267.
Brandes, Georg, *Friedrich Nietzsche*, tr. by A. G. Chater. New York,
1914.
Castiglioni, M., *Il poema eroico di Federico Nietzsche*. Torino, 1924.
Ellis, Havelock, *Affirmations*. Second series. Boston, 1915, pp. 1–85.
Fairley, Barker, "Nietzsche and Goethe," *Bulletin* of the John Ryland
Library, XVIII, 298–334 (1934).
——, "Nietzsche and the Poetic Impulse," *Bulletin* of the John Ryland
Library, XIX, 344–361 (1936). Subtle analysis delineating (1) the
incompatibility of the poetic impulse in Nietzsche with the philo-
sophical and the resultant "vulnerability" of *Zarathustra;* and (2)
this cleavage in his works as a possible clue to his peculiar tension
of character.
Filser, Benno, *Die Aesthetik Nietzsches in der Geburt der Tragödie*. Passau,
[1915].
Graff, W. L., "Nietzsche and Goethe," *Open Court*, L, 193–210 (1936).
Knight, A. H. J., *Some Aspects of the Life and Work of Nietzsche*, and par-
ticularly of his connection with Greek literature and thought. Cam-
bridge [England], 1933. See especially chap. IV, "The Philosophy of
Dionysus," pp. 67–92.
Kennedy, J. M., *The Quintessence of Nietzsche*. New York, 1910.
Ludovici, Anthony, *Nietzsche and Art*. Boston, 1912.
Rehder, Helmut, "Leben und Geist in Nietzsches Lyrik," *Dichtung und
Volkstum* (Euphorion) XXXVII, 187–219 (1936).
Shestov, Leo, *Dostojewski und Nietzsche*. Cologne, 1924.
——, *Tolstoi and Nietzsche*. London, 1923.

THE BIRTH OF TRAGEDY (*selections*)[1]

1871

I

We shall do a great deal for the science of aesthetics, once we
perceive not merely by logical inference, but with the immediate

[1]Reprinted by courtesy of The Modern Library. The translation is by Clifton
Fadiman.

certainty of intuition, that the continuous development of art is bound up with the *Apollonian* and *Dionysian* duality: just as procreation depends on the duality of the sexes, involving perpetual strife with only periodically intervening reconciliations. The terms Dionysian and Apollonian we borrow from the Greeks, who disclose to the discerning mind the profound mysteries of their view of art, not, to be sure, in concepts, but in the impressively clear figures of their gods. Through Apollo and Dionysus, the two art-deities of the Greeks, we come to recognize that in the Greek world there existed a sharp opposition, in origin and aims, between the Apollonian art of sculpture, and the non-plastic, Dionysian, art of music. These two distinct tendencies run parallel to each other, for the most part openly at variance; and they continually incite each other to new and more powerful births, which perpetuate an antagonism, only superficially reconciled by the common term "Art"; till at last, by a metaphysical miracle of the Hellenic will, they appear coupled with each other, and through this coupling eventually generate the art-product, equally Dionysian and Apollonian, of Attic tragedy.

In order to grasp these two tendencies, let us first conceive of them as the separate art-worlds of *dreams* and *drunkenness*. These physiological phenomena present a contrast analogous to that existing between the Apollonian and the Dionysian. It was in dreams, says Lucretius, that the glorious divine figures first appeared to the souls of men; in dreams the great shaper beheld the splendid corporeal structure of superhuman beings; and the Hellenic poet, if questioned about the mysteries of poetic inspiration, would likewise have suggested dreams and he might have given an explanation like that of Hans Sachs in the *Mastersingers:*

> *"Mein Freund, das grad' ist Dichters Werk,*
> *dess er sein Träumen deut' und merk'.*
> *Glaubt mir, des Menschen wahrster Wahn*
> *wird ihm im Traume aufgethan:*
> *all' Dichtkunst und Poëterei*
> *ist nichts als Wahrtraum-Deuterei."* [2]

[2] "My friend, that is exactly the poet's task, to mark his dreams and to attach meanings to them. Believe me, man's most profound illusions are revealed to him in dreams; and all versifying and poetizing is nothing but an interpretation of them" (Clifton P. Fadiman's translation)

The beautiful appearance of the dream-worlds, in creating which every man is a perfect artist, is the prerequisite of all plastic art, and in fact, as we shall see, of an important part of poetry also. In our dreams we delight in the immediate apprehension of form; all forms speak to us; none are unimportant, none are superfluous. But, when this dream-reality is most intense, we also have, glimmering through it, the sensation of its appearance: at least this is my experience, as to whose frequency, aye normality, I could adduce many proofs, in addition to the sayings of the poets. Indeed, the man of philosophic mind has a presentiment that underneath this reality in which we live and have our being, is concealed another and quite different reality, which, like the first, is an appearance; and Schopenhauer actually indicates as the criterion of philosophical ability the occasional ability to view men and things as mere phantoms or dream-pictures. Thus the aesthetically sensitive man stands in the same relation to the reality of dreams as the philosopher does to the reality of existence; he is a close and willing observer, for these pictures afford him an interpretation of life, and it is by these processes that he trains himself for life. . . .

This joyful necessity of the dream-experience has been embodied by the Greeks in their Apollo; for Apollo, the god of all plastic energies, is at the same time the soothsaying god. He, who (as the etymology of the name indicates) is the "shining one," the deity of light, is also ruler over the fair appearance of the inner world of fantasy. The higher truth, the perfection of these states in contrast to the incompletely intelligible everyday world, this deep consciousness of nature, healing and helping in sleep and dreams, is at the same time the symbolical analogue of the soothsaying faculty and of the arts generally, which make life possible and worth living. But we must also include in our picture of Apollo that delicate boundary, which the dream-picture must not overstep—lest it act pathologically (in which case appearance would impose upon us as pure reality). We must keep in mind that measured restraint, that freedom from the wilder emotions, that philosophical calm of the sculptor god. His eye must be "sunlike," as befits his origin; even when his glance is angry and distempered, the sacredness of his beautiful appearance must still be there. And so, in one sense, we might apply to Apollo the words of Schopenhauer when he speaks of the man wrapped in the veil of Mâyâ:

"Just as in a stormy sea, unbounded in every direction, rising and falling with howling mountainous waves, a sailor sits in a boat and trusts in his frail barque: so in the midst of a world of sorrows the individual sits quietly, supported by and trusting in his *principium individuationis*." [3]   In fact, we might say of Apollo, that in him the unshaken faith in this *principium* and the calm repose of the man wrapped therein receive their sublimest expression; and we might consider Apollo himself as the glorious divine image of the *principium individuationis*, whose gestures and expression tell us of all the joy and wisdom of "appearance," together with its beauty.

In the same work Schopenhauer has depicted for us the terrible *awe* which seizes upon man when he is suddenly unable to account for the cognitive forms of a phenomenon, when the principle of reason in some one of its manifestations seems to admit of an exception. If we add to this awe the blissful ecstasy which rises from the innermost depths of man, aye, of nature, at this very collapse of the *principium individuationis*, we shall gain an insight into the nature of the *Dionysian*, which is brought home to us most intimately perhaps by the analogy of *drunkenness*. It is either under the influence of the narcotic draught, which we hear of in the songs of all primitive men and peoples, or with the potent coming of spring penetrating all nature with joy, that these Dionysian emotions awake, which, as they intensify, cause the subjective to vanish into complete self-forgetfulness. . . .

Under the charm of the Dionysian not only is the union between man and man reaffirmed, but Nature which has become estranged, hostile, or subjugated celebrates once more her reconciliation with her prodigal son, man. Freely earth proffers her gifts, and peacefully the beasts of prey approach from desert and mountain. The chariot of Dionysus is bedecked with flowers and garlands; panthers and tigers pass beneath his yoke. . . .

2

Thus far we have considered the Apollonian and its antithesis, the Dionysian, as artistic energies which burst forth from nature herself, *without the mediation of the human artist;* energies in which nature's art impulses are satisfied in the most immediate and direct way: first, on the one hand, in the pictorial world of

---

[3] *Welt als Wille und Vorstellung*, I, 416.

dreams, whose completeness is not dependent upon the intellectual attitude or the artistic culture of any single being; and,
on the other hand, as drunken reality, which likewise does not
heed the single unit, but even seeks to destroy the individual
and redeem him by a mystic feeling of Oneness. With reference
to these immediate art-states of nature, every artist is an "imitator," that is to say, either an Apollonian artist in dreams, or a
Dionysian artist in ecstasies, or finally—as for example in Greek
tragedy—at once artist in both dreams and ecstasies: so we may
perhaps picture him sinking down in his Dionysian drunkenness and mystical self-abnegation, alone, and apart from the
singing revelers, and we may imagine how now, through Apollonian dream-inspiration, his own state, i.e., his oneness with
the primal nature of the universe, is revealed to him in a *symbolical dream-picture.* . . .

3

The Greek knew and felt the terror and horror of existence.
That he might endure this terror at all, he had to interpose
between himself and life the radiant dream-birth of the Olympians. That overwhelming dismay in the face of the titanic
powers of nature, the Moira enthroned inexorably over all
knowledge, the vulture of the great lover of mankind, Prometheus, the terrible fate of the wise Oedipus, the family curse of the
Atridae which drove Orestes to matricide: in short, that entire
philosophy of the sylvan god, with its mythical exemplars,
which caused the downfall of the melancholy Etruscans—all
this was again and again overcome by the Greeks with the aid
of the Olympian *middle world* of art; or at any rate it was veiled
and withdrawn from sight. It was out of the direst necessity to
live that the Greeks created these gods. Perhaps we may picture
the process to ourselves somewhat as follows: out of the original
Titan thearchy of terror the Olympian thearchy of joy gradually
evolved through the Apollonian impulse towards beauty,
just as roses bud from thorny bushes. How else could this people,
so sensitive, so vehement in its desires, so singularly constituted
for *suffering*, how could they have endured existence if it had
not been revealed to them in their gods, surrounded with a
higher glory? The same impulse which calls art into being,
as the complement and consummation of existence, seducing
one to a continuation of life, was also the cause of the Olympian

world which the Hellenic "will" made use of as a transfiguring mirror. Thus do the gods justify the life of man, in that they themselves live it—the only satisfactory theodicy! Existence under the bright sunshine of such gods is regarded as desirable in itself, and the real *grief* of the Homeric men is caused by parting from it, especially by early parting: so that now, reversing the wisdom of Silenus, we might say of the Greeks that "to die early is worst of all for them, the next worst—some day to die at all." Once heard, it will ring out again; forget not the lament of the short-lived Achilles, mourning the leaflike change and vicissitude of the race of men and the decline of the heroic age. It is not unworthy of the greatest hero to long for a continuation of life, aye, even though he live as a slave. At the Apollonian stage of development, the "will" longs so vehemently for this existence, the Homeric man feels himself so completely at one with it, that lamentation itself becomes a song of praise.

Here we should note that this harmony which is contemplated with such longing by modern man, in fact, this oneness of man with nature (to express which Schiller introduced the technical term "naïve"), is by no means a simple condition, resulting naturally, and as if inevitably. It is not a condition which, like a terrestrial paradise, *must* necessarily be found at the gate of every culture. Only a romantic age could believe this, an age which conceived of the artist in terms of Rousseau's *Émile* and imagined that in Homer it had found such an artist Émile, reared in Nature's bosom. Wherever we meet with the "naïve" in art, we recognize the highest effect of the Apollonian culture, which in the first place has always to overthrow some Titanic empire and slay monsters, and which, through its potent dazzling representations and its pleasurable illusions, must have triumphed over a terrible depth of world-contemplation and a most keen sensitivity to suffering. But how seldom do we attain to the naïve—that complete absorption in the beauty of appearance! And hence how inexpressibly sublime is *Homer*, who, as individual being, bears the same relation to this Apollonian folk-culture as the individual dream-artist does to the dream-faculty of the people and of nature in general. The Homeric "naïveté" can be understood only as the complete victory of the Apollonian illusion: an illusion similar to those which Nature so frequently employs to achieve her own ends. The true goal

is veiled by a phantasm: and while we stretch out our hands for
the latter, Nature attains the former by means of your illusion.
In the Greeks the "will" wished to contemplate itself in the
transfiguration of genius and the world of art; in order to glorify
themselves, its creatures had to feel themselves worthy of glory;
they had to behold themselves again in a higher sphere, without
this perfect world of contemplation acting as a command or a
reproach. Such is the sphere of beauty, in which they saw their
mirrored images, the Olympians. With this mirroring of beauty
the Hellenic will combated its artistically correlative talent
for suffering and for the wisdom of suffering: and, as a monument
of its victory, we have Homer, the naïve artist.

10

The tradition is undisputed that Greek tragedy in its earliest
form had for its sole theme the sufferings of Dionysus, and that
for a long time the only stage hero was simply Dionysus himself.
With equal confidence, however, we can assert that, until
Euripides, Dionysus never once ceased to be the tragic hero;
that in fact all the celebrated figures of the Greek stage—
Prometheus, Oedipus, etc.—are but masks of this original hero,
Dionysus. There is godhead behind all these masks; and that
is the one essential cause of the typical "ideality," so often
wondered at, of these celebrated characters. I know not who
it was maintained that all individuals as such are comic and
consequently untragic: whence we might infer that the Greeks
in general *could* not endure individuals on the tragic stage. And
they really seem to have felt this: as, in general, we may note
in the Platonic distinction, so deeply rooted in the Hellenic
nature, of the "idea" in contrast to the "eidolon," or image.
Using Plato's terms, we should have to speak of the tragic
figures of the Hellenic stage somewhat as follows: the one truly
real Dionysus appears in a variety of forms, in the mask of a fighting hero and entangled, as it were, in the net of the individual
will. In the latter case the visible god talks and acts so as to
resemble an erring, striving, suffering individual. That, generally speaking, he *appears* with such epic precision and clarity
is the work of the dream-reading Apollo, who through this
symbolic appearance indicates to the chorus its Dionysian
state. In reality, however, and behind this appearance, the hero
is the suffering Dionysus of the mysteries, the god experiencing

in himself the agonies of individuation, of whom wonderful myths tell that as a boy he was torn to pieces by the Titans and has been worshiped in this state as Zagreus: whereby is intimated that this dismemberment, the properly Dionysian *suffering*, is like a transformation into air, water, earth, and fire, that we are therefore to regard the state of individuation as the origin and prime cause of all suffering, as something objectionable in itself. From the smile of this Dionysus sprang the Olympian gods, from his tears sprang man. In this existence as a dismembered god, Dionysus possesses the dual nature of a cruel barbarized demon and a mild, gentle-hearted ruler. But the hope of the epopts looked towards a new birth of Dionysus, which we must now in anticipation conceive as the end of individuation. It was for this coming third Dionysus that the epopts' stormy hymns of joy resounded. And it is this hope alone that casts a gleam of joy upon the features of a world torn asunder and shattered into individuals: as is symbolized in the myth of Demeter, sunk in eternal sorrow, who *rejoices* again only when told that she may *once more* give birth to Dionysus. This view of things already provides us with all the elements of a profound and pessimistic contemplation of the world, together with the *mystery doctrine of tragedy:* the fundamental knowledge of the oneness of everything existent, the conception of individuation as the prime cause of evil, and of art as the joyous hope that the bonds of individuation may be broken in augury of a restored oneness. . . .

II

Greek tragedy met an end different from that of her older sister arts: she died by suicide, in consequence of an irreconcilable conflict. Accordingly she died tragically, while all the others passed away calmly and beautifully at a ripe old age. If it be consonant with a happy natural state to take leave of life easily, leaving behind a fair posterity, the closing period of these older arts exhibits such a happy natural state: slowly they sink from sight, and before their dying eyes already stand their fairer progeny, who impatiently, with a bold gesture, lift up their heads. But when Greek tragedy died, there rose everywhere the deep feeling of an immense void. Just as the Greek sailors in the time of Tiberius once heard upon a lonesome island the thrilling cry, "Great Pan is dead": so now through the Hellenic world there sounded the grievous lament: "Tragedy is dead! Poetry itself has perished with her! Away with you, ye pale, stunted epigones! Away to Hades, that ye may for once eat your fill of the crumbs of your former masters!"

And when after this death a new Art blossomed forth which revered tragedy as her ancestress and mistress, it was observed with horror that she did indeed bear the features of her mother, but that they were the very features the latter had exhibited in her long death-struggle. It was Euripides who fought this death-struggle of tragedy; the later art is known as the *New Attic Comedy*. In it the degenerate form of tragedy lived on as a monument of its painful and violent death.

This connection helps to explain the passionate attachment that the poets of the New Comedy felt for Euripides; so that we are no longer surprised at the wish of Philemon, who would have let himself be hanged at once, merely that he might visit Euripides in the lower world: if he could only be certain that the deceased still had possession of his reason. But if we desire, as briefly as possible and without claiming to say anything exhaustive, to characterize what Euripides has in common with Menander and Philemon, and what appealed to them so strongly as worthy of imitation, it is sufficient to say that Euripides brought the *spectator* upon the stage.[4] He who has perceived the material out of which the Promethean tragic writers prior to Euripides formed their heroes, and how remote from their purpose it was to bring the true mask of reality on the stage, will also be able to explain the utterly opposite tendency of Euripides. Through him the average man forced his way from the spectators' benches on to the stage itself; the mirror in which formerly only grand and bold traits were represented now showed the painful fidelity that conscientiously reproduces even the abortive outlines of nature. Odysseus, the typical Hellene of the older art, now sank in the hands of the new poets to the figure of the Graeculus, who, as the good-naturedly cunning houseslave, henceforth occupies the center of dramatic interest. What Euripides claims credit for in Aristophanes' *Frogs*, namely, that his household medicines have freed tragic art from its pompous corpulency, is apparent above all in his tragic heroes. The spectator now actually saw and heard his double on the Euripidean stage, and rejoiced that he could talk

[4] Cf. Schiller's Preface to the *Bride of Messina*.

so well. But this joy was not all: you could even learn of Euripides how to speak. He prides himself upon this in his contest with Aeschylus: from him the people have learned how to observe, debate, and draw conclusions according to the rules of art and with the cleverest sophistries. In general, through this revolution of the popular speech, he had made the New Comedy possible. For henceforth it was no longer a secret, how—and with what wise maxims—the commonplace was to express itself on the stage. Civic mediocrity, on which Euripides built all his political hopes, was now given a voice, while heretofore the demigod in tragedy and the drunken satyr, or demiman, in comedy, had determined the character of the language. And so the Aristophanean Euripides prides himself on having portrayed the common, familiar, everyday life and activities of the people about which all are qualified to pass judgment. If now the entire populace philosophizes, manages land and goods and conducts lawsuits with unheard-of circumspection, the glory is all his, together with the spendid results of the wisdom with which he has inoculated the rabble. . . .

15

. . . Socrates . . . [was] the type of the *theoretical man.* Our next task will be to obtain an insight into the meaning and purpose of this theoretical man. Like the artist, the theorist finds an infinite satisfaction in the present, and, like the former also, this satisfaction protects him from the practical ethics of pessimism with its lynx eyes shining only in the dark. Whenever the truth is unveiled, the artist will always cling with rapt gaze to whatever still remains veiled after the unveiling; but the theoretical man gets his enjoyment and satisfaction out of the cast-off veil. He finds his highest pleasure in the process of a continuously successful unveiling effected through his own unaided efforts. There would have been no science if it had been concerned only with that *one* naked goddess and nothing else. For then its disciples would have felt like those who wished to dig a hole straight through the earth: each one of them perceives that with his utmost lifelong efforts he can excavate but a very small portion of the enormous depth, and this is filled up again before his eyes by the labors of his successor, so that a third man seems to be doing a sensible thing in selecting a new spot for his attempts at tunneling. Now suppose someone shows conclusively that the antipodal goal cannot be attained thus directly. Who will then still care to toil on in the old depths, unless in the meantime he has learned to content himself with finding precious stones or discovering natural laws? For this reason Lessing, the most honest of theoretical men, boldly said that he cared more for the search after truth than for truth itself: in saying which, he revealed the fundamental secret of science, to the astonishment, and indeed, to the anger of scientists. Well, to be sure, beside this detached perception there stands, with an air of great frankness, if not presumption, a profound *illusion* which first came to birth in the person of Socrates. This illusion consists in the imperturbable belief that, with the clue of logic, thinking can reach to the nethermost depths of being, and that thinking cannot only perceive being but even modify it. This sublime metaphysical illusion is added as an instinct to science and again and again leads the latter to its limits, where it must change into *art; which is really the end to be attained by this mechanism.* . . .

WALTER HORATIO PATER

(1839–1894)

oᏇoooᏇo

WALTER PATER WAS AN OXFORD SCHOLAR, a Victorian aesthete, and a prominent member of the movement which produced, in England, Oscar Wilde and the decadents, and in France, Mallarmé and the symbolists. Pater did not actively found any of these schools, but he carried Ruskin's aestheticism to a height far removed from the moral purpose which Ruskin championed, he supplied a critical theory for the latter-day paganism which was springing up as a reaction against Victorianism, and the famous conclusion to his *Studies in the History of the Renaissance* (1873)—reprinted below—encouraged the development of the movement which later came to be known as the "Art for art's sake" school.

In his early essay on Winckelmann (1867) Pater revealed a prophetic admiration for the poor man who found his destiny in the study and interpretation of Greek art. Pater became in a sense a nineteenth-century Winckelmann, and like Winckelmann he saw antiquity through the impressionable eyes of his own age.

Studies in the History of the Renaissance is not a history but a series of enthusiastic interpretations of characters whom Pater thought represented the Renaissance spirit, not all of whom lived in the historical age of the Renaissance. This work contains both the theory and the method of Pater's criticism. In his Preface to *The Renaissance* we find this definition of the "aesthetic critic":

> The aesthetic critic, then, regards all the objects with which he has to do, all works of art, and the fairer forms of nature and human life as powers or forces producing pleasurable sensations, each of a more or less peculiar or unique kind. . . . To him, the picture, the landscape, the engaging personality in life or in a book . . . [is valuable] for the property each has of affecting one with a special, a unique, impression of pleasure. . . .

> What is important, then, is not that the critic should possess a correct abstract definition of beauty for the intellect, but a certain kind of temperament, the power of being deeply moved by the presence of beautiful objects. . . .

In a review Pater defines this "imaginative criticism" as "that criticism which is itself a kind of construction, or creation, as it penetrates through the given literary or artistic product into the mental and inner constitution of the producer, shaping his work. . . ." [1]

In the autobiographical *The Child in the House* (1894) Pater reveals the traits of character out of which grew his aesthetics and his critical method. The boy is delicately sensitive to all beautiful impressions, to the sensations of sound, touch, smell, and sight, and out of this disposition grew the hedonism of *Marius the Epicurean* (1885). But *The Child in the House* also reveals the *macabre* as well as the healthily stimulating aspect of Pater's acute awareness. One passage in particular reminds one of Novalis or Poe and indicates a latent decadence:

> He would think of Julian, fallen into incurable sickness, as spoiled in the sweet blossoms of his skin like pale amber, and his honey-like hair; of Cecil, early dead, as cut off from the lilies, from golden summer days, from women's voices; and then what comforted him a little was the thought of the turning of the child's flesh to violets in the turf above him.

Marius the Epicurean is the culmination, we might say the reducing to a philosophy, of this cult of beauty and sense impressionism. The hero of the book begins as a neopagan, but he very nearly ends as a Christian mystic, thus indicating the nearness of Pater to the Catholic and symbolistic writers of the end of the century.

Walter Pater was never a professional book reviewer, but in the latter part of his career he did write a number of reviews. In commenting on these, Benson says, "What strikes one most in reading them is, in the first place, a marked tenderness for the feelings of the author whom he is reviewing . . . he enters into the intentions of the writer with a great catholicity of sympathy." [2] Pater is thus one of the best examples of the imaginative, impressionistic, and sympathetic critics, and in some ways he reminds us of that supreme impressionist, Anatole France. [3]

BIBLIOGRAPHY

TEXT

Appreciations; with an essay on Style. Library edition. London, 1910.
Essays from "The Guardian." Library edition. London, 1910.
Greek Studies; a series of essays. Library edition. London, 1910.

[1]From a review in the *Guardian*, quoted by A. C. Benson, *Walter Pater* (London, 1926), p. 49.   [2]Benson, *op. cit.*, p. 119.   [3]See pp. 580–585.

The Renaissance; studies in art and poetry. Library edition. London, 1910.
Works. 10 vols. Library edition. London, 1910.

BIOGRAPHY AND CRITICISM

Benson, A. C., *Walter Pater.* New York, 1906. (English Men of Letters.)
Beyer, Arthur, *Walter Paters Beziehungen zur französischen Literatur und Kultur.* Halle, 1931.
Chandler, Zilpha Emma, *An Analysis of the Stylistic Technique of Addison, Hazlitt, and Pater.* University of Iowa, [1928].
Child, Ruth C., *The Aesthetic of Walter Pater.* New York, 1940.
Dowden, Edward, "Walter Pater," in *Essays Modern and Elizabethan.* New York, 1910, pp. 1–25.
Greenslet, Ferris, *Walter Pater.* New York, 1903.
Symons, Arthur, *A Study of Walter Pater.* London, 1902.
——, *Studies in Prose and Verse.* London, 1904.
Wright, Thomas, *Life of Walter Pater.* 2 vols. New York, 1907.
Young, Helen Hawthorne, *The Writings of Walter Pater; a Reflection of British Philosophical Opinion from 1860–1890.* Lancaster, Pennsylvania, 1933. (A Bryn Mawr Ph. D. Thesis.)

CONCLUSION TO "STUDIES IN THE HISTORY OF THE RENAISSANCE"[1]

1873

Λέγει που Ἡράκλειτος ὅτι πάντα χωρεῖ καὶ οὐδὲν μένει.[2]

To regard all things and principles of things as inconstant modes or fashions has more and more become the tendency of modern thought. Let us begin with that which is without— our physical life. Fix upon it in one of its more exquisite intervals—the moment, for instance, of delicious recoil from the flood of water in summer heat. What is the whole physical life in that moment but a combination of natural elements to which science gives their names? But these elements, phosphorus and lime and delicate fibers, are present not in the human body alone: we detect them in places most remote from it. Our physical life is a perpetual motion of them—the passage of the blood, the wasting and repairing of the lenses of the

---

[1] This now famous "Conclusion" to the first edition of *Studies in the History of the Renaissance* (1873) was so violently condemned by the conservative element at Oxford, and elsewhere, that Pater omitted it from the second edition (1877) but restored it in the 1888 edition of the *Studies,* with some slight changes.

[2] "Heraclitus says that all things give way and nothing remains" (Plato's *Cratylus*).

eye, the modification of the tissues of the brain by every ray
of light and sound—processes which science reduces to simpler and more elementary forces. Like the elements of which
we are composed, the action of these forces extends beyond us;
it rusts iron and ripens corn. Far out on every side of us those
elements are broadcast, driven by many forces; and birth and
gesture and death and the springing of violets from the grave
are but a few out of ten thousand resultant combinations. That
clear, perpetual outline of face and limb is but an image of ours,
under which we group them—a design in a web, the actual
threads of which pass out beyond it. This at least of flame-
like our life has, that it is but the concurrence, renewed from
moment to moment, of forces parting sooner or later on
their ways.

Or if we begin with the inward whirl of thought and feeling,
the whirlpool is still more rapid, the flame more eager and
devouring. There it is no longer the gradual darkening of the
eye and fading of color from the wall,—the movement of the
shore side, where the water flows down indeed, though in
apparent rest,—but the race of the mid-stream, a drift of
momentary acts of sight and passion and thought. At first
sight experience seems to bury us under a flood of external
objects, pressing upon us with a sharp and importunate reality,
calling us out of ourselves in a thousand forms of action. But
when reflection begins to act upon those objects they are dis-
sipated under its influence; the cohesive force seems suspended
like a trick of magic; each object is loosed into a group of impressions—color, odor, texture—in the mind of the observer. And
if we continue to dwell in thought on this world, not of objects
in the solidity with which language invests them, but of impressions unstable, flickering, inconsistent, which burn and are
extinguished with our consciousness of them, it contracts still
further; the whole scope of observation is dwarfed to the narrow
chamber of the individual mind. Experience, already reduced
to a swarm of impressions, is ringed round for each one of us
by that thick wall of personality through which no real voice
has ever pierced on its way to us, or from us to that which we can
only conjecture to be without. Every one of those impressions
is the impression of the individual in his isolation, each mind
keeping as a solitary prisoner its own dream of a world.[3]

[3]Cf. Bergson, below, pp. 614 ff.

Analysis goes a step farther still and assures us that those impressions of the individual mind to which, for each one of us, experience dwindles down, are in perpetual flight; that each of them is limited by time, and that as time is infinitely divisible, each of them is infinitely divisible also; all that is actual in it being a single moment, gone while we try to apprehend it, of which it may ever be more truly said that it has ceased to be than that it is. To such a tremulous wisp constantly reforming itself on the stream, to a single sharp impression, with a sense in it—a relic more or less fleeting—of such moments gone by, what is real in our life fines itself down. It is with this movement, with the passage and dissolution of impressions, images, sensations, that analysis leaves off—that continual vanishing away, that strange, perpetual weaving and unweaving of ourselves.

Philosophiren, says Novalis, *ist dephlegmatisiren, vivificiren.*[4] The service of philosophy, of speculative culture, towards the human spirit is to rouse, to startle it into sharp and eager observation. Every moment some form grows perfect in hand or face; some tone on the hills or the sea is choicer than the rest; some mood of passion or insight or intellectual excitement is irresistibly real and attractive for us,—but for that moment only. Not the fruit of experience, but experience itself, is the end. A counted number of pulses only is given to us of a variegated, dramatic life. How may we see in them all that is to be seen in them by the finest senses? How shall we pass most swiftly from point to point, and be present always at the focus where the greatest number of vital forces unite in their purest energy?

To burn always with this hard, gemlike flame, to maintain this ecstasy, is success in life. In a sense it might even be said that our failure is to form habits: for, after all, habit is relative to a stereotyped world, and meantime it is only the roughness of the eye that makes any two persons, things, situations, seem alike. While all melts under our feet, we may well catch at any exquisite passion, or any contribution to knowledge that seems by a lifted horizon to set the spirit free for a moment, or any stirring of the senses, strange dyes, strange colors, and curious odors, or work of the artist's hands, or the face of one's friend.

---

[4]"To be a philosopher is to cease to be sluggish, to become alive." Novalis was the pseudonym of Friedrich von Hardenberg (1772–1801).

Not to discriminate every moment some passionate attitude
in those about us, and in the brilliancy of their gifts some
tragic dividing of forces on their ways, is, on this short day of
frost and sun, to sleep before evening. With this sense of the
splendor of our experience and of its awful brevity, gathering
all we are into one desperate effort to see and touch, we shall
hardly have time to make theories about the things we see and
touch. What we have to do is to be forever curiously testing
new opinions and courting new impressions, never acquiescing
in a facile orthodoxy of Comte, or of Hegel, or of our own.
Philosophical theories or ideas, as points of view, instruments of
criticism, may help us to gather up what might otherwise pass
unregarded by us. "Philosophy is the microscope of thought."
The theory or idea or system which requires of us the sacrifice
of any part of this experience, in consideration of some interest
into which we cannot enter or some abstract theory we have not
identified with ourselves or what is only conventional, has no real
claim upon us.

One of the most beautiful passages in the writings of Rousseau is that in the sixth book of the *Confessions*, where he describes the awakening in him of the literary sense. An undefin-
able taint of death had always clung about him, and now in
early manhood he believed himself smitten by mortal disease.
He asked himself how he might make as much as possible of
the interval that remained; and he was not biased by anything
in his previous life when he decided that it must be by intellectual excitement, which he found just then in the clear, fresh
writings of Voltaire. Well! we are all *condamnés*, as Victor
Hugo says: we are all under sentence of death but with a sort
of indefinite reprieve—*les hommes sont tous condamnés à mort
avec des sursis indéfinis:* we have an interval, and then our place
knows us no more. Some spend this interval in listlessness,
some in high passions, the wisest—at least among "the children
of this world"—in art and song. For our one chance lies in
expanding that interval, in getting as many pulsations as possible
into the given time. Great passions may give us this quickened
sense of life, ecstasy and sorrow of love, the various forms of
enthusiastic activity, disinterested or otherwise, which come
naturally to many of us. Only be sure it is passion—that it
does yield you this fruit of a quickened, multiplied consciousness.
Of this wisdom, the poetic passion, the desire of beauty, the love

of art for art's sake, has most; for art comes to you professing frankly to give nothing but the highest quality to your moments as they pass, and simply for those moments' sake.

[ROMANTICISM][1]

1876

The words "classical" and "romantic," although, like many other critical expressions, sometimes abused by those who have understood them too vaguely or too absolutely, yet define two real tendencies in the history of art and literature. Used in an exaggerated sense, to express a greater opposition between those tendencies than really exists, they have at times tended to divide people of taste into opposite camps. But in that House Beautiful which the creative minds of all generations—the artists and those who have treated life in the spirit of art—are always building together, for the refreshment of the human spirit, these oppositions cease; and the Interpreter of the House Beautiful, the true aesthetic critic, uses these divisions only so far as they enable him to enter into the peculiarities of the objects with which he has to do. The term "classical," fixed, as it is, to a well-defined literature and a well-defined group in art, is clear, indeed; but then it has often been used in a hard and merely scholastic sense by the praisers of what is old and accustomed, at the expense of what is new, by critics who would never have discovered for themselves the charm of any work, whether new or old, who value what is old in art or literature, for its accessories, and chiefly for the conventional authority that has gathered about it—people who would never really have been made glad by any Venus fresh-risen from the sea, and who praise the Venus of old Greece and Rome only because they fancy her grown now into something staid and tame.

And as the term "classical" has been used in a too absolute, and therefore in a misleading sense, so the term "romantic" has been used much too vaguely, in various accidental senses. The sense in which Scott is called a romantic writer is chiefly this—that, in opposition to the literary tradition of the last century, he loved strange adventure, and sought it in the Mid-

[1]This essay forms the Postscript to the volume of essays titled *Appreciations* (1889). It was first published in *Macmillan's Magazine*, November, 1876.

dle Age. Much later, in a Yorkshire village, the spirit of romanticism bore a more really characteristic fruit in the work of
a young girl, Emily Brontë, the romance of *Wuthering Heights;*
the figures of Hareton Earnshaw, of Catherine Linton, and of
Heathcliffe—tearing open Catherine's grave, removing one
side of her coffin that he may really lie beside her in death—
figures so passionate, yet woven on a background of delicately
beautiful moorland scenery, being typical examples of that
spirit. . . . In Germany and France, within the last hundred
years, the term has been used to describe a particular school of
writers; and consequently, when Heine criticizes the "Romantic School" in Germany, that movement which culminated in
Goethe's *Goetz von Berlichingen,* or when Théophile Gautier criticizes the romantic movement in France, where, indeed, it bore
its most characteristic fruits, and its play is hardly yet over—
where by a certain audacity or *bizarrerie* of motive, united with
faultless literary execution, it still shows itself in imaginative
literature—they use the word with an exact sense of special
artistic qualities indeed, but use it, nevertheless, with a limited
application to the manifestation of those qualities at a particular period. But the romantic spirit is, in reality, an ever-present,
an enduring principle, in the artistic temperament; and the
qualities of thought and style which that and other similar uses
of the word "romantic" really indicate are indeed but symptoms
of a very continuous and widely working influence.

Though the words "classical" and "romantic," then, have
acquired an almost technical meaning, in application to certain
developments of German and French taste, yet this is but one
variation of an old opposition, which may be traced from the
very beginning of the formation of European art and literature.
From the first formation of anything like a standard of taste in
these things, the restless curiosity of their more eager lovers
necessarily made itself felt in the craving for new motives, new
subjects of interest, new modifications of style. Hence the
opposition between the classicists and romanticists—between
the adherents, in the culture of beauty, of the principles of
liberty and authority respectively—of strength and order—or
what the Greeks called κοσμιότης.[2]

. . . The charm, therefore, of what is classical in art or literature is that of the well-known tale, to which we can never-

[2]Decorum.

theless listen over and over again because it is told so well.
To the absolute beauty of its artistic form is added the accidental, tranquil charm of familiarity. There are times, indeed,
at which these charms fail to work on our spirits at all, because
they fail to excite us. "Romanticism," says Stendhal, "is the
art of presenting to people the literary works which, in the
actual state of their habits and beliefs, are capable of giving
them the greatest possible pleasure; classicism, on the contrary, of presenting them with that which gave the greatest
possible pleasure to their grandfathers." But then, beneath
all changes of habits and beliefs, our love of that mere abstract
proportion—of music—which what is classical in literature
possesses, still maintains itself in the best of us, and what pleased
our grandparents may at least tranquilize us. The "classic"
comes to us out of the cool and quiet of other times, as the
measure of what a long experience has shown will at least never
displease us. And in the classical literature of Greece and Rome,
as in the classics of the last century, the essentially classical
element is that quality of order in beauty, which they possess
indeed in a pre-eminent degree, and which impresses some minds
to the exclusion of everything else in them.

It is the addition of strangeness to beauty that constitutes
the romantic character in art; and the desire of beauty being
a fixed element in every artistic organization, it is the addition
of curiosity to this desire of beauty that constitutes the romantic temper. Curiosity and the desire of beauty have each their
place in art, as in all true criticism. When one's curiosity is
deficient, when one is not eager enough for new impressions
and new pleasures, one is liable to value mere academical proprieties too highly to be satisfied with worn-out or conventional types, with the insipid ornament of Racine, or the pretti-
ness of that later Greek sculpture which passed so long for true
Hellenic work; to miss those places where the handiwork of
nature or of the artist has been most cunning; to find the
most stimulating products of art a mere irritation. And when
one's curiosity is in excess, when it overbalances the desire of
beauty, then one is liable to value in works of art what is inartistic in them—to be satisfied with what is exaggerated in
art, with productions like some of those of the romantic school
in Germany—not to distinguish jealously enough between
what is admirably done and what is done not quite so well,

in the writings, for instance, of Jean Paul.[3] And if I had to give instances of these defects, then I should say that Pope, in common with the age of literature to which he belonged, had too little curiosity, so that there is always a certain insipidity in the effect of his work, exquisite as it is; and, coming down to our own time, that Balzac had an excess of curiosity—curiosity not duly tempered with the desire of beauty.

But, however falsely those two tendencies may be opposed by critics or exaggerated by artists themselves, they are tendencies really at work at all times in art, molding it, with the balance sometimes a little on one side, sometimes a little on the other; generating, respectively, as the balance inclines on this side or on that, two principles, two traditions, in art, and in literature so far as it partakes of the spirit of art. If there is a great overbalance of curiosity, then, we have the grotesque in art; if the union of strangeness and beauty, under very difficult and complex conditions, be a successful one, then the resultant beauty is very exquisite, very attractive. With a passionate care of beauty, the romantic spirit refuses to have it unless the condition of strangeness be first fulfilled. Its desire is for a beauty born of unlikely elements, by a profound alchemy, by a difficult initiation, by the charm which wrings it even out of terrible things; and a trace of distortion, of the grotesque, may perhaps linger, as an additional element of expression, about its ultimate grace. Its eager, excited spirit will have strength, the grotesque, first of all—the trees shrieking as you tear off the leaves; for Jean Valjean,[4] the long years of convict life; for Redgauntlet,[5] the quicksands of Solway Moss; then, incorporate with this strangeness, and intensified by restraint, as much sweetness, as much beauty, as is compatible with that . . .

The essential elements, then, of the romantic spirit are curiosity and the love of beauty; and it is only as an illustration of these qualities that it seeks the Middle Age, because, in the overcharged atmosphere of the Middle Age, there are unworked sources of romantic effect, of a strange beauty, to be won, by strong imagination, out of things unlikely or remote. . . .

In his book on *Racine and Shakespeare*, Stendhal argues that all good art was romantic in its day, and this is perhaps true in

---

[3]Jean Paul Richter (1763–1825). [4]A character in Hugo's *Les Misérables*.
[5]A character in Scott's novel of the same name.

Stendhal's sense. That little treatise, full of "dry light" and fertile ideas, was published in the year 1823, and its object is to defend an entire independence and liberty in the choice and treatment of subject, both in art and literature, against those who upheld the exclusive authority of precedent. In pleading the cause of romanticism, therefore, it is the novelty, both of form and of motive, in writings like the *Hernani* of Victor Hugo (which soon followed it, raising a storm of criticism) that he is chiefly concerned to justify. To be interesting and really stimulating, to keep us from yawning even, art and literature must follow the subtle movements of that nimbly shifting Time-Spirit, or *Zeitgeist*, understood by French not less than by German criticism, which is always modifying men's taste as it modifies their manners and their pleasures. This, he contends, is what all great workmen had always understood. Dante, Shakespeare, Molière, had exercised an absolute independence in their choice of subject and treatment. To turn always with that ever-changing spirit, yet to retain the flavor of what was admirably done in past generations, in the classics, as we say, is the problem of true romanticism. "Dante," he observes, "was pre-eminently the romantic poet. He adored Vergil, yet he wrote the *Divine Comedy*, with the episode of Ugolino, which is as unlike the *Aeneid* as can possibly be. And those who thus obey the fundamental principle of romanticism, one by one become classical, and are joined to that ever-increasing common league, formed by men of all countries, to approach nearer and nearer to perfection."

Romanticism, then, although it has its epochs, is in its essential characteristics rather a spirit which shows itself at all times, in various degrees, in individual workmen and their work, and the amount of which criticism has to estimate in them taken one by one, than the peculiarity of a time or a school. Depending on the varying proportion of curiosity and the desire of beauty, natural tendencies of the artistic spirit at all times, it must always be partly a matter of individual temperament. The eighteenth century in England has been regarded as almost exclusively a classical period; yet William Blake, a type of so much which breaks through what are conventionally thought the influences of that century, is still a noticeable phenomenon in it, and the reaction in favor of naturalism in poetry begins in that century, early. There are, thus, the born ro-

manticists and the born classicists. There are the born classicists who start with *form*, to whose minds the comeliness of
the old, immemorial, well-recognized types in art and literature
have revealed themselves impressively; who will entertain
no matter which will not go easily and flexibly into them;
whose work aspires only to be a variation upon, or study from,
the older masters. " 'T is art's decline, my son!" they are always
saying to the progressive element in their own generation—
to those who care for that which in fifty years' time everyone
will be caring for. On the other hand, there are the born romanticists, who start with an original, untried *matter*, still in fusion;
who conceive this vividly, and hold by it as the essence of their
work; who, by the very vividness and heat of their conception,
purge away sooner or later all that is not organically appropriate
to it, till the whole effect adjusts itself in clear, orderly, propor-
tionate form; which form, after a very little time, becomes
classical in its turn.

The romantic or classical character of a picture, a poem, a
literary work, depends, then, on the balance of certain qualities in it; and in this sense a very real distinction may be drawn
between good classical and good romantic work. But all critical terms are relative; and there is at least a valuable suggestion
in that theory of Stendhal's, that all good art was romantic in
its day. In the beauties of Homer and Phidias, quiet as they
now seem, there must have been, for those who confronted them
for the first time, excitement and surprise, the sudden, unforeseen satisfaction of the desire of beauty. Yet the *Odyssey*, with
its marvelous adventure, is more romantic than the *Iliad*, which
nevertheless contains, among many other romantic episodes,
that of the immortal horses of Achilles, who weep at the death
of Patroclus. . . .

Classicism, then, means for Stendhal, for that younger enthusiastic band of French writers whose unconscious method
he formulated into principles, the reign of what is pedantic,
conventional, and narrowly academical in art; for him, all
good art is romantic. To Sainte-Beuve, who understands the
term in a more liberal sense, it is the characteristic of certain
epochs, of certain spirits in every epoch, not given to the exercise of original imagination, but rather to the working out of
refinements of manner on some authorized matter; and who
bring to their perfection, in this way, the elements of sanity, of

order and beauty in manner. In general criticism, again, it means the spirit of Greece and Rome, of some phases in literature and art that may seem of equal authority with Greece and Rome, the age of Louis Fourteenth, the age of Johnson; though this is at best an uncritical use of the term, because in Greek and Roman work there are typical examples of the romantic spirit. But explain the terms as we may, in application to particular epochs, there are these two elements always recognizable; united in perfect art—in Sophocles, in Dante, in the highest work of Goethe, though not always absolutely balanced there; and these two elements may be not inappropriately termed the classical and romantic tendencies.

Material for the artist, motives of inspiration, are not yet exhausted: our curious, complex, aspiring age still abounds in subjects for aesthetic manipulation by the literary as well as by other forms of art. For the literary art, at all events, the problem just now is, to induce order upon the contorted, proportionless accumulation of our knowledge and experience, our science and history, our hopes and disillusion, and, in effecting this, to do consciously what has been done hitherto for the most part too unconsciously—to write our English language as the Latins wrote theirs, as the French write, as scholars should write. Appealing, as he may, to precedent in this matter, the scholar will still remember that if "the style is the man"[6] it is also the age: that the nineteenth century too will be found to have had its style, justified by necessity—a style very different, alike from the baldness of an impossible "Queen Anne" revival, and an incorrect, incondite exuberance, after the mode of Elizabeth: that we can only return to either at the price of an impoverishment of form or matter, or both, although, an intellectually rich age such as ours being necessarily an eclectic one, we may well cultivate some of the excellences of literary types so different as those: that in literature as in other matters it is well to unite as many diverse elements as may be: that the individual writer or artist, certainly, is to be estimated by the number of graces he combines, and his power of interpenetrating them in a given work. To discriminate schools, of art, of literature, is of course part of the obvious business of literary criticism; but in the work of literary production it is easy to

[6] Buffon, *Discours de réception.*

be overmuch occupied concerning them. For, in truth, the legitimate contention is, not of one age or school of literary art against another, but of all successive schools alike against the stupidity which is dead to the substance, and the vulgarity which is dead to form.

HENRY JAMES

(1843–1916)

o◯ooo◯o

HENRY JAMES IS NOT ONLY A DISTINGUISHED master of fiction but a
voluminous literary critic and theorist of peculiar subtlety, especially
in matters of form. His basic assumption is that "the main object of
the novel is to represent life,"[1] and not merely to entertain. The novel,
he said, is "the most magnificent form of art" distinguished for "its
large, free character of an immense and exquisite correspondence with
life." The life of a human being, as distinct from that of an animal, he
argues, embraces not only the body, but also the mind and spirit—
moral values—and therefore he argues that, other things being equal,
the novelist who deals with the mind and spirit as well as the body is
greater than he who confines himself to the body, to physical surfaces.
Since reflection "is a part of disciplined manhood," he censures Maupassant for skipping "the whole reflective part of his men and women—
that reflective part which governs conduct and produces character."[2]
He disposes of the "famous question of the morality, the decency, of
the novel," by arguing that "our fiction will always be decent enough
if it be sufficiently general," sufficiently inclusive of *all* the distinctively
human attributes. He pleads for liberalism, inclusiveness, and argues
that Trollope tells us "more about life than the 'naturalists' in our sister
republic," France, because he shares the English ability to be "more at
home in the moral world." Yet James would like to have the English
learn certain skills from the French, to whom the English are
"inferior in audacity, in neatness, in acuteness, in intellectual vivacity, in the arrangement of material, in the art of characterizing visible
things."[3]

Every good story, he says, should be "both a picture and an idea."[4]

[1]*Partial Portraits* (1905 ed.), p. 227. He in this passage disagrees with C. D. Warner's essay on "Modern Fiction" (*Atlantic Monthly*, April, 1883), which argued that
"the main object in the novel is to entertain."

[2]*Ibid.*, pp. 285; 402.

[3]*Ibid.*, p. 124. Cf. p. 238, where he concludes that "Daudet's imagination fails
him when he begins to take the soul into account. . . . He has no high imagination,
and, as a consequence, no ideas."

[4]*Ibid.*, p. 269.

James, it will be remembered, wrote the *Hawthorne* for the English Men of Letters Series, and he greatly admired the New England master of symbolism. "Imaginative writers," he says, "of the first order always give us an impression that they have a kind of philosophy."[5] James himself paid tribute to Emerson, the "wisest American," because he saw that "the prize was within,"[6] because he saw life as an inward struggle between the "law for thing" and the "law for man." And James carried on much of the Emersonian doctrine according to which "the beautiful is the highest," beauty being "the mark God sets upon virtue." As Stuart Pratt Sherman has shown, James, at bottom, "is not an historian of manners; he is a trenchant idealistic critic of life from the aesthetic point of view," a prophet of "the possible amenity of human intercourse in a society aesthetically disciplined and controlled."[7]

Like Emerson, James set great store by manners, as telltale signs and indexes of character; like Ruskin, he thought that the houses we live in and the things with which we surround ourselves reveal our characters. In civilized society he thought that the most well-bred people reveal themselves indirectly, and he argued that it is chiefly by indirection that we find direction out. Thus he developed an intricate form by which people show themselves by externals and by "reflectors." For example, in his preface explaining *The Awkward Age*, he shows how he had his central character surrounded by other characters, "small rounds represent[ing] so many distinct lamps, as I liked to call them, the function of each of which would be to light with all due intensity one of its aspects."[8] As he grew older, his interest in ultra-subtle matters of form and management of plot increased, although such matters were really subservient to his central interest in ethics and the common denominator of all his novels, the renunciation of something of price for something spiritually priceless.[9] In his old age, his admirer and disciple, Edith Wharton, confessed that "his literary judgments had long been hampered by his increasing preoccupation with the structure of the novel, and his unwillingness to concede that the vital center (when there was any) could lie elsewhere. . . . As time passed, and the intricate problem of form and structure engrossed him more deeply, it became almost impossible to persuade him that there might be merit in the work of writers apparently insensible to

[5]*Ibid.*, p. 238. But see *North American Review* (January, 1880), p. 56.   [6]*Ibid.*, p. 9.
[7]S. P. Sherman, "The Aesthetic Idealism of Henry James," in his book *On Contemporary Literature* (New York, 1917), p. 253.
[8]R. P. Blackmur, *The Art of the Novel: Critical Prefaces* (New York, 1934), p. 110.
[9]Cf. Pelham Edgar, *Henry James* (Boston, 1927), p. 250.

these sterner demands of the art."[10]   But this overemphasis on form is not apparent in James's basic statement of his principles in middle life in his essay on "The Art of Fiction," which he described as a plea for freedom, and which embraces his central doctrine of representative inclusiveness. "Art is essentially selection, but it is a selection whose main care is to be typical, to be inclusive . . ."[11] to avoid that artificial "rearrangement" which would exclude the "ugly" and the "illusion of life." "The cultivation of this success, the study of this process, form, to my taste, the beginning and the end of the art of the novelist."

These, then, were James's general criteria in criticizing the novel. He may be called the Walter Pater of American criticism because of his special interest in appreciation and expressionism. He set forth his theory in his essay entitled "Criticism": "To lend himself, to project himself and steep himself, to feel and feel till he understand and to understand so well that he can say, to have perception at the pitch of passion and expression as embracing as the air, to be infinitely curious and incorrigibly patient, and yet plastic and inflammable and determinable, stooping to conquer and serving to direct—these are fine chances for an active mind, chances to add the idea of independent beauty to the conception of success. Just in proportion as he is sentient and restless, just in proportion as he reacts and reciprocates and penetrates, is the critic a valuable instrument."[12]   James's own criticism, which steadily developed from a somewhat stiff use of yardsticks to a peculiar subtlety under the influence of James's master, Sainte-Beuve, is an excellent illustration of the truth of his self-characterization: "I have to the last point the instinct and the sense for fusions and interrelations, for framing and encircling . . . every part of my stuff in every other."[13]

BIBLIOGRAPHY

TEXT

Essays in London and Elsewhere. London, 1893.
French Poets and Novelists. London, 1878.
Hawthorne. London, 1879.
Partial Portraits. London, 1888.
Notes on Novelists. London, 1914.
Notes and Reviews. Cambridge, 1921.
View and Reviews. Boston, 1908.

[10]Edith Wharton, *A Backward Glance* (New York, 1934), p. 323; her chapter on Henry James is here reprinted from the *Quarterly Review* for July, 1920. Mrs. Wharton's own theories of the novel, which have much in common with those of James, will be found ably set forth in her book, *The Writing of Fiction* (New York, 1925).
[11]*Partial Portraits*, p. 348.   [12]*Essays in London* (1893 ed.), p. 276.   [13]*Letters*, II, 347.

The Art of the Novel: Critical Prefaces, ed., with an introduction by R. P.
Blackmur. New York, 1934. Contains the Prefaces provided for the
New York edition of his novels.
The Letters of Henry James. 2 vols. Ed. by P. Lubbock. New York, 1920.

BIOGRAPHY AND CRITICISM

Beach, J. W., *The Method of Henry James.* Yale University Press, 1918.
Bethurum, D., "Morality and Henry James," *Sewanee Review*, XXXI,
324–330 (1923).
Bosanquet, Theodora, "Henry James as a Literary Artist," *Bookman*,
XLV, 571–581 (1917).
Brownell, W. C., *American Prose Masters.* New York, 1909, pp. 339–400.
De Mille, George E., "James," in *Literary Criticism in America.* New
York, 1931, pp. 158–181.
Edgar, Pelham, *Henry James, Man and Author.* Boston, 1927.
Egan, M. F., "The Revelation of an Artist in Literature," *Catholic
World*, CXI, 289–300 (1920).
Hale, E. E., "The Impressionism of Henry James," *Faculty Papers of
Union College* (1931), II, 3–17.
Harvitt, H., "How Henry James Revised *Roderick Hudson*," *Publica-
tions of the Modern Language Association*, XXXIX, 203–227 (1924).
Hughes, H. L., *Theory and Practice in Henry James.* Ann Arbor, 1926.
Kelley, Cornelia P., *The Early Development of Henry James.* University
of Illinois Studies in Language and Literature, XV (1930), nos. 1–2.
Lubbock, P., *The Craft of Fiction.* London, 1921.
Marsh, E. C., "James: Auto-Critic," *Bookman*, XXX, 138–143 (1909).
Pallache, J. C., "The Critical Faculty of Henry James," *University of
California Chronicle*, XXVI, 399–410 (1924).
Roberts, Morris, *Henry James's Criticism.* Harvard University Press, 1929.
Sherman, S. P., "The Aesthetic Idealism of Henry James," in *On
Contemporary Literature.* New York, 1917, pp. 226–255.

THE ART OF FICTION [1]
1884

I should not have affixed so comprehensive a title to these few
remarks, necessarily wanting in any completeness upon a subject
the full consideration of which would carry us far, did I not seem
to discover a pretext for my temerity in the interesting pamphlet
lately published under this name by Mr. Walter Besant. Mr.

[1]Appeared originally in *Longman's Magazine* (September, 1884); in 1885 it was
reprinted with Walter Besant's "The Art of Fiction"; and in 1888 it was included
in *Partial Portraits*. The text is that of 1888, and is here reprinted by permission of
The Macmillan Company.

Besant's lecture at the Royal Institution—the original form of his pamphlet—appears to indicate that many persons are interested in the art of fiction, and are not indifferent to such remarks, as those who practice it may attempt to make about it. I am therefore anxious not to lose the benefit of this favorable association, and to edge in a few words under cover of the attention which Mr. Besant is sure to have excited. There is something very encouraging in his having put into form certain of his ideas on the mystery of storytelling.

It is a proof of life and curiosity—curiosity on the part of the brotherhood of novelists as well as on the part of their readers. Only a short time ago it might have been supposed that the English novel was not what the French call *discutable*. It had no air of having a theory, a conviction, a consciousness of itself behind it—of being the expression of an artistic faith, the result of choice and comparison. I do not say it was necessarily the worse for that: it would take much more courage than I possess to intimate that the form of the novel as Dickens and Thackeray (for instance) saw it had any taint of incompleteness. It was, however, *naïf* (if I may help myself out with another French word); and evidently if it be destined to suffer in any way for having lost its *naïveté* it has now an idea of making sure of the corresponding advantages. During the period I have alluded to there was a comfortable, good-humored feeling abroad that a novel is a novel, as a pudding is a pudding, and that our only business with it could be to swallow it. But within a year or two, for some reason or other, there have been signs of returning animation—the era of discussion would appear to have been to a certain extent opened. Art lives upon discussion, upon experiment, upon curiosity, upon variety of attempt, upon the exchange of views and the comparison of standpoints; and there is a presumption that those times when no one has anything particular to say about it, and has no reason to give for practice or preference, though they may be times of honor, are not times of development—are times, possibly even, a little of dullness. The successful application of any art is a delightful spectacle, but the theory too is interesting; and though there is a great deal of the latter without the former I suspect there has never been a genuine success that has not had a latent core of conviction. Discussion, suggestion, formulation, these things are fertilizing when they are frank and sincere. Mr. Besant has set an excellent example in saying what he thinks, for his part, about the way in which fiction should be written, as well as about the way in which it should be published; for his view of the "art," carried on into an appendix, covers that too. Other laborers in the same field will doubtless take up the argument, they will give it the light of their experience, and the effect will surely be to make our interest in the novel a little more what it had for some time threatened to fail to be—a serious, active, inquiring interest, under protection of which this delightful study may, in moments of confidence, venture to say a little more what it thinks of itself.

It must take itself seriously for the public to take it so. The old superstition about fiction being "wicked" has doubtless died out in England; but the spirit of it lingers in a certain oblique regard directed toward any story which does not more or less admit that it is only a joke. Even the most jocular novel feels in some degree the weight of the proscription that was formerly directed against literary levity: the jocularity does not always succeed in passing for orthodoxy. It is still expected, though perhaps people are ashamed to say it, that a production which is after all only a "make-believe" (for what else is a "story"?) shall be in some degree apologetic—shall renounce the pretension of attempting really to represent life. This, of course, any sensible, wide-awake story declines to do, for it quickly perceives that the tolerance granted to it on such a condition is only an attempt to stifle it disguised in the form of generosity. The old evangelical hostility to the novel, which was as explicit as it was narrow, and which regarded it as little less favorable to our immortal part than a stage play, was in reality far less insulting. The only reason for the existence of a novel is that it does attempt to represent life. When it relinquishes this attempt, the same attempt that we see on the canvas of the painter, it will have arrived at a very strange pass. It is not expected of the picture that it will make itself humble in order to be forgiven; and the analogy between the art of the painter and the art of the novelist is, so far as I am able to see, complete. Their inspiration is the same, their process (allowing for the different quality of the vehicle) is the same, their success is the same. They may learn from each other, they may explain and sustain each other. Their cause is the same, and the honor of one is the honor of another. The Mahometans think a picture an unholy thing, but it is a long time since any Christian did, and it is therefore the more odd that in the Christian mind the traces (dissimulated though they may be) of a suspicion of the sister art should linger to this day. The only effectual way to lay it to rest is to emphasize the analogy to which I just alluded—to insist on the fact that as the picture is reality, so the novel is history. That is the only general description (which does it justice) that we may give of the novel. But history also is allowed to represent life; it is not, any more than painting, expected to apologize. The subject matter of fiction is stored up likewise in documents and records, and if it will not give itself away, as they say in California, it must speak with assurance, with the tone of the historian. Certain accomplished novelists have a habit of giving themselves away which must often bring tears to the eyes of people who take their fiction seriously. I was lately struck, in reading over many pages of Anthony Trollope, with his want of discretion in this particular. In a digression, a parenthesis or an aside, he concedes to the reader that he and this trusting friend are only "making believe." He admits that the events he narrates have not really happened, and that he can give his narrative any turn the reader may like best. Such a betrayal of a sacred office seems to me, I confess, a terrible crime; it is what I mean by the attitude of apology, and it shocks me every whit as much in Trollope as it would have shocked me in Gibbon or Macaulay. It implies that the novelist is less occupied in looking for the truth (the truth, of course I mean, that he assumes, the premises that we must grant him, whatever they may be) than the historian, and in doing so it deprives him at a stroke of all his standing room. To represent and illustrate the past, the actions of men, is the task of either writer, and the only difference that I can see is, in proportion as he succeeds, to the honor of the novelist, consisting as it does in his having more difficulty in collecting his evidence, which is so far from being purely literary. It seems to me to give him a great character, the fact that he has at once so much in common with the philosopher and the painter; this double analogy is a magnificent heritage.

It is of all this evidently that Mr. Besant is full when he insists upon the fact that fiction is one of the *fine* arts, deserving in its turn of all the honors and emoluments that have hitherto been reserved for the successful profession of music, poetry, painting, architecture. It is impossible to insist too much on so important a truth, and the place that Mr. Besant demands for the work of the novelist may be represented, a trifle less abstractly, by saying that he demands not only that it shall be reputed artistic, but that it shall be reputed very artistic indeed. It is excellent that he should have struck this note, for his doing so indicates that there was need of it, that his proposition may be to many people a novelty. One rubs one's eyes at the thought; but the rest of Mr. Besant's essay confirms the revelation. I suspect in truth that it would be possible to confirm it still further, and that one would not be far wrong in saying that in addition to the people to whom it has never occurred that a novel ought to be artistic, there are a great many others who, if this principle were urged upon them, would be filled with an indefinable mistrust. They would find it difficult to explain their repugnance, but it would operate strongly to put them on their guard. "Art," in our Protestant communities, where so many things have got so strangely twisted about, is supposed in certain circles to have some vaguely injurious effect upon those who make it an important consideration, who let it weigh in the balance. It is assumed to be opposed in some mysterious manner to morality, to amusement, to instruction. When it is embodied in the work of the painter (the sculptor is another affair!) you know what it is: it stands there before you, in the honesty of pink and green and a gilt frame; you can see the worst of it at a glance, and you can be on your *guard*. But when it is introduced into literature it becomes more insidious—there is danger of its hurting you before you know it. Literature should be either instructive or amusing, and there is in many minds an impression that these artistic preoccupations, the search for form, contribute to neither end, interfere indeed with both. They are too frivolous to be edifying, and too serious to be diverting; and they are moreover priggish and paradoxical and superfluous. That, I think, represents the manner in which the latent thought of many people who read novels as an exercise in skipping would explain itself if it were to become articulate. They would argue, of course, that a novel ought to be "good," but they would interpret this term in a fashion of their own, which indeed would vary considerably from one critic to another. One would say that being good means representing virtuous and aspiring characters, placed in prominent positions; another would say that it depends on a "happy ending," on a distribution at the last of prizes, pensions, husbands, wives, babies, millions, appended paragraphs, and cheerful remarks. Another still would say that it means being full of incident and movement, so that we shall wish to jump ahead, to see who was the mysterious stranger, and if the stolen will was ever found, and shall not be distracted from this pleasure by any tiresome analysis or "description." But they would all agree that the "artistic" idea would spoil some of their fun. One would hold it accountable for all the description, another would see it revealed in the absence of sympathy. Its hostility to a happy ending would be evident, and it might even in some cases render any ending at all impossible. The "ending" of a novel is, for many persons, like that of a good dinner, a course of dessert and ices, and the artist in fiction is regarded as a sort of meddlesome doctor who forbids agreeable aftertastes. It is therefore true that this conception of Mr. Besant's of the novel as a superior form encounters not only a negative but a positive indifference. It matters little that as a work of art it should really be as little or as much of its essence to supply happy endings, sympathetic characters, and an objective tone, as if it were a work of mechanics: the association of ideas, however incongruous, might easily be too much for it if an eloquent voice were not sometimes raised to call attention to the fact that it is at once as free and as serious a branch of literature as any other.

Certainly this might sometimes be doubted in presence of the enormous number of works of fiction that appeal to the credulity of our generation, for it might easily seem that there could be no great character in a commodity so quickly and easily produced. It must be admitted that good novels are much compromised by bad ones, and that the field at large suffers discredit from overcrowding. I think, however, that this injury is only superficial, and that the superabundance of written fiction proves nothing against the principle itself. It has been vulgarized, like all other kinds of literature, like everything else today, and it has proved more than some kinds accessible to vulgarization. But there is as much difference as there ever was between a good novel and a bad one: the bad is swept with all the daubed canvases and spoiled marble into some unvisited limbo, or infinite rubbish yard beneath the back windows of the world, and the good subsists and emits its light and stimulates our desire for perfection. As I shall take the liberty of making but a single criticism of Mr. Besant, whose tone is so full of the love of his art, I may as well have done with it at once. He seems to me to mistake in attempting to say so definitely beforehand what sort of an affair the good novel will be. To indicate the danger of such an error as that has been the purpose of these few pages; to suggest that certain traditions on the subject, applied *a priori*, have already had much to answer for, and that the good health of an art which undertakes so immediately to reproduce life must demand that it be perfectly free. It lives upon exercise, and the very meaning of exercise is freedom. The only obligation to which in advance we may hold a novel, without incurring the accusation of being arbitrary, is that it be interesting. That general responsibility rests upon it, but it is the only one I can think of. The ways in which it is at liberty to accomplish this result (of interesting us) strike me as innumerable, and such as can only suffer from being marked out or fenced in by prescription. They are as various as the temperament of man, and they are successful in proportion as they reveal a particular mind, different from others. A novel is in its broadest definition a personal, a direct impression of life: that, to begin with, constitutes its value, which is greater or less according to the intensity of the impression. But there will be no intensity at all, and therefore no value, unless there is freedom to feel and say. The tracing of a line to be followed, of a tone to be taken, of a form to be filled out, is a limitation of that freedom and a suppression of the very thing that we are most curious about. The form, it seems to me, is to be appreciated after the fact: then the author's choice has been made, his standard has been indicated; then we can follow lines and directions and compare tones and resemblances. Then in a word we can enjoy one of the most charming of pleasures, we can estimate quality, we can apply the test of execution. The execution belongs to the author alone; it is what is most personal to him, and we measure him by that. The advantage, the luxury, as well as the torment and responsibility of the novelist, is that there is no limit to what he may attempt as an executant—no limit to his possible experiments, efforts, discoveries, successes. Here it is especially that he works, step by step, like his brother of the brush, of whom we may always say that he has painted his picture in a manner best known to himself. His manner is his secret, not necessarily a jealous one. He cannot disclose it as a general thing if he would; he would be at a loss to teach it to others. I say this with a due recollection of having insisted on the community of method of the artist who paints a picture and the artist who writes a novel. The painter *is* able to teach the rudiments of his practice, and it is possible, from the study of good work (granted the aptitude), both to learn how to paint and to learn how to write. Yet it remains true, without injury to the *rapprochement*, that the literary artist would be obliged to say to his pupil much more than the other, "Ah, well, you must do it as you can!" It is a question of degree, a matter of delicacy. If there are exact sciences, there are also exact arts, and the grammar of painting is so much more definite that it makes the difference.

I ought to add, however, that if Mr. Besant says at the beginning of his essay that the "laws of fiction may be laid down and taught with as much precision and exactness as the laws of harmony, perspective, and proportion," he mitigates what might appear to be an extravagance by applying his remark to "general" laws, and by expressing most of these rules in a manner with which it would certainly be unaccommodating to disagree. That the novelist must write from his experience, that his "characters must be real and such as might be met with in actual life"; that "a young lady brought up in a quiet country village should avoid descriptions of garrison life," and "a writer whose friends and personal experiences belong to the lower middle class should carefully avoid introducing his characters into society"; that one should enter one's notes in a common-place book; that one's figures should be clear in outline; that making them clear by some trick of speech or of carriage is a bad method, and "describing them at length" is a worse one; that English fiction should have a "conscious moral purpose"; that "it is almost impossible to estimate too highly the value of careful workmanship—that is, of style"; that "the most important point of all is the story," that "the story is everything": these are principles with most of which it is surely impossible not to sympathize. That remark about the lower middle-class writer and his knowing his place is perhaps rather chilling; but for the rest I should find it difficult to dissent from any one of these recommendations. At the same time, I should find it difficult positively to assent to them, with the exception, perhaps, of the injunction as to entering one's notes in a common-place book. They scarcely seem to me to have the quality that Mr. Besant

attributes to the rules of the novelist—the "precision and exactness" of "the laws of harmony, perspective, and proportion."
They are suggestive, they are even inspiring, but they are not
exact, though they are doubtless as much so as the case admits
of: which is a proof of that liberty of interpretation for which
I just contended. For the value of these different injunctions—
so beautiful and so vague—is wholly in the meaning one attaches
to them. The characters, the situation, which strike one as real
will be those that touch and interest one most, but the measure
of reality is very difficult to fix. The reality of Don Quixote or of
Mr. Micawber is a very delicate shade; it is a reality so colored
by the author's vision that, vivid as it may be, one would hesitate
to propose it as a model: one would expose one's self to some
very embarrassing questions on the part of a pupil. It goes
without saying that you will not write a good novel unless you
possess the sense of reality; but it will be difficult to give you a
recipe for calling that sense into being. Humanity is immense,
and reality has a myriad forms; the most one can affirm is that
some of the flowers of fiction have the odor of it, and others have
not; as for telling you in advance how your nosegay should be
composed, that is another affair. It is equally excellent and
inconclusive to say that one must write from experience; to our
supposititious aspirant such a declaration might savor of mockery.
What kind of experience is intended, and where does it begin
and end? Experience is never limited, and it is never complete;
it is an immense sensibility, a kind of huge spiderweb of the
finest silken threads suspended in the chamber of consciousness,
and catching every air-borne particle in its tissue. It is the very
atmosphere of the mind; and when the mind is imaginative—
much more when it happens to be that of a man of genius—it
takes to itself the faintest hints of life, it converts the very pulses
of the air into revelations. The young lady living in a village
has only to be a damsel upon whom nothing is lost to make it
quite unfair (as it seems to me) to declare to her that she shall
have nothing to say about the military. Greater miracles have
been seen than that, imagination assisting, she should speak
the truth about some of these gentlemen. I remember an English
novelist, a woman of genius, telling me that she was much commended for the impression she had managed to give in one of
her tales of the nature and way of life of the French Protestant
youth. She had been asked where she learned so much about

this recondite being, she had been congratulated on her peculiar
opportunities. These opportunities consisted in her having once,
in Paris, as she ascended a staircase, passed an open door where,
in the household of a *pasteur*, some of the young Protestants were
seated at table round a finished meal. The glimpse made a
picture; it lasted only a moment, but that moment was experience.   She had got her direct personal impression, and she
turned out her type. She knew what youth was, and what
Protestantism; she also had the advantage of having seen what
it was to be French, so that she converted these ideas into a
concrete image and produced a reality. Above all, however,
she was blessed with the faculty which when you give it an inch
takes an ell, and which for the artist is a much greater source of
strength than any accident of residence or of place in the social
scale. The power to guess the unseen from the seen, to trace the
implication of things, to judge the whole piece by the pattern,
the condition of feeling life in general so completely that you are
well on your way to knowing any particular corner of it—this
cluster of gifts may almost be said to constitute experience, and
they occur in country and in town, and in the most differing
stages of education. If experience consists of impressions, it may
be said that impressions *are* experience, just as (have we not
seen it?) they are the very air we breathe. Therefore, if I should
certainly say to a novice, "Write from experience and experience only," I should feel that this was rather a tantalizing moni-
tion if I were not careful immediately to add, "Try to be one of
the people on whom nothing is lost!"

I am far from intending by this to minimize the importance
of exactness—of truth of detail. One can speak best from one's
own taste, and I may therefore venture to say that the air of
reality (solidity of specification) seems to me to be the supreme
virtue of a novel—the merit on which all its other merits (including that conscious moral purpose of which Mr. Besant
speaks) helplessly and submissively depend. If it be not there,
they are all as nothing, and if these be there, they owe their
effect to the success with which the author has produced the
illusion of life. The cultivation of this success, the study of this
exquisite process, form, to my taste, the beginning and the end
of the art of the novelist. They are his inspiration, his despair,
his reward, his torment, his delight. It is here in very truth that
he competes with life; it is here that he competes with his

brother the painter in *his* attempt to render the look of things, the look that conveys their meaning, to catch the color, the relief, the expression, the surface, the substance of the human spectacle. It is in regard to this that Mr. Besant is well inspired when he bids him take notes. He cannot possibly take too many, he cannot possibly take enough. All life solicits him, and to "render" the simplest surface, to produce the most momentary illusion, is a very complicated business. His case would be easier, and the rule would be more exact, if Mr. Besant had been able to tell him what notes to take. But this, I fear, he can never learn in any manual; it is the business of his life. He has to take a great many in order to select a few, he has to work them up as he can, and even the guides and philosophers who might have most to say to him must leave him alone when it comes to the application of precepts, as we leave the painter in communion with his palette. That his characters "must be clear in outline," as Mr. Besant says—he feels that down to his boots; but how he shall make them so is a secret between his good angel and himself. It would be absurdly simple if he could be taught that a great deal of "description" would make them so, or that on the contrary the absence of description and the cultivation of dialogue, or the absence of dialogue and the multiplication of "incident," would rescue him from his difficulties. Nothing, for instance, is more possible than that he be of a turn of mind for which this odd, literal opposition of description and dialogue, incident and description, has little meaning and light. People often talk of these things as if they had a kind of internecine distinctness, instead of melting into each other at every breath, and being intimately associated parts of one general effort of expression. I cannot imagine composition existing in a series of blocks, nor conceive, in any novel worth discussing at all, of a passage of description that is not in its intention narrative, a passage of dialogue that is not in its intention descriptive, a touch of truth of any sort that does not partake of the nature of incident, or an incident that derives its interest from any other source than the general and only source of the success of a work of art—that of being illustrative. A novel is a living thing, all one and continuous, like any other organism, and in proportion as it lives will it be found, I think, that in each of the parts there is something of each of the other parts. The critic who over the close texture of a finished work shall pretend to trace a geography of items will mark some frontiers as artificial, I fear, as any that have been known to history. There is an old-fashioned distinction between the novel of character and the novel of incident which must have cost many a smile to the intending fabulist who was keen about his work. It appears to me as little to the point as the equally celebrated distinction between the novel and the romance—to answer as little to any reality. There are bad novels and good novels, as there are bad pictures and good pictures; but that is the only distinction in which I see any meaning, and I can as little imagine speaking of a novel of character as I can imagine speaking of a picture of character. When one says picture one says of character, when one says novel one says of incident, and the terms may be transposed at will. What is character but the determination of incident? What is incident but the illustration of character? What is either a picture or a novel that is *not* of character? What else do we seek in it and find in it? It is an incident for a woman to stand up with her hand resting on a table and look out at you in a certain way; or if it be not an incident I think it will be hard to say what it is. At the same time it is an expression of character. If you say you don't see it (character in *that—allons donc!*), this is exactly what the artist who has reasons of his own for thinking he *does* see it undertakes to show you. When a young man makes up his mind that he has not faith enough after all to enter the church as he intended, that is an incident, though you may not hurry to the end of the chapter to see whether perhaps he doesn't change once more. I do not say that these are extraordinary or startling incidents. I do not pretend to estimate the degree of interest proceeding from them, for this will depend upon the skill of the painter. It sounds almost puerile to say that some incidents are intrinsically much more important than others, and I need not take this precaution after having professed my sympathy for the major ones in remarking that the only classification of the novel that I can understand is into that which has life and that which has it not.

The novel and the romance, the novel of incident and that of character—these clumsy separations appear to me to have been made by critics and readers for their own convenience, and to help them out of some of their occasional queer predicaments, but to have little reality or interest for the producer, from whose point of view it is of course that we are attempting to consider the art of fiction. The case is the same with another shadowy category which Mr. Besant apparently is disposed to set up— that of the "modern English novel"; unless indeed it be that in this matter he has fallen into an accidental confusion of stand-points. It is not quite clear whether he intends the remarks in which he alludes to it to be didactic or historical. It is as difficult to suppose a person intending to write a modern English as to suppose him writing an ancient English novel: that is a label which begs the question. One writes the novel, one paints the picture, of one's language and of one's time, and calling it modern English will not, alas! make the difficult task any easier. No more, unfortunately, will calling this or that work of one's fellow artist a romance—unless it be, of course, simply for the pleasantness of the thing, as for instance when Hawthorne gave this heading to his story of *Blithedale*. The French, who have brought the theory of fiction to remarkable completeness, have but one name for the novel, and have not attempted smaller things in it, that I can see, for that. I can think of no obligation to which the "romancer" would not be held equally with the novelist; the standard of execution is equally high for each. Of course it is of execution that we are talking—that being the only point of a novel that is open to contention. This is perhaps too often lost sight of, only to produce interminable confusions and cross purposes. We must grant the artist his subject, his idea, his *donnée:* our criticism is applied only to what he makes of it. Naturally I do not mean that we are bound to like it or find it interesting: in case we do not, our course is perfectly simple—to let it alone. We may believe that of a certain idea even the most sincere novelist can make nothing at all, and the event may perfectly justify our belief; but the failure will have been a failure to execute, and it is in the execution that the fatal weakness is recorded. If we pretend to respect the artist at all, we must allow him his freedom of choice, in the face, in particu-lar cases, of innumerable presumptions that the choice will not fructify. Art derives a considerable part of its beneficial exercise from flying in the face of presumptions, and some of the most interesting experiments of which it is capable are hidden in the bosom of common things. Gustave Flaubert has written a story about the devotion of a servant girl to a parrot, and the produc-tion, highly finished as it is, cannot on the whole be called a success. We are perfectly free to find it flat, but I think it might have been interesting; and I, for my part, am extremely glad he should have written it; it is a contribution to our knowledge of what can be done—or what cannot. Ivan Turgenev has written a tale about a deaf and dumb serf and a lap dog, and the thing is touching, loving, a little masterpiece. He struck the note of life where Gustave Flaubert missed it—he flew in the face of a presumption and achieved a victory.

Nothing, of course, will ever take the place of the good old fashion of "liking" a work of art or not liking it: the most improved criticism will not abolish that primitive, that ultimate test. I mention this to guard myself from the accusation of intimating that the idea, the subject, of a novel or a picture, does not matter. It matters, to my sense, in the highest degree, and if I might put up a prayer it would be that artists should select none but the richest. Some, as I have already hastened to admit, are much more remunerative than others, and it would be a world happily arranged in which persons intending to treat them should be exempt from confusions and mistakes. This fortunate condition will arrive only, I fear, on the same day that critics become purged from error. Meanwhile, I repeat, we do not judge the artist with fairness unless we say to him, "Oh, I grant you your starting point, because if I did not I should seem to prescribe to you, and heaven forbid I should take that responsibility. If I pretend to tell you what you must not take, you will call upon me to tell you then what you must take; in which case I shall be prettily caught. Moreover, it isn't till I have accepted your data that I can begin to measure you. I have the standard, the pitch; I have no right to tamper with your flute and then criticize your music. Of course I may not care for your idea at all; I may think it silly, or stale, or unclean; in which case I wash my hands of you altogether. I may content myself with believing that you will not have succeeded in being interesting, but I shall, of course, not attempt to demonstrate it, and you will be as indifferent to me as I am to you. I needn't remind you that there are all sorts of tastes: who can know it better? Some people, for excellent reasons, don't like to read about carpenters; others, for reasons even better, don't like to read about courtesans. Many object to Americans. Others (I believe they are mainly editors and publishers) won't look at Italians. Some readers don't like quiet subjects; others don't like bustling ones. Some enjoy a complete illusion, others the consciousness of large concessions.

They choose their novels accordingly, and if they don't care about your idea they won't, *a fortiori*, care about your treatment."

So that it comes back very quickly, as I have said, to the liking: in spite of M. Zola, who reasons less powerfully than he represents, and who will not reconcile himself to this absoluteness of taste, thinking that there are certain things that people ought to like, and that they can be made to like. I am quite at a loss to imagine anything (at any rate in this matter of fiction) that people *ought* to like or to dislike. Selection will be sure to take care of itself, for it has a constant motive behind it. That motive is simply experience. As people feel life, so they will feel the art that is most closely related to it. This closeness of relation is what we should never forget in talking of the effort of the novel. Many people speak of it as a factitious, artificial form, a product of ingenuity, the business of which is to alter and arrange the things that surround us, to translate them into conventional, traditional molds. This, however, is a view of the matter which carries us but a very short way, condemns the art to an eternal repetition of a few familiar *clichés*, cuts short its development, and leads us straight up to a dead wall. Catching the very note and trick, the strange irregular rhythm of life, that is the attempt whose strenuous force keeps Fiction upon her feet. In proportion as in what she offers us we see life *without* rearrangement do we feel that we are touching the truth; in proportion as we see it *with* rearrangement do we feel that we are being put off with a substitute, a compromise and convention. It is not uncommon to hear an extraordinary assurance of remark in regard to this matter of rearranging, which is often spoken of as if it were the last word of art. Mr. Besant seems to me in danger of falling into the great error with his rather unguarded talk about "selection." Art is essentially selection, but it is a selection whose main care is to be typical, to be inclusive. For many people art means rose-colored windowpanes, and selection means picking a bouquet for Mrs. Grundy. They will tell you glibly that artistic considerations have nothing to do with the disagreeable, with the ugly; they will rattle off shallow commonplaces about the province of art and the limits of art till you are moved to some wonder in return as to the province and the limits of ignorance. It appears to me that no one can ever have made a seriously artistic attempt without becoming conscious of an immense increase—a kind of revelation—of freedom. One perceives in that case—by the light of a heavenly ray—that the province of art is all life, all feeling, all observation, all vision. As Mr. Besant so justly intimates, it is all experience. That is a sufficient answer to those who maintain that it must not touch the sad things of life, who stick into its divine unconscious bosom little prohibitory inscriptions on the end of sticks, such as we see in public gardens—"It is forbidden to walk on the grass; it is forbidden to touch the flowers; it is not allowed to introduce dogs or to remain after dark; it is requested to keep to the right." The young aspirant in the line of fiction whom we continue to imagine will do nothing without taste, for in that case his freedom would be of little use to him; but the first advantage of his taste will be to reveal to him the absurdity of the little sticks and tickets. If he have taste, I must add, of course he will have ingenuity, and my disrespectful reference to that quality just now was not meant to imply that it is useless in fiction. But it is only a secondary aid; the first is a capacity for receiving straight impressions.

Mr. Besant has some remarks on the question of "the story" which I shall not attempt to criticize, though they seem to me to contain a singular ambiguity, because I do not think I understand them. I cannot see what is meant by talking as if there were a part of a novel which is the story and part of it which for mystical reasons is not—unless indeed the distinction be made in a sense in which it is difficult to suppose that anyone should attempt to convey anything. "The story," if it represents anything, represents the subject, the idea, the *donnée* of the novel; and there is surely no "school"—Mr. Besant speaks of a school— which urges that a novel should be all treatment and no subject. There must assuredly be something to treat; every school is intimately conscious of that. This sense of the story being the idea, the starting point, of the novel, is the only one that I see in which it can be spoken of as something different from its organic whole; and since in proportion as the work is successful the idea permeates and penetrates it, informs and animates it, so that every word and every punctuation point contribute directly to the expression, in that proportion do we lose our sense of the story being a blade which may be drawn more or less out of its sheath. The story and the novel, the idea and the form, are the needle and thread, and I never heard of a guild of tailors who recommended the use of the thread without the needle, or the needle without the thread. Mr. Besant is not the only critic who may be observed to have spoken as if there were certain things in life which constitute stories, and certain others which do not. I find the same odd implication in an entertaining article in the *Pall Mall Gazette*, devoted, as it happens, to Mr. Besant's lecture. "The story is the thing!" says this graceful writer, as if with a tone of opposition to some other idea. I should think it was, as every painter who, as the time for "sending in" his picture looms in the distance, finds himself still in quest of a subject—as every belated artist not fixed about his theme will heartily agree. There are some subjects which speak to us and others which do not, but he would be a clever man who should undertake to give a rule—an index expurgatorius—by which the story and the no-story should be known apart. It is impossible (to me at least) to imagine any such rule which shall not be altogether arbitrary. The writer in the *Pall Mall* opposes the delightful (as I suppose) novel of *Margot la Balafrée* to certain tales in which "Bostonian nymphs" appear to have "rejected English dukes for psychological reasons." I am not acquainted with the romance just designated, and can scarcely forgive the *Pall Mall* critic for not mentioning the name of the author, but the title appears to refer to a lady who may have received a scar in some heroic adventure. I am inconsolable at not being acquainted with this episode, but am utterly at a loss to see why it is a story when the rejection (or acceptance) of a duke is not, and why a reason, psychological or other, is not a subject when a cicatrix is. They are all particles of the multitudinous life with which the novel deals, and surely no dogma which pretends to make it lawful to touch the one and unlawful to touch the other will stand for a moment on its feet. It is the special picture that must stand or fall, according as it seem to possess truth or to lack it. Mr. Besant does not, to my sense, light up the subject by intimating that a story must, under penalty of not being a story, consist of "adventures." Why of adventures more than of green spectacles? He mentions a category of impossible things, and among them he places "fiction without adventure." Why without adventure, more than without matrimony, or celibacy, or parturition, or cholera, or hydropathy, or Jansenism? This seems to me to bring the novel back to the hapless little role of being an artificial, ingenious thing—bring it down from its large, free character of an immense and exquisite correspondence with life. And what *is* adventure, when it comes to that, and by what sign is the listening pupil to recognize it? It is an adventure—an immense one—for me to write this little article; and for a Bostonian nymph to reject an English duke is an adventure only less stirring, I should say, than for an English duke to be rejected by a Bostonian nymph. I see dramas within dramas in that, and innumerable points of view. A psychological reason is, to my imagination, an object adorably pictorial; to catch the tint of its complexion—I feel as if that idea might inspire one to Titianesque efforts. There are few things more exciting to me, in short, than a psychological reason, and yet, I protest, the novel seems to me the most magnificent form of art. I have just been reading, at the same time, the delightful story of *Treasure Island*, by Mr. Robert Louis Stevenson and, in a manner less consecutive, the last tale from M. Edmond de Goncourt, which is entitled *Chérie*. One of these works treats of murders, mysteries, islands of dreadful renown, hairbreadth escapes, miraculous coincidences, and buried doubloons. The other treats of a little French girl who lived in a fine house in Paris, and died of wounded sensibility because no one would marry her. I call *Treasure Island* delightful because it appears to me to have succeeded wonderfully in what it attempts; and I venture to bestow no epithet upon *Chérie*, which strikes me as having failed deplorably in what it attempts—that is, in tracing the development of the moral consciousness of a child. But one of these productions strikes me as exactly as much of a novel as the other, and as having a "story" quite as much. The moral consciousness of a child is as much a part of life as the islands of the Spanish Main, and the one sort of geography seems to me to have those "surprises" of which Mr. Besant speaks quite as much as the other. For myself (since it comes back in the last resort, as I say, to the preference of the individual), the picture of the child's experience has the advantage that I can at successive steps (an immense luxury, near to the "sensual pleasure" of which Mr. Besant's critic in the *Pall Mall* speaks) say Yes or No, as it may be, to what the artist puts before me. I have been a child in fact, but I have been on a quest for a buried treasure only in supposition, and it is a simple accident that with M. de Goncourt I should have for the most part to say No. With George Eliot, when she painted that country with a far other intelligence, I always said Yes.

The most interesting part of Mr. Besant's lecture is unfortunately the briefest passage—his very cursory allusion to the "conscious moral purpose" of the novel. Here again it is not very clear whether he be recording a fact or laying down a principle; it is a great pity that in the latter case he should not have developed his idea. This branch of the subject is of immense importance, and Mr. Besant's few words point to considerations of the widest reach, not to be lightly disposed of. He will have treated the art of fiction but superficially who is not prepared to go every inch of the way that these considerations will carry him. It is for this reason that at the beginning of these remarks I was careful to notify the reader that my reflections on so large a theme have no pretension to be exhaustive. Like Mr. Besant, I have left the question of the morality of the novel till the last, and at the last I find I have used up my space. It is a question surrounded with difficulties, as witness the very first that meets us, in the form of a definite question, on the threshold. Vagueness, in such a discussion, is fatal, and what is the meaning of your morality and your conscious moral purpose? Will you not define your terms and explain how (a novel being a picture) a picture can be either moral or immoral? You wish to paint a moral picture or carve a moral statue: will you not tell us how you would set about it? We are discussing the Art of Fiction; questions of art are questions (in the widest sense) of execution; questions of morality are quite another affair, and will you not let us see how it is that you find it so easy to mix them up? These things are so clear to Mr. Besant that he has deduced from them a law which he sees embodied in English fiction, and which is "a truly admirable thing and a great cause for congratulation." It is a great cause for congratulation indeed when such thorny problems become as smooth as silk. I may add that in so far as Mr. Besant perceives that in point of fact English fiction has addressed itself preponderantly to these delicate questions he will appear to many people to have made a vain discovery. They will have been positively struck, on the contrary, with the moral timidity of the usual English novelist; with his (or with her) aversion to face the difficulties with which on every side the treatment of reality bristles. He is apt to be extremely shy (whereas the picture that Mr. Besant draws is a picture of boldness), and the sign of his work, for the most part, is a cautious silence on certain subjects. In the English novel (by which of course I mean the American as well), more than in any other, there is a traditional difference between that which people know and that which they agree to admit that they know, that which they see and that which they speak of, that which they feel to be a part of life and that which they allow to enter into literature. There is the great difference, in short, between what they talk of in conversation and what they talk of in print. The essence of moral energy is to survey the whole field, and I should directly reverse Mr. Besant's remark and say not that the English novel has a purpose, but that it has a diffidence. To what degree a purpose in a work of art is a source of corruption I shall not attempt to inquire; the one that seems to me least dangerous is the purpose of making a perfect work. As for our novel, I may say lastly on this score that as we find it in England today it strikes me as addressed in a large degree to "young people," and that this in itself constitutes a presumption that it will be rather shy. There are certain things which it is generally agreed not to discuss, not even to mention, before young people. That is very well, but the absence of discussion is not a symptom of the moral passion. The purpose of the English novel—"a truly admirable thing, and a great cause for congratulation"—strikes me therefore as rather negative.

There is one point at which the moral sense and the artistic sense lie very near together; that is in the light of the very obvious truth that the deepest quality of a work of art will always be the quality of the mind of the producer. In proportion as that intelligence is fine will the novel, the picture, the statue partake of the substance of beauty and truth. To be constituted of such elements is, to my vision, to have purpose enough. No good novel will ever proceed from a superficial mind; that seems to me an axiom which, for the artist in fiction, will cover all needful moral ground: if the youthful aspirant take it to heart it will illuminate for him many of the mysteries of "purpose." There are many other useful things that might be said to him, but I have come to the end of my article, and can only touch them as I pass. The critic in the *Pall Mall Gazette*, whom I have already quoted, draws attention to the danger, in speaking of the art of fiction, of generalizing. The danger that he has in mind is rather, I imagine, that of particularizing, for there are some comprehensive remarks which, in addition to those embodied in Mr. Besant's suggestive lecture, might without fear of misleading him be addressed to the ingenuous student. I should remind him first of the magnificence of the form that is open to him, which offers to sight so few restrictions and such innumerable opportunities. The other arts, in comparison, appear confined and hampered; the various conditions under which they are exercised are so rigid and definite. But the only condition that I can think of attaching to the composition of the novel is, as I have already said, that it be sincere. This freedom is a splendid privilege, and the first lesson of the young novelist is to learn to be worthy of it. "Enjoy it as it deserves," I should say to him; "take possession of it, explore it to its utmost extent, publish it, rejoice in it. All life belongs to you, and do not listen either to those who would shut you up into corners of it and tell you that it is only here and there that art inhabits, or to those who would persuade you that this heavenly messenger wings her way outside of life altogether, breathing a superfine air, and turning away her head from the truth of things. There is no impression of life, no manner of seeing it and feeling it, to which the plan of the novelist may not offer a place; you have only to remember that talents so dissimilar as those of Alexandre Dumas and Jane Austen, Charles Dickens and Gustave Flaubert have worked in this field with equal glory. Do not think too much about optimism and pessimism; try and catch the color of life itself. In France today we see a prodigious effort (that of Emile Zola,[2] to whose solid and serious work no explorer of the capacity of the novel can allude without respect), we see an extraordinary effort vitiated by a spirit of pessimism on a narrow basis. M. Zola is magnificent, but he strikes an English reader as ignorant; he has an air of working in the dark; if he had as much light as energy, his results would be of the highest value. As for the aberrations of a shallow optimism, the ground (of English fiction especially) is strewn with their brittle particles as with broken glass. If you must indulge in conclusions, let them have the taste of a wide knowledge. Remember that your first duty is to be as complete as possible—to make as perfect a work. Be generous and delicate and pursue the prize."

[2]See James's study of Zola, in *Notes on Novelists* (New York, 1914), pp. 26–64.

WILLIAM DEAN HOWELLS

(1837–1920)

o◯ooo◯o

WILLIAM DEAN HOWELLS is America's best representative of realism in both fiction and criticism. He was one of our most voluminous authors, and as editor of the *Atlantic Monthly* and later as chief reviewer for *Harper's* he exerted great influence as an arbiter of literary taste. With little formal education, he lacked scholarly knowledge of the great literary masters of the past (a fact which may help to explain his general disrespect for them), but as a good journalist he had a wide knowledge of contemporary literature,[1] and he served as an excellent mirror of the time-spirit which was dominated by two great forces—democracy and science. These twin forces explain much of his realistic theory.

He defined realism as "nothing more and nothing less than the truthful treatment of material," as involving "fidelity to experience and probability of motive."[2] He would have the novelist "interpret the common feelings of commonplace people."[3] He found the lack of distinction in democratic America, which seemed ominous to Arnold (his *bête noire*), a source of inspiration. "The pride of caste," he said, "is becoming the pride of taste; but as before, it is averse to the mass of men. . . . Democracy in literature is the reverse of all this."[4] He would have "our American novelists be as American as they unconsciously can. . . . The arts must become democratic, and then we shall have the expression of art in America."[5] Believing in evolutionary

---

[1]The record of his reading is partially covered in his book, *My Literary Passions.* Cervantes is about the only major older writer he greatly admired. He says that it was Heine who "showed me that this ideal of literature [should be different from life] was false; that the life of literature was from the springs of the best common speech, and that the nearer it could be made to conform, in voice, look, and gait, to graceful, easy, picturesque and humorous or impassioned talk, the better it was" (pp. 128–129 of the Library edition). He was also strongly influenced by Goldsmith, Irving, and Tolstoi. He especially admired "the almost ideal perfection in the art of Jane Austen." (See his introduction to *Pride and Prejudice*, New York, 1919.) In critical principles he took hints from Canon Farrar and Valdes—see *Criticism and Fiction* (Library edition), pp. 214–229.

[2]*My Literary Passions and Criticism and Fiction* (Library edition), pp. 229, 200.
[3]Cf. below, p. 573.   [4]*My Literary Passions and Criticism and Fiction*, p. 282.
[5]*Ibid.*, pp. 257, 258.

progress and regarding traditionalism as mere "paralysis,"[6] he had a strong antipathy toward novelists like Scott, whom he found "false and mistaken" in "his medieval ideals, his blind Jacobitism, his intense devotion to aristocracy and royalty."[7] "At least three fifths of the literature called classic, in all languages, . . . is as dead as the people who wrote it," and it is preserved merely by "a superstitious piety."[8] His debt to democracy was equaled by his debt to science, which also reinforced his contempt for tradition. The truth on which his realism was based was essentially non-qualitative and scientific rather than imaginative, as in the case of Emerson and Lowell who followed Coleridge and Plato. "The true realist," Howells said, "cannot look upon human life and declare this thing or that thing unworthy of notice, any more than the scientist can declare a fact of the material world beneath the dignity of his inquiry. . . ." He quotes with approval his master Valdes' saying, "In nature there is neither great nor small; all is equal. . . . because it is equally divine. Let not the novelists then endeavor to add anything to reality, to turn it and twist it, to restrict it."[9] He would thus, in theory, minimize selection and even the ordering and focusing of material which constitutes plot. It is odd to discover Howells, who as a socialist deified a planned economy, saying, "Ought we not to praise (the novelist) where his work confesses itself, as life confesses itself, without a plan?" Whereas followers of Aristotle and Plato had urged that the artist imitate an imaginative synthesis re-created from reality selected in the interest of a representative type, something universal derived from particulars, Howells ridiculed this doctrine of idealization as analogous to reproducing a cardboard grasshopper when a "real grasshopper" was available. Idealizing characters meant to him taking "the lifelikeness out of them and put[ting] the booklikeness into them."[10] "Do not trouble yourselves about standards and ideals; but try to be faithful and natural." "The greatest achievement of fiction, in its highest sense, is to present a picture of life; and the deeper the sense of something desultory, unfinished, imperfect it gives, even in the region of conduct, the more admirable it seems."[11] Ultimately, perhaps, his view that the impersonal and unfocused record of unselected experi-

---

[6]*Ibid.*, p. 200.   [7]*Ibid.*, pp. 203–204.   [8]*Ibid.*, p. 261.
[9]*Ibid.*, pp. 201; 228. But compare his reaction to Whitman, *ibid.*, p. 54: "I had an instinctive doubt whether formlessness was really better than formality. Something, it seems to me, may be contained and kept alive in formality, but in formlessness everything spills and wastes away. This is what I find the fatal defect of our American Ossian, Walt Whitman, whose way is where artistic madness lies." He goes on to praise Whitman's "beautiful and noble thoughts."
[10]*Ibid.*, p. 198.   [11]Quoted by De Mille, *Literary Criticism in America*, p. 186.

ence will fulfill the aim of literature, which is to make "the race better and kinder," rests on the religious faith of the Victorian evolutionists that "the beast-man will be so far subdued and tamed in us that the memory of him in literature shall be left to perish."[12] Once he said that "a great gulf, never to be bridged, divides the ethical and the aesthetic intention." But his more characteristic (and Victorian?) view is expressed in connection with Tolstoi: "If he had represented the fact truly, as in his conscience and intelligence he had known it really to be, he had treated it ethically and of necessity aesthetically; for as you cannot fail to feel in every piece of his fiction, the perfect aesthetics result from the perfect ethics. . . . Where the artist and the moralist work together for righteousness, there is the true art."[13]

In line with Taine, Howells accepted a deterministic interpretation of literature and demanded that the critic should proceed as a botanist treats a plant. Continuing his general break with tradition, Howells claimed that "much if not most current criticism as practiced among the English and Americans is bad, is falsely principled, and is conditioned in evil."[14] In the first place, one must realize in the light of determinism that literature is like a plant, that it couldn't be otherwise than it is, and therefore that one has no right to evaluate it: one can only describe it and "place a book in such a light that the reader shall know its class, its function, its character."[15] The true critic, he argues, will be a "gentle, dispassionate, scientific student of current literature who never imagines that he can direct literature, but realizes that it is a plant which springs from the nature of a people,[16] and draws its forces from their life, that its root is in their character, and that it takes form from their will and taste."[17] Criticism, hitherto judicial, must "altogether reconceive its office." "It must reduce this to the business of observing, recording, and comparing; to analyzing the material before it, and then synthesizing its impressions." "There is a measure of the same absurdity," Howells says, in the critic's "trampling on a poem, a novel, or an essay that does not please him as in the botanist's grinding a plant underfoot because he does not find it pretty. . . . It is his business rather to identify the species and then explain how and where

[12]*My Literary Passions* (1895), p. 54.
[13]*North American Review*, CLXXXVIII, 847.
[14]*My Literary Passions and Criticism and Fiction*, p. 215.
[15]Cooke, *Howells*, p. 50, emphasizes the view that "The general method of criticism, Howells believed, should be in a word the method of science."
[16]Compare Whitman's theory of literature, and also that of Van Wyck Brooks today in the Conclusion to *The Flowering of New England* (New York, 1936).
[17]Quoted by Cooke, *Howells*, p. 51.

the specimen is imperfect and irregular."[18] Howells has been much censured[19] for narrowing criticism by trying to deprive it of its immemorial right to judge; indeed, he himself violated his principle in this respect as much as anyone, for no one judged people like Scott and Thackeray and Poe, and indeed "three fifths" of all the great masters, more harshly. He was followed by many theorists, however, who saw in science the gateway to a better criticism.[20]

In actual critical practice, Howells's best work is doubtless his essays on Longfellow and Lowell and Mark Twain. Here, as a more dignified Boswell, with impeccable good taste he mingles personal reminiscence with literary appreciation of a broad sort, enabling us to see the authors in their habit as they lived, revealing their characters in action. Historically his critical claim to fame rests on his work as a pioneer in "discovering" Emily Dickinson, Hamlin Garland, Stephen Crane, and Frank Norris when most critics were shocked at such books as *Maggie, A Girl of the Streets*.[21] Howells has been much laughed at for saying that our novelists "concern themselves with the more smiling aspects of life, which are the more American,"[22] but such a remark should be countered, in one's memory, by his championship of the rancid realism of Crane and Norris, and by his plea, at the end of *Criticism and Fiction*, that our writers should "see how even here vast masses of men are sunk in misery that must grow every day more hopeless, or embroiled in a struggle for life that must end in enslaving and imbruting them."[23] We must remember that he courageously "presented, for the first time in the American novel, an economic criticism definitely based on collectivism instead of the older order of competitive, individual effort."[24] He recognized very realistically the aspects of American life which were unsmiling in his socialistic novels after *A Hazard of New Fortunes* (1890).

[18]*Ibid.*, pp. 50–51.

[19]See especially the study of J. M. Robertson, listed in the following bibliography.

[20]See Hamlin Garland's *Crumbling Idols* (1894); H. H. Boyesen's many books of criticism; C. D. Warner's *The Relation of Literature to Life* (1896); W. M. Payne, "American Literary Criticism and the Doctrine of Evolution," *The International Monthly*, II, 26–46; 127–153 (1900); and H. W. Mabie, "The Significance of Modern Criticism," in *Essays in Literary Interpretation* (New York, 1892), pp. 46–70.

[21]See his "Poems of Emily Dickinson," *Harper's Magazine*, LXXXII, 318–321 (1891); his preface to Hamlin Garland's *Main-Travelled Roads* (Chicago, 1893) and "Mr. Garland's Books," *North American Review*, CLXXXXVI, 523 ff.; "Frank Norris," *North American Review*, CLXXV, 769 ff. (1902).

[22]*My Literary Passions and Criticism and Fiction*, p. 252.   [23]*Ibid.*, p. 280.

[24]W. F. Taylor, "William Dean Howells and the Economic Novel," *American Literature*, IV, 113 (1932).

BIBLIOGRAPHY

TEXT

Modern Italian Poets: Essays and Versions. New York, 1887.
Criticism and Fiction. New York, 1891.
My Literary Passions. New York, 1895.
Literary Friends and Acquaintance: A Personal Retrospect of American Author-ship. New York, 1900.
Heroines of Fiction. 2 vols. New York, 1901.
Literature and Life: Studies. New York, 1902.
My Mark Twain: Reminiscences and Criticisms. New York, 1910.
Imaginary Interviews. New York, 1910.

BIBLIOGRAPHY

Cooke, D. G., *William Dean Howells.* New York, 1922. (Pages 257–272 contain the best bibliography available, although it is admittedly incomplete. A considerable list of Howells's contributions to periodicals is given, as well as a list of his critical introductions to some twenty books by others.)

BIOGRAPHY AND CRITICISM

Cooke, D. G., *William Dean Howells.* New York, 1922.
De Mille, George E., "Howells," in *Literary Criticism in America.* New York, 1931, pp. 182–206.
Edwards, Herbert. "Howells and the Controversy over Realism in America," *American Literature*, III, 237–248 (1931).
Firkins, O. W., *William Dean Howells.* Harvard University Press, 1924.
Matthews, Brander, "Mr. Howells as a Critic," *Forum*, XXXII, 629–638 (1902).
Robertson, J. M., "Howells," in *Essays Toward a Critical Method.* London, 1889, pp. 149–199.
Taylor, W. F., "William Dean Howells and the Economic Novel," in *American Literature*, IV, 103–113 (1932).
Trent, W. P., *The Authority of Criticism.* New York, 1899, pp. 259–267.
Wilkinson, W. C., *Some New Literary Valuations.* New York, 1909.

CRITICISM AND FICTION (*selections*)[1]

1886–1891

II

. . . "As for those called critics," the author [Burke] says, "they have generally sought the rule of the arts in the wrong

---

[1]From *Criticism and Fiction*, copyright 1891, Harper and Brothers; copyright 1918, Mildred Howells and John Mead Howells. The text used is that of the Library edition (1910), which differs slightly from earlier versions.

place; they have sought among poems, pictures, engravings, statues, and buildings; but art can never give the rules that make an art. This is, I believe, the reason why artists in general, and poets principally, have been confined in so narrow a circle; they have been rather imitators of one another than of nature. Critics follow them, and therefore can do little as guides. I can judge but poorly of anything while I measure it by no other standard than itself. The true standard of the arts is in every man's power; and an easy observation of the most common, sometimes of the meanest, things in nature will give the truest lights, where the greatest sagacity and industry that slights such observation must leave us in the dark, or, what is worse, amuse and mislead us by false lights.''

If this should happen to be true—and it certainly commends itself to acceptance—it might portend an immediate danger to the vested interests of criticism, only that it was written a hundred years ago; and we shall probably have the "sagacity and industry that slights the observation" of nature long enough yet to allow most critics the time to learn some more useful trade than criticism as they pursue it. Nevertheless, I am in hopes that the communistic era in taste foreshadowed by Burke is approaching, and that it will occur within the lives of men now overawed by the foolish old superstition that literature and art are anything but the expression of life, and are to be judged by any other test than that of their fidelity to it. The time is coming, I hope, when each new author, each new artist, will be considered, not in his proportion to any other author or artist, but in his relation to the human nature, known to us all, which it is his privilege, his high duty, to interpret. "The true standard of the artist is in every man's power" already, as Burke says; Michelangelo's "light of the piazza," the glance of the common eye, is and always was the best light on a statue; Goethe's "boys and blackbirds" have in all ages been the real connoisseurs of berries; but hitherto the mass of common men have been afraid to apply their own simplicity, naturalness, and honesty to the appreciation of the beautiful. They have always cast about for the instruction of someone who professed to know better, and who browbeat wholesome common sense into the self-distrust that ends in sophistication. They have fallen generally to the worst of this bad species, and have been "amused and misled" (how pretty that quaint old use of amuse is!) "by the false lights" of critical vanity and self-righteousness. They have been taught to compare what they see and what they read, not with the things that they have observed and known, but with the things that some other artist or writer has done. Especially if they have themselves the artistic impulse in any direction they are taught to form themselves, not upon life, but upon the masters who became masters only by forming themselves upon life. The seeds of death are planted in them, and they can produce only the still-born, the academic. They are not told to take their work into the public square and see if it seems true to the chance passer, but to test it by the work of the very men who refused and decried any other test of their own work. The young writer who attempts to report the phrase and carriage of everyday life, who tries to tell just how he has heard men talk and seen them look, is made to feel guilty of something low and unworthy by the stupid people who would like to have him show how Shakespeare's men talked and looked, or Scott's, or Thackeray's, or Balzac's, or Hawthorne's, or Dickens's; he is instructed to idealize his personages, that is, to take the lifelikeness out of them, and put the booklikeness into them. He is approached in the spirit of the pedantry into which learning, much or little, always decays when it withdraws itself and stands apart from experience in an attitude of imagined superiority, and which would say with the same confidence to the scientist: "I see that you are looking at a grasshopper there which you found in the grass, and I suppose you intend to describe it. Now don't waste your time and sin against culture in that way. I've got a grasshopper here, which has been evolved at considerable pains and expense out of the grasshopper in general; in fact, it's a type. It's made up of wire and cardboard, very prettily painted in a conventional tint, and it's perfectly indestructible. It isn't very much like a real grasshopper, but it's a great deal nicer, and it's served to represent the notion of a grasshopper ever since man emerged from barbarism. You may say that it's artificial. Well, it is artificial; but then it's ideal too; and what you want to do is to cultivate the ideal. You'll find the books full of my kind of grasshopper, and scarcely a trace of yours in any of them. The thing that you are proposing to do is common-place; but if you say that it isn't commonplace, for the very reason that it hasn't been done before, you'll have to admit that it's photographic."

As I said, I hope the time is coming when not only the artist, but the common, average man, who always "has the standard of the arts in his power," will have also the courage to apply it, and will reject the ideal grasshopper wherever he finds it, in science, in literature, in art, because it is not "simple, natural, and honest," because it is not like a real grasshopper. But I will own that I think the time is yet far off, and that the people who have been brought up on the ideal grasshopper, the heroic grasshopper, the impassioned grasshopper, the self-devoted, adventureful, good old romantic cardboard grasshopper, must die out before the simple, honest, and natural grasshopper can have a fair field. I am in no haste to compass the end of these good people, whom I find in the meantime very amusing. It is delightful to meet one of them, either in print or out of it— some sweet elderly lady or excellent gentleman whose youth was pastured on the literature of thirty or forty years ago—and to witness the confidence with which they preach their favorite authors as all the law and the prophets. They have commonly read little or nothing since, or, if they have, they have judged it by a standard taken from these authors, and never dreamed of judging it by nature; they are destitute of the documents in the case of the later writers; they suppose that Balzac was the beginning of realism and that Zola is its wicked end; they are quite ignorant, but they are ready to talk you down, if you differ from them, with an assumption of knowledge sufficient for any occasion. The horror, the resentment, with which they receive any question of their literary saints is genuine; you descend at once very far in the moral and social scale, and anything short of offensive personality is too good for you; it is expressed to you that you are one to be avoided, and put down even a little lower than you have naturally fallen.

These worthy persons are not to blame; it is part of their intellectual mission to represent the petrifaction of taste, and to preserve an image of a smaller and cruder and emptier world than we now live in, a world which was feeling its way towards the simple, the natural, the honest, but was a good deal "amused and misled" by lights now no longer mistakable for heavenly luminaries. They belong to a time, just passing away, when certain authors were considered authorities in certain kinds, when they must be accepted entire and not questioned in any particular. Now we are beginning to see and to say that no author is an authority except in those moments when he held his ear close to Nature's lips and caught her very accent. These moments are not continuous with any authors in the past, and they are rare with all. Therefore I am not afraid to say now that the greatest classics are sometimes not at all great, and that we can profit by them only when we hold them, like our meanest contemporaries, to a strict accounting, and verify their work by the standard of the arts which we all have in our power, the simple, the natural, and the honest.

Those good people must always have a hero, an idol of some sort, and it is droll to find Balzac, who suffered from their sort such bitter scorn and hate for his realism while he was alive, now become a fetich in his turn, to be shaken in the faces of those who will not blindly worship him. But it is no new thing in the history of literature: whatever is established is sacred with those who do not think. At the beginning of the century, when romance was making the same fight against effete classicism which realism is making today against effete romanticism, the Italian poet Monti declared that "the romantic was the cold grave of the Beautiful," just as the realistic is now supposed to be. The romantic of that day and the real of this are in certain degree the same. Romanticism then sought, as realism seeks now, to widen the bounds of sympathy, to level every barrier against aesthetic freedom, to escape from the paralysis of tradition. It exhausted itself in this impulse; and it remained for realism to assert that fidelity to experience and probability of motive are essential conditions of a great imaginative literature. It is not a new theory, but it has never before universally characterized literary endeavor. When realism becomes false to itself, when it heaps up facts merely, and maps life instead of picturing it, realism will perish too. Every true realist instinctively knows this, and it is perhaps the reason why he is careful of every fact, and feels himself bound to express or to indicate its meaning at the risk of over-moralizing. In life he finds nothing insignificant; all tells for destiny and character; nothing that God has made is contemptible. He cannot look upon human life and declare this thing or that thing unworthy of notice, any more than the scientist can declare a fact of the material world beneath the dignity of his inquiry. He feels in every nerve the equality of things and the unity of men; his soul is exalted, not by vain shows and shadows and ideals, but by realities, in which alone the truth lives. In criticism it is his business to break the images of false gods and misshapen heroes, to take away the poor silly toys that many grown people would still like to play with. He cannot keep terms with "Jack the Giantkiller" or "Puss in Boots," under any name or in any place, even when they reappear as the convict Vautrec, or the Marquis de Montrivaut, or the Sworn Thirteen Noblemen. He must say to himself that Balzac, when he imagined these monsters, was not Balzac, he was Dumas; he was not realistic, he was romanticistic.

XV

Which brings us again, after this long way about, to Jane Austen and her novels, and that troublesome question about them. She was great and they were beautiful, because she and they were honest, and dealt with nature nearly a hundred years ago as realism deals with it today. Realism is nothing more and nothing less than the truthful treatment of material, and Jane Austen was the first and the last of the English novelists to treat material with entire truthfulness. Because she did this, she remains the most artistic of the English novelists, and alone worthy to be matched with the great Scandinavian and Slavic and Latin artists. It is not a question of intellect, or not wholly that. The English have mind enough; but they have not taste enough; or, rather, their taste has been perverted by their false criticism, which is based upon personal preference, and not upon principle; which instructs a man to think that what he likes is good, instead of teaching him first to distinguish what is good before he likes it. The art of fiction, as Jane Austen knew it, declined from her through Scott, and Bulwer, and Dickens, and Charlotte Brontë, and Thackeray, and even George Eliot, because the mania of romanticism had seized upon all Europe, and these great writers could not escape the taint of their time; but it has shown few signs of recovery in England, because English criticism, in the presence of the Continental masterpieces, has continued provincial and special and personal, and has expressed a love and a hate which had to do with the quality of the artist rather than the character of his work. It was inevitable that in their time the English romanticists should treat, as Señor Valdés says, "the barbarous customs of the Middle Ages, softening and disfiguring them, as Walter Scott and his kind did"; that they should "devote themselves to falsifying nature, refining and subtilizing sentiment, and modifying psychology after their own fancy," like Bulwer and Dickens, as well as like Rousseau and Madame de Staël, not to mention Balzac, the worst of all that sort at his worst. This was the natural course of the disease; but it really seems as if it were their criticism that was to blame for the rest: not, indeed, for the performance of this writer or that, for criticism can never affect the actual doing of a thing; but for the esteem in which this writer or that is held through the perpetuation of false ideals. The only observer of English middle-class life since Jane Austen worthy to be named with her was not George Eliot, who was first ethical and then artistic, who transcended her in everything but the form and method most essential to art, and there fell hopelessly below her. It was Anthony Trollope who was most like her in simple honesty and instinctive truth, as unphilosophized as the light of common day; but he was so warped from a wholesome ideal as to wish at times to be like Thackeray, and to stand about in his scene, talking it over with his hands in his pockets, interrupting the action, and spoiling the illusion in which alone the truth of art resides. Mainly, his instinct was too much for his ideal, and with a low view of life in its civic relations and a thoroughly bourgeois soul, he yet produced works whose beauty is surpassed only by the effect of a more poetic writer in the novels of Thomas Hardy. Yet if a vote of English criticism even at this late day, when all continental Europe has the light of aesthetic truth, could be taken, the majority against these artists would be overwhelmingly in favor of a writer who had so little artistic sensibility that he never hesitated on any occasion, great or small, to make a foray among his characters, and catch them up to show them to the reader and tell him how beautiful or ugly they were; and cry out over their amazing properties. . . .

XXI

. . . I would have our American novelists be as American as they unconsciously can. Matthew Arnold complained that he found no "distinction" in our life, and I would gladly persuade all artists intending greatness in any kind among us that the recognition of the fact pointed out by Mr. Arnold ought to be a source of inspiration to them, and not discouragement. We have been now some hundred years building up a state on the affirma-

tion of the essential equality of men in their rights and duties, and
whether we have been right or been wrong the gods have taken
us at our word, and have responded to us with a civilization in
which there is no "distinction" perceptible to the eye that loves
and values it.   Such beauty and such grandeur as we have is
common beauty, common grandeur, or the beauty and grandeur
in which the quality of solidarity so prevails that neither distinguishes itself to the disadvantage of anything else.   It seems
to me that these conditions invite the artist to the study and the
appreciation of the common, and to the portrayal in every art
of those finer and higher aspects which unite rather than sever
humanity, if he would thrive in our new order of things.   The
talent that is robust enough to front the everyday world and
catch the charm of its workworn, careworn, brave, kindly face,
need not fear the encounter, though it seems terrible to the sort
nurtured in the superstition of the romantic, the bizarre, the
heroic, the distinguished, as the things alone worthy of painting
or carving or writing.   The arts must become democratic, and
then we shall have the expression of America in art; and the
reproach which Mr. Arnold was half right in making us shall
have no justice in it any longer; we shall be "distinguished." . . .

XXIII

One of the great newspapers the other day invited the prominent American authors to speak their minds upon a point in the
theory and practice of fiction which had already vexed some of
them.   It was the question of how much or how little the American novel ought to deal with certain facts of life which are not
usually talked of before young people, and especially young
ladies.   Of course the question was not decided, and I forget
just how far the balance inclined in favor of a larger freedom in
the matter.   But it certainly inclined that way; one or two
writers of the sex which is somehow supposed to have purity in
its keeping (as if purity were a thing that did not practically
concern the other sex, preoccupied with serious affairs) gave it
a rather vigorous tilt to that side.   In view of this fact it would
not be the part of prudence to make an effort to dress the balance;
and indeed I do not know that I was going to make any such
effort.   But there are some things to say, around and about the
subject, which I should like to have someone else say, and which
I may myself possibly be safe in suggesting.

One of the first of these is the fact, generally lost sight of by those who censure the Anglo-Saxon novel for its prudishness, that it is really not such a prude after all; and that if it is sometimes apparently anxious to avoid those experiences of life not spoken of before young people, this may be an appearance only. Sometimes a novel which has this shuffling air, this effect of truckling to propriety, might defend itself, if it could speak for itself, by saying that such experiences happened not to come within its scheme, and that, so far from maiming or mutilating itself in ignoring them, it was all the more faithfully representative of the tone of modern life in dealing with love that was chaste, and with passion so honest that it could be openly spoken of before the tenderest society bud at dinner. It might say that the guilty intrigue, the betrayal, the extreme flirtation even, was the exceptional thing in life, and unless the scheme of the story necessarily involved it, that it would be bad art to lug it in, and as bad taste as to introduce such topics in a mixed company. It could say very justly that the novel in our civilization now always addresses a mixed company, and that the vast majority of the company are ladies, and that very many, if not most, of these ladies are young girls. If the novel were written for men and for married women alone, as in continental Europe, it might be altogether different. But the simple fact is that it is not written for them alone among us, and it is a question of writing, under cover of our universal acceptance, things for young girls to read which you would be put out-of-doors for saying to them, or frankly giving notice of your intention, and so cutting yourself off from the pleasure—and it is a very high and sweet one—of appealing to these vivid, responsive intelligences, which are none the less brilliant and admirable because they are innocent.

One day a novelist who liked, after the manner of other men, to repine at his hard fate, complained to his friend, a critic, that he was tired of the restriction he had put upon himself in this regard; for it is a mistake, as can be readily shown, to suppose that others impose it. "See how free those French fellows are!" he rebelled. "Shall we always be shut up to our tradition of decency?"

"Do you think it's much worse than being shut up to their tradition of indecency?" said his friend.

Then that novelist began to reflect, and he remembered how sick the invariable motive of the French novel made him. He perceived finally that, convention for convention, ours was not only more tolerable, but on the whole was truer to life, not only to its complexion, but also to its texture. No one will pretend that there is not vicious love beneath the surface of our society; if he did, the fetid explosions of the divorce trials would refute him; but if he pretended that it was in any just sense characteristic of our society, he could be still more easily refuted. Yet it exists, and it is unquestionably the material of tragedy, the stuff from which intense effects are wrought. The question, after owning this fact, is whether these intense effects are not rather cheap effects. I incline to think they are, and I will try to say why I think so, if I may do so without offense. The material itself, the mere mention of it, has an instant fascination; it arrests, it detains, till the last word is said, and while there is anything to be hinted. This is what makes a love intrigue of some sort all but essential to the popularity of any fiction. Without such an intrigue the intellectual equipment of the author must be of the highest, and then he will succeed only with the highest class of readers. But any author who will deal with a guilty love intrigue holds all readers in his hand, the highest with the lowest, as long as he hints the slightest hope of the smallest potential naughtiness. He need not at all be a great author; he may be a very shabby wretch, if he has but the courage or the trick of that sort of thing. The critics will call him "virile" and "passionate"; decent people will be ashamed to have been limed by him; but the low average will only ask another chance of flocking into his net. If he happens to be an able writer, his really fine and costly work will be unheeded, and the lure to the appetite will be chiefly remembered. There may be other qualities which make reputations for other men, but in his case they will count for nothing. He pays this penalty for his success in that kind; and everyone pays some such penalty who deals with some such material.

But I do not mean to imply that his case covers the whole ground. So far as it goes, though, it ought to stop the mouths of those who complain that fiction is enslaved to propriety among us. It appears that of a certain kind of impropriety it is free to give us all it will, and more. But this is not what serious men and women writing fiction mean when they rebel against the limitations of their art in our civilization. They have no desire to deal with nakedness, as painters and sculptors freely do in the worship of beauty; or with certain facts of life, as the stage does, in the service of sensation. But they ask why, when the conventions of the plastic and histrionic arts liberate their followers to the portrayal of almost any phase of the physical or of the emotional nature, an American novelist may not write a story on the lines of *Anna Karénina* or *Madame Bovary*. They wish to touch one of the most serious and sorrowful problems of life in the spirit of Tolstoi and Flaubert, and they ask why they may not. At one time, they remind us, the Anglo-Saxon novelist did deal with such problems—Defoe in his spirit, Richardson in his, Goldsmith in his. At what moment did our fiction lose this privilege? In what fatal hour did the Young Girl arise and seal the lips of Fiction, with a touch of her finger, to some of the most vital interests of life?

Whether I wished to oppose them in their aspiration for greater freedom, or whether I wished to encourage them, I should begin to answer them by saying that the Young Girl had never done anything of the kind. The manners of the novel have been improving with those of its readers; that is all. Gentlemen no longer swear or fall drunk under the table, or abduct young ladies and shut them up in lonely country houses, or so habitually set about the ruin of their neighbors' wives, as they once did. Generally, people now call a spade an agricultural implement; they have not grown decent without having also grown a little squeamish, but they have grown comparatively decent; there is no doubt about that. They require of a novelist whom they respect unquestionable proof of his seriousness, if he proposes to deal with certain phases of life; they require a sort of scientific decorum. He can no longer expect to be received on the ground of entertainment only; he assumes a higher function, something like that of a physician or a priest, and they expect him to be bound by laws as sacred as those of such professions; they hold him solemnly pledged not to betray them or abuse their confidence. If he will accept the conditions, they give him their confidence, and he may then treat to his greater honor, and not at all to his disadvantage, of such experiences, such relations of men and women as George Eliot treats in *Adam Bede*, in *Daniel Deronda*, in *Romola*, in almost all her books; such as Hawthorne treats in *The Scarlet Letter;* such as Dickens treats in *David Copperfield;* such as Thackeray treats in *Pendennis*, and glances at in every one of his fictions; such as most of the masters of English fiction have at some time treated more or less openly. It is quite false or quite mistaken to suppose that our novels have left untouched these most important realities of life. They have only not made them their stock in trade; they have kept a true perspective in regard to them; they have relegated them in their pictures of life to the space and place they occupy in life itself, as we know it in England and America. They have kept a correct proportion, knowing perfectly well that unless the novel is to be a map, with everything scrupulously laid down in it, a faithful record of life in far the greater extent could be made to the exclusion of guilty love and all its circumstances and consequences.

I justify them in this view not only because I hate what is cheap and meretricious, and hold in peculiar loathing the cant of the critics who require "passion" as something in itself admirable and desirable in a novel, but because I prize fidelity in the historian of feeling and character. Most of these critics who demand "passion" would seem to have no conception of any passion but one. Yet there are several other passions: the passion of grief, the passion of avarice, the passion of pity, the passion of ambition, the passion of hate, the passion of envy, the passion of devotion, the passion of friendship; and all these have a greater part in the drama of life than the passion of love, and infinitely greater than the passion of guilty love. Wittingly or unwittingly, English fiction and American fiction have recognized this truth, not fully, not in the measure it merits, but in greater degree than most other fiction.

XXVII

But if the humanitarian impulse has mostly disappeared from Christmas fiction, I think it has never so generally characterized all fiction. One may refuse to recognize this impulse; one may deny that it is in any greater degree shaping life than ever before, but no one who has the current of literature under his eye can fail to note it there. People are thinking and feeling generously, if not living justly, in our time; it is a day of anxiety to be saved from the curse that is on selfishness, of eager question how others shall be helped, of bold denial that the conditions in which we would fain have rested are sacred or immutable. Especially in America, where the race has gained a height never reached before, the eminence enables more men than ever before to see how even here vast masses of men are sunk in misery that must grow every day more hopeless, or embroiled in a struggle for mere life that must end in enslaving and imbruting them.

Art, indeed, is beginning to find out that if it does not make friends with Need it must perish. It perceives that to take itself from the many and leave them no joy in their work, and to give itself to the few whom it can bring no joy in their idleness, is an error that kills. The men and women who do the hard work of the world have learned that they have a right to pleasure in their toil, and that when justice is done them they will have it. In all ages poetry has affirmed something of this sort, but it remained for ours to perceive it and express it somehow in every form of literature. But this is only one phase of the devotion of the best literature of our time to the service of humanity. No book written with a low or cynical motive could succeed now, no matter how brilliantly written; and the work done in the past to the glorification of mere passion and power, to the deification of self, appears monstrous and hideous. The romantic spirit worshiped genius, worshiped heroism, but at its best, in such a man as Victor Hugo, this spirit recognized the supreme claim of the lowest humanity. Its error was to idealize the victims of society, to paint them impossibly virtuous and beautiful; but truth, which has succeeded to the highest mission of romance, paints these victims as they are, and bids the world consider them not because they are beautiful and virtuous, but because they are ugly and vicious, cruel, filthy, and only not altogether loathsome because the divine can never wholly die out of the human. The truth does not find these victims among the poor alone, among the hungry, the houseless, the ragged; but it also finds them among the rich, cursed with the aimlessness, the satiety, the despair of wealth, wasting their lives in a fool's paradise of shows and semblances, with nothing real but the misery that comes of insincerity and selfishness.

I do not think the fiction of our own time even always equal to this work, or perhaps more than seldom so. But as I once expressed, to the long-reverberating discontent of two continents, fiction is now a finer art than it has been hitherto, and more nearly meets the requirements of the infallible standard. I have hopes of real usefulness in it, because it is at last building on the only sure foundation; but I am by no means certain that it will be the ultimate literary form, or will remain as important as we believe it is destined to become. On the contrary, it is quite imaginable that when the great mass of readers, now sunk in the foolish joys of mere fable, shall be lifted to an interest in the meaning of things through the faithful portrayal of life in fiction, then fiction the most faithful may be superseded by a still more faithful form of contemporaneous history. I willingly leave the precise character of this form to the more robust imagination of readers whose minds have been nurtured upon romantic novels, and who really have an imagination worth speaking of, and confine myself, as usual, to the hither side of the regions of conjecture.

The art which in the meantime disdains the office of teacher is one of the last refuges of the aristocratic spirit which is disappearing from politics and society and is now seeking to shelter itself in aesthetics. The pride of caste is becoming the pride of taste; but, as before, it is averse to the mass of men; it consents to know them only in some conventionalized and artificial guise. It seeks to withdraw itself, to stand aloof; to be distinguished, and not to be identified. Democracy in literature is the reverse of all this. It wishes to know and to tell the truth, confident that consolation and delight are there; it does not care to paint the marvelous and impossible for the vulgar many, or to sentimentalize and falsify the actual for the vulgar few. Men are more like than unlike one another: let us make them know one another better, that they may be all humbled and strengthened with a sense of their fraternity. Neither arts, nor letters, nor sciences, except as they somehow, clearly or obscurely, tend to make the race better and kinder, are to be regarded as serious interests; they are all lower than the rudest crafts that feed and house and clothe, for except they do this office they are idle; and they cannot do this except from and through the truth.

ANATOLE FRANCE

(1844–1924)

o◯ooo◯o

ANATOLE FRANCE (Jacques Anatole Thibault), the son of an antiquarian book dealer and a devout Catholic mother, was a strange combination of dreamer and disillusioned realist. As a child his imaginative mind was deeply stirred by religious mysticism, but after reading Taine,[1] attending Renan's lectures, and being imbued with Darwinism, he became a cynical and skeptical young man.

The Parnassian group attracted Anatole France in 1867, and his first book, published when he was twenty-four, was a biographical study of Alfred de Vigny, the father of the Parnassius school. At this early age he came to the pessimistic conclusion that the originality of literary genius consisted in the assimilation of borrowings from other writers. In 1873 he published his first volume of verse, *Les Poèmes dorés*, representing a fatalistic, epicurean view of life. Darwinism had only awakened in him a revived neo-Greek pantheism, somewhat anticipating Bergson's *élan vital*.[2]

Very early Anatole France had shown an implacable hatred for Christianity, but in the Preface to *Les Noces corinthiennes* (1876) he admits that, though "there is nothing certain outside the realm of science," yet science can never take the place of religion in men's lives:

> As long as man is suckled at a woman's breast, he will be conse-crated in the temple and initiated into some mystery of the divine. He will have his dream. And what matter if the dream be false, provided it be fair? Is it not the destiny of man to be sunk in an everlasting illusion? And is not this illusion the very condition of life?

When he wrote this, he was already well along on the road of his "escape" theory of art and his subjective practice of criticism.

In his naturalistic fiction, *Jocaste et le chat maigre* (1879), Anatole France shows a bleak determinism, under the dual influence of Flaubert and Taine, but by the time he wrote *Sylvestre Bonnard* (1881) he had lost

[1]Cf. pp. 481–493.

[2]*L'élan vital* is Bergson's term for the vital impulse, or creative urge, in his theory of evolution, set forth in *L'Évolution créatrice* (1907).

confidence in science. In the final chapters of *Le Livre de mon ami* (1885) he declares that even the scientist is "vainly driven about by dreams."

Not by the faculty of laughter does man rise above the animals, but by the gift of dreaming. The storyteller remakes the world after his own fashion, and gives to lesser men, to the simple, to children, a chance to make it over in theirs.

His "escape" philosophy has now become almost a creed.

In 1887 Anatole France became a literary critic on *Le Temps*. After the mild success of his first book (the critical study of de Vigny), the publisher Lemerre had commissioned him to write prefaces for editions of the French classics—these were later collected under the title of *Génie latin* (1913)—and no doubt gave Anatole France valuable practice. Out of his writing for *Le Temps* grew his critical volumes, *La Vie littéraire* (1888–1893)—translated as *Life and Letters*,— and in these he is revealed as a completely subjective critic. Skeptical of all values, he ends by amusing himself. Beauty is a universal illusion. The Preface to the first volume contains that famous definition: "The good critic is the one who relates the adventures of his soul among masterpieces." To be honest, he says, the critic should announce: "Gentlemen, I am going to speak of myself in connection with Shakespeare, Racine, or Goethe." Brunetière, the conservative humanist and disciple of Taine, replied vigorously in *La Revue des deux mondes* (January 1, 1891), but Anatole France's maliciously clever rejoinder (preserved in the fourth series of *Life and Letters*) left no doubt of the inequality of the combatants.

Anatole France's American follower, James Branch Cabell, championed the "escape" philosophy in his many novels of Poictesme, and especially in his critical volume, *Beyond Life*, but today the escapists are far outnumbered by the Marxist and sociological critics. Whether or not the movement is ever revived, however, Anatole France will probably always remain the most brilliant of the subjective critics.

BIBLIOGRAPHY

TEXT

Œuvres complètes, illustrées. Paris, 1925.
On Life and Letters . . . tr. by A. W. Evans. First series. London, 1911.
La Vie littéraire. 4th ed. 4 vols. Paris, 1889–1892.

CRITICISM

Ahlström, Alvida, *Le Moyen âge dans l'œuvre d'Anatole France*. Paris, 1930.
Belis, Alexandre, *La Critique française à la fin du XIXe siècle: Ferdinand Brunetière, Émile Faguet, Jules Lemaître, Anatole France*. Paris, 1926.

Cerf, Barry, *Anatole France, the Degeneration of a Great Artist.* New York, 1926.

Deuschamps, Gaston, . . . *La Vie et les livres.* Second series. Paris, 1895.

Masson, Georges Armand, *Anatole France, son œuvre, portrait et autographe,* document pour l'histoire de la littérature française. Paris, 1923. Bibliography, pp. 51–64.

Michaut, Gustave, *Anatole France: étude psychologique.* Paris, 1913.

Shanks, Lewis Piaget, *Anatole France.* Chicago, 1919.

Sherman, Stuart P., "The Skepticism of Anatole France," in *On Contemporary Literature.* New York, 1917.

Truc, Gonzague, *Anatole France; l'artiste et le penseur.* Paris, 1924.

UNSUBSTANTIALITY OF AESTHETICS (*selections*)[1]

1889

. . . In aesthetics, that is, in the clouds, one can argue more and better than in any other subject. It is in this connection that we must be distrustful. In this connection we must fear everything; indifference as much as partiality, coldness as much as passion, knowledge as much as ignorance, art, intellect, subtlety, and innocence more dangerous than cunning. In matters of aesthetics you will be chary of sophisms, above all when they are pretty ones, and some of them are admirable. You will not even believe in the mathematical spirit; for mathematics, so complete, so sublime, is yet so delicate a machine that it can work only in a vacuum, and a grain of sand in the wheels will suffice to throw it out of gear. One shudders on reflecting whither this grain of sand may lead a mathematical brain. Think of Pascal!

Aesthetics is based upon nothing solid. It is a castle in the air. Some have sought to base it upon ethics. But there is no such thing as ethics. There is no such thing as sociology. Nor is there such thing as biology. The completion of the sciences never existed save in the mind of M. Auguste Comte, whose work is a prophecy. When biology has been created, that is in a few million years' time, we shall perhaps be able to construct a sociology. It will be the work of a great many centuries; after which it will be permissible to create an aesthetic science on solid foundations. But then our planet will be very aged, and near the limits of its destiny. The sun, whose black spots, not

[1] From the Preface to *Life and Letters,* fourth series, published by Dodd, Mead and Company, 1924. Translated by Bernard Miall.

without reason, already cause us anxiety, will show the earth only a dull red fuliginous disk half covered with opaque scoriae, and the last human beings, withdrawn to the depths of the mines, will be less anxious to discuss the essence of the beautiful than to burn their last morsels of coal in the darkness before perishing in the midst of the eternal ice.

In order to give a basis to criticism we speak of tradition and universal consent. There are no such things. It is true that an almost general opinion favors certain works. But this is by virtue of a prepossession; not in the least as a matter of choice or as the result of a spontaneous preference. The works that everybody admires are those that no one examines. We receive them as a precious burden which we pass on to others without glancing at them. Do you really imagine that there is any great degree of liberty in the approbation which we extend to the Greek and Latin classics—or even to our own? Is the taste that attracts us to one work of art and repels us from another really free? Is it not determined by a great number of circumstances alien to the content of the work, the principal among which is the spirit of imitation, so powerful in men and animals? This spirit of imitation is a necessity if we are to live without going too far astray; we import it into all our actions and it dominates our aesthetic sense. Without it our opinions in the province of art would be far more various than they are already. It is because of this tendency that a work of art which has, to begin with, for whatever reason, obtained the acceptance of a few persons is thereupon accepted by a larger number. The first alone were free; all the rest do no more than obey. Their opinions have neither spontaneity nor value, nor are they founded on judgment or capacity of any sort. And by their number they establish fame. All depends on a very small beginning. Thus we see that works of art which are undervalued at their birth have little chance of pleasing later; while, on the other hand, works that have been celebrated from the first retain their reputation for a long time and are valued even after they have become unintelligible. What proves that agreement is purely the result of prepossession is that it ceases with the latter. One might give many examples of this. I will record only one. Fifteen years ago in an examination for admission to one year's voluntary service in the army the military examiners gave the candidates a page of dictation, unsigned, which, being quoted in various newspapers, was derided with a great deal of spirit and excited the gaiety of highly cultivated readers.—Where, it was asked, did these officers find such uncouth and ridiculous phrases?— Nevertheless, they had taken the passage from a very fine book. It was Michelet and the best Michelet; Michelet of the best period. The officers had taken the text of their dictation from that brilliant description of France with which the great writer closes the first volume of his *History*, one of the most admired passages in the book: "In latitude the belts of France are easily identified by their products. In the north the rich low-lying plains of Belgium and Flanders with their fields of flax and colza, and hops, and bitter vine of the north, etc." I have seen critics laughing at this style, which they believed that of some old army captain. The man who laughed loudest was an ardent admirer of Michelet. This is an admirably written page, but in order to be admired by unanimous consent it would have had to be signed. It is the same with every page written by the hand of man. On the other hand, anything covered by a great name has the good fortune to be blindly praised. Victor Cousin discovered sublimities in Pascal which have been recognized as the errors of the copyist. He went into ecstasies, for example, over certain "raccourcis d'abîme" that were the result of careless proof reading. One cannot imagine M. Cousin admiring these "raccourcis d'abîme" in the work of a contemporary. The rhapsodies of a Vrain-Lucas were favorably accepted by the Academy of Sciences under the names of Pascal and Descartes. Ossian, when he was believed to be ancient, was thought the equal of Homer. He is despised now he is known to be Macpherson.

When men exhibit a common admiration and give one another the reasons for it, concord is changed into discord. In a single book they approve of contrary things which cannot exist together.

A very interesting work would be the history of the varying criticisms of one of those works to which humanity has paid the greatest attention: *Hamlet*, the *Divine Comedy*, or the *Iliad*. The *Iliad* delights us today by a barbaric and primitive quality which many of us discover in it in all good faith. In the seventeenth century Homer was praised for having observed the rules of the epic.

"Be assured," said Boileau, "that if Homer has employed the word *dog* it is because that word is noble in Greek." These ideas are ridiculous to us. Ours will perhaps appear equally ridiculous in two hundred years' time, for after all we cannot rank the statements that Homer is barbaric and that barbarism is admirable among the eternal truths. In questions of literature there is not a single opinion that cannot easily be opposed by a contrary opinion. Who could ever terminate the disputes of the flute players?

ÉMILE ZOLA

(1840–1902)

oᏅooᏅo

New and revolutionary scientific discoveries and theories were to a large extent responsible for the "naturalistic" literary movement in the last half of the nineteenth century, and Zola was perhaps the most powerful single writer in this school. The son of a civil engineer, he was himself a student of science at Aix and Paris, and was only nineteen years old when Darwin published his *Origin of Species*.[1] As a young man he read Rousseau and other romanticists who deprecated civilization and preached a "return to nature." Later Darwin, Laplace, and Dr. Prosper Lucas, who wrote a *Treatise on Natural Heredity*, converted Zola to the worship of nature, which he considered the great source of poetry. "Naturalism" meant to him simply the return to Nature— "as she is." Rousseauism and Darwinism, therefore, are the twin sources of his "naturalism."

Two of the chief scientific ideas of the age exerted an especially great influence on Zola's critical theory. One was scientific determinism, the belief that all acts of the human will are the results of heredity and environment, that man, in the popular idiom, is a victim of circumstances. The second of these scientific doctrines was *laissez faire*, or the belief that nature unchecked does all things for the best—a theory destined to run its rampant course in the American "naturalism" of the Frank Norris school.

So much has been said about Zola's determinism, and his later humanitarianism, that his essential pantheism is often overlooked, but his rhapsody on fecundity sounds almost like Walt Whitman: "Yes, I desire to lose myself in thee [Whitman's primitive urge]; I feel thee down there, under my limbs pressing and arousing me; it is thou alone who shalt be as a pristine force in my works, the end and the means at once of all things."[2] Thus do romanticism and naturalism join forces.

The great work of Zola's life was his twenty volumes, including twelve

[1] *The Origin of Species* was translated into French in 1862.
[2] Quoted by Matthew Josephson, *Zola and His Time* (New York, 1928), p. 13.

hundred characters, of the Rougon-Macquart cycle, an attempted scientific study of heredity in family history. His famous essay on *The Experimental Novel* is sometimes thought to be the foundation of this cycle, but he did not know the Claude Bernard work so freely quoted in this essay until he had completed a substantial part of the Rougon-Macquart structure. As Professor Muller says, "*The Experimental Novel* was one of a number of polemical treatises designed to present a striking exposition of his creed, and by their very violence to attract customers and trumpet his novels."[3] In fact, "His creed was largely an afterthought, a rationalization of his instinctive practices." But, whatever his intention, certainly it is a fact that, as Sidney Lanier pointed out, "nothing is clearer than that Zola's conception of an experiment is an evolving, from the inner consciousness, of what the author thinks the experimental subjects would do under given circumstances."[4]

About the time that Zola finished his Rougon-Macquart cycle, some young writers issued their "Manifesto of Five," ridiculing the famous novelist's obesity, condemning his sordidness, and accusing him of being obsessed with sex because of his own impotence. This attack seems to have made a deep impression on Zola, for he promptly began dieting, took a mistress—who bore him a child,—and turned humanitarian. Hence, "The new, thin Zola, the father of a child, overflowed with energy, optimism, joy."[5] He became "the poet of human 'fecundity' and of Utopianism."[6]

But to give the "Manifesto" full credit for Zola's change seems hardly fair, for humanitarianism was implied in his youthful Rousseauistic tendencies, as well as his social determinism, and this final period in his career also coincides with the symbolistic movement under the leadership of Mallarmé. Zola never became a Catholic, an "escapist," or an outright mystic, like many other writers of the period, but the rarefied spiritual atmosphere undoubtedly had some effect upon him.

Zola's great contribution to the history of ideas and literary theories, however, remains his earlier "naturalism," and *The Experimental Novel*, even though it may be exaggerated, is a convenient introduction to his doctrines.

[3] Herbert J. Muller, *Modern Fiction: A Study of Values* (New York, 1937), p. 166.
[4] *The English Novel* (New York, 1883), p. 70. Jules Lemaître also "unmasked" Zola; see Josephson, *op. cit.*, p. 375. The best discussion of Zola's experimental method is Josephson's chapter on "Aesthetics," pp. 366–376.
[5] Muller, *op. cit.*, p. 179—based on Josephson, *op. cit.*, chap. XIII.
[6] Josephson, *op. cit.*, p. 380.

BIBLIOGRAPHY

TEXT

The Experimental Novel and Other Essays, tr. by Belle M. Sherman. New York, 1893.
Le Roman expérimental. Paris, 1902.
Les Romanciers naturalistes. Paris, 1893.

BIOGRAPHY AND CRITICISM

D'aureuilly, Jules Amédée Barbey, *Le Roman contemporain.* Paris, 1902.
Biencourt, Marius, *Une Influence du naturalisme français en Amérique: Frank Norris.* Paris, 1933.
Bonnamour, Georges, *Le Procès Zola: Impressions d'audience.* Paris, [1898].
Brandes, Georg Morris Cohen, *Menschen und Werke.* Berlin, 1894.
Carrére, Jean, *Degeneration in the Great French Masters.* London, 1922.
Croce, Benedetto, *European Literature in the Nineteenth Century.* New York, 1924.
Doumic, René, *Portraits d'écrivains.* Paris, [1892].
De Goncourt, Edmond and Jules, *Journal.* Paris, 1887–1895.
Doucet, Ferdinand, *L'Esthétique d'Émile Zola et son application à la critique.* The Hague, 1923.
Edwards, Herbert, "Zola and the American Critics," *American Literature,* IV, 114–129 (1932).
Ellis, Havelock, *Affirmations.* London, 1898.
France, Anatole, *La Vie littéraire.* Paris, 1889.
——, *Funérailles de Zola.* Paris, 1903.
Frye, Prosser Hall, *Literary Reviews and Criticisms.* New York, 1908.
Grand, John, *Carteret, Zola en images.* Paris, 1908.
Hennequin, Émile, *Études de critique scientifique.* Paris, 1890.
Huret, J., *Enquête sur l'évolution littéraire.* Paris, 1896.
James, Henry, *Notes on Novelists.* New York, 1914.
Josephson, Matthew, *Zola and His Time.* New York, 1928.
Laporte, Antoine, *Le Naturalisme ou l'immoralité littéraire.* Paris, 1894.
Lemaître, Jules, *Les Contemporains.* Vols. I, IV. Paris, 1888.
Lepelletier, Edmond, *Émile Zola: sa vie—son œuvre.* Paris, 1908.
Martineau, Henri, *Le Roman scientifique de Zola.* Paris, 1907.
Martino, P., *Le Roman réaliste sous le second empire.* Paris, 1931.
——, *Le Naturalisme français.* Paris, 1923.
Massis, Henri, *Comment Émile Zola composait ses romans.* Paris, 1906.
Oehlert, Richard, *E. Zola als Theaterdichter, mit einer Einleitung über den Naturalismus im französischen Drama.* Berlin, 1920.
Ricca, Vincenzo, *Emilio Zola e il romanzo sperimentale.* Catania, 1902.
Root, Winthrop Hegeman, *German Criticism of Zola.* Columbia University Press, 1931.
Tolstoy, Count Leo, *Émile Zola, Novelist and Reformer.* London, 1904.

THE EXPERIMENTAL NOVEL (*selections*) [1]
1893

In my literary essays I have often spoken of the application of the experimental method to the novel and to the drama. The return to nature, the naturalistic evolution which marks the century, drives little by little all the manifestation of human intelligence into the same scientific path. Only the idea of a literature governed by science is doubtless a surprise, until explained with precision and understood. It seems to me necessary, then, to say briefly and to the point what I understand by the experimental novel.

I really only need to adapt, for the experimental method has been established with strength and marvelous clearness by Claude Bernard in his *Introduction à l'étude de la médecine expérimentale*. This work, by a savant whose authority is unquestioned, will serve me as a solid foundation. I shall here find the whole question treated, and I shall restrict myself to irrefutable arguments and to giving the quotations which may seem necessary to me. This will then be but a compiling of texts, as I intend on all points to intrench myself behind Claude Bernard. It will often be but necessary for me to replace the word "doctor" by the word "novelists," to make my meaning clear and to give it the rigidity of a scientific truth.

What determined my choice, and made me choose *L'Introduction* as my basis, was the fact that medicine, in the eyes of a great number of people, is still an art, as is the novel. Claude Bernard all his life was searching and battling to put medicine in a scientific path. In his struggle we see the first feeble attempts of a science to disengage itself little by little from empiricism,[2] and to gain a foothold in the realm of truth, by means of the experimental method. Claude Bernard demonstrates that this method, followed in the study of inanimate bodies in chemistry and in physics, should be also used in the study of living bodies, in physiology and medicine. I am going to try and prove for my part that if the experimental method leads to the knowledge of physical life, it should also lead to the knowledge of

---

[1] Translated by Belle M. Sherman.

[2] Zola uses empiricism in this essay in the sense of "haphazard observation" in contrast with a scientific experiment undertaken to prove a certain truth. (Translator's note.)

the passionate and intellectual life. It is but a question of degree in the same path which runs from chemistry to physiology, then from physiology to anthropology and to sociology. The experimental novel is the goal.

To be more clear, I think it would be better to give a brief résumé of *L'Introduction* before I commence. The applications which I shall make of the texts will be better understood if the plan of the work and the matters treated are explained.

Claude Bernard, after having declared that medicine enters the scientific path with physiology as its foundation and by means of the experimental method, first explains the differences which exist between the sciences of observation and the sciences of experiment. He concludes, finally, that experiment is but provoked observation. All experimental reasoning is based on doubt, for the experimentalist should have no preconceived idea, in the face of nature, and should always retain his liberty of thought. He simply accepts the phenomena which are produced, when they are proved.

In the second part he reaches his true subject and shows that the spontaneity of living bodies is not opposed to the employment of experiment. The difference is simply that an inanimate body possesses merely the ordinary, external environment, while the essence of the higher organism is set in an internal and perfected environment endowed with constant physico-chemical properties exactly like the external environment; hence there is an absolute determinism in the existing conditions of natural phenomena, for the living as for the inanimate bodies. He calls determinism the cause which determines the appearance of these phenomena. This nearest cause, as it is called, is nothing more than the physical and material condition of the existence or manifestation of the phenomena. The end of all experimental method, the boundary of all scientific research, is then identical for living and for inanimate bodies; it consists in finding the relations which unite a phenomenon of any kind to its nearest cause, or, in other words, in determining the conditions necessary for the manifestation of this phenomenon. Experimental science has no necessity to worry itself about the "why" of things; it simply explains the "how."

After having explained the experimental considerations common to living beings and to inanimate, Claude Bernard passes to the experimental considerations which belong specially

to living beings. The great and only difference is this, that there
is presented to our consideration, in the organism of living
beings, a harmonious group of phenomena. He then treats
of practical experiments on living beings, of vivisection, of the
preparatory anatomical conditions, of the choice of animals,
of the use of calculation in the study of phenomena, and lastly
of the physiologist's laboratory.

Finally, in the last part of *L'Introduction*, he gives some
examples of physiological experimental investigations in support
of the ideas which he has formulated. He then furnishes some
examples of experimental criticism in physiology. In the end
he indicates the philosophical obstacles which the experimental
doctor encounters. He puts in the first rank the false application of physiology to medicine, the scientific ignorance as well
as certain illusions of the medical mind. Further, he concludes
by saying that empirical medicine and experimental medicine,
not being incompatible, ought, on the contrary, to be inseparable
one from the other. His last sentence is that experimental
medicine adheres to no medical doctrine nor any philosophical
system.

This is, very broadly, the skeleton of *L'Introduction* stripped
of its flesh. I hope that this rapid exposé will be sufficient to fill
up the gaps which my manner of proceeding is bound to produce; for, naturally, I shall cite from the work only such passages
as are necessary to define and comment upon the experimental
novel. I repeat that I use this treatise merely as a solid foundation on which to build, but a foundation very rich in arguments
and proofs of all kinds. Experimental medicine, which but lisps
as yet, can alone give us an exact idea of experimental literature, which, being still unhatched, is not even lisping.

I

The first question which presents itself is this: Is experiment
possible in literature, in which up to the present time observation
alone has been employed?

Claude Bernard discusses observation and experiment at
great length. There exists, in the first place, a very clear line of
demarcation, as follows: "The name of 'observer' is given to
him who applies the simple or complex process of investigation
in the study of phenomena which he does not vary, and which
he gathers, consequently, as nature offers them to him; the

name of 'experimentalist' is given to him who employs the simple and complex process of investigation to vary or modify, for an end of some kind, the natural phenomena, and to make them appear under circumstances and conditions in which they are not presented by nature." For instance, astronomy is a science of observation, because you cannot conceive of an astronomer acting upon the stars; while chemistry is an experimental science, as the chemist acts upon nature and modifies it. This, according to Claude Bernard, is the only true and important distinction which separates the observer from the experimentalist.

I cannot follow him in his discussion of the different definitions given up to the present time. As I have said before, he finishes by coming to the conclusion that experiment is but provoked observation. I repeat his words: "In the experimental method the search after facts, that is to say, investigation, is always accompanied by a reason, so that ordinarily the experimentalist makes an experiment to confirm and verify the value of an experimental idea. In this case you can say that experiment is an observation instigated for the purpose of verification."

To determine how much observation and experimenting there can be in the naturalistic novel, I only need to quote the following passages:

> The observer relates purely and simply the phenomena which he has under his eyes. . . . He should be the photographer of phenomena, his observation should be an exact representation of nature. . . . He listens to nature and he writes under its dictation. But once the fact is ascertained and the phenomenon observed, an idea or hypothesis comes into his mind, reason intervenes, and the experimentalist comes forward to interpret the phenomenon. The experimentalist is a man who, in pursuance of a more or less probable, but anticipated, explanation of observed phenomena, institutes an experiment in such a way that, according to all probability, it will furnish a result which will serve to confirm the hypothesis or preconceived idea. The moment that the result of the experiment manifests itself, the experimentalist finds himself face to face with a true observation which he has called forth and which he must ascertain, as all observation, without any preconceived idea. The experimentalist should then disappear, or rather transform himself instantly into the observer, and it is not until after he has ascertained the absolute results of the experiment, like that of an ordinary observation, that his mind

comes back to reasoning, comparing, and judging whether the experimental hypothesis is verified or invalidated by these same results.

The mechanism is all there. It is a little complicated, it is true, and Claude Bernard is led on to say:

> When all this passes into the brain of a savant who has given himself up to the study of a science as complicated as medicine still is, then there is such an entanglement between the result of observation and what belongs to experiment that it will be impossible and, besides, useless to try to analyze, in their inextricable *mélange*, each of these terms.

In one word, it might be said that observation "indicates" and that experiment "teaches."

Now, to return to the novel, we can easily see that the novelist is equally an observer and an experimentalist. The observer in him gives the facts as he has observed them, suggests the point of departure, displays the solid earth on which his characters are to tread and the phenomena to develop. Then the experimentalist appears and introduces an experiment, that is to say, sets his characters going in a certain story so as to show that the succession of facts will be such as the requirements of the determinism of the phenomena under examination call for. Here it is nearly always an experiment *"pour voir,"* as Claude Bernard calls it. The novelist starts out in search of a truth. I will take as an example the character of the Baron Hulot, in *Cousine Bette*, by Balzac. The general fact observed by Balzac is the ravages that the amorous temperament of a man makes in his home, in his family, and in society. As soon as he has chosen his subject, he starts from known facts; then he makes his experiment, and exposes Hulot to a series of trials, placing him amid certain surroundings in order to exhibit how the complicated machinery of his passions works. It is then evident that there is not only observation there, but that there is also experiment; as Balzac does not remain satisfied with photographing the facts collected by him, but interferes in a direct way to place his character in certain conditions, and of these he remains the master. The problem is to know what such a passion, acting in such a surrounding and under such circumstances, would produce from the point of view of an individual and of society; and an experimental novel, *Cousine*

Bette, for example, is simply the report of the experiment that the novelist conducts before the eyes of the public. In fact, the whole operation consists in taking facts in nature, then in studying the mechanism of these facts, acting upon them by the modification of circumstances and surroundings without deviating from the laws of nature. Finally, you possess knowledge of the man, scientific knowledge of him, in both his individual and social relations.

Doubtless we are still far from certainties in chemistry and even physiology. Nor do we know any more the reagents which decompose the passions, rendering them susceptible of analysis. Often, in this essay, I shall recall in similar fashion this fact, that the experimental novel is still younger than experimental medicine, and the latter is but just born. But I do not intend to exhibit the acquired results, I simply desire to clearly expose a method. If the experimental novelist is still groping in the most obscure and complex of all the sciences, this does not prevent this science from existing. It is undeniable that the naturalistic novel, such as we understand it today, is a real experiment that a novelist makes on man by the help of observation.

Besides, this opinion is not only mine, it is Claude Bernard's as well. He says in one place: "In practical life men but make experiments on one another." And again, in a more conclusive way, he expresses the whole theory of the experimental novel:

> When we reason on our own acts we have a certain guide, for we are conscious of what we think and how we feel. But if we wish to judge of the acts of another man, and know the motives which make him act, that is altogether a different thing. Without doubt we have before our eyes the movements of this man and his different acts, which are, we are sure, the modes of expression of his sensibility and his will. Further, we even admit that there is a necessary connection between the acts and their cause; but what is this cause? We do not feel it, we are not conscious of it, as we are when it acts in ourselves; we are therefore obliged to interpret it, and to guess at it, from the movements which we see and the words which we hear. We are obliged to check off this man's actions one by the other; we consider how he acted in such a circumstance, and, in a word, we have recourse to the experimental method.

All that I have spoken of further back is summed up in this last phrase, which is written by a savant.

I shall still call your attention to another illustration of Claude Bernard, which struck me as very forcible: "The experimentalist is the examining magistrate of nature." We novelists are the examining magistrates of men and their passions.

But see what splendid clearness breaks forth when this conception of the application of the experimental method to the novel is adequately grasped and is carried out with all the scientific rigor which the matter permits today. A contemptible reproach which they heap upon us naturalistic writers is the desire to be solely photographers. We have in vain declared that we admit the necessity of an artist's possessing an individual temperament and a personal expression; they continue to reply to us with these imbecile arguments, about the impossibility of being strictly true, about the necessity of arranging facts to produce a work of art of any kind. Well, with the application of the experimental method to the novel that quarrel dies out. The idea of experiment carried with it the idea of modification. We start, indeed, from the true facts, which are our indestructible basis; but to show the mechanism of these facts it is necessary for us to produce and direct the phenomena; this is our share of invention, here is the genius in the book. Thus without having recourse to the questions of form and of style, which I shall examine later, I maintain even at this point that we must modify nature, without departing from nature, when we employ the experimental method in our novels. If we bear in mind this definition, that "observation indicates and experiment teaches," we can even now claim for our books this great lesson of experiment.

The writer's office, far from being lessened, grows singularly from this point of view. An experiment, even the most simple, is always based on an idea, itself born of an observation. As Claude Bernard says: "The experimental idea is not arbitrary, nor purely imaginary; it ought always to have a support in some observed reality, that is to say, in nature." It is on this idea and on doubt that he bases all the method. "The appearance of the experimental idea," he says further on, "is entirely spontaneous and its nature absolutely individual, depending upon the mind in which it originates; it is a particular sentiment, a *quid proprium*, which constitutes the originality, the invention, and the genius of each one." Further, he makes doubt the great scientific lever. "The doubter is the true savant; he doubts only himself and his interpretations; he believes in science; he even admits in the experimental sciences a criterion or a positive principle, the determinism of phenomena, which is absolute in living beings as in inanimate bodies." Thus, instead of confining the novelist within narrow bounds, the experimental method gives full sway to his intelligence as a thinker, and to his genius as a creator. He must see, understand, and invent. Some observed fact makes the idea start up of trying an experiment, of writing a novel, in order to attain to a complete knowledge of the truth. Then when, after careful consideration, he has decided upon the plan of his experiment, he will judge the results at each step with the freedom of mind of a man who accepts only facts conformable to the determinism of phenomena. He set out from doubt to reach positive knowledge; and he will not cease to doubt until the mechanism of the passion, taken to pieces and set up again by him, acts according to the fixed laws of nature. There is no greater, no more magnificent work for the human mind. We shall see, further on, the miseries of the scholastics, of the makers of systems, and those theorizing about the ideal, compared with the triumph of the experimentalists.

I sum up this first part by repeating that the naturalistic novelists observe and experiment, and that all their work is the offspring of the doubt which seizes them in the presence of truths little known and phenomena unexplained, until an experimental idea rudely awakens their genius some day, and urges them to make an experiment, to analyze facts, and to master them.

V

. . . Let us clearly define now what is meant by an experimental novelist. Claude Bernard gives the following definition of an artist: "What is an artist? He is a man who realizes in a work of art an idea or a sentiment which is personal to him." I absolutely reject this definition. On this basis if I represented a man as walking on his head, I should have made a work of art, if such happened to be my personal sentiments. But in that case I should be a fool and nothing else. So one must add that the personal feeling of the artist is always subject to the higher law of truth and nature. We now come to the question of hypothesis. The artist starts out from the same point as the savant; he places himself before nature, has an idea apriori, and works according to this idea. Here alone he separates himself from the savant.

if he carries out his idea to the end without verifying its truth by the means of observation and experiment. Those who make use of experiment might well be called experimental artists; but then people will tell us that they are no longer artists, since such people regard art as the burden of personal error which the artist has put into his study of nature. I contend that the personality of the writer should only appear in the idea apriori and in the form, not in the infatuation for the false. I see no objection, besides, to its showing in the hypothesis, but it is necessary to clearly understand what you mean by these words.

It has often been said that writers ought to open the way for savants. This is true, for we have seen in *L'Introduction* that hypothesis and empiricism precede and prepare for the scientific state which is established finally by the experimental method. Man commenced by venturing certain explanations of phenomena, the poets gave expression to their emotions, and the savants ended by mastering hypotheses and fixing the truth. Claude Bernard always assigns the role of pioneers to the philosophers. It is a very noble role, and today it is the writers who should assume it and who should endeavor to fill it worthily. Only let it be well understood that each time that a truth is established by the savants the writers should immediately abandon their hypothesis to adopt this truth; otherwise they will remain deliberately in error without benefiting anyone. It is thus that science, as it advances, furnishes to us writers a solid ground upon which we should lean for support, to better enable us to shoot into new hypotheses. In a word, every phenomenon, once clearly determined, destroys the hypothesis which it replaces, and it is then necessary to transport your hypothesis one step further into the new unknown which arises. I will take a very simple example in order to make myself better understood; it has been proved that the earth revolves around the sun; what would you think of a poet who should adopt the old belief that the sun revolves around the earth? Evidently the poet, if he wishes to risk a personal explanation of any fact, should choose a fact whose cause is not already known. This, then, illustrates the position hypothesis should occupy for experimental novelists; we must accept determined facts, and not attempt to risk about them our personal sentiments, which would be ridiculous, building throughout on the territory that science has conquered; then before the unknown, but only then, exercising our intuition and suggesting the way to science, free to make mistakes, happy if we produce any data toward the solution of the problem. Here I stand at Claude Bernard's practical program, who is forced to accept empiricism as a necessary forerunner. In our experimental novel we can easily risk a few hypotheses on the questions of heredity and surroundings, after having respected all that science knows today about the matter. We can prepare the ways, we can furnish the results of observation, human data which may prove very useful. A great lyrical poet has written lately that our century is a century of prophets. Yes, if you wish it; only let it be well understood that these prophets rely neither upon the irrational nor the supernatural. If the prophets thought best to bring up again the most elementary notions, to serve up nature with a strange religious and philosophical sauce, to hold fast to the metaphysical man, to confound and obscure everything, the prophets, notwithstanding their genius in the matter of style, would never be anything but great gooses ignorant whether they would get wet if they jumped into the water. In our scientific age it is a very delicate thing to be a prophet, as we no longer believe in the truths of revelation, and in order to be able to foresee the unknown we must begin by studying the known.

The conclusion to which I wish to come is this: If I were to define the experimental novel I should not say, as Claude Bernard says, that a literary work lies entirely in the personal feeling, for the reason that in my opinion the personal feeling is but the first impulse. Later nature, being there, makes itself felt, or at least that part of nature of which science has given us the secret, and about which we have no longer any right to romance. The experimental novelist is therefore the one who accepts proven facts, who points out in man and in society the mechanism of the phenomena over which science is mistress, and who does not interpose his personal sentiments, except in the phenomena whose determinism is not yet settled, and who tries to test, as much as he can, this personal sentiment, this idea apriori, by observation and experiment.

I cannot understand how our naturalistic literature can mean anything else. I have only spoken of the experimental novel, but I am fairly convinced that the same method, after having triumphed in history and in criticism, will triumph everywhere, on the stage and in poetry even. It is an inevitable evolution.

Literature, in spite of all that can be said, does not depend merely upon the author; it is influenced by the nature it depicts and by the man whom it studies. Now if the savants change their ideas of nature, if they find the true mechanism of life, they force us to follow them, to precede them even, so as to play our role in the new hypotheses. The metaphysical man is dead; our whole territory is transformed by the advent of the physiological man. No doubt "Achilles' Anger," "Dido's Love," will last forever on account of their beauty; but today we feel the necessity of analyzing anger and love, of discovering exactly how such passions work in the human being. This view of the matter is a new one; we have become experimentalists instead of philosophers. In short, everything is summed up in this great fact: the experimental method in letters, as in the sciences, is in the way to explain the natural phenomena, both individual and social, of which metaphysics, until now, has given only irrational and supernatural explanations.

FERDINAND BRUNETIÈRE

(1849–1906)

oᏅoooᏅo

BRUNETIÈRE MUST BE RANKED as one of the major critics of France, a nation famous for critical masterpieces. He first gained recognition as a contributor to *La Révue des deux mondes*, later serving on the editorial staff. He became professor of French language and literature at the École Normale in 1886, a position which he filled with distinction. In 1893 he was elected to the French Academy. His chief critical works include his six series of *Études critiques* (1880–1898); *Le Roman naturaliste* (1883); *Histoire et littérature*, three series (1884–1886); *Questions de critique* (1888–1890); the first volume of *L'Évolution de genres dans l'histoire de la littérature* (1890), in which he attempted to classify literary types on the analogy of the Darwinian hypothesis; and a monograph on *Honoré de Balzac* (1906).

A Catholic and a conservative, Brunetière tended to codify and to pronounce reactionary judgments. But, as Professor Hocking has demonstrated in his recent book,[1] Brunetière passed through an evolutionary development, and it is incorrect to label him by any one of his single works. He was more conservative in his first period than in his last. During his first period he was deeply concerned with the morality of literature, and like his American contemporary, Sidney Lanier, he found his ideal morality represented in the works of George Eliot.[2] In the *Roman naturaliste* he objected to the lack of universality in the naturalists. He believed that naturalism was lowering the artistic standards to the level of the democratic masses; "scientific art" he regarded as unthinkable.[3] Even in *Honoré de Balzac* he insisted that "Balzac . . . is not a Realist. . . . He used reality only to transform it."[4]

Again like Lanier,[5] Brunetière thought that literature should express love for humanity (cf. *Histoire et littérature*). In the words of Hocking, "The history of civilization thus becomes the history of the struggle between man and nature, and progress is defined as the conquest of

---

[1]Elton Hocking, *Ferdinand Brunetière; the Evolution of a Critic*, Studies in Language and Literature, University of Wisconsin, no. 36 (Madison, 1936).

[2]Cf. Hocking, *op. cit.*, p. 79; Lanier's *English Novel*, p. 94, *passim*.

[3]*Roman naturaliste*, pp. 7 ff.   [4]*Ibid.*   [5]A main theme in *The English Novel*.

nature by man."[6] Consequently, Brunetière found an aesthetic value in sympathy, again reminding us of Lanier—and Ruskin. "If the function of art is not moral, it is social, which is about the same thing,"[7] he declares. He was both social and reactionary in his belief that the purpose of art is "to maintain among men the consciousness of their solidarity."[8] Therefore, he had no patience with confessions and memoirs, because literature must be social rather than personal.

Possibly Brunetière's theory that the evolution of each genre determines the laws for that genre led him finally, in his monograph on Balzac, to the conclusion that novels should be a-moral, or no more moral than history and life.[9] His idea of a classic likewise changed, until he finally believed that since the mental outlook changes during the various ages, the classic also changes, i.e., it has different meanings in different ages.

Brunetière's genius for abstracting critical laws from the literary genres is brilliantly illustrated in his essay, "The Law of the Drama," which was first published as a preface to the *Annales de théâtre et de la musique* (1894), but he formulated the theory in his lectures at the Odéon in 1891–1892, *Les Époques du théâtre française*. Brunetière's presentation of the theory is entirely original, but it perhaps owes something to the doctrine of "tragic conflict" which Schlegel and Coleridge adapted from Hegel, and of course the idea that the essence of tragedy is struggle goes back to Aristotle. Brunetière's special contribution is that the struggle must be a volitional one, and thus his theory may be applied to all forms of drama.

Brunetière's essay is considerably clarified by William Archer's attack in his *Playmaking*[10] and Henry Arthur Jones's "agreeable reconciliation" of Brunetière and Archer in his Introduction to the English translation of the *Law of the Drama*.[11]

BIBLIOGRAPHY

TEXT

Art and Morality, tr. with introduction by Arthur Beatty. New York, 1899.
Études critiques sur l'histoire de la littérature française. Paris, 1880.
Essais sur la littérature contemporaine. 2d ed. Paris, 1892.
Études sur la XVIIIe siècle. Paris, 1911.

---

[6]Translated quotation of Hocking, *op. cit.*, p. 99.
[7]*Discours de combats*, I, 108.   [8]*Nouvelle questions de critique*, p. 214.
[9]*Honoré de Balzac*, p. 224.   [10]New York, 1923, pp. 23–33.
[11]Published by the Brander Matthews Dramatic Museum of Columbia University (New York, 1914).

L'Évolution de la poésie lyrique en France au dix-neuvième siècle. 2 vols. Paris, 1894.
L'Évolution des genres dans l'histoire de la littérature. Paris, 1890.
Histoire de la littérature française classique (1515–1830). 4 vols. Paris, 1904–1917.
Honoré de Balzac, tr. by Robert Louis Sanderson. Philadelphia, 1906.
Nouveaux essais sur la littérature contemporaine. 5th ed. Paris, 1910.
Questions de critique. 2nd ed. Paris, 1889.
Le Roman naturaliste. New ed. Paris, 1893.

CRITICISM

Babbitt, Irving, *Masters of Modern French Criticism.* Boston, 1912, pp. 298–338.
Basch, Victor, *Essais d'esthétique, de philosophie et de littérature.* Paris, 1934.
Belis, Alexandre, *La Critique française à la fin du XIXᵉ siècle: Ferdinand Brunetière, Émile Faguet, Jules Lemaître, Anatole France.* Paris, 1926.
Bondy, Louis Joseph, *Le Classicisme de Ferdinand Brunetière.* Baltimore, 1930.
Hocking, Elton, *Ferdinand Brunetière; the Evolution of a Critic.* University of Wisconsin, Madison, 1936.
Nonteuil, Jacques, *Ferdinand Brunetière.* Paris, 1933.

THE LAW OF THE DRAMA (*selections*)[1]

1894

. . . Observe, if you please, that I ask only one [characteristic] of the drama—no more—and that I leave the dramatist complete freedom in development. That is where I depart from the old school of criticism that believed in the mysterious power of "Rules" in their inspiring virtues; and consequently we see the old-school critics struggling and striving, exercising all their ingenuity to invent additional Rules; read, for example, the *Cours de littérature analytique* by Népomucène Lemercier. But the truth is that there are no Rules in that sense; there never will be. There are only conventions, which are necessarily variable, since their only object is to fulfill the essential aim of the dramatic work, and the means of accomplishing this vary with the piece, the time, and the man. Must we, like Corneille, regularly subordinate character to situation; invent, construct the situations first, and then, if I may so express it, put the characters inside? We may do so,

---

[1] Reprinted by permission of the Brander Matthews Dramatic Museum; translated by Philip M. Hayden.

certainly, since he did it, in the *Cid* and in *Horace*, in *Polyeucte* and in *Rodogune*. Or shall we, like Racine, subordinate situation to character, find the characters first, study them, master them, and then seek the situations which will best bring out their different aspects? We may do so, and that is what he did, as you know, in *Andromaque*, in *Britannicus*, in *Bajazet*, in *Phèdre*. There is an example, then, of a Rule which may be violated, and Racine's dramaturgy is none the less dramatic for being the opposite of Corneille's dramaturgy. Take another Rule. Shall we oblige the dramatic author to observe the Three Unities? I reply that he will not be hampered by them if he can choose, like Racine, subjects which properly or necessarily adjust themselves of their own accord, so to speak, to the rule: *Bérénice, Iphigénie, Esther.* . . . But if he chooses, like Shakespeare, subjects which are checked by it in their free development, or diverted merely, we will relieve him of the Rule: and *Othello, Macbeth, Hamlet*, will still be drama. This is another example of a Rule which can be turned in various ways. Or again, shall we mingle tragic and comic, tears and laughter, terror and joy, the sublime and the grotesque, Ariel and Caliban, Bottom and Titania, Triboulet and François I,[2] Don Guritan and Ruy Blas?[3] Shakespeare and Hugo have done it, but Euripides and Sophocles seem to have carefully avoided it; and who will deny that they were both right? We do not feel the need of a comic element to enliven or vary the severe beauty of Oedipus at Colonus, but we should certainly be sorry to have King Lear deprived of his Fool. It is unnecessary to continue. Evidently, all these alleged Rules effect or express only the most superficial characteristics of the drama. Not only are they not mysterious, they are not in the least profound. Whether we observe them or not, drama is drama with them or without them. They are only devices which may at any time give place to others. It all depends on the subject, the author, and the public. This is the point to add that there is something which does not depend on them.

To convince ourselves of that fact, let us examine more carefully two or three works whose dramatic value is universally recognized, and let us take them from species as different as the *Cid*, the *École des femmes*,[4] and *Célimare le bien-aimé*.[5] Chimène

---

[2]Triboulet was the fool of Louis XII and François I.
[3]Don Guritan and Ruy Blas, from Hugo's historical comedy, *Ruy Blas* (1838).
[4]*École des femmes*, comedy by Molière (1662).
[5]*Célimare le bien-aimé*, comedy by Labiche (1851).

wants to avenge her father; and the question is how she will succeed. Arnolphe *wants* to marry Agnès, whose stupidity will guarantee her fidelity; and the question is whether he will succeed. Célimare *wants* to get rid of the widowers of his former mistresses; and the question is what means he will employ. But Célimare is hampered in the execution of his *will* by his fear of the vengeance of his friends. Arnolphe is disturbed in the execution of his *will* by the young madcap Horace, who arouses love, and with love a *will*, in Agnès' heart. Chimène is betrayed in the execution of her *will* by the love which she feels for Rodrigue. On the other hand, Chimène's *will* is checked and broken by the insurmountable obstacle which she encounters in a *will* superior to her own. Arnolphe, who is far from being a fool, sees all the plans of his *will* tricked by the conspiracy of youth and love. And Célimare by the power of his *will* triumphs over the widowers of his mistresses. Nothing would be easier than to multiply examples. Take the *Tour de Nelse*,[6] the *Demi-monde*,[7] and the *Chapeau de paille d'Italie*.[8] Fadinard *wants* to obtain a Leghorn hat to replace that of Mme. Beauperthuis; and the whole farce consists in the remarkable character of the means which he employs. Suzanne d'Ange *wants* to marry M. de Nanjac; and the whole drama consists only in the means which she formulates. Buridan *wants* to exploit the monstrous secret which exists between him and Marguerite de Bourgogne; and the whole melodrama consists only of the succession of the means which he invents. Buridan's *will* is opposed in its work by Marguerite's pride. Suzanne's *will* is countered by that of Olivier de Jalin. And Fadinard's *will* becomes entangled in the means which he seeks to satisfy it. But chance, more powerful than Fadinard's *will*, brings success at the moment when he least expects it. Olivier's *will* wins out over Suzanne's. And by the exercise of their *will*, Marguerite and Buridan fall into the trap set by their own *will*. Is it not easy now to draw the conclusion? In drama or farce, what we ask of the theater is the spectacle of a *will* striving towards a goal, and conscious of the means which it employs.

This essential characteristic of dramatic composition distinguishes it, in the first place, from lyric composition, which I

[6]Minor French comedy, unidentified.
[7]*Le Demi-monde*, comedy by Alexandre Dumas, *fils* (1855).
[8]Minor French comedy.

shall not discuss, in order not to complicate the question unnecessarily and from the composition of the novel, with which,
especially in our day, it has so often been confused. "Who is not
for us is against us"—you know the phrase. The drama and the
novel are not the same thing; or rather, each is exactly the
opposite of the other. Read *Gil Blas*[9] again, or go again to see
the *Mariage de Figaro*.[10] The setting and the character are the
same. Beaumarchais made a trip to Spain, but Le Sage's novel
was none the less his principal model. I have shown elsewhere
that we find in the monologue of Figaro whole sentences from
Gil Blas. Only, whereas nothing happens to Gil Blas that he has
actually willed, it is on the contrary Figaro's *will* that conducts
the plot of his marriage. Let us pursue this point of comparison.

Gil Blas, like everybody else, wants to live, and if possible to
live agreeably. That is not what we call having a will. But
Figaro wants a certain definite thing, which is to prevent Count
Almaviva from exercising on Suzanne the seigneurial privilege.
He finally succeeds, and I grant, since the statement has been
made, that it is not exactly through the means which he had
chosen, most of which turn against him; but nevertheless he has
constantly willed what he willed. He had not ceased to devise
means of attaining it, and when these means have failed, he has
not ceased to invent new ones. That is what may be called *will*,
to set up a goal, and to direct everything toward it, to strive to
bring everything into line with it. Gil Blas really has no goal.
Highway robber, doctor's assistant, servant to a canon, to an
actress, or to a nobleman, all the positions which he occupies one
after another, come to him from fortune or chance. He has no
plan, because he has no particular or definite aim. He is subject
to circumstances; he does not try to dominate them. He does
not *act;* he is *acted upon.* Is not the difference evident? The proper
aim of the novel, as of the epic—of which it is only a secondary
and derived form, what the naturalists call a subspecies or a
variety—the aim of the *Odyssey*, as of *Gil Blas*, of the *Knights of the
Round Table*, as of *Madame Bovary*, is to give us a picture of the
influence which is exercised upon us by all that is outside of ourselves. The novel is therefore the contrary of the drama; and if
I have successfully set forth this opposition, do you not see the
consequences which result from it?

[9]*Gil Blas*, picaresque novel by Le Sage (1715–1735).
[10]*Le Mariage de Figaro*, comedy by Beaumarchais (1784).

It is thus that one can distinguish action from motion or agitation; and that is certainly worth while. Is it action to move about? Certainly not, and there is no true action except that of a will conscious of itself, conscious, as I was saying, of the means which it employs for its fulfillment, one which adapts them to its goal, and all other forms of action are only imitations, counterfeits, or parodies. The material or the subject of a novel or of a play may therefore be the same at bottom; but they become drama or novel only by the manner in which they are treated; and the manner is not merely different, it is opposite. One will never be able, therefore, to transfer to the stage any novels except those which are already dramatic; and note well that they are dramatic only to the extent to which their heroes are truly the architects of their destiny. It follows that one could make a novel of the *Mariage de Figaro*, but one will never make a drama or a comedy of *Gil Blas*. One might make a novel of Corneille's *Rodogune*, one will never make a drama of Rousseau's *Héloïse*. The general law of the theater, thus defined, gives us, then, in the first place, a sure means of perceiving what in any subject there is of the novel or the drama. The fact is that people do not know this well enough; and the naturalist school in France has committed no worse error than confusing the conditions of the two species.

The same law provides, further, the possibility of defining with precision the dramatic species—about as one does the biological species; and for that it is only necessary to consider the particular obstacle against which the will struggles. If these obstacles are recognized to be insurmountable or reputed to be so, as were, for example, in the eyes of the ancient Greeks, the decrees of fate, or in the eyes of the Christians, the decrees of Providence; as are for us the laws of nature or the passions aroused to frenzy and becoming thus the internal fatality of Phaedra and of Roxane, of Hamlet or of Othello;—it is tragedy. The incidents are generally terrifying, and the conclusion sanguinary, because in the struggle which man undertakes to make against fate, he is vanquished in advance, and must perish. Suppose now that he has a chance of victory, just one, that he still has in himself the power to conquer his passion; or suppose that, the obstacles which he is striving to overcome being the work of his fellowmen, as prejudice, for example, or social conventions, a man is for that very reason capable of surmounting them—that is the drama, properly speaking, romantic drama or social drama, *Hernani*[11] or *Antony*,[12] the *Fils naturel*,[13] or *Madame Caverlet*.[14] Change once more the nature of the obstacle, equalize, at least in appearance, the conditions of the struggle, bring together two opposing wills, Arnolphe and Agnès, Figaro and Almaviva, Suzanne d'Ange and Olivier de Jalin—this is comedy. *Don Sanche d'Aragon*,[15] heroic comedy,—you know this title of one of Corneille's plays. Bérénice, for the same reason, is hardly a tragedy. But instead of locating the obstacle in an opposing will, conscious and mistress of its acts, in a social convention, or in the fatality of destiny, let us locate it in the irony of fortune, or in the ridiculous aspect of prejudice, or again in the disproportion between the means and the end,—that is farce, that is the *Légataire universel*,[16] the *Chapeau de paille d'Italie*.

I do not say after that, that the types are always pure. In the history of literature or of art, as in nature, a type is almost never anything but an ideal, and consequently a limit. Where is the man among us, where is the woman, who embodies the perfection of the sex and of the species? There is moreover a natural relationship, we might say a consanguinity between adjoining species. Is a mulatto or a quadroon white or black? They are related to both. Likewise there may be an alliance or mixture of farce and comedy, of drama and tragedy. *Célimare* is almost a comedy; the *Cid* is almost a melodrama. It is nevertheless useful to have carefully defined the species; and if the law should only teach authors not to treat a subject of comedy by the devices of farce, that would be something. The general law of the theater is defined by the action of a will conscious of itself; and the dramatic species are distinguished by the nature of the obstacles encountered by this will.

And the quality of will measures and determines, in its turn, the dramatic value of each work in its species. Intelligence rules in the domain of speculation, but the will governs in the field of action, and consequently in history. It is the will which gives power; and power is hardly ever lost except by a failure or relaxation of the will. But that is also the reason why men think

[11]*Hernani*, tragedy by Victor Hugo (1830).
[12]*Antony*, romantic drama by Alexandre Dumas, *père* (1831).
[13]*Le Fils naturel*, comedy by Alexandre Dumas, *fils* (1858).
[14]*Madame Caverlet*, comedy by Augier (1876).
[15]*Don Sanche d'Aragon*, comedy by Corneille (1650).
[16]*Le Légataire universel*, comedy by Regnard (1708).

there is nothing grander than the development of the will, whatever the object, and that is the reason for the superiority of tragedy over the other dramatic forms. One may prefer for one's own taste a farce to a tragedy; one ought even to prefer a good farce to a mediocre tragedy, that goes without saying; and we do it every day. One cannot deny that tragedy is superior to farce: *Athalie* [17] to the *Légataire universel*, and *Ruy Blas* to the *Trois epiciers*. [18] Another reason sometimes given is that it implies indifference to death, but that is the same reason, if the supreme effort of the will is to conquer the horror of death. But shall we say that comedy is superior to farce, and why? We will say that, and for the same reason, because the obstacles against which Crispin contends in the *Légataire universel* do not exist, strictly speaking; they are only an invention of Regnard; and so the will is exerting itself to no effect. The goal is only a lure, so that the action is only a game. And we will say in con- clusion that one drama is superior to another drama according as the quantity of will exerted is greater or less, as the share of chance is less, and that of necessity greater. Who doubts that *Bajazet* is very much superior to *Zaïre?* [19] If you seek the true reason, you will find it here, *Zaïre* would not finish if Voltaire did not intervene at every moment in his work; but given the characters of Bajazet and Roxane, they develop as if of them- selves; and does it not really seem as if Racine confined himself to observing their action?

I will not continue. But I cannot refrain from noting the remarkable confirmation that this law finds in the general history of the theater. As a matter of fact, it is always at the exact moment of its national existence when the will of a great people is exalted, so to speak, within itself, that we see its dra- matic art reach also the highest point of its development, and produce its masterpieces. Greek tragedy is contemporary with the Persian wars. [20] Aeschylus fought the Mede; and while the fleets were engaged in the waters of Salamis, on that very day, the legend has it, Euripides was born. Legend is perhaps not more true, but it is often more profound than history. Con- sider the Spanish theater: Cervantes, Lope de Vega, Calderon

[17]*Athalie*, tragedy by Racine (1691).
[18]Evidently a minor French comedy, unidentified.
[19]*Zaïre*, tragedy by Voltaire (1733), inspired by *Othello*.
[20]Cf. A. W. Schlegel, p. 187, above.

belong to the time when Spain was extending over all of Europe, as well as over the New World, the domination of her will, or rather, as great causes do not always produce their literary effects at once, they are of the time immediately following. And France in the seventeenth century? The greatest struggle that our fathers made to maintain, within as without, the unity of the French nation, or to bring it to pass, was at the end of the sixteenth century, and was under Henry IV, under Richelieu, under Mazarin. The development of the theater followed immediately. I see, indeed, that great strengthenings of the national will have not always been followed by a dramatic renaissance, in England in the eighteenth century, for example, or in Germany today; but what I do not see, is a dramatic renaissance whose dawn has not been announced, as it were, by some progress, or some arousing of the will. Think of the theater of Lessing, of Schiller, of Goethe and remember what Frederick the Great had done, a few years before, without knowing it perhaps, to give to the Germany of the eighteenth century a consciousness of herself and of her national genius. The converse is no less striking. If it is extremely rare that a great development of the novel is contemporary even with a great development of the theater—if in France in particular, when the Molières, the Corneilles, the Racines have appeared, we have seen the *Artamènes*,[21] the *Faramons*,[22] the *Astrées*,[23] sink gently into oblivion, or again if *Gil Blas, Manon Lescaut*,[24] *Marianne*[25] are contemporary, at the beginning of the eighteenth century, with an exhaustion only too certain of the dramatic vein,—it is because in literature as in nature, the competition is always keenest between the neighboring species; and the soil is rarely rich enough for two rival varieties to prosper, develop, and multiply in peace. But it is also because, being, as we have seen, the contrary each of the other, drama and novel do not answer to the same conception of life. *Gil Blas* and *Figaro*, I repeat, belong to the same family; they cannot belong to the same time; and between them, if you take the trouble to examine carefully, there is all the interval that separates the relaxation of the will in the time of the Regency, from the vigorous recovery that it makes on the

---

[21]*Artamène*, novel by Mlle de Scudéry (1650).   [22]*Faramon*, unidentified.
[23]*Astrée*, pastoral novel by Honoré d'Urfé (1610–1624).
[24]*Manon Lescaut*, novel by Prévost (1731).
[25]*Marianne*, unfinished novel by Marivaux (1731–1741).

eve of the Revolution. What can be more singular? But if the theater has for its object to present the development of the will, what can be more natural? The Orientals have no drama, but they have novels. That is because they are fatalists, or determinists if you prefer, which amounts to the same thing, for today at least; and when the Greeks had a drama, they no longer had novels, I mean epics; they no longer had an *Odyssey*.

You see the reason, don't you? Are we free agents? Or are we not? Are we the masters of events? Or are we only their dupes, their playthings, their victims? I don't know; at this moment I don't care to know, and you may believe that I am not going to dabble in metaphysics here. But in any case it appears that our belief in our freedom is of no small assistance in the struggle that we undertake against the obstacles which prevent us from attaining our object. And I grant that in order to succeed in dominating nature, or even in reforming society, it is not necessary to believe one's self capable of it. There is always an acquired momentum of the human race that aids the insufficiency of individual effort. But that is not without value either; for one does not attempt the impossible. The bond between the belief in free will and the exertion of the will explains therefore pretty well the favor or the moral support given, at certain epochs, to an art whose essential object is the representation of the power of the will. A question of fitness, or, as we say, of adaption to environment. The belief in determinism is more favorable to the progress of the novel, but the belief in free will is more favorable to the progress of dramatic art. Men of action, Richelieu, Condé, Frederick, Napoleon, have always been fond of the theater. . . .

HENRI BERGSON

(1859–1941)

o◯oo◯o

BERGSON IS KNOWN primarily as a philosopher, but probably no one
else except Freud has had a wider influence on contemporary literature.
He taught philosophy at several schools in France, including the
École Normale Supérieure and the Collège de France. In 1918 he was
elected to the Académie Française. In 1928 he was awarded the Nobel
Prize in Literature. His *Creative Evolution* (*L'Évolution créatrice*, 1907) is
his most widely known work, but he laid the philosophical foundation
in *Time and Free Will* and *Introduction to Metaphysics*. As early as 1900
he applied his philosophical theories to art, in *Laughter: An Essay on the
Meaning of the Comic* (French, *Le Rire*).

Professor Leighton has given an excellent concise summary of
Bergson's theory of evolution:

> Bergson develops his own theory that evolution is a continuously
> creative vital and psychical process. The true reality is the vital
> impetus (*l'élan vital*); it is the creative current of being, the urge
> towards increase of individuality. But there is a counter current,
> the downward tendency towards inertia, sameness, immobility,
> exemplified in habit. This is matter; life and matter are thus two
> opposing tendencies, the one driving towards creativity and in-
> dividuality, the other dragging it down towards immobility and
> mechanism which is death.[1]

Thus the world "is the theater of the cosmical struggle of the dynamic
and the static. The life force is mind. For the vital impetus, the moving
spring of all evolution, is immaterial."[2] Bergson is, therefore, an anti-
mechanist and an antirationalist; in fact, he leans heavily on intuition
and is something of a mystic.

The doctrine of life as a "continuous process indefinitely pursued, an
indivisible progress, on which each visible organism rides during the
short interval of the time given it to live"[3] has been a major inspiration
to many recent novelists, especially the "impressionistic" ones, who

---

[1]Joseph A. Leighton, *The Field of Philosophy* (New York, 1923), p. 316.
[2]*Ibid.*, p. 329.
[3]*Creative Evolution*, tr. by Arthur Mitchell (New York, 1911), p. 27.

reduce existence to a continuous flux, and most of these writers make use of the introspective "stream-of-consciousness" stylistic technique.

Creative Evolution clarifies Bergson's theory of art, as expressed below in the extract from *Laughter*. If we could come into direct contact with reality, thinks Bergson, if we could "enter into immediate communion with things and with ourselves, probably art would be useless, or we should all be artists, for then our soul would continually vibrate in perfect accord with nature."[4] Artists are those rare people, especially gifted in the intuition of reality, who come nearest to perceiving "all things in their native purity: the forms, colors, sounds of the physical world as well as the subtlest movements of the inner life."[5] But the artist is "usually wedded to art" through only one of his senses, "and through that sense alone. . . ."[6] "So art, whether it be painting or sculpture, poetry or music, has no other object than to brush aside the utilitarian symbols, the conventional and socially accepted generalities . . . [and] to bring us face to face with reality itself."[7]

But the average person is bound by habit and convention; matter outweighs spirit; inertia is stronger than creativity. "This tendency," says Bergson, "has become even more pronounced under the influence of speech; for words—with the exception of proper nouns—all denote genera."[8] Thus "not only external objects, but even our own mental states, are screened from us in their inmost, their personal aspect, in the original life they possess."[9] Bergson's aesthetic, therefore, somewhat resembles Emerson's transcendentalism, and his theory has inspired the host of modern writers who are striving to become more and more *aware* of life. Of course, this philosophy lends itself readily to the mysticism of a Charles Morgan, the sentimentalism of a Sherwood Anderson, or the romantic "realism" of a William Faulkner. But whether the theory be studied historically to explain some of these modern writers, or as an intrinsic contribution to the literature of criticism, the student will find it interesting and illuminating.

BIBLIOGRAPHY

TEXT

L'Évolution créatrice. 5th ed. Paris, 1909.
Le Rire; Essai sur la signification du comique. 5th ed. Paris, 1908.

TRANSLATIONS

Creative Evolution, tr. by Arthur Mitchell. London, 1911.
Laughter; an Essay on the Meaning of the Comic, tr. by Cloudesley Brereton and Fred Rothwell. London, 1911.

[4]See p. 613. [5]See p. 615. [6]See *ibid.* [7]See p. 616. [8]See p. 614. [9]See p. 615.

CRITICISM

Dodson, George Rowland, *Bergson and the Modern Spirit; an Essay in Constructive Thought*. London, 1914.

Gunn, John Alexander, *Bergson and His Philosophy*, with an introduction by Alexander Mair. London, [1920].

Hager, Wilhelm, *Bergson als Neu-Romantiker mit besonderer Berücksichtigung, von M. Maeterlinck*. München, 1916.

Kallen, Horace Meyer, *William James and Henri Bergson; a Study in Contrasting Theories of Life*. University of Chicago Press [c.1914].

Lovejoy, Arthur O., *Bergson and Romantic Evolutionism*. University of California Press, 1914.

Maire, Gilbert, *Henri Bergson, son œuvre* . . . Paris, [1926].

Mathewson, Louise, *Bergson's Theory of the Comic in the Light of English Comedy*. University of Nebraska, 1920.

Santayana, George, *Winds of Doctrine; Studies in Contemporary Opinion*. New York, [1913].

Szathmary, A., *The Aesthetic Theory of Bergson*. Harvard University Press, 1937.

Turquet-Milnes, Gladys Rosaleen, *From Pascal to Proust, Studies in the Genealogy of a Philosophy*. New York, 1926.

[THE OBJECT OF ART][1]

1900

What is the object of art? Could reality come into direct contact with sense and consciousness, could we enter into immediate communion with things and with ourselves, probably art would be useless, or rather we should all be artists, for then our soul would continually vibrate in perfect accord with nature. Our eyes, aided by memory, would carve out in space and fix in time the most inimitable of pictures. Hewn in the living marble of the human form, fragments of statues, beautiful as the relics of antique statuary, would strike the passing glance. Deep in our souls we should hear the strains of our inner life's unbroken melody—a music that is ofttimes gay, but more frequently plaintive and always original. All this is around and within us, and yet no whit of it do we distinctly perceive. Between nature and ourselves, nay, between ourselves and our own consciousness a veil is interposed: a veil that is dense and

[1]Extract from chap. III, "The Comic in Character," in *Laughter; an Essay on the Meaning of the Comic*. The translation is by Cloudesley Brereton and Fred Rothwell. Reprinted by special arrangement with The Macmillan Company.

opaque for the common herd—thin, almost transparent, for the artist and the poet. What fairy wove that veil? Was it done in malice or in friendliness? We had to live, and life demands that we grasp things in their relations to our own needs. Life is action. Life implies the acceptance only of the *utilitarian* side of things in order to respond to them by appropriate reactions: all other impressions must be dimmed or else reach us vague and blurred. I look and I think I see, I listen and I think I hear, I examine myself and I think I am reading the very depths of my heart. But what I see and hear of the outer world is purely and simply a selection made by my senses to serve as a light to my conduct; what I know of myself is what comes to the surface, what participates in my actions. My senses and my consciousness, therefore, give me no more than a practical simplification of reality. In the vision they furnish me of myself and of things, the differences that are useless to man are obliterated, the resemblances that are useful to him are emphasized; ways are traced out for me in advance along which my activity is to travel. These ways are the ways which all mankind has trod before me. Things have been classified with a view to the use I can derive from them. And it is this classification I perceive, far more clearly than the color and the shape of things. Doubtless man is vastly superior to the lower animals in this respect. It is not very likely that the eye of a wolf makes any distinction between a kid and a lamb; both appear to the wolf as the same identical quarry, alike easy to pounce upon, alike good to devour. We, for our part, make a distinction between a goat and a sheep; but can we tell one goat from another, one sheep from another? The *individuality* of things or of beings escapes us, unless it is materially to our advantage to perceive it. Even when we do take note of it—as when we distinguish one man from another—it is not the individuality itself that the eye grasps, i.e. an entirely original harmony of forms and colors, but only one or two features that will make practical recognition easier.

In short, we do not see the actual things themselves; in most cases we confine ourselves to reading the labels affixed to them. This tendency, the result of need, has become even more pronounced under the influence of speech; for words—with the exception of proper nouns—all denote genera. The word, which only takes note of the most ordinary function and com-

monplace aspect of the thing, intervenes between it and ourselves, and would conceal its form from our eyes, were that form
not already masked beneath the necessities that brought the
word into existence. Not only external objects, but even our
own mental states, are screened from us in their inmost, their
personal aspect, in the original life they possess. When we feel
love or hatred, when we are gay or sad, is it really the feeling
itself that reaches our consciousness with those innumerable
fleeting shades of meaning and deep resounding echoes that
make it something altogether our own? We should all, were it
so, be novelists or poets or musicians. Mostly, however, we
perceive nothing but the outward display of our mental state.
We catch only the impersonal aspect of our feelings, that aspect
which speech has set down once for all because it is almost the
same, in the same conditions, for all men. Thus, even in our
own individual, individuality escapes our ken. We move
amidst generalities and symbols, as within a tiltyard in which
our force is effectively pitted against other forces; and fascinated
by action, tempted by it, for our own good, on to the field it has
selected, we live in a zone midway between things and ourselves,
externally to things, externally also to ourselves. From time to
time, however, in a fit of absentmindedness, nature raises up
souls that are more detached from life. Not with that inten-
tional, logical, systematical detachment—the result of reflection and philosophy—but rather with a natural detachment,
one innate in the structure of sense or consciousness, which at
once reveals itself by a virginal manner, so to speak, of seeing,
hearing, or thinking. Were this detachment complete, did the
soul no longer cleave to action by any of its perceptions, it
would be the soul of an artist such as the world has never yet
seen. It would excel alike in every art at the same time; or
rather, it would fuse them all into one. It would perceive all
things in their native purity: the forms, colors, sounds of the
physical world as well as the subtlest movements of the inner
life. But this is asking too much of nature. Even for such of us
as she has made artists, it is by accident, and on one side only,
that she has lifted the veil. In one direction only has she forgotten to rivet the perception to the need. And since each
direction corresponds to what we call a *sense*—through one of
his senses, and through that sense alone, is the artist usually
wedded to art. Hence, originally, the diversity of arts. Hence

also the speciality of predispositions. This one applies himself to colors and forms, and since he loves color for color and form for form, since he perceives them for their sake and not for his own, it is the inner life of things that he sees appearing through their forms and colors. Little by little he insinuates it into our own perception, baffled though we may be at the outset. For a few moments at least, he diverts us from the prejudices of form and color that come between ourselves and reality. And thus he realizes the loftiest ambition of art, which here consists in revealing to us nature. Others, again, retire within themselves. Beneath the thousand rudimentary actions which are the outward and visible signs of an emotion, behind the commonplace, conventional expression that both reveals and conceals an individual mental state, it is the emotion, the original mood, to which they attain in its undefiled essence. And then, to induce us to make the same effort ourselves, they contrive to make us see something of what they have seen: by rhythmical arrangement of words, which thus become organized and animated with a life of their own, they tell us—or rather suggest—things that speech was not calculated to express. Others delve yet deeper still. Beneath these joys and sorrows which can, at a pinch, be translated into language, they grasp something that has nothing in common with language, certain rhythms of life and breath that are closer to man than his inmost feelings, being the living law—varying with each individual—of his enthusiasm and despair, his hopes and regrets. By setting free and emphasizing this music, they force it upon our attention; they compel us, willy-nilly, to fall in with it, like passers-by who join in a dance. And thus they impel us to set in motion, in the depths of our being, some secret chord which was only waiting to thrill. So art, whether it be painting or sculpture, poetry or music, has no other object than to brush aside the utilitarian symbols, the conventional and socially accepted generalities, in short, everything that veils reality from us, in order to bring us face to face with reality itself. It is from a misunderstanding on this point that the dispute between realism and idealism in art has risen. Art is certainly only a more direct vision of reality. But this purity of perception implies a break with utilitarian convention, an innate and specially localized disinterestedness of sense or consciousness, in short, a certain immateriality of life, which is what has always been called idealism. So that we might say, without in any way playing upon the meaning of the words, that realism is in the work when idealism is in the soul, and that it is only through ideality that we can resume contact with reality.

Dramatic art forms no exception to this law. What drama goes forth to discover and brings to light is a deep-seated reality that is veiled from us, often in our own interests, by the necessities of life. What is this reality? What are these necessities? Poetry always expresses inward states. But amongst these states some arise mainly from contact with our fellowmen. They are the most intense as well as the most violent. As contrary electricities attract each other and accumulate between the two plates of the condenser from which the spark will presently flash, so, by simply bringing people together, strong attractions and repulsions take place followed by an utter loss of balance, in a word, by that electrification of the soul known as passion. Were man to give way to the impulse of his natural feelings, were there neither social nor moral law, these outbursts of violent feeling would be the ordinary rule in life. But utility demands that these outbursts should be foreseen and averted. Man must live in society, and consequently submit to rules. And what interest advises, reason commands: duty calls, and we have to obey the summons. Under this dual influence has perforce been formed an outward layer of feelings and ideas which make for permanence, aim at becoming common to all men, and cover, when they are not strong enough to extinguish it, the inner fire of individual passions. The slow progress of mankind in the direction of an increasingly peaceful social life has gradually consolidated this layer, just as the life of our planet itself has been one long effort to cover over with a cool and solid crust the fiery mass of seething metals. But volcanic eruptions occur. And if the earth were a living being, as mythology has feigned, most likely when in repose it would take delight in dreaming of these sudden explosions whereby it suddenly resumes possession of its innermost nature. Such is just the kind of pleasure that is provided for us by drama. Beneath the quiet humdrum life that reason and society have fashioned for us, it stirs something within us which luckily does not explode, but which it makes us feel in its inner tension. It offers nature her revenge upon society. Sometimes it makes straight for the goal, summoning up to the surface, from the depths below, passions that produce a general upheaval. Sometimes it follows a flank movement, as is often the case in contemporary drama; with a skill that is frequently sophistical it shows up the inconsistencies of society; it exaggerates the shams and shib-boleths of the social law, and so indirectly, by merely dissolving or corroding the outer crust, it again brings us back to the inner core. But, in both cases, whether it weakens society or strength-ens nature, it has the same end in view: that of laying bare a secret portion of ourselves, what might be called the tragic element in our character. This is indeed the impression we get after seeing a stirring drama. What has just interested us is not so much what we have been told about others as the glimpse we have caught of ourselves—a whole host of ghostly feelings, emotions, and events that would fain have come into real exist-ence, but, fortunately for us, did not. It also seems as if an appeal had been made within us to certain ancestral memories belong-ing to a faraway past—memories so deep-seated and so foreign to our present life that this latter, for a moment, seems some-thing unreal and conventional, for which we shall have to serve a fresh apprenticeship. So it is indeed a deeper reality that drama draws up from beneath our superficial and utilitarian at-tainments; and this art has the same end in view as all the others.

Hence it follows that art always aims at what is *individual*. What the artist fixes on his canvas is something he has seen at a certain spot, on a certain day, at a certain hour, with a coloring that will never be seen again. What the poet sings of is a certain mood which was his, and his alone, and which will never return. What the dramatist unfolds before us is the life-history of a soul, a living tissue of feelings and events—something, in short, which has once happened and can never be repeated. We may, indeed, give general names to these feelings, but they cannot be the same thing in another soul. They are *individualized*. Thereby, and thereby only, do they belong to art; for generalities, symbols, or even types form the current coin of our daily perception. How, then, does a misunderstanding on this point arise?

The reason lies in the fact that two very different things have been mistaken for each other: the generality of things and that of the opinions we come to regarding them. Because a feeling is generally recognized as true, it does not follow that it is a general feeling. Nothing could be more unique than the character of Hamlet. Though he may resemble other men in some respects,

it is clearly not on that account that he interests us most. But
he is universally accepted and regarded as a living character. In
this sense only is he universally true. The same holds good of all
the other products of art. Each of them is unique, and yet, if it
bear the stamp of genius, it will come to be accepted by everybody. Why will it be accepted? And if it is unique of its kind, by
what sign do we know it to be genuine? Evidently by the very
effort it forces us to make against our predispositions in order to
see sincerely. Sincerity is contagious. What the artist has seen we
shall probably never see again, or at least never see in exactly
the same way; but if he has actually seen it, the attempt he has
made to lift the veil compels our imitation. His work is an example which we take as a lesson. And the efficacy of the lesson
is the exact standard of the genuineness of the work. Consequently, truth bears within itself a power of conviction, nay, of
conversion, which is the sign that enables us to recognize it. The
greater the work and the more profound the dimly apprehended
truth, the longer may the effect be in coming; but, on the other
hand, the more universal will that effect tend to become. So the
universality here lies in the effect produced, and not in the cause.

Altogether different is the object of comedy. Here it is in
the work itself that the generality lies. Comedy depicts characters we have already come across and shall meet with again.
It takes note of similarities. It aims at placing types before our
eyes. It even creates new types, if necessary. In this respect it
forms a contrast to all the other arts.

The very titles of certain classical comedies are significant in
themselves. *Le Misanthrope*,[2] *L'Avare*,[3] *Le Joueur*,[4] *Le Distrait*,[5]
etc., are names of whole classes of people; and even when a
character comedy has a proper noun as its title, this proper noun
is speedily swept away, by the very weight of its contents, into
the stream of common nouns. We say "a Tartufe,"[6] but we
should never say "a Phèdre"[7] or "a Polyeucte."[8]

[2]A comedy by Molière, produced in 1666; ideal of classical comedy—chief interest
is in the development of various pairs of opposing characters.

[3]A comedy by Molière (1668); plot borrowed from Plautus. Fielding's *Miser* is
based on it.

[4]A comedy by Regnard (1696). Mrs. Centlivre's *Gamester* is based on it.

[5]A comedy by Regnard (1697), amusing character study.

[6]Chief character in Molière's *Tartufe* (1667); Tartufe is a hypocritical religious
devotee.

[7]Chief character in Racine's great tragedy, *Phèdre* (1677).

[8]Principal character, a Christian martyr, in Corneille's tragedy, *Polyeucte* (1643).

Above all, a tragic poet will never think of grouping around the chief character in his play secondary characters to serve as simplified copies, so to speak, of the former. The hero of a tragedy represents an individuality unique of its kind. It may be possible to imitate him, but then we shall be passing, whether consciously or not, from the tragic to the comic. No one is like him, because he is like no one. But a remarkable instinct, on the contrary, impels the comic poet, once he has elaborated his central character, to cause other characters, displaying the same general traits, to revolve as satellites round him. Many comedies have either a plural noun or some collective term as their title. *Les Femmes savantes,*[9] *Les Précieuses ridicules,*[10] *Le Monde où l'on s'ennuie,*[11] etc., represent so many rallying points on the stage adopted by different groups of characters, all belonging to one identical type. It would be interesting to analyze this tendency in comedy. Maybe dramatists have caught a glimpse of a fact recently brought forward by mental pathology, viz., that cranks of the same kind are drawn by a secret attraction, to seek each other's company. Without precisely coming within the province of medicine, the comic individual, as we have shown, is in some way absentminded, and the transition from absentmindedness to crankiness is continuous. But there is also another reason. If the comic poet's object is to offer us types, that is to say, characters capable of self-repetition, how can he set about it better than by showing us, in each instance, several different copies of the same model? That is just what the naturalist does in order to define a species. He enumerates and describes its main varieties.

This essential difference between tragedy and comedy, the former being concerned with individuals, and the latter with classes, is revealed in yet another way. It appears in the first draft of the work. From the outset it is manifested by two radically different methods of observation.

Though the assertion may seem paradoxical, a study of other men is probably not necessary to the tragic poet. We find that some of the great poets have lived a retiring, homely sort of life, without having a chance of witnessing around them an outburst of the passions they have so faithfully depicted. But, supposing

[9]Comedy by Molière (1672), adapted from *Les Précieuses ridicules.*
[10]Comedy by Molière (1659).
[11]Comedy by Pailleron (1881).

even they had witnessed such a spectacle, it is doubtful whether they would have found it of much use. For what interests us in the work of the poet is the glimpse we get of certain profound moods or inner struggles. Now, this glimpse cannot be obtained from without. Our souls are impenetrable to one another. Certain signs of passion are all that we ever apperceive externally. These we interpret—though always, by the way, defectively—only by analogy with what we have ourselves experienced. So what we experience is the main point, and we cannot become thoroughly acquainted with anything but our own heart—supposing we ever get so far. Does this mean that the poet has experienced what he depicts, that he has gone through the various situations he makes his characters traverse, and lived the whole of their inner life? Here, too, the biographies of poets would contradict such a supposition. How, indeed, could the same man have been Macbeth, Hamlet, Othello, King Lear, and many others? But then a distinction should perhaps here be made between the personality *we have* and all those we might have had. Our character is the result of a choice that is continually being renewed. There are points—at all events there seem to be—all along the way, where we may branch off, and we perceive many possible directions though we are unable to take more than one. To retrace one's steps and follow to the end the faintly distinguishable directions appears to be the essential element in poetic imagination. Of course, Shakespeare was neither Macbeth, nor Hamlet, nor Othello; still, he *might have been* these several characters, if the circumstances of the case on one hand, and the consent of his will on the other, had caused to break out into explosive action what was nothing more than an inner prompting. We are strangely mistaken as to the part played by poetic imagination if we think it pieces together its heroes out of fragments filched from right and left, as though it were patching together a harlequin's motley. Nothing living would result from that. Life cannot be recomposed; it can only be looked at and reproduced. Poetic imagination is but a fuller view of reality. If the characters created by a poet give us the impression of life, it is only because they are the poet himself—a multiplication or division of the poet—the poet plumbing the depths of his own nature in so powerful an effort of inner observation, that he lays hold of the potential in the real, and takes up what nature has left as a mere outline or sketch in his soul in order to make of it a finished work of art.

Altogether different is the kind of observation from which comedy springs. It is directed outwards. However interested a dramatist may be in the comic features of human nature, he will hardly go, I imagine, to the extent of trying to discover his own. Besides, he would not find them, for we are never ridiculous except in some point that remains hidden from our own consciousness. It is on others, then, that such observation must perforce be practiced. But it will, for this very reason, assume a character of generality that it cannot have when we apply it to ourselves. Settling on the surface, it will not be more than skin-deep, dealing with persons at the point at which they come into contact and become capable of resembling one another. It will go no farther. Even if it could, it would not desire to do so, for it would have nothing to gain in the process. To penetrate too far into the personality, to couple the outer effect with causes that are too deep-seated, would mean to endanger, and in the end to sacrifice all that was laughable in the effect. In order that we may be tempted to laugh at it, we must localize its cause in some intermediate region of the soul. Consequently, the effect must appear to us as an average effect, as expressing an average of mankind. And, like all averages, this one is obtained by bringing together scattered data, by comparing analogous cases and extracting their essence; in short by a process of abstraction and generalization similar to that which the physicist brings to bear upon facts with the object of grouping them under laws. In a word, method and object are here of the same nature as in the inductive sciences in that observation is always external and the result always general.

And so we come back, by a roundabout way, to the double conclusion we reached in the course of our investigations. On the one hand, a person is never ridiculous except through some mental attribute resembling absentmindedness, through something that lives upon him without forming part of his organism, after the fashion of a parasite; that is the reason this state of mind is observable from without and capable of being corrected. But, on the other hand, just because laughter aims at correcting, it is expedient that the correction should reach as great a number of persons as possible. This is the reason comic observation instinctively proceeds to what is general. It chooses such peculiarities as admit of being reproduced, and consequently are not indissolubly bound up with the individuality of a single person,—a possibly common sort of uncommonness, so to say— peculiarities that are held in common. By transferring them to the stage, it creates works that doubtless belong to art in that their only visible aim is to please, but that will be found to contrast with other works of art by reason of their generality, and also of their scarcely confessed or scarcely conscious intention to correct and instruct. So we were probably right in saying that comedy lies midway between art and life. It is not disinterested as genuine art is. By organizing laughter, comedy accepts social life as a natural environment; it even obeys an impulse of social life. And in this respect it turns its back upon art, which is a breaking away from society and a return to pure nature.

BENEDETTO CROCE

(1866-   )

o◯oo◯o

FIRST PUBLISHED in 1936,[1] when the author was seventy years of age,
Poetry gives the result of the long meditation of a thinker who issued
a book on the subject when he was twenty-eight.   Its first part deals
with "Poetry and Literature," showing the nature of poetic expression
in the true sense of the word and distinguishing it from other types of
expression often confused with it.   For example, it is not sentimental
expression, it is not oratory or rhetoric, it is not the sophisticated expression of literature, it is not even "pure poetry."   Poetry shows most
obviously the quality of inspiration that appears in all human experience, because in poetry the relation of the individual to the universal,
the finite to the infinite, is more evident than in the world of action.
The Greek word *poiein*[2] is properly applied to an activity in which
knowing appears as doing.   The second part is called "The Life of
Poetry"; one of its most important ideas is the re-evocation of poetry,
on which Croce says:

> Several years, months, days, or even hours after a poetic expres-
> sion has been formed, the author, by reason of the passage of time
> or a change in conditions, may find that he is quite unlike his
> earlier self. Yet he may then repeat his own words or reread them
> if they have been written. If the poetic expression has at such
> times a new birth in the author himself, in spite of changes in his
> nature, it equally has a new birth in others who are also truly the
> author himself, since they are joined with him in a common hu-
> manity, his contemporaries or his successors throughout the ages.
> This is the eternal rebirth or re-evocation that poetry undergoes.
> Such re-evocation cannot become actual otherwise than as the
> retracing of the creative process of that expression.[3]

Here is found also something on the structural parts of a poem. Croce's
earlier discussions had been interpreted, chiefly by hostile critics, to

---

[1]After considerable, though not exhaustive, comparison I have found no changes
in the second edition (1937) except in the index. (Translator's note.)

[2]Cf. e.g., Gilbert, *Literary Criticism: Plato to Dryden*, pp. 270; 411.

[3]*La poesia*, p. 65.

mean that the framework of the poem, such as Dante's journey in the *Divine Comedy*, was unpoetical and that the truly poetical parts were found only in episodes, as that of Francesca in the *Inferno;* he now explains that for spirits full of intellectual and moral as well as poetical life, the structure "was a vital part of the spirit, distinct from and yet joined with the poetry, which drew nutriment from it, in a union not static but dialectical. It cannot be regarded with indifference by one who wishes to understand the spirit of the poets or the physiognomy of their works; but like all other structures it ought to be indifferent to us in so far as absolutely in it we do not hear their poetry sing." Chapters of the third part are included in the present volume. The last part deals with the "Formation and Education of the Poet." It affirms the necessity for discipline, though not the discipline of the schools, but still more asserts the artist's independence. He need not, for example, be fettered by the notions of the literary genera, as epic and dramatic. In the last chapter Croce presents his belief that all the arts are subject to the same general aesthetic principles. Postscripts, giving informal remarks, quotations, etc., and forming a charming addition to the volume, occupy almost as much space as the primary text. Paraphrases and translations of parts of them (indicated by the abbreviation Ps.) appear in the notes.

This work reveals the development and clarification of the author's views, often probably as the result of objections. Yet one familiar with his writings will find little that can be called new and strange; the *Poetry of Dante* expresses or implies, or at least prepares one to read without surprise, many of the ideas of *Poetry*. The book, however, will be understood in proportion as it is considered in connection with his other writings, though Croce does not think himself the founder of a system:

> Many of my friends, when I had published the whole of the *Philosophy of Spirit*, advised me to rest now that I had, as they said, completed my "system"; but I knew that I had completed nothing, closed nothing, but only written a few volumes about the problems which ever since my youth had been by degrees accumulating in my spirit. And I went on living my life, and reading not so much the philosophers as the poets and historians; and soon I found growing up within me of themselves, my . . . essays on the *Theory and History of Historical Thought* [and other works]. I shall do the same thing over again; I shall go on philosophizing, even if, as I sometimes allow myself to think, not without pleasure, I one day give up "philosophy," philosophy ordinarily so called

in the narrow or scholastic sense of the word, treatises, dissertations, debates, historical inquiries into the doctrines of so-called
philosophers; for the unity of philosophy and history means just
this, that all thought is philosophy, whatever it is about and in
whatever form it is cast. Indeed the highest form of philosophy
consists, as I believe, in overcoming the provisional form of abstract "theory" and thinking the philosophy of particular facts, nar-
rating history; a history that is not merely narrated but thought.[4]

In such a life Croce's opponents see the Protean writhings of one determined to escape those able to convict him of error; his friends see
unwearied pursuit of truth.

As he himself points out, even his all-important conception of "lyrical
intuition" has not remained constant. Possibly the following, on
scenes of Trojan life recalled by Aeneas (*Aeneid*, III, 294 ff.), would still
be acceptable to him:

. . . Through them all there runs a feeling, a feeling which is our
own no less than the poet's, a human feeling of bitter memories,
of shuddering horror, of melancholy, of homesickness, of tenderness, of a kind of childish *pietas* that could prompt this vain revival
of things perished, these playthings fashioned by a religious devotion, the *parva Troia*, the *Pergama simulata magnis*, the *arentem Xan-
thi cognomine rivum:* something inexpressible in logical terms, which
only poetry can express in full. Moreover, these two elements
may appear as two in a first abstract analysis, but they cannot be
regarded as two distinct threads, however intertwined; for, in
effect, the feeling is altogether converted into images, into this
complex of images, and is thus a feeling that is contemplated and
therefore resolved and transcended. Hence poetry must be called
neither feeling, nor image, nor yet the sum of the two, but "contemplation of feeling" or "lyrical intuition" or (which is the same
thing) "pure intuition"—pure, that is, of all historical and critical
reference to the reality or unreality of the images of which it is
woven, and apprehending the pure throb of life in its ideality.[5]

Most literary critics of the past thirty-five years, for example Lascelles
Abercrombie, have been influenced by Croce's theory and practice.

BIBLIOGRAPHY

TEXT AND TRANSLATIONS

Aesthetic, tr. by Douglas Ainslie. London, 1929. From the fourth
Italian edition. The last Italian edition is the sixth.

[4]Benedetto Croce, *An Autobiography*, trans. by R. G. Collingwood, pp. 108–109.
[5]Benedetto Croce, "Aesthetics," in the *Encyclopaedia Britannica*, 14th edition.

"Aesthetics" (tr. not indicated), in the *Encyclopaedia Britannica*, 14th ed. An admirable brief account. But Croce would not wish any statement of his views to be taken as final.
Ariosto, Shakespeare, and Corneille, tr. by Douglas Ainslie. New York, 1920.
Autobiography, tr. by R. G. Collingwood. Oxford, 1927.
The Breviary of Aesthetic. Rice Institute Pamphlets, II (1915), 223–310.
The Defence of Poetry, Variations on the Theme of Shelley, tr. by E. F. Carritt. Oxford, 1933.
The Essence of Aesthetics, tr. by Douglas Ainslie. London, 1921. Same as the preceding.
Goethe, tr. by Emily Anderson, with an introduction by Douglas Ainslie. New York, 1923.
History, Its Theory and Practice, tr. by Douglas Ainslie. New York, 1921.
The Poetry of Dante, tr. by Douglas Ainslie. New York, 1922.
La poesia. Bari, 1937.

CRITICISM

Borgese, G. A., *On Dante Criticism*, Annual Reports of the Dante Society. Harvard University Press, 1936. A criticism of Croce's view.
Bosanquet, Bernard, "Croce's Aesthetic" in *Science and Philosophy*. London, 1927, pp. 407–437.
Carritt, E. F., *What Is Beauty?* Oxford, 1932, pp. 87–111.
Dodds, Mrs. Annie Edwards [Powell], *The Romantic Theory of Poetry, an Examination in the Light of Croce's Aesthetic*. New York, 1926.
Gilbert, Allan H., Review of *La poesia*, in *Italica*, XIV (1937), 28.
Gilbert, Katharine, "The One and the Many in Croce's Aesthetic," in *Studies in Recent Aesthetic*. Chapel Hill, 1927. According to the author "the development of Croce's thought as shown in his recent writings removes some of the force of the imputation of fundamental contradiction in his views."
Smith, J. A., "Croce," in the *Encyclopaedia Britannica*, 14th ed.
Spingarn, Joel E., *The New Criticism*. Columbia University Press, 1911. (Reprinted in *Creative Criticism: Essays on the Unity of Genius and Taste*. New York, 1917; in *Criticism in America: Its Function and Status*. New York, 1924; and in Edwin Berry Burgum, *The New Criticism: An Anthology of Modern Aesthetics and Literary Criticism*. New York, 1930.) An excellent account of Croce's thought up to 1911 by the best-known American exponent. It cannot now be taken as adequate; for example, characterization, as explained in the present selections, is not mentioned.

POETRY (*selections*)[1]

1937

III, ii

Beauty, the sole category of aesthetic judgment

Great and varied must be the labor, thought, and effort of the man who undertakes to "give names to things,"[2] to the things of poetry and literature; yet in the course of this treatise we have already used those names many times in speaking of their chief exponents. The judgment of poetry has a single indivisible category, that of beauty. According to this category it applies the words beautiful and ugly to works re-evoked[3] by the imagination, and classifies them as fully or poetically beautiful, or as beautiful in a literary way,[4] and divides these last, according to the varied sentimental, intellectual, or volitional content which they clothe with beautiful form, into works of emotion, prose or instruction, oratory, pleasing literature, and art for art's sake. These delicate discriminations cannot be mechanical or easy; they require the theoretical distinctions of philosophy as necessary instruments, and imply the obligation to use these distinctions properly, that is, not to abuse them.[5] The abuse and foolish use of these instruments by the unwise and inexpert cause complaint about them, and they are indeed dangerous; we forget the saying of Jacobi on a similar occasion, namely that what cannot be abused is of no use.

[1]Translated for this volume by Allan H. Gilbert, from the second edition of *La poesia* (Bari, 1937), with the permission of The Macmillan Company, which plans to issue a complete translation.

[2]Cicero, *Tusculan Disputations*, I, 25. Cf. Milton's Adam, on the naming of the animals:

> I named them as they passed, and understood
> Their nature, with such knowledge God endued
> My sudden apprehension.
>
> *Paradise Lost*, VIII, 352–354.

[3]On re-evocation see the introduction to this selection, above.

[4]In earlier chapters (I, vi–vii) Croce deals with literature as distinguished from poetry. Beside poetry, literature appears like a friend of smaller stature who has no desire to grow to the height of her companion. Literature comes only in a time of culture; she speaks well and beautifully, but without the intuition and ecstasy of poetry.

[5]In a postscript Croce speaks of disciples who mechanize the methods of their master, and of the dislike of the expositor of truth for seeing his name reduced to an abstraction ending in -*ism*. This is a protest against Croceanism and the attitude of the Croceans.

The category of beauty, then, is one and indivisible, its single manifestations are infinite and can be grouped into classes; these classes, however, like all such groups, are merely empirical and have nothing in common with speculative divisions made by the rational powers. At one time aestheticians spoke of various manifestations of the beautiful, such as the sublime, the tragic, the comic, the humorous,[6] the gracious, and so on, yet when one examines these forms which have been presented as speculative divisions of the beautiful, one finds that they are nothing but abstractions formed from single groups of beautiful works and referable to their matter, to their matter and not to their form, for beauty is in form alone. For example, the conception of the humorous has been refined and given the subtlety of a speculative idea, purified from its special matter; it then appears to some theorists as a kind of synthesis of the tragic, the sublime, the comic, the pleasing, and every other aspect of art. But when this is done we get a synonym of beauty which embraces all the other manifestations of the spirit and is therefore a resolution of the contrasts into the fullness of humanity.

The same conclusion is reached through the examination of another system of groups, also at first formed empirically by abstracting certain contents and forms from single groups, namely from the three supreme and fundamental genera, the lyric, epic, and dramatic, which have been elevated to the position of eternal categories of poetry. According to this theory, the poet either sings his personal sentiments or narrates the deeds of other men, or so handles his matter that the actions of others are presented on the stage without any intervention by the narrator; he is expected to enter one of these three roads and continue along it without deviating into either of the others. But when the three roads are more closely considered they do not appear absolutely three; some would cast doubts on the second, that of narrative, and unify it with the first or abolish it, because mere narration is not poetic or dramatic presentation.

---

[6]"The humorous will be laughter amid tears, bitter laughter, the sudden spring from the comic to the tragic and from the tragic to the comic, the romantic comic, the opposite of the sublime, war declared against every attempt at insincerity, compassion ashamed to weep, a laugh, not at the fact, but at the ideal itself; and what you will beside, according as it is wished to get a view of the physiognomy of this or that poet, or this or that poem, which in its uniqueness, is its own definition, and though momentary and circumscribed, is alone adequate" (Croce, *Aesthetic*, tr. by Douglas Ainslie, pp. 90–91).

Others make the first and second into two byways which lead to
the third, the main highway, which is the drama, a type that
from the Greeks to the romantics has often been idolized as the
single form that fulfills the ideal of poetry.[7] But the truth is that
the lyric poet dramatizes his feeling and the dramatic poet
lyricizes his action; if the lyric poet does not do this he will be
emotional but not lyrical, and if the dramatic writer does not do
this he will be a writer for the theater but not a poet.[8] When the
trinity is reduced from the three necessary forms to the duality
of lyric and drama, and this duality is reduced to distinction and
opposition, what is found at bottom except the relation of
matter with poetic expression, of sentiment with intuition?

The same is true of the famous division of poetry into classical
and romantic.[9] These adjectives have some empirical and
lexicographical value when the first designates the ancient
poetry of Greece and Rome, and the second applies to modern
and Christian poetry, but unhappily they have been and still
are used to make a speculative distinction between two diverse
categories of poetry. The immediate originator of the latter
meaning was Goethe, who ever afterwards regretted that he had
set up this dichotomy, which was taken over by Schiller and
exaggerated by the romantics. This scission of the indivisible
concept of poetry and beauty was intolerable because it caused
the romantics to reject the poetry of classicism as cold, or unpoetical, and the classicists to reject romantic poetry as unformed
and therefore also inartistic and unpoetical. The sole division
that should be considered in this case is not a division but an
antinomy, namely the contrast between the beautiful and the
ugly. When romanticism and classicism are thoroughly studied
and their full meaning developed, it appears that their relation

[7] See Aristotle's discussion in *The Poetics*, chap. XXVI. Certain German aestheticians have attempted to give a metaphysical explanation of the superiority of the
drama, making it unite the objectivity of the epic and the subjectivity of the lyric.
Croce thinks such ideas troublesome dreams produced by the incubus of the belief
in the literary types as fundamental critical classes (Ps.).

[8] In a postscript on "the impossibility of distinguishing lyric, epic, and dramatic,"
Croce refers to Goethe (*Ueber epische und dramatische Dichtung*, 1797, in *Werke*,
XXVII, 139–141), who said that the epic writer presented the action as past, the
dramatic as present. This in Croce's opinion is merely an empirical distinction
at times helpful to the composer.

[9] The category of the sentimental and romantic has always served to admit among
the poets those of small poetical power, and owes its origin to Schiller's attempt to
defend his own work. Croce quotes from Goethe: "The classical is the sane, the
romantic the sick" (*Conversations with Eckermann*, April 2, 1829, p. 149, above) (Ps.).

to each other is the same as that of dramaticism and lyricism, intuition and sentiment, form and matter; namely, truth can be found only in their synthesis. The truth does not reside in one of two mutually exclusive abstractions; one of them must be resolved into the other and thus subordinated and preserved. Hence to classicism and romanticism there is opposed classic quality, a phrase which has the defect, which is in the end a merit, of signifying nothing, and which implies no judgment, either abstract or based on matter, because it suggests only excellent expression, perfect expression, beauty.[10]

It would be possible to continue with other divisions less famous or varying little from the preceding, such as that of primitive and sophisticated art and poetry,[11] with the preference given now to the first, now to the second, but by these divisions art, which is a unit composed at once of primitiveness and culture, is broken into fragments.[12] The danger in cutting in two the concept of beauty, which was the true spiritual heresy of Germany (I refer to that in the field of aesthetics and not to the other in the field of religion, which aided the progress of the European mind) is not that men will vainly knock together two empty ideas, such as abstract classicism and abstract romanticism,[13] or abstract primitivism and abstract sophistication, with resulting quarrels over words and with loss of time; the danger is that these pseudoaesthetic conceptions will be turned into practical attitudes, so that such working distinctions come to be thought of as forms of poetry, and poetry becomes to those con-

---

[10]By etymology the word *classical* means *of the highest class*. There is also the sense that refers to the Greco-Roman world, which when applied by the writers of history loses clarity and moves over into vague imaginings. The word *Greek* is used as a symbol of the beautiful. In contrast with *classical* as *excellent*, *romantic* in the theory of poetry can have only a negative sense of inferiority, such as results from sentimentalism (Pss.).

[11]There is an erroneous belief that with the variations of ages and peoples there may be change in the idea of what poetry is, and that therefore it must be judged according to these various ideas. "What changes is the meaning of the word *poetry*, but poetry itself does not change nor does its conception, which always remains as the perpetual premise, expressed or implied, of every aesthetic judgment." Poetry should not be judged according to the narrow ideas of our own time, nor according to the narrow ideas of the time of its composition, but the critic should "rise to the critical ideal" (Ps.).

[12]Most ages appear primitive to their successors, and "what is most nearly perfected in the present age will in its turn become primitive" (Ps.).

[13]Such divisions of poetry as realism and idealism come to much the same thing as classicism and romanticism. To all such divisions is opposed the "image at once substantial and airy of complete and true poetry" (Ps.).

cerned as practical as their philosophies, hedonistic, utilitarian, and materialistic. Striking in this respect is the rise in Germany today of a new ideal form added to the other two, namely the baroque.[14] This ideal form is derived from an aesthetically negative conception and yet has been used to mark off a particular attitude of poetry and literature; we may expect that before long, by another step forward, the critics will decide on another form which will be absolutely that of poetic and literary ugliness, asserting that this too is a particular spiritual attitude; the formation and acceptance of false appearances through vanity or greed really brings about such an attitude, but it is essentially a negation of poetry.

Such a practical notion of poetry was prepared to submit to political and social divisions. On the one side, these pseudo-aesthetic forms tend to be maintained as genuinely ideal and to be affirmed as necessary to the human race, so that we hear of a romanticism not merely modern but also Greek or Roman, of a baroque not merely of sixteenth-century Europe but of Hellenistic or late Roman culture, of a classicism not merely of the golden age of Greece or Rome, but French and German, and so on. On the other hand, they tend to be fixed as individual and peculiar to individual peoples and races. Poetry of the classical type has been identified with the poetic mode of the Roman and Neo-Latin peoples; the romantic, in spite of the etymology of the name, which seems to say the opposite, has been identified with that of the Germanic peoples, but now it appears that its place has been taken by the baroque, which seems to some northern theorists a grander and more vigorous and virile type to assign to the Germans, even in the earliest times. But now such ideal modes have been discarded, and peoples, races, and social classes have been provided with their own peculiar forms of poetry; each of these forms is completely separated from every other; they are unknown to one another, and strive against one another in the same way as do the same peoples, races, and classes in the sphere of practical life. Thus we now have, among the others, a Germanic poetry, composed by pure Germans and to be perceived and judged only by them; there is also a proletarian poetry, especially in Russia, which

---

[14]See Croce's *Storia dell' età barocca in Italia.* He illustrates the arbitrary and confusing use of the word *baroque* by examples of German references to Raphael and Plautus as baroque (Ps.).

only the proletariat are in a position to produce and understand and about which the middle classes ought not to open
their mouths, even in admiration. Not only is beauty no longer
one and indivisible, but its divisions are no longer those of
dramatic and lyric, ingenuous and sentimental, classical and
romantic, which though arbitrary were in intention universally
human. Its divisions are now the peoples themselves and the
social classes, with whose doings the work of poetry is identified;
hence the category of judgment is by turns Germany, France,
England, Russia, Italy, or bourgeoisie, democracy, sickle and
hammer, hooked cross, and so forth.

Such divisions not merely, like the older ones, break up the
aesthetic unity of the human race, but they destroy humanity
itself by confining it to regions that are foreign to one another
and irreconcilably and perpetually hostile. We must therefore
be the more active in affirming against them the indivisibility of
beauty as the only category of aesthetic judgment.

III, iii

The characterization of poetry and the completion
of the interpretative-critical process

If the taste for poetry attracts the beautiful and repels the
ugly, the aesthetic judgment indicates the qualities of both. It
has often been a cause for wonder that aesthetics is so poor in
distinctive terms for the varieties of beauty and so rich in terms
for the ugly. This condition is attributed to natural malice,
which has a hundred eyes open for evil and looks on the good
with but one, and that almost closed, yet it is but a natural consequence of what has just been set forth: namely, that there are
no distinctions or divisions of the beautiful in the strict sense of
the word. The terminology of the beautiful should be called
not poor but monotonous, because it is one continual series of
synonyms, in which the single concept of beautiful expression is
repeated in such words as harmony, truth, simplicity, unity in
variety, naturalness, sincerity, imaginative vigor, lyric intensity,
delicacy, serenity, sublimity, and the like. On the other hand,
since the ugly arises from the destruction of aesthetic coherence
for a practical end or convenience, its concept is specified in all
the ways in which, in various extensions and according to various
circumstances, that incoherence is manifested. These ways are

numerous and give rise to a terminology that continually en-
riches itself with new words: incorrect, redundant, negligent,
awkward, miserable, swelling, declamatory, charlatanesque,
affected, buffoonish, baroque, sentimental, sensual, frivolous,
obscene, rude, crude, violent, abortive, vulgar, plebeian, languid, pedestrian, conventional, mechanical, banal, hard, heavy,
precious, distorted, overdone, and so on infinitely.

But in distinguishing among attractions and repugnances of
taste, the aesthetic judgment remains bound to taste and inseparable from it. This is in accord with the nature of all true
and concrete judging, for it is the identification of intuition and
category, of intuitive subject and conceptual predicate; good
judgment is never occupied with a mere abstract relation of
concepts except in appearance or rather when superficially
considered.[15] The didactic form in which the critic sets forth
his judgment shows this clearly, because, like the critic of the
graphic arts, who always presupposes the sight of the original
picture or statue or piece of architecture, and aids the exposition
of his judgments with drawings or photographs of the originals,
the critic of poetry uses paraphrases or quotations from the
pieces of poetry he examines. His discourse is empty for the
reader who does not enter into relation with the original, and
becomes empty for the critic himself when he loses the original
from sight and wanders about in generalities or bewilders
himself in subtleties.

All the same, the work of the critic does not consist wholly in
distinguishing the various kinds of beauty and ugliness as soon
as they are recognized, but is properly considered unsatisfactory
when it is limited to pointing out and naming the parts that are
beautiful and those that are not. He who does only this is called
a man of taste rather than a critic; his criticism goes but half
way, and the other half must be added if judgment is to be
perfect and complete. The missing half is not what has been
demanded of the critic by some theories, namely that in addition to an aesthetic judgment the critic, as *"artifex additus
artifici,"* should produce an aesthetic revision or re-rendering
of the work formed by the poet; the reason is this: such a revision

---

[15]"Just as the theory of poetry cannot take the place of genius, so the theory of
criticism is unable to take the place of taste, and taste is the genius of the critic.
It is said that the poet is born; the critic is born too; the critic has inborn abilities
given him by nature" (Ps. from Croce's *Saggio sopra un dramma di G. Gattinelli*).

or rendering may be an aesthetic orgy, wholly to be deprecated, and improperly celebrated over the work of art; or it may be an indiscrete song on the part of the critic, often forced and out of tune, which accompanies or mixes with that of the poet himself; or it may be a translation, in the sense and within the limits that have been determined.[16] But the translation, if analytic and prosaic, pertains to the philological preparation for reading and not to the criticism of poetry. If it is synthetic and artistic, it does not pertain to criticism at all because it is a variation from the poetic work. The critic, however, is attached to the individual reality of the poem and cannot detach himself from it without ceasing to be a critic. Though allowing that it does not consist in furnishing an intuitive substitute for a poem, some require that it furnish a logical equivalent. If such a logical equivalent could exist, poetry would not have come into the world, or would quickly have been dismissed as superfluous, for it would be possible to obtain its equivalent and to receive logic in addition, as though one got a sum of money not in paper but in minted gold. This is a rather playful confutation but is at bottom a serious response: namely that a logical equivalent of the intuitive is contrary to the natural logic of the judgment, because it will annul one of the terms of the relation which is its very life.

The critic does not offer as his completed judgment either intuitive remakings or logical equivalents of poetry, but does something very different: he gives a characterization of it.[17] For the reasons given above, this determination of character has nothing to do with the form of poetry, for that is something single, indivisible, and identical in all the poets, because it is the form of beauty. Whenever anybody says that poetry pleases through this or that particular characteristic, he either falls into the ingenuous illusion of attributing what is wholly concrete and living to a particularity that is abstract and dead, or he repeats tautologically, though in varying verbal forms, that

[16]In Pt. II, chap. v, Croce explains that translations may be simple instruments for the understanding of originals, as are literal versions in prose that may be made of ancient poems or even of those in our own language. When their limitations are recognized, these may be useful means to an ultimate appreciation of a poem. There are also translations of a second sort, the poetical, which set out from an original but become something quite different from it.

[17]The titles given to their works by poets are often first attempts to furnish the reader some indication of the content. This is an indication that the attempt to give the qualities of a work results from a need of the human mind (Ps.).

beauty is beauty.[18]   Still less can criticism consist in hybrid rhetorical and lexical labor halfway between aesthetic and grammatical study, such as some positivist philologues carry on; their product, like all hybrids, is sterile. To break the forms of poetry into words and metaphors, comparisons, figures, syntactic connections, rhythmic schemes, and so forth, is not to grasp the character of poetry, which can be revivified and contemplated only in its total and unique intuition; on the contrary, it ends in getting together a pitiable heap of lifeless bits, to be thrown away at last as stuff that is of no use.[19]

Characterization is properly based on the content of poetry, the sentiment that the poem has expressed and in expression has amplified by transference to the poetic atmosphere. The critic must abstract himself from such idealization to consider the poetic sentiment in its various forms and as it is characteristic, for the characteristic, according to the saying of Goethe already quoted,[20] is the point of departure of the beautiful. All that has not become the content of poetry, but remains outside it though united materially to the work or pertaining to the person of the poet, is of no value to the investigator who sets out to grasp and define the generating motive which shapes and animates all parts of the poem.

But the object of this last investigation is human reality in its completeness, in all its infinite subdivisions, all of which from time to time rise so high as to become generating motives of poetic expressions. Hence the critic must possess knowledge of the human heart, and we esteem critics who are expert not merely in beauty of form but also in "human vices and virtue."[21] Hence also, on the other side, the impatience we feel toward those who

[18]In a postscript on the nonexistence of particular characteristics of beauty, Croce quotes from his *Nuovi saggi di estetica* (2d ed., p. 284): "It is possible to say, 'I am in love with this lady because she is good, because she has black eyes, because she has little hands, etc.' But how many other ladies have little hands, and black eyes, and are good, etc., and yet we do not for those reasons fall in love with them. One loves because one loves, say the theorists of the subject; the critics ought to say that a work is beautiful because it is beautiful."

[19]There is no value in merely statistical studies in literature, such as one on the modes of death in Grillparzer and other dramatists (Ps.). This does not mean that Croce rejects grammatical and lexical studies that, like the translation mentioned on the preceding page, form part of the necessary philological preparation for understanding a work of art. The studies mentioned in the text pretend to be criticism and are not.

[20]*Der Sammler und die Seiningen*, Letter 5 (Croce's note to the reference on p. 81 of *La poesia*).   [21]Dante, *Inferno*, xx, 99.

discourse on poetry without having loved and dreamed and experienced the tempest of the different passions and endured their strife, or without having encountered them by proxy and grown in experience through understanding and sympathy; I mean impatience toward the *normaliens*, as poets and artists say in France, or toward the professors, as we say in Italy. For these reasons some think, with correct intention but unsuitable idea, that the true critic of poetry should be something of a moralist. The critic should be not a moralist but a philosopher, who has meditated on the human spirit in its distinctions and oppositions and in its dialectic. He is not a philosopher in the sense that he employs his thoughts in judgments of philosophy, science, politics, morals, and everything else, but rather as he orders the immense material of his formed judgments in classes or types of the various perceptions and activities of the mind and thus changes himself into a psychologist. To characterize a poetical work means to determine its content or fundamental moving force, and to assign what has been determined to the psychological class or type best suited to include it. In this procedure the critic exercises his acuteness and shows his skill and delicacy; in this labor he is satisfied only when, after reading and rereading and considering, he finally succeeds in seizing the fundamental trait and in defining it in a formula which announces the successful inclusion of the feeling of the single work of poetry in the most suitable class he knows or has thought out for the occasion.

But the most satisfactory class is always nothing but a class or a general concept, and a poetical work, on the contrary, is not general but individual-universal, finite-infinite; hence the formula, however close it comes to the work of poetry in question, never coincides with it, but there is always an abyss between the two. Compared to the poetic work, the formula for its characterization always appears more or less rigid and harsh. For this reason, after momentary satisfaction, we are always discontented with the most elaborate critical formulas, even with our own, which have been produced with such great tension of mind, so much labor of brain, such scrupulous delicacy.[22] From this comes an impulse to turn one's back on criti-

---

[22]Croce himself has always been conscious of the limits of criticism in his writings on Ariosto, Dante, and others; he has not believed that he was furnishing by his aesthetic formulas an equivalent of poetry, or that he could exhaust the concrete and living poet, nor has he forgotten that even the authentic image of the poet

cism and immerse oneself completely in individual and living poetry. So Goethe said that it was not at all possible to discourse on Shakespeare, because every discourse was insufficient, that he had convinced himself by trying it in his *Meister* but had not come out very well;[23] and similarly Wilhelm von Humboldt, speaking of the works, as it happened, of Goethe and describing some of their characteristics, interrupted himself to say that he wished merely to touch on such things, because to speak or write about a poet is nothing other than to go wandering around in the ineffable ("als ein Herumgehen um das Unaussprechliche").[24] Nevertheless the critic who understands his function and the theory of his function realizes the conditions and knows that the formula does not coincide with the poetry, that it is not possible to express in general terms what has already been expressed by itself in intuitive terms, and that what is in itself effable becomes in the new conditions ineffable. And all the same he labors tirelessly because he knows he is doing necessary work; and he strives to think out classes always nearer the original poetry, though always divided from it by an interval that can be crossed only by a leap. If he becomes angry at anything, it is when he sees that instead of taking up the work where he laid it down and striving to carry it further, other critics are using classes not of the right sort or too general, though he himself has already excluded them and replaced them with a more correct class. If anything annoys and torments him,

presented by the critic must be inadequate and prosaic, if not always brought back by the reader to the ample spaces of the poetry itself (Ps.).

"Critical monographs always contain either briefly or at length the history of preceding characterizations, to which the new and more precise delimitation or clarification is attached. Nor can anything else be done; still the incompetent have marveled that the monographs of the author on Dante, Ariosto, Shakespeare, Corneille (to mention his chief works of the sort) are taken up in great part with a reconstruction of the history of the criticism of Dante, Ariosto, Shakespeare, and Corneille. Those who without this presume to indulge in criticism and say that they study directly the work of poetry, without caring how much has been chattered about it, utter a half truth, in other words an error; certainly the direct and unprejudiced intuition of the work of art is indispensable and essential, but the labor of characterization is always prejudged, that is, it rises from other preceding judgments and opposes itself to them; in order to come into being it asks from them criticism, or the history of earlier pronouncements, because the successive steps, as it were, in the process of scientific study are not prejudices and obstacles to progress. In short, those who think to free themselves from prejudices by leaping over them still remain their slaves" (Ps.).

[23]*Gespräche mit Eckermann*, 25 December, 1825 (Croce's note).

[24]W. V. Humboldt, in his essay on the *Italienische Reise* of Goethe, in *Ausgew. phil. Schriften*, ed. Schubert (Leipzig, 1910), p. 74 (Croce's note).

it is to find his formulas in the mouths of men who have made them rigid and dogmatized them instead of receiving them with the wise and valuable skepticism that the affair demands. If he discusses with anybody (and surely he is always discussing with both individuals and groups), he discusses with another critic or with other critics, but not with poetry, because he knows that criticism, when in characterization it has reached its highest point, is by nature criticism of criticism. In the critical effort the element that must be changed for the sake of accuracy is not poetry, which is definitive, but the form of the characterizations, which is always indefinite; it must be indefinite because the motion of the human spirit is always proposing new difficulties and giving rise to new problems. The critic has formed an instrument that is better than those that formerly existed and he wishes to make it still more perfect and to have others go on improving it, because he knows its value and use.

He understands its value when he reflects that in the final product—the formula—is gathered up all the long process that he passed through in obtaining his grasp of poetry, from the philological preparation to the intuitive re-evocation, and from this to the judgment it has prepared for. Therefore, though the critic's formula is not the living process, it is the most efficacious means for repetition of that process without repetition of the labor already undergone; it profits by what is past and economizes forces for new activity. The critic who has studied a work of poetic expression and by interpreting similar works has trained the special capacity with which nature has endowed him, thus obtaining special cultivation and undergoing special discipline, can confidently interpret and judge the work and indicate to his hearers the point of view from which it must be regarded. In other words, he communicates to them the characterization contained in the formula he has worked out. In addition, he dispels the inertness and uncertainty as to where to begin, that beset men on confronting expression new to them; he also frees them from long wandering with other and inferior formulas among classes that are distant and diverse or too general when compared with the one best suited to the poetry. Without doubt the critic confers a great benefit by this activity of his, even though he is unable to confer the other of making men perceive and enjoy poetry, because that is something we can accomplish only for ourselves alone. If in spite of the aids the critic furnishes, we persist in inertness, the fault is our own. It is the benefit to which Sainte-Beuve refers when in his famous saying, perhaps more profound than he himself thought, he said that criticism is the art of teaching to read. That is what we owe to the great critics: they have taught us to read the poets. In what a confused and bewildering world we should find ourselves if we were thrown all at once into the midst of the songs of the poets, the words chanted in poetic manner by the non-poets, and the false songs of the bad poets! How grateful we should be that criticism has arranged for us the world of the mind, divided the poetic voices from the non-poetic, and both of them from the falsely poetic, distinguished the greater voices and those worth hearing from the lesser ones, and settled for us the significance of each! Critical effort has made the poetical world as familiar to us as our homes, the dwellings of our hearts and our phantasies. This is what the critics have done with their labors through the ages, and of their efforts we enjoy the fruits, often, as is normal, ignorant of it and ungrateful toward those who have done it for us.

III, iv

The aesthetic judgment as the history of poetry

Let us now take up and examine the aesthetic judgment of poetry to ascertain its relation to the historical statement or affirmation from which, as from a parent cell, springs every more complex history that can be thought of and written. Such examination and comparison make plain to us that the aesthetic judgment is nothing else than a perfect historical statement. It says, in fact, that at a definite moment there appeared and took its place in the sequence of events an a, which is a work of poetry that may be characterized in one way or another. The construction of any other history is not different, though the a, instead of being a work of poetry, may be a philosophical statement, an institution, a military action, a religious belief, and so on. We can do nothing else than conclude with certainty that with the aesthetic judgment of a poetical work its history is also given to us, or, to speak more exactly, that the aesthetic judgment is that history.[25]

[25]On the reform of the history of poetry, see *La riforma della storia artistica e letteraria,* in Croce's *Nuovi saggi di estetica,* 2d ed., pp. 157–197.

Over the simple clarity of this truth is the shadow of the conception of reality as divided into facts and values. According to this notion there can be history without values and values without history; therefore it is first needful to settle the reality of a fact and then to determine whether it has value or not, to see whether its being corresponds with its ought-to-be. This is a metaphysical concept that sublimates in philosophical terminology the superficial and popular mode of representing dualistically the relation of fact to value; and since it is superficial and popular, one should be astonished on encountering it, even outside the severely reasoned systematizations (such as that of Herbart),[26] in positivism and psychologism, and in seeing it commonly accepted in the schools. In the schools, or in many of them, flourishes also the distinction between, on the one hand, "development" or the historical unfolding of poetry—which is a matter of science—and, on the other hand, judgment, which is a subjective and personal reaction with which science should not concern itself but which it can permit as a pardonable expression of sentiment, a pleasure of the fancy, or a desperate and vain attempt at a conclusion after careful and solid researches into the nature of historical evolution. But fact and value in the work of poetry are the same, as they are in every human work. Hence there is still value in thought to which no value is assigned, if it is thought and not a pretense of thought. The same is true of action, if it is genuine action and not mere desire for action. Consequently the judgment of value is the judgment of the fact itself, and since a fact cannot be thought of except as a process of being acted, and therefore as history, it is the judgment of history. In estimating poetry, throughout the re-evocation[27] which is included in it and the included process of interpretation, all the genesis of the work is made present and thought out.

It may seem that the identification of the judgment of poetry with its history gets rid of history, resolving it into a multiplicity of single narratives, placed one beside the other, and so destroying the order of succession that is indispensable to historical thought. However, the judgment of poetry does not deny this

[26]For Croce's censure of Herbart, see his *Aesthetic*, Pt. II, chap. x: "Herbart restates the mechanical view, restores the duality [of theory of beauty and theory of art], and presents a capricious, narrow, barren mysticism, devoid of all breath of artistic feeling."
[27]See the introduction to this selection, above.

order; it does not even preclude it, but on the contrary continually presupposes and reaffirms it.   Who would be able
seriously to comprehend the *Divine Comedy* and arrange it in his
thought if he should put it at the same time as the *Iliad* or earlier,
the *Orlando Furioso* if he made it contemporary with or earlier
than the *Chanson de Roland?*   Every work is well interpreted or
well re-evoked only in its historical position, where all the preceding works, together with all the preceding history of which
it is a part, converge.

Of course this reply, crushing as it is, is not wholly satisfactory
to those tenacious of the obsolete conceptions, because at the
bottom of their minds there is an idea of a history of poetry which
not merely considers the single works in their succession, but
establishes among them a direct connection, making one of
them generate the next; in comparison with this the succession
which is here admitted appears a discontinuous and extrinsic
series.[28]   Now if the works of poetry are generated one from
another, they are ultimately seen to form a single process;
hence they make up a single work of poetry, which in practice
never exists, because it is always in process of elaboration and
never evocable and comprehensible as a whole; yet any work is
an object of enjoyment and intelligence only when considered as
an individual whole.   Individual women may be loved and
embraced; but how is it possible to love and embrace the single
woman who is perpetually being formed, womanhood infinitely
in process of becoming?   This serves to demonstrate the impossibility of that pretended history.   The origin of the error about it
becomes clear when one considers that the connection between
the single works, though it cannot be denied, yet resides in the
whole of history and not in the direct connection with one
another of facts of a certain sort, as though they could come
into being and grow without any relation to others of different
quality.   Poetry does not generate poetry, as philosophy does
not generate philosophy and action does not generate action,
unless each of these passes through all the other forms.   A new
action has as its necessary condition new imaginings and new
conceptions; imagination demands new philosophy, new facts,

---

[28]Tolstoi said: "One genius is not derived from another; geniuses are always
independent" (Ps.).

One of the best instances in England of such a poetic family as those of which
Croce speaks in a postscript is furnished by the "sons of Ben." Yet Herrick, though
in some respects similar to Ben Jonson, is essentially independent.

and new actions; new poetry requires new thoughts and new actions, and above all new perception. The history of poetry which is developed within the confines of the subject is, in the last analysis, an imaginary thing devised by the philologists; they abstract similarities and kinships between poetical works, dispose them in a chain, and imagine that into the chain constructed by them they have breathed a generative force that has transformed them into a Biblical order of generations.

The objection is also made that in conceiving the history of poetry as the mere judgment of single works an essential conception of history is lost, namely that of progress, because every work of poetry would be looked on as perfect in itself, and as having its individual progress merely in the travail of its own coming into being. But the same is true of every other human work, because a truth that is thought out, a good act that is completed, has in itself its own progress and its own perfection. General historical progress is not progress of the categories and spiritual forms; they are the causes of general progress and would not be such if they did not have constancy and did not continually generate definite and concrete beauties, truths, moral actions. General progress is the motion of the spirit in the dialectic of all its forms. And this progress, this spiritual enrichment, this spiritual increase, escapes no one who understands poetry as it passes from Homer to Dante, from Dante to Shakespeare, from Shakespeare to Goethe, since he sees clearly that Shakespeare would not have understood Goethe, nor Dante Shakespeare, nor Homer Dante, though Dante included Homer in himself when he saluted him as sovereign poet, and Goethe included Shakespeare, whose work he had before him as "the enormous volume of destiny." [29] In short the poetic work of each of these is beautiful and perfect in itself and is not, in so far as it is poetry, made perfect by the poetry of its successor.[30]

This reaffirmed perfection of each work in itself seems to shake also another principle of historical constructions, to wit, the relation of importance that exists between works, their hierarchy; but surely if this can be established only by submitting poems

[29] *Lehrjahre des Meisters*, Bk. III, chap. XI (Croce's note).

[30] In denying that there is progress in poetry, Croce makes clear that he is not concerned with the ever increasing number of works of art but with the specific action of the spirit on individual poems; the beautiful and the ugly are opposed now just as they have been in the past and will be in the future. The work of art begins and ends in itself (Ps.).

to a criterion that is extraneous and repugnant (philosophical, moral, utilitarian, or whatever else it is), it should be resolutely renounced. Without recourse to judgment by an extraneous criterion, the importance of each work is determined in a spontaneous manner, and the hierarchy establishes itself spontaneously, by the very character of each work, which takes in the mind of its readers a certain place and no other. And because, in the strict sense, each man establishes among these works the hierarchy that best suits him, works of poetry generally detach themselves from works of literature, because of the growing consciousness that literature is one thing and poetry another. In the sphere of poetry itself a line, though an uncertain one, divides elementary or popular poetry from the complex poetry that is assigned to art.[31] There is a similar line dividing the poetry of art which shows some pride of virtuosity from that in which the mutual penetration of content and form is perfect, and the most exquisite elaboration is united with the greatest simplicity. In various classes are arranged the works that are variations of the same fundamental motive and those that are creations of new fundamental motives, and the less and the greater are arranged according to their growing complexity. Every people raises one or more poets above the others; Italy, closing that period of its literature that ran from the thirteenth to the eighteenth century, decided on four, "the four poets," [32] and with further selection Europe has fixed on four or five that it considers the greatest of those born among all its peoples. No reason can be seen why the beauty of things that are beautiful should be denied or diminished, or their nature distorted by measuring them with an extraneous criterion, in order to obtain this hierarchical order that forms itself and varies of itself, according to the preponderance of one or another spiritual interest, and for which there is no necessary and rational criterion.

The monographic character that the history of poetry assumes when it identifies itself with the judgment of each work of poetry is to be understood in its logical essence and not to be confused (and this is the last objection to be brought forward and an-

---

[31]One of Croce's books is entitled *Popular Poetry and the Poetry of Art* (not translated into English).

[32]Dante, Petrarch, Ariosto, Tasso. Volumes containing their chief works were issued under the title of *The Four Poets*.

swered here) with the pedagogical literary forms used in treating the history of poetry; the historian has the utmost liberty to do what he wishes in the use of the most various tags or labels. The following groups are all acceptable: nation and language (for example, Greek, Roman, Italian, or German poetry), century or other chronological division (medieval, sixteenth-century, or seventeenth-century poetry), various combinations of the preceding two (French medieval poetry, or French poetry in the sixteenth century), ideal affinity (Dante, Goethe, and Shakespeare, etc.), contrast (Shakespeare vs. Corneille, or Boiardo vs. Ariosto), ruling idea (popular poetry, baroque poetry, etc.); and there are many others. What is of importance is merely that the treatment of poetry should be intrinsically or logically monographic,[33] depending always on the individual work in the concrete.

After these explanations, if anybody is not satisfied with the history of poetry as the judgment of poetry itself, there is nothing to do but to allow him to apply himself to one of the various schemes we possess for the false history of poetry and of literature, with which we shall now deal briefly.[34]

[33]"Monographs on poets attain their end when they are not mere collections of scattered observations or aesthetic comments on single works, but when they succeed in giving the characteristic quality of the motive or fundamental state of mind of the poet, and in some way correct and enrich what we already possess on the subject" (*La poesia*, pp. 149–150). The good history, written according to the principles of criticism, would be a series of such monographs.

[34]In the following chapter he gives several types of the false history of poetry: (1) poetry as the expression of society; (2) poetry as a national product; (3) poetry as illustrating some historical or metaphysical construct. In general see Croce's *History, Its Theory and Practice*, tr. by Douglas Ainslie.

GENERAL BIBLIOGRAPHY

o◯ooo◯o

Note: All the bibliographies are necessarily selective, but this is especially true of the general list; however, we have attempted to give a comprehensive and representative selection, particularly including the newer trends and schools in English and American literary criticism.

ANTHOLOGIES

Alden, Raymond Macdonald, ed., *Critical Essays of the Early Nineteenth Century*. New York, 1921.

Burgum, Edwin Berry, ed., *The New Criticism, An Anthology of Modern Aesthetics and Literary Criticism*. New York, 1930.

Clark, Barrett H., ed., *European Theories of the Drama*, with bibliographies. Rev. ed. New York, 1929.

Cooper, Lane, ed., *Theories of Style*. New York, 1907.

Durham, Willard Higley, ed., *Critical Essays of the Eighteenth Century, 1700–1725*. Yale University Press, 1915.

Foerster, Norman, ed., *American Critical Essays, Nineteenth and Twentieth Centuries*. Oxford, 1930.

Gilbert, Allan H., *Literary Criticism: Plato to Dryden*. New York, 1940.

Jones, Edmund David, ed., *English Critical Essays* (Sixteenth, Seventeenth, and Eighteenth Centuries). London, 1922.

——, *English Critical Essays of the Nineteenth Century*. London, 1922.

Jones, Phyllis M., ed., *English Critical Essays, Twentieth Century*, with an introduction by the editor. London, 1932.

Ker, William Paton, ed., *Collected Essays*, with an introduction by Charles Whibley. 2 vols. London, 1925.

Lewisohn, Ludwig, ed., *A Modern Book of Criticism*. New York, 1919.

Payne, William Morton, ed., *American Literary Criticism*. London, 1904.

Pollak, Gustav, ed., *International Perspective in Criticism: Goethe, Grillparzer, Sainte-Beuve, Lowell*. New York, 1914.

Putnam, Samuel, and others, ed., *European Caravan: An Anthology of the New Spirit in European Literature*. New York, 1931.

Saintsbury, George Edward, comp., *Loci Critici;* Passages Illustrative of Critical Theory and Practice from Aristotle Downward. Boston, 1903.

Smith, James Harry, and Parks, Edd Winfield, eds., *The Great Critics, an Anthology of Literary Criticism*. New York, 1939.

Vaughan, C. E., ed., *English Literary Criticism, An Anthology*. London, 1906.

History and Treatise

Abercrombie, Lascelles, *Principles of Literary Criticism.* London, 1932.

Allen, Beverly Sprague, *Tides in English Taste, 1619–1800; A Background for the Study of Literature.* 2 vols. Harvard University Press, 1937.

Altamira y Crevea, Rafael, *Psicología y literatura.* Barcelona, 1905.

Audiat, Pierre, *La Biographie de l'œuvre littéraire; esquisse d'une méthode critique.* Paris, 1924.

Babbitt, Irving, *Rousseau and Romanticism.* Boston, 1919.

Brandes, Georg Morris Cohen, *Liv og Kunst.* København, 1929.

——, *Main Currents in Nineteenth Century Literature.* 6 vols. New York, 1923.

——, *Menschen und Werke.* Frankfurt a. M., 1894.

Bodkin, Maud, *Archetypal Patterns in Poetry; Psychological Studies of Imagination.* Oxford, 1934.

Bosker, A., *Literary Criticism in the Age of Johnson.* New York, 1930.

Bray, Jeremiah Wesley, *A History of English Critical Terms.* Boston, 1898.

Brightfield, Myron Franklin, *The Issue in Literary Criticism* [apropos of Aristotle's *Poetics*]. University of California Press, 1932.

Brownell, William Crary, *Criticism.* New York, 1914.

Bruggen, Carry van, *Prometheus.* 2 vols. Rotterdam, 1919. "An attempt to trace the development of individualism in literature."

Buck, Gertrude, *The Social Criticism of Literature.* Yale University Press, 1916.

Buck, Philo M., *The Golden Thread.* New York, 1931.

——, *Literary Criticism, a Study of Values in Literature.* New York, 1930.

Calverton, Victor F., *The Newer Spirit: A Sociological Criticism of Literature.* New York, 1925.

Carton, Henri, *Histoire de la critique littéraire en France.* Paris, 1886.

Cazamian, Louis François, *Criticism in the Making.* New York, 1929.

Chadwick, Hector M., and Chadwick, Nora, *The Growth of Literature.* 3 vols. New York, 1932.

Charrier, Pierre, *Les Droits du critique.* Paris, 1910.

Charvat, William, *The Origins of American Critical Thought, 1810–1835.* University of Pennsylvania Press, 1936.

Clark, A., *Boileau and the French Classical Critics in England (1660–1830).* Paris, 1925.

Cline, Thomas Lucian, *Critical Opinion in the Eighteenth Century.* University of Michigan Press, 1926.

Criticism in America, Its Function and Status. New York, 1924. Essays by Ernest Boyd, Van Wyck Brooks, W. C. Brownell, Irving Babbitt, T. S. Eliot, H. L. Mencken, Stuart P. Sherman, J. E. Spingarn, and G. E. Woodberry.

De Mille, George E., *Literary Criticism in America; a Preliminary Survey.* New York, [c. 1931].

Dewey, John, *Construction and Criticism*. Columbia University Press, 1930.

Downey, June Etta, *Creative Imagination; Studies in the Psychology of Literature*. New York, 1929.

Eliot, Thomas Stearns, *The Sacred Wood; Essays on Poetry and Criticism*. London, [1920].

Elton, Oliver, *The Nature of Literary Criticism*. Manchester University Press, 1935.

Ermatinger, Emil, *Philosophie der Literaturwissenschaft*. Berlin, 1930.

Farinelli, Arturo, *Ensayos y discursos de crítica literaria hispano-Europea*. 2 vols. in one. Rome, 1925.

Fernández y González, Francisco, *Historia de la crítica literaria en España*. Madrid, 1867.

Foerster, Norman, *American Criticism, a Study in Literary Theory from Poe to the Present*. Boston, 1928.

——, *Humanism and America*. New York, [c. 1930].

——, *Towards Standards; a Study of the Present Critical Movement in American Letters*. New York, [c. 1930].

Garrod, H. W., *Poetry and the Criticism of Life*. Harvard University Press, 1931.

Gayley, Charles Mills, and Scott, F. N., *An Introduction to the Methods and Materials of Literary Criticism, the Bases in Aesthetics and Poetics*. Boston, 1899.

Gilbert, Katharine and Kuhn, Helmut, *A History of Esthetics*. New York, 1939.

Grattan, Clinton Hartley, ed., *The Critique of Humanism; A Symposium*. New York, 1930. A reply to Foerster's *Humanism and America*.

Green, Clarence C., *The Neo-Classic Theory of Tragedy in England during the Eighteenth Century*. Harvard University Press, 1934.

Greenlaw, Edwin A., *The Province of Literary History*. Johns Hopkins Press, [c. 1931].

Guérard, Albert Léon, *Literature and Society*. Boston, 1935.

Haskins, John Preston, *Biological Analogy in Literary Criticism*. University of Chicago Press, 1909.

Hasselblatt, Emil, *Dikt och Diktare: Studien och Kritiker*. Helsinfors, 1918.

Hazlitt, Henry, *The Anatomy of Criticism, a Trialogue*. New York, 1933.

Hennequin, Émile, *Études de critique scientifique*. Paris, 1890.

Hoops, Reinald, *Der Einfluss der Psychoanalyse auf die englische Literatur*. Heidelberg, 1934.

Hulme, Thomas Ernest, *Speculations; Essays on Humanism and the Philosophy of Art*, ed. by Herbert Read. New York, 1924.

Huxley, Aldous Leonard, *Vulgarity in Literature*. London, 1930.

Ichowicz, Marc, *La Littérature à la lumière du matérialisme historique*. Paris, 1929.

Ingenieros, José, *La Psicopatología en el arte*. Buenos Aires, 1920.

Kallen, Horace Meyer, *Indecency and the Seven Arts and Other Adventures of a Pragmatist in Aesthetics.* New York, 1930.

Krutch, Joseph Wood, *Experience and Art; Some Aspects of the Esthetics of Literature.* New York, 1932.

Landsberger, Franz, *Impressionismus und Expressionismus.* Leipzig, 1922.

Lewisohn, Ludwig, *The Creative Life.* New York, 1924.

Lockhart, John Gibson, *Literary Criticism*, with introduction and bibliography by M. Clive Hildyard. New York, 1931.

Lucas, Frank Laurence, *The Decline and Fall of the Romantic Ideal.* New York, 1936.

Machen, Arthur, *Hieroglyphics, A Note upon Ecstasy in Literature.* New York, 1923.

Maier, Norman R. F., and Reninger, H. Willard, *A Psychological Approach to Literary Criticism.* New York, 1933. An attempt to apply Gestalt psychology to literary criticism.

Matthews, Brander, *Aspects of Fiction and Other Ventures in Criticism.* 3rd ed., rev. New York, 1902.

Marshall, Elizabeth Glass, *Poetical Theories and Criticisms of the Chief Romantic Poets as Expressed in Their Personal Letters.* Ann Arbor, 1926.

Marx, Karl, and Engels, F., *Sur la littérature et l'art*, choisis, traduits et présentés par Jean Fréville. Paris, 1936.

Maszynski, Georg, *Die Methode des Expressionismus, Studien zur seiner Psychologie.* Leipzig, 1921.

Miller, George M., *The Historical Point of View in English Literary Criticism, 1570–1770.* Heidelberg, 1913.

Monk, Samuel Holt, *The Sublime; a Study of Critical Theories in Eighteenth Century England.* New York, 1935.

More, Paul Elmer, *The Demon of the Absolute.* Princeton University Press, 1928.

——, *The Greek Tradition.* 5 vols. Princeton University Press, 1917–1927.

——, *On Being Human.* Oxford, 1906.

Murry, John Middleton, *Aspects of Literature.* New York, 1920.

——, *Countries of the Mind, Essays in Literary Criticism.* London, 1931.

——, *Discoveries in Literary Criticism.* London, [c. 1924].

——, *The Problem of Style.* New York, 1922.

Omond, Thomas Stewart, *English Metrists*, being a sketch of English prosodical criticism from Elizabethan times to the present day. Oxford, 1921.

Pell, Orlie Anna Haggerty, *Value-Theory and Criticism.* New York, 1930.

Pfister, Oskar, *Der psychologische und biologische Untergrund expressionistischer Bilder.* Bern, 1920.

——, *Expressionism in Art, Its Psychological and Biological Basis.* New York, 1923.

Plekhanov, Georgiï V., *Art and Society* [a Marxist analysis], tr. by Paul S. Leitner, Alfred Goldstein, C. H. Crout. New York, 1936.

Pound, Ezra Loomis, *A B C of Reading*. London, 1934.

Quigley, Hugh, *Italy and the Rise of a New School of Criticism in the Eighteenth Century*. Perth, 1921.

Quinlan, Michael A., *Poetic Justice in the Drama;* the history of an ethical principal in literary history. Notre Dame University Press, 1912.

Raleigh, Sir Walter Alexander, *Style*. London, 1897.

Rank, Otto, *Der Kuenstler, und andere Beiträge zur Psychoanalyse des dichterischen Schaffens*. Leipzig, 1925.

Ransom, John Crowe, *The World's Body; Foundations for Literary Criticism*. New York, 1938.

Read, Herbert, *Reason and Romance*. London, 1926.

Renard, Georges François, *La Méthode scientifique de l'histoire littéraire*. Paris, 1900.

Ricardou, A., *La Critique littéraire, étude philosophique;* avec une préface de M. F. Brunetière. Paris, 1896.

Richards, Ivor Armstrong, *Practical Criticism, a Study of Literary Judgment*. New York, 1929.

——, *Principles of Literary Criticism*. New York, 1925.

Robertson, John M., *New Essays toward a Critical Method*. London, 1897.

Rosenblatt, Louise, *L'Idée de l'art pour l'art dans la littérature anglaise pendant la période victorienne*. Paris, 1931.

Rubow, Paul V., *Dansk literaer Kritik i det nittende Aarhundrede indtil 1870*. København, 1921.

——, *Georg Brandes og den kritiske Tradition i det nittende Aarhundrede*. København, 1931.

Rudler, Gustave, *Les Techniques de la critique et de l'histoire littéraires en littérature française moderne*. Oxford, 1923.

Saintsbury, George, *A History of Criticism and Literary Taste in Europe from the Earliest Texts to the Present Day*. 3 vols. Edinburgh, 1900–1904.

——, *A History of English Criticism*, being the English chapters of *A History of Criticism and Literary Taste in Europe*, revised, adapted, and supplemented. New York, 1911.

Santayana, George, *The Sense of Beauty*. New York, 1896.

——, *Reason in Art*. New York, 1906.

Sinclair, Upton Beall, *Mammonart, an Essay in Economic Interpretation*. Pasadena, California, 1925.

Spingarn, Joel Elias, *Creative Criticism; Essays on the Unity of Genius and Taste*. New ed. New York, 1931.

——, *A Note on Dramatic Criticism*. Oxford, 1913.

Strachey, John, *Literature and Dialectical Materialism*. New York, [c. 1934].

Symonds, John Addington, *Essays, Speculative and Suggestive*. 2 vols. London, 1890.

Thibaudet, Albert, *Physiologie de la critique*. Paris, 1930.

Tolstoi, Leo, *What is Art?* tr. by Aylmer Maude. London, 1925.

Trotsky, Leon, *Literature and Revolution*, tr. by Rose Strunsky. New York, 1925.

Turquet-Milnes, Gladys Rosaleen, *From Pascal to Proust, Studies in the Genealogy of a Philosophy*. New York, 1926.

Vaihinger, H., *The Philosophy of "As-if,"* tr. by C. K. Ogden. New York, 1924.

Valéry, Paul, *Littérature*. Paris, 1929.

——, *Variety*, tr. by Malcolm Cowley. New York, 1927.

Walzel, Oskar Franz, *Gehalt und Gestalt im Kunstwerk des Dichters*. Berlin, 1923.

Woodberry, George Edward, *Two Phases of Criticism, Historical and Aesthetic*. New York, 1914.

Wylie, Laura Johnson, *Studies in the Evolution of English Criticism*. Boston, 1894.

Zabel, Morton D., *Literary Opinion in America; essays illustrating the status, methods, and problems of criticism in the United States since the War*. New York, 1937.

Index

INDEX

o◯ooo◯o

In order to avoid a bulky and inconvenient index, the editors have included in it only the important references to proper names, literary titles, and critical terms. The dozens of mere allusions to Homer, Milton, and Shakespeare, for example, are not indicated, but all discussions of the men or their works are indexed, and practically all the comments on sources and influences.

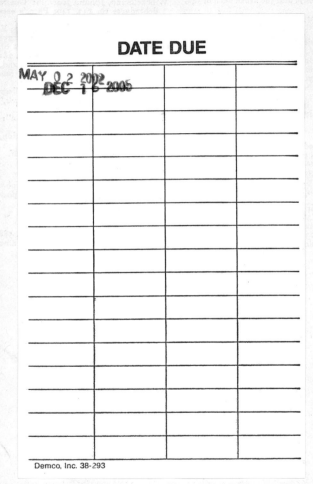

DATE DUE

MAY 0 2 2002 DEC 1 6 2005			